Business Law offers comprehensive co
stand for both law and non-law stuc

Established legal topics such as
areas such as health and safety and e
new edition has been thoroughly u
such as the Equalities Act, occupiers

Key learning features include:

- new Law in Context boxes that cc
- diagrams and tables to illustrate
- newly updated key cases boxes
- revision summaries at the end c
- an attractive two-colour text de
- an up-to-date and easy-to-use
  learning and track your progres

Business Law offers a topical overview
business studies undergraduates.

David Kelly was formerly Principal
the best-selling textbook *The English*

Ruby Hammer, LLB (Hons), LLM, M
Law at Staffordshire University and subject leader for Environmental Law. She is research active within the fields of Environmental Law and Stress at Work claims.

John Hendy is a Director of In Touch Learning Ltd and is an Education Consultant specialising in the development of LLB, LLM and MBA awards for online learning. He has expertise in International Business Law and Employment Law, International Environmental Law and Health and Safety.

business law

Second Edition

David Kelly, Ruby Hammer
and John Hendy

LONDON AND NEW YORK

This edition published 2014
by Routledge
2 Park Square, Milton Park, Abingdon, Oxon, OX14 4RN

and by Routledge
711 Third Avenue, New York, NY 10017

Routledge is an imprint of the Taylor & Francis Group, an informa business

First published by Cavendish Publishing 1995

First published by Routledge 2011

British Library Cataloguing in Publication Data
A catalogue record for this book is available from the British Library

Library of Congress Cataloging-in-Publication Data
Kelly, David, 1950- author.
Business law / David Kelly, Ruby Hammer, John Hendy.—Second edition.
pages cm
ISBN 978-0-415-72307-7 (hardback)—ISBN 978-0-415-72306-0 (pbk)—
ISBN 978-1-315-85790-9 (ebk) 1. Commercial law—England. 2. Business enterprises—Law and legislation—England. 3. Labor laws and legislation—England. I. Hammer, Ruby (Law teacher) author. II. Hendy, John, 1980- author.
III. Title.
KD1629.6.K45 2014
346.4207—dc23

2013044932

ISBN: 978-0-415-72307-7 (hbk)
ISBN: 978-0-415-72306-0 (pbk)
ISBN: 978-1-315-85790-9 (ebk)

Typeset in Joanna
by RefineCatch Limited, Bungay, Suffolk

Printed and bound in Great Britain by
TJ International Ltd, Padstow, Cornwall

Outline Contents

Detailed Contents

Preface

One of the problems facing the person studying business activity, and one that is specifically addressed in this book, is the fact that business enterprise takes place within a general and wide-ranging legal environment, but the student is required to have more than a passing knowledge of the legal rules and procedures which impact on business activity. The difficulty lies in acquiring an *adequate* knowledge of the many areas that govern such business activity. Law students may legitimately be expected to focus their attention on the minutiae of the law, but those studying law within, and as merely a component part of, a wider sphere of study cannot be expected to have the same detailed level of knowledge as law students. Nonetheless, they are expected to have a more than superficial knowledge of various legal topics.

For the author of a business law textbook, the difficulty lies in pitching the material considered at the appropriate level so that those studying the subject acquire a sufficient grasp to understand law as it relates *generally* to business enterprise, and of course to equip the student to pass the requisite exams. To achieve this goal, the text must not be too specialised and focus on too small a part of what is contained in most business law syllabuses. For example, although contract law is central to any business law course, to study it on its own, or with a few ancillary topics, is not sufficient. (With three subject specialists involved, each with a favouritism to advance, not to say an axe to grind, it can be well imagined that the final text was a matter of some serious debate.) Nor, however, should the text be so wide-ranging as to provide the student with no more than a superficial general knowledge of most of the possible interfaces between law and business enterprise. A selection has to be made and it is hoped that this text has made the correct one. No attempt has been made to cover all the areas within the potential scope of business law, but it is hoped that attention has been focused on the most important of these, without excluding any area of major importance. Additionally, it is hoped that the material provided deals with the topics selected in as thorough a way as is necessary.

We have taken the decision that anyone conducting a business today can no longer deny, or ignore, the impact of their activity on the physical environment and the legal rules that constrain such activity. Consequently, we have included a section on environmental law and its impact on business. Perhaps this may seem an unusual topic for the moment, but we are sure that we are merely beating a path that others will follow in the future. As is only to be expected, we have made every effort to ensure that the text is as up to date as we can make it.

David Kelly
Ruby Hammer
John Hendy
February 2014

Guide to Using the Book

Business Law is rich with features designed to support and reinforce your learning. This Guided Tour shows you how to make the most of your textbook by illustrating each of the features used by the authors.

12.1 Introduction

One of the commonest transactions made b
businesses or consumers. However, goods r
a hire contract. There the owner of goods t
ship; common examples are television rent
A person may also be supplied with
defects in the goods can, in some circumst
Furthermore, the sale and supply
criminal liability, the latter being of pa

Chapter Overviews

These overviews are a brief introduction to the core themes and issues you will encounter in each chapter.

Law in Context: The

In the following chapter you will dev
every aspect of social order within soci
regulation of business activities. The En
law and legislative legal rules, but one
deregulation of the legal profession v
2007 effectively introduced the conc
outcome has been that for the first t

Law in Context

A new feature at the start of each chapter to contextualise the aspects of law under discussion in order to enhance your understanding of the relationship between the law and the business world.

❖ **KEY CASE** *Cumbrian and Westr Co Ltd (19*

Facts:
Following a merger between the plain
cles were altered so as to give the plair
to appoint a director, so long as it held

Key Cases

A variety of landmark cases are highlighted in text boxes for ease of reference. The facts and decisions are presented to help you reach an understanding of how and why the court reached the conclusion it did.

Diagrams and Flowcharts

Diagrams, tables and flowcharts provide a clear visual representation of important or complex points.

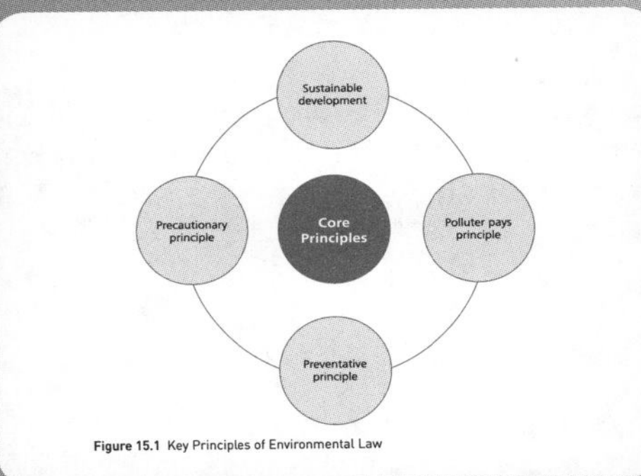

Figure 15.1 Key Principles of Environmental Law

Cross-References

Related material is linked together by a series of clearly marked cross-references.

will reasonably and promptly afford a
of any grievance they may have.

There is generally no requireme
former employee. However, in certai
employer open to a claim c
discrimination legislation –
Yorkshire Police v Khan (2001).
tion.) Also, if a reference is provided
accurate reflection of the employee's
Assurance plc (1995), the employer ma

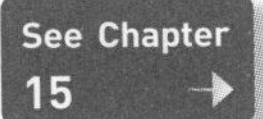

Chapter Summaries

The essential points and concepts covered in each chapter are distilled into bulleted summaries at the end of each chapter in order to provide you with an at-a-glance reference point for each topic.

Summary

Individual Employment Rights

An employee is employed under a contrac
independent contractor is employed unde
because many employment rights only acc

- An express term in a document which
  is conflict between them – *Stevedoring &*

Further Reading

There are a number of further reading mat
the general nature of Tort Law. The classic

Jones, MA and Dugdale, AM (eds), *Clerk &*
Maxwell

For general textbooks on Tort Law the follo

Harpwood, VH, *Modern Tort Law*, 7th edn, 2

Further Reading

Selected further reading is included at the end of each chapter to provide a pathway for further study.

Guide to the Companion Website

www.routledge.com/textbooks/kelly

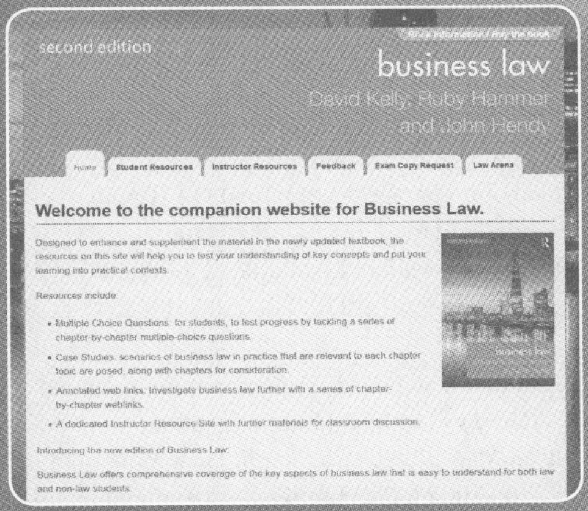

Visit *Business Law*'s Companion Website to discover a comprehensive range of resources designed to enhance the learning and teaching experience for both students and lecturers.

On this accompanying website, you'll find the following resources with which you can engage with *Business Law*:

Chapter Questions and Suggested Answers

Questions around the key topics discussed in the book are provided, with sample and suggested discussion points also shown to demonstrate full and accurate answers.

Multiple Choice Questions

Ordered by chapter, these MCQs have been written to test your knowledge and understanding of each subject in the book.

Diagrams

A full set of PowerPoints of the diagrams contained within the text should be of use for lecturers and students alike.

Weblinks

Make use of a series of website links, ordered by Part, to related websites.

Case Studies

Scenarios presenting business law in practice are posed, relating to the key topics discussed in the chapters. Sample answers and points of discussion are then provided for your consideration.

Table of Cases

B

C

E

F

G

H

I

J

K

P

Q

R

S

T

U

V

W

X

Y

Z

Table of Statutes

F

R

S

T

U

W

Y

Table of Statutory Instruments

D

E

F

T

U

W

Table of Conventions, Treaties and EC Legislation

European Treaties and Conventions

Directives

Regulations

List of Abbreviations

ACAS	Advisory, Conciliation and Arbitration Service
ADR	Alternative Dispute Resolution
BNA	Business Names Act 1985
CA	Companies Act 1862/1985/1989
CAA	Criminal Appeal Act 1968/1995
C(AICE)A	Companies (Audit, Investigations and Community Enterprise) Act 2004
CDDA	Company Directors Disqualification Act 1986
CFREU	Charter of Fundamental Rights of the European Union
CIB	Companies Investigations Branch (of the Department of Trade and Industry)
CIC	Community Interest Company
CJA	Criminal Justice Act 1972/1988/1993
CPA	Consumer Protection Act 1987
CPIA	Criminal Procedure and Investigations Act 1996
CPR	Civil Procedure Rules
CPS	Crown Prosecution Service
DCOA	Deregulation and Contracting Out Act 1994
DDA	Disability Discrimination Act 1995/2004
EAT	Employment Appeal Tribunal
EC	European Community
ECJ	European Court of Justice
ECHR	European Convention on Human Rights
ECtHR	European Court of Human Rights
EEC	European Economic Community
EOC	Equal Opportunities Commission
EPA	Equal Pay Act 1970
ERA	Employment Rights Act 1996
EU	European Union
FRC	Finance Reporting Council
FRRP	Financial Reporting Review Panel
GPSR	General Product Safety Regulations 1994/2005
HRA	Human Rights Act 1998
IA	Insolvency Act 1986
LLP	Limited Liability Partnership
LLPA	Limited Liability Partnership Act 2000
LLPR	Limited Liability Partnership Regulations 2001
MA	Misrepresentation Act 1967
NICA	Northern Ireland Court of Appeal
NMWA	National Minimum Wage Act 1998
PA	Partnership Act 1890
RRA	Race Relations Act 1976
SDA	Sex Discrimination Act 1975/1986

SEA	Single European Act 1986
SGSA	Supply of Goods and Services Act 1982
SoGA	Sale of Goods Act 1979
TDA	Trade Descriptions Act 1968
TEU	Treaty on European Union
TFEU	Treaty on the Functioning of the European Union
TULR(C)A	Trade Union and Labour Relations (Consolidation) Act 1992
TURERA	Trade Union Reform and Employment Rights Act 1993
UCTA	Unfair Contract Terms Act 1977
YJCEA	Youth Justice and Criminal Evidence Act 1999

Part 1

Law, Legal Sources and Dispute Resolution

Business activity takes place in the context of a legal environment that structures, regulates and controls its operation. The greater part of this book will focus on the substantive legal rules and procedures that apply to such business activity. However, in order to understand the content of 'business' law as such, it is necessary to have a general understanding of the legal context. It is the purpose of the first part of this book to supply this necessary general introduction to the level required to allow the business student to understand and deal with specific legal rules. It has to be emphasised that no business related modules, courses or indeed text books look to make lawyers of those who study them, but they do look to make their students aware of the inescapable interface between law and business activity.

This part of our book introduces the reader to the study of law and provides the basis for the later study of more detailed specific areas of business law. The first chapter addresses what law is and where it comes from. In doing so it looks to explain different types of law, particularly legislation and the judge-made common law. The chapter also introduces two further aspects of law that must constantly be borne in mind by businesses: the first of these is the Human Rights Act 1998, the provisions and principles of which apply pervasively throughout all aspects of business. The second specific area of attention is the impact of the UK's membership of the European Union – which is now the source of many of the legal regulations that apply to business activity.

Where legal problems arise they are usually dealt with in the courts and chapter 2 introduces the reader to the courts, both criminal and civil, and explains the relationship between them.

However, it is not always in the parties' interest to take disputes to court and chapter 3 looks at the alternatives to taking court action and the reasons why such alternative dispute resolution procedures are sometimes preferred.

Chapter 1

Law and Legal Sources

Chapter Contents

Law in Context: The Provision of Legal Services

In the following chapter you will develop an understanding of how law regulates nearly every aspect of social order within society, and the impact it has upon the organisation and regulation of business activities. The English legal system is a rich tapestry of both common law and legislative legal rules but one of the biggest changes in recent times has been the deregulation of the legal profession which interprets such rules. The Legal Services Act 2007 effectively introduced the concept of 'alternative business structures' (ABS). The outcome has been that for the first time in history law firms can operate with capital investment from non-legal investors. Many law firms are already inviting investment from non-lawyers and several brand names have entered the legal service marketplace. This has revolutionised the availability of legal advice to both the private and business sectors, but not without criticism. Many argue that the quality of service and integrity of the legal profession will suffer. Students embarking on a study of business law should remain alert to how the changes work out, as they will have considerable implications for business and commerce.

1.1 The Nature of Law

To a great extent, business activity across the world is carried on within a capitalist, market-based system. With regard to such a system, law provides and maintains an essential framework within which such business activity can take place, and without which it could not operate. In maintaining this framework, law establishes the rules and procedures for what is to be considered legitimate business activity and, as a corollary, what is not legitimate. It is essential, therefore, for the businessperson to be aware of the nature of the legal framework within which they have to operate. Even if they employ legal experts to deal with their legal problems, they will still need to be sufficiently knowledgeable to be able to recognise when to refer matters to those experts. It is the intention of this textbook to provide business students with an understanding of the most important aspects of law as they impinge on various aspects of business activity.

One of the most obvious and most central characteristics of all societies is that they must possess some degree of order, in order to permit their members to interact over a sustained period of time. Different societies, however, have different forms of order. Some societies are highly regimented with strictly enforced social rules, whereas others continue to function in what outsiders might consider a very unstructured manner, with apparently few strict rules being enforced.

Order is, therefore, necessary, but the form through which order is maintained is certainly not universal, as many anthropological studies have shown (see Mansell and Meteyard, *A Critical Introduction to Law*, 1999).

In our society, law plays an important part in the creation and maintenance of social order. We must be aware, however, that law as we know it is not the only means of creating order. Even in our society, order is not solely dependent on law, but also involves questions of a more general moral and political character. This book is not concerned with providing a general explanation of the form of order. It is concerned, more particularly, with describing and explaining the key institutional aspects of that particular form of order that is legal order.

The most obvious way in which law contributes to the maintenance of social order is the way in which it deals with disorder or conflict. This book, therefore, is particularly concerned with the institutions and procedures, both civil and criminal, through which law operates to ensure a particular form of social order by dealing with various conflicts when they arise.

Law is a formal mechanism of social control and, as such, it is essential that the student of law is fully aware of the nature of that formal structure. There are, however, other aspects to law that are less immediately apparent but of no less importance, such as the inescapably political nature of law. Some textbooks focus more on this particular aspect of law than others and these differences become evident in the particular approach adopted by the authors. The approach favoured by the authors of this book is to recognise that studying English law is not just about learning legal rules; it is also about considering a social institution of fundamental importance.

There is an ongoing debate about the relationship between law and morality and as to what exactly that relationship is or should be. Should all laws accord with a moral code, and, if so, which one? Can laws be detached from moral arguments? Many of the issues in this debate are implicit in much of what follows in the text, but the authors believe that, in spite of claims to the contrary, there is no simple causal relationship of dependency or determination, either way, between morality and law. We would rather approach both morality and law as ideological, in that they are manifestations of, and seek to explain and justify, particular social and economic relationships. This essentially materialist approach to a degree explains the tensions between the competing ideologies of law and morality and explains why they sometimes conflict and why they change, albeit asynchronously, as underlying social relations change.

1.2 Categories of Law

There are various ways of categorising law, which initially tends to confuse the non-lawyer and the new student of law. What follows will set out these categorisations in their usual dual form whilst, at the same time, trying to overcome the confusion inherent in such duality. It is impossible to avoid the confusing repetition of the same terms to mean different things and, indeed, the purpose of this section is to make sure that students are aware of the fact that the same words can have different meanings, depending upon the context in which they are used.

1.2.1 Common law and civil law

In this particular juxtaposition, these terms are used to distinguish two distinct legal systems and approaches to law. The use of the term 'common law' in this context refers to all those legal systems which have adopted the historic English legal system. Foremost amongst these is, of course, the US, but many other Commonwealth and former Commonwealth countries retain a common law system. The term 'civil law' refers to those other jurisdictions which have adopted the European continental system of law, which is derived essentially from ancient Roman law but owes much to the Germanic tradition.

The usual distinction to be made between the two systems is that the former, the common law system, tends to be case centred and, hence, judge centred, allowing scope for a discretionary, *ad hoc*, pragmatic approach to the particular problems that appear before the courts, whereas the latter, the civil law system, tends to be a codified body of general abstract principles which control the exercise of judicial discretion. In reality, both of these views are extremes, with the former overemphasising the extent to which the common law judge can impose his discretion and the latter underestimating the extent to which continental judges have the power to exercise judicial discretion. It is perhaps worth mentioning at this point that the Court of Justice of the European Union (CJEU), which was established, in theory, on civil law principles, is in practice increasingly recognising the benefits of establishing a body of case law.

It has to be recognised, and indeed the English courts do so, that although the CJEU is not bound by the operation of the doctrine of *stare decisis* (see 1.6 below), it still does not decide individual cases on an *ad hoc* basis and, therefore, in the light of a perfectly clear decision of the CJEU, national courts will be reluctant to refer similar cases to its jurisdiction. Thus, after the CJEU decided in *Grant v South West Trains Ltd* (1998) that Community law did not cover discrimination on grounds of sexual orientation, the High Court withdrew a similar reference in *R v Secretary of State for Defence ex p Perkins* (No 2) (1998) (see 1.4.3 below, for a detailed consideration of the CJEU).

1.2.2 Common law and equity

In this particular juxtaposition, these terms refer to a particular division within the English legal system.

The common law has been romantically and inaccurately described as 'the law of the common people of England'. In fact, the common law emerged as the product of a particular struggle for political power. Prior to the Norman Conquest of England in 1066, there was no unitary, national legal system. The emergence of the common law represented the imposition of such a unitary system under the auspices and control of a centralised power in the form of a sovereign king; in that respect, it represented the assertion and affirmation of that central sovereign power.

Traditionally, much play is made about the circuit of judges who travelled around the country establishing the King's peace and, in so doing, selected the best local customs and making them the basis of the law of England by means of a piecemeal but totally altruistic procedure. The reality of this process was that the judges were asserting the authority of the central State and its legal forms and institutions over the disparate and fragmented State and legal forms of the earlier feudal period. Hence, the common law was common *to* all in application, but certainly was not common *from* all. By the end of the 13th century, the central authority had established its precedence at least partly through the establishment of the common law. Originally, courts had been no more than an adjunct of the King's Council, the *Curia Regis*, but, gradually, the common law courts began to take on a distinct institutional existence in the form of the Courts of Exchequer, Common Pleas and King's Bench. With this institutional autonomy, however, there developed an institutional sclerosis, typified by a reluctance to deal with matters that were not, or could not be, processed in the proper form of action. Such a refusal to deal with substantive injustices, because they did not fall within the particular parameters of procedural and formal constraints, by necessity led to injustice and the need to remedy the perceived weaknesses in the common law system. The response was the development of equity.

Plaintiffs who were unable to gain access to the three common law courts might appeal directly to the Sovereign, and such pleas would be passed for consideration and decision to the Lord Chancellor, who acted as the 'King's conscience'. As the common law courts became more formalistic and more inaccessible, pleas to the Chancellor correspondingly increased and, eventually, this resulted in the emergence of a specific court which was constituted to deliver equitable or fair decisions in cases with which the common law courts declined to deal. As had happened with the common law, the decisions of the courts of equity established principles which were used to decide later cases, so it should not be thought that the use of equity meant that judges had discretion to decide cases on the basis of their personal ideas of what was just in each case.

The division between the common law courts and the courts of equity continued until they were eventually combined by the Judicature Acts 1873–75. Prior to this legislation, it was essential for a party to raise their action in the appropriate court; for example, the courts of law would not implement equitable principles. The Judicature Acts, however, provided that every court had the power and the duty to decide cases in line with common law and equity, with the latter being paramount in the final analysis.

Some would say that as equity was never anything other than a gloss on common law, it is perhaps appropriate, if not ironic, that both systems have now effectively been subsumed under the one term: common law.

Common law remedies

Common law remedies are available as of right. The classic common law remedy of damages can be subdivided into the following types:

- *Compensatory damages*: these are the standard awards, intended to achieve no more than to recompense the injured party to the extent of the injury suffered. Damages in contract can only be compensatory.
- *Aggravated damages*: these are compensatory in nature but are additional to ordinary compensatory awards and are awarded in relation to damage suffered to the injured party's dignity and pride. They are, therefore, akin to damages being paid in relation to mental distress. In *Khodaparast v Shad* (2000), the claimant was awarded aggravated damages after the defendant had been found liable for the malicious falsehood of distributing fake pictures of her in a state of undress, which resulted in her losing her job.
- *Exemplary damages*: these are awarded in tort in addition to compensatory damages. They may be awarded where the person who committed the tort intended to make a profit from their tortious action. The most obvious area in which such awards might be awarded is in libel cases where the publisher issues the libel to increase sales. An example of exemplary awards can be seen in the award of £50,000 (originally £275,000) to Elton John as a result of his action against *The Mirror* newspaper (*John v MGN Ltd* (1996)).
- *Nominal damages*: these are awarded in the few cases which really do involve 'a matter of principle' but where no loss or injury to reputation is involved. There is no set figure in relation to nominal damages; it is merely a very small amount.
- *Contemptuous damages*: these are extremely small awards made where the claimant wins their case, but has suffered no loss and has failed to impress the court with the standard of their own behaviour or character. In *Reynolds v Times Newspapers Ltd* (1998), the former Prime Minister of Ireland was awarded one penny in his libel action against *The Times* newspaper; this award was actually made by the judge after the jury had awarded him no damages at all. Such an award can be considered nothing if not contemptuous.

The whole point of damages is compensatory, to recompense someone for the wrong they have suffered. There are, however, different ways in which someone can be compensated. For example, in contract law the object of awarding damages is to put the wronged person in the situation they would have been in had the contract been completed as agreed: that is, it places them in the position in which they would have been *after the event*. In tort, however, the object is to compensate the wronged person, to the extent that a monetary award can do so, for injury sustained; in other words to return them to the situation they were in *before the event*.

Equitable remedies

Remedies in equity are discretionary; in other words, they are awarded at the will of the court and depend on the behaviour and situation of the party claiming such remedies. This means that, in effect, the court does not have to award an equitable remedy where it considers that the conduct of the party seeking such an award does not deserve such an award (*D & C Builders Ltd v Rees* (1965)). The usual equitable remedies are as follows:

- *Injunction* – this is a court order requiring someone to do something or, alternatively, to stop doing something (*Warner Bros v Nelson* (1937)).
- *Specific performance* – this is a court order requiring one of the parties to a contractual agreement to complete their part of the contract. It is usually only awarded in respect of contracts relating to specific individual articles, such as land, and will not be awarded where the court cannot supervise the operation of its order (*Ryan v Mutual Tontine Westminster Chambers Association* (1893)).

- *Rectification* – this order relates to the alteration, under extremely limited circumstances, of contractual documents (*Joscelyne v Nissen* (1970)).
- *Rescission* – this order returns parties to a contractual agreement to the position they were in before the agreement was entered into. It is essential to distinguish this award from the common law award of damages, which is intended to place the parties in the position they would have been in had the contract been completed.

1.2.3 Common law and statute law

This particular conjunction follows on from the immediately preceding section, in that 'common law' here refers to the substantive law and procedural rules that have been created by the judiciary, through their decisions in the cases they have heard. Statute law, on the other hand, refers to law that has been created by Parliament in the form of legislation. Although there was a significant increase in statute law in the 20th century, the courts still have an important role to play in creating and operating law generally, and in determining the operation of legislation in particular. The relationship of this pair of concepts is of central importance and is considered in more detail below, at 1.5 and 1.6.

1.2.4 Private law and public law

There are two different ways of understanding the division between private and public law.

At one level, the division relates specifically to actions of the State and its functionaries vis à vis the individual citizen, and the legal manner in which, and form of law through which, such relationships are regulated; that is, public law. In the 19th century, it was at least possible to claim, as Dicey did, that there was no such thing as public law in this distinct administrative sense, and that the power of the State with regard to individuals was governed by the ordinary law of the land, operating through the normal courts. Whether such a claim was accurate when it was made, which is unlikely, there certainly can be no doubt now that public law constitutes a distinct and growing area of law in its own right. The growth of public law, in this sense, has mirrored the growth and increased activity of the contemporary State, and has seen its role as seeking to regulate such activity. The crucial role of judicial review in relation to public law will be considered below, at 1.5.6.

There is, however, a second aspect to the division between private and public law. One corollary of the divide is that matters located within the private sphere are seen as purely a matter for individuals themselves to regulate, without the interference of the State, whose role is limited to the provision of the forum for deciding contentious issues and mechanisms for the enforcement of such decisions. Matters within the public sphere, however, are seen as issues relating to the interest of the State and general public and are, as such, to be protected and prosecuted by the State. It can be seen, therefore, that the category to which any dispute is allocated is of crucial importance to how it is dealt with. Contract may be thought of as the classic example of private law, but the extent to which this purely private legal area has been subjected to the regulation of public law in such areas as consumer protection should not be underestimated. Equally, the most obvious example of public law in this context would be criminal law. Feminists have argued, however, that the allocation of domestic matters to the sphere of private law has led to a denial of a general interest in the treatment and protection of women. By defining domestic matters as private, the State and its functionaries have denied women access to its power to protect themselves from abuse. In doing so, it is suggested that, in fact, such categorisation has reflected and maintained the social domination of men over women.

1.2.5 Civil law and criminal law

Civil law is a form of private law and involves the relationships between individual citizens. It is the legal mechanism through which individuals can assert claims against others and have those rights adjudicated and enforced. The purpose of civil law is to settle disputes between individuals and to provide remedies; it is not concerned with punishment as such. The role of the State in relation to civil law is to establish the general framework of legal rules and to provide the legal institutions for operating those rights, but the activation of the civil law is strictly a matter for the individuals concerned. Contract, tort and property law are generally aspects of civil law.

Criminal law, on the other hand, is an aspect of public law and relates to conduct which the State considers with disapproval and which it seeks to control and/or eradicate. Criminal law involves the enforcement of particular forms of behaviour, and the State, as the representative of society, acts positively to ensure compliance. Thus, criminal cases are brought by the State in the name of the Crown and cases are reported in the form of *Regina v . . .* (*Regina* is simply Latin for 'Queen' and case references are usually abbreviated to *R v . . .*), whereas civil cases are referred to by the names of the parties involved in the dispute, for example, *Smith v Jones*.

Decisions to prosecute in relation to criminal cases are taken by the Crown Prosecution Service (CPS), which is a legal agency operating independently of the police force.

In distinguishing between criminal and civil actions, it has to be remembered that the same event may give rise to both. For example, where the driver of a car injures someone through their reckless driving they will be liable to be prosecuted under the road traffic legislation but, at the same time, they will also be responsible to the injured party in the civil law relating to the tort of negligence.

In June 2009 relatives of the victims of the Omagh bombing in Northern Ireland, which killed 29 people in 1998, won the right to take a civil case against members of the Real IRA, following the failure of a criminal prosecution to secure any convictions. Damages of £1.6 million were awarded against four men. Subsequently, in 2013 a retrial of two of the men was held after they had succeeded on appeal in challenging the original decision. At the retrial they were once again found liable with the other two men, whose original appeal had failed.

A crucial distinction between criminal and civil law is the level of proof required in the different types of cases. In a criminal case, the prosecution is required to prove that the defendant is guilty beyond reasonable doubt, whereas in a civil case the degree of proof is much lower and has only to be on the balance of probabilities. This difference in the level of proof raises the possibility of someone being able to succeed in a civil case although there may not be sufficient evidence for a criminal prosecution. Indeed, this strategy has been used successfully in a number of cases against the police where the CPS has considered there to be insufficient evidence to support a criminal conviction for assault.

It is essential not to confuse the standard of proof with the burden of proof. The latter refers to the need for the person making an allegation, be it the prosecution in a criminal case or the claimant in a civil case, to prove the facts of the case. In certain circumstances, once the prosecution/claimant has demonstrated certain facts, the burden of proof may shift to the defendant/respondent to provide evidence to prove their lack of culpability. The reverse burden of proof may be either *legal* or *evidential*, which in practice indicates the degree of evidence they have to provide in order to meet the burden they are under.

It should also be noted that the distinction between civil and criminal responsibility is further blurred in cases involving what may be described as hybrid offences. These are situations where a court awards a civil order against an individual, but with the attached sanction that any breach of the order will be subject to punishment as a criminal offence. As examples of this procedure may be cited the Protection from Harassment Act 1997 and the provision for the making of Anti-Social Behaviour Orders originally made available under s 1(1) of the Crime and Disorder Act 1998.

Although prosecution of criminal offences is usually the prerogative of the CPS as the agent of the State, it remains open to the private individual to initiate a private prosecution in relation to a criminal offence. It has to be remembered, however, that, even in the private prosecution, the test of the standard of proof remains the criminal one – requiring the facts to be proved beyond reasonable doubt. An example of the problems inherent in such private actions can be seen in the case of Stephen Lawrence, the young black man who was gratuitously stabbed to death by a gang of white racists whilst standing at a bus stop in London. Although there was strong suspicion, and indeed evidence, against particular individuals, the CPS declined to press the charges against them on the basis of insufficiency of evidence. When the lawyers of the Lawrence family mounted a private prosecution against the suspects, the action failed for want of sufficient evidence to convict. As a consequence of the failure of the private prosecution, the then rule against double jeopardy meant that the accused could not be re-tried for the same offence at any time in the future, even if the police subsequently acquired sufficient new evidence to support a conviction. The report of the Macpherson Inquiry into the manner in which the Metropolitan Police dealt with the Stephen Lawrence case gained much publicity for its finding of 'institutional racism' within the service, but it also made a clear recommendation that the removal of the rule against double jeopardy be considered. Subsequently, a Law Commission report recommended the removal of the double jeopardy rule and provision to remove it, under particular circumstances and subject to strict regulation, was contained in ss 75–79 of the Criminal Justice Act 2003.

In considering the relationship between civil law and criminal law, it is sometimes thought that criminal law is the more important in maintaining social order, but it is at least arguable that, in reality, the reverse is the case. For the most part, people come into contact with the criminal law infrequently, whereas everyone is continuously involved with civil law, even if it is only the use of contract law to make some purchase. The criminal law of theft, for example, may be seen as simply the cutting edge of the wider and more fundamental rights established by general property law. In any case, there remains the fact that civil and criminal law each has its own distinct legal system.

1.3 The Human Rights Act 1998

The UK was one of the initial signatories to the European Convention on Human Rights (ECHR) in 1950, which was set up in post-War Europe as a means of establishing and enforcing essential human rights. In 1966, it recognised the power of the European Commission on Human Rights to hear complaints from individual UK citizens and, at the same time, recognised the authority of the European Court of Human Rights (ECtHR) to adjudicate on such matters. It did not, however, at that time incorporate the European Convention into UK law.

The consequence of non-incorporation was that the Convention could not be directly enforced in English courts (*R v Secretary of State for the Home Department ex p Brind* (1991)). That situation was remedied, however, by the passing of the Human Rights Act 1998 (HRA), which came into force in England and Wales in October 2000 and was by then already in effect in Scotland. The HRA incorporates the ECHR into UK law. The Articles incorporated into UK law and listed in Sched 1 to the Act cover the following matters:

- The right to life. Article 2 states that 'everyone's right to life shall be protected by law'.
- Prohibition of torture. Article 3 actually provides that 'no one shall be subjected to torture or inhuman or degrading treatment or punishment'.
- Prohibition of slavery and forced labour (Art 4).
- The right to liberty and security. After stating the general right, Art 5 is mainly concerned with the conditions under which individuals can lawfully be deprived of their liberty.
- The right to a fair trial. Article 6 provides that 'everyone is entitled to a fair and public hearing within a reasonable time by an independent and impartial tribunal established by law'.
- The general prohibition of the enactment of retrospective criminal offences. Article 7 does, however, recognise the *post hoc* criminalisation of previous behaviour where it is 'criminal according to the general principles of law recognised by civilised nations'.

- The right to respect for private and family life. Article 8 extends this right to cover a person's home and their correspondence.
- Freedom of thought, conscience and religion (Art 9).
- Freedom of expression. Article 10 extends the right to include 'freedom . . . to receive and impart information and ideas without interference by public authority and regardless of frontiers'.
- Freedom of assembly and association. Article 11 specifically includes the right to form and join trade unions.
- The right to marry (Art 12).
- Prohibition of discrimination (Art 14).
- The right to peaceful enjoyment of possessions and protection of property (Art 1 of Protocol 1).
- The right to education (subject to a UK reservation) (Art 2 of Protocol 1).
- The right to free elections (Art 3 of Protocol 1).
- The right not to be subjected to the death penalty (Arts 1 and 2 of Protocol 6).

The rights listed can be relied on by any person, non-governmental organisation, or group of individuals. Importantly, they also apply, where appropriate, to companies, which are incorporated entities and hence legal persons. However, they cannot be relied on by governmental organisations, such as local authorities.

The rights listed above are not all seen in the same way. Some are absolute and inalienable and cannot be interfered with by the State. Others are merely contingent and are subject to derogation, that is, signatory States can opt out of them in particular circumstances. The absolute rights are those provided for in Arts 2, 3, 4, 7 and 14. All of the others are subject to potential limitations; in particular, the rights provided for under Arts 8, 9, 10 and 11 are subject to legal restrictions, such as are:

> . . . necessary in a democratic society in the interests of national security or public safety, for the prevention of crime, for the protection of health or morals or the protection of the rights and freedoms of others. [Art 11(2)]

In deciding the legality of any derogation, courts are required not just to be convinced that there is a need for the derogation, but they must also be sure that the State's action has been proportionate to that need. In other words, the State must not overreact to a perceived problem by removing more rights than is necessary to effect the solution. The UK entered such a derogation in relation to the extended detention of terrorist suspects without charge under the Prevention of Terrorism (Temporary Provisions) Act 1989, subsequently replaced and extended by the Terrorism Act 2000. Those powers had been held to be contrary to Art 5 of the Convention by the ECtHR in **Brogan v United Kingdom** (1989). The UK also entered a derogation with regard to the Anti-Terrorism, Crime and Security Act 2001, which was enacted in response to the attack on the World Trade Center in New York on 11 September that year. The Act allowed for the detention without trial of foreign citizens suspected of being involved in terrorist activity.

With further regard to the possibility of derogation, s 19 of the 1998 Act requires a minister, responsible for the passage of any Bill through Parliament, either to make a written declaration that it is compatible with the Convention or, alternatively, to declare that although it may not be compatible, it is still the Government's wish to proceed with it.

1.3.1 The structure of the Human Rights Act 1998

The HRA has profound implications for the operation of the English legal system. However, to understand the structure of the HRA, it is essential to be aware of the nature of the changes introduced by the Act, especially in the apparent passing of fundamental powers to the judiciary. Under the doctrine of parliamentary sovereignty, the legislature could pass such laws at it saw fit, even to the extent of removing the rights of its citizens. The 1998 Act reflects a move towards the entrenchment of rights recognised under the ECHR but, given the sensitivity of the relationship between the elected Parliament and the unelected judiciary, it has been thought expedient to minimise the change in the constitutional relationship of Parliament and the judiciary.

Section 2 of the Act requires future courts to take into account any previous decision of the ECtHR. This provision impacts on the operation of the doctrine of precedent within the English legal system, as it effectively sanctions the overruling of any previous English authority that was in conflict with a decision of the ECtHR.

Section 3 requires all legislation to be read, so far as possible, to give effect to the rights provided under the ECHR. As will be seen, this section provides the courts with new and extended powers of interpretation. It also has the potential to invalidate previously accepted interpretations of statutes which were made, by necessity, without recourse to the ECHR (see *Ghaidan v Godin-Mendoza* (2004) below at 1.3.2).

Section 4 empowers the courts to issue a declaration of incompatibility where any piece of primary legislation is found to conflict with the rights provided under the ECHR. This has the effect that the courts cannot invalidate primary legislation, essentially Acts of Parliament but also Orders in Council, which is found to be incompatible; they can only make a declaration of such incompatibility, and leave it to the legislature to remedy the situation through new legislation. Section 10 provides for the provision of remedial legislation through a fast track procedure, which gives a minister of the Crown the power to alter such primary legislation by way of statutory instrument.

Section 5 requires the Crown to be given notice where a court considers issuing a declaration of incompatibility, and the appropriate Government minister is entitled to be made a party to the case.

Section 6 declares it unlawful for any public authority to act in a way that is incompatible with the ECHR, and consequently the Human Rights Act does not *directly* impose duties on private individuals or companies unless they are performing public functions. Whether or not a private company is performing a public function is problematic, there are instances where they clearly would be considered as doing so, such as in regard to the privitised utility companies providing essential services, equally if a private company were to provide prison facilities then clearly it would be operating as a public authority. However, at the other end of an uncertain spectrum, it has been held that, where a local authority fulfils its statutory duty to arrange the provision of care and accommodation for an elderly person through the use of a private care home, the functions performed by the care home are not to be considered as of a public nature. At least that was the decision of the House of Lords by a majority of three to two in *YL v Birmingham City Council* (2007), a rather surprisingly conservative decision, and one that met with no little dismay, given that it was the expectation that the public authority test would be applied generously. Where a public authority is acting under the instructions of some primary legislation which is itself incompatible with the ECHR, the public authority will not be liable under s 6.

Section 6(3), however, *indirectly* introduces the possibility of horizontal effect into private relationships. As s 6(3)(a) specifically states that courts and tribunals are public authorities they must therefore act in accordance with the Convention. The consequence of this is that, although the HRA does not introduce new causes of action between private indivuduals the courts, as public authorities, are required to to recognise and give effect to their Convention rights in any action that can be raised.

Section 7 allows the 'victim of the unlawful act' to bring proceedings against the public authority in breach. However this is interpreted in such a way as to permit relations of the actual victim to initiate proceedings.

Section 8 empowers the court to grant such relief or remedy against the public authority in breach of the Act as it considers just and appropriate.

Section 19 of the Act requires that the minister responsible for the passage of any Bill through Parliament must make a written statement that the provisions of the Bill are compatible with ECHR rights. Alternatively, the minister may make a statement that the Bill does not comply with ECHR rights but that the Government nonetheless intends to proceed with it.

Reactions to the introduction of the HRA have been broadly welcoming, but some important criticisms have been raised. First, the ECHR is a rather old document and does not address some of the issues that contemporary citizens might consider as equally fundamental to those rights actually contained in the document. For example, it is silent on the rights to substantive equality relating to such issues as welfare and access to resources. Also, the actual provisions of the ECHR are uncertain in the extent of their application, or perhaps more crucially in the area where they can be derogated from, and at least to a degree they are contradictory. The most obvious difficulty arises from the need to reconcile Art 8's right to respect for private and family life with Art 10's freedom of expression. Newspaper editors have expressed their concern in relation to this particular issue, and fear the development, at the hands of the court, of an overly limiting law of privacy, which would prevent investigative journalism. This leads to a further difficulty: the potential politicisation, together with a significant enhancement in the power, of the judiciary. Consideration of this issue will be postponed until some cases involving the HRA have been examined.

Perhaps the most serious criticism of the HRA was the fact that the Government did not see fit to establish a Human Rights Commission to publicise and facilitate the operation of its procedures. Many saw the setting up of such a body as a necessary step in raising human rights awareness and assisting individuals, who might otherwise be unable to use the Act, to enforce their rights. However, on 1 October 2007, a new Equality and Human Rights Commission (EHRC) came into operation. The new commission brought together and replaced the former Commission for Racial Equality, the Equal Opportunities Commission and the Disability Rights Commission, with the remit of promoting 'an inclusive agenda, underlining the importance of equality for all in society as well as working to combat discrimination affecting specific groups'.

1.3.2 Cases decided under the Human Rights Act 1998

Proportionality

The way in which States can interfere with rights, so long as they do so in a way that is proportionate to the attainment of a legitimate end, can be seen in *Brown v Advocate General for Scotland* (2001).

❖ KEY CASE *Brown v Advocate General for Scotland* (2001)

Facts:

Brown had been arrested at a supermarket in relation to the theft of a bottle of gin. When the police officers noticed that she smelled of alcohol, they asked her how she had travelled to the superstore. Brown replied that she had driven and pointed out her car in the supermarket car park. Later, at the police station, the police used their powers under s 172(2)(a) of the Road Traffic Act 1988 to require her to say who had been driving her car at about 2.30 am; that is, at the time when she would have travelled in it to the supermarket. Brown admitted that she had been driving. After a positive breath test, Brown was charged with drunk driving, but appealed to the Scottish High Court of Justiciary for a declaration that the case could not go ahead on the grounds that her admission, as required under s 172, was contrary to the right to a fair trial under Art 6 of the ECHR.

Decision:
The High Court of Justiciary supported her claim on the basis that the right to silence and the right not to incriminate oneself at trial would be worthless if an accused person did not enjoy a right of silence in the course of the criminal investigation leading to the court proceedings. If this were not the case, then the police could require an accused person to provide an incriminating answer which subsequently could be used in evidence against them at their trial. Consequently, the use of evidence obtained under s 172 of the Road Traffic Act 1988 infringed Brown's rights under Art 6(1).

However, on 5 December 2000, the Privy Council reversed the judgment of the Scottish appeal court. The Privy Council reached its decision on the grounds that the rights contained in Art 6 of the ECHR were not themselves absolute and could be restricted in certain limited conditions. Consequently, it was possible for individual States to introduce limited qualification of those rights so long as they were aimed at 'a clear public objective' and were 'proportionate to the situation' under consideration. The ECHR had to be read as balancing community rights with individual rights. With specific regard to the Road Traffic Act 1998, the objective to be attained was the prevention of injury and death from the misuse of cars, and s 172 was not a disproportionate response to that objective.

Subsequently, in a majority decision in *O'Halloran v UK* (2007), the European Court of Human Rights approved the use of s 172 in order to require owners to reveal who had been driving cars caught on speed cameras.

Section 3: duty to interpret legislation in line with the ECHR

It has long been a matter of concern that, in cases where rape has been alleged, the common defence strategy employed by lawyers has been to attempt to attack the credibility of the woman making the accusation. Judges had the discretion to allow questioning of the woman as to her sexual history where this was felt to be relevant, and in all too many cases this discretion was exercised in a way that allowed defence counsel to abuse and humiliate women accusers. Section 41 of the Youth Justice and Criminal Evidence Act 1999 (YJCEA) placed the court under a restriction that seriously limited evidence that could be raised in cross-examination of a sexual relationship between a complainant and an accused. Under s 41(3) of the 1999 Act, such evidence was limited to sexual behaviour 'at or about the same time' as the event giving rise to the charge that was 'so similar' in nature that it could not be explained as a coincidence.

In *R v A* (2001), the defendant in a case of alleged rape claimed that the provisions of the YJCEA were contrary to Art 6 of the ECHR to the extent that they prevented him from putting forward a full and complete defence. In reaching its decision, the House of Lords emphasised the need to protect women from humiliating cross-examination and prejudicial but valueless evidence in respect of their previous sex lives. It nonetheless held that the restrictions in s 41 of the 1999 Act were *prima facie* capable of preventing an accused from putting forward relevant evidence that could be crucial to his defence.

However, rather than make a declaration of incompatibility, the House of Lords preferred to make use of s 3 of the HRA to allow s 41 of the YJCEA to be read as permitting the admission of evidence or questioning relating to a relevant issue in the case where it was considered necessary by the trial judge to make the trial fair. The test of admissibility of evidence of previous sexual relations between an accused and a complainant under s 41(3) of the 1999 Act was whether the evidence was so relevant to the issue of consent that to exclude it would be to endanger the fairness of the trial under Art 6 of the Convention. Where the line is to be drawn is left to the judgment of trial judges. In reaching its decision, the House of Lords was well aware that its interpretation of s 41 did a violence to its actual meaning, but it nonetheless felt it within its power so to do.

In *Re S* (2002), the Court of Appeal used s 3 of the HRA in such a way as to create new guidelines for the operation of the Children Act 1989, which increased the courts' powers to intervene in the interests of children taken into care under the Act. This extension of the courts' powers in the pursuit of the improved treatment of such children was achieved by reading the Act in such a way as to allow the courts increased discretion to make interim rather than final care orders, and to establish what were referred to as 'starred milestones' within a child's care plan. If such starred milestones were not achieved within a reasonable time, then the courts could be approached to deliver fresh directions. In effect, what the Court of Appeal was doing was setting up a new and more active regime of court supervision in care cases.

The House of Lords, however, although sympathetic to the aims of the Court of Appeal, felt that it had exceeded its powers of interpretation under s 3 of the HRA and, in its exercise of judicial creativity, it had usurped the function of Parliament.

Lord Nicholls explained the operation of s 3:

> The Human Rights Act reserves the amendment of primary legislation to Parliament. By this means the Act seeks to preserve parliamentary sovereignty. The Act maintains the constitutional boundary. Interpretation of statutes is a matter for the courts; the enactment of statutes, are matters for Parliament . . . [but that any interpretation which] departs substantially from a fundamental feature of an Act of Parliament is likely to have crossed the boundary between interpretation and amendment.

Unfortunately, the Court of Appeal had overstepped that boundary.

In *Ghaidan v Godin-Mendoza*, the Court of Appeal used s 3 to extend the rights of same-sex partners to inherit a statutory tenancy under the Rent Act 1977. In *Fitzpatrick v Sterling Housing Association Ltd* (1999), the House of Lords had extended the rights of such individuals to inherit the lesser assured tenancy by including them within the deceased person's family. It declined to allow them to inherit statutory tenancies, however, on the grounds that they could not be considered to be the wife or husband of the deceased as the Act required. In *Ghaidan v Godin-Mendoza*, the Court of Appeal held that the Rent Act 1977, as it had been construed by the House of Lords in *Fitzpatrick*, was incompatible with Art 14 of the ECHR on the grounds of its discriminatory treatment of surviving same-sex partners. The court, however, decided that the failing could be remedied by reading the words 'as his or her wife or husband' in the Act as meaning 'as if they were his or her wife or husband'. The Court of Appeal's decision and reasoning were subsequently confirmed by the House in 2004 in *Ghaidan v Godin-Mendoza*. *Mendoza* is of particular interest in the fact that it shows how the HRA can permit lower courts to avoid previous and otherwise binding decisions of the House of Lords. It also clearly shows the extent to which s 3 increases the powers of the judiciary in relation to statutory interpretation. In spite of this potential increased power, the House of Lords found itself unable to use s 3 in *Bellinger v Bellinger* (2003). The case related to the rights of transsexuals and the court found itself unable, or at least unwilling, to interpret s 11(c) of the Matrimonial Causes Act 1973 in such a way as to allow a male to female transsexual to be treated in law as a female. Nonetheless, the court did issue a declaration of incompatibility (see below for explanation).

Declarations of incompatibility

Where a court cannot interpret a piece of primary legislation in such a way as to make it compatible with the ECHR, it cannot declare the legislation invalid, but it can make a declaration that the legislation in question is not compatible with the rights provided by the Convention. The first declaration of incompatibility was issued in *R v (1) Mental Health Review Tribunal, North & East London Region (2) Secretary of State for Health ex p H* in March 2001. In that case, the Court of Appeal held that ss 72 and

73 of the Mental Health Act 1983 were incompatible with Art 5(1) and (4) of the ECHR, inasmuch as they reversed the normal burden of proof by requiring the detained person to show that they should not be detained, rather than placing the burden on the authorities to show that they should be detained.

Wilson v First County Trust (2000) was, however, the first case in which a court indicated its likelihood of its making a declaration of incompatibility under s 4 of the HRA.

❖ KEY CASE *Wilson v First County Trust* (2000)

Facts:

Section 127(3) of Consumer Credit Act (CCA) 1974, proscribed the enforcement of any consumer credit agreement which did not comply with the requirements of the Act. Wilson had borrowed £5,000 from First County Trust (FCT) and had pledged her car as security for the loan. Wilson was to be charged a fee of £250 for drawing up the loan documentation but asked FCT to add it to the loan, which they agreed to do. The effect of this was that the loan document stated that the amount of the loan was £5,250. This, however, was inaccurate, as in reality the extra £250 was not part of the loan as such; rather, it was part of the charge for the loan. The loan document had therefore been drawn up improperly and did not comply with the requirement of s 61 of the CCA 1974. When Wilson subsequently failed to pay the loan at the end of the agreed period, FCT stated their intention of selling the car unless she paid £7,000. Wilson brought proceedings: (a) for a declaration that the agreement was unenforceable by reason of s 127(3) of the 1974 Act because of the misstatement of the amount of the loan; and (b) for the agreement to be reopened on the basis that it was an extortionate credit bargain.

At first instance the judge rejected Wilson's first claim but reopened the agreement and substituted a lower rate of interest, and Wilson subsequently redeemed her car on payment of £6,900. However, she then successfully appealed against the judge's decision as to the enforceability of the agreement, the Court of Appeal holding that s 127(3) clearly and undoubtedly had the effect of preventing the enforcement of the original agreement and Wilson was entitled to the repayment of the money she had paid to redeem her car. Consequently, Wilson not only got her car back but also retrieved the money she paid to FCT, who lost their money completely. In reaching its decision, however, the Court of Appeal expressed the opinion that it was at least arguable that s 127(3) was incompatible with Art 6(1) and/or Protocol 1 of Art 1 of the ECHR. First, the absolute prohibition of enforcement of the agreement appeared to be a disproportionate restriction on the right of the lender to have the enforceability of its loan determined by the court contrary to Art 6(1); and secondly, to deprive FCT of its property – that is, the money which it had lent to Wilson – appeared to be contrary to Protocol 1 of Art 1. The Court of Appeal's final decision to issue a declaration of incompatibility was taken on appeal to the House of Lords.

Decision:

The House of Lords overturned the earlier declaration of incompatibility. In reaching its decision, the House of Lords held that the Court of Appeal had wrongly used its powers retrospectively to cover an agreement that had been entered into before the HRA itself had come into force. This ground in itself was enough to overturn the immediate decision of the Court of Appeal. Nonetheless, the House of Lords went on to consider the compatibility question, and once again it disagreed with the lower court's decision. In the view of the House of Lords, the provision of the CCA 1974 was extremely severe in its consequences for the lender, to the extent that its provisions might even appear unreasonable on occasion. However, once again the court recognised a powerful social interest in the need to protect unsophisticated borrowers from potentially unscrupulous lenders. In seeking to protect this interest, the legislature could not be said to have acted in a disproportionate manner. Consequently, s 127(3) and (4) of the CCA 1974 was not incompatible with Art 1 of the First Protocol to the ECHR.

1.4 The European Union: Law and Institutions

This section examines the various ways in which law comes into existence. Although it is possible to distinguish domestic and European sources of law, it is necessary to locate the former firmly within its wider European context; in line with that requirement, this section begins with an outline of that context.

1.4.1 European Union

Ever since the UK joined the European Economic Community (EEC), subsequently the European Community (EC) and now the European Union (EU) it has progressively, but effectively, passed the power to create laws which have effect in this country to the wider European institutions. In effect, the UK's legislative, executive and judicial powers are now controlled by, and can only be operated within, the framework of EU law. It is essential, therefore, that the contemporary student of business law is aware of the operation of the legislative and judicial powers of the EU.

Before the UK joined the EU, its law was just as foreign as law made under any other jurisdiction. On joining the EU, however, the UK and its citizens accepted and became subject to EU law. This subjection to European law remains the case even where the parties to any transaction are themselves both UK subjects. In other words, in areas where it is applicable, EU law supersedes any existing UK law to the contrary.

An example of EU law invalidating the operation of UK legislation can be found in the first *Factortame* case.

❖ KEY CASE ***Factortame Ltd v Secretary of State for Transport (No 1)*** **(1989)**

Facts:

The common fishing policy, established by the EEC, as it then was, had placed limits on the amount of fish that any member country's fishing fleet was permitted to catch. In order to gain access to British fish stocks and quotas, Spanish fishing boat owners formed British companies and re-registered their boats as British. In order to prevent what it saw as an abuse and an encroachment on the rights of indigenous fishermen, the UK Government introduced the Merchant Shipping Act 1988, which provided that any fishing company seeking to register as British must have its principal place of business in the UK and at least 75% of its shareholders must be British nationals. This effectively debarred the Spanish boats from taking up any of the British fishing quota. Some 95 Spanish boat owners applied to the British courts for judicial review of the Merchant Shipping Act 1988 on the basis that it was contrary to EU law.

The High Court decided to refer the question of the legality of the legislation to the European Court of Justice (ECJ) under what is currently Art 267 of the Treaty on the Functioning of the European Union (TFEU) (formerly Art 234 and Art 177 of previous versions of the treaty), but in the meantime granted interim relief, in the form of an injunction disapplying the operation of the legislation, to the fishermen. On appeal, the Court of Appeal removed the injunction, a decision confirmed by the House of Lords. However, the House of Lords referred the question of the relationship of Community law and contrary domestic law to the ECJ. Effectively, they were asking whether the domestic courts should follow the domestic law or Community law.

Decision:

The ECJ ruled that the Treaty of Rome, the TFEU as it now is, requires domestic courts to give effect to the directly enforceable provisions of EU law and, in doing so, such courts are required to ignore any national law that runs counter to EU law.

The House of Lords then renewed the interim injunction. The ECJ later ruled that, in relation to the original referral from the High Court, the Merchant Shipping Act 1988 was contrary to EU law and therefore the Spanish fishing companies should be able to sue for compensation in the UK courts. The subsequent claims also went all the way to the House of Lords before it was finally settled in October 2000 that the UK was liable to pay compensation, which has been estimated at between £50 million and £100 million.

The long-term process leading to the, as yet still to be attained, establishment of an integrated European Union was a response to two factors: the disasters of the Second World War; and the emergence of the Soviet Bloc in Eastern Europe. The aim was to link the separate European countries, particularly France and Germany, together in such a manner as to prevent the outbreak of future armed hostilities. The first step in this process was the establishment of a European Coal and Steel Community. The next step towards integration was the formation of the European Economic Community (EEC) under the Treaty of Rome in 1957. The UK joined the EEC in 1973. The Treaty of Rome has subsequently been amended in the further pursuit of integration as the Community has expanded. Thus, the Single European Act (SEA) 1986 established a single economic market within the EC and widened the use of majority voting in the Council of Ministers. The Maastricht Treaty further accelerated the move towards a federal European supranational State, in the extent to which it recognised Europe as a social and political – as well as an economic – community. Previous Conservative Governments of the UK resisted the emergence of the EU as anything other than an economic market and objected to, and resiled from, various provisions aimed at social, as opposed to economic, affairs. Thus, the UK was able to opt out of the Social Chapter of the Treaty of Maastricht. The new Labour administration in the UK had no such reservations and, as a consequence, the Treaty of Amsterdam 1997 incorporated the European Social Charter into the EC Treaty which, of course, applies to the UK.

As the establishment of the single market within the European Community progressed, it was suggested that its operation would be greatly facilitated by the adoption of a common currency, or at least a more closely integrated monetary system. Thus, in 1979, the European Monetary System (EMS) was established, under which individual national currencies were valued against a nominal currency called the ECU and allocated a fixed rate within which they were allowed to fluctuate to a limited extent. Britain was a member of the EMS until 1992, when financial speculation against the pound forced its withdrawal. Nonetheless, other members of the EC continued to pursue the policy of monetary union, now entitled European Monetary Union (EMU), and January 1999 saw the installation of the new european currency, the euro, which has now replaced national currencies within what is now known as the Eurozone. The UK did not join the EMU at its inception and there is little chance that membership will appear on the political agenda for the foreseeable future.

The general aim of the EU was set out in Art 2 of the Treaty of Rome, the founding treaty of the EEC.

Among the policies originally detailed in Art 3 were included:

- the elimination between Member States of customs duties and of quantitative restrictions on the import and export of goods;
- the establishment of a common customs tariff and a common commercial policy towards third countries;
- the abolition between Member States of obstacles to the freedom of movement for persons, services and capital;
- the adoption of a common agricultural policy;
- the adoption of a common transport policy;
- the harmonisation of laws of Member States to the extent required to facilitate the proper functioning of the single market;
- the creation of a European Social Fund in order to improve the employment opportunities of workers in the Community and to improve their standard of living.

These essentially economic imperatives were subsequently extended to cover more social, as opposed to purely economic, matters and now incorporate policies relating to education, health, consumer protection, the environment and culture generally.

1.4.2 Sources of EU law

EU law, depending on its nature and source, may have direct effect on the domestic laws of its various members; that is, it may be open to individuals to rely on it, without the need for their particular State to have enacted the law within its own legal system (see *Factortame (No 1)* (1989)).

There are two types of direct effect. Vertical direct effect means that the individual can rely on EU law in any action in relation to their government, but cannot use it against other individuals. Horizontal direct effect allows the individual to use an EU provision in an action against other individuals. Other EU provisions take effect only when they have been specifically enacted within the various legal systems within the EU.

The sources of EU law are fourfold:

- internal treaties and protocols;
- international agreements;
- secondary legislation; and
- decisions of the CJEU.

Internal treaties

Internal treaties govern the Member States of the EU and, as has been seen, anything contained therein supersedes domestic legal provisions.

As long as Treaties are of a mandatory nature and are stated with sufficient clarity and precision, they have both vertical and horizontal effect (*Van Gend en Loos v Nederlandse Administratie der Belastingen* (1963)).

As has previously been mentioned, the originating treaty of the EU was the Treaty of Rome, which was subsequently altered and supplemented by a number of subsequent treaties. The most recent of these treaties is the Lisbon Treaty, which led to significant changes in the constitution and operation of the EU. The origin of the Lisbon Treaty lay in *The Convention on the Future of Europe*, which was established in February 2002 by the then members to consider the establishment of a European

Constitution. The Convention produced a draft constitution, which it was hoped would provide a more simple, streamlined and transparent procedure for internal decision-making within the Union and to enhance its profile on the world stage. Among the proposals for the new constitution were the following:

- the establishment of a new office of President of the European Union. This is currently Herman Van Rompuy of Belgium;
- the appointment of High Representative for Foreign Affairs. This position, effectively that of EU foreign minister, is currently held by Baroness Catherine Ashton from the UK;
- the shift to a two-tier Commission;
- fewer national vetoes;
- increased power for the European Parliament;
- simplified voting power;
- the establishment of an EU defence force by 'core members';
- the establishment of a charter of fundamental rights.

In the months of May and June 2005 the move towards the European Constitution came to a juddering halt when first the French and then the Dutch electorates voted against its implementation. However, as with most EU initiatives, the new constitution did not disappear and re-emerged as the Treaty of Lisbon, signed by all the members in December 2007. In legal form, the Lisbon Treaty merely amended the existing treaties, rather than replacing them as the previous constitution had proposed. In practical terms, however, all the essential changes that would have been delivered by the constitution were contained in the treaty.

The necessary alterations to the fundamental treaties governing the EU, brought about by the Lisbon Treaty, were published at the end of March 2010. As a result there are three newly consolidated treaties:

- *The Treaty on European Union* (TEU)
  Article 1 of this treaty makes it clear that 'The Union shall be founded on the present Treaty and on the Treaty on the Functioning of the European Union (hereinafter referred to as 'the Treaties'). Those two Treaties shall have the same legal value. *The Union shall replace and succeed the European Community*.'
- *The Treaty on the Functioning of the European Union* (TFEU)
  Article 2 of this treaty provides that:

  > 'When the Treaties confer on the Union exclusive competence in a specific area, only the Union may legislate and adopt legally binding acts, the Member States being able to do so themselves only if so empowered by the Union or for the implementation of Union acts.'

  Article 3 specifies that the Union shall have exclusive competence in the following areas:

  (a) customs union;
  (b) the establishing of the competition rules necessary for the functioning of the internal market;
  (c) monetary policy for the Member States whose currency is the euro;
  (d) the conservation of marine biological resources under the common fisheries policy;
  (e) common commercial policy.

  Additionally Art 3 provides that the Union shall also have exclusive competence for the conclusion of an international agreement when its conclusion is provided for in a legislative act of the Union or is necessary to enable the Union to exercise its internal competence, or in so far as its conclusion may affect common rules or alter their scope.

- *The Charter of Fundamental Rights of the European Union* (CFREU)
  Many Member States, including the UK, have negotiated opt outs from some of the provisions of the charter.

Upon the UK joining the EU, the Treaty of Rome was incorporated into UK law by the European Communities Act 1972 and it remains bound by all the subsequent provisions it has not opted out of.

International treaties

International treaties are negotiated with other nations by the European Commission on behalf of the EU as a whole and are binding on the individual members of the EU.

Secondary legislation

Three types of legislation may be introduced by the European Council and Commission. These are as follows:

- *Regulations* apply to, and within, Member States generally, without the need for those States to pass their own legislation. They are binding and enforceable from the time of their creation, and individual States do not have to pass any legislation to give effect to regulations. Thus, in *Macarthys Ltd v Smith* (1979), on a referral from the Court of Appeal to the ECJ, it was held that Art 141 (formerly Art 119) entitled the claimant to assert rights that were not available to her under national legislation (the Equal Pay Act 1970) which had been enacted before the UK had joined the EEC. Whereas the national legislation clearly did not include a comparison between former and present employees, Art 141's reference to 'equal pay for equal work' did encompass such a situation. Smith was consequently entitled to receive a similar level of remuneration to that of the former male employee who had done her job previously.

  Regulations must be published in the Official Journal of the EU. The decision as to whether or not a law should be enacted in the form of a regulation is usually left to the Commission, but there are areas where the TFEU requires that the regulation form must be used. These areas relate to: the rights of workers to remain in Member States of which they are not nationals; the provision of State aid to particular indigenous undertakings or industries; the regulation of EU accounts; and budgetary procedures.
- *Directives*, on the other hand, state general goals and leave the precise implementation in the appropriate form to the individual Member States. Directives, however, tend to state the means as well as the ends to which they are aimed and the ECJ will give direct effect to directives which are sufficiently clear and complete (see *Van Duyn v Home Office* (1974)). Directives usually provide Member States with a time limit within which they are required to implement the provision within their own national laws. If they fail to do so, or implement the directive incompletely, then individuals may be able to cite and rely on the directive in their dealings with the State in question. Further, *Francovich v Italy* (1991) established that individuals who have suffered as a consequence of a Member State's failure to implement EU law may seek damages against that State.

  In contract law, the provisions in the Unfair Terms in Consumer Contracts Regulations 1994 (SI 1994/3159), repealed and replaced by the Unfair Terms in Consumer Contracts Regulations 1999 (SI 1999/2083), are an example of UK law being introduced in response to EU directives, and company law is continuously subject to the process of European harmonisation through directives.
- *Decisions* on the operation of European laws and policies are not intended to have general effect but are aimed at particular States or individuals. They have the force of law under TFEU Art 288 (formerly Art 249). On the other hand, neither recommendations nor opinions in relation to the operation of Union law have any binding force (Art 288), although they may be taken into account in trying to clarify any ambiguities in domestic law.

Judgments of the CJEU

The Court of Justice of the European Union (CJEU, formerly ECJ) is the judicial arm of the EU and, in the field of EU law its judgments overrule those of national courts. Under Art 267 (formerly Art 234) of the TFEU, national courts have the right to apply to the CJEU for a preliminary ruling on a point of Union law before deciding a case.

The mechanism through which EU law becomes immediately and directly effective in the UK is provided by s 2(1) of the European Communities Act 1972. Section 2(2) gives power to designated ministers or departments to introduce Orders in Council to give effect to other non-directly effective Union law.

1.4.3 The institutions of the EU

The major institutions of the EU are: the Council of Ministers; the European Parliament; the European Commission; and the European Court of Justice.

The Council of Ministers

The Council is made up of ministerial representatives of each of the 27 Member States of the EU. The actual composition of the Council varies, depending on the nature of the matter to be considered: when considering economic matters, the various States will be represented by their finance ministers; if the matter before the Council relates to agriculture, the various agriculture ministers will attend. The Council of Ministers is the supreme decision-making body of the EU and, as such, has the final say in deciding upon EU legislation. Although it acts on recommendations and proposals made to it by the Commission, it does have the power to instruct the Commission to undertake particular investigations and to submit detailed proposals for its consideration.

At present Council decisions are taken on a mixture of voting procedures. Some measures only require a simple majority; in others, a procedure of qualified majority voting is used; in yet others, unanimity is required. Qualified majority voting is the procedure in which the votes of the 27 Member countries are weighted in proportion to their population from 29 down to three votes each and a specific number of votes is required to pass any specific proposal.

However, the Lisbon Treaty introduces changes to this procedure. As a consequence, although the present system will continue until November 2014, after that date the qualified majority voting procedure will be fundamentally changed, with the Council, from then on, adopting a 'double majority' system under which a proposal must be supported by both 55% of the EU Member States, i.e. 15 of the current 27 members, and at least 65% of the population of the EU. In addition for a blocking minority to prevent the adoption of a proposal, that majority must include the votes of at least four Member States. However, between November 2014 and March 2017 any Member State may request that the current voting system be applied instead of the new double majority system.

The European Parliament

The European Parliament is the directly elected European institution and, to that extent, it can be seen as the body which exercises democratic control over the operation of the EU. As in national Parliaments, members are elected to represent constituencies, the elections being held every five years. Following the Lisbon Treaty there is a maximum total of 751 members, divided amongst the 27 Member States in approximate proportion to the size of their various populations. The Treaty also provides that that no Member State can have fewer than 6 or more than 86 seats (from 2014). Members of the European Parliament do not sit in national groups but operate within political groupings.

The European Parliament's General Secretariat is based in Luxembourg and, although the Parliament sits in plenary session in Strasbourg for one week in each month, its detailed and preparatory work is carried out through 18 permanent committees, which usually meet in Brussels.

These permanent committees consider proposals from the Commission and provide the full Parliament with reports of such proposals for discussion.

Originally, the powers of the Parliament were merely advisory and supervisory, but its role and functions have increased over time and as a consequence of the changes introduced by the Lisbon Treaty, the previous 'co-decision procedure' under which proposals required to be approved by both the Parliament and the Council have been extended to a further 40 areas, to greatly enhance the power and prestige of the Parliament. In its supervisory role, the Parliament scrutinises the activities of the Commission and has the power to remove the Commission by passing a motion of censure against it by a two-thirds majority.

The Parliament, together with the Council of Ministers, is the budgetary authority of the EU. The budget is drawn up by the Commission and is presented to both the Council and the Parliament. As regards what is known as obligatory expenditure, the Council has the final say but, in relation to non-obligatory expenditure, the Parliament has the final decision as to whether to approve the budget or not.

The European Commission

The European Commission is the executive of the EU and, in that role, is responsible for the administration of EU policies. There are 27 Commissioners, chosen from the various Member States to serve for renewable terms of four years. Commissioners are appointed to head departments with specific responsibility for furthering particular areas of EU policy. Once appointed, Commissioners are expected to act in the general interest of the EU as a whole, rather than in the partial interest of their own home country.

In pursuit of EU policy, the Commission is responsible for ensuring that Treaty obligations between the Member States are met and that EU laws relating to individuals are enforced. In order to fulfil these functions, the Commission has been provided with extensive powers in relation to both the investigation of potential breaches of EU law and the subsequent punishment of offenders. The classic area in which these powers can be seen in operation is in the area of competition law. Under Arts 101 and 102 (formerly Arts 81 and 82) of the TFEU, the Commission has substantial powers to investigate and control potential monopolies and anti-competitive behaviour. It has used these powers to levy what, in the case of private individuals, would amount to huge fines where breaches of EU competition law have been discovered. In November 2001, the Commission imposed a then record fine of £534 million on a cartel of 13 pharmaceutical companies that had operated a price-fixing scheme within the EU in relation to the market for vitamins. The highest individual fine was against the Swiss company Roche, which had to pay £288 million, while the German company BASF was fined £185 million. The lowest penalty levelled was against Aventis, which was only fined £3 million due to its agreement to provide the Commission with evidence as to the operation of the cartel. Otherwise its fine would have been £70 million. The Commission took two years to investigate the operation of what it classified as a highly organised cartel, holding regular meetings to collude on prices, exchange sales figures and co-ordinate price increases.

In the following month, December 2001, Roche was again fined a further £39 million for engaging in another cartel, this time in the citric acid market. The total fines imposed in this instance amounted to £140 million.

In 2004 the then EU Competition Commissioner, Mario Monti, levied an individual record fine of €497 million (£340 million) on Microsoft for abusing its dominant position in the PC operating systems market. In addition, the Commissioner required Microsoft to disclose 'complete and accurate' interface documents to allow rival servers to operate with the Microsoft windows system, or face penalties of €2 million (£1.4 million) for each day of non-compliance. In January 2006 Microsoft offered to make available part of its source code – the basic instructions for the Windows operating system. In an assertion of its complete compliance with Mario Monti's decision, Microsoft insisted it had actually gone beyond the Commission's remedy by opening up part of the source code behind Windows to rivals willing to pay a licence fee.

The offer, however, was dismissed by many as a public relations exercise. As a lawyer for Microsoft's rivals explained, 'Microsoft is offering to dump a huge load of source code on companies that have not asked for source code and cannot use it. Without a road map that says how to use the code, a software engineer will not be able to design inter-operable products.'

In February 2006 Microsoft repeated its claim that it had fully complied with the Commission's requirements. It also announced that it wanted an oral hearing on the allegations before national competition authorities and senior EU officials, a proposal that many saw as merely a delaying tactic postponing the imposition of the threatened penalties until the court of first instance has heard the company's appeal against the original allegation of abuse of its dominant position and, of course, the related €497 million fine. In July 2006, the Commission fined Microsoft an additional €280.5 million, €1.5 million per day from 16 December 2005 to 20 June 2006. On 17 September 2007, Microsoft lost their appeal and in October 2007, it announced that it would comply with the rulings.

In May 2009 the Commission levied a new record individual fine against the American computer chip manufacturer Intel for abusing its dominance of the microchip market. Intel was accused of using discounts to squeeze its nearest rival, Advanced Micro Devices, (AMD), out of the market. The amount of the fine was €1.06 billion, equivalent to £950 million, or $1.45 billion. Intel appealed against the finding and the fine in September 2009. As yet, the appeal has not been decided.

In addition to these executive functions, the Commission also has a vital part to play in the EU's legislative process. The Council can only act on proposals put before it by the Commission. The Commission, therefore, has a duty to propose to the Council measures that will advance the achievement of the EU's general policies.

The Court of Justice of the European Union (CJEU)

The CJEU is the judicial arm of the EU and, in the field of Union law, its judgments overrule those of national courts. It consists of 27 judges, assisted by 8 Advocates General, and sits in Luxembourg. The role of the Advocate General is to investigate the matter submitted to the CJEU and to produce a report, together with a recommendation for the consideration of the Court. The CJEU is free to accept the report or not, as it sees fit. A Court of First Instance, separate from the CJEU, was introduced by the Single European Act 1986. Under the Treaty of Lisbon it was renamed the General Court. It has jurisdiction in first instance cases, with appeals going to the CJEU on points of law. The former jurisdiction of the Court of First Instance, in relation to internal claims by EU employees was transferred to a newly created European Union Civil Service Tribunal in 2004. Together the three distinct courts constitute *the Court of Justice of the European Union*. The aim of introducing the two latter courts was to reduce the burden of work on the CJEU, but there is a right of appeal, on points of law only, to the full CJEU. In July 2000, an appeal against a fine imposed by the Commission in 1998 against Europe's biggest car producer, Volkswagen (VW), was successful to the extent that the CJEU reduced the amount of the fine by £7.5 million. Unfortunately for VW, it upheld the essential finding of the Commission and imposed a fine of £57 million on it, then a record for any individual company. VW was found guilty of 'an infringement which was particularly serious, the seriousness being magnified by the size of the Volkswagen group'. What the company had done was to prevent customers, essentially those in Germany and Austria, from benefiting from the weakness of the Italian lire between 1993 and 1996 by instructing the Italian dealers not to sell to foreign customers on the false basis that different specifications and warranty terms prevented cross-border sales. Not only had VW instructed that this should happen, but it threatened that Italian dealers would lose their franchises if they failed to comply.

The CJEU performs two key functions, as follows:

(a) It decides whether any measures adopted, or rights denied, by the Commission, Council or any national government are compatible with Treaty obligations. In October 2000, the ECJ (as it was then) annulled EC Directive 98/43, which required Member States to impose a ban on advertising and sponsorship relating to tobacco products, because it had been adopted on the basis of the wrong provisions of the EC Treaty. The Directive had been adopted on the basis of the provisions relating to the elimination of obstacles to the completion of the internal market, but the Court decided that, under the circumstances, it was difficult to see how a ban on tobacco advertising or sponsorship could facilitate the trade in tobacco products.

Although a partial prohibition on particular types of advertising or sponsorship might legitimately come within the internal market provisions of the Treaty, the Directive was clearly aimed at protecting public health, and it was therefore improper to base its adoption on freedom to provide services (*Germany v European Parliament and EU Council* (Case C-376/98)).

A Member State may fail to comply with its Treaty obligations in a number of ways. It might fail, or indeed, refuse, to comply with a provision of the Treaty or a regulation; alternatively, it might refuse to implement a directive within the allotted time provided for. Under such circumstances, the State in question will be brought before the CJEU, either by the Commission or by another Member State or, indeed, by individuals within the State concerned.

In 1996, following the outbreak of 'mad cow disease' (BSE) in the UK, the European Commission imposed a ban on the export of UK beef. The ban was partially lifted in 1998 and, subject to conditions relating to the documentation of an animal's history prior to slaughter, from 1 August 1999 exports satisfying those conditions were authorised for despatch within the Community. When the French Food Standards Agency continued to raise concerns about the safety of British beef, the Commission issued a protocol agreement, which declared that all meat and meat products from the UK would be distinctively marked as such. However, France continued in its refusal to lift the ban. Subsequently, the Commission applied to the CJEU for a declaration that France was in breach of Community law for failing to lift the prohibition on the sale of correctly labelled British beef in French territory. In December 2001, in *Commission of the European Communities v France*, the CJEU held that the French Government had failed to put forward a ground of defence capable of justifying the failure to implement the relevant decisions and was therefore in breach of Community law.

France was also fined in July 2005 for breaching EU fishing rules. On that occasion the CJEU imposed the first ever 'combination' penalty, under which a lump-sum fine was payable, but in addition France is liable to a periodic penalty for every six months until it has shown it is fully complying with EU fisheries laws. The CJEU set the lump sum fine at €20 million and the periodic penalty at €57.8 million.

The Court held that it is was possible and appropriate to impose both types of penalty at the same time, in circumstances where the breach of obligations has both continued for a long period and is inclined to persist.

(b) It provides authoritative rulings at the request of national courts under Art 267 (formerly Art 234) of the EC Treaty on the interpretation of points of Community law. When an application is made under Art 234, the national proceedings are suspended until such time as the determination of the point in question is delivered by the CJEU. Whilst the case is being decided by the CJEU, the national court is expected to provide appropriate interim relief, even if this involves going against a domestic legal provision (as in the *Factortame* case).

The question of the extent of the CJEU's authority arose in *Arsenal Football Club plc v Reed* (2003), which dealt with the sale of football souvenirs and memorabilia bearing the name of the football club and consequently infringing its registered trademarks. On first hearing, the Chancery Division of the High Court referred the question of the interpretation of the Trade Marks Directive (89/104) in relation to the issue of trademark infringement to the CJEU. After the CJEU had made its decision, the case came before Laddie J for application, who declined to follow its decision. The ground for so doing was that the ambit of the CJEU's powers was clearly set out in Art 234. Consequently, where, as in this case, the ECJ makes a finding of fact which reverses the finding of a national court on those facts, it exceeds its jurisdiction, and it follows that its decisions are not binding on the national court.

The Court of Appeal later reversed Laddie J's decision on the ground that the ECJ had not disregarded the conclusions of fact made at the original trial and, therefore, he should have followed its ruling and decided the case in the favour of Arsenal. Nonetheless, Laddie J's general point as to the ECJ's authority remains valid.

1.5 Domestic Legislation

If the institutions of the EU are sovereign within its boundaries then, within the more limited boundaries of the UK, the sovereign power to make law lies with Parliament. Under UK constitutional law, it is recognised that Parliament has the power to enact, revoke or alter such, and any, law as it sees fit. Coupled to this wide power is the convention that no one Parliament can bind its successors in such a way as to limit their absolute legislative powers. Although we still refer to our legal system as a common law system, and although the courts still have an important role to play in the interpretation of statutes, it has to be recognised that legislation is the predominant method of law making in contemporary society. It is necessary, therefore, to have a knowledge of the workings of the legislative procedure through which law is made.

1.5.1 The legislative process

As an outcome of various historical political struggles, Parliament, and in particular the House of Commons, has asserted its authority as the ultimate source of law making in the UK. Parliament's prerogative to make law is encapsulated in the notion of the supremacy of Parliament.

Parliament consists of three distinct elements: the House of Commons, the House of Lords and the Monarch. Before any legislative proposal, known at that stage as a Bill, can become an Act of Parliament, it must proceed through and be approved by both Houses of Parliament and must receive the royal assent.

Before the formal law making procedure is started, the Government of the day, which in practice decides and controls what actually becomes law, may enter into a process of consultation with concerned individuals or organisations.

Green Papers are consultation documents issued by the Government which set out and invite comments from interested parties on particular proposals for legislation.

After considering any response, the Government may publish a second document in the form of a White Paper, in which it sets out its firm proposals for legislation.

A Bill must be given three readings in both the House of Commons and the House of Lords before it can be presented for the royal assent. It is possible to commence the procedure in either House, although money Bills must be placed before the Commons in the first instance.

Before it can become law, any Bill introduced in the Commons must go through five distinct procedures:

- *First reading*
  This is a purely formal procedure, in which the Bill's title is read and a date is set for its second reading.

- *Second reading*
  At this stage, the general principles of the Bill are subject to extensive debate. The second reading is the critical point in the process of a Bill. At the end, a vote may be taken on its merits and, if it is approved, it is likely that it will eventually find a place in the statute book.
- *Committee stage*
  After its second reading, the Bill is passed to a standing committee, whose job is to consider the provisions of the Bill in detail, clause by clause. The committee has the power to amend it in such a way as to ensure that it conforms with the general approval given by the House at its second reading.
- *Report stage*
  At this point, the standing committee reports the Bill back to the House for consideration of any amendments made during the committee stage.
- *Third reading*
  Further debate may take place during this stage, but it is restricted solely to matters relating to the content of the Bill; questions relating to the general principles of the Bill cannot be raised.

When a Bill has passed all of these stages, it is passed to the House of Lords for consideration. After this, the Bill is passed back to the Commons, which must then consider any amendments to the Bill that might have been introduced by the Lords. Where one House refuses to agree to the amendments made by the other, Bills can be repeatedly passed between them; since Bills must complete their process within the life of a particular parliamentary session, however a failure to reach agreement within that period might lead to the total failure of the Bill.

Since the Parliament Acts of 1911 and 1949, the blocking power of the House of Lords has been restricted as follows:

- a 'Money Bill', that is, one containing only financial provisions, can be enacted without the approval of the House of Lords after a delay of one month;
- any other Bill can be delayed by one year by the House of Lords.

The royal assent is required before any Bill can become law. The procedural nature of the royal assent was highlighted by the Royal Assent Act 1967, which reduced the process of acquiring royal assent to a formal reading out of the short titles of any Act in both Houses of Parliament.

An Act of Parliament comes into effect on the date that royal assent is given, unless there is any provision to the contrary in the Act itself.

1.5.2 Types of legislation

Legislation can be categorised in a number of ways. For example, distinctions can be drawn between:

- *public Acts*, which relate to matters affecting the general public. These can be further subdivided into either Government Bills or Private Members' Bills;
- *private Acts*, which relate to the powers and interests of particular individuals or institutions, although the provision of statutory powers to particular institutions can have a major effect on the general public. For example, companies may be given the power to appropriate private property through compulsory purchase orders; and
- *enabling legislation*, which gives power to a particular person or body to oversee the production of the specific details required for the implementation of the general purposes stated in the parent Act. These specifics are achieved through the enactment of statutory instruments. (See 1.5.3 below, for a consideration of delegated legislation.)

Acts of Parliament can also be distinguished on the basis of the function that they are designed to carry out. Some are unprecedented and cover new areas of activity previously not governed by legal rules, but other Acts are aimed at rationalising or amending existing legislative provisions:

- *Consolidating legislation* is designed to bring together provisions previously contained in a number of different Acts, without actually altering them. The Companies Act 1985 is an example of a consolidation Act. It brought together provisions contained in numerous amending Acts which had been introduced since the previous Consolidation Act 1948.
- *Codifying legislation* seeks not just to bring existing statutory provisions under one Act, but also looks to give statutory expression to common law rules. The classic examples of such legislation are the Partnership Act 1890 and the Sale of Goods Act 1893, now 1979.
- *Amending legislation* is designed to alter some existing legal provision. Amendment of an existing legislative provision can take one of two forms:
    - *textual amendments*, where the new provision substitutes new words for existing ones in a legislative text or introduces completely new words into that text. Altering legislation by means of textual amendment has one major drawback, in that the new provisions make very little sense on their own without the contextual reference of the original provision that it is designed to alter; or
    - *non-textual amendments* do not alter the actual wording of the existing text, but alter the operation or effect of those words. Non-textual amendments may have more immediate meaning than textual alterations, but they too suffer from the problem that, because they do not alter the original provisions, the two provisions have to be read together to establish the legislative intention.

  Neither method of amendment is completely satisfactory, but the Renton Committee on the Preparation of Legislation (1975, Cmnd 6053) favoured textual amendments over non-textual amendments.

1.5.3 Delegated legislation

In contemporary practice, the full scale procedure detailed above is usually only undergone in relation to enabling Acts. These Acts set out general principles and establish a framework within which certain individuals or organisations are given power to make particular rules designed to give practical effect to the enabling Act. The law produced through this procedure is referred to as 'delegated legislation'.

As has been stated, delegated legislation is law made by some person or body to whom Parliament has delegated its general law-making power. A validly enacted piece of delegated legislation has the same legal force and effect as the Act of Parliament under which it is enacted; equally, however, it only has effect to the extent that its enabling Act authorises it. Any action taken in excess of the powers granted is said to be *ultra vires* and the legality of such legislation can be challenged in the courts, as considered below.

In previous editions of this book the authors have, to a greater or lesser degree, focused on the increase in the power of Ministers of State to alter Acts of Parliament by means of statutory instruments in the pursuit of economic, business and regulatory efficiency.

The first of these (dis)empowering Acts of Parliament that brought this situation about was the Deregulation and Contracting Out Act (DCOA) 1994, introduced by the last Conservative Government. It was a classic example of the wide-ranging power that enabling legislation can extend to ministers in the attack on such primary legislation as was seen to impose unnecessary burdens on any trade, business or profession. Although the DCOA 1994 imposed the requirement that ministers should consult with interested parties to any proposed alteration, it nonetheless gave them extremely wide powers to alter primary legislation without the necessity of having to follow the same procedure as was required to enact that legislation in the first place. For that reason, deregulation orders were subject to a far more rigorous procedure (sometimes referred to as 'super-affirmative') than ordinary statutory instruments. The powers were extended in its first term in office by the former Labour Government under the Regulatory Reform Act (RRA) 2001.

It was, however, only with the proposed Legislative and Regulatory Reform Bill 2006 that alarm bells started to ring generally. This critical reaction was based on the proposed power contained in the Act for ministers to create new criminal offences, punishable with less than two years imprisonment, without the need for a debate in Parliament. However as a result of much opposition, the Government amended the legislation to ensure that its powers could only be used in relation to business and regulatory efficiency.

It should also be remembered that s 10 of the HRA allows ministers to amend primary legislation by way of statutory instrument where a court has issued a declaration of incompatibility (see 1.3 above).

The output of delegated legislation in any year greatly exceeds the output of Acts of Parliament. For example, in 2011, Parliament passed just 25 general public Acts, in comparison to over 3,000 statutory instruments. In statistical terms, therefore, it is at least arguable that delegated legislation is actually more significant than primary Acts of Parliament.

There are various types of delegated legislation, as follows:

- *Orders in Council* permit the Government, through the Privy Council, to make law. The Privy Council is nominally a non-party political body of eminent parliamentarians, but in effect it is simply a means through which the Government, in the form of a committee of ministers, can introduce legislation without the need to go through the full parliamentary process. Although it is usual to cite situations of State emergency as exemplifying occasions when the Government will resort to the use of Orders in Council, in actual fact a great number of Acts are brought into operation through Orders in Council. Perhaps the widest scope for Orders in Council is to be found in relation to EU law, for, under s 2(2) of the European Communities Act 1972, ministers can give effect to provisions of Community law which do not have direct effect.
- *Statutory instruments* are the means through which government ministers introduce particular regulations under powers delegated to them by Parliament in enabling legislation. Examples have already been considered in relation to the DCOA 1994.
- *Bylaws* are the means through which local authorities and other public bodies can make legally binding rules. Bylaws may be made by local authorities under such enabling legislation as the Local Government Act 1972, and public corporations are empowered to make regulations relating to their specific sphere of operation. *Court rule committees* are empowered to make the rules which govern procedure in the particular courts over which they have delegated authority under such acts as the Supreme Court Act 1981, the County Courts Act 1984 and the Magistrates' Courts Act 1980.
- *Professional regulations* governing particular occupations may be given the force of law under provisions delegating legislative authority to certain professional bodies which are empowered to regulate the conduct of their members. An example is the power given to The Law Society, under the Solicitors Act 1974, to control the conduct of practising solicitors.

1.5.4 Advantages of the use of delegated legislation

The advantages of using delegated legislation are as follows:

- *Timesaving*
  Delegated legislation can be introduced quickly where necessary in particular cases and permits rules to be changed in response to emergencies or unforeseen problems.
  The use of delegated legislation, however, also saves parliamentary time generally. Given the pressure on debating time in Parliament and the highly detailed nature of typical delegated legislation, not to mention its sheer volume, Parliament would not have time to consider each individual piece of law that is enacted in the form of delegated legislation.
- *Access to particular expertise*
  Related to the first advantage is the fact that the majority of Members of Parliament (MPs) simply do not have sufficient expertise to consider such provisions effectively. Given the highly specialised and extremely technical nature of many of the regulations that are introduced through delegated legislation, it is necessary that those who are authorised to introduce the legislation should have access to the external expertise required to formulate such regulations. With regard to bylaws, it practically goes without saying that local and specialist knowledge should give rise to more appropriate rules than reliance on the general enactments of Parliament.
- *Flexibility*
  The use of delegated legislation permits ministers to respond on an *ad hoc* basis to particular problems as and when they arise, and provides greater flexibility in the regulation of activity which is subject to the ministers' overview.

1.5.5 Disadvantages in the prevalence of delegated legislation

Disadvantages in the prevalence of delegated legislation are as follows:

- *Accountability*
  A key issue in the use of delegated legislation concerns the question of accountability and the erosion of the constitutional role of Parliament. Parliament is presumed to be the source of legislation but, with respect to delegated legislation, individual MPs are not the source of the law. Certain people, notably government ministers and the civil servants who work under them to produce the detailed provisions of delegated legislation, are the real source of such - regulations. Even allowing for the fact that they are in effect operating on powers delegated to them from Parliament, it is not beyond questioning whether this procedure does not give them more power than might be thought appropriate or, indeed, constitutionally correct.
- *Scrutiny*
  The question of general accountability raises the need for effective scrutiny, but the very form of delegated legislation makes it extremely difficult for ordinary MPs to fully understand what is being enacted and, therefore, to effectively monitor it. This difficulty arises in part from the tendency for such regulations to be highly specific, detailed and technical. This problem of comprehension and control is compounded by the fact that regulations appear outside the context of their enabling legislation but only have any real meaning in that context.
- *Bulk*
  The problems faced by ordinary MPs in effectively keeping abreast of delegated legislation are further increased by the sheer mass of such legislation, and if parliamentarians cannot keep up with the flow of delegated legislation, the question has to be asked as to how the general public can be expected to do so.

1.5.6 Control over delegated legislation

The foregoing difficulties and potential shortcomings in the use of delegated legislation are, at least to a degree, mitigated by the fact that specific controls have been established to oversee the use of delegated legislation. These controls take two forms:

- *Parliamentary control over delegated legislation*
  Power to make delegated legislation is ultimately dependent upon the authority of Parliament, and Parliament retains general control over the procedure for enacting such law. New regulations, in the form of delegated legislation, are required to be laid before Parliament. This procedure takes one of two forms, depending on the provision of the enabling legislation. Some regulations require a positive resolution of one or both of the Houses of Parliament before they become law. Most Acts, however, simply require that regulations made under their auspices be placed before Parliament. They automatically become law after a period of 40 days, unless a resolution to annul them is passed. The problem with the negative resolution procedure is that it relies on Members of Parliament being sufficiently aware of the content, meaning and effect of the detailed provisions laid before them. Given the nature of such statutory legislation, such reliance is unlikely to prove secure.

  Since 1973, there has been a Joint Select Committee on Statutory Instruments, whose function it is to consider statutory instruments. This committee scrutinises statutory instruments from a technical point of view as regards drafting and has no power to question the substantive content or the policy implications of the regulation. Its effectiveness as a general control is, therefore, limited.

  The House of Commons has its own *Select Committee on Statutory Instruments*, which is appointed to consider all statutory instruments laid *only* before the House of Commons.

  EU legislation is overseen by a specific committee, as are local authority bylaws.
- *Judicial control of delegated legislation*
  It is possible for delegated legislation to be challenged through the procedure of judicial review, on the basis that the person or body to whom Parliament has delegated its authority has acted in a way that exceeds the limited powers delegated to them. Any provision which does not have this authority is *ultra vires* and void. Additionally, there is a presumption that any power delegated by Parliament is to be used in a reasonable manner and the courts may, on occasion, hold particular delegated legislation to be void on the basis that it is unreasonable. The power of the courts to scrutinise and control delegated legislation has been greatly increased by the introduction of the HRA. As has been noted previously, that Act does not give courts the power to strike down primary legislation as being incompatible with the rights contained in the ECHR. However, as – by definition – delegated legislation is not primary legislation, it follows that the courts now do have the power to declare invalid any such legislation which conflicts with the ECHR.

1.6 Case Law

The foregoing has highlighted the increased importance of legislation in today's society but, even allowing for this and the fact that case law can be overturned by legislation, the UK is still a common law system, and the importance and effectiveness of judicial creativity and common law principles and practices cannot be discounted. 'Case law' is the name given to the creation and refinement of law in the course of judicial decisions.

1.6.1 The meaning of precedent

The doctrine of binding precedent, or *stare decisis*, lies at the heart of the English common law system. It refers to the fact that, within the hierarchical structure of the English courts, a decision of a higher court will be binding on any court which is lower than it in that hierarchy. In general terms, this means that, when judges try cases, they will check to see whether a similar situation has already come before a court. If the precedent was set by a court of equal or higher status to the court deciding the new case, then the judge in that case should follow the rule of law established in the earlier case. Where the precedent is set by a court lower in the hierarchy, the judge in the new case does not have to follow it, but he will certainly consider it and will not overrule it without due consideration.

The operation of the doctrine of binding precedent depends on the existence of an extensive reporting service to provide access to previous judicial decisions. The earliest summaries of cases appeared in the Year Books but, since 1865, cases have been reported by the Council of Law Reporting, which produces the authoritative reports of cases. Modern technology has resulted in the establishment of Lexis, a computer-based store of cases.

For reference purposes, the most commonly referenced law reports are cited as follows:

- *Law reports*
  Appeal Cases (AC)
  Chancery Division (Ch D)
  Family Division (Fam)
  King's/Queen's Bench (KB/QB)
- *Other general series of reports*
  All England Law Reports (All ER)
  Weekly Law Reports (WLR)
  Solicitors Journal (SJ)
  European Court Reports (ECR)
- *CD-ROMs and Internet facilities*
  As in most other fields, the growth of information technology has revolutionised law reporting and law finding. Many of the law reports mentioned above are both available on CD-ROM and on the Internet. See, for example, Justis, Lawtel, Lexis-Nexis and Westlaw UK, amongst others. Indeed, members of the public can now access law reports directly from their sources in the courts, both domestically and in Europe. The first major electronic cases database was the Lexis system, which gave immediate access to a huge range of case authorities, some unreported elsewhere. The problem for the courts was that lawyers with access to the system could simply cite lists of cases from the database without the courts having access to paper copies of the decisions. The courts soon expressed their displeasure at this indiscriminate citation of unreported cases trawled from the Lexis database (see *Stanley v International Harvester Co of Great Britain Ltd* (1983)).

In line with the ongoing modernisation of the whole legal system, the way in which cases are to be cited has been changed. Thus, from January 2001, following *Practice Direction (Judgments: Form and Citation)* [2001] 1 WLR 194, a neutral system was introduced; it was extended in a further Practice Direction in April 2002. Cases in the various courts are now cited as follows:

Supreme Court	[year]	UKSC case no
House of Lords	[year]	UKHL case no
Court of Appeal (Civil Division)	[year]	EWCA Civ case no
Court of Appeal (Criminal Division)	[year]	EWCA Crim case no
High Court		
Queen's Bench Division	[year]	EWHC case no (QB)
Chancery Division	[year]	EWHC case no (Ch)
Patents Court	[year]	EWHC case no (Pat)
Administrative Court	[year]	EWHC case no (Admin)
Commercial Court	[year]	EWHC case no (Comm)

Admiralty Court	[year]	EWHC case no (Admlty)
Technology & Construction Court	[year]	EWHC case no (TCC)
Family Division	[year]	EWHC case no (Fam)

Within the individual case, the paragraphs of each judgment are numbered consecutively and, where there is more than one judgment, the numbering of the paragraphs carries on sequentially.

1.6.2 The hierarchy of the courts and the setting of precedent

Supreme Court

Perhaps the most significant change to have taken place in the English legal system since the previous edition of this book is the replacement of the Judicial Committee of the House of Lords

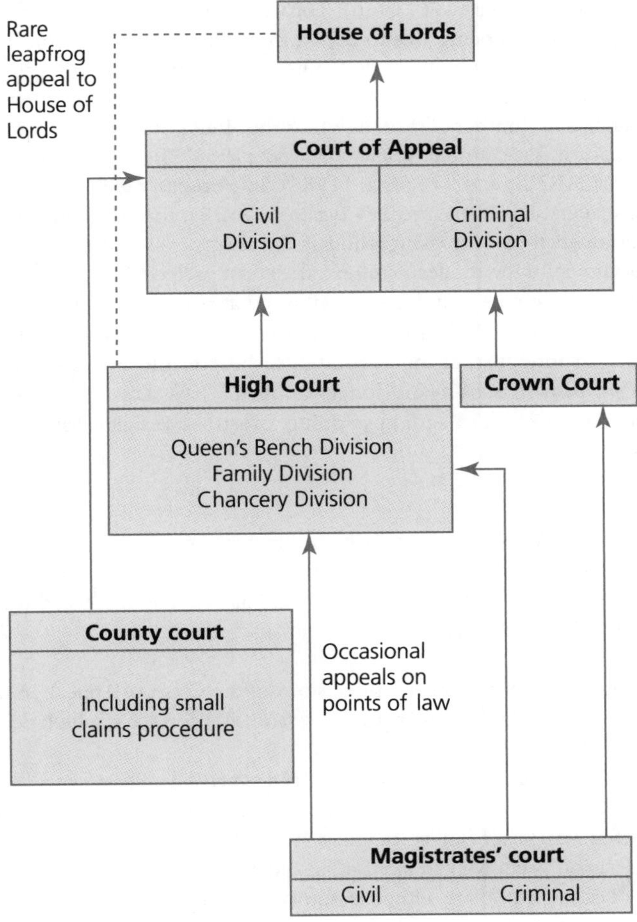

Figure 1.1 The hierarchy of the courts

by the Supreme Court. The Supreme Court began its work on 1 October 2009 and was officially opened by the Queen on 16 October of that year. The Court will be considered in more detail in later chapters, but as the replacement for the House of Lords it now clearly sits at the pinnacle of the English court hierarchy and as such its future decisions will have the same effect and binding power as those of its predecessor. Given the relative novelty of the Supreme Court, with the related lack of actual judgments, the decision has been taken that it would be wrong simply to delete references to the House of Lords and tedious to continually refer to the House of Lords as the House of Lords/Supreme Court. Consequently all future reference to the House of Lords and its powers will be assumed to apply to the Supreme Court. It should also be mentioned that the Supreme Court carries on the previous double existence of the House of Lords and the Privy Council as a distinct institution.

Supreme Court/House of Lords

Until its replacement by the Supreme Court, the House of Lords stood at the summit of the English court structure and its decisions were and still are binding on all courts below it in the hierarchy. It must be recalled, however, that the CJEU is superior to the House of Lords in matters relating to EU law. As regards its own previous decisions, until 1966, the House of Lords regarded itself as bound by such decisions. In a *Practice Statement* (1966), Lord Gardiner indicated that the House of Lords would in future regard itself as being free to depart from its previous decisions where it appeared to be right to do so. Given the potentially destabilising effect on existing legal practice based on previous decisions of the House of Lords, this is not a discretion that the court exercises lightly. There have, however, been a number of cases in which the House of Lords has overruled or amended its own earlier decisions, for example: *Conway v Rimmer* (1968); *Herrington v BRB* (1972); *Miliangos v George Frank (Textiles) Ltd* (1976); and *R v Shivpuri* (1986). In *Herrington v BRB*, the House of Lords overturned the previous rule, established in *Addie v Dumbreck* (1929), that an occupier was only responsible for injury sustained to a trespassing child if the injury was caused either intentionally or recklessly by the occupier. In the modern context, the court preferred to establish responsibility on the basis of whether the occupier had done everything that a humane person should have done to protect the trespasser. Further, in *Miliangos v George Frank (Textiles) Ltd*, the House of Lords decided that, in the light of changed foreign exchange conditions, the previous rule that damages in English courts could only be paid in sterling no longer applied. They allowed payment in the foreign currency as specified in the contract and, in so doing, overruled *Re United Railways of the Havana & Regla Warehouses Ltd* (1961).

Court of Appeal

In civil cases, the Court of Appeal is generally bound by previous decisions of the House of Lords.

The Court of Appeal is also bound by its own previous decisions in civil cases. There are, however, a number of exceptions to this general rule. Lord Greene MR listed these exceptions in *Young v Bristol Aeroplane Co Ltd* (1944). They arise where:

- there is a conflict between two previous decisions of the Court of Appeal. In this situation, the later court must decide which decision to follow and, as a corollary, which decision to overrule (*Tiverton Estates Ltd v Wearwell Ltd* (1974));
- a previous decision of the Court of Appeal has been overruled, either expressly or impliedly, by the House of Lords. In this situation, the Court of Appeal is required to follow the decision of the House of Lords (*Family Housing Association v Jones* (1990)); or
- the previous decision was given *per incuriam*, in other words, that previous decision was taken in ignorance of some authority, either statutory or judge made, that would have led to a different conclusion. In this situation, the later court can ignore the previous decision in question (*Williams v Fawcett* (1985)).

There is also the possibility that, as a consequence of s 3 of the European Communities Act 1972, the Court of Appeal can ignore a previous decision of its own which is inconsistent with EU law or with a later decision of the ECJ.

The Court of Appeal may also make use of ss 2 and 3 of the HRA to overrule precedents no longer compatible with the rights provided under that Act (see 1.3 above). As has been seen in *Ghaidan v Godin-Mendoza* (2004), it extended the rights of same-sex partners to inherit tenancies under the Rent Act 1977 in a way that the House of Lords had not felt able to do in *Fitzpatrick v Sterling Housing Association Ltd* (1999), a case decided before the HRA had come into force. Doubtless the Court of Appeal would use the same powers to overrule its own previous decisions made without regard to rights provided by the 1998 Act.

Although, on the basis of *R v Spencer* (1985), it would appear that there is no difference, in principle, in the operation of the doctrine of *stare decisis* between the Criminal and Civil Divisions of the Court of Appeal, it is generally accepted that, in practice, precedent is not followed as strictly in the former as it is in the latter. Courts in the Criminal Division are not bound to follow their own previous decisions which they subsequently consider to have been based on either a misunderstanding or a misapplication of the law. The reason for this is that the criminal courts deal with matters which involve individual liberty and which, therefore, require greater discretion to prevent injustice.

High Court

The Divisional Courts, each located within the three divisions of the High Court, hear appeals from courts and tribunals below them in the hierarchy. They are bound by the doctrine of *stare decisis* in the normal way and must follow decisions of the House of Lords and the Court of Appeal. Each Divisional Court is usually also bound by its own previous decisions, although in civil cases it may make use of the exceptions open to the Court of Appeal in *Young v Bristol Aeroplane Co Ltd* (1944) and, in criminal appeal cases, the Queen's Bench Divisional Court may refuse to follow its own earlier decisions where it considers the earlier decision to have been made wrongly.

The High Court is also bound by the decisions of superior courts. Decisions by individual High Court judges are binding on courts which are inferior in the hierarchy, but such decisions are not binding on other High Court judges, although they are of strong persuasive authority and tend to be followed in practice.

Crown Courts cannot create precedent and their decisions can never amount to more than persuasive authority.

County courts and magistrates' courts do not create precedents.

1.6.3 The nature of precedent

Previous cases establish legal precedents which later courts must either follow or, if the decision was made by a court lower in the hierarchy, at least consider. It is essential to realise, however, that not every part of the case as reported in the law reports is part of the precedent. In theory, it is possible to divide cases into two parts: the *ratio decidendi* and *obiter dicta*:

- *Ratio decidendi*
  The *ratio decidendi* of a case may be understood as the statement of the law applied in deciding the legal problem raised by the concrete facts of the case. It is essential to establish that it is not the actual decision in a case that sets the precedent – it is the *rule of law on which that decision is founded* that does this. This rule, which is an abstraction from the facts of the case, is known as the *ratio decidendi* of the case.
- *Obiter dicta*
  Any statement of law that is not an essential part of the *ratio decidendi* is, strictly speaking, superfluous, and any such statement is referred to as *obiter dictum* (*obiter dicta* in the plural), that is, 'said

by the way'. Although *obiter dicta statements* do not form part of the binding precedent, they are of persuasive authority and can be taken into consideration in later cases.

The division of cases into these two distinct parts is a theoretical procedure. It is the general misfortune of all those who study law that judges do not actually separate their judgments into the two clearly defined categories. It is the particular misfortune of a student of business law, however, that they tend to be led to believe that case reports are divided into two distinct parts: the *ratio*, in which the judge states what he takes to be the law; and *obiter* statements, in which the judge muses on alternative possibilities. Such is not the case: there is no such clear division and, in reality, it is actually later courts which effectively determine the *ratio* in any particular case. Indeed, later courts may declare *obiter* what was previously felt to be part of the *ratio*. One should never overestimate the objective, scientific nature of the legal process.

Students should always read cases fully; although it is tempting to rely on the headnote at the start of the case report, it should be remembered that this is a summary provided by the case reporter and merely reflects what he or she thinks the *ratio* is. It is not unknown for headnotes to miss an essential point in a case.

1.6.4 Evaluation

The foregoing has set out the doctrine of binding precedent as it operates, in theory, to control the ambit of judicial discretion. It has to be recognised, however, that the doctrine does not operate as stringently as it appears to at first sight, and there are particular shortcomings in the system that must be addressed in weighing up the undoubted advantages with the equally undoubted disadvantages.

1.6.5 Advantages of case law

There are numerous perceived advantages of the doctrine of *stare decisis*, amongst which are the following:

- *Consistency*
  This refers to the fact that like cases are decided on a like basis and are not apparently subject to the whim of the individual judge deciding the case in question. This aspect of formal justice is important in justifying the decisions taken in particular cases.
- *Certainty*
  This follows from, and indeed is presupposed by, the previous item. Lawyers and their clients are able to predict the likely outcome of a particular legal question in the light of previous judicial decisions. Also, once the legal rule has been established in one case, individuals can orient their behaviour with regard to that rule relatively secure in the knowledge that it will not be changed by some later court.
- *Efficiency*
  This particular advantage follows from the preceding one. As the judiciary are bound by precedent, lawyers and their clients can be reasonably certain as to the likely outcome of any particular case on the basis of established precedent. As a consequence, most disputes do not have to be re-argued before the courts. With regard to potential litigants, it saves them money in court expenses because they can apply to their solicitor/barrister for guidance as to how their particular case is likely to be decided in the light of previous cases on the same or similar points.
- *Flexibility*
  This refers to the fact that various mechanisms enable the judges to manipulate the common law in such a way as to provide them with an opportunity to develop law in particular areas

without waiting for Parliament to enact legislation. It should be recognised that judges do have a considerable degree of discretion in electing whether or not to be bound by a particular authority.

Flexibility is achieved through the possibility of previous decisions being either overruled or distinguished, or the possibility of a later court extending or modifying the effective ambit of a precedent. The main mechanisms through which judges alter or avoid precedents are overruling and distinguishing:

- *Overruling*
  This is the procedure whereby a court which is higher in the hierarchy sets aside a legal ruling established in a previous case. It is somewhat anomalous that, within the system of *stare decisis*, precedents gain increased authority with the passage of time. As a consequence, courts tend to be reluctant to overrule long-standing authorities, even though they may no longer accurately reflect contemporary practices. In addition to the wish to maintain a high degree of certainty in the law, the main reason for the judicial reluctance to overrule old decisions would appear to be the fact that overruling operates retrospectively and the principle of law being overruled is held never to have been law. Overruling a precedent, therefore, might have the consequence of disturbing important financial arrangements made in line with what were thought to be settled rules of law. It might even, in certain circumstances, lead to the imposition of criminal liability on previously lawful behaviour. It has to be emphasised, however, that the courts will not shrink from overruling authorities where they see them as no longer representing an appropriate statement of law. The decision in R v R (1992) to recognise the possibility of rape within marriage may be seen as an example of this, although, even here, the House of Lords felt constrained to state that it was not actually altering the law but was merely removing a misconception as to the true meaning and effect of the law. As this demonstrates, the courts are rarely ready to challenge the legislative prerogative of Parliament in an overt way.

  Overruling should not be confused with reversing, which is the procedure whereby a court higher in the hierarchy reverses the decision of a lower court in the same case.
- *Distinguishing*
  The main device for avoiding binding precedents is distinguishing. As has been previously stated, the *ratio decidendi* of any case is an abstraction from the material facts of the case. This opens up the possibility that a court may regard the facts of the case before it as significantly different from the facts of a cited precedent and, consequentially, it will not find itself bound to follow that precedent. Judges use the device of distinguishing where, for some reason, they are unwilling to follow a particular precedent, and the law reports provide many examples of strained distinctions where a court has quite evidently not wanted to follow an authority that it would otherwise have been bound by.

1.6.6 Disadvantages of case law

It should be noted that the advantage of flexibility at least potentially contradicts the alternative advantage of certainty, but there are other disadvantages in the doctrine which have to be considered. Amongst these are the following:

- *Uncertainty*
  This refers to the fact that the degree of certainty provided by the doctrine of *stare decisis* is undermined by the absolute number of cases that have been reported and can be cited as authorities. This uncertainty is compounded by the ability of the judiciary to select

which authority to follow, through use of the mechanism of distinguishing cases on their facts.

- *Fixity*
  This refers to the possibility that the law, in relation to any particular area, may become ossified on the basis of an unjust precedent, with the consequence that previous injustices are perpetuated. An example of this was the long delay in the *recognition* of the possibility of rape within marriage, which was only recognised some twenty years ago (*R v R* (1992)).
- *Unconstitutionality*
  This is a fundamental question that refers to the fact that the judiciary are in fact overstepping their theoretical constitutional role by actually making law, rather than restricting themselves to the role of simply *applying* it. It is now probably a commonplace of legal theory that judges do make law. Due to their position in the constitution, however, judges have to be circumspect in the way in which, and the extent to which, they use their powers to create law and impose values. To overtly assert or exercise the power would be to challenge the power of the legislature. For an unelected body to challenge a politically supreme Parliament would be unwise, to say the least.

1.6.7 Case study

Carlill v Carbolic Smoke Ball Co Ltd (1892) is one of the most famous examples of the case law in this area. A summary of the case is set out below.

❖ KEY CASE *Carlill v Carbolic Smoke Ball Co Ltd* (1892)

Facts:

Mrs Carlill made a retail purchase of one of the defendant's medicinal products: the Carbolic Smoke Ball. It was supposed to prevent people who used it in a specified way (three times a day for at least two weeks) from catching influenza. The company was very confident about its product and placed an advertisement in a newspaper, the *Pall Mall Gazette*, which praised the effectiveness of the smoke ball and promised to pay £100 (a huge sum of money at that time) to:

> . . . any person who contracts the increasing epidemic influenza, colds, or any disease caused by taking cold, having used the ball three times daily for two weeks according to the printed directions supplied with each ball.

The advertisement went on to explain that the company had deposited £1,000 with the Alliance Bank (on Regent Street in London) as a sign of its sincerity in the matter. Any proper claimants could get their payment from that sum. On the faith of the advertisement, Mrs Carlill bought one of the balls at a chemist and used it as directed, but she caught influenza. She claimed £100 from the company but was refused it, so she sued for breach of contract. The company said that, for several reasons, there was no contract, the main reasons being that:

- the advert was too vague to amount to the basis of a contract;
- there was no time limit and no way of checking the way in which the customer used the ball;
- Mrs Carlill did not give any legally recognised value to the company; one cannot legally make an offer to the whole world, so the advert was not a proper offer;

- even if the advert could be seen as an offer, Mrs Carlill had not given a legal acceptance of that offer because she had not notified the company that she was accepting; and
- the advert was a mere puff, that is, a piece of insincere rhetoric.

Decision:
The Court of Appeal found that there was a legally enforceable agreement – a contract – between Mrs Carlill and the company. The company would have to pay damages to Mrs Carlill.

Ratio decidendi: The three Lords Justice of Appeal who gave judgments in this case all decided in favour of Mrs Carlill. Each, however, used slightly different reasoning, arguments and examples. The process, therefore, of distilling the reason for the decision of the court is quite a delicate art. The *ratio* of the case can be put as follows.

Offers must be sufficiently clear in order to allow the courts to enforce agreements that follow from them. The offer here was a distinct promise, expressed in language which was perfectly unmistakable. It could not be a mere puff in view of the £1,000 deposited specially to show good faith. An offer *may* be made to the world at large, and the advert was such an offer. It was accepted by any person, like Mrs Carlill, who bought the product and used it in the prescribed manner. Mrs Carlill had accepted the offer by her conduct when she did as she was invited to do and started to use the smoke ball. She had not been asked to let the company know that she was using it.

Obiter dicta: In the course of his reasoning, Bowen LJ gave the legal answer to a set of facts which were not in issue in this case. They are thus *obiter dicta*. He did this because it assisted him in clarifying the answer to Mrs Carlill's case. He said:

> If I advertise to the world that my dog is lost, and that anybody who brings the dog to a particular place will be paid some money, are all the police or other persons whose business it is to find lost dogs to be expected to sit down and write me a note saying that they have accepted my proposal? Why, of course, they at once look [for] the dog, and as soon as they find the dog they have performed the condition.

If such facts were ever subsequently in issue in a court case, the words of Bowen LJ could be used by counsel as persuasive precedent.

Carlill was applied in *Peck v Lateu* (1973) but was distinguished in *AM Satterthwaite & Co v New Zealand Shipping Co* (1972).

1.7 Statutory Interpretation

The two previous sections have tended to present legislation and case law in terms of opposition: legislation being the product of Parliament and case law the product of the judiciary in the courts. Such stark opposition is, of course, misleading, for the two processes come together when consideration is given to the necessity for judges to interpret statute law in order to apply it.

1.7.1 Problems in interpreting legislation

In order to apply legislation, judges must ascertain its meaning and, in order to ascertain that meaning, they are faced with the difficulty of interpreting the legislation. Legislation, however, shares the general problem of uncertainty, which is inherent in any mode of verbal communication. Words can have more than one meaning and the meaning of a word can change, depending on its context.

One of the essential requirements of legislation is generality of application – the need for it to be written in such a way as to ensure that it can be effectively applied in various circumstances without the need to detail those situations individually. This requirement, however, can give rise to particular problems of interpretation; the need for generality can only really be achieved at the expense of clarity and precision of language.

Legislation, therefore, involves an inescapable measure of uncertainty, which can only be made certain through judicial interpretation. However, to the extent that the interpretation of legislative provisions is an active process, it is equally a creative process, and it inevitably involves the judiciary in creating law through determining the meaning and effect being given to any particular piece of legislation.

There are, essentially, two contrasting views as to how judges should go about determining the meaning of a statute – the restrictive, literal approach and the more permissive, purposive approach:

1 *The literal approach*
The literal approach is dominant in the English legal system, although it is not without critics, and devices do exist for circumventing it when it is seen as too restrictive. This view of judicial interpretation holds that the judge should look primarily to the words of the legislation in order to construe its meaning and, except in the very limited circumstances considered below, should not look outside of, or behind, the legislation in an attempt to find its meaning.

2 *The purposive approach*
The purposive approach rejects the limitation of the judges' search for meaning to a literal construction of the words of legislation itself. It suggests that the interpretative role of the judge should include, where necessary, the power to look beyond the words of statute in pursuit of the reason for its enactment, and that meaning should be construed in the light of that purpose and so as to give it effect. This purposive approach is typical of civil law systems found on the European mainland. In these jurisdictions, legislation tends to set out general principles and leaves the fine details to be filled in later by the judges who are expected to make decisions in the furtherance of those general principles.

European Union (EU) legislation tends to be drafted in the continental, civil law, manner. Its detailed effect, therefore, can only be determined on the basis of a purposive approach to its interpretation. This requirement, however, runs counter to the literal approach that was the dominant approach in the English system. The need to interpret such legislation, however, has forced a change in that approach in relation to EU legislation and even with respect to domestic legislation designed to implement EU legislation. Thus, in *Pickstone v Freemans plc* (1988), the House of Lords held that it was permissible, and indeed necessary, for the court to read words into inadequate domestic legislation in order to give effect to EU law in relation to provisions relating to equal pay for work of equal value.

As a consequence of the foregoing there has been, even in the English legal system, a move away from the over-reliance on the literal approach to statutory interpretation to a more purposive approach. As Lord Griffiths put it in *Pepper v Hart* (1993):

> The days have long passed when the court adopted a strict constructionist view of interpretation which required them to adopt the literal meaning of the language. The courts now adopt a purposive approach which seeks to give effect to the true purpose of legislation and are prepared to look at much extraneous material that bears on the background against which the legislation was enacted.

However, it is still necessary to consider the traditional and essentially literally based approaches to statutory interpretation. Additionally, what follows should be read within the context of the Human Rights Act (HRA) 1998, which requires all legislation to be construed in such a way as, if at all possible, to bring it within the ambit of the European Convention on Human Rights (ECHR). The effect of this requirement is to provide the judiciary with powers of interpretation much wider than those afforded to them by the more traditional rules of interpretation, as can be seen from *R v A* (2001), considered above at 1.3.2.

1.7.2 Rules of interpretation

In attempting to decide upon the precise meaning of any statute, judges use well established rules of interpretation, of which there are three primary ones, together with a variety of other secondary aids to construction.

The rules of statutory interpretation are as follows:

- *Literal rule*
  Under this rule, the judge is required to consider what the legislation actually says, rather than considering what it might mean. In order to achieve this end, the judge should give words in legislation their literal meaning; that is, their plain, ordinary, everyday meaning, even if the effect of this is to produce what might be considered an otherwise unjust or undesirable outcome. *Inland Revenue Commissioners v Hinchy* (1960) concerned s 25(3) of the Income Tax Act 1952, which stated that any taxpayer who did not complete their tax return was subject to a fixed penalty of £20 plus *treble the tax which he ought to be charged under the Act*. The question that had to be decided was whether the additional element of the penalty should be based on the total amount that should have been paid, or merely the unpaid portion of that total. The House of Lords adopted a literal interpretation of the statute and held that any taxpayer in default should have to pay triple their original tax bill.

  In *Fisher v Bell* (1961), the court, in line with general contract principles, decided that the placing of an article in a window did not amount to offering but was merely an invitation to treat, and thus the shopkeeper could not be charged with 'offering the goods for sale'. In this case, the court chose to follow the contract law literal interpretation of the meaning of 'offer' in the Act in question, and declined to consider the usual non-legal literal interpretation of the word. (The executive's attitude to the courts' legal-literal interpretation in *Fisher v Bell*, and the related case of *Partridge v Crittenden* (1968), can be surmised from the fact that later legislation, such as the Trade Descriptions Act 1968, has effectively legislated that invitations to treat are to be treated in the same way as offers for sale.)

  A problem in relation to the literal rule arises from the difficulty that judges face in determining the literal meaning of even the commonest of terms. In *R v Maginnis* (1987), the judges differed amongst themselves as to the literal meaning of the common word 'supply' in relation to a charge of supplying drugs. *Attorney General's Reference* (No 1 of 1988) (1989) concerned the meaning of 'obtained' in s 1(3) of the Company Securities (Insider Dealing) Act 1985, since replaced by the Criminal Justice Act 1993, and led to similar disagreement as to the precise meaning of an everyday word.
- *Golden rule*
  This rule is generally considered to be an extension of the literal rule. It is applied in circumstances where the application of the literal rule is likely to result in an obviously absurd result. An example of the application of the golden rule is *Adler v George* (1964). In this case, the court held that the literal wording of the statute ('in the vicinity of') covered the action committed by the defendant who carried out her action within the area concerned.

  Another example of this approach is to be found in *Re Sigsworth* (1935), in which the court introduced common law rules into legislative provisions, which were silent on the matter, to prevent the estate of a murderer from benefiting from the property of the party he had murdered.

- *Mischief rule*
  This rule, sometimes known as the rule in *Heydon's Case* (1584), operates to enable judges to interpret a statute in such a way as to provide a remedy for the mischief that the statute was enacted to prevent. Contemporary practice is to go beyond the actual body of the legislation to determine what mischief a particular Act was aimed at redressing. The example usually cited of the use of the mischief rule is *Corkery v Carpenter* (1951), in which a man was found guilty of being drunk in charge of a 'carriage', although he was in fact only in charge of a bicycle. A much more controversial application of the rule is to be found in *Royal College of Nursing v DHSS* (1981), where the courts had to decide whether the medical induction of premature labour to effect abortion, under the supervision of nursing staff, was lawful.

1.7.3 Aids to construction

In addition to the three main rules of interpretation, there are a number of secondary aids to construction. These can be categorised as either intrinsic or extrinsic in nature:

- *Intrinsic assistance*
  This is help which is actually derived from the statute which is the object of interpretation. The judge uses the full statute to understand the meaning of a particular part of it. Assistance may be found from various parts of the statute, such as: the title, long or short; any preamble, which is a statement preceding the actual provisions of the Act; and schedules, which appear as detailed additions at the end of the Act. Section headings or marginal notes may also be considered, where they exist.
- *Extrinsic assistance*
  Sources outside of the Act itself may, on occasion, be resorted to in determining the meaning of legislation. For example, judges have always been entitled to refer to dictionaries in order to find the meaning of non-legal words. The Interpretation Act 1978 is also available for consultation with regard to the meaning of particular words generally used in statutes.

  Judges are also allowed to use extrinsic sources to determine the mischief at which particular legislation is aimed. For example, they are able to examine earlier statutes and they have been entitled for some time to look at Law Commission reports, Royal Commission reports and the reports of other official commissions.

Until fairly recently, *Hansard*, the verbatim report of parliamentary debate, literally remained a closed book to the courts. In *Pepper v Hart* (1993), however, the House of Lords decided to overturn the previous rule. In a majority decision it was held that, where the precise meaning of legislation was uncertain or ambiguous, or where the literal meaning of an Act would lead to a manifest absurdity, the courts could refer to *Hansard's Reports of Parliamentary Debates and Proceedings* as an aid to construing the meaning of the legislation.

The operation of the principle in *Pepper v Hart* was extended in *Three Rivers DC v Bank of England (No 2)* (1996) to cover situations where the legislation under question was not in itself ambiguous but might be ineffective in its intention to give effect to some particular EC directive. Applying the wider powers of interpretation open to it in such circumstances, the court held that it was permissible to refer to *Hansard* in order to determine the actual purpose of the statute.

The *Pepper v Hart* principle only applies to statements made by ministers at the time of the passage of legislation, and the courts have declined to extend it to cover situations where ministers subsequently make some statement as to what they consider the effect of a particular Act to be (*Melluish (Inspector of Taxes) v BMI (No 3) Ltd* (1995)).

1.7.4 Presumptions

In addition to the rules of interpretation, the courts may also make use of certain presumptions. As with all presumptions, they are rebuttable, which means that the presumption is subject to being overturned in argument in any particular case. The presumptions operate in the following ways:

- *Against the alteration of the common law*
  Parliament can alter the common law whenever it decides to do so. In order to do this, however, it must expressly enact legislation to that end. If there is no express intention to that effect, it is assumed that statute does not make any fundamental change to the common law. With regard to particular provisions, if there are alternative interpretations, one of which will maintain the existing common law situation, then that interpretation will be preferred.
- *Against retrospective application*
  As the War Crimes Act 1990 shows, Parliament can impose criminal responsibility *retrospectively, where particular* and extremely unusual circumstances dictate the need to do so, but such effect must be clearly expressed.
- *Against the deprivation of an individual's liberty, property or rights*
  Once again, the presumption can be rebutted by express provision and it is not uncommon for legislation to deprive people of their rights to enjoy particular benefits. Nor is it unusual for individuals to be deprived of their liberty under the Mental Health Act 1983.
- *Against application to the Crown*
  Unless the legislation contains a clear statement to the contrary, it is presumed not to apply to the Crown.
- *Against breaking international law*
  Where possible, legislation should be interpreted in such a way as to give effect to existing international legal obligations.
- *In favour of the requirement that* mens rea *(a guilty mind) be a requirement in any criminal offence*
  The classic example of this presumption is *Sweet v Parsley* (1969), in which a landlord was eventually found not guilty of allowing her premises to be used for the purpose of taking drugs, as she had absolutely no knowledge of what was going on in her house. Offences which do not require the presence of *mens rea* are referred to as strict liability offences.
- *In favour of words taking their meaning from the context in which they are used*
  This final presumption refers back to, and operates in conjunction with, the major rules for interpreting legislation considered previously. The general presumption appears as three distinct sub-rules, each of which carries a Latin tag:

  - the *noscitur a sociis* rule is applied where statutory provisions include a list of examples of what is covered by the legislation. It is presumed that the words used have a related meaning and are to be interpreted in relation to each other (see *IRC v Frere* (1965));
  - the *eiusdem generis* rule applies in situations where general words are appended to the end of a list of specific examples. The presumption is that the general words have to be interpreted in line with the prior restrictive examples. Thus, a provision which referred to a list that included horses, cattle, sheep and other animals would be unlikely to apply to domestic animals such as cats and dogs (see *Powell v Kempton Park Racecourse* (1899)); and
  - the *expressio unius exclusio alterius* rule simply means that, where a statute seeks to establish a list of what is covered by its provisions, then anything not expressly included in that list is specifically excluded (see *R v Inhabitants of Sedgley* (1831)).

1.8 Custom

The traditional view of the development of the common law tends to adopt an overly romantic view as regards its emergence. This view suggests that the common law is no more than the crystallisation of ancient common customs, this distillation being accomplished by the judiciary in the course of their historic travels around the land in the middle ages. This view, however, tends to ignore the political process that gave rise to this procedure. The imposition of a common system of law represented the political victory of a State that had fought to establish and assert its central authority. Viewed in that light, the emergence of the common law can perhaps better be seen as the invention of the judges as representatives of the State and as representing what they wanted the law to be, rather than what people generally thought it was.

One source of customary practice that undoubtedly did find expression in the form of law was business and commercial practice. These customs and practices were originally constituted in the distinct form of the Law Merchant but, gradually, this became subsumed under the control of the common law courts and ceased to exist apart from the common law.

Notwithstanding the foregoing, it is still possible for specific local customs to operate as a source of law. In certain circumstances, parties may assert the existence of customary practices in order to support their case. Such local custom may run counter to the strict application of the common law and, where they are found to be legitimate, they will effectively replace the common law. Even in this respect, however, reliance on customary law as opposed to common law, although not impossible, is made unlikely by the stringent tests that have to be satisfied (see *Egerton v Harding* (1974)). The requirements that a local custom must satisfy in order to be recognised are as follows:

- it must have existed from time immemorial, that is, 1189;
- it must have been exercised continuously within that period;
- it must have been exercised peacefully and without opposition;
- it must also have been felt to be obligatory;
- it must be capable of precise definition;
- it must have been consistent with other customs; and
- it must be reasonable.

Given this list of requirements, it can be seen why local custom is not an important source of law.

1.8.1 Books of authority

In the very unusual situation of a court being unable to locate a precise or analogous precedent, it may refer to legal textbooks for guidance. Such books are subdivided, depending on when they were written. In strict terms, only certain works are actually treated as authoritative sources of law. Legal works produced after *Blackstone's Commentaries* of 1765 are considered to be of recent origin and, although they cannot be treated as authoritative sources, the courts may consider what the most eminent works by accepted experts in particular fields have said in order to help determine what the law is or should be.

1.9 Law Reform

At one level, law reform is a product of either parliamentary or judicial activity, as has been considered previously. Parliament tends, however, to be concerned with particularities of law reform and the judiciary are constitutionally and practically disbarred from reforming the law on anything other than an opportunistic and piecemeal basis. Therefore, there remains a need for the question of law reform to be considered generally and a requirement that such consideration be conducted in an informed but disinterested manner.

Reference has already been made to the use of consultative Green Papers by the Government as a mechanism for gauging the opinions of interested parties to particular reforms. More formal advice may be provided through various advisory standing committees. Amongst these is the Law Reform Committee. The function of this Committee is to consider the desirability of changes to the civil law which the Lord Chancellor may refer to it. The Criminal Law Revision Committee performs similar functions in relation to criminal law.

Royal Commissions may be constituted to consider the need for law reform in specific areas. For example, the Commission on Criminal Procedure (1980) led to the enactment of the Police and Criminal Evidence Act (PACE) 1984.

Committees may be set up in order to review the operation of particular areas of law, the most significant recent example being the Woolf review of the operation of the civil justice system. (Detailed analysis of the consequences flowing from the implementation of the recommendations of the Woolf Report will be considered subsequently.) Similarly, Sir Robin Auld conducted a review of the whole criminal justice system and Sir Andrew Leggatt carried out a similar task in relation to the tribunal system.

If a criticism is to be levelled at these committees and commissions, it is that they are all *ad hoc* bodies. Their remit is limited and they do not have the power either to widen the ambit of their investigation or initiate reform proposals.

The Law Commission fulfils the need for some institution to concern itself more generally with the question of law reform. Its general function is to keep the law as a whole under review and to make recommendations for its systematic reform.

Although the scope of the Commission is limited to those areas set out in its programme of law reform, its ambit is not unduly restricted, as may be seen from the range of matters covered in its eleventh programme set out in July 2011, which includes reviews of charity law, contempt of court, electoral law, European contract law, misconduct in a public office, and the modernisation of the law on wildlife management (www.justice.gov.uk/lawcommission/docs/lc330_eleventh_programme.pdf). In addition, ministers may refer matters of particular importance to the Commission for its consideration. As was noted above at 1.2.5, it was just such a referral by the Home Secretary, after the Macpherson Inquiry into the Stephen Lawrence case, that gave rise to the Law Commission's recommendation that the rule against double jeopardy be removed in particular circumstances. An extended version of that recommendation was included in the Criminal Justice Act 2003.

Summary

Law and Legal Sources

The nature of law

Legal systems are particular ways of establishing and maintaining social order. Law is a formal mechanism of social control.

Categories of law

Law can be categorised in a number of ways, although the various categories are not mutually exclusive, as follows:

- Common law and civil law relate to distinct legal systems. The English legal system is a common law one.
- Common law and equity distinguish the two historical sources and systems of English law.
- Common law is judge made; statute law is produced by Parliament.

- Private law relates to individual citizens; public law relates to institutions of government.
- Civil law facilitates the interaction of individuals; criminal law enforces particular standards of behaviour.

The Human Rights Act 1998

The Human Rights Act 1998 incorporates the European Convention on Human Rights into UK law. The Articles of the Convention cover:

- the right to life (Art 2);
- the prohibition of torture (Art 3);
- the prohibition of slavery and forced labour (Art 4);
- the right to liberty and security (Art 5);
- the right to a fair trial (Art 6);
- the general prohibition of the enactment of retrospective criminal offences (Art 7);
- the right to respect for private and family life (Art 8);
- freedom of thought, conscience and religion (Art 9);
- freedom of expression (Art 10);
- freedom of assembly and association (Art 11);
- the right to marry (Art 12);
- the prohibition of discrimination (Art 14); and
- the political activity of aliens may be restricted (Art 16).

The incorporation of the Convention into UK law means that UK courts can decide cases in line with the above Articles. This has the potential to create friction between the judiciary and the executive/legislature.

European Union Law

Sources:

- internal treaties and protocols;
- international agreements;
- secondary legislation; and
- decisions of the CJEU.

Institutions:

- Council of Ministers
- European Parliament
- Commission
- Court of Justice of the European Union.

Domestic sources of law

- Legislation is the law produced through the parliamentary system; then it is given royal assent. The House of Lords has only limited scope to delay legislation.
- Delegated legislation is a sub-classification of legislation. It appears in the form of: Orders in Council; statutory instruments; bylaws; and professional regulations.
  Advantages of delegated legislation:
  - speed of implementation;
  - the saving of parliamentary time;

- access to expertise; and
- flexibility.

The disadvantages relate to:

- the lack of accountability;
- the lack of scrutiny of proposals for such legislation; and
- the sheer amount of delegated legislation.

Controls over delegated legislation:

- Joint Select Committee on Statutory Instruments;
- *ultra vires* provisions may be challenged in the courts;
- judges may declare secondary legislation invalid if it conflicts with the provisions of the Human Rights Act.

Case law

- Created by judges in the course of deciding cases.
- The doctrine of *stare decisis*, or binding precedent, refers to the fact that courts are bound by previous decisions of courts which are equal or above them in the court hierarchy.
- The *ratio decidendi* is binding. Everything else is *obiter dicta*.
- Precedents may be avoided through either overruling or distinguishing. The advantages of precedent are:
  - saving the time of all parties concerned;
  - certainty; and
  - flexibility.

  The disadvantages are:

  - uncertainty;
  - fixity; and
  - unconstitutionality.

Statutory interpretation

This is the way in which judges give practical meaning to legislative provisions, using the following rules:

- The *literal rule* gives words everyday meaning, even if this leads to an apparent injustice.
- The *golden rule* is used in circumstances where the application of the literal rule is likely to result in an obviously absurd result.
- The *mischief rule* permits the court to go beyond the words of the statute in question to consider the mischief at which it was aimed.

There are rebuttable presumptions against:

- the alteration of the common law;
- retrospective application;
- the deprivation of an individual's liberty, property or rights; and
- application to the Crown.

And in favour of:

- the requirement of *mens rea* in relation to criminal offences; and
- deriving the meaning of words from their contexts.

Judges may seek assistance from:

- intrinsic sources as the title of the Act, any preamble or any schedules to it; and
- extrinsic sources such as: dictionaries; textbooks; reports; other parliamentary papers; and, since *Pepper v Hart* (1993), *Hansard*.

Custom

Custom is of very limited importance as a contemporary source of law, although it was important in the establishment of business and commercial law in the form of the old Law Merchant.

Law reform

The need to reform the law may be assessed by a number of bodies:

- Royal Commissions;
- standing committees;
- *ad hoc* committees; and
- the Law Commission.

Further Reading

Barnett, H, *Constitutional & Administrative Law*, 10th edn, 2013, Abingdon: Routledge
Bennion, F, *Statutory Interpretation*, 2nd edn, 1992, London: Butterworths
Bennion, F, 'Statute law: obscurity and drafting parameters' (1978) 5 BR JLS 235
Cross, R (Sir) and Harris, JW, *Precedent in English Law*, 4th edn, Oxford: Clarendon Press
Davies, K, *Understanding European Union Law*, 4th edn, London: Routledge
Fenwick, H and Phillipson, G, *Text, Cases and Materials on Public Law and Human Rights*, 3rd edn, London: Routledge
Hart, HLA and Bulloch, PA, *The Concept of Law*, 2nd edn, Oxford: Clarendon Press
Sedley, S (Sir), 'Human rights: a 21st century agenda' [1995] PL 386
Simpson, A, 'The *ratio decidendi* of a case' (1957) 20 MLR 413
Slapper, G and Kelly, D, *English Legal System*, 15th edn, 2014, Abingdon: Routledge

Websites

www.justice.gov.uk/ – Justice Ministry
www.opsi.gov.uk/acts.htm
www.statutelaw.gov.uk
www.supremecourt.gov.uk
www.bailii.org
www.lawreports.co.uk – Incorporate Council of Law Reporting
www.judiciary.gov.uk
http://eur-lex.europa.eu/en/index.htm
http://curia.europa.eu/ – European Court of Justice
www.echr.coe.int/echr/Homepage_EN – European Court of Justice

Chapter 2

The Criminal and Civil Courts

Chapter Contents

Law in Context: The Court System and the Technological Age

Traditionally, accessing information and judgments from both the criminal and civil justice court systems in England and Wales was dependent upon officially reported law reports and the interpretation of these by solicitors and barristers. Nowadays, in the age of social media, the business law student, or indeed any member of the public, can access websites to find out more about the work of the various courts in England and Wales. Access to law reports direct from the key court websites allows everyone to keep up to date with reported cases and also debates about justice issues. Social media has also caught up with the English legal system, with key courts now operating Facebook and Twitter accounts. With this in mind, the news that a UK law firm was granted permission to serve legal documents via Facebook came as no surprise, and heralds the modernisation of the court system. Such an approach follows a precedent already used in both Australia and New Zealand, whereby court approval will be granted when a judge is satisfied that the correct individual has been tracked down and that the use of social networking sites is the most appropriate way to serve documents when conventional means of service are not available.

2.1 Introduction

In the UK, the structure of the court system is divided into two distinct sectors, following the division between criminal and civil law. This chapter locates particular courts within the general hierarchical structure in ascending order of authority. It is essential not just to be aware of the role and powers of the individual courts, but also to know the paths of appeal from one court to another within the hierarchy.

2.2 The Criminal Court Structure

Crimes are offences against the law of the land and are usually prosecuted by the State. Criminal cases are normally cited in the form *R v Brown*. Cases are heard in different courts, depending on their seriousness. Offences can be divided into three categories, as follows:

- *Summary offences* are the least serious and are tried by magistrates, without recourse to a jury.
- *Indictable offences* are the most serious and are required to be tried before a judge and jury in the Crown Court.
- *Either way offences*, as their title suggests, are open to trial in either of the preceding ways. At the moment, the decision as to whether the case is heard in the magistrates' court or the Crown Court is decided by the accused. The previous Labour Government twice attempted to introduce legislation to remove the defendant's right to elect for jury trial in relation to either way offences. On both occasions, the proposed Bills were defeated in the House of Lords.

2.3 Magistrates' Courts

The office of magistrate or justice of the peace (JP) dates from 1195, when Richard I appointed keepers of the peace to deal with those who were accused of breaking the King's peace. The JPs originally acted as local administrators for the King, in addition to carrying out their judicial responsibilities.

There are approximately 330 magistrates' courts in England and Wales, staffed by some 30,000 part time lay magistrates. In addition, there are 140 full time professional district judges (magistrates' courts) who sit in cities and large towns. The latter used to be known as stipendiary magistrates. Magistrates are empowered to hear and decide a wide variety of legal matters, and the amount and importance of the work they do should not be underestimated. It has been estimated that up to 97% of all criminal cases are dealt with by the magistrates' courts.

Lay magistrates are not usually legally qualified and sit as a bench of three. District judges are legally qualified and decide cases on their own.

A bench of lay magistrates is legally advised by a justices clerk, who is legally qualified and guides the justices on matters of law, sentencing and procedure, even when not specifically invited to do so. The clerk should not give any opinion on matters of fact. Magistrates are independent of the clerks and the latter should not instruct the magistrates as to what decision they should reach.

2.3.1 Powers of magistrates' courts

Magistrates' courts have considerable power. In relation to criminal law, they are empowered to try summary cases, that is, cases which are triable without a jury. Additionally, with the agreement of the accused, they may deal with triable either way cases, that is, cases which can either be tried summarily by the magistrates or on indictment before a jury in the Crown Court.

The maximum sentence that magistrates can normally impose is a £5,000 fine and/or a six month prison sentence. The sentencing powers of magistrates were potentially increased by the CJA 2003. When section 154 of that Act is eventually brought onto effect it will enable magistrates to impose a custodial sentence of up to 12 months for any one offence, and s 155 will allow for a custodial sentence of up to 65 weeks for two or more offences. The maximum sentences for many summary offences, however, are much less than these limits. Where a defendant is convicted of two or more offences at the same hearing, consecutive sentences amounting to more than six months are not permitted, although this can rise to 12 months in cases involving offences triable either way. If the magistrates feel that their sentencing powers are insufficient to deal with the defendant, then the offender may be sent to the Crown Court for sentencing.

Magistrates can impose alternative sentences, such as community service orders or probation orders. They can also discharge offenders either conditionally or absolutely. In addition, they can issue compensation orders. Such orders are used not as a means of punishing the offender, but as a way of compensating the victims of the offender without them having to sue the offender in the civil courts. The maximum payment under any such order is £5,000.

Where magistrates decide that an offence triable either way should be tried in the Crown Court, they hold committal proceedings. These proceedings are also held where the defendant has been charged with an indictable offence. Acting in this way, the justices become examining magistrates. The object of these proceedings is to determine whether there is a *prima facie* case against the defendant. If the justices decide that there is a *prima facie* case, they must commit the defendant to a Crown Court for trial; if not, they must discharge him. Section 44 of the Criminal Procedure and Investigations Act (CPIA) 1996 repeals s 44 of the Criminal Justice and Public Order Act 1994 and, in effect, introduces a new, streamlined version of committal proceedings, in which no oral evidence can be given. The new system of committals is governed by s 47 and Sched 1 to the CPIA 1996. The effect of this law is to abolish the old style mini-trial committals and the right of the defendant to have witnesses called and cross-examined at the magistrates' court. Now, defendants may only use written evidence at committal stage.

Magistrates sit in youth courts to try children and young persons. A child is someone who has not reached his 14th birthday and young people are taken to be below the age of 18. These tribunals are not open to the public and sit separately from the ordinary magistrates' court in order to protect the young defendants from publicity.

2.4 The Crown Court

The Crown Court, unlike the magistrates' court, is not a local court, but a single court, which sits in over 90 centres. The Crown Court is part of the Senior courts of England and Wales, which is defined as including the Court of Appeal, the High Court of Justice and the Crown Court. For the purposes of the operation of the Crown Court, England and Wales are divided into six circuits, each with its own headquarters and staff. The centres are divided into three tiers. In first tier centres, High Court judges hear civil and criminal cases, whereas circuit judges and recorders hear only criminal cases. Second tier centres are served by the same types of judge but hear criminal cases only. At third tier centres, recorders and circuit judges hear criminal cases only.

2.4.1 Jurisdiction

The Crown Court hears all cases involving trial on indictment. It also hears appeals from those convicted summarily in the magistrates' courts. At the conclusion of an appeal hearing, the Crown Court has the power to confirm, reverse or vary any part of the decision under appeal (s 48(2) of the Supreme Court Act 1981). If the appeal is decided against the accused, the Crown Court has the power to impose any sentence which the magistrates could have imposed, including one which is harsher than that originally imposed on the defendant.

Criminal offences are divided into four classes according to their gravity. Class 1 offences are the most serious, including treason and murder, and are usually tried by a High Court judge; exceptionally he may transfer a murder case (including attempts) to be heard by a circuit judge approved for this purpose by the Lord Chief Justice. Class 2 offences include manslaughter and rape and are subject to similar provisions. Class 3 offences include all remaining offences, triable only on indictment, and are usually tried by a High Court judge, although releases of cases to circuit judges are more common here. Class 4 offences include robbery, grievous bodily harm and all offences triable 'either way', and are not normally tried by a High Court judge.

2.5 Criminal Appeals

The process of appeal depends upon how a case was originally tried, that is, whether it was tried summarily or on indictment. The following sets out the various routes and procedures involved in appealing against the decisions of particular courts.

Changes to the system of criminal appeals introduced in the CJA 2003 were brought into effect in 2005.

2.5.1 Appeals from Magistrates' Courts

Two routes of appeal are possible. The first route allows only a defendant to appeal. The appeal is to a judge and between two and four magistrates sitting in the Crown Court, and can be:

- against conviction (only if the defendant pleaded not guilty) on points of fact or law; or
- against sentence.

Such an appeal will take the form of a new trial (a trial *de novo*).

Alternatively, either the defendant or the prosecution can appeal by way of case stated to the High Court (the Divisional Court of the Queen's Bench Division). This court consists of two or more judges (but usually two), of whom one will be a Lord Justice of Appeal. This appeal is limited to matters relating to:

- points of law; or
- a claim that the magistrates acted beyond their jurisdiction.

Appeal from the Divisional Court is to the House of Lords. Either side may appeal, but only on a point of law and only if the Divisional Court certifies the point to be one of general public importance. Leave to appeal must also be granted either by the Court of Appeal or the House of Lords.

2.5.2 Appeals from the Crown Court

Appeals from this court lie to the Court of Appeal (Criminal Division), which hears appeals against conviction and sentence. The court hears around 8,000 applications for appeals and substantives appeals each year.

Appeals may be made by the defence against conviction, but the prosecution cannot appeal against an acquittal. Under s 36 of the CJA 1972, the Attorney General can refer a case which has resulted in an acquittal to the Court of Appeal where he believes the decision to have been questionable on a point of law. The Court of Appeal only considers the point of law and, even if its finding is contrary to the defendant's case, the acquittal is not affected. This procedure merely clarifies the law for future cases.

The Criminal Appeal Act (CAA) 1995 introduced significant changes to the criminal appeal system. Section 1 of this Act amended the CAA 1968 so as to bring appeals against conviction, appeals against a verdict of not guilty by reason of insanity and appeals against a finding of disability on a question of law alone into line with other appeals against conviction and sentence (that is, those involving questions of fact, or mixtures of law and fact). Now, all appeals against conviction and sentence must first have leave of the Court of Appeal or a certificate of fitness for appeal from the trial judge before the appeal can be taken. Before the new Act came into force, it was possible to appeal without the consent of the trial judge or Court of Appeal on a point of law alone.

The law now requires the Court of Appeal to allow an appeal against conviction if it thinks that the conviction, verdict or finding is unsafe (as opposed to the previous law, which used the formula unsafe or unsatisfactory).

Where there is an appeal against sentence, the court may confirm or alter the original sentence by way of changing the terms or substituting a new form of punishment. It cannot increase the sentence on appeal. However, under the CJA 1988, the Attorney General may refer indictable only cases to the Court of Appeal, where the sentence at trial is regarded as unduly lenient. In such circumstances, the court may impose a harsher sentence.

2.5.3 The Criminal Justice Act 2003

The CJA 2003 made significant changes to the prosecution's right to appeal as follows:

Section 57: introduction

This section sets out certain basic criteria for a prosecution appeal under this Part of the Act. The right of appeal arises only in trials on indictment and lies to the Court of Appeal.

Section 57(2) sets out two further limitations on appeals under this Part. It prohibits the prosecution from appealing rulings on discharge of the jury and those rulings that may be appealed by the prosecution under other legislation, for example, appeals from preparatory hearings against rulings on admissibility of evidence and other points of law.

Section 57(4) provides that the prosecution must obtain leave to appeal, either from the judge or the Court of Appeal.

Section 58: general right of appeal

This section sets out the procedure that must be followed when the prosecution wishes to appeal against a terminating ruling. The section covers both rulings that are formally terminating and those that are *de facto* terminating in the sense that they are so fatal to the prosecution case that, in the absence of a right of appeal, the prosecution would offer no or no further evidence. It applies to rulings made at an applicable time during a trial (which is defined in s 58(13) as any time before the start of the judge's summing up to the jury).

Where the prosecution fails to obtain leave to appeal or abandons the appeal, the prosecution must agree that an acquittal follow by virtue of s 58(8) and (9).

Section 59: expedited and non-expedited appeals

This section provides two alternative appeal routes: an expedited (fast) route and a non-expedited (slower) route. The judge must determine which route the appeal will follow (s 59(1)). In the case of an expedited appeal, the trial may be adjourned (s 59(2)). If the judge decides that the appeal should follow the non-expedited route, he may either adjourn the proceedings or discharge the jury, if one has been sworn (s 59(3)). Section 59(4) gives both the judge and the Court of Appeal power to reverse a decision to expedite an appeal, thus transferring the case to the slower non-expedited route. If a decision is reversed under this sub-section, the jury may be discharged.

Section 61: determination of appeal by Court of Appeal

This section sets out the powers of the Court of Appeal when determining a prosecution appeal. This needs to be read in conjunction with s 67.

Section 61(1) authorises the Court of Appeal to confirm, reverse or vary a ruling which has been appealed against. The section is drafted to ensure that, after the Court of Appeal has ordered one or other of these disposals, it must then always make it clear what is to happen next in the case.

When the Court of Appeal confirms a ruling, s 61(3) and (7) provides that it must then order the acquittal of the defendant(s) for the offence(s) which are the subject of the appeal.

When the Court of Appeal reverses or varies a ruling, s 61(4) and (8) provides that it must either order a resumption of the Crown Court proceedings or a fresh trial, or order the acquittal of the defendant(s) for the offence(s) under appeal. By virtue of s 61(5) and (8), the Court of Appeal will order the resumption of the Crown Court proceedings or a fresh trial only where it considers it necessary in the interests of justice to do so.

Section 68: appeals to the Supreme Court

Section 68(1) amends s 33(1) of the CAA 1968 to give both the prosecution and defence a right of appeal to the House of Lords from a decision by the Court of Appeal on a prosecution appeal against a ruling made under this Part of the Act.

Section 68(2) amends s 36 of the CAA 1968 to prevent the Court of Appeal from granting bail to a defendant who is appealing, or is applying for leave to appeal, to the Supreme Court from a Court of Appeal decision made under this Part of the Act. Bail will continue to be a matter for the trial court.

2.6 The Supreme Court

By virtue of the Constitutional Reform Act 2005, the Supreme Court replaced the House of Lords as the highest court in the UK in October 2009. The Judicial Committee of the Privy Council remains as a distinct entity, but follows the Supreme Court to its new location.

Consequently the Supreme Court is the final court of appeal for all United Kingdom civil cases, and criminal cases from England, Wales and Northern Ireland and hears appeals on arguable points of law of general public importance.

Following the determination of an appeal by the Court of Appeal or the Divisional Court, either the prosecution or the defence may appeal to the Supreme Court. Leave from the court below or the

Supreme Court itself must be obtained and two other conditions must be fulfilled, according to s 33 of the CAA 1968:

- the court below must certify that a point of law of general public importance is involved; and
- either the court below or the Supreme Court must be satisfied that the point of law is one which ought to be considered by the Supreme Court.

2.7 Judicial Committee of the Privy Council

The Privy Council is the final court of appeal for certain Commonwealth countries that have retained this option, and for some independent members and associate members of the Commonwealth. The Committee comprises Privy Councillors who hold (or have held) high judicial office and five Lords of Appeal in Ordinary, sometimes assisted by a judge from the country concerned.

Most of the appeals heard by the Committee are civil cases. In the rare criminal cases, it is only on matters involving legal questions that appeals are heard; the Committee does not hear appeals against criminal sentence.

2.8 The Civil Court Structure

Civil actions are between individuals. The State merely provides the legal framework within which they determine and seek to enforce their mutual rights and obligations. Civil cases are cited in the form *Smith v Jones*.

2.9 Magistrates' Courts

Although they deal mainly with criminal matters, the magistrates' courts have a significant civil jurisdiction. They hear family proceedings under the Domestic Proceedings and Magistrates' Courts Act 1978 and the Children Act 1989. Under such circumstances, the court is termed a 'family proceedings court'. A family proceedings court must normally be composed of not more than three justices, including, as far as is practicable, both a man and a woman. Justices who sit on such benches must be members of the family panel, which comprises people specially appointed and trained to deal with family matters. Under the Children Act 1989, the court deals with adoption proceedings, applications for residence and contact orders, and maintenance relating to spouses and children. Under the Magistrates' Courts Act 1978, the court also has the power to make personal protection orders and exclusion orders in cases of matrimonial violence.

The magistrates' courts have powers of recovery in relation to the community charge and its replacement, council tax. They also have the power to enforce charges for water, gas and electricity. Although no longer licensing courts as such, Magistrates' courts hear appeals against licensing decisions of local authorities.

2.10 The Woolf Reforms to the Civil Justice System

Before considering the two most important civil courts, the county court and the High Court, it is necessary to have some understanding of the radical way in which civil law procedure has altered in the fairly recent past. In 1994, Lord Woolf was invited to review the operation of the entire civil justice system and, in his *Interim Report* in 1995, he stated that:

> . . . the key problems facing civil justice today are cost, delay and complexity. These three are interrelated and stem from the uncontrolled nature of the litigation process. In particular, there is no clear judicial responsibility for managing individual cases or for the overall administration of the civil courts [*Access to Justice – Interim Report*, 1995].

Lord Woolf's recommendations, which formed the basis of major changes to the system, were given effect by the Civil Procedure Act 1997 and Civil Procedure Rules (CPR) 1998, supplemented by a series of new practice directions and pre-action protocols. The new system came into effect in April 1999.

There are four main aspects to the reforms, which are as follows.

2.10.1 Judicial case management

The judge is a case manager under the new regime. The new system allocates cases to one of three tracks, depending upon the complexity and value of the dispute. Previously, lawyers from either side were permitted to wrangle almost endlessly with each other about who should disclose what information and documents to whom and at what stage. Now, the judge is under an obligation to actively manage cases. This includes:

- encouraging parties to co-operate with each other;
- identifying issues in the dispute at an early stage;
- disposing of summary issues which do not need full investigation;
- helping the parties to settle the whole or part of the case;
- fixing timetables for the case hearing and controlling the progress of the case; and
- considering whether the benefits of a particular method of hearing the dispute justify its costs.

If the parties refuse to comply with the new rules, practice directions or protocols, the judge will be able to exercise disciplinary powers. These include:

- using costs sanctions against parties (that is, refusing to allow the lawyers who have violated the rules to recover their costs from their client or the other side of the dispute);
- striking out;
- refusal to grant extensions of time; and
- refusal to allow documents not previously disclosed to the court and the other side to be relied upon.

2.10.2 Pre-action protocols

Part of the problem in the past arose from the fact that the courts could only start to exercise control over the progress of a case, and the way it was handled, once proceedings had been issued. Before that stage, lawyers were at liberty to take inordinate amounts of time to do things related to the case, to write to lawyers on the other side to the dispute, and so forth. Now, a mechanism allows new pre-action requirements to be enforced. The objects of the protocols are:

- to encourage greater contact between the parties at the earliest opportunity;
- to encourage a better exchange of information;
- to encourage better pre-action investigation;
- to put parties in a position where they can settle cases fairly and early; and
- to reduce the need for the case to go all the way to court.

2.10.3 Alternatives to going to court

Rule 4.1 of the CPR 1998 requires the court, as a part of its active case management, to encourage and facilitate the use of alternative dispute resolution (ADR), and r 26.4 allows the court to stay proceedings (that is, halt them) in order to allow the parties to go to ADR either where the parties themselves request it or where the court of its own initiative considers it appropriate. The Commercial Court has already used this policy with notable success. It often acts to send cases to ADR where, for example, one side applies for a lengthy extension of time for the case to be heard.

2.10.4 Allocation to track (Pt 26 of the CPR 1998)

Allocation will be to one of three tracks: the small claims track; the fast track; or the multi-track. Each of the tracks offers a different degree of case management.

Small claims track

There is no longer any automatic reference to the small claims track. Claims are allocated to this track in exactly the same way as to the fast track or multi-track. The concept of an arbitration, therefore, disappears and is replaced by a small claims hearing. The jurisdiction for small claims is increased to £5,000 (with the exception of claims for personal injury and actions for housing disrepair, where the limit is £1,000). Parties can consent to use the small claims track even if the value of their claim exceeds the normal value for that track, but this is subject to the court's approval.

Fast track

The fast track procedure handles cases with a value of more than £5,000 but less than £15,000. Amongst the features of the procedure which aim to achieve this are:

- standard directions for trial preparation which avoid complex procedures and multiple experts, with minimum case management intervention by the court;
- a maximum of one day (five hours) for trial; and
- normally, no oral expert evidence is to be given at trial, and costs allowed for the trial are fixed, and vary depending on the level of advocate acting for the parties in the case.

Multi-track

The multi-track handles cases of higher value and more complexity, that is, those cases with a value of over £15,000.

This track does not provide any standard procedure, unlike those for small claims or claims in the fast track. Instead, it offers a range of case management tools, standard directions, case management conferences and pre-trial reviews, which can be used in a 'mix and match' way to suit the requirements of individual cases.

2.11 County Courts

There are approximately 218 county courts, served by some 665 circuit judges and 447 district judges, and every county court has at least one specifically assigned circuit judge. District judges can try cases where the amount involved is £5,000 or less. A *Practice Direction* (1991) has stated that any case involving issues of particular importance or complexity should, as far as possible, be heard by a circuit judge. An appeal from the district judges' decision lies to the circuit judge.

Before the 1999 civil justice reforms, jurisdiction of the county courts was separated from that of the High Court on a strict financial limit basis; for example, a district judge heard cases where the amount was £5,000 or less. The CPR 1998 operate the same processes irrespective of whether the case forum is the High Court or the county court. Broadly, however, county courts will hear small claims and fast track cases, while the more challenging multi-track cases will be heard in the High Court. The changes brought about by the civil justice reforms are likely to put a considerable burden of work on the county courts.

A *Practice Direction* (1991) stated that certain types of actions set down for trial in the High Court are considered to be too important for transfer to a county court. These are cases involving:

- professional negligence;
- fatal accidents;
- allegations of fraud or undue influence;
- defamation;
- malicious prosecution or false imprisonment; and
- claims against the police.

The county courts have an important role to play in the resolution of small claims, through their operation of an arbitration scheme. Consideration of the operation of this scheme will be undertaken below in Chapter 3.

2.12 The High Court of Justice

The High Court has three administrative Divisions: the Court of Chancery; the Queen's Bench Division; and the Family Division. In addition, each Division has a confusingly named Divisional Court, which hears appeals from other legal forums.

The majority of High Court judges sit in the Courts of Justice in the Strand, London, although it is possible for the High Court to sit anywhere in England and Wales.

2.12.1 The Queen's Bench Division

The main civil work of the Queen's Bench Division (QBD) is in contract and tort cases. The Commercial Court is part of this Division. It is staffed by judges with specialist experience in commercial law.

2.12.2 The Queen's Bench Divisional Court

The Queen's Bench Divisional Court, as distinct from the QBD, exercises appellate jurisdiction. Here, two, or sometimes three, judges sit to hear cases relating to the following circumstances:

- appeals on a point of law by way of case stated from magistrates' courts, tribunals and the Crown Court;
- applications for judicial review of the decisions made by governmental and public authorities, inferior courts and tribunals; and
- applications for the writ of habeas corpus from persons who claim that they are being unlawfully detained.

2.12.3 The Chancery Division

The Chancery Division is the modern successor to the old Court of Chancery, that is, the Lord Chancellor's court from which equity was developed. Its jurisdiction includes matters relating to:

- the sale or partition of land and the raising of charges on land;
- the redemption or foreclosure of mortgages;
- the execution or declaration of trusts;
- the administration of the estates of the dead;
- bankruptcy;
- contentious probate business, for example, the validity and interpretation of wills;
- company law and partnerships; and
- revenue law.

Like the QBD, Chancery contains specialist courts: these are the Patents Court and the Companies Court.

2.12.4 The Chancery Divisional Court

Comprising one or two Chancery judges, the Chancery Divisional Court hears appeals from the Commissioners of Inland Revenue on income tax cases and from county courts on matters such as bankruptcy.

2.12.5 The Family Division

The Family Division of the High Court deals with all matrimonial matters, both at first instance and on appeal. It also considers proceedings relating to minors under the Children Act 1989 and issues under the Domestic Violence and Matrimonial Proceedings Act 1976 and s 30 of the Human Fertilisation and Embryology Act 1990.

2.12.6 The Family Divisional Court

The Family Divisional Court, which consists of two High Court judges, hears appeals from decisions of magistrates' courts and county courts in family matters. Commonly, these involve appeals against orders made about financial provision under the Domestic Proceedings and Magistrates' Courts Act 1978.

2.12.7 Specialist courts

In addition to the Divisions within the High Court, there also are two specialist courts which, although not actually part of the High Court, are equivalent in status. These are:

- the Restrictive Practices Court, established by statute in 1956, which hears cases relating to the area of commercial law concerned with whether an agreement is unlawful owing to the extent to which it restricts the trading capabilities of one of the parties. One QBD judge sits with specialist laypersons to hear these cases; and
- the Employment Appeal Tribunal, which is presided over by similar panels, hearing appeals from employment tribunals.

2.13 The Court of Appeal (Civil Division)

Appeals from decisions made by a judge in one of the three High Court Divisions will usually go to the Court of Appeal (Civil Division). An exception to this rule allows an appeal to miss out, or leapfrog, a visit to the Court of Appeal and go straight to the House of Lords. In order for this to happen, the trial judge must grant a certificate of satisfaction and the House of Lords must give permission to appeal. In order for the judge to grant a certificate, he must be satisfied that the case involves a point of law of general public importance which is concerned mainly with statutory interpretation. Alternatively, the court might find that it was bound by a previous Court of Appeal or House of Lords decision which appears to be in conflict with contemporary circumstances. Also, both parties must consent to the procedure.

The Court of Appeal hears appeals from the three Divisions of the High Court, the Divisional Courts, the county courts and various tribunals (considered at 3.3 below). Usually, three judges will sit to hear an appeal, although five may sit for very important cases.

The appeal procedure takes the form of a rehearing of the case through the medium of the transcript of the case, together with the judge's notes. Witnesses are not re-examined and fresh evidence is not usually allowed.

2.13.1 The Civil Procedure Rules

From 2 May 2000, a new Pt 52 of the CPR 1998 combined with the Access to Justice Act 1999 to make new civil appeal rules covering the Court of Appeal, the High Court and the county court. The general rule is that permission to appeal in virtually all cases is mandatory. It should be obtained immediately following the judgment from the lower court or appellate court. Permission will only be given where the court considers that the appellant shows a real prospect of success or there is some other compelling reason.

All appeals will now be limited to a review rather than a complete rehearing, and the appeal will only be allowed if the decision of the lower court was wrong or unjust due to a serious procedural or other irregularity.

The rule now is that there should be only one appeal. An application for a second or subsequent appeal (from High Court or county court) must be made to the Court of Appeal, which will not allow it unless the appeal would raise an important point of principle or practice, or there is some other compelling reason.

The route of appeal has also been altered. The general rule is that the appeal lies to the next level of judge in the court hierarchy, that is, district judge to county court judge to High Court judge. The main exception relates to an appeal against a final decision in a multi-track claim, which will go straight to the Court of Appeal.

Great emphasis is placed on ensuring that cases are dealt with promptly and efficiently, and on weeding out and deterring unjustified appeals. The result is that the opportunity to appeal a decision at first instance in a lower court is much more restricted. It is vital, therefore, that practitioners be properly prepared at the initial hearing.

2.14 The Supreme Court

The Supreme Court is the final court of appeal in civil as well as criminal law. For most cases, five justices will sit to hear the appeal, but courts of seven or more are sometimes convened to hear very important cases.

2.15 Judicial Committee of the Privy Council

As with criminal law, the Privy Council is the final court of appeal for certain Commonwealth countries which have retained this option and from some independent members and associate members of the Commonwealth. In practice, most of the appeals heard by the Committee are civil cases.

The decisions of the Privy Council are very influential in English courts because they concern points of law that are applicable in this jurisdiction and are pronounced upon by the Justices of the Supreme Court in a way which is thus tantamount to a Supreme Court ruling. Technically, however, these decisions are of persuasive authority only, although they are normally followed by English courts.

2.16 The Court of Justice of the European Union

The function of the Court of Justice of the European union (CJEU), which sits in Luxembourg, is to ensure that 'in the interpretation and application of this Treaty the law is observed' (Art 19 of the Treaty on European Union, formerly Art 220 of the EC Treaty). The CJEU is the ultimate authority on European Union law. As the Treaty is often composed in general terms, the court is often called upon to provide the necessary detail for EU law to operate. By virtue of the European Communities Act 1972, EC law has been enacted into English law, so the decisions of the court have direct authority in the English jurisdiction.

See Chapter 1

The court hears disputes between nations and between nations and the institutions of the European Union (EU), such as the European Commission. Individuals, however, can only bring an action if they are challenging a decision which affects them personally.

2.17 The European Court of Human Rights

This Court (the ECtHR) is the supreme court of the Council of Europe, that is, those States within Europe which have accepted to be bound by the European Convention on Human Rights. It has to be established, and emphasised, from the outset that the substance of this section has absolutely nothing to do with the EU as such; the Council of Europe is a completely distinct organisation and, although membership of the two organisations overlap, they are not the same. The Council of Europe is concerned not with economic matters but with the protection of civil rights and freedoms.

It is gratifying, at least to a degree, to recognise that the Convention and its Court are no longer a matter of mysterious external control, the Human Rights Act (HRA) 1998 having incorporated the Convention into UK law and having rendered the ECtHR the supreme court in matters related to its jurisdiction. Much attention was paid to the Convention and the HRA 1998 in Chapter 1 (see above, 1.3), so it only remains to consider the structure and operation of the ECtHR.

The Convention originally established two institutions:

- The European Commission of Human Rights: this body was charged with the task of examining and, if need be, investigating the circumstances of petitions submitted to it. If the Commission was unable to reach a negotiated solution between the parties concerned, it referred the matter to the ECtHR.
- The ECtHR: the European Convention on Human Rights provides that the judgment of the Court shall be final and that parties to it will abide by the decisions of the Court. This body, sitting in Strasbourg, was, and remains, responsible for all matters relating to the interpretation and application of the current Convention.

However, in the 1980s, as the Convention and its Court became more popular and widely known as a forum for asserting human rights, so its workload increased. This pressure was exacerbated by the break-up of the old Communist Eastern Bloc and the fact that the newly independent countries, in both senses of the words, became signatories to the Convention. The statistics support the view of the incipient sclerosis of the original structure:

Applications registered with the Commission

Year	Number of applications registered
1981	404
1993	2,037
1997	4,750

Cases referred to the ECtHR

Year	Number of cases referred
1981	7
1993	52
1997	119

As a consequence of such pressure it became necessary to streamline the procedure by amalgamating the two previous institutions into one Court. In pursuit of this aim, Protocol 11 of the Convention was introduced in 1994. The new ECtHR came into operation on 1 November 1998, although the Commission continued to deal with cases which had already been declared admissible for a further year. Following the reconstruction, however, applications to the new court continued to rise and it is widely recognised that its present structure and procedure need to be radically altered to allow it to manage its current, and apparently ever expanding, case load.

Structure of the Court

The ECtHR consists of 46 judges, representing the number of signatories to the Convention, although they do not have to be chosen from each State and, in any case, they sit as individuals rather than representatives of their State. Judges are generally elected, by the Parliamentary Assembly of the Council of Europe, for six years, but arrangements have been put in place so that one half of the membership of the judicial panel will be required to seek renewal every three years.

The Plenary Court elects its President, two Vice-Presidents and two Presidents of Section for a period of three years. The Court is divided into four Sections, whose composition, fixed for three years, is geographically and gender balanced, and takes account of the different legal systems of the Contracting States. Each Section is presided over by a President, two of the Section Presidents being at the same time Vice-Presidents of the Court. Committees of three judges within each Section deal with preliminary issues, and to that extent they do the filtering formerly done by the Commission. Cases are actually heard by Chambers of seven members, who are chosen on the basis of rotation. Additionally, there is a Grand Chamber of 17 judges, made up of the President, Vice-Presidents and Section Presidents and other judges by rotation. The Grand Chamber deals with the most important cases that require a reconsideration of the accepted interpretations of the Convention.

Judgments

Chambers decide by a majority vote and, usually, reports give a single decision. However, any judge in the case is entitled to append a separate opinion, either concurring or dissenting.

Within three months of delivery of the judgment of a Chamber, any party may request that a case be referred to the Grand Chamber if it raises a serious question of interpretation or application, or a serious issue of general importance. Consequently, the Chamber's judgment only becomes final at the expiry of a three month period, or earlier if the parties state that they do not intend to request a referral. If the case is referred to the Grand Chamber, its decision, taken on a majority vote, is final. All final judgments of the Court are binding on the respondent States concerned. Responsibility for supervising the execution of judgments lies with the Committee of Ministers of the Council of

Europe, which is required to verify that States have taken adequate remedial measures in respect of any violation of the Convention.

Margin of appreciation and derogation

This refers to the fact that the court recognises that there may well be a range of responses to particular crises or social situations within individual States which might well involve some legitimate limitation on the rights established under the Convention. The Court recognises that in such areas, the response should be decided at the local level rather than being imposed centrally. The most obvious, but by no means the only, situations that involve the recognition of the margin of appreciation are the fields of morality and State security.

❖ KEY CASE *Wingrove v United Kingdom* (1996)

Facts:

The British Board of Film Classification refused to give a certificate of classification to the video-film *Visions of Ecstasy* on the ground that it was blasphemous, thus effectively banning it. The applicant, the director of the film, claimed that the refusal to grant a certificate of classification to the film amounted to a breach of his rights to free speech under Art 10 of the Convention.

Decision:

The ECtHR rejected the claim, holding that the offence of blasphemy, by its very nature, did not lend itself to precise legal definition. Consequently, national authorities 'must be afforded a degree of flexibility in assessing whether the facts of a particular case fall within the accepted definition of the offence'.

In *Civil Service Union v United Kingdom* (1987), it was held that national security interests were of such paramount concern that they outweighed individual rights of freedom of association. Hence, the unions had no response under the Convention to the removal of their members' rights to join and be members of a trade union.

It should also be borne in mind that states can enter a derogation from particular provisions of the Convention, or the way in which they operate in particular areas or circumstances. The UK entered such derogation in relation to the extended detention of terrorist suspects without charge under the Terrorism Act 2000 and the Anti-Terrorism, Crime and Security Act 2001.

Even where states avail themselves of the margin of appreciation, they are not at liberty to interfere with rights to any degree beyond what is required as a minimum to deal with the perceived problem within the context of a democratic society. In other words, the doctrine of proportionality requires that there must be a relationship of necessity between the end desired and the means used to achieve it.

An example of the way in which the system operates may be seen in the case of *R v Saunders* (1996). Ernest Saunders was one of the original defendants in the Guinness fraud trial of 1990. Prior to his trial, Saunders had been interviewed by Department of Trade and Industry (DTI) inspectors and was required, under the provisions of the companies legislation, to answer questions without the right to silence. It was claimed that interviews under such conditions, and their subsequent use at the trial leading to his conviction, were in breach of the Convention on Human Rights. In October 1994, the Commission decided in Saunders' favour and the ECtHR confirmed that decision in 1996, although Saunders was not awarded damages. As a result, the Government recognised that the powers given to DTI inspectors breached the Convention, and altered them, but not in a retrospective way that would have benefited Mr Saunders.

The ECtHR subsequently followed its *Saunders* ruling in the case of three others found guilty in the Guinness fraud trials: *IJL, GMR and AKP v United Kingdom* (2000) (see further 7.6.3 below).

Summary

The Criminal and Civil Courts

Criminal courts

Trials take place in either the magistrates' courts or the Crown Court, depending on the nature of the offence, as follows:

- Summary offences cover less serious criminal activity and are decided by the magistrates.
- Indictable offences are the most serious and are tried before a jury in the Crown Court.
- Offences triable either way may be tried by magistrates with the agreement of the defendant; otherwise, they go to the Crown Court.

Appeals

- Appeals from magistrates' courts are to the Crown Court or the High Court (specifically, the Queen's Bench Divisional Court), by way of case stated.
- Appeals from the Crown Court are to the Court of Appeal, and may be as to sentence or conviction.
- Appeals from the Court of Appeal or the Queen's Bench Divisional Court are to the Supreme Court, but only on a point of law of general public importance.

Civil courts

- *Magistrates' courts* have limited but important civil jurisdiction in licensing and, especially, as a family proceedings court under the Children Act 1989.
- *County courts* try personal injuries cases worth up to £50,000. Other actions up to £25,000 should normally be heard by them. Whether actions between £25,000 and £50,000 are heard in the county court or the High Court depends upon the substance, importance and complexity of the case.
- *The High Court* consists of three Divisions:
  - the Queen's Bench Division deals with contract and tort, amongst other things. Its Divisional Court hears applications for judicial review;
  - Chancery deals with matters relating to commercial matters, land, bankruptcy, probate, etc. Its Divisional Court hears taxation appeals; and
  - the Family Division hears matrimonial and child related cases. Its Divisional Court hears appeals from lower courts on these issues.
- *The Court of Appeal (Civil Division)*, usually consisting of three judges, hears appeals from the High Court and county court and, in most cases, is the ultimate court of appeal.
- *The Supreme Court* hears appeals on points of law of general importance. Appeals are heard from the Court of Appeal and may rarely, under the 'leapfrog' provision, hear appeals from the High Court.
- *The Judicial Committee of the Privy Council* is the final court of appeal for those Commonwealth countries which have retained it as the head of their national legal systems.

- *The European Court of Justice* interprets and determines the application of EC law throughout the Community. In such matters, its decisions bind all national courts.
- *The European Court of Human Rights* decides cases in the light of the European Convention on Human Rights. It has no mechanism for directly enforcing its decisions against Member States. However, the Human Rights Act 1998 has incorporated the Convention into UK law; consequently, UK courts are bound to decide cases in line with its provisions.

Further Reading

Flemming, J, 'Judge airs concerns over Woolf reforms' (2000) Law Soc Gazette, 10 February
Harrison, R, 'Appealing prospects' (2000) NLJ 1175–76
Harrison, R, 'Cry Woolf' (1999) 149 NLJ 1011
Harrison, R, 'Why have two types of civil court?' (1999) 149 NLJ 65
Slapper, G and Kelly, D, *English Legal System*, 15th edn, 2014, Abingdon: Routledge

Websites

www.hmcourts-service.gov.uk/index.htm
www.justice.gov.uk/civil/procrules_fin/ – Civil Procedure Rules

Chapter 3

Alternative Dispute Resolution

Chapter Contents

Law in Context: Arbitration

Arbitration developed as a mechanism to resolve business and commercial disputes outside the formal court system. Certain business sectors would agree to appoint an individual who was a respected member of that sector to try and resolve their disputes. By adopting arbitration as the mechanism to resolve a dispute, both parties would generally abide by the decision of the arbitrator and the courts were little involved in monitoring or supervising the process. This process considerably reduced the potential legal costs of litigation. It is suggested that increasingly arbitration has moved closer to litigation and has become less of an alternative to it. In the construction industry, in particular, arbitration is used regularly to resolve disputes and conflict, but has increasingly become more formalised and also services a whole industry dedicated to the provision of arbitration experts.

3.1 Introduction

Although attention tends to be focused on the courts as the forum for resolving conflicts when they arise, the court system is not necessarily the most effective way of deciding disputes, especially those which arise between people, or indeed businesses, which have enjoyed a close relationship. The problem with the court system is that it is essentially an antagonistic process, designed ultimately to determine a winner and a loser in any particular dispute. As a consequence, court procedure tends to emphasise and heighten the degree of conflict between the parties, rather than seek to produce a compromise solution. For various reasons, considered below, it is not always in the best long term interests of the parties to enter into such hostile relations as are involved in court procedure. In recognition of this fact, a number of alternative procedures to court action have been developed for dealing with such disputes.

In its 1999 Consultation Paper, *Alternative Dispute Resolution*, the then Lord Chancellor's Department redefined 'access to justice' as meaning:

> [W]here people need help there are effective solutions that are proportionate to the issues at stake. In some circumstances, this will involve going to court, but in others, that will not be necessary. *For most people most of the time, litigation in the civil courts, and often in tribunals too, should be the method of dispute resolution of last resort.*

That extremely useful Consultation Paper also set out the following list of types of alternative dispute resolution (ADR) mechanisms:

- *Arbitration* is a procedure whereby both sides to a dispute agree to let a third party, the arbitrator, decide. In some instances, there may be a panel. The arbitrator may be a lawyer or may be an expert in the field of the dispute. He will make a decision according to the law. The arbitrator's decision, known as an award, is legally binding and can be enforced through the courts.
- *Early neutral evaluation* is a process in which a neutral professional, commonly a lawyer, hears a summary of each party's case and gives a non-binding assessment of the merits. This can then be used as a basis for settlement or for further negotiation.
- *Expert determination* is a process where an independent third party who is an expert in the subject matter is appointed to decide the dispute. The expert's decision is binding on the parties.
- *Mediation* is a way of settling disputes in which a third party, known as a mediator, helps both sides to come to an agreement that each considers acceptable. Mediation can be 'evaluative',

where the mediator gives an assessment of the legal strength of a case, or 'facilitative', where the mediator concentrates on assisting the parties to define the issues. When mediation is successful and an agreement is reached, it is written down and forms a legally binding contract unless the parties state otherwise.

- *Conciliation* is a procedure like mediation but where the third party, the conciliator, takes a more interventionist role in bringing the two parties together and in suggesting possible solutions to help achieve an agreed settlement. The term 'conciliation' is gradually falling into disuse and the process is regarded as a form of mediation.
- *Med-Arb* is a combination of mediation and arbitration where the parties agree to mediate, but if that fails to achieve a settlement, the dispute is referred to arbitration. The same person may act as mediator and arbitrator in this type of arrangement.
- *Neutral fact finding* is a non-binding procedure used in cases involving complex technical issues. A neutral expert in the subject matter is appointed to investigate the facts of the dispute and make an evaluation of the merits of the case. This can form the basis of a settlement or a starting point for further negotiation.
- *Ombudsmen* are independent office-holders who investigate and rule on complaints from members of the public about maladministration in government and, in particular, services in both the public and private sectors. Some Ombudsmen use mediation as part of their dispute resolution procedures. The powers of Ombudsmen vary. Most Ombudsmen are able to make recommendations; only a few can make decisions which are enforceable through the courts.
- *Utility regulators* are watchdogs appointed to oversee the privatised utilities such as water or gas. They handle complaints from customers who are dissatisfied by the way a complaint has been dealt with by their supplier.

While ADR is usually regarded as referring to arbitration and mediation this chapter will extend this meaning to allow an examination of the role of the various administrative tribunals that exercise so much power in contemporary society.

3.2 Mediation and Conciliation

A number of alternatives to court proceedings have already been listed, but the two most common, or certainly the two that most immediately spring to mind when the topic of ADR is raised, are mediation and conciliation, and as a consequence, although distinct, they are dealt with together.

3.2.1 Mediation

Mediation is the process whereby a third party acts as the conduit through which two disputing parties communicate and negotiate, in an attempt to reach a common resolution to a problem. The mediator may move between the parties, communicating their opinions without their having to meet, or alternatively the mediator may operate in the presence of the parties, but in either situation, the emphasis is on the parties themselves working out a shared agreement as to how the dispute in question is to be settled.

In his Hamlyn Lecture, Lord Mackay considered three alternative systems of mediation and examined the possibility of annexing such schemes to the existing court system. One, involving lawyers advising parties as to the legal strengths of their relative positions, he rejected on the grounds that it merely duplicated, without replacing or extending, what was already available in the courts. A second, based on judges adopting the role of mediators, he rejected on the ground that it might be seen as undermining the traditional impartiality of the judiciary. The third type, and the one that found most favour with him, broadened the issues beyond the legal, to explore solutions that were not available to the court. His approval, however, did not extend to financing such a system; the implication being that public money should, and does, finance the civil justice system and that any benefits that flow from a different system should be financed privately.

In March 1998, the LCD reported that take-up of voluntary mediation procedures offered in pilot schemes had been fairly low. As regards the pilot scheme established in the Central London County Court, a monitoring report found that only 5% of cases referred to the ADR scheme actually took it up. However, in a more positive mode, the report did find that, in cases that did go to mediation, 62% settled during the process without going on to court. The conclusion of the report was that mediation was capable of dealing with a wider range of cases than might have been expected, including personal injury cases. It also reported that those who participated found the process satisfying and led to outcomes that the parties generally thought acceptable.

The way in which mediation operates will become clear from the cases considered below. General information about the operation of mediation may be found at the National Mediation Helpline at www.nationalmediationhelpline.com, which is in itself an indication of the current importance of ADR as a means of resolving disputes. Equally helpful, with excellent flow diagrams on the relationship of ADR and court processes, is the Civil Court Mediation Service Manual produced by the Judicial studies Board at www.jsboard.co.uk/downloads/civil_court_mediation_service_manual_v3_mar09.pdf.

3.2.2 Mediation in divorce

Mediation has an important part to play in family matters, where it is felt that the adversarial approach of the traditional legal system has tended to emphasise, if not increase, existing differences of view between individuals and has not been conducive to amicable settlements. Thus, in divorce cases, mediation has traditionally been used to enable the parties themselves to work out an agreed settlement rather than having one imposed on them from outside by the courts.

This emphasis on mediation was strengthened in the Family Law Act 1996, but it is important to realise that there are potential problems with mediation. The assumption that the parties freely negotiate the terms of their final agreement in a less than hostile manner may be deeply flawed, to the extent that it assumes equality of bargaining power and knowledge between the parties to the negotiation. Mediation may well ease pain, but unless the mediation procedure is carefully and critically monitored, it may gloss over and perpetuate a previously exploitative relationship, allowing the more powerful participant to manipulate and dominate the more vulnerable and force an inequitable agreement. Establishing entitlements on the basis of clear legal advice may be preferable to apparently negotiating those entitlements away in the non-confrontational, therapeutic, atmosphere of mediation.

Before receiving legal aid for representation in a divorce case a person is supposed to have a meeting with a mediator to assess whether mediation is a suitable alternative to court proceedings. The only exception to this requirement is in relation to allegations of domestic abuse. However, excluding those exempted for reasons of domestic abuse, only 20% of people publicly funded in divorce proceedings actually get involved in mediation. In March 2007 the National Audit Office (NAO), an independent body responsible for scrutinising public spending on behalf of Parliament, published the results of an investigation into this low take-up of mediation in this area. It was entitled *Legal aid and mediation for people involved in family breakdown*. Its findings were based on an 18-month period, from October 2004 to March 2006 and related to 4,000 people who had received legal aid in relation to marital breakdown proceedings. Those involved were also asked where they had first sought advice and whether their adviser had discussed mediation. Where mediation had been mentioned they were asked why they had either chosen or rejected mediation.

The report confirmed the statistic that at present only 20% of people funded by legal aid for family breakdown cases currently opt for mediation and further found that:

- 33% of those who did not try mediation said that their adviser had not told them about it. The NAO was particularly concerned at the proportion of legal advisers who failed to tell their clients about mediation, suggesting that the motivation for such failure was financial;
- 42% of those who were not told about mediation would have been willing to try it had they known about it;
- the average cost of legal aid in mediated cases is £752, compared with £1,682 for non-mediated cases. Consequently, if all cases had been mediated the cost to the taxpayer would have been £74 million less, and if 14% of the cases that proceeded to court had been resolved through mediation, there would have been resulting savings equivalent to some £10 million a year;
- mediated cases are quicker to resolve, taking on average 110 days, compared with 435 days for non-mediated cases.

The report makes several key recommendations to the Legal Services Commission (LSC) including:

- the LSC should actively promote mediation to solicitors and their clients;
- contracts between the LSC and solicitors should reflect a presumption that mediation should normally be attempted before other remedies are tried;
- the exemptions from using mediation should be reviewed;
- the LSC should consider paying for both parties to use mediation where only one party is eligible for legal aid;
- the provision of mediation should be extended to areas of the country that are not well covered, either by supporting extension of the existing provision of outreach services or by providing reasonable travel expenses to those living in areas with less access to a mediator.

Interestingly, the LSC's own strategy papers on family law, and the family fee consultation (both published in March 2007), also proposed a review of the exemptions from mediation and that mediators, rather than solicitors, should assess whether domestic violence is an issue and whether mediation is or is not suitable.

3.2.3 Conciliation

Conciliation takes mediation a step further and gives the mediator the power to suggest grounds for compromise and the possible basis for a conclusive agreement. Both mediation and conciliation have been available in relation to industrial disputes under the auspices of the government-funded ACAS. One of the statutory functions of ACAS is to try to resolve industrial disputes by means of discussion and negotiation or, if the parties agree, the Service might take a more active part as arbitrator in relation to a particular dispute.

The essential weakness in the procedures of mediation and conciliation lies in the fact that, although they *may* lead to the resolution of a dispute, they do not *necessarily* achieve that end. Where they operate successfully, they are excellent methods of dealing with problems, as essentially the parties to the dispute determine their own solutions and therefore feel committed to the outcome. The problem is that they have no binding power and do not always lead to an outcome.

3.3 The Courts and Mediation

The increased importance of alternative dispute resolution mechanisms has been signalled in both legislation and court procedures. For example, the Commercial Court issued a *Practice Statement* in 1993, stating that it wished to encourage ADR, and followed this in 1996 with a further *Direction* that allows judges to consider whether a case is suitable for ADR at its outset, and to invite the parties to attempt a neutral, non-court settlement of their dispute. In cases in the Court of Appeal, the Master of the Rolls now writes to the parties, urging them to consider ADR and asking them for their reasons for declining to use it. Also, as part of the civil justice reforms, r 26.4 of the Civil Procedure Rules (CPR) 1998 enables judges, either on their own account or with the agreement of both parties, to stop court proceedings where they consider the dispute to be better suited to solution by some alternative procedure, such as arbitration or mediation.

In *Cowl v Plymouth CC* (2001), the Court of Appeal, with Lord Woolf as a member of the panel, made it perfectly clear that lawyers for both parties are under a heavy duty only to resort to litigation if it is unavoidable and the dispute cannot be settled by some other non-court based mechanism. In *Kinstreet Ltd v Bamargo Corp Ltd* (1999), the court actually ordered ADR against the wishes of one of the parties to the action, requiring that:

> [T]he parties shall take such serious steps as they may be advised to resolve their disputes by ADR procedures before the independent mediator . . . [and] if the actions are not finally settled by 30 October 1999 the parties are to inform the court by letter within three working days what steps towards ADR have been taken and why such steps have failed.

If, subsequently, a court is of the opinion that an action it has been required to decide could have been settled more effectively through ADR then, under r 45.5 of the CPR 1998, it may penalise the party who insisted on the court hearing by awarding them reduced (or no) costs should they win the case. The potential consequences of not abiding by a recommendation to use ADR may be seen in *Dunnett v Railtrack plc* (2002).

❖ KEY CASE — *Dunnett v Railtrack plc* (2002)

Facts:

Dunnett won a right to appeal against a previous court decision, the court granting the appeal recommended that the dispute should be put to arbitration. Railtrack, however, refused Dunnett's offer of arbitration and insisted on the dispute going back to a full court hearing.

Decision:

Although Railtrack was successful in the subsequent hearing the Court of Appeal, however, held that if a party rejected ADR out of hand, when it had been suggested by the court, they would suffer the consequences when costs came to be decided. In this case, Railtrack had refused even to contemplate ADR at a stage prior to the costs of the appeal beginning to flow and consequently were not entitled to their full costs.

In his judgment in *Dunnett*, Brooke LJ set out the modern approach to ADR:

> Skilled mediators are now able to achieve results satisfactory to both parties in many cases which are quite beyond the power of lawyers and courts to achieve. This court has knowledge of cases where intense feelings have arisen, for instance in relation to clinical negligence claims. But when the parties are brought together on neutral soil with a skilled mediator to help them resolve their differences, it may very well be that the mediator is able to achieve a result by which the parties shake hands at the end and feel that they have gone away having settled the dispute on terms with which they are happy to live. A mediator may be able to

provide solutions which are beyond the powers of the court to provide . . . It is to be hoped that any publicity given to this part of the judgment of the court will draw the attention of lawyers to their duties to further the overriding objective in the way that is set out in Part 1 of the Rules and to the possibility that, if they turn down out of hand the chance of alternative dispute resolution when suggested by the court, as happened on this occasion, they may have to face uncomfortable costs consequences.

The Court of Appeal subsequently applied *Dunnett* in *Leicester Circuits Ltd v Coates Bros plc* (2003), where, although it found for Coates, it did not award it full costs on the grounds that it had withdrawn from a mediation process. The Court of Appeal also dismissed Coates' claim that there was no realistic prospect of success in the mediation. As Judge LJ stated:

> We do not for one moment assume that the mediation process would have succeeded, but certainly there is a prospect that it would have done if it had been allowed to proceed. That therefore bears on the issue of costs.

It is possible to refuse to engage in mediation without subsequently suffering in the awards of costs. The test, however, is an objective rather than a subjective one and a difficult one to sustain, as was shown in *Hurst v Leeming* (2002).

❖ KEY CASE *Hurst v Leeming* (2002)

Facts:

Hurst, a solicitor, started legal proceedings against his former partners. He instructed Leeming, a barrister, to represent him. When the action proved unsuccessful, Hurst sued Leeming in professional negligence. When that action failed, Hurst argued that Leeming should not be awarded costs, as he, Hurst, had offered to mediate the dispute but Leeming had rejected the offer. Leeming cited five separate justifications for his refusal to mediate. These were:

- the heavy costs he had already incurred in meeting the allegations;
- the seriousness of the allegation made against him;
- the lack of substance in the claim;
- the fact that he had already provided Hurst with a full refutation of his allegation; and
- the fact that, given Hurst's obsessive character, there was no real prospect of a successful outcome to the litigation.

Decision:

Only the fifth justification was accepted by the court, although even in that case it was emphasised that the conclusion had to be supported by an objective evaluation of the situation. However, in the circumstances, given Hurst's behaviour and character, the conclusion that mediation would not have resolved the complaint could be sustained objectively.

In *Halsey v Milton Keynes General NHS Trust* (2004), the Court of Appeal emphasised that the criterion was the reasonableness of the belief that there was no real prospect of success through ADR.

In the *Halsey* appeal, the only ground of appeal was that the judge at first instance had been wrong to award the defendant, the Milton Keynes General NHS, its costs, since it had refused a number of invitations by the claimant to mediate. As the court emphasised, in deciding whether to deprive a successful party of some or all of their costs on the grounds that they have refused to agree to ADR, it must be borne in mind that such an order is an exception to the general rule that costs should follow the event. In demonstrating such exceptional circumstances, in the view of the Court of Appeal, the burden is to be placed on the unsuccessful party to the substantive action to show why there should be any departure from that general rule. Lord Justice Dyson said (para 28):

> It seems to us that a fair . . . balance is struck if the burden is placed on the unsuccessful party to show that there was a reasonable prospect that mediation would have been successful. This is not an unduly onerous burden to discharge: he does not have to prove that a mediation would *in fact* have succeeded. It is significantly easier for the unsuccessful party to prove that there was a reasonable prospect that a mediation would have succeeded than for the successful party to prove the contrary.

In taking such a stance, the Court of Appeal was sensitive to the possibility, as it implicitly suggested was the case in relation to the claimants in the *Halsey* case, that (para 18):

> . . . there would be considerable scope for a claimant to use the threat of costs sanctions to extract a settlement from the defendant even where the claim is without merit. Courts should be particularly astute to this danger. Large organisations, especially public bodies, are vulnerable to pressure from claimants who, having weak cases, invite mediation as a tactical ploy. They calculate that such a defendant may at least make a nuisance-value offer to buy off the cost of a mediation and the risk of being penalised in costs for refusing a mediation even if ultimately successful . . .

As regards the power of the courts to order mediation, the Court of Appeal declined to accept such a proposition, finding it to be contrary to both domestic and ECHR law.

In *Swain Mason v Mills & Reeve* (2011), the Court of Appeal reaffirmed the decision in *Halsey* that, under certain circumstances, parties could refuse to engage in mediation. In reaching its decision, the Court of Appeal provided a gloss on *Halsey v Milton Keynes General NHS Trust*, holding that it was authority for the following:

- parties should not be compelled to mediate;
- mediation and other ADR processes do not offer a panacea, and can have disadvantages as well as advantages, and are not appropriate for every case;
- a party's reasonable belief that it has a strong case is a factor in deciding whether it was unreasonable to refuse mediation;
- where a party reasonably believes that they have a watertight case, that may well be a sufficient justification for a refusal to mediate;
- account needs to be taken of whether meditation would succeed, given the parties' stances;
- the court should be astute to the danger of parties being wrongly put under costs pressure as regards mediation.

3.3.1 A case study in how not to do it: *Burchell v Bullard* (2005)

This unfortunate case, for everyone apart perhaps from the lawyers engaged to pursue it, can be taken as a signal example of the dangers and inappropriateness of pursuing legal action in the courts when ADR is available and a better way of deciding the contended issue.

❖ KEY CASE *Burchell v Bullard* (2005)

Facts:
The appellant in the case was a builder who had contracted to build two large extensions on to the defendants' home. The dispute arose because the Bullards claimed that some of the work carried out by Burchell's subcontractor was substandard. As a result they refused to make a payment, due under the contract, until the allegedly defective work had been rectified. As a result, Burchell left the site. In an attempt to resolve the dispute Burchell suggested that the dispute be referred to mediation, but on the advice of their chartered surveyor the Bullards refused to mediate, claiming that due to the complexity of the issues the case was not appropriate for mediation.

At first instance the judge, District Judge Tennant, was clear that (para 20):

> There are faults on both sides . . . [o]n balance however, I am satisfied that quite apart from the net amount actually recovered by the claimant, the defendants are more at fault than the claimant in the sense that they have conducted the litigation more unreasonably.

Nonetheless, he decided that each of the parties should pay the costs of the other in relation to the main claim in the action. Burchell subsequently appealed against those costs orders.

Decision:
The attitude of the Court of Appeal is scathingly evident in the judgment of Ward LJ. As to the offer of mediation he stated that (para 3):

> [Burchell's] solicitors wrote sensibly suggesting that to avoid litigation the matter be referred for alternate dispute resolution through 'a qualified construction mediator'. *The sorry response* from the respondents' chartered building surveyor was that 'the matters complained of are technically complex and as such mediation is not an appropriate route to settle matters.' (emphasis added)

However, as Ward LJ pointed out, 'All the Bullards wanted was for the builder to complete the contract and rectify the defective work'. So what was the underlying 'technically complex' issue that prevented mediation?

As Ward LJ examined the facts of the case he found things, regrettably but not unexpectedly, getting worse (para 23):

> As we had expected, *an horrific picture emerges*. In this comparatively small case where ultimately only about £5,000 will pass from defendants to claimant, the claimant will have spent about £65,000 up to the end of the trial and he will also have to pay the subcontractor's costs of £27,500. We were told that the claimant might recover perhaps only 25 per cent of his trial costs, say £16,000, because most of the contest centred on the counterclaim. The defendants' costs of trial are estimated at about £70,000 and it was estimated the claimant would have to pay about 85 per cent, i.e. £59,500. *Recovery of £5,000 will have cost him about £136,000. On the other hand the defendants who lost in the sense that they have to pay the claimant £5,000 are only a*

> *further £26,500 out of pocket in respect of costs*. Then there are the costs of the appeal – £13,500 for the appellant and over £9,000 for the respondents. *A judgment of £5,000 will have been procured at a cost to the parties of about £185,000. Is that not horrific*? (emphases added)

In examining the situation, Ward LJ emphasised the fact that the appellant's offer to mediate was made long before the action started, and long before the crippling costs had been incurred. The issue to be decided, therefore, was whether the respondents had acted unreasonably in refusing the offer of mediation. While Ward LJ recognised that *Halsey v The Milton Keynes General NHS Trust* had set out the manner in which such a question should be answered, he declined to follow it in the immediate case. His reasoning was as follows (para 42):

> It seems to me, therefore, that the *Halsey* factors are established in this case and that the court should mark its disapproval of the defendants' conduct by imposing some costs sanction. Yet I draw back from doing so. This offer was made in May 2001. The defendants rejected the offer on the advice of their surveyor, not of their solicitor. The law had not become as clear and developed as it now is following the succession of judgments from this court of which *Halsey* and *Dunnett v Railtrack plc (Practice Note)* [2002] 1 WLR 2434 are prime examples. To be fair to the defendants one must judge the reasonableness of their actions against the background of practice a year earlier than *Dunnett*. In the light of the knowledge of the times and in the absence of legal advice, I cannot condemn them as having been so unreasonable that a costs sanction should follow many years later.

However, Ward LJ was as emphatic as he was admonitory in his assessment of the present case and his view as to how future cases should be treated. As he put it (paras 41–43):

> *. . . a small building dispute is par excellence the kind of dispute which, as the recorder found, lends itself to ADR*. Secondly, the merits of the case favoured mediation. The defendants behaved unreasonably in believing, if they did, that their case was so watertight that they need not engage in attempts to settle. They were counterclaiming almost as much to remedy *some* defective work as they had contracted to pay for the whole of the stipulated work. There was clearly room for give and take. *The stated reason for refusing mediation that the matter was too complex for mediation is plain nonsense*. Thirdly, the costs of ADR would have been a drop in the ocean *compared with the fortune that has been spent on this litigation*. Finally, the way in which the claimant modestly presented his claim and readily admitted many of the defects, allied with the finding that he was transparently honest and more than ready to admit where he was wrong and to shoulder responsibility for it augured well for mediation. The claimant has satisfied me that mediation would have had a reasonable prospect of success. The defendants cannot rely on their own obstinacy to assert that mediation had no reasonable prospect of success . . . *The profession must, however, take no comfort from this conclusion. Halsey has made plain not only the high rate of a successful outcome being achieved by mediation but also its established importance as a track to a just result running parallel with that of the court system*. Both have a proper part to play in the administration of justice. The court has given its stamp of approval to mediation and *it is now the legal profession which must become fully aware of*

> *and acknowledge its value*. The profession can no longer with impunity shrug aside reasonable requests to mediate . . . These defendants have escaped the imposition of a costs sanction in this case *but defendants in a like position in the future can expect little sympathy if they blithely battle on regardless of the alternatives*. (emphases added)

In the final analysis the Court of Appeal directed the defendants to pay 60% of the claimant's costs of the original claim and counterclaim and related proceedings. However, there was still a sting in the tail, for as Ward LJ stated (para 47):

> We have not heard argument on the costs of this appeal. In order that more costs are not wasted, I say that my preliminary view is that costs of the appeal should follow the event. The appellant has been successful and as at present advised and having regard to the checklist of relevant considerations set out in CPR 44.3, I can see no justification for his not having the costs of the appeal.

So the Bullards faced even more costs for their failure to take advantage of the earlier offer of mediation.

3.4 Arbitration

The first and oldest of these alternative procedures is arbitration. This is the procedure whereby parties in dispute refer the issue to a third party for resolution, rather than taking the case to the ordinary law courts. Studies have shown a reluctance on the part of commercial undertakings to have recourse to the law to resolve their disputes. At first sight, this appears to be paradoxical. The development of contract law can, to a great extent, be explained as the law's response to the need for regulation in relation to business activity, and yet businesses decline to make use of its procedures. To some degree, questions of speed and cost explain this peculiar phenomenon, but it can be explained more fully by reference to the introduction to this chapter. It was stated there that informal procedures tend to be most effective where there is a high degree of mutuality and interdependency, and that is precisely the case in most business relationships. Businesses seek to establish and maintain long term relationships with other concerns. The problem with the law is that the court case tends to terminally rupture such relationships. It is not suggested that, in the final analysis, where the stakes are sufficiently high, recourse to the law will not be had; such action, however, does not represent the first, or indeed the preferred, option. In contemporary business practice it is common, if not standard, practice for commercial contracts to contain express clauses referring any future disputes to arbitration. This practice is well established and its legal effectiveness has long been recognised by the law.

3.4.1 Arbitration procedure

The Arbitration Act 1996 repeals Pt 1 of the Arbitration Act 1950 and the whole of the Arbitration Acts of 1975 and 1979. As the Act is a relatively new piece of legislation, it is necessary to consider it in some detail.

Section 1 of the 1996 Act states that it is founded on the following principles:

(a) the object of arbitration is to obtain the fair resolution of disputes by an impartial tribunal without necessary delay or expense;

(b) the parties should be free to agree how their disputes are resolved, subject only to such safeguards as are necessary in the public interest;
(c) in matters governed by this part of the Act, the court should not intervene except as provided by this part.

This provision of general principles, which should inform the reading of the later detailed provisions of the Act, is unusual for UK legislation, but may be seen as reflecting the purposes behind the Act, a major one of which was the wish to ensure that London did not lose its place as a leading centre for international arbitration. As a consequence of the demand-driven nature of the new legislation, it would seem that court interference in the arbitration process has had to be reduced to a minimum and replaced by party autonomy. Under the 1996 Act, the role of the arbitrator has been increased and that of the court has been reduced to the residual level of intervention where the arbitration process either requires legal assistance or is seen to be failing to provide a just settlement.

The Act follows the Model Arbitration Law, which was adopted in 1985 by the United Nations Commission on International Trade Law.

While it is possible for there to be an oral arbitration agreement at common law, s 5 provides that Pt 1 of the Arbitration Act 1996 only applies to agreements in writing. What this means in practice, however, has been extended by s 5(3), which provides that, where the parties agree to an arbitration procedure which is in writing, that procedure will be operative, even though the agreement between the parties is not itself in writing. An example of such a situation would be where a salvage operation was negotiated between two vessels on the basis of Lloyds' standard salvage terms. It would be unlikely that the actual agreement would be reduced to written form but, nonetheless, the arbitration element in those terms would be effective.

In analysing the Arbitration Act 1996, it is useful to consider it in four distinct parts: autonomy of the parties; arbitrators and their powers; powers of the court; and appellate rights.

Autonomy of the parties

It is significant that most of the provisions set out in the Arbitration Act 1996 are not compulsory. As is clearly stated in s 1, it is up to the parties to an arbitration agreement to agree on what procedures to adopt. The main purpose of the Act is to empower the parties to the dispute and to allow them to decide how it is to be decided. In pursuit of this aim, the mandatory parts of the Act only take effect where the parties involved do not agree otherwise. It is actually possible for the parties to agree that the dispute should not be decided in line with the strict legal rules; rather, it should be decided in line with commercial fairness, which might be a different thing altogether.

Arbitrators and their powers

The arbitration tribunal may consist of either a single arbitrator or a panel, as the parties decide (s 15). If one party fails to appoint an arbitrator, then the other party's nominee may act as sole arbitrator (s 17). Under s 20(4) of the Arbitration Act 1996, where there is a panel and it fails to reach a majority decision, the decision of the chair shall prevail.

The tribunal is required to fairly and impartially adopt procedures which are suitable to the circumstances of each case. It is also for the tribunal to decide all procedural and evidential matters. Parties may be represented by a lawyer or any other person, and the tribunal may appoint experts or legal advisers to report to it.

Arbitrators will be immune from action being taken against them, except in situations where they have acted in bad faith.

Section 30 provides that, unless the parties agree otherwise, the arbitrator can rule on questions relating to jurisdiction, that is, in relation to:

a. whether there actually is a valid arbitration agreement;
b. whether the arbitration tribunal is properly constituted; and
c. what matters have been submitted to arbitration in accordance with the agreement.

Section 32 allows any of the parties to raise preliminary objections to the substantive jurisdiction of the arbitration tribunal in court, but provides that they may only do so on limited grounds, which require either: the agreement of the parties concerned; the permission of the arbitration tribunal; or the agreement of the court. Permission to appeal will only be granted where the court is satisfied that the question involves a point of law of general importance.

Section 28 expressly provides that the parties to the proceedings are jointly and severally liable to pay the arbitrators such reasonable fees and expenses as are appropriate. Previously, this was only an implied term.

Section 29 of the Arbitration Act 1996 provides that arbitrators are not liable for anything done or omitted in the discharge of their functions unless the act or omission was done in bad faith.

Section 33 provides that the tribunal has a general duty:

a. to act fairly and impartially between the parties, giving each a reasonable opportunity to state their case; and
b. to adopt procedures suitable for the circumstance of the case, avoiding unnecessary delay or expense.

Section 35 provides that, subject to the parties agreeing to the contrary, the tribunal shall have the power:

a. to order parties to provide security for costs (previously a power reserved to the courts);
b. to give directions in relation to property subject to the arbitration; and
c. to direct that a party or witness be examined on oath, and to administer the oath.

The parties may also empower the arbitrator to make provisional orders (s 39 of the Arbitration Act 1996).

Powers of the court

Where one party seeks to start a court action in the face of a valid arbitration agreement to the contrary, then the other party may request the court to stay the litigation in favour of the arbitration agreement under ss 9–11 of the Arbitration Act 1996. Where, however, both parties agree to ignore the arbitration agreement and seek recourse to litigation, then, following the party consensual nature of the Act, the agreement may be ignored.

The courts may order a party to comply with an order of the tribunal and may also order parties and witnesses to attend and to give oral evidence before tribunals (s 43).

The court has power to revoke the appointment of an arbitrator, on application of any of the parties, where there has been a failure in the appointment procedure under s 18, but it also has powers to revoke authority under s 24. This power comes into play on the application of one of the parties in circumstances where the arbitrator:

a. has not acted impartially;
b. does not possess the required qualifications;
c. does not have either the physical or mental capacity to deal with the proceedings;
d. has refused or failed to properly conduct the proceedings; or has been dilatory in dealing with the proceedings or in making an award, to the extent that it will cause substantial injustice to the party applying for their removal.

Under s 45, the court may, on application by one of the parties, decide any preliminary question of law arising in the course of the proceedings.

Appellate rights

Once the decision has been made, there are limited grounds for appeal. The first ground arises under s 67 of the Arbitration Act 1996, in relation to the substantive jurisdiction of the arbitral panel, although the right to appeal on this ground may be lost if the party attempting to make use of it took part in the arbitration proceedings without objecting to the alleged lack of jurisdiction. The second ground for appeal to the courts is on procedural grounds, under s 68, on the basis that some serious irregularity affected the operation of the tribunal. Serious irregularity means either:

- failure to comply with the general duty set out in s 33;
- failure to conduct the tribunal as agreed by the parties;
- uncertainty or ambiguity as to the effect of the award; or
- failure to comply with the requirement as to the form of the award.

Parties may also appeal on a point of law arising from the award under s 69 of the Arbitration Act 1996. However, the parties can agree beforehand to preclude such a possibility and, where they agree to the arbitral panel making a decision without providing a reasoned justification for it, they will also lose the right to appeal.

The issue of rights to appeal under s 69 has been considered in a number of cases by the Court of Appeal. In March 2002, in *North Range Shipping Ltd v Seatrams Shipping Corp* (2002), the court confirmed that there was no further right of appeal against a judge's refusal to grant permission for an appeal against an arbitrator's decision, except on the grounds of unfairness. In *CMA CGM SA v Beteiligungs KG* (2002), it insisted that judges in the High Court should not be too hasty in allowing appeals. In the case in point, the Court of Appeal decided that the present appeal should not have been allowed. In reaching this decision, the court set out the new standard that had to be met to justify an appeal, that 'the question should be one of general importance and the decision of the arbitrators should be at least open to serious doubt'. This standard was higher than that applied under the previous test as stated in *Antaios Compania Naviera SA v Salen Redereierna AB* (1985).

In *BLCT Ltd v J Sainsbury plc* (2003), the Court of Appeal held that not only had the appellant no real prospect of succeeding in its appeal but also rejected the argument that, by curtailing the right of appeal, s 69 was incompatible with Art 6 of the European Convention on Human Rights.

The sensitivity with which the court considers appeals may be seen in in the approach of Mrs Justice Gloster in *Soeximex SAS v Agrocorp International PTE Ltd* (2011). While allowing the appeal, she was nonetheless at pains to justify her/his action:

> The Commercial Court is very sensitive to the fact that parties have chosen to have their disputes resolved by an industry or trade arbitral tribunal, rather than by the Courts. As a matter of general approach, it tries to uphold arbitration awards and to read them in a sensible and commercial way. It is very mindful that the Court's role on a s 68 application is not to pick holes in an award, or to indulge in an over-nice analysis of what may be understandably brief reasons given by commercial men in areas with which they are far more familiar than the Court. However, in this case, there were clearly legal issues which had to be addressed and were not . . . [T]his failure amounted to a serious irregularity which has caused the buyers substantial injustice, since . . . they have been deprived of the opportunity of having their arguments on these important points resolved, whether by the board, or on an appeal under s 69.

3.4.2 Relationship to ordinary courts

In general terms, the courts have no objection to individuals settling their disputes on a voluntary basis but, at the same time, they are careful to maintain their supervisory role in such procedures. Arbitration agreements are no different from other terms of a contract and, in line with the normal rules of contract law, courts will strike out any attempt to oust their ultimate jurisdiction as being contrary to public policy. Thus, as has been stated above, arbitration proceedings are open to challenge, through judicial review, on the ground that they were not conducted in a judicial manner.

The Arbitration Act 1950 allowed for either party to the proceedings to have questions of law authoritatively determined by the High Court through the procedure of case stated. The High Court could also set aside the decision of the arbitrator on grounds of fact, law or procedure. Whereas the arbitration process was supposed to provide a quick and relatively cheap method of deciding disputes, the availability of the appeals procedures meant that parties could delay the final decision and, in so doing, increase the costs. In such circumstances, arbitration became the precursor to a court case, rather than a replacement of it. The Arbitration Act 1979 abolished the case stated procedure and curtailed the right to appeal and, as has been seen, the Arbitration Act 1996 has reduced the grounds for appeal to the court system even further.

In February 2008 the Archbishop of Canterbury, Rowan Williams, caused a furore when, in a speech, he suggested that the eventual use of Sharia law to deal with disputes was inevitable in the United Kingdom. His comment was taken out of context, but as some commentators pointed out it was already possible for Sharia Councils to decide disputes on an informal non-compulsory basis using Sharia principles. Similarly, Jewish people are able to use their own system of courts, the Beth Din, to decide issues on a voluntary basis.

3.4.3 Advantages

There are numerous advantages to be gained from using arbitration rather than the court system:

- *Privacy*
  Arbitration tends to be a private procedure. This has the twofold advantage that outsiders do not get access to any potentially sensitive information and the parties to the arbitration do not run the risk of any damaging publicity arising out of reports of the proceedings. The issue of privacy was considered by the Court of Appeal in *Department of Economic Policy and Development of the City of Moscow v Bankers Trust* (2004), in which the decision of an arbitration panel was challenged in the High Court under s 68 of the Arbitration Act 1996. The details of the original arbitration had remained confidential between the parties and in the High Court Cooke J decided that the details of his judgment against the appellants should also remain confidential. On appeal, Cooke J's decision not to publish his judgment in full was confirmed, although the Court of Appeal did allow the publication of a Lawtel summary of the case.
- *Informality*
  The proceedings are less formal than a court case and they can be scheduled more flexibly than court proceedings.
- *Speed*
  Arbitration is generally much quicker than taking a case through the courts. Where, however, one of the parties makes use of the available grounds to challenge an arbitration award, the prior costs of the arbitration will have been largely wasted.
- *Cost*
  Arbitration is generally a much cheaper procedure than taking a case to the normal courts. Nonetheless, the costs of arbitration and the use of specialist arbitrators should not be underestimated.

- *Expertise*
  The use of a specialist arbitrator ensures that the person deciding the case has expert knowledge of the actual practice within the area under consideration and can form their conclusion in line with accepted practice.

It can be argued that arbitration represents a privatisation of the judicial process. It may be assumed, therefore, that, of all its virtues, perhaps the greatest (at least as far as the Government is concerned) is the potential reduction in costs for the State in providing the legal framework within which disputes are resolved.

3.4.4 The small claims track (Pt 27 of the CPR 1998)

After 1973, an arbitration service was available within the county court specifically for the settlement of relatively small claims. This small claims procedure, known as arbitration, was operated by county court district judges. However, under the civil justice reforms, there is no longer any automatic reference to arbitration, which is replaced by reference to the small claims track (see 2.10.4 above). Claims are allocated to this track in exactly the same way as they are allocated to the fast track or multi-track. The concept of an arbitration therefore disappears and is replaced by a small claims hearing. Aspects of the old small claims procedure that are retained include their informality, the interventionist approach adopted by the judiciary, the limited costs regime and the limited grounds for appeal (misconduct of the district judge or an error of law made by the court).

Parties can consent to use the small claims track even if the value of their claim exceeds the normal value for that track, although subject to the court's approval. The limited cost regime will not apply to these claims. But costs will be limited to the costs that might have been awarded if the claim had been dealt with in the fast track. Parties will also be restricted to a maximum one day hearing.

3.4.5 Arbitration under codes of conduct

When it was first established in 1973, the small claims procedure was seen as a mechanism through which consumers could enforce their rights against recalcitrant traders. In reality, the arbitration procedure has proved to be just as useful for, and used just as much by, traders and businesses as consumers. There remains one area of arbitration, however, that is specifically focused on the consumer: arbitration schemes that are run under the auspices of particular trade associations. As part of the regulation of trade practices and in the pursuit of effective measures of consumer protection, the Office of Fair Trading has encouraged the establishment of voluntary codes of practice within particular areas. It is usual to find that such codes of practice provide arbitration schemes to resolve particularly intractable problems between individual consumers and members of the association. Such schemes are never compulsory and do not seek to replace the consumers' legal rights, but they do provide a relatively inexpensive mechanism for dealing with problems without the need even to bother the county court. Such schemes are numerous; the most famous one is probably the travel industry scheme operated under the auspices of the Association of British Travel Agents, but other associations run similar schemes in such areas as car sales, shoe retailing, dry cleaning, etc. Again, the point of such schemes is to provide a quick, cheap means of dealing with problems without running the risk of completely alienating the consumer from the trade in question.

Although many of the trade arbitration schemes offered consumers distinct advantages, some did not and, in order to remedy any abuses, the Consumer Arbitration Act 1988 was introduced. This statute provides that, in the case of consumer contracts, no prior agreement between the parties that subsequent disputes will be referred to arbitration can be enforced. However, consumers will be bound by arbitration procedures where they have already entered into them as a consequence of a prior agreement, or have agreed to them subsequently.

3.5 Administrative Tribunals

Although attention tends to be focused on the operation of the courts as the forum within which legal decisions are taken, it is no longer the case that the bulk of legal and quasi-legal questions are determined within that court structure. There are, as an alternative to the court system, a large number of tribunals that have been set up under various Acts of Parliament to rule on the operation of the particular schemes established under those Acts. Almost one million cases are dealt with by tribunals each year, and as the Royal Commission on Legal Services (Cmnd 7648) pointed out in 1979, the number of cases then being heard by tribunals was six times greater than the number of contested civil cases dealt with by the High Court and county court combined. It is evident, therefore, that tribunals are of major significance as alternatives to traditional courts in dealing with disputes.

The generally accepted explanation for the establishment and growth of tribunals in Britain since 1945 was the need to provide a specialist forum to deal with cases involving conflicts between an increasingly interventionist welfare state, its functionaries and the rights of private citizens. It is certainly true that, since 1945, the welfare state has intervened more and more in every aspect of people's lives. The intention may have been to extend various social benefits to a wider constituency, but in so doing, the machinery of the welfare state, and in reality those who operate that machinery, have been granted powers to control access to its benefits, and as a consequence have been given the power to interfere in and control the lives of individual subjects of the State. By its nature, welfare provision tends to be discretionary and dependent upon the particular circumstance of a given case. As a consequence, State functionaries were extended discretionary power over the supply/withdrawal of welfare benefits. As the interventionist State replaced the completely free market as the source of welfare for many people, so access to the provisions made by the State became a matter of fundamental importance, and a focus for potential contention, especially given the discretionary nature of its provision. At the same time as welfare state provisions were being extended, the view was articulated that such provisions and projects should not be under the purview and control of the ordinary courts. It was felt that the judiciary reflected a culture that tended to favour a more market-centred, individualistic approach to the provision of rights and welfare and that their essentially formalistic approach to the resolution of disputes would not fit with the operation of the new projects.

3.5.1 Tribunals and courts

There is some debate as to whether tribunals are merely part of the machinery of administration of particular projects, or whether their function is the distinct one of adjudication. The Franks Committee (Cmnd 218, 1957) favoured the latter view, but others have disagreed, and have emphasised the administrative role of such bodies. Parliament initiated various projects and schemes, and included within those projects specialist tribunals to deal with the problems that they inevitably generated. On that basis, it is suggested that tribunals are merely adjuncts to the parent project, and that this therefore defines their role as more administrative than adjudicatory.

If the foregoing has suggested the theoretical possibility of distinguishing courts and tribunals in relation to their administrative or adjudicatory role, in practice it is difficult to implement such a distinction, for the reason that the members of tribunals may be, and usually are, acting in a judicial capacity. Thus, in *Pickering v Liverpool Daily Post and Echo Newspapers* (1991), it was held that a mental health review tribunal was a court whose proceedings were subject to the law of contempt. Although a newspaper was entitled to publish the fact that a named person had made an application to the tribunal, together with the date of the hearing and its decision, it was not allowed to publish the reasons for the decision or any conditions that applied.

If the precise distinction between tribunals and courts is a matter of uncertainty, what is certain is that tribunals are inferior to the normal courts. One of the main purposes of the tribunal system is to prevent the ordinary courts of law from being overburdened by cases, but a tribunal is still subject to judicial review on the basis of breach of natural justice, or where it acts in an *ultra vires* manner, or indeed where it goes wrong in relation to the application of the law when deciding cases.

In addition to the control of the courts, tribunals are also subject to the supervision of the Administrative Justice and Tribunals Council. Members of the Council are appointed by the Lord Chancellor and its role is to keep the general operation of the system under review.

3.5.2 The Leggatt Review of Tribunals

In May 2000, the then Lord Chancellor, Lord Irvine, appointed Sir Andrew Leggatt to review the operation of the tribunal system. The attendant Consultation Paper stated that:

> There are signs . . . that the complexity of the system (if indeed it amounts to a system at all), its diversity, and the separateness within it of most tribunals, may be creating problems for the user and an overall lack of coherence.

As Sir Andrew found, there were 70 different administrative tribunals in England and Wales, leaving aside regulatory bodies, and between them they dealt with nearly one million cases a year. However, of those 70 tribunals, only 20 heard more than 500 cases a year and many were, in fact, defunct. Sir Andrew's task was to rationalise and modernise the tribunal structure, and to that end, he made a number of proposals, including the following:

- *Making the 70 tribunals into one tribunals system*
  He suggested that the existing 'system' did not really merit that title and that combining the administration of the different tribunals was necessary to generate a collective standing to match that of the court system.
- *Ensuring that the tribunals were independent of their sponsoring departments by having them administered by one Tribunals Service*
  He thought that, as happened, where a Department of State may provide the administrative support for a tribunal, pay its fees and expenses, appoint some of its members, provide its IT support and possibly promote legislation prescribing the procedure that the tribunal was to follow, the tribunal neither appeared to be independent, nor was it independent in fact.
- *Improving the training of chairpersons and members in the interpersonal skills peculiarly required by tribunals*
  He saw the prime necessity for improved training in the interpersonal skills peculiar to tribunals so as to enable the users of the tribunals to cope on their own without the need for legal representation.
- *Ensuring that unrepresented users could participate effectively and without apprehension in tribunal proceedings*
  Following on from the previous finding, he felt that every effort should be made to reduce the number of cases in which legal representation was needed. He recognised, however, that there would always be a residual category of complex cases in which legal representation was necessary. Voluntary and community bodies should be funded so that they could provide such representation and only as a last resort should it be provided by public funding.
- *Providing a coherent appeal system*
  He found the current system to be confusing and some tribunals to have too many appeal stages, leading to long delays in reaching finality.
- *Reconsidering the position of lay members*
  He considered that there was no justification for any members to sit, whether expert or lay, unless they have a particular function to fulfil, as they do in the employment tribunal.

Subsequently, in March 2003, the Lord Chancellor's Office, as it then was, announced its intention to follow the Leggatt recommendation in establishing a new unified Tribunal Service. The details of the proposal were set out in a White Paper, *Transforming Public Services: Complaints, Redress and Tribunals*, in July 2004, and at its heart was the plan for a unified service, replacing the existing fragmented arrangement. The new organisation formally came into being in April 2005 and was launched operationally in April 2006.

According to its mission statement the Tribunals Service was focused on delivering real benefits to tribunal users, including:

- ensuring that tribunals are manifestly independent from those whose decisions are being reviewed;
- helping to provide better information to users and potential users;
- delivering greater consistency in practice and procedure; and
- making better use of existing tribunal resources.

On 1 April 2011 Her Majesty's Courts Service and the Tribunals Service were amalgamated into a single integrated agency, Her Majesty's Courts and Tribunals Service (HMCTS), providing support for the administration of justice in courts (up to and including the Court of Appeal) and most tribunals, but importantly not Employment Tribunals. The new Service operates as an agency of the Justice Ministry.

3.5.3 The Tribunals, Court and Enforcement Act 2007

In further pursuance of the Leggatt review, the stated intention of this piece of legislation (TCEA 2007) was the creation of a new, simplified, statutory framework for tribunals, which was to be achieved not just by the bringing together of existing tribunal jurisdictions but by provision of a new structure of jurisdiction and new appeal rights.

- *Unified structure*

  The Act provides for the establishment of a new unified structure to subsume all tribunals, except for the Employment tribunals, which will remain independent. This unification is to be achieved through the creation of two new tribunals, the First-tier Tribunal and the Upper Tribunal, and in pursuit of that end the Act gives the Lord Chancellor power to transfer the jurisdiction of existing tribunals to the two new tribunals. The Act also provides for the establishment within each tier of 'chambers', so that existing jurisdictions may be grouped together appropriately. Chambers at the first-tier level will hear cases initially and the role of the upper chambers will be mainly, but not exclusively, to hear appeals from the first tier. Each chamber will be headed by a Chamber President and the tribunals' judiciary, as the legal members of tribunals will now be entitled, will be headed by a Senior President of Tribunals.
- *Appeals*

  The Act specifically recognises and attempts to deal with the previous unclear and unsatisfactory routes of appeal in relation to tribunals' decisions. Under its provisions, in most cases, a decision of the First-tier Tribunal may be appealed to the Upper Tribunal and a decision of the Upper Tribunal may be appealed to the Court of Appeal. The grounds of appeal must always relate to a point of law. However, an appeal will not be allowed if such procedure is excluded by the specific Act or in any order made by the Lord Chancellor. However, it also provides that any such appeal must relate to a point of law and may only be exercised with permission from the tribunal being appealed from or the tribunal or court being appealed to.

- *Administration*
  The Act restated the role of the Tribunals Service, subsequently replaced by the amalgamated HMCTS, in the successful operation of the new unified system.
- *Supervision*
  Whereas previous tribunals came under the preview of the Council of Tribunals, the new Act replaced that body with the Administrative Justice and Tribunals Council (AJTC), an important new institution with responsibility not just for tribunals, as was the remit of the previous body, but with a wider overview and input into the operation of the administrative justice system as a whole.
- *Enforcement*
  In relation to enforcement, at present, tribunals have no enforcement powers of their own. Consequently, if a monetary award is not paid then the claimant must register the claim in the county court before seeking enforcement. Under the TCEA 2007, claimants will be able to go directly to the county court or High Court for enforcement.

Progress on the TCEA 2007

Sir Robert Carnwath, a Court of Appeal Judge, was appointed as the first Senior President of Tribunals. He has responsibility for representing the views of the tribunal judiciary to Ministers, Parliament and for training, guidance and welfare. In addition to the powers under the Act, the Lord Chief Justice has delegated to the Senior President some of his powers under the Constitutional Reform Act, particularly in relation to judicial discipline of most tribunal judges and members.

The following Chambers within the First-tier are operational:

- **General Regulatory Chamber**
  The General Regulatory Chamber (GRC) was established within the First-tier Tribunal on 1 September 2009. The GRC brings together tribunals that hear appeals on regulatory issues relating to the following specific areas:

  (a) Charity: the role of this tribunal is to hear appeals against the decisions of the Charity Commission and to consider references from the Attorney General or the Charity Commission on points of law.
  (b) Claims Management Services: the role of this tribunal is to hear appeals from businesses and individuals who provide claims management services in areas including:

    - personal injury;
    - criminal injuries compensation;
    - employment matters;
    - housing disrepair;
    - financial products and services;
    - industrial injury disablement benefits.

  The Tribunal considers cases where the Claims Management Regulator has refused them authorisation or imposed sanctions on them.
  (c) Consumer Credit: this tribunal hears appeals against decisions of the Office of Fair Trading relating to:

    - licensing decisions of the Office of Fair Trading made under the Consumer Credit Act 1974;
    - the imposition of requirements or a civil penalty on licensees under the Consumer Credit Act 1974;
    - the refusal to register, cancellation of registration, or imposition of a penalty under the Money Laundering Regulations 2007.

(d) Estate Agents: this tribunal hears appeals against decisions made by the Office of Fair Trading relating to, for example, orders prohibiting a person from acting as an estate agent where a person has been convicted of an offence involving fraud or other dishonesty.

(e) Gambling: this tribunal hears appeal on issues such as the granting of operating licences by the Gambling Commission.

(f) Immigration Services: this tribunal hears appeals against decisions made by the Office of the Immigration Services Commissioner and considers disciplinary charges brought against immigration advisors by the Commission.

(g) Information Rights: this tribunal hears appeals from notices issued by the Information Commissioner under:

- the Freedom of Information Act 2000;
- the Environmental Information Regulations 2004;
- the INSPIRE Regulations 2009 (these are the result of an EU Directive to establish an infrastructure for spatial information in Europe);
- the Data Protection Act 1998;
- the Privacy and Electronic Communications Regulations 2003;
- the Data Protection Monetary Penalty Regulations 2010.

(h) Local Government Standards in England: established to decide references and appeals about the conduct of members of local authorities.

(i) Transport Functions: this tribunal decides appeals against decisions of the Registrar of Approved Driving Instructors. These appeals concern approved driving instructors, trainee driving instructors, and training provider appeals. It can also hear appeals for London service permits against decisions of Transport for London and resolve disputes over postal charges.

- **Social Entitlement Chamber**
  The SEC Chamber deals with the following areas:

  (a) Asylum Support (it does not deal with asylum claims or other immigration matters).
  (b) Criminal Injuries Compensation.
  (c) Social Security and Child Support.

- **Health, Education and Social Care Chamber**

  (a) Care Standards (i.e. appeals from people who have received a decision issued by organisations concerned with children and vulnerable adults, and those which regulate the provision of social, personal and health care).
  (b) Special Education Needs and Disability.
  (c) Mental Health Review.
  (d) Primary Health Lists: this tribunal hears appeals/applications resulting from decisions made by Primary Care Trusts as part of the local management of such lists, which medical practitioners must be on in order to function.

- **Tax Chamber**
  This Chamber has two specific areas of competence:

  (a) Tax, where it hears appeals against decisions relating to tax made by Her Majesty's Revenue and Customs (HMRC).
  (b) MPs' expenses, where it hears appeals against certain decisions made by the Compliance Officer. The Compliance Officer is appointed by the Independent Parliamentary Standards Authority (IPSA) and is responsible for determining and paying MPs' expenses. Appeals can be made by MPs under the Parliamentary Standards Act 2009.

- **War Pensions and Armed Forces Compensation Chamber**
  As its title suggests this Chamber hears appeals from ex-servicemen or women who have had their claims for a war pension rejected by the Secretary of State for Defence.

The following is a list of the **Chambers within the Upper Tribunal** already operating:

- **Administrative Appeals Chamber**
  This Chamber hears appeals from the present First-tier Tribunals; the General Regulatory Chamber, the Health, Education and Social Care Chamber, Social Entitlement Chamber, and the War Pensions and Armed Forces Compensation Chamber.
- **Tax and Chancery Chamber**
  This Chamber hears appeals from the First-tier Tax Chamber Tribunal. This brought together the four existing tax tribunals to hear the full range of direct and indirect tax cases.
- **Lands Chamber (Lands Tribunal)**
  In June 2009 the Lands Tribunal joined the tribunal system established by the TCEA when it became the Lands Chamber of the Upper Tribunal. As its functions have not changed, for the time being, the Lands Chamber of the Upper Tribunal is still known as the Lands Tribunal.
- **Immigration and Asylum Chamber**
  In February 2010, Immigration and Asylum Chambers were established in both tiers of the Unified Tribunals framework. The Upper Tribunal is a superior court of record dealing with appeals against decisions made by the First-tier Immigration and Asylum Chamber Tribunal.

Employment Tribunals

The Employment Tribunals, and the Employment Appeal Tribunal continue largely unchanged as a separate 'pillar' of the new system. They are subject to the authority of the Senior President for training and welfare purposes and are treated as having the same status as Chambers in the First-tier and Upper Tribunals.

Employment tribunals are governed by the Employment Tribunals Act 1996, which sets out their composition, major areas of competence and procedure. In practice, such tribunals are normally made up of a legally qualified chairperson, a representative chosen from a panel representing employers and another representative chosen from a panel representing the interests of employees. However, s 4(3) ETA details proceedings which may be heard by an Employment Judge sitting alone. In 2012 the list was extended to include actions in relation to unfair dismissal.

Employment tribunals have jurisdiction in relation to a number of statutory provisions relating to employment issues. The majority of issues arise in relation to such matters as disputes over the meaning and operation of particular terms of employment, disputes relating to redundancy payments, disputes involving issues of unfair dismissal, and disputes as to the provision of maternity pay.

They also have authority in other areas under different legislation. Thus, they deal with: complaints about racial discrimination in the employment field under the Race Relations Act 1976; complaints about sexual discrimination in employment under the Sex Discrimination Act 1975; complaints about equal pay under the Equal Pay Act 1970, as amended by the Sex Discrimination Act; complaints under the Disability Discrimination Act 1995; complaints about unlawful deductions from wages under the Wages Act 1986; and appeals against the imposition of improvement notices under the Health and Safety at Work Act 1974. There are, in addition, various ancillary matters relating to trade union membership and activities that employment tribunals have to deal with.

The tribunal hearing is relatively informal. As in arbitration hearings, the normal rules of evidence are not applied and parties can represent themselves or be represented by solicitors or barristers. And, as appropriate in an employment context, they may also be represented by trade union officials or representatives, or indeed by any other person they wish to represent them.

Appeal, on a point of law only, is to the Employment Appeal Tribunal, which also sits with lay representatives (see below, at 4.5.1).

Although less formal than ordinary courts, the process of taking a case to, or defending a case in, an employment tribunal can be time-consuming and expensive, and employers' representatives have complained about the increased use of tribunals. As an alternative to the formal hearing Employment Tribunals offer a Judicial Mediation scheme. This was introduced as a pilot in 2006, and is now available throughout England and Wales. Judicial Mediation involves bringing the parties together for a Mediation Case Management Discussion before an employment judge who remains neutral and tries to assist the parties in resolving their disputes.

In a further attempt to remedy the alleged shortcomings in the Employment Tribunal process, the Advisory, Conciliation and Arbitration Service (ACAS) initiated a voluntary arbitration process for dealing with unfair dismissal claims as an alternative to using the employment tribunals. In the guide to the new scheme, ACAS states that:

> The intention is that the resolution of disputes under the Scheme will be confidential, relatively fast and cost efficient. Procedures under the Scheme are non-legalistic and far more informal and flexible than the employment tribunal. The process is inquisitorial rather than adversarial with no formal pleadings or cross-examination by parties or representatives. Instead of applying strict law or legal tests the arbitrator will have regard to general principles of fairness and good conduct in employment relations including, for example, principles referred to in the ACAS Code of Practice Disciplinary and Grievance Procedures and the ACAS Handbook *Discipline at Work* which were current at the time of the dismissal. In addition, as it is only possible to appeal or otherwise challenge an arbitrator's award (decision) in very limited circumstances, the Scheme should also provide quicker finality of outcome for the parties to an unfair dismissal dispute.

However, even before it was introduced, the scheme came under attack from the Industrial Society. In a pamphlet entitled *Courts or Compromise? Routes to Resolving Disputes*, it argued that the new alternative to employment tribunals could well become as rigid, formal and almost as expensive as current tribunal and court processes, and claimed that in any event, the impact on the tribunal system was likely to be slight. While it recognised the advantages in such schemes, that they were faster, cheaper, more informal and flexible than tribunals, it also foresaw inherent risks. The pamphlet argued that ADR does not guarantee fairness or consistency in outcomes. In particular, it highlighted dangers where there is no appeal process, in lack of precedent, and where confidentiality is unjustifiable. It also pointed out the risk that compensation awarded through ADR might be less than in a tribunal or court. In conclusion, it warned that people who opt for ADR need to make sure that they understand the implications, for example, where the decision is binding and leaves no route to appeal.

Resolving workplace disputes

In January 2011 the Coalition Government set out proposals for reforming the operation of the Employment Tribunal system. Such reforms were designed to address business concerns that Employment Tribunals had become too costly and time-consuming. One proposal that gave rise to particular concern amongst employee representatives was the suggestion that the qualifying period for unfair dismissal should be raised to two years, from the current one year. As yet there has been no response to the consultation exercise.

3.5.4 Composition of tribunals

Tribunals are usually made up of three members, only one of whom (the chair) is expected to be legally qualified. The other two members are lay representatives. The lack of legal training is not considered a drawback, given the technical, administrative, as opposed to specifically legal, nature of the provisions the members have to consider. Indeed, the fact of there being two lay representatives on tribunals provides them with one of their perceived advantages over courts. The non-legal members may provide specialist knowledge and thus they may enable the tribunal to base its decision on actual practice as opposed to abstract legal theory or mere legal formalism. An example of this can be seen with regard to the tribunals having responsibility for determining issues relating to employment, which usually have a trade union representative and an employers' representative sitting on the panel and are therefore able to consider the immediate problem from both sides of the employment relationship.

The procedure for nominating tribunal members is set out in the parent statute, but generally it is the minister of State with responsibility for the operation of the statute in question who ultimately decides the membership of the tribunal. As tribunals are established to deal largely with conflicts between the general public and government departments, this raises at least the possibility of suspicion that the members of tribunals are not truly neutral. In response to such doubts, the 1957 Franks Committee recommended that the appointment of the chairmen of tribunals should become the prerogative of the Lord Chancellor and that the appointment of the other members should become the responsibility of a Council on Tribunals. This recommendation was not implemented and ministers by and large still retain the power to appoint tribunal members. As a compromise, however, the minister selects the chairperson from a panel appointed by the Lord Chancellor.

3.5.5 Domestic tribunals

The foregoing has focused on public administrative tribunals set up under particular legislative provisions to deal with matters of public relevance. The term 'tribunal', however, is also used in relation to the internal, disciplinary procedures of particular institutions. Whether these institutions are created under legislation or not is immaterial; the point is that domestic tribunals relate mainly to matters of private rather than public concern, although at times the two can overlap. Examples of domestic tribunals are the disciplinary committees of professional institutions such as the Bar, the Law Society or the British Medical Association; trade unions; and universities. The power that each of these tribunals has is very great and it is controlled by the ordinary courts through ensuring that the rules of natural justice are complied with and that the tribunal does not act *ultra vires*, that is, beyond its powers. Matters relating to trade union membership and discipline are additionally regulated by the Employment Rights Act 1996.

3.5.6 Advantages of tribunals

Advantages of tribunals over courts relate to such matters as:

- *Speed*
  The ordinary court system is notoriously dilatory in hearing and deciding cases. Tribunals are much quicker to hear cases. A related advantage of the tribunal system is the certainty that it will be heard on a specific date and not subject to the vagaries of the court system. This being said, there have been reports that the tribunal system is coming under increased pressure and is falling behind in relation to its caseload.
- *Cost*
  Tribunals are a much cheaper way of deciding cases than using the ordinary court system. One factor that leads to a reduction in cost is the fact that no specialised court building is required to hear the cases. Also, the fact that those deciding the cases are less expensive to employ than judges, together with the fact that complainants do not have to rely on legal representation,

makes the tribunal procedure considerably less expensive than using the traditional court system. These reductions are further enhanced by the additional facts that there are no court fees involved in relation to tribunal proceedings and that costs are not normally awarded against the loser.

- *Informality*
  Tribunals are supposed to be informal in order to make them less intimidating than full-blown court cases. The strict rules relating to evidence, pleading and procedure that apply in courts are not binding in tribunal proceedings. The lack of formality is strengthened by the fact that proceedings tend not to be inquisitorial or accusatorial, but are intended to try to encourage and help participants to express their views of the situation before the tribunal. Informality should not, however, be mistaken for a lack of order, and the Franks Committee Report itself emphasised the need for clear rules of procedure. The provision of this informal situation and procedure tends to suggest that complainants do not need to be represented by a lawyer in order to present their grievance. They may represent themselves or be represented by a more knowledgeable associate such as a trade union representative or some other friend. This contentious point will be considered further below.
- *Flexibility*
  Tribunals are not bound by the strict rules of precedent, although some pay more regard to previous decisions than others. It should be remembered that, as tribunals are inferior and subject to the courts, they are governed by the precedents made in the courts.
- *Expertise*
  Reference has already been made to the advantages to be gained from the particular expertise that is provided by the lay members of tribunals, as against the more general legal expertise of the chairperson.
- *Accessibility*
  The aim of tribunals is to provide individuals with a readily accessible forum in which to air their grievances, and gaining access to tribunals is certainly not as difficult as getting a case into the ordinary courts.
- *Privacy*
  The final advantage is the fact that proceedings can be taken before a tribunal without necessarily triggering the publicity that might follow from a court case.

3.5.7 Disadvantages of tribunals

It is important that the supposed advantages of tribunals are not simply taken at face value. They represent significant improvements over the operation of the ordinary court system, but it is at least arguable that some of them are not as advantageous as they appear at first sight, and that others represent potential, if not actual, weaknesses in the tribunal system.

Tribunals are cheap, quick, flexible and informal, but their operation should not be viewed with complacency. These so-called advantages could be seen as representing an attack on general legal standards, and the tribunal system could be portrayed as providing a second-rate system of justice for those who cannot afford to pay to gain access to 'real law' in the court system. Vigilance is required on the part of the general community to ensure that such does not become an accurate representation of the tribunal system.

In addition to this general point, there are particular weaknesses in the system of tribunal adjudication. Some of these relate to the following:

- *Appeals procedures*
  Prior to the Franks Committee Report, tribunals were not required to provide reasons for their decisions and this prevented appeals in most cases. Subsequent to the Franks Report, however,

most tribunals, although still not all of them, are required to provide reasons for their decisions under s 10 of the Tribunals and Inquiries Act 1992. The importance of this provision was that in cases where a tribunal had erred in its application of the law, the claimant could apply to the High Court for judicial review to have the decision of the tribunal set aside for error of law on the face of the record.

The previous confusion and complexity relating to means and routes of appeal noted by Sir Andrew Leggatt have been remedied by the TCEA 2007.

- *Publicity*
  It was stated above that lack of publicity in relation to tribunal proceedings was a potential advantage of the system. A lack of publicity, however, may be a distinct disadvantage because it has the effect that cases involving issues of general public importance are not given the publicity and consideration that they might merit.
- *The provision of public funding*
  It was claimed previously that one of the major advantages of the tribunal system is its lack of formality and non-legal atmosphere. Research has shown, however, that individual complainants fare better where they are represented by lawyers. Additionally, as a consequence of the Franks recommendations, the fact that chairpersons have to be legally qualified has led to an increase in the formality of tribunal proceedings. As a result, non-law experts find it increasingly difficult in practice to represent themselves effectively. This difficulty is compounded when the body that is the object of the complaint is itself legally represented; although the parties to hearings do not have to be legally represented, there is nothing to prevent them from being so represented.

Summary

Alternative Dispute Resolution

Alternative dispute resolution

ADR has many features that make it preferable to the ordinary court system in many areas.

Its main advantage is that it is less antagonistic than the ordinary legal system, and is designed to achieve agreement between the parties involved.

Mediation and conciliation

- Mediation: the third party only acts as a go-between. The Family Law Act 1996 proposed a greater role for mediation in relation to divorce. However, following adverse trials, the Lord Chancellor announced in January 2001 that Part II of the Family Law Act would be repealed.
- Conciliation: the third party is more active in facilitating a reconciliation or agreement between the parties.

Arbitration

This is the procedure whereby parties in dispute refer the issue to a third party for resolution, rather than take the case to the ordinary law courts. Arbitration procedures can be contained in the original contract or agreed after a dispute arises. The procedure is governed by the Arbitration Act 1996. The Act follows the Model Arbitration Law adopted by the United Nations Commission on International Trade Law (UNCITRAL). Arbitration awards are enforceable in the ordinary courts. They must be carried out in a judicial manner and are subject to judicial review.

Advantages over the ordinary court system are: privacy; informality; speed; lower cost; expertise; and it is less antagonistic.

Administrative tribunals

These deal with cases involving conflicts between the State, its functionaries and private citizens. Domestic tribunals deal with private internal matters within institutions. Tribunals may be seen as administrative, but they are also adjudicative in that they have to act judicially when deciding particular cases. Tribunals are subject to the supervision of the Council on Tribunals, but are subservient to, and under the control of, the ordinary courts.

Usually, only the chair of a tribunal is legally qualified.

Examples of tribunals are the: employment tribunal; social security appeals tribunal; mental health review tribunal; Lands Tribunal; Rent Assessment Committee.

Advantages of tribunals over ordinary courts relate to: speed; cost; informality; flexibility; expertise; accessibility; privacy.

Disadvantages relate to: the appeals procedure; lack of publicity; the lack of public funding in most cases.

Further Reading

Abel, R, 'The Comparative Study of Dispute Institutions in Society' (1973) 8 Law and Society Rev 217

Chatterjee, C, *Alternative Dispute Resolution: A Practical Guide*, 2008, London, Routledge

Frenkel, J, 'Offers to settle and payments into court' (1999) 149 NLJ 458

Genn, H and Genn, Y, *The Effectiveness of Representation at Tribunals*, 1989, London: LCD

McGrath, P, 'Appeals against small claims track decisions' (1999) 149 NLJ 748

Pearl, P and Goodman, A, *Small Claims Procedure in the County Court: A Practical Guide to Mediation and Litigation*, 5th edn, London: Wildy, Simmonds and Hill Publishing

Slapper, G and Kelly, D, *English Legal System*, 15th edn, 2014, Abingdon: Routledge

Trent, M, 'ADR and the new Civil Procedure Rules' (1999) 149 NLJ 410

Websites

www.adrnow.org.uk/go/Default.html

www.tribunals.gov.uk/

Part 2

Business Transactions

Ours is a market system. This means that economic activity takes place through the exchange of commodities. Individual possessors of commodities meet in the market place and freely enter into negotiations to arrange the terms on which they are willing to exchange those commodities. Contract law may be seen as the mechanism for facilitating, regulating and enforcing such market activities.

It is usual for textbooks to cite how all our daily transactions, from buying a newspaper or riding on a bus to buying a house, are all examples of contracts, but the point is nonetheless valid and well made. We are all players in the contract game, even if we do not realise it. In fact, we probably will have no need to recognise that particular contractual version of reality until we enter into some transaction that goes wrong, or at least does not go as we hoped it would. Then, we seek to assert rights and to look for remedies against the person with whom we have come into dispute. It is at this time that the analytical framework of contract law principles comes to bear on the situation, to determine what, if any, rights can be enforced and what, if any, remedies can be recovered. It is perhaps paradoxical that students of contract law have to approach their study of the subject from the opposite end to that at which the layperson begins. The layperson wants a remedy and focuses on that above all else; the student, or practitioner, realises that the availability of the remedy depends upon establishing contractual responsibility and, hence, their focus is on the establishment of the contractual relationship and the breach of that relationship, before any question of remedies can be considered. Such is the nature and relationship of law and ordinary, everyday reality.

Although people have always exchanged goods, even in the UK market transactions only came to be the dominant form of economic activity during the 19th century. The general law of contract as it now operates is essentially the product of the common law, and emerged in the course of the 19th century. It has been suggested that the general principles of contract law, or of the 'classical model of contract', as they are known, are themselves based on an idealised model of how the market operates.

As the following chapters will evidence, there is much tension between the fit of the theoretical classical model and the practical demands of everyday business activity. Equally of note is the extent to which statutory inroads have been made into the common law, particularly in the area of consumer protection. For example, notable pieces of legislation that will require close attention are the Unfair Contract Terms Act 1977, which restricts the use of exclusion clauses in contracts, and the Contracts (Rights of Third Parties) Act 1999, which has made inroads into the common law doctrine of privity. The extent to which employment contracts are a matter of statutory regulation will be considered in detail in Chapter 16, below.

In any event, in order to lessen the possibility of the expense and damage to business reputation of legal proceedings, businesses need to be aware of the legal significance and the consequences of their transactions. Accordingly, Part 3 will examine the general legal principles of the law of contract, and specific rules relating to contracts for the sale and supply of goods. Consideration will also be given to further possible consequences of business transactions, such as criminal liability.

However, before going on to consider the substance of contract law, it is necessary to issue a warning in relation to examinations. Together with company law, contract forms the main component in most syllabuses. It is not possible to select particular areas as being more important and, therefore, more likely to be examined than others. Unfortunately, any aspect of contract may be asked about, so candidates must be familiar with most, if not all, aspects of the subject. For example, it may be legitimate to expect a question on the vitiating factors in relation to contracts (see below, Chapter 6). It is not possible, however, to predict with any confidence which particular vitiating factor will be selected. To restrict one's study would be extremely hazardous. The candidate may have learned mistake and misrepresentation very well, but that will be worthless if the question asked actually relates to duress, as it might very well do. The warning, therefore, is to study contract thoroughly. Equally, students should be aware that knowledge of remedies is of particular importance to all contractual topics; for example, an examination question on offer and acceptance or on misrepresentation may also require reference to appropriate remedies.

Chapter 4

Contract (1): Formation of a Contract

Chapter Contents

Law in Context: The Rise of Email

One of the key issues in contract law is determining whether an offer has been accepted or not. Traditionally, where the parties have agreed acceptance of an offer can be concluded via post, the contract is deemed to be accepted at the point the letter is properly addressed, stamped and posted. Known as 'the postal rule', this applies even if the letter fails to arrive and goes astray. In recent years, the courts have had to grapple with the issue of 'instantaneous' communication such as email. As will be seen below, the courts have developed various principles to determine when such offers can be accepted via email, and when they cannot. In such cases, to avoid confusion, businesses should communicate the exact method of acceptance to be used and provide timescales for responses. This avoids disputes arising in connection with the postal rule.

4.1 Introduction

The simplest definition of a contract is a '**legally binding agreement**'. It must be understood, however, that, although all contracts result from agreements, not all agreements are contracts. To be a contract, the agreement must be legally enforceable in a court of law; it must comply with certain legal requirements:

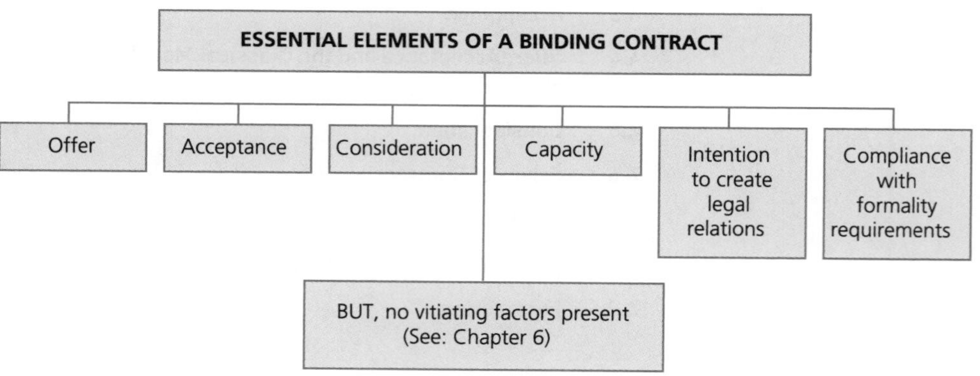

Figure 4.1

Though not all agreements are recognised as contracts in law, even those agreements which are contracts, may not be given full effect by the courts. The legal effect of particular agreements may be distinguished as follows:

- *Valid contracts* are agreements which the law recognises as being fully binding. By entering such agreements, the parties establish rights and responsibilities which the courts will enforce, either by insisting on performance of the promised action or awarding damages to the innocent party.

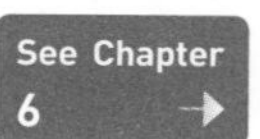
See Chapter 6

- *Void contracts* are a contradiction in terms, for this type of agreement does not constitute a contract: it has no legal effect. Agreements may be void for various reasons, including mistake and illegality.

- *Voidable contracts* are agreements which may be avoided, that is, set aside by one of the parties. However, if no steps are taken to avoid the agreement, a valid contract ensues. Examples of contracts which may be avoided are those entered into on the basis of fraud or misrepresentation.

- *Unenforceable contracts* are agreements which, though legal, cannot be sued on for some reason, such as expiry of the time limit for enforcement.

The emphasis placed on agreement highlights the consensual nature of contracts. It is sometimes said that contract is based on *consensus ad idem*, that is, a meeting of minds. This is slightly misleading, however, for the reason that English contract law applies an objective test in determining whether or not a contract exists. It is not so much a matter of what the parties actually had in mind, as what their behaviour would lead others to conclude as to their state of mind. Consequently, contracts may be found and enforced, even though the parties themselves might not have thought that they had entered into such a relationship.

4.2 Offer

An offer is a promise to be bound on particular terms, and it must be capable of acceptance. The person who makes the offer is the offeror; the person who receives the offer is the offeree. The offer sets out the terms upon which the offeror is willing to enter into contractual relations with the offeree. To be capable of acceptance, the offer must not be too vague; if the offeree accepts, each party should know what their rights and obligations are.

In *Scammel v Ouston* (1941), Ouston ordered a van from Scammel on the understanding that the balance of the purchase price could be paid on hire purchase terms over two years. Scammel used several different hire purchase terms and the specific terms applying were never actually fixed. When Scammel failed to deliver the van, Ouston sued for breach of contract. The action failed because no contract could be established, due to the uncertainty of the terms; no specific hire purchase terms had been identified.

4.2.1 Identifying an offer

An offer, through acceptance by the offeree, may result in a legally enforceable contract. So, it is important to be able to distinguish what the law will treat as an offer from other statements which will not form the basis of an enforceable contract. An offer must be distinguished from the following:

NOT OFFERS	Examples
Statement of Intent	
Supply of Information	
Invitation to Treat	• Display of goods in shop window • Display of goods on self-service shelves • Public advertisement • Share prospectus

Figure 4.2

- *A mere statement of intention* cannot form the basis of a contract, even though the party to whom it is made acts on it. For example, in *Re Fickus* (1900), a father informed his prospective son-in-law that his daughter would inherit under his will. It was held that the father's words were simply a statement of present intention, which he could alter as he wished in the future; they were not an offer. Therefore, the father could not be bound by them.
  Another, more business-related example of a statement of intention is the '*letter of conform*', which will be considered later at 4.4.2.
- *A mere supply of information* was demonstrated in *Harvey v Facey* (1893). The plaintiff telegraphed to the defendants: 'Will you sell us Bumper Hall Pen? Telegraph lowest cash price.' The defendant answered, 'Lowest price for Bumper Hall Pen £900'. The plaintiff then telegraphed, 'We agree to buy Bumper Hall Pen for £900', and sued for specific performance when the defendants declined to transfer the property. It was held that the defendants' telegram was not an offer capable of being accepted by the plaintiff; it was simply a statement of information. This clearly has similarities with asking the price of goods in a retail outlet.
- *An invitation to treat* means requesting others to make offers. The person extending the invitation is not bound to accept any offers made to him, he can choose whether to accept or not. The courts have drawn the distinction between offers and invitations to treat in everyday business transactions:

  - *The display of goods in a shop window*. In the classic case of *Fisher v Bell* (1961), a shopkeeper was prosecuted for offering offensive weapons for sale, by having flick-knives on display in his window. He was found not guilty, as the display in the shop window was not an offer for sale; it was only an invitation to treat.
  - *The display of goods on the shelf of a self-service shop*. The exemplary case is:

❖ KEY CASE — *Pharmaceutical Society of Great Britain v Boots Cash Chemists* (1953)

Facts:
The defendants were charged with breaking a law which provided that certain drugs could only be sold under the supervision of a qualified pharmacist. They had placed the drugs on open display in their self-service store and, although a qualified person was stationed at the cash desk, it was alleged that the contract of sale had been formed when the customer removed the goods from the shelf, the display being an offer to sell.

Decision:
It was held that Boots were not guilty; the display was only an invitation to treat. In law, the customer offered to buy the goods at the cash desk where the pharmacist was stationed.

Comment: This decision is clearly practical, as the alternative would mean that, once customers had placed goods in their shopping baskets, they would be bound to accept them and could not change their minds and return the goods to the shelves.

  - *A public advertisement* does not amount to an offer. In *Partridge v Crittenden* (1968), a person was charged with offering a wild bird for sale, contrary to the Protection of Birds Act 1954, when he advertised the sale of such birds in a magazine. It was held he could not be guilty of *offering* the bird for sale, as the advertisement was no more than an invitation to treat. In *Harris v Nickerson* (1873), the plaintiff failed to recover damages for the cost of attending an advertised auction which was cancelled. In deciding against him, the court stated that he was attempting 'to make a mere declaration of intention a binding contract'. As a general rule, in auctions the bids are offers to buy.

However, there are exceptional circumstances where an advertisement may be an offer; where the advertisement specifies performance of a task in return for a 'reward' and, on its terms, does not admit any room for negotiation, it may be treated as an offer. In *Carlill v Carbolic Smoke Ball Co* (1893), the facts of which are given in 4.2.2 below, the advertisement was held to be an offer, not an invitation to treat, because it specified performance of the task of using the smoke ball as directed and catching influenza in return for the reward of £100. Furthermore, there was no room to negotiate these terms, unlike the usual advertisement (such as the one in *Partridge*), where one would commonly expect to be able to negotiate on price.

- Advertisements of goods on websites (internet shopping) are of particular interest. The legal issue is whether the advertisements are offers (in which case the customer ordering the goods accepts the offer and then a binding contract is made) or invitations to treat, so that the customer's order is an offer to buy, which the advertiser can accept or reject. Readers may remember the widely reported dispute involving Argos in 1999, where the Argos website advertised Sony televisions at £2.99 instead of £299. Customers placing orders at £2.99, argued that they had accepted Argos' offer and that there was a binding contract to supply the goods for £2.99. It is probable that Argos could have escaped contractual liability on the basis of fundamental unilateral mistake. Such problems are addressed by the Electronic Commerce (EC Directive) Regulations 2002 (SI 2002/2013). Regulation 9 requires Member States to ensure that certain information is given by the 'service provider' to the recipient of the service. Unless otherwise agreed by parties who are not consumers, the relevant information is:

See Chapter 6

(a) the different technical steps to follow to conclude the contract;
(b) whether or not the concluded contract will be filed by the service provider;
(c) the technical means for identifying and correcting input errors before placing the order;
(d) the languages available for conclusion of the contract; and
(e) reference to any relevant codes of conduct and how they can be accessed.

These rules do not apply where the contract is conducted exclusively by email. The Regulations also require that:

(a) the contract terms and general conditions provided to the recipient can be stored and reproduced by him/her; and
(b) the service provider acknowledges receipt of the order, without delay and by electronic means.

- *A share prospectus*. Contrary to common understanding, such a document is not an offer; it is merely an invitation to treat, inviting people to make offers to subscribe for shares in the company.

It can be seen that the decisions in both *Fisher* and *Partridge* run contrary to the common, non-legal understanding of the term 'offer'. It is interesting to note that later legislation, such as the Trade Descriptions Act 1968, was specifically worded to ensure that invitations to treat were subject to the same legal regulation as offers, where the aim was to protect consumers from being misled.

4.2.2 Offers to particular people

An offer may be made to a particular person, group of people, or to the world at large. If the offer is restricted, then only those to whom it is addressed may accept it; if the offer is made to the public at large, however, it can be accepted by anyone. In *Boulton v Jones* (1857), the defendant sent an order to a shop, not knowing the shop had been sold to the plaintiff. The plaintiff supplied the goods, the defendant consumed them but did not pay, as he had a right to offset the debt against money the former owner owed him. The plaintiff sued for the price of the goods. The defendant argued there was no contract obliging him to pay because his offer was made *only* to the former owner (because of the right of offset and lack of knowledge of the sale of the business), so only the former owner could accept, not the plaintiff. The court agreed with the defendant's argument; there was no contract, and so no contractual obligation to pay.

❖ KEY CASE *Carlill v Carbolic Smoke Ball Co* (1893)

Facts:

The company advertised that it would pay £100 to anyone catching influenza after using their smoke ball as directed. Mrs Carlill used the smoke ball but still caught influenza and sued the company for the promised £100. Amongst the many defences argued for the defendants, it was suggested that the advertisement could not be an offer, as it was addressed to the whole world, not particularly to Mrs Carlill. It was held that the advertisement was an offer to the whole world, which Mrs Carlill had accepted by her conduct. Therefore, there was a valid contract obliging the company to pay.

The case considered other issues which are of real significance; accordingly the case will be referred to again, in the context of such issues.

Decision:

Carlill is an example of a unilateral contract – a 'reward' is offered in return for an action. The person(s) to whom the offer is made can choose whether to respond by performing the task stated in the advertisement. A current example of the *Carlill* type advertisement would be a newspaper promising free cinema tickets in return for vouchers printed in the newspaper (see: *O'Brien v MGN Ltd* (2001)). These type of advertisements often contain phrases like 'subject to availability' or 'whilst stocks last'; thus, the offer is automatically withdrawn if, for example, the offeror's stock of the promised 'reward' runs out.

4.2.3 Knowledge of the offer

A person cannot accept an offer he is not aware of. Thus, if a person offers a reward for the return of a lost watch and someone returns it without knowing about the offer, he cannot claim the reward. Motive for accepting is not important, as long as the person accepting knows about the offer. In *Williams v Carwadine* (1883), a person was held to be entitled to receive a reward, although that was not the reason why he provided the information requested. (Acceptance is considered 4.3 below.)

4.2.4 Rejection of offers

Express rejection of an offer terminates it, and the offeree cannot subsequently accept the original offer. A counter-offer, where the offeree tries to change the terms of the offer, has the same effect.

In *Hyde v Wrench* (1840), Wrench offered to sell his farm for £1,000. Hyde offered £950, which Wrench rejected. Hyde then informed Wrench that he accepted the original offer. It was held that there was no contract. Hyde's counter-offer had effectively ended the original offer and it was no longer open to him to accept it; Hyde was now making a new offer to buy for £1,000, which Wrench could accept or reject.

A counter-offer must not be confused with a request for further information. Such a request does not end the offer, which can still be accepted after the new information has been elicited. Such requests are common in business, to clarify aspects of the offer. In *Stevenson v McLean* (1880), it was held that a request by the offeree about the length of time that the offeror would give for payment did not terminate the original offer, which he was entitled to accept prior to revocation. The issue was considered and clarified in *Society of Lloyds v Twinn* (2000) (see 4.3.1 below).

4.2.5 Revocation of offers

Revocation (cancellation), occurs when the offeror withdraws the offer. There are a number of points to bear in mind in relation to revocation, namely:

- *An offer may be revoked at any time before acceptance*
  Once revoked, it is no longer open to the offeree to accept the original offer. In *Routledge v Grant* (1828), Grant offered to buy Routledge's house and gave him six weeks to accept the offer. Within that period, however, he withdrew the offer. It was held that Grant was entitled to withdraw the offer at any time before acceptance and, upon withdrawal, Routledge could no longer create a contract by purporting to accept it.
- *Revocation is not effective until it is actually received by the offeree*
  This means that the offeror must ensure that the offeree is made aware of the withdrawal of the offer; otherwise it might still be open to the offeree to accept the offer. In *Byrne v Van Tienhoven* (1880), the defendant offerors conducted their business in Cardiff and the plaintiff offerees in New York. On 1 October, an offer was made by post. On 8 October, a letter of revocation was posted, seeking to withdraw the offer. On 11 October, the plaintiffs telegraphed their acceptance of the offer. On 20 October, the letter of revocation was received by the plaintiffs. It was held that the revocation did not take effect until it arrived and the defendants were bound by the contract, which had been formed by the plaintiffs' earlier acceptance (which was effective on *sending* under the postal rule: see 4.3.2 below).
- *Communication of revocation may be made through a reliable third party*
  Where the offeree finds out about the withdrawal of the offer from a reliable third party, the revocation is effective and the offeree can no longer accept the original offer. In *Dickinson v Dodds* (1876), Dodds offered to sell property to Dickinson, telling him that the offer would be open until Friday. On Thursday, the plaintiff was informed by a reliable third party, acting as an intermediary, that Dodds intended selling the property to someone else. Dickinson still attempted to accept the offer on Friday, by which time the property had already been sold. It was held that the sale of the property amounted to revocation, which had been effectively communicated by the third party. It must be noted that, the mere fact of sale to another is not revocation – communication is necessary. Thus, if an offer to sell property is made to two people, the offeror may find he contracts to sell to both of them, if he does not communicate withdrawal of offer to one person when he sells to the other.
- *A promise to keep an offer open is only binding where there is a separate contract to that effect, known as an option contract*
  The offeree/promisee must provide consideration (see 4.5 below) for the promise to keep the offer open. If no consideration is provided for the offer to be kept open, then the original offeror is at liberty to withdraw the offer at any time, as was seen in *Routledge*, above.

- *Revocation is not permissible once the offeree has started performing the task requested in a unilateral contract*
  A unilateral contract is one where one party promises something in return for some action on the part of another party. Rewards for finding lost property are examples of such unilateral promises, as was the advertisement in *Carlill* (see 4.2.2 above). There is no compulsion placed on the party undertaking the action, but it would be unfair if the promisor was entitled to revoke the offer just before the offeree was about to complete their part of the contract; for example, withdrawing a 'free gift for labels' offer before the expiry date, whilst customers were still collecting labels. Thus, in *Errington v Errington and Woods* (1952), a father promised his son and daughter-in-law that he would convey a house to them when they had paid off the outstanding mortgage. After the father's death, his widow sought to revoke the promise. It was held that the promise could not be withdrawn as long as the mortgage payments continued to be met. A more recent examination of the issue can be found in *Soulsbury v Soulsbury* (2007), where the Court of Appeal enforced a husband's promise to bequeath a lump sum to his former wife, rather than pay her annual maintenance. The court determined there to be a classic unilateral agreement, under which the promise could not be withdrawn whilst maintenance was not claimed.

4.2.6 Lapse of offers

Offers lapse and are no longer capable of acceptance in the following circumstances:

- *At the end of a stated period* It is possible for the parties to agree, or for the offeror to set, a time limit within which acceptance has to take place. If the offeree has not accepted the offer within that period, it lapses and can no longer be accepted.
- *After a reasonable time* Where no time limit is set, an offer will lapse after the passage of a reasonable time. What amounts to a reasonable time is, of course, dependent upon the particular circumstances of each case.
- *Where the offeree dies* This automatically brings the offer to a close.
- *Where the offeror dies and the contract was one of a personal nature* In such circumstances, the offer automatically ends, but the outcome is less certain in relation to contracts that are not of a personal nature. See *Bradbury v Morgan* (1862) for example, where it was held that the death of an offeror did not invalidate the offeree's acceptance.

It should be noted that the effect of death after acceptance also depends on whether or not the contract was one of a personal nature. In the case of a non-personal contract (for example, the sale of a car), the contract can be enforced by and against the representatives of the deceased. On the other hand, if performance of the contract depended upon the personal qualification or capacity of the deceased, then the contract will be frustrated (see 7.4 below).

4.3 Acceptance

Acceptance of the offer is necessary to form a contract. Once the offeree has assented to the terms offered, a contract comes into effect. Both parties are bound: the offeror cannot withdraw his offer and the offeree cannot withdraw his acceptance.

4.3.1 Form of acceptance

In order to form a binding agreement, the acceptance must correspond with the terms of the offer. Thus, the offeree must not seek to introduce new contractual terms by way of the acceptance.

In *Neale v Merrett* (1930), one party offered to sell property for £280. The other party purported to accept by sending £80 and promising to pay the remainder by monthly instalments. This purported acceptance was ineffective, as the offeree had not accepted the original offer as stated.

As was seen in *Hyde v Wrench* (1840), a counter-offer does not constitute acceptance. Analogously, it may also be stated that a conditional acceptance cannot create a contractual relationship. Thus, any agreement 'subject to contract' is not binding, but merely signifies the fact that the parties are in the process of finalising the terms on which they will be willing to be bound (*Winn v Bull* (1877)). However, the mere fact that a person adds a 'qualification' to their acceptance may not prevent acceptance from taking place:

❖ KEY CASE *Society of Lloyds v Twinn* (2000)

Facts:
A dispute arose from a settlement arrangement offered to Lloyd's 'names' in July 1996. Mr and Mrs Twinn indicated that they accepted the settlement agreement but added that they were unsure of their ability to actually carry out its terms; they queried whether any 'indulgence' would be granted them in such circumstances. Subsequently, the defendants argued that their acceptance had been conditional, so there was no contract enforceable against them.

Decision:
It was decided that it was a question of fact in each case whether there was an unconditional acceptance plus a collateral offer (which there was in the present case) or a counter-offer (that is, a conditional acceptance – 'I only accept the offer if . . .') which rejected the offer.

Acceptance may be by express words, either oral or written, or may be implied from conduct. Thus, in *Brogden v Metropolitan Railway Co* (1877), the plaintiff, having supplied the company with coal for several years, suggested that they should enter into a written contract. The company agreed and sent Brogden a draft contract. He altered some points and returned it, marked 'approved'. The company did nothing further about the document, but Brogden continued to deliver coal on the terms included in the draft contract. When a dispute arose, Brogden denied the existence of any contract. It was held that the draft became a full contract when both parties acted on it. A counter-offer may also be accepted by conduct, as in *Pickfords Ltd v Celestica Ltd* (2003). Acceptance by conduct was examined in:

❖ KEY CASE *IRC v Fry* (2001)

Facts:
The defendant owed the Inland Revenue £100,000 and her husband sent a cheque for £10,000 to them, stating that cashing the cheque would be acceptance of his offer that it was 'full and final settlement' of the debt. As was normal practice, the Inland Revenue postroom sent the cheque for immediate banking and the accompanying letter to an inspector. The inspector informed the defendant that the cheque could not be full settlement; the defendant argued that cashing the cheque was acceptance of her husband's offer, so the debt was now fully settled. It should be noted here that part payment of a debt by a third party is an exception to the rule in *Pinnel's Case* (1602) (see

4.5.5 below), so the only issue was whether the husband's offer had been accepted. Jacobs J stated:

> Cashing a cheque is always strong evidence of acceptance, especially if it is not accompanied by an immediate rejection of the offer. Retention of the cheque without rejection is also strong evidence of acceptance, depending on the length of delay. But neither of these factors are conclusive and it would, I think, be artificial to draw a hard and fast line between cases where payment is accompanied by immediate rejection of the offer and cases where objection comes within a day or a few days.

Decision:
It was decided that cashing the cheque raised a *rebuttable presumption* of acceptance of the offer, but the fact that the Inland Revenue did not know of the offer at the time that the cheque was cashed, rebutted the presumption of acceptance (see 4.2.3 above).

4.3.2 Communication of acceptance

The general rule is that acceptance must be communicated to the offeror. As a consequence of this rule, silence cannot amount to acceptance. The classic case is *Felthouse v Bindley* (1863), where an uncle was negotiating the purchase of his nephew's horse. He eventually wrote to the nephew, offering to buy it at a particular price, stating: 'If I hear no more about him I shall consider the horse mine.' The nephew made no reply. When the horse was mistakenly sold by an auctioneer, the uncle sued the auctioneer in conversion. It was held that the uncle had no cause of action, as the horse did not belong to him. Acceptance could not be imposed on the offeree on the basis of his silence.

There are, however, exceptions to the general rule that acceptance must be communicated:

- *Where the offeror has waived the right to receive communication* In unilateral contracts, such as that in *Carlill*, or general reward cases, acceptance occurs when the offeree performs the required act. Thus, in *Carlill*, Mrs Carlill did not have to inform the defendants that she had used their treatment. Nor, in reward cases, do those seeking to benefit have to inform the person offering the reward that they have begun to perform the task that will lead to the reward.
- *Where acceptance is through the postal service*

POSTAL RULE ISSUES	
When is appropriate to accept by post?	e.g. did parties contemplate acceptance by post?
Can postal rule be applied to 'instantaneous' communication methods?	e.g. fax, email, telephone
Meaning of 'posting'?	e.g. letter incorrectly addressed
Relationship with revocation of offer by post?	

Figure 4.3

Acceptance is complete as soon as the letter, properly addressed and stamped, is posted. The contract is concluded, even if the letter fails to reach the offeror. In *Adams v Lindsell* (1818), the defendant made an offer to the plaintiff on 2 September, but the letter was delayed, arriving on 5 September. Adams immediately posted an acceptance. On 8 September, Lindsell sold the merchandise to a third party. On 9 September, the letter of acceptance from Adams arrived. It was held that a valid acceptance took place when Adams posted the letter. Lindsell was, therefore, liable for breach of contract. The revocation came *after* acceptance as it could only be effective on receipt (see 4.2.5 above).

As already seen in *Byrne v Van Tienhoven* (1880), the postal rule applies equally to telegrams. It does not apply, however, when instantaneous means of communication are used (see *Entores v Far East Corp* (1955) for a consideration of this point). It follows that, when acceptance is made by means of telephone, fax or telex, the offeror must actually receive the acceptance. This also raises issues concerning acceptance by email; it has been argued that this situation should be treated as a 'face to face' situation where receipt only occurs when the recipient reads the email. This argument would be in line with the decision in *Brinkibon Ltd v Stahag Stahl und Stahlwarenhandelsgesellshaft mbH* (1983). This, of course, begs the question of the effect of culpability in not reading emails quickly. It is suggested that, as a result of the decisions in *The Brimnes* (1975) and *Mondial Shipping and Chartering BV v Astarte Shipping Ltd* (1995), a court would take account of when the sender might reasonably expect the message to be received. Where the agreement is conducted on the Internet, reg 11 of the Electronic Commerce (EC Directive) Regulations 2002 (SI 2002/2013) indicates that the contract is concluded when the service provider's acknowledgment of receipt of acceptance is received by electronic means.

It should be noted that the postal rule will apply only where it is in the contemplation of the parties that the post will be used as the means of acceptance. If the parties have negotiated either face to face, for example in a shop, or over the telephone, then it might not be reasonable for the offeree to use the post as a means of communicating their acceptance and they would not gain the benefit of the postal rule (see *Henthorn v Fraser* (1892)).

In order to expressly exclude operation of the postal rule, the offeror can insist that acceptance is only effective upon receipt (see *Holwell Securities v Hughes* (1974)). The offeror can also require that acceptance be communicated in a particular manner. Where the offeror does not actually insist that acceptance can only be made in the stated manner, then acceptance is effective if it is communicated in a way that is no less advantageous to the offeror (see *Yates Building Co v J Pulleyn & Sons* (1975)). From a business point of view, it is probably advisable to avoid the possible application of the postal rule, by indicating clearly when and how a contract will be deemed to be concluded.

4.3.3 Tenders

These arise where one party wishes work to be done and issues a statement requesting interested parties to submit the terms on which they are willing to carry out the work. In the case of tenders, the person who invites the tender is making an invitation to treat. The person who submits a tender is the offeror, and the other party can choose whether to accept or reject the offer (see *Spencer v Harding* (1870)).

It is important for businesses to realise that the effect of acceptance depends upon the wording of the invitation to tender. If the invitation states that the potential purchaser requires that a certain quantity of goods are supplied to him, then acceptance of a tender will form a contract and he will be in breach if he fails to order the stated quantity of goods from the tenderer.

If, on the other hand, the invitation states only that the potential purchaser *may* require goods, acceptance of a tender gives rise to a standing offer. There is no obligation on the purchaser to take any goods, but he must not deal with any other supplier. Each order given forms a separate contract and the supplier must deliver any goods required within the time stated in the tender. The supplier can revoke the standing offer, but he must supply any goods already ordered. In *Great Northern Railway v Witham* (1873), the defendant successfully tendered to supply the company with 'such quantities as the company may order from time to time'. After fulfilling some orders, Witham refused to supply any more goods. It was held that he was in breach of contract in respect of the goods already ordered but, once these were supplied, he was at liberty to revoke his standing offer.

4.4 Offer, Acceptance and the Classical Model of Contract

The foregoing has presented the legal principles of offer and acceptance in line with the 'classical model' of contract. Underlying that model is the operation of the market in which individuals freely negotiate the terms on which they are to be bound. The offeror sets out terms which he is willing to be bound to and, if the offeree accepts those terms, then a contract is formed. If, however, the offeree alters the terms, then the parties reverse their roles: the former offeree now becomes the offeror and the former offeror becomes the offeree, able to accept or reject the new terms as he chooses. This process of role reversal continues until an agreement is reached or the parties decide that there are no grounds on which they can form an agreement. Thus, the classical model of contract insists that there must be a correspondence of offer and acceptance, and that failure to match acceptance to offer will not result in a binding contract.

Commercial reality, however, tends to differ from this theoretical model, and lack of genuine agreement as to terms in a commercial contract can leave the courts with the difficulty of determining whether there *was* a contract in the first place and, if so, upon precisely which, or whose, terms it was entered into. This difficulty may be seen in relation to what is known as 'the battle of the forms', in which the parties do not actually enter into real negotiations but simply exchange standard form contracts, setting out their usual terms of trade. The point is that the contents of these standard form contracts might not agree and, indeed, might actually be contradictory. The question then arises as to whose terms are to be taken as forming the basis of the contract, if, indeed, a contract has actually been concluded. The difficulty of pinpointing offer and acceptance in commercial negotiations was shown in *ProForce Recruit Ltd v Rugby Group Ltd* (2006).

Some judges, notably Lord Denning, have felt themselves to be too restricted by the constraints of the classical model of contract and have argued that, rather than being required to find, or construct, a correspondence of offer and acceptance, they should be able to examine the commercial reality of the situation in order to decide whether or not the parties had intended to enter into contractual relations. As Lord Denning would have had it, judges should not be restricted to looking for a precise matching of offer and acceptance, but should be at liberty to:

> . . . look at the correspondence as a whole, and at the conduct of the parties, and see therefrom whether the parties have come to an agreement on everything that was material [*Gibson v Manchester CC* (1979)].

Gibson concerned the sale of a council house to a tenant, who had entered into negotiations with his local council about purchasing his house. Before he had entered into a binding contract, the political make-up of the council changed and the policy of selling houses was reversed. It was clear that, under the classical model of contract, there was no correspondence of offer and acceptance, but the Court of Appeal nonetheless decided that the tenant could insist on the sale.

The status quo was restored by the House of Lords, overturning the Court of Appeal's decision. Lord Diplock expressed the view that:

> . . . there may be certain types of contract, though they are exceptional, which do not easily fit into the normal analysis of a contract as being constituted by offer and acceptance, but a contract alleged to have been made by an exchange of correspondence by the parties in which the successive communications other than the first are in reply to one another is not one of these.

With this clear re-affirmation of the classical model, even Lord Denning was cowed in deciding *Butler Machine Tool Co Ltd v Ex-Cell-O Corp (England) Ltd* (1979). Although he did not hesitate to repeat his claim as to the unsuitability of the traditional offer/acceptance analysis in the particular case, which involved a clear battle of the forms, he did feel it necessary to frame his judgment in terms of the traditional analysis. It has been argued that Lord Denning's questioning of the classical model was revitalised by the Court of Appeal in *Trentham Ltd v Archital Luxfer* (1993), another battle of the forms case, where Steyn LJ was:

> . . . satisfied that in this fully executed contract transaction a contract came into existence during performance, even if it cannot be precisely analysed in terms of offer and acceptance.

However, that case involved a completed contract and, therefore, the court faced the problem of giving retrospective effect to the parties' interactions and business relationship. So, the case may not be as significant an attack on the classical model of contract as appears at first sight. The same approach was taken by the Supreme Court in *RTS Flexible Systems Ltd v Molkerei Alois Muller Gmbh and Company KG (UK Production)* (2010). A contract was found to exist, though the written draft contract remained unexecuted, because the work had been completed.

The decisions in *Balmoral Group Ltd v Borealis (UK) Ltd* (2006) and *Sterling Hydraulics Ltd v Dichtomatik Ltd* (2007), demonstrate judicial adherence to the classical model of offer and acceptance, by a detailed analysis of the parties' exchanges of their terms of contracting and their responses to such exchanges. The end result may well have been different from what the parties intended, but that only goes to confirm the necessity for businesses to be legally aware in conducting their transactions.

4.5 Consideration

English law does not enforce gratuitous promises unless they are made by deed. Consideration can be understood as the price paid for a promise. The element of bargain implicit in the idea of consideration is evident in Sir Frederick Pollock's definition, adopted by the House of Lords in *Dunlop v Selfridge* (1915):

> An act or forbearance of one party, or the promise thereof, is the price for which the promise of the other is bought, and the promise thus given for value is enforceable.

It is sometimes said that consideration consists of some benefit to the promisor or detriment to the promisee. Not both elements stated in that definition are required to be present to support a legally enforceable agreement though, in practice, they usually are. If the promisee acts to their detriment, it is immaterial that the action does not directly benefit the promisor. However, that detriment must be suffered at the request of the promisor; for example, in *Carlill* (see 4.2.2 above), Mrs Carlill gave consideration by way of detriment, by undertaking the inconvenience of using the smoke ball as requested by the company in their advertisement.

Forbearance involves non-action or the relinquishing of some right. An example is forbearance from suing. If two parties, A and B, believe that A has a cause of legal action against B, then, if B promises to pay a sum of money to A if A will give up the right to pursue the action, there is a valid contract to that effect: A has provided consideration by giving up his right to have recourse to law. Such action would not amount to consideration if A knew that the claim was either hopeless or invalid, as in *Wade v Simeon* (1846), where it transpired that the plaintiff had no legal claim for breach of the original contract.

4.5.1 Types of consideration

Consideration can be categorised as follows:

- *Executory consideration*
  This is the promise to perform an action at some future time. A contract can be made on the basis of an exchange of promises as to future action. Such a contract is known as an executory contract.
- *Executed consideration*
  In unilateral contracts, where the offeror promises something in return for the offeree's doing something, the promise only becomes enforceable when the offeree has actually performed the required act. If A offers a reward for the return of a lost watch, the reward only becomes enforceable once it is returned.
- *Past consideration* is not valid consideration; that is, it is insufficient to make any agreement which is based on it a binding contract. Normally, consideration is provided either at the time of the creation of a contract or at a later date. In the case of past consideration, however, the action is performed before the promise for which it is supposed to be the consideration. Such action is not sufficient to support a promise, as consideration cannot consist of any action already wholly performed before the promise was made. The consideration must be given *because of or in return for the other's promise*, as in:

❖ KEY CASE *Re McArdle* (1951)

Facts:

Several children were entitled to a house on their mother's death. While the mother was alive, her son and his wife had lived with her, and the wife had made improvements to the house. The children later promised that they would pay the wife £488 for the improvements.

Decision:

It was held that, as the work was completed before the promise was given, it was past consideration, and the promise could not be enforced; she had not carried out the work *because* of a promise of reimbursement.

However, the case should be compared with the situation, where the claimant performs the action at the request of the defendant and payment *was expected* but not mentioned. In such a case any subsequent promise to pay will be enforceable, as can be seen in *Re Casey's Patents* (1892), where the joint owners of patent rights asked Casey to find licensees to work the patents. After he had done as requested, they promised to reward him. When one of the patent holders died, his executors denied the enforceability of the promise made to Casey on the basis of past consideration. It was held that the promise made to Casey was enforceable. There had been an implied promise to reward him, before he had performed his action, and the later payment simply fixed the extent of that reward.

Comment: In practical terms, it is usually implied that you are promising to pay where you ask a person to undertake work which is within the course of his/her trade or profession even though you do not actually promise to pay.

4.5.2 Rules relating to consideration

It has already been seen that consideration must not be past, but that is only one of the many rules that govern the legal definition and operation of consideration. Thus:

- *Performance must be legal*
  The courts will not countenance a claim to enforce a promise to pay for any criminal act.
- *Performance must be possible*
  It is generally accepted that a promise to perform an impossible act cannot form the basis of a binding contractual agreement.
- *Consideration must move from the promisee*
  If A promises B £1,000 if B gives his car to C, then C cannot usually enforce B's promise, because C is not the party who has provided the consideration for the promise. In *Tweddle v Atkinson* (1861), on the occasion of the marriage of A and B, their respective fathers entered into a contract to pay money to A. When one of the parents died without having made the payment, A tried to enforce the contract against his estate. It was held that A could not enforce the contract, as he personally provided no consideration for the promise. (This point should be considered in the context of the doctrine of privity, and its exceptions: see 4.6 below.)
- *Consideration must be sufficient but need not be adequate*
  It is up to the parties to decide the terms of their contract. The court will not intervene to require equality in the value exchanged; as long as the agreement has been freely entered into, the consideration exchanged need not be adequate. In *Thomas v Thomas* (1842), the executors of a man's will promised to let his widow live in his house, in return for rent of £1 per year. It was held that £1 was sufficient consideration to validate the contract, although it did not represent an adequate rent in economic terms. In *Chappell & Co v Nestlé Co* (1959), a chocolate wrapper was adequate consideration to form a contract, even though it had no economic value and was thrown away after it was returned to Nestlé. However, the consideration must be *sufficient*; that is, something which the law recognises as amounting to consideration, examined below in 4.5.3.

4.5.3 Sufficiency of consideration

CONSIDERATION TO SUPPORT A CONTRACT	
INSUFFICIENT	SUFFICIENT
Discharge of public duty	Exceeding public duty
Performance of existing contractual duty	• Performance of such duty, with practical benefits accruing to promisor (subject to fraud or duress)
	• Performance of such duty owed to one person, in return for promise of a third party

Figure 4.4

It is generally accepted that performance of an existing duty does not provide valid consideration. The rules relating to existing duty are as follows:

- *The discharge of a public duty*
  As a matter of public policy, in order to forestall the possibility of corruption or extortion, it has long been held that those required to perform certain public duties cannot claim the

performance of those duties as consideration for a promised reward. In *Collins v Godefroy* (1831), the plaintiff was served with a subpoena, which meant he was legally required to give evidence in a court case. Additionally, however, the defendant promised to pay him for giving his evidence. When the plaintiff tried to enforce the promised payment, it was held that there was no binding agreement, as he had not provided consideration by simply fulfilling his existing duty.

Where, however, a promisee does more than his duty, he can claim on the promise. See, for example, *Glasbrook v Glamorgan CC* (1925), where the police authority provided more protection than their public duty required; and *Harris v Sheffield United FC* (1987), where the defendant football club was held liable to pay police costs for controlling crowds at their matches.

In cases where there is no possibility of corruption and no evidence of coercion, the courts have stretched the understanding of what is meant by 'consideration' in order to fit the facts of the case in question within the framework of the classical model of contract. See, for example, *Ward v Byham* (1956), in which a mother was held to provide consideration by looking after her child well; and *Williams v Williams* (1957), in which the consideration for a husband's promise of maintenance to his estranged wife seemed to be the fact of her staying away from him. In both cases, Lord Denning's *obiter dicta* directly questioned the reason why the performance of an existing duty should not amount to consideration, but the cases were ultimately decided on the basis that sufficient consideration was provided.

- *The performance of a contractual duty*

Lord Denning's challenge to the formalism of the classical model of contract is particularly pertinent when considered in the context of commercial contracts, where the mere performance of a contract may provide a benefit, or at least avoid a loss, for a promisor. The long-established rule, however, was that the performance of a contractual duty already owed to the promisor could not be consideration for a new promise. In *Stilk v Myrick* (1809), when two members of his crew deserted, a ship's captain promised the remaining members of the crew the deserters' wages if they completed the voyage. On completion of the voyage, the owners refused to honour the promise and it was held that it could not be legally enforced, since the sailors had only done what they were already obliged to do by their contracts of employment.

Although *Stilk* is cited as an authority in relation to consideration, it would appear that the public policy issue, in the perceived need to preclude even the possibility of sailors in distant parts exerting coercive pressure to increase their rewards, was just as important. Thus, although the reason for the decision was a matter of public policy, its legal justification was in terms of consideration.

As in the case of a public duty, so performance of more than the existing contractual duty will be valid consideration for a new promise. Thus, in *Hartley v Ponsonby* (1857), the facts of which were similar to those in *Stilk v Myrick*, it was decided that the crew had done more than they previously had agreed to do, because the number of deserters had been so great as to make the voyage unusually hazardous. On that basis, they were entitled to enforce the agreement to increase their wages. Again, one finds in this case, a reluctance to deny the theoretical application of the classical model of contract, whilst at the same time undermining its operation in practice.

The continued relevance and application of *Stilk v Myrick* in commercial cases was placed in doubt in more recent years by a potentially extremely important decision of the Court of Appeal:

❖ KEY CASE *Williams v Roffey Bros* (1990)

Facts:
Roffey Bros had entered into a contract to refurbish a block of flats and sub-contracted with Williams to carry out carpentry work, for a fixed price of £20,000. It became apparent that Williams was in such financial difficulties that he might not be able to complete his work on time, with the consequence that Roffey Bros would be subject to a penalty clause in the main contract. As a result, Roffey Bros offered to pay Williams an additional £575 for each flat he completed. On that basis, Williams carried on working but, when it seemed that Roffey Bros were not going to pay him, he stopped work and sued for the additional payment in relation to the eight flats he had completed after the promise of additional payment.

Decision:
The Court of Appeal held that Roffey Bros had enjoyed practical benefits as a consequence of their promise to increase Williams' payment: the work would be completed on time; they would not have to pay any penalty; and they would not suffer the bother and expense of getting someone else to complete the work. In the circumstances, these benefits were sufficient to provide consideration for the promise of extra money and Williams was held to be entitled to recover the extra money owed to him.

It should be emphasised that the Court of Appeal in *Williams v Roffey* made it clear that they were not to be understood as disapproving the *ratio* in *Stilk*. They distinguished the present case but, in so doing, effectively limited the application of the *ratio* in *Stilk*. As the owners in *Stilk* would appear to have enjoyed similar practical benefits to those enjoyed by Roffey Bros, it would seem that the reason for distinguishing the cases rests on the clear absence of any fraud, economic duress or other improper pressure. This was emphasised by the Court of Appeal in *Williams*, where it was indicated that **Williams did not put pressure on Roffey Bros for extra payment; it was Roffey Bros who approached Williams with the suggestion**.

Comment: Thus, the legal situation would seem to be that the performance of an existing contractual duty can amount to consideration for a new promise in circumstances where there is no question of fraud or duress, and where practical benefits accrue to the promisor. Such a conclusion not only concurs with the approach suggested by Lord Denning in *Ward v Byham* and *Williams v Williams*, but also reflects commercial practice, where contracts are frequently renegotiated in the course of their performance. However, it is important to note that in *Williams v Roffey Bros*, the court still felt constrained to find that consideration existed on the part of Williams, though some might consider such a finding artificial. It has been suggested that the court paid 'lip service' to the concept of consideration, not being prepared to depart entirely from its constraints in the interests of commercial reality.
However, that there has been judicial criticism of the *Roffey* judgment; see, for example, *South Carribean Trading Ltd v Trafigura Beheer* (2005). The real difficulty is to reconcile business practice and interest with accepted legal principles.

The foregoing has considered the situation between parties to an existing contract. It has long been recognised that the performance of a contractual duty owed to one person can amount to valid consideration for the promise made by another person.

In *Shadwell v Shadwell* (1860), the plaintiff had entered into a contract to marry. His uncle promised that, if he went ahead with the marriage, he would pay him £150 per year, until his earnings reached a certain sum. When the uncle died, owing several years' payment, the nephew successfully sued his estate for the outstanding money. It was held that going through with the marriage was sufficient consideration for the uncle's promise, even though the nephew was already contractually bound to his fiancée.

4.5.4 Consideration in relation to the waiver of existing rights

At common law, if A owes B £10 but B agrees to accept £5 in full settlement of the debt, B's promise to give up existing rights must be supported by consideration on the part of A. A business creditor might well be prepared to agree to such a settlement on the basis that some money is better than none. However, *Pinnel's Case* (1602), determined that payment of a lesser sum cannot be satisfaction for the whole. This opinion was approved in *Foakes v Beer* (1884), where Mrs Beer had obtained a judgment in debt against Dr Foakes for £2,091. She agreed in writing to accept payment of this amount in instalments. When payment was complete, she claimed a further £360 as interest due on the judgment debt. It was held that she was entitled to the interest, as her promise to accept the bare debt was not supported by any consideration from Foakes.

It can be appreciated that there are some similarities between the rules in *Foakes v Beer* and *Stilk v Myrick* (1809) in respect of the way in which promisors escape liability for their promises. In the former case, however, the promisor was being asked to give up what she was legally entitled to insist on, whereas, in the latter case, the promisors were being asked to provide more than they were legally required to provide.

As has been considered in 4.5.3 above, the rule in *Stilk* has been subsequently modified and made less strict in its application by *Williams v Roffey Bros*. However, no corresponding modification has taken place in relation to *Foakes*; indeed, the Court of Appeal has rejected the argument that it should be so modified. In *Re Selectmove Ltd* (1994), during negotiations relating to money owed to the Inland Revenue, the company had agreed with the collector of taxes that it would pay off the debt by instalments. The company began paying off the debt, only to be faced with a demand from the Revenue that the total be paid off immediately, on threat of liquidation. It was argued for the company, on the basis of *Williams v Roffey Bros*, that its payment of the debt was sufficient consideration for the promise of the Revenue to accept it in instalments. It was held that situations relating to the payment of debt were distinguishable from those relating to the supply of goods and services, and that, in the case of the former, the court was bound to follow the clear authority of the House of Lords in *Foakes v Beer*.

The practical validity of the distinction drawn by the Court of Appeal is, to say the least, arguable. It ignores the fact that payment by instalments, and indeed part payment, is substantially better than no payment at all, which is a possible, if not likely, outcome of liquidating businesses in an attempt to recover the full amount of a debt. It is surely unnecessarily harsh to deny legal enforceability to renegotiated agreements in relation to debt where the terms have been renegotiated freely and without any suggestion of fraud or coercion. Nonetheless, the Court of Appeal clearly felt itself constrained by the doctrine of binding precedent and had less scope to distinguish *Foakes* than it had with regard to *Stilk*. Indeed, the Court of Appeal upheld the rule in *Pinnel's Case* in *Collier v P & MJWright (Holdings) Ltd* (2007), rejecting an attempt to create a further exception to that rule.

There are a number of situations in which the rule in *Pinnel's case* does not apply. The following actions, which are clearly commercially significant, will operate to fully discharge an outstanding debt:

- *Payment in kind*
  Money's worth is just as capable of satisfying a debt as money. So, A may clear a debt if B agrees to accept something instead of money. As considered previously, consideration does not have to be adequate; thus, A can discharge a £10 debt by giving B £5 and a bar of chocolate. Payment by cheque is no longer treated as substitute payment in this respect (see *D & C Builders Ltd v Rees* (1966)).
- *Payment of a lesser sum before the due date of payment*
  The early payment has, of course, to be acceptable to the creditor.
- *Payment at a different place*
  This, also, must be at the wish of the creditor.
- *Payment of a lesser sum by a third party*
  See *Welby v Drake* (1825).
- *A composition arrangement*
  This is an agreement between creditors to the effect that they will accept part payment of their debts. The individual creditors cannot subsequently seek to recover the unpaid element of the debt (see *Good v Cheesman* (1831)).

4.5.5 Promissory estoppel

It has been seen that, generally, English law will not enforce gratuitous promises, that is, promises which are not supported by consideration coming from the promisee. The equitable doctrine of promissory estoppel, however, can sometimes be relied upon to prevent promisors from going back on their promises to forgo their strict contractual rights. Its application may well protect a business, which has been promised some leeway in performance of contractual terms, from the other party seeking to apply strict legal principles to ignore that promise. The doctrine first appeared in *Hughes v Metropolitan Railway Co* (1877) and was revived by Lord Denning in:

❖ KEY CASE *Central London Pty Trust Ltd v High Trees House Ltd* (1947)

Facts:

The plaintiffs let a block of flats to the defendants in 1937 at a fixed rent. During the Second World War, it became difficult to let the flats and the parties renegotiated the rent to half of the original amount. No consideration was provided for this agreement. By 1945, all the flats were let and the plaintiffs sought to return to the terms of the original agreement. They claimed that they were entitled to the full rent in the future and enquired as to whether they were owed additional rent for the previous period.

Decision:

It was held that the plaintiffs were entitled to the full rent in the future but were estopped from claiming the full rent for the period 1941–45.

Note: The precise scope of the doctrine of promissory estoppel is far from certain. There are a number of conflicting judgments on the point, with some judges adopting a wide understanding of its operation, whilst others prefer to keep its effect narrowly constrained.

However, some points should be noted:

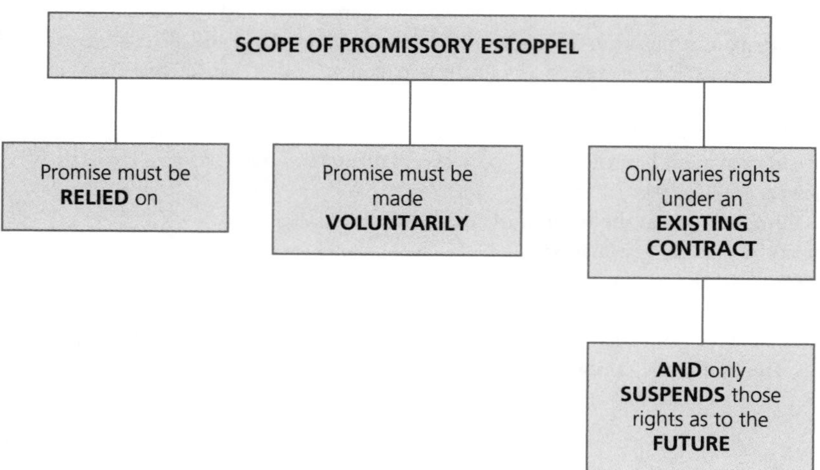

Figure 4.5

- *Promissory estoppel only arises where a party relies on the promise*
  The promise must have been made with the intention that it be acted upon, and it must actually have been acted on. It was once thought that the promisee must have acted to their detriment, but such detriment is no longer considered necessary (see *WJ Alan & Co v El Nasr Export and Import Co* (1972)).
- *Promissory estoppel only varies or discharges rights within an existing contract*
  Promissory estoppel does not apply to the formation of contract and, therefore, does not avoid the need for consideration to establish a contract in the first instance. This point is sometimes made by stating that promissory estoppel is 'a shield and not a sword'. Thus in *Combe v Combe* (1951), it was held that the doctrine could only be used as a defence, when sued on the terms of the original agreement, and not as a cause of action (see also: *Baird Textile Holdings Ltd v Marks & Spencer plc* (2001)).
- *Promissory estoppel normally only suspends rights*
  It is usually open to the promisor, on the provision of reasonable notice, to retract the promise and revert to the original terms of the contract for the future (see *Tool Metal Manufacturing Co v Tungsten Electric Co* (1955)). Rights may be extinguished, however, in the case of a non-continuing obligation or where the parties cannot resume their original positions. (Consider *D & C Builders v Rees* (1966), below; it is clear that, had the defendants been able to rely on promissory estoppel, the plaintiffs would have permanently lost their right to recover the full amount of the original debt.)
- *The promise relied upon must be given voluntarily*
  As an equitable remedy, the benefit of promissory estoppel will not be extended to those who behaved in an inequitable manner. Thus, if the promise has been extorted through fraud, duress, or any other inequitable act, it cannot be relied on and the common law rules will apply. In *D & C Builders Ltd v Rees* (1966), the defendants owed the plaintiffs £482 but would agree to pay only £300. As the plaintiffs were in financial difficulties, they accepted the £300 in full settlement of the account. The plaintiffs later successfully claimed the outstanding balance on the ground that they had been forced to accept the lesser sum. As the defendants had not acted

in an equitable manner, they were denied the protection of the equitable remedy and the case was decided on the basis of the rule in *Pinnel's Case* (1602).

- *Promissory estoppel might only apply to future rights*
  It is not entirely clear whether the doctrine can apply to forgoing existing rights as well as future rights, but it should be noted that, in *Re Selectmove Ltd* (1994), it was stated that promissory estoppel could not be applied where the promise related to forgoing an existing debt; it only related to debts accruing in the future, such as rent due *after* the promise was made.

It is likely that the decision in *Williams v Roffey Bros*, has reduced the need for reliance on promissory estoppel in cases involving the renegotiation of contracts for the supply of goods or services, since performance of existing duties may now provide consideration for new promises. As stated previously with regard to *Re Selectmove Ltd*, however, the same claim cannot be made in relation to partial payments of debts. Those situations are still subject to the rule in *Foakes v Beer* (1884), as modified, uncertainly, by the operation of promissory estoppel. As estoppel is generally only suspensory in effect, it is always open to the promisor, at least in the case of continuing debts, to reimpose the original terms by withdrawing their new promise.

4.6 Privity of Contract

There is some debate as to whether privity is a principle in its own right, or whether it is simply a conclusion from the more general rules relating to consideration. In any case, it is a general rule that a contract can only impose rights or obligations on those who are actually parties to it. This is the doctrine of privity and its operation may be seen in:

❖ KEY CASE *Dunlop v Selfridge* (1915)

Facts:
Dunlop sold tyres to a distributor, Dew & Co, on terms that the distributor would not sell them at less than the manufacturer's list price and that they would extract a similar undertaking from anyone whom they supplied with tyres. Dew & Co resold the tyres to Selfridge, who agreed to abide by the restrictions and to pay Dunlop £5 for each tyre they sold in breach of them. When Selfridge sold tyres at below Dunlop's list price, Dunlop sought to recover the promised £5 per tyre.

Decision:
It was held that Dunlop could not recover damages on the basis of the contract between Dew and Selfridge, to which they were not a party.

However, there are circumstances in which the strict rule of privity may be avoided, to allow a third party to enforce a contract, for example:

- *The beneficiary sues in some other capacity*
  Although someone may not be a party to a particular contract, they may, nonetheless, acquire the power to enforce the contract where they are legally appointed to administer the affairs of one of the original parties. An example of this is *Beswick v Beswick* (1967), where a coal merchant sold his business to his nephew in return for a consultancy fee of £6 10s during his lifetime, and thereafter an annuity of £5 per week, payable to his widow. After the uncle died, the

nephew stopped paying the widow. When she became administratrix of her husband's estate, she sued the nephew for specific performance of the agreement in that capacity, as well as in her personal capacity. It was held that, although she was not a party to the contract, and therefore could not be granted specific performance in her personal capacity, such an order could be awarded to her as the administratrix of the deceased's estate. However, she *only* benefited personally because she was the beneficiary of the deceased's estate.

- *The situation involves a collateral contract*

  A collateral contract arises where one party promises something to another party if that other party enters into a contract with a third party; for example, A promises to give B something if B enters into a contract with C. In such a situation, the second party can enforce the original promise, that is, B can insist that A complies with the original promise. It may be seen from this that, although treated as an exception to the privity rule, a collateral contract conforms with the requirements relating to the establishment of any other contract, consideration for the original promise being the making of the second contract. An example of the operation of a collateral contract will demonstrate, however, the way in which the courts tend to construct collateral contracts in order to achieve what they see as fair dealing.

  In *Shanklin Pier v Detel Products Ltd* (1951), the plaintiffs contracted to have their pier repainted. On the basis of promises as to its quality, the defendants persuaded the pier company to insist that a particular paint produced by Detel be used. The painters used the paint but it proved unsatisfactory. The plaintiffs sued for breach of the original promise as to the paint's suitability. The defendants countered that the only contract that they had entered into was with the painters to whom they had sold the paint, and that, as the pier company was not a party to that contract, they had no right of action against Detel. The pier company was successful. It was held that, in addition to the contract for the sale of paint, there was a second, collateral, contract between the plaintiffs and the defendants, by which the latter guaranteed the suitability of the paint in return for the pier company specifying that the painters used it.

- *There is a valid assignment of the benefit of the contract*

  A contracting party can transfer the benefit of that contract to a third party through the formal process of assignment. The assignment must be in writing, and gives no better rights under the contract than those which the assignor possessed. The burden of a contract cannot be assigned without the consent of the other party to the contract.

- *Where it is foreseeable that damage caused by breach of contract will cause a loss to a third party*

  In *Linden Gardens Trust Ltd v Lenesta Sludge Disposals Ltd* (1994), the original parties had entered into a contract for work to be carried out on a property, knowing that the property was likely to be subsequently transferred to a third party. The defendants' poor work, amounting to a breach of contract, only became apparent after the property was transferred. There had been no assignment of the original contract and, normally, under the doctrine of privity, the new owners would have no contractual rights against the defendants and the original owners of the property would have suffered only a nominal breach, as they had sold it at no loss to themselves. Nonetheless, the House of Lords held that, under such circumstances and within a commercial context, the original promisee should be able to claim full damages on behalf of the third party for the breach of contract. The issue was examined subsequently by the House of Lords, in *Alfred McAlpine Construction Ltd v Panatown Ltd* (2002).

- *One of the parties has entered the contract as a trustee for a third party*

  There exists the possibility that a party to a contract can create a contract specifically for the benefit of a third party. In such limited circumstances, the promisee is considered as a trustee of the contractual promise for the benefit of the third party. In order to enforce the contract, the third party must act through the promisee by making them a party to any action, as in *Les Affréteurs Réunis SA v Leopold Walford (London) Ltd* (1919).

Another exception to the privity rule is agency, where the agent brings about contractual relations between two other parties, even where the existence of the agency has not been disclosed.

See Chapter 12

4.6.1 Contracts (Rights of Third Parties) Act 1999

Significant inroads into the operation of the doctrine of privity have been made by the Contracts (Rights of Third Parties) Act 1999, which establishes the circumstances in which third parties can enforce terms of contracts. In order for the third party to gain enforcement rights, the contract in question must either expressly confer such a right on the third party or clearly have been made for their benefit (s 1(1)). For example, *Tweddle v Atkinson* (above), would be differently decided today because the contract expressly named the son as beneficiary *and* stated that he could enforce the contract. In *Nisshin Shipping Co Ltd v Cleaves & Co Ltd & Others* (2003), the Commercial Court examined the application of s 1(1). It was decided that, though there was no express provision for third parties to enforce the contract for their own benefit, that intention could be inferred; however, the lack of an express provision did not automatically raise an inference that the third party could enforce clauses of the contract. It would be a matter of construction whether there was a mutual intention that a third party could enforce or rely on the contractual clauses (see also: *Prudential Assurance Co Ltd v Ayres* (2007)). Section 1(3), examined in *Avraamides v Colwill* (2006), limits the third party rights of s 1(1). The third party must be expressly identified in the contract – by name, as a member of a class of persons or as answering a particular description. However, the third person need not be in existence when the contract was made, so it is possible for parties to make contracts for the benefit of unborn children or a future marriage partner. The third party may exercise the right to any remedy which would have been available had they been a party to the contract. Such rights are, however, subject to the terms and conditions contained in the contract; the third party can get no better rights than the original promisee; and the actual parties to the contract can place conditions on the rights of the third party.

Under s 2 of the Act, where a third party has rights by virtue of the Act, the original contracting parties cannot agree to rescind or vary the contract terms without the consent of the third party, unless the original contract contained an express term to that effect.

Section 3 allows the promisor to make use of any defences or rights of set-off that they might have against the promisee in any action by the third party. Additionally, the promisor can rely on any such rights against the third party. These rights are subject to any express provision in the contract to the contrary.

Section 5 removes the possibility of the promisor suffering from double liability in relation to the promisor and the third party. It provides, therefore, that any damages awarded to a third party for a breach of the contract be reduced by the amount recovered by the promisee in any previous action relating to the contract.

Section 6 specifically states that it does not alter the existing law relating to, and confers no new rights on third parties in relation to, for example, negotiable instruments, contracts of employment or contracts for the carriage of goods. However, a third party stated as benefiting from an exclusion clause in a contract for the carriage of goods by sea may rely on such a clause if sued. So, an independent firm of stevedores damaging a cargo during loading might claim the protection of a clause in the contract of carriage between the cargo owner and the shipowner.

4.7 Capacity

Capacity refers legal ability to enter into a contract. The scope of a company's capacity to contract is examined in Chapter 14. In general, all adults of sound mind have full capacity. However, the capacity of certain individuals is limited.

See Chapter 14

4.7.1 Minors

Minors are persons under the age of 18, whom the law tries to protect by restricting their contractual capacity and, thus, preventing them from entering into disadvantageous agreements. Accordingly, businesses may be at a disadvantage when contracting with minors. The rules which apply are a mixture of common law and statute. Agreements entered into by minors may be classified as follows:

MINORS' CONTRACTS	
Valid (enforceable by and against minor)	• Contract for necessaries • Beneficial contract of service
Voidable (binding, subject to repudiation by minor)	For example; • contracts for shares • leases of property • partnership agreements
Other contracts (enforceable against minor, unless ratifies at age of 18)	For example; • contract made in course of minor's trade or profession

Figure 4.6

Valid contracts

Contracts can be enforced against minors where they relate to the following:

- *Contracts for necessaries*
  A minor is bound to pay for necessaries, that is, things that are necessary to maintain the minor. Necessaries are defined in s 3 of the Sale of Goods Act 1979 as goods 'suitable to the condition in life of the minor and their actual requirements at the time of sale'. The operation of this section is demonstrated in *Nash v Inman* (1908), where a tailor sued a minor to whom he had supplied clothes, including 11 fancy waistcoats. The minor was an undergraduate at Cambridge University at the time. It was held that, although the clothes were suitable according to the minor's station in life, they were not necessary, as he already had sufficient clothing. The minor is, in any case, only required to pay a reasonable price for any necessaries purchased.
- *Beneficial contracts of service*
  A minor is bound by a contract of apprenticeship or employment, as long as it is, on the whole, for their benefit.

  In *Doyle v White City Stadium* (1935), Doyle, a minor, obtained a professional boxer's licence, which was treated as a contract of apprenticeship. The licence provided that he would be bound by the rules of the Boxing Board of Control, which had the power to retain any prize money if he was ever disqualified in a fight. He claimed that the licence was void, as it was not for his benefit, but it was held that the conditions of the licence were enforceable. In spite of the penal clause, it was held that, taken as whole, it was beneficial to him.

  There has to be an element of education or training in the contract. Thus, a contract made by Wayne Rooney, when 15, appointing an agent to represent him, was not a beneficial contract of service (*Proform Sports Management Ltd v Proactive Sports Management Ltd* (2006)).

Voidable contracts

These are binding on the minor, unless they are repudiated by the minor during the period of minority or within a reasonable time after reaching the age of majority. These are generally transactions in which the minor acquires an interest of a permanent nature with continuing obligations.

If the minor has made payments prior to repudiation of the contract, such payment cannot be recovered unless there is a total failure of consideration and the minor has received no benefit whatsoever. In *Steinberg v Scala (Leeds)* (1923), Miss Steinberg, while still a minor, applied for, and was allotted, shares in the defendant company. After paying some money on the shares, she defaulted on payment and repudiated the contract. The company agreed that her name be removed from its register of members but refused to return the money she had already paid. It was held that Miss Steinberg was not entitled to recover the money paid. She had benefited from membership rights in the company; thus, there had not been a complete failure of consideration.

Other contracts

By virtue of the Minors' Contracts Act 1987, contracts not falling within the previous two categories are unenforceable against the minor, unless the minor ratifies on attaining the age of 18. Equally, a minor can so ratify a voidable contract. Ratification means a confirmation by the minor of the contractual obligation.

The Act has given the courts wide powers to order restoration of property acquired by a minor. They are not restricted to cases where the minor has acquired the property through fraud; they can order restitution where they think it just and equitable to do so.

Minors' liability in tort

As there is no minimum age limit in relation to claims in tort, minors may be liable under a tortious action. The courts, however, will not permit a party to enforce a contract indirectly by substituting a claim in tort or quasi-contract for a claim in contract.

In *Leslie v Shiell* (1914), Shiell, a minor, obtained a loan from Leslie by lying about his age. Leslie sued to recover the money as damages in an action for the tort of deceit. It was held, however, that the action must fail, as it was simply an indirect means of enforcing the otherwise void contract.

4.7.2 Mental incapacity and intoxication

A contract made by a party who is of unsound mind or under the influence of drink or drugs is *prima facie* valid. In order to avoid a contract, such a person must show:

- that their mind was so affected at the time that they were incapable of understanding the nature of their actions; and
- that the other party either knew or ought to have known of their disability.

The person claiming such incapacity, nonetheless, must pay a reasonable price for necessaries sold and delivered to them. The Sale of Goods Act 1979 specifically applies the same rules to such people as those that are applicable to minors.

4.8 Intention to Create Legal Relations

Though all of the aspects considered previously are present in a particular agreement, there still may not be a contract. In order to limit the number of cases that might otherwise be brought, the courts will only enforce those agreements which the parties intended to have legal effect. Although expressed in terms of the parties' intentions, the test for the presence of such intention is objective, rather than subjective. For the purposes of this topic, agreements can be divided into categories, where different presumptions apply:

4.8.1 Domestic and social agreements

In this type of agreement, there is a presumption that the parties do not intend to create legal relations.

In *Balfour v Balfour* (1919), a husband returned to Ceylon to take up employment and he promised his wife, who could not return with him due to health problems, that he would pay her £30 per month as maintenance. When the marriage later ended in divorce, the wife sued for the promised maintenance. It was held that the parties had not intended the original promise to be binding and, therefore, it was not legally enforceable.

It is essential to realise that the intention not to create legal relations in such relationships is only a presumption and that, as with all presumptions, it may be rebutted by the actual facts and circumstances of a particular case. A case in point is *Merritt v Merritt* (1970). After a husband had left the matrimonial home, he met his wife and promised to pay her £40 per month, from which she undertook to pay the outstanding mortgage on their house. The husband, at the wife's insistence, signed a note, agreeing to transfer the house into the wife's sole name when the mortgage was paid off. The wife paid off the mortgage but the husband refused to transfer the house. It was held that the agreement was enforceable, as, in the circumstances, the parties had clearly intended to enter into a legally enforceable agreement.

'Social' agreements, such as lottery syndicates, have also been the subject of legal dispute. In *Simpkins v Pays* (1955), a relatively vague agreement about contribution to postage and sharing of any winnings in competitions made between a lodger, a landlady and her granddaughter was alleged not to be a contract for lack of intention to create legal relations. However, the court decided that there was a binding contract to share winnings, despite the apparently social nature of the agreement. The agreement was commercial in nature and related to a matter unconnected with the running of a household; there was a degree of *mutuality* in the agreement which indicated an intention that it was binding. In *Albert v Motor Insurers' Bureau* (1971), an agreement between colleagues in relation to lifts to work was held to be a contract because there was intention to create legal relations. It was said to be unnecessary to show whether the parties had thought about whether there was a contract, nor did it matter that, if asked, they would have said that they would not have sued if the arrangement failed. Clearly, therefore, the presumption does not purport to find the *actual* intention of the parties. Perhaps the best advice, particularly in relation to lottery syndicates, is to reduce the agreement to writing so that there is written evidence that the parties did intend the agreement to be a binding contract.

4.8.2 Commercial agreements

In commercial situations, the strong presumption is that the parties intend to enter into a legally binding relationship in consequence of their dealings. *Judge v Crown Leisure Ltd* (2005), considered the meaning of 'commercial situation'.

In *Edwards v Skyways* (1964), employers undertook to make an *ex gratia* payment to an employee whom they had made redundant. It was held that, in such a situation, the use of the term '*ex gratia*' was not sufficient to rebut the presumption that the establishment of legal relations had been intended. The former employee was, therefore, entitled to the promised payment.

As with other presumptions, this is open to rebuttal. In commercial situations, however, the presumption is so strong that it will usually take express wording to the contrary to avoid its operation. In *Rose & Frank Co v Crompton Bros* (1925), it was held that an express clause which stated that no legal relations were to be created by a business transaction was effective. In *Jones v Vernons Pools*

Ltd (1938), the plaintiff claimed to have submitted a correct pools forecast, which the defendants denied receiving, and relied on a clause in the coupon which stated that the transaction was binding in honour only. Under such circumstances, it was held that the plaintiff had no cause of action in contract, as no legal relations had been created.

Conversely, it is usually presumed that commercial advertisements, often making exaggerated claims, are not intended to create legal relations. However, *Carlill* (see 4.2.2 above) shows that, given specific wording, a public advertisement may show intention to create legal relations. Accordingly, businesses should consider the possible legal implications of their advertising materials before publication and distribution.

4.8.3 Collective agreements

Agreements between employers and trade unions may be considered as a distinct category of agreement for, although they are commercial agreements, they are presumed not to give rise to legal relations and, therefore, are not normally enforceable in the courts. Such was the outcome of *Ford Motor Co v AUEFW* (1969), in which it was held that Ford could not take legal action against the defendant trade union, which had ignored previously negotiated terms of a collective agreement.

This presumption became conclusive by virtue of s 179 of the Trade Union and Labour Relations (Consolidation) Act 1992, unless the agreement was in writing and expressly stated that it was a binding agreement.

4.8.4 Letters of comfort

Letters of comfort are generally used by parent companies to encourage potential lenders to extend credit to their subsidiary companies by stating their intention to provide financial backing for those subsidiaries. It is generally the case that such letters merely amount to statements of present intention on the part of the parent company and, therefore, do not amount to offers that can be accepted by the creditors of any subsidiary companies. Given the operation of the doctrine of separate personality, this effectively leaves the creditors with no legal recourse against the parent company for any loans granted to the subsidiary.

See Chapter 14

❖ KEY CASE *Kleinwort Benson v Malaysian Mining Corp* (1989)

Facts:

The defendant company had issued a letter of comfort to the plaintiffs in respect of its subsidiary company, MMC Metals. However, when MMC Metals went into liquidation, the defendant failed to make good its debts to the plaintiffs.

Decision:

At first instance, the judge decided in favour of the plaintiffs, holding that, in such commercial circumstances, the defendants had failed to rebut the presumption that there had been an intention to create legal relations. On appeal, it was held that, in the circumstances of the instant case, the letter of comfort did not amount to an offer; it was a statement of intention which could not bind the defendants contractually. Therefore, the Malaysian Mining Corp was not legally responsible for the debt of its subsidiary.

Note: Kleinwort opens up the possibility that, under different circumstances, letters of comfort might be considered to constitute offers capable of being accepted and leading to contractual relations. Under such circumstances, the presumption as to the intention to create legal relations as they normally apply in commercial situations will operate, though it is almost inconceivable that a court would decide that a letter of comfort amounted to an offer without also finding an intention to create legal relations.

4.9 Formalities

There is no general requirement for contracts to be in writing. They can also be created orally or by action. Contracts made in any of these ways are called *parol* or *simple* contracts, whereas those made by deed are known as *speciality* contracts. Usually the parties can decide the form of the contract but, sometimes formalities are required:

- *Contracts that must be made by deed* Essentially, this requirement applies to conveyances of land and leases of more than three years. A conveyance is the legal process to transfer land. It is distinct from a contract to sell land, which is an agreement to transfer the land, not the actual transfer, which comes later. A promise made by deed, though without consideration, will be enforced by the courts.
- *Contracts that must be in writing (but not necessarily by deed)*, for example, cheques and contracts of marine insurance. Some agreements in this category, such as hire purchase, must also be signed by both parties. Increasingly, contracts are made electronically, and the Electronic Communications Act 2000 gives legal recognition to electronic signatures; such signatures, accompanied by certification of authenticity, are admissible as evidence in legal proceedings.
- *Contracts which must be evidenced in writing* This category covers contracts of guarantee, derived from the Statute of Frauds 1677. In *Pereira (J) Fernandes SA v Metha* (2006), an email offering a personal guarantee, was held to be sufficient evidence 'in writing' for the purposes of s 4.

Summary

Contract (1): Formation of a Contract

Definition

- A contract is a **legally binding agreement** – it is enforceable in court if it complies with legal requirements.
- In order to create a contract, the following factors have to be present:

Offer

- An offer is a promise, which is capable of acceptance, to be bound on particular terms.
- An offer may be restricted to a particular person(s) or made to the public at large.
- A person can only accept an offer they are aware of.
- An offer may be revoked *before* acceptance or may come to an end in other ways.
- An offer must be distinguished from an invitation to treat, a statement of intention and a supply of information.

Acceptance

- Acceptance must correspond with the terms of the offer.
- Acceptance must be communicated to the offeror (subject to exceptions such as the *postal rule*).

Consideration

- Consists of some benefit to the promisor or detriment to the promisee.
- Consideration can be *executed* or *executory*, but not *past*.
- Consideration must be *sufficient*, but need not be *adequate*.

Promissory estoppel

- The doctrine may prevent a person from going back on a promise to forgo strict contractual rights.
- The doctrine operates as a defence, not a cause of action.

Privity

- Only a party to a contract can sue or be sued on it.
- There are common law and statutory exceptions to the doctrine of privity, notably the Contracts (Rights of Third Parties) Act 1999.

Capacity

- Minors, those of unsound mind or under the influence of drugs or alcohol have limited capacity to make binding contracts; nevertheless, contracts for necessaries bind them.
- Minors are also bound by beneficial contracts of service.
- Some contracts made by minors are voidable and only bind them if not repudiated by them before or within a reasonable time after reaching the age of majority.
- Other contracts are not binding on minors unless ratified by the minor on attaining majority.

Intention to create legal relations

- In social/domestic agreements, there is a rebuttable presumption that legal relations were not intended.
- In commercial/business agreements, there is a rebuttable presumption that legal relations were intended.
- Collective agreements are usually presumed not to create legal relations.

Formalities

- Not normally required for simple/parol contracts.
- Some simple contracts need to be in writing/evidenced in writing.

Further Reading

Capps, D, 'You've got mail' (2003) NLJ 906 – (consideration of the postal rule in relation to email acceptance)

Furmston, MP, *Cheshire, Fifoot and Furmston's Law of Contract*, 16th edn, 2012, Oxford: OUP

Kramer, A, 'The many doctrines of promissory estoppel' (2002) 37 Student Law Review 17 – (relationship of promissory estoppel and consideration)

MacQueen and Azim-Khan, 'The Argos Free TV Debacle: Two Legal Opinions' [1999] 1 Electronic Business Law 9 – (offer and invitation to treat in the context of internet shopping)

Peel, E, *Treitel on the Law of Contract*, 13th edn, 2011, London: Sweet & Maxwell

Phang, A, 'Consideration at the Crossroads' [1991] 107 LQR 21 – (discussion of *Williams v Roffey*)

Poole, J, *Casebook on Contract Law*, 10th edn, 2010, Oxford: OUP
Richards, P, *The Law of Contract*, 11th edn, 2013, Harlow: Pearson Longman
Stone, R, 'Re Selectmove: Issues on Contract Formation' (1995) Student Law Review (Autumn) 19 – (aspects of contract formation raised in the case)

Websites

www.lawreports.co.uk (daily summaries of new cases)
www.statutelaw.gov.uk (for text of Contracts (Rights of Third Parties) Act 1999; Electronic Communications Act 2000)

Chapter 5

Contract (2): Contents of a Contract

Chapter Contents

Law in Context: Conditions and Warranties

Once a contract is created, attention turns to its contents, and one of the distinctions which students find difficult to apply is the actual difference between contractual terms. Such terms are classified into a condition, warranty or innominate term (the latter category was introduced in a case called *Hong Kong Fir Shipping*). A condition is a major term of the contract which goes to the root of the contract. If a condition is breached, the innocent party is entitled to repudiate (i.e. bring to an end) the contract and claim damages. In contrast, a warranty is a minor term within a contract and not central to the existence of the contract. If a warranty is breached the innocent party may claim damages but cannot end the contract. It is a useful exercise for students of business law to examine sample contracts to see if they can determine what wording constitutes a condition and what aspects of the contract amount to warranties.

5.1 Introduction

The previous chapter examined how a binding contract was formed; this chapter will consider what the parties have agreed. What they have agreed to do forms the *terms* of the contract.

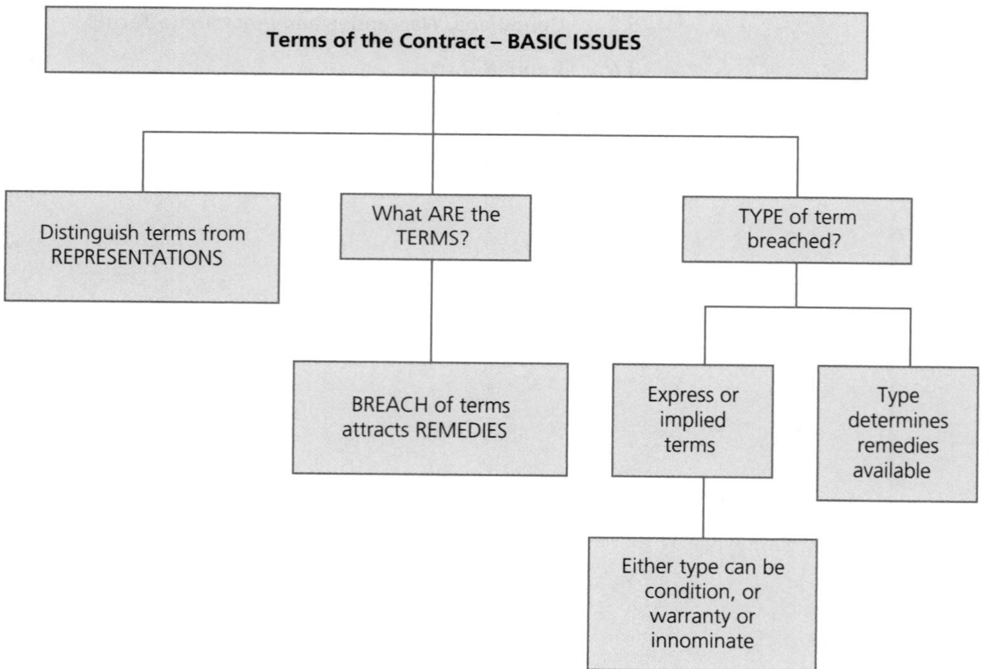

Figure 5.1

5.2 Contract Terms and Mere Representations

As the parties are normally bound to perform any promise that they have contracted to undertake, it is important to decide precisely what promises are included in the contract. Some statements do not form part of a contract, even though they might have induced the other party to make the contract. These pre-contractual statements are called *representations*. The consequences of such representations being false will be considered later (see 10.3 below) but, for the moment, it is sufficient to distinguish them from contractual terms, which are statements which *do* form part of the contract. There are four tests for distinguishing a contractual term from a mere representation:

- Where the statement is of such major importance that the promisee would not have made the agreement without it, it will be construed as a term. In *Bannerman v White* (1861), the defendant wanted to buy hops for brewing purposes and asked the plaintiff if they had been treated with sulphur. On the basis of the plaintiff's false statement that they had not been so treated, he agreed to buy the hops. When he discovered that they had been treated with sulphur, he refused to accept them. It was held that the plaintiff's statement about the sulphur was a fundamental term (the contract would not have been made *but for* the statement) of the contract and, since it was untrue, the defendant was entitled to repudiate (see 7.11 below) the contract.
- Where there is a time gap between the statement and making the contract, the statement is likely to be treated as a representation. In *Routledge v McKay* (1954), on 23 October, the defendant told the plaintiff that a motorcycle was a 1942 model. On 30 October, a written contract for the sale of the bike was made, without reference to its age. The bike was actually a 1930 model. It was held that the statement about the date was a pre-contractual representation and the plaintiff could not sue for damages for breach of contract. However, this rule is not a hard and fast one. In *Schawell v Reade* (1913), the court held that a statement made three months *before the final* agreement was part of the contract.
- Where the statement is oral and the agreement is subsequently drawn up in writing, its exclusion from the written document will suggest that the statement was not meant to be a contractual term. *Routledge* (above), may also be cited as authority for this proposition.
- Where one of the contracting parties has special knowledge or skill, then statements made by them will be terms, but statements made *to* them will not. In *Dick Bentley Productions Ltd v Harold Smith (Motors) Ltd* (1965), the plaintiff bought a Bentley car from the defendant, after being assured that it had only travelled 20,000 miles since its engine and gearbox were replaced. When this statement proved to be untrue, the plaintiff sued for breach of contract. *It was held that the statement was a term of the contract* and the plaintiff recovered damages.

  In *Oscar Chess Ltd v Williams* (1957), Williams traded in one car when buying another from the plaintiffs. He told them that his trade-in was a 1948 model, but it was a 1939 model. The company's claim for breach of contract failed. The statement of age was merely a representation, and the right to sue for misrepresentation (see 6.3 below) had been lost, due to delay.

5.3 Conditions, Warranties and Innominate Terms

Once it is decided that a statement is a term, rather than merely a pre-contractual representation, it is necessary to determine which type of term it is, in order to decide what remedies are available for its breach. Terms can be conditions, warranties or innominate.

5.3.1 Conditions

A condition is a fundamental part of the agreement, something which goes to the root of the contract. Breach of a condition gives the innocent party the right either to terminate the contract and refuse to perform their part of it or to go through with the agreement and sue for damages.

5.3.2 Warranties

A warranty is a subsidiary obligation which is not vital to the overall agreement, breach of which does not totally destroy its efficacy. Breach of warranty does not give the right to terminate the agreement. The innocent party has to complete their part of the agreement and can only sue for damages.

5.3.3 Distinction between conditions and warranties

The difference between the two types of term can be seen in the following cases:

- In *Poussard v Spiers and Pond* (1876), the plaintiff had contracted with the defendants to sing in an opera that they were producing. Due to illness, she was unable to appear on the first night and for some nights thereafter. When Mme Poussard recovered, the defendants refused her services, as they had hired a replacement for the whole run of the opera. It was held that her failure to appear on the opening night had been a breach of a condition and the defendants could treat the contract as discharged.
- In *Bettini v Gye* (1876), the plaintiff had contracted with the defendants to complete a number of engagements. He had also agreed to be in London for rehearsals six days before his opening performance. Due to illness, he only arrived three days before the opening night and the defendants refused his services. It was decided that there was only a breach of warranty. The defendants could recover damages but could not treat the contract as discharged.

The distinction between the effects of a breach of condition as against the effects of a breach of warranty is enshrined in s 11 of the Sale of Goods Act (SoGA) 1979. For some time, it was thought that these were the only two types of term possible, the nature of the remedy available being prescribed by the particular type of term concerned. This simple classification was subsequently rejected by the courts as being too restrictive, and a third type of term has emerged: the innominate or intermediate term (see *Hong Kong Fir Shipping Co Ltd v Kawasaki Kisen Kaisha Ltd* (1962)).

5.3.4 Innominate terms

In this case, the remedy is not prescribed in advance simply by whether the term breached is a condition or a warranty, but depends on **the consequence of the breach**.

If the breach substantially deprives the innocent party of the whole benefit of the contract, then the right to repudiate follows, even if the term might otherwise appear to be a mere warranty.

If, however, the innocent party does not lose the whole benefit of the contract, then they cannot repudiate but must settle for damages, even if the term might otherwise appear to be a condition.

❖ KEY CASE *Cehave v Bremer (The Hansa Nord)* (1976)

Facts:
A contract for the sale of a cargo of citrus pulp pellets, for animal feed, provided that they were to be delivered in good condition. On delivery, the buyers rejected the cargo as not complying with this provision and claimed back the price paid from the sellers. The buyers then obtained the pellets when the cargo was sold off and used them for animal feed.

Decision:
It was held that, since the breach had not been serious (the buyers could use the goods for their intended purpose), the buyers should not have rejected the cargo and the sellers acted lawfully in retaining the money paid.

Comment: Not all judges are wholly in favour of this third category of term, feeling that, in the world of commerce, **certainty as to the outcome of breach** is necessary at the outset and should not be dependent on a court's findings after breach has occurred (see *Bunge Corp v Tradax Export SA* (1981) and *The Mihalis Angelos* (1970)).

5.4 Implied Terms

So far, the cases considered in this chapter have involved express terms: statements actually made by one of the parties, either orally or in writing. Implied terms, however, are not actually stated but are introduced into the contract by implication. There are three types of implied terms:

5.4.1 Terms implied by statute

For example, under the SoGA 1979, terms relating to description, quality and fitness for purpose are all implied into sale of goods contracts. (For consideration of these implied terms, see 8.2.4 below.)

5.4.2 Terms implied by custom

An agreement may be subject to customary terms not actually specified by the parties. For example, in *Hutton v Warren* (1836), it was held that customary usage permitted a farm tenant to claim an allowance for seed and labour on quitting his tenancy. However, custom cannot override the express terms of an agreement (*Les Affréteurs Réunis v Walford* (1919)).

5.4.3 Terms implied by the courts

Generally, it is for the parties concerned to decide the terms of a contract, but sometimes the court will presume that the parties intended to include a term which is not expressly stated. It will do so where it is necessary to give business efficacy to the contract.

Whether a term may be implied is decided by the 'officious bystander' test. Imagine two parties, A and B, negotiating a contract. A third party, C, interrupts to suggest a particular provision. A and B reply that that particular term is understood. In such a way, the court will decide that a term should be implied into a contract.

In *The Moorcock* (1889), the appellants, the owners of a wharf, contracted with the respondents to permit them to discharge their ship at the wharf. It was apparent to both parties that, when the tide was out, the ship would rest on the river bed. When the tide was out, the ship sustained damage by settling on a ridge. It was held that there was an implied warranty in the contract that the place of anchorage should be safe for the ship, and the shipowner was entitled to damages for breach of that term.

5.5 The Parol Evidence Rule

If all the terms of a contract are in writing, then there is a strong presumption that no evidence supporting a different oral agreement will be permitted to vary those terms.

In *Hutton v Watling* (1948), on the sale of a business and its goodwill, a written agreement was drawn up and signed by the vendor. In an action to enforce one of the clauses in the agreement, the vendor claimed that it did not represent the whole contract. It was held that the vendor was not entitled to introduce evidence on this point, as the written document represented a true record of the contract.

The presumption against introducing contrary oral evidence can be rebutted, however, where it is shown that the document was not intended to set out all of the terms agreed by the parties.

In *Re SS Ardennes* (1951), a ship's bill of lading stated that it might proceed by any route directly or indirectly. The defendants promised that the ship would proceed directly to London from Spain with its cargo of tangerines. However, the ship called at Antwerp before heading for London and, as a result, the tangerines had to be sold at a reduced price. The shippers successfully sued for damages, as it was held that the bill of lading did not constitute the contract between the parties but merely evidenced their intentions. The verbal promise was part of the final contract.

The effect of the parol evidence rule has also been avoided by the willingness of the courts to find collateral contracts which import different, not to say contradictory, terms into the written contract. An example of this is *City and Westminster Properties (1934) Ltd v Mudd* (1959), where, although the written contract expressly provided that the defendant had no right to live on particular premises, the court recognised the contrary effect of a verbal collateral contract to allow him to do so. In return for agreeing to sign the new lease, the tenant (who had previously resided on the premises) was promised that he could continue to do so, despite the term of the new lease. Thus, both parties provided consideration to support the collateral contract. (See 4.6 above, for the use of collateral contracts to avoid the strict operation of the doctrine of privity.)

The *Mudd* case suggests that the courts will find justification for avoiding the strict application of the parol evidence rule, where they wish to do so. On that basis, it has been suggested that it should be removed from contract law entirely. However, a Law Commission Report (No 154) took the opposite view, stating that there was no need for legislation to remove the rule, as it was already a dead letter in practice. For businesses, perhaps the best advice is to ensure that a written contract encompasses the whole of the agreement.

5.6 Exemption or Exclusion Clauses

In a sense, an exemption clause is no different from any other clause, in that it seeks to define the rights and obligations of the contracting parties. However, an exemption clause is a term which tries to exempt, or limit, the liability of a party in breach of the agreement. Such clauses give rise to most concern when they are included in standard form contracts, in which a party in a position of commercial dominance imposes their terms on the other party, who has no choice (other than to take it or leave it) as far as the terms of the contract go. Such standard form contracts are contrary to the ideas of consensus and negotiation underpinning contract law; for this reason, they have received particular attention from both the judiciary and the legislature, in an endeavour to counteract their perceived unfairness. A typical example of a standard form agreement would be a holiday booking, made on the terms printed in a travel brochure.

The law relating to exclusion clauses is complicated by the interplay of the common law, the Unfair Contract Terms Act (UCTA) 1977 and the various Acts which imply certain terms into particular contracts. However, the following questions should always be asked with regard to exclusion clauses:

- Has the exclusion clause been incorporated into the contract?
- Does the exclusion clause effectively cover the breach?
- What effect do UCTA 1977 and the Unfair Terms in Consumer Contracts Regulations 1999 have on the exclusion clause?

5.6.1 Has the exclusion clause been incorporated into the contract?

An exclusion clause cannot be effective unless it is actually a term of a contract. There are three ways in which such a term may be incorporated into a contractual agreement:

By signature

If a person signs a contractual document then they are bound by its terms, even if they do not read it.

In *L'Estrange v Graucob* (1934), a café owner bought a vending machine, signing a contract (without reading it), which took away all her rights under the SoGA 1893. When the machine proved faulty, she sued the vendors, but it was held there was no cause of action; she had signified her consent to the terms of the contract by signing it and the exclusion clause effectively exempted liability for breach.

The rule in *L'Estrange* may be avoided where the party seeking to rely on the exclusion clause misled the other party into signing the contract by a misleading oral explanation of the clause (*Curtis v Chemical Cleaning and Dyeing Co* (1951)).

By notice

Apart from the above, an exclusion clause will not be incorporated into a contract unless the party affected **actually knew** of it or **was given sufficient notice** of it. In order for notice to be adequate, the document bearing the exclusion clause must be an integral part of the contract and must be given at the time that the contract is made.

In *Chapelton v Barry UDC* (1940), the plaintiff hired a deck chair and received a ticket, which stated on its back that the council would not be responsible for injuries arising from hire of the chairs. After he was injured when the chair collapsed, Chapelton successfully sued the council. It was held that the ticket was merely a receipt, the contract already having been made, and could not be used effectively to communicate the exclusion clause.

In *Olley v Marlborough Court Hotel Ltd* (1949), a couple contracted and paid for a hotel room on arrival. On reaching their room, they found a notice purporting to exclude the hotel's liability for theft of goods not handed in to the manager. The wife's purse was stolen. The hotel did not escape liability, since the disclaimer was made *after* the contract had been formed. In *Sterling Hydraulics Ltd v Dichtomatik* (2007), contractual terms were only made available *on delivery* of regular orders. They were not incorporated into the contracts of sale as they were not available to be referred to at the time of making the contracts.

The notice given must be **sufficient for the average person to be aware of it**; if it is sufficient, it matters not that this contracting party was unaware of it. In *Thompson v LM & S Railway* (1930), a woman who could not read was bound by a printed clause referred to on a railway timetable and ticket because the average person could have been aware of it before booking a ticket.

Whether the degree of notice given is sufficient is a matter of fact but, in *Thornton v Shoe Lane Parking Ltd* (1971), it was stated that the greater the exemption, the greater the degree of notice required.

❖ KEY CASE *Interfoto Picture Library Ltd v Stiletto Programmes Ltd* (1988)

Facts:

The Court of Appeal decided that a particular clause was not imported into a contract, even though it had been available for inspection before the contract was made. The clause in question sought to impose almost £4,000 liability for any delay in returning the photographic negatives which were rented under the contract.

Decision:

It was held, following *Thornton*, that this penalty was so severe that it could not be fairly brought to the attention of the other party by indirect reference; explicit notification was necessary where a clause was particularly **onerous and unusual**. This is sometimes referred to as the *red ink* or *red hand* principle, and was recently re-examined in relation to scratch cards in *O'Brien v MGN Ltd* (2001).

Further consideration of such clauses can be found in *Ocean Chemical Transport Inc v Exnor Craggs* (2000) and *Sumukan Ltd v Commonwealth Secretariat* (2007), where it was determined that such clauses need only be **either** onerous **or** unusual.

By custom (previous dealings)

Where the parties have had previous dealings on the basis of an exclusion clause, that clause may be included in later contracts (*Spurling v Bradshaw* (1956)), but it has to be shown that the party affected had actual knowledge of the exclusion clause.

In *Hollier v Rambler Motors* (1972), on each of the previous occasions that the plaintiff had had his car repaired at the defendants' garage, he had signed a form containing an exclusion clause. On the last occasion, he had not signed such a form. When the car was damaged by fire through negligence, the defendants sought to rely on the exclusion clause. It was held that there was no evidence that Hollier had been aware of the clause to which he had been agreeing and, therefore, it could not be considered to be a part of his last contract. In *Sterling Hydraulics* (above 4.4), the court was unwilling to incorporate the terms by virtue of the parties' previous dealings, because the terms had never been referred to *at the time of making* any of the regular contracts, only at the time of delivery.

5.6.2 Does the exclusion clause effectively cover the breach?

As a consequence of the disfavour with which the judiciary have looked on exclusion clauses, a number of rules of construction have been developed which operate to restrict the effectiveness of exclusion clauses. For example:

- *The construction of the clause*

  The court will determine whether the clause, on its construction, covers what has occurred. In *Andrews v Singer* (1934), the plaintiffs contracted to buy some new Singer cars from the defendant. A clause excluded all conditions, warranties and liabilities *implied* by statute, common law or otherwise. One car supplied was not new. It was held that the requirement that the cars be new was an *express condition* of the contract and, therefore, was not covered by the exclusion clause, which only referred to implied clauses.

- *The contra proferentem rule*
  This requires that any uncertainties or ambiguities in the exclusion clause are interpreted against the person seeking to rely on it. In *Hollier* (above), it was stated that as the exclusion clause in question could be interpreted as applying only to non-negligent accidental damage or, alternatively, as including damage caused by negligence, it should be restricted to the former, narrower interpretation. As a consequence, the plaintiff could recover for damages caused to his car by the defendants' negligence.

  A more recent example of the operation of the *contra proferentem* rule may be seen in *Bovis Construction (Scotland) Ltd v Whatlings Construction Ltd* (1995). The details of the contract between the two parties were based on a standard form and a number of letters. One of the letters introduced a term which limited the defendants' liability in respect of time related costs to £100,000. The plaintiffs terminated the contract on the basis of the defendants' lack of diligence in carrying out the contracted work. When they subsequently sued for £2,741,000, the defendants relied on the limitation clause. The House of Lords decided that as the defendants had introduced the limitation clause, it had to be interpreted strictly, although not as strictly as a full exclusion clause. It was held that the term 'time related costs' applied to losses arising as a consequence of delay in performance, and not non-performance. The defendants had been guilty of the latter and were, therefore, fully liable for the consequences of their repudiatory breach. Another ambiguous clause was considered by the Court of Appeal in *The University of Keele v Price Waterhouse* (2004). The appellant accountants claimed they were not liable to pay damages to the university, which had suffered loss of anticipated savings under a profit-related pay scheme. The appellants had given negligent financial advice in relation to the scheme. A clause of the contract between the appellants and the university indicated that, subject to a cap on liability of twice the anticipated savings, the appellants accepted 'liability to pay damages in respect of loss or damage suffered by the university as a direct result of our providing the Services'. The clause continued, 'All other liability is expressly excluded, in particular consequential loss, failure to realise anticipated savings or benefits and a failure to obtain registration of the Scheme'. The appellants contended that the second part of the clause protected them from liability. Clearly, the clause, taken as a whole, appeared contradictory; the first part limited liability in relation to anticipated savings, whilst the second part excluded any such liability. The Court of Appeal interpreted the clause as meaning that the second part applied only to exclude liability which exceeded the cap on liability in the first part. The later case of *Decoma UK Ltd v Haden Drysys International Ltd* (2005), examined whether a clause *should* be considered ambiguous, where the contracting parties were commercial undertakings, regularly negotiating such contracts.
- *The doctrine of fundamental breach*
  In a series of complicated and conflicting cases, culminating in the House of Lords' decision in *Photo Production v Securicor Transport* (1980), some courts attempted to develop a rule that it was impossible to exclude liability if a fundamental breach of the contract had occurred, that is, where the party in breach had failed altogether to perform the contract. In *Photo Production* (affirmed in *George Mitchell (Chesterhall) Ltd v Finney Lock Seeds* (1983)), the defendants had entered into a contract with the plaintiffs to guard their factory. An exclusion clause exempted Securicor from liability, even if one of their employees caused damage to the factory. Later, one of the guards deliberately set fire to the factory. Securicor claimed the protection of the exclusion clause. Ultimately, the House of Lords decided that whether an exclusion clause could operate after a fundamental breach was a matter of construction. There was no absolute rule that total failure of performance rendered such clauses inoperative. The exclusion clause in this particular case was wide enough to cover the events that took place, and so Photo Production's action failed.

5.6.3 What effect does the Unfair Contract Terms Act 1977 have on the exclusion clause?

This Act represents the statutory attempt to control exclusion clauses. In spite of its title, it is really aimed at unfair exclusion/exemption clauses, rather than contract terms generally. Thus:

Main Provisions of UCTA 1977	
Liability excluded/restricted	Valid?
Negligence • causing death/injury • causing property damage over £275 or other loss	 • No • Yes, subject to 'reasonableness'
Breach of Contract • implied undertakings as to title in contracts of sale/supply of goods • other implied undertakings in contracts of sale/supply of goods • other breaches of any contract where one party deals as a 'consumer' or on the other party's standard terms of contracting	 • No • No, in 'consumer' contracts (other than hire) • Yes, subject to 'reasonableness' in hire contracts and non-consumer contracts • Yes, subject to 'reasonableness'

Figure 5.2

Negligence

There is an absolute prohibition on exemption of liability for negligence resulting in **death or injury** (s 2(1)). An exemption of liability for other damage (e.g. to goods) caused by negligence will only be enforced to the extent it satisfies the requirement of **reasonableness** (s 2(2)). Section 2 clearly has implications for businesses, such as shops, allowing the public to enter the premises. Furthermore, as the provision *also* applies to *contractual* terms, it would be of real significance to, for example, a business installing gas boilers.

In *Smith v Bush* (1989), the plaintiff bought a house on the basis of a valuation report carried out for her building society by the defendant. The surveyor had included a disclaimer of liability for negligence in his report to the building society and sought to rely on that fact when the plaintiff sued after the chimneys of the property collapsed. The House of Lords held that the disclaimer was an exemption clause and that it failed the requirement that such terms should be reasonable.

Contract

The general rule of the Act (s 3), is that an exclusion (or limitation of liability) clause imposed on a consumer, or by standard terms of business (which could include one business dealing with another), is **not binding** unless it satisfies the Act's **requirement of reasonableness**. Effectively, the Act is dealing with clauses imposed by a person acting **in the course of business**.

The elements of s 3 needing clarification are:

- *'Consumer'* – s 12(1), (as amended by the Sale and Supply of Goods to Consumers Regulations 2002), states that a person deals as a consumer (so that he does *not act in the course of business*) if he neither makes the contract in the course of business nor holds himself out as so doing and the other party does make the contract in the course of business. Additionally, where goods are supplied under the contract, they must be of a type normally supplied for private consumption and they must be so used.

- *'Acting in the course of business'* – was considered in *R & B Customs Brokers Co Ltd v UDT* (1988). In deciding that the sellers of a car to a company could not rely on an exclusion clause contained in the contract, as the transaction had not been in the course of business, the Court of Appeal stated that the purchase had been:

  > . . . at highest, only incidental to the carrying on of the relevant business [and] . . . a degree of regularity is required before it can be said that they are an integral part of the business carried on and so entered into in the course of business.

  In reaching this decision, the Court of Appeal followed the House of Lords' decision in *Davies v Sumner* (1984), which dealt with a similar provision in the Trade Descriptions Act 1968. This interpretation of s 12(1) was confirmed in *Feldaroll Foundry plc v Hermes Leasing (London) Ltd* (2004). On facts similar to *R & B Customs Brokers Co Ltd v UDT*, a company was held not to act 'in the course of business', even though the contract stated the car was acquired for use in the business. It would seem, however, that the meaning of selling 'in the course of business' for the purposes of s 14 of the SoGA 1979 is different. Section 14, which implies conditions of satisfactory quality and fitness for purpose into contracts for the sale of goods, applies where the seller 'sells in the course of business'. The meaning of selling 'in the course of business' under s 14 of the SoGA 1979 is wide enough to cover incidental sales by, for example, the professions, local and central government departments and public authorities. The meaning of selling 'in the course of business' in the context of s 14 was examined in *Stevenson v Rogers* (1999).
- *'Reasonableness'* – it has already been shown that this term is relevant to exclusion of negligence and to s 3. It is also an element of other provisions of UCTA 1977, and so will be considered (below), when these provisions have been examined.

UCTA 1977 applies more **specific rules to contracts for the sale of goods**; which rules apply depends on whether the seller sells to a person 'dealing as a consumer' (as defined in s 12(1) of UCTA 1977; such sales are commonly referred to as 'consumer sales'). Under s 6(1) of UCTA 1977, the implied term of s 12(1) of the SoGA 1979 (transfer of title) cannot be excluded in consumer or non-consumer sales.

See Chapter 8

The other implied terms, namely, those as to description, fitness, satisfactory quality and sample, cannot be excluded in a consumer contract (s 6(2)); in a non-consumer transaction, any restriction is subject to the requirement of reasonableness (s 6(3)). Under s 7, similar rules apply to other contracts under which goods are supplied (for example, hire contracts) by virtue of the Supply of Goods and Services Act 1982. Amendments to UCTA 1977, in so far as its provisions apply to contracts for the sale and supply of goods, are made by the Sale and Supply of Goods to Consumers Regulations 2002.

Indemnity clauses are covered by s 4 of UCTA 1977. These are provisions in contracts by means of which one party agrees to compensate the other for any liability incurred by them in the course of carrying out the contract. Although these may be legitimate ways of allocating risk and insurance responsibilities in a commercial context, they are of more dubious effect in consumer transactions and are, therefore, required to satisfy the requirement of reasonableness.

As stated already, 'reasonableness' plays a role in determining the validity of clauses in several situations:

'**The requirement of reasonableness** means fair and reasonable . . . having regard to the circumstances . . . [s 11].' Schedule 2 to UCTA 1977 provides guidelines for the application of the reasonableness test in regard to non-consumer transactions, but it is likely that similar considerations will be taken into account by the courts in consumer transactions. Amongst these considerations are:

- the relative strength of the parties' bargaining power;
- whether any inducement was offered in return for the limitation on liability;

- whether the customer knew, or ought to have known, about the existence or extent of the exclusion; and
- whether the goods were manufactured or adapted to the special order of the customer.

In *George Mitchell (Chesterhall) Ltd v Finney Lock Seeds Ltd* (1983), the respondents planted 63 acres with cabbage seed supplied by the appellants. The crop failed, due partly to the fact that the wrong type of seed had been supplied and partly to the fact it was of inferior quality. When the respondents claimed damages, the sellers relied on a clause in their standard conditions of sale, which limited their liability to replacing the seeds supplied or refunding payment. It was held, however, that the respondents were entitled to compensation for the loss of the crop. The House of Lords decided that although the limitation clause was sufficiently clear and unambiguous to be effective at common law, it failed the test of reasonableness under UCTA 1977.

The defendants' **ability to meet potential liability and to obtain insurance cover for** liability, was considered in relation to the 'reasonableness' of a limitation clause in *St Albans City and District Council v International Computers Ltd* (1996). The **'relative strength of the parties' bargaining power'** was in issue in *Watford Electronics Ltd v Sanderson CFL Ltd* (2001). A contract between two businesses for the purchase of integrated software systems stated that:

- the parties agreed no pre-contractual representations had been made;
- liability for indirect/consequential loss was excluded; and
- liability for breach of contract was limited to the contract price of £104,596.

The system being unsatisfactory, the buyer claimed damages for breach of contract, misrepresentation and negligence, totalling (including loss of expected profits) £5.5 million. The seller sought to rely on the clauses to limit/escape liability; the buyer alleged that they were unreasonable under UCTA 1977. The Court of Appeal held that the clauses were reasonable because the contract was negotiated between two experienced businesses, both of which (on the facts) were of equal bargaining strength.

The decisions in *Granville Oil and Chemicals Ltd v Davies Turner and Co Ltd* (2003); *Overland Shoes Ltd v Schenkers Ltd* (1998); *Regus (UK) Ltd v Epcot Solutions Ltd* (2008) reinforce the courts' reluctance to find clauses 'unreasonable', where the contracting businesses have equal bargaining power. The Court of Appeal, in *Regus*, examined the history of the parties' negotiations, their business experience, awareness of the standard terms, and previous experience of contracting on standard terms generally, to reach the conclusion that the parties' had equality of bargaining power. Other issues examined, to determine that an exclusion and a limitation clause were reasonable, were *liability insurance* and *whether the contract could have been made with another party*. However, in:

❖ KEY CASE — *Kingsway Hall Hotel Ltd v Red Sky IT (Hounslow) Ltd* (2010)

Facts:

A clause excluding liability for satisfactory quality, under the SoGA 1979 and the Supply of Goods and Services Act 1982, was not upheld. The claimant purchased an 'off the shelf' software system to manage, *inter alia* room reservations and payments. The purchase was made on Red Sky's standard terms, after demonstrations and Red Sky's advice that the software was suitable for the claimant's purposes. After installation, there were major problems with the system. Consequently, the claimant incurred considerable expense (including buying a replacement system), and loss of profit and goodwill. The claimant rejected the system and sought damages.

Decision:

Toulmin J found that the system was not of satisfactory quality, nor fit for its purpose, entitling the claimant to reject and claim damages. Red Sky had sought to rely on limitation and exclusion clauses in their standard terms. They argued that, though s 3 of the UCTA 1977 applied, the 'reasonableness' test was satisfied.

On the facts, the clauses were found not to be 'reasonable' within the meaning of s 11 of the UCTA 1977, because:

- they allowed the seller to supply unsatisfactory software with no benefit accruing to the buyer (for example, the buyer did not receive any *inducement* to contract on these terms);
- the parties' did not have *equal bargaining power*; Red Sky was the *specialist* and, having supplied the software to other hotels, was in the best position to determine its suitability;
- the defendants had control of the contract in respect of maintenance and support; as they withdrew this, the claimants had *no choice* but to purchase a new system;
- the terms of the contract, other than the price, were not discussed and there was no evidence the claimants knew of the exclusion/limitation clauses. In effect there was *no negotiation*, except on price;
- there was *no long course of previous dealing*, which could have made the claimants aware of the existence and scope of the clauses; and
- it was a reasonable inference, given Red Sky's specialist knowledge, that they were in a *better position to insure* the risk of defects in the system.

Comment: Though, as previously stated, courts might be reluctant to find clauses 'unreasonable', where the parties *have* equal bargaining power, specialist businesses should be very careful when seeking to impose exemptions on small or non-specialist businesses.

It is likely that many of the situations in the cases considered under the common law prior to UCTA 1977 would now be decided under that Act. It is still important, however, to understand the common law principles, for the very good reason that (*inter alia*), UCTA 1977 does not apply in many important situations. Amongst these are transactions relating to insurance; interests in land; patents and other intellectual property; the transfer of securities; and the formation of companies or partnerships. It is evident from *Ailsa Craig Fishing Co Ltd v Malvern Fishing Co Ltd* (1983) that UCTA 1977 does not supersede common law rules. Furthermore, in *Red Sky*, one exclusion clause was construed *contra proferentem* because of ambiguity.

5.6.4 The Unfair Terms in Consumer Contracts Regulations

The current Regulations (SI 1999/2083) were intended to reflect closely the wording of the original regulations of 1994, but they also introduced significant alterations. Concern was expressed as to the precise way in which UCTA 1977 and the 1994 Regulations impacted on one another and how their interaction would affect consumer law generally. Unfortunately, the 1999 Regulations have done nothing to improve this general problem.

The 1999 Regulations apply to **any** term in a contract concluded between a seller or supplier and a consumer which has not been individually negotiated. It should be noted that:

- The Regulations are wider in scope than UCTA 1977, which only covers exclusion and limitation clauses.

- Under reg 1, the 'consumer' is 'any natural person . . . acting for purposes outside his trade, business or profession'.
- Under reg 3(1), a 'seller or supplier' is 'any natural or legal person . . . acting for purposes relating to his trade, business or profession, whether publicly or privately owned'. So, as under s 14 of the UCTA 1977, professions and activities of government departments and local authorities are within its scope.
- Under reg 5(1), the Regulations *only* apply to express standard form contracts. It was confirmed in *Baybut v Eccle Riggs Country Park Ltd* (2006), that the Regulations had no application to terms implied at common law.

By virtue of reg 5, a term is unfair if, contrary to the requirements of good faith, it causes a significant imbalance in the parties' rights and obligations arising under the contract, to the detriment of the consumer. Schedule 2 gives a long, indicative, but non-exhaustive, list of terms which may be regarded as unfair. Examples of terms in this list are: a term which excludes or limits liability in the event of the supplier or seller causing the death or injury of the consumer; inappropriately excluding or limiting the legal rights of the consumer in the event of total or partial non-performance or inadequate performance; a term requiring any consumer who fails to fulfil his obligations to pay a disproportionately high sum in compensation; and a term enabling the seller or supplier to alter the terms of the contract unilaterally without a valid reason which is specified in the contract.

Any such term as outlined above will be assumed to be unfair and, under reg 8, if a term is found to be unfair, it will not be binding on the consumer, although the remainder of the contract will continue to operate if it can do so after the excision of the unfair term. Regulation 6(2) states that, apart from the requirement of plain language (see below, reg 7), neither the core provisions of a consumer contract, which set out its subject matter, nor the adequacy of the price are open to assessment of fairness. The Supreme Court, in *OFT v Abbey National plc* (2009), determined that bank charges for unauthorised overdrafts were exempt from review under reg 6(2)(b). Thus, it appears that the Regulations focus on the formal procedure through which contracts are made, rather than the substantive content of contracts.

Two further provisions of the Regulations, worth mentioning, were taken from the previous Regulations. First, there is the requirement that all contractual terms be in plain, intelligible language and that, when there is any doubt as to the meaning of any term, it will be construed in favour of the consumer (reg 7). This is somewhat similar to the *contra proferentem* rule in English common law.

Secondly, although the Regulations will be most used by consumers to defeat particular unfair terms, regs 10–12 give the Director-General of Fair Trading the power to take action against the use of unfair terms by obtaining an injunction to prohibit the use of such terms (see, for example, *OFT v Foxtons Ltd* (2009)). It should be noted that the Enterprise Act 2002 abolished the office of Director-General and his powers were transferred to the Office of Fair Trading. The power to seek injunctions to control unfair contract terms has been extended to other qualifying bodies. These qualifying bodies are listed in Sched 1 to the Regulations and include the various regulatory bodies controlling the previous public utilities sector of the economy, the Data Protection Registrar and every weights and measures authority in Great Britain.

Various aspects of the original Regulations, which have implications for the current Regulations, were examined by the House of Lords in *Director General of Fair Trading v First National Bank* (2001).

In 2005 the Law Commission of England and Wales and the Scottish Law Commission issued a joint recommendation that the over-complexity of regulation of consumer transactions, arising as a result of the co-existence of the two overlapping schemes of regulation, should be simplified by the introduction of a new unitary regime. That recommendation was repeated, following a further consultation exercise in 2012.

Summary

Contract (2): Contents of a Contract

Contract terms and mere representations

A pre-contract statement is likely to be a term if:

- the contract would not have been made but for the statement;
- the time gap between the statement and the contract is short; or
- the statement is made by a person with special skill/knowledge.

A pre-contract statement is likely to be a representation only, if:

- there is a long time gap between the statement and the contract;
- the statement is oral and the written contract does not refer to it; or
- the person making the statement had no special skill/knowledge.

Terms

- A *condition* is a fundamental term, going to the root of the contract, breach of which gives a right to repudiate the contract.
- A *warranty* is a subsidiary term, breach of which gives a right to claim damages.
- If a term is *innominate*, the seriousness of the breach determines the remedies available.

Express and implied terms

- Express terms are those specifically agreed by the parties.
- Implied terms are not specifically agreed by the parties, but are implied into the contract by statute or custom or the courts.

The parol evidence rule

- Where there is a written contract, it is *presumed* that evidence cannot be adduced to show a differing oral agreement.

Exemption or exclusion clauses

The validity of such a clause depends on:

- whether it was incorporated into the contract;
- whether, on its wording, it covers the breach;
  whether a common law rule of construction, such as the *contra proferentem* rule, restricts its effect; and
- the effect of statutory provision.

Statutory regulation of exemption clauses

Under the Unfair Contract Terms Act 1977

- Liability for negligence causing death or injury cannot be excluded.
- Liability for negligence causing damage other than death or injury, can be excluded, subject to the requirement of 'reasonableness'.

- Liability for breach of the implied terms of the Sale of Goods Act 1979 cannot be excluded in consumer sales.
- Liability for breach of s 12(1) of the Sale of Goods Act 1979 cannot be excluded in non-consumer sales, but liability for breach of the other implied terms may be excluded, subject to the requirement of reasonableness.

Under the Unfair Terms in Consumer Contracts Regulations 1999

- Contract clauses not made in good faith are void.
- Authorised bodies may obtain injunctions to prevent the use of unfair terms.

Further Reading

Barker, D, 'A return to freedom of contract?' (2001) NLJ 344 (consideration of s 11 of UCTA 1977)
Colbey, R, 'Banking on unfair terms' (2000) NLJ 254 (discussion of *Director-General of Fair Trading v First National Bank*)
Furmston, MP, *Cheshire, Fifoot and Furmston's Law of Contract*, 16th edn, 2012, Oxford: OUP
Howell, A and Beauchamp, B, 'Know your limitations' (2005) NLJ 1747 (ambiguous limitation clauses)
Peel, E, *Treitel on the Law of Contract*, 13th edn, 2011, London: Sweet & Maxwell
Poole, J, *Casebook on Contract Law*, 10th edn, 2010, Oxford: OUP
Richards, P, *The Law of Contract*, 11th edn, 2013, Harlow: Pearson Longman
Stone, R, 'Exclusion Clauses' (2001) Student Law Review (Summer) 20 (guidelines on answering questions involving exclusion clauses)
Wilkinson, HW, 'Unfair Contract Terms – not again?' (2000) NLJ 1778 (OFT in relation to unfair contract terms)

Websites

www.oft.gov.uk (information on work and powers of OFT)
www.lawreports.co.uk (daily summaries of new cases)
www.statutelaw.gov.uk (for text of Unfair Contract Terms Act 1977; Unfair Terms in Consumer Contracts Regulations 1999)

Chapter 6

Contract (3): Vitiating Factors

Chapter Contents

Law in Context: Misrepresentation

Misrepresentation is an interesting area of contract law, as on the one hand a carelessly made statement inducing someone to enter a contract can void the contract, but it may also amount to negligent misstatement, which can be dealt with via negligence (see later). For business law students the study of misrepresentation and negligent misstatement provides students with an opportunity to explore the relative merits of pursuing an action for misrepresentation compared to an action for negligent misstatement. This is particularly relevant where provision of financial advice or related contracts is in question. Liability for negligent misstatement developed to cover situations where the recipient of such advice fell outside the contractual relationship. Developing knowledge and understanding of both helps business students to appreciate the subtle differences in the remedies available.

6.1 Introduction

Vitiating factors are those elements which make an agreement either void or voidable, depending on which vitiating factor is present. The vitiating factors are:

- mistake;
- misrepresentation;
- duress;
- undue influence; and
- public policy, rendering contracts void/illegal.

6.2 Mistake

Generally speaking, contracting parties are not relieved from their contractual obligations because they make a mistake. If one party makes a bad bargain, such as agreeing to pay too high a price for goods, that is not a reason to set the contract aside.

At *common law*, few mistakes affect the validity of a contract, because a mistake must be **operative** to render the contract void. If a contract is void for operative mistake, property transferred under it is recoverable, even from an innocent third party transferee.

However, if the mistake is *not operative, an equitable remedy such as rescission* may be available. The grant of such remedies is in the court's discretion and subject to the principles of equity. In *Leaf v International Galleries* (1950), there was a contract for the sale of a painting of Salisbury Cathedral, which both parties believed to be by Constable. Five years later, the buyer discovered that the painting was not by Constable but was refused rescission because of the lapse of time since purchase.

However, a mistake cannot affect a contract unless it *exists at the time of contracting*. In *Amalgamated Investment & Property Co Ltd v John Walker & Sons Ltd* (1976), a company purchased property for redevelopment. Just after the contract, the property was given listed building status, which would restrict the intended development. The purchaser could not rescind the contract on the basis of a mistake that the property could be redeveloped as intended, because at the time of sale it could have been so developed.

Furthermore, mistakes of **law**, rather than just mistakes of **fact**, may now affect contractual validity. In *Kleinwort Benson v Lincoln City Council* (1999), the House of Lords allowed recovery of money paid under mistake of **law**. The Court of Appeal considered previous authorities (such as *Bell v Lever Bros* (below), and *Great Peace Shipping Ltd v Tsavliris Salvage Ltd* (2001)), in *Brennan v Bolt Burden* (2004), concluding that a mistake of law could render a contract void (see also *Champion Investments Ltd v Ahmed* (2004); *EIC Services Ltd v Phipps* (2004)).

It is usual to categorise mistakes as follows:

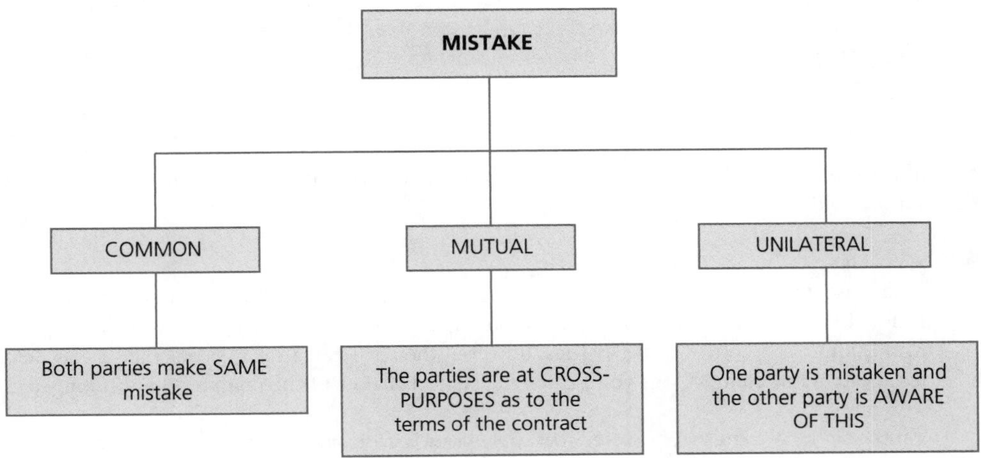

Figure 6.1

6.2.1 Common mistake

Here, both parties to an agreement share the **same mistake** about the circumstances surrounding the transaction. In order for the mistake to be **operative**, it must be **fundamental**.

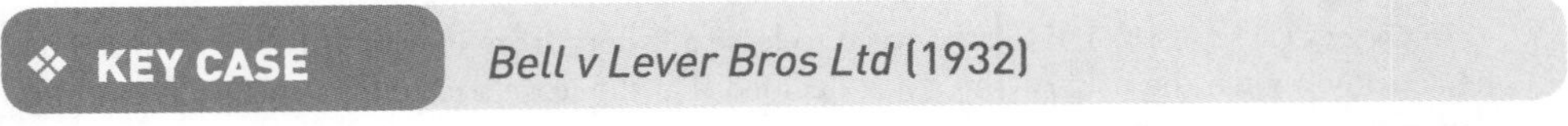

Bell v Lever Bros Ltd (1932)

Facts:

Bell had been employed as chairman of the company by Lever Bros. When he became redundant, they paid off the remaining part of his service contract. Only then did they discover that Bell had been guilty of offences which would have permitted them to dismiss him without compensation. They claimed to have the payment set aside on the basis of the common mistake that neither party had considered the possibility of Bell's dismissal for breach of duty.

Decision:

It was held that the action must fail. The mistake was *as to quality* and *not sufficiently fundamental* to render the contract void. Similarly, in *Leaf v International Galleries* (1950) (above), the mistake was held to be one of quality; the court found that the contract was for the sale of a painting of Salisbury Cathedral (the value of which was mistaken) rather than a painting by Constable, and as such the mistake could not render the contract void.

Comment: However, though *Bell* and *Leaf* appear to restrict the circumstances in which a common mistake will render a contract void, it should be noted that not all judges agree that mistakes of quality cannot be operative. Two of the judges, in *Bell*, thought mistakes of quality could render the contract void; paying £50,000, when no payment needed to be made to dismiss, rendered the contract *fundamentally different from what was intended*. In *Associated Japanese Bank v Credit du Nord* (1988), Steyn J (*obiter*, at first instance) supported the view that a mistake as to quality might, in exceptional circumstances, render a contract void if it made the subject matter of the contract essentially and radically different from what the parties believed it to be. These views were approved by the Court of Appeal in *Great Peace* (above), though the mistake, relating to the hire of a salvage tug, was not sufficiently different from what the parties intended to render the contract void.

Nevertheless, there are two situations where is clearly established that common mistake will render the contract void:

- *Res extincta*
  In this case, the mistake is as to the existence of the subject matter of the contract. In *Couturier v Hastie* (1856), a contract was made in London for the sale of some corn that was being shipped from Salonica. Unknown to the parties, however, the corn had already been sold. It was held that the London contract was void, since the subject matter of the contract was no longer in existence.
  It should be recognised, however, that in *Associated Japanese Bank* (above), a contract was treated as void for common mistake on the basis of the non-existence of some gaming machines, although the agreement in point actually related to a contract of guarantee in relation to the non-existent machines. It might also be noted that there could be an argument, on the facts of *Leaf* (above), for saying that the mistake was not one of quality but as to the existence of the subject matter of the contract; that is, the contract was for the sale of a painting by Constable. Such a finding would mean that the common mistake rendered the contract void.
- *Res sua*
  In this case, the mistake is that one of the parties to the contract already owns what they are contracting to receive.
  In *Cooper v Phibbs* (1867), Cooper agreed to lease a fishery from Phibbs. It later transpired that he actually owned the fishery. The court decided that the lease had to be set aside at common law. In equity, however, Phibbs was given a lien over the fishery in respect of the money he had spent on improving it, permitting him to hold the property against payment.
  In *Solle v Butcher* (1950) and *Magee v Pennine Insurance Co* (1969) Lord Denning had interpreted *Bell v Lever Brothers* in such a way as to suggest the existence of an equitable doctrine of common mistake. This would allow a contract to be to set aside even if it were binding in common law. This equitable doctrine was subsequently struck down by a later Court of Appeal in *Great Peace Shipping v Tsavliris Salvage* (2002), which categorically declared that where the contract is valid at common law, there is no jurisdiction to set it aside in Equity. Although the doctrine of precedent prevented the later court from overruling Lord Denning's decisions, it nonetheless made it emphatically clear that they were wrong and not to be followed in future.
  In the *Great Peace* case, the defendant owned a ship, the *Cape Providence* which was in severe trouble at sea. The claimant offered the salvage service of the *Great Peace*. However, both parties wrongly believed that the *Great Peace* was close to the ship in trouble. When the defendants discovered that the *Great Peace* was much further away than they had thought, they cancelled the contract. The claimant demanded a cancellation fee, which the defendant refused to pay. The Court of Appeal refused to set aside the contract due to the common mistake as to the location of the *Great Peace* and upheld the claimant's right to the fee. The contract was capable of performance and contained no warranty as to the time when the Great Peace would reach the stricken ship. It would therefore be enforced.

6.2.2 Mutual mistake

This occurs where the parties are at **cross-purposes**. They have different views on the facts of the situation, but they do not realise it. However, an agreement will not necessarily be void simply because the parties to it are at cross-purposes. In order for mutual mistake to be **operative**, that is, to make the contract void, the terms of agreement must comply with **an objective test**. The court must decide which of the competing views of the situation a reasonable person would support, and the contract will be enforceable or unenforceable on such terms.

In *Smith v Hughes* (1871), the plaintiff offered to sell oats to the defendant, Hughes. Hughes wrongly believed that the oats were old, and on discovering that they were new oats he refused to complete the contract. The defendant's mistake as to the age of the oats did not make the contract void; he had not been misled by the plaintiff and the contract did not indicate it was for the sale of 'old oats'.

In *Scriven Bros v Hindley & Co* (1913), the defendants bid at an auction for two lots, believing both to be hemp. In fact, one was tow, an inferior and cheaper substance. Although the auctioneer had not induced the mistake, it was not normal practice to sell hemp and tow together. It was decided that, in such circumstances, where one party thought that he was buying hemp and the other thought that he was selling tow, the contract was not enforceable. Effectively, offer and acceptance did not coincide.

If the court is unable to decide the outcome on the basis of an objective 'reasonable person' test, then the contract will be void, as was illustrated in *Raffles v Wichelhaus* (1864), where the defendants agreed to buy cotton from the plaintiffs. The cotton was to arrive *ex Peerless* from Bombay. There were, however, two ships called *Peerless* sailing from Bombay, the first in October and the second in December. Wichelhaus thought that he was buying from the first, but Raffles thought that he was selling from the second. Under the exceptional circumstances, it was impossible for the court to decide which party's view was the correct one. It was decided, therefore, that the agreement was void for mutual mistake.

In respect of mutual mistake, **equity follows the common law**. In *Tamplin v James* (1879), James purchased a public house at auction, believing it included a field the previous publican had used. The sale particulars stated the property for sale correctly, but James did not read them. On discovering his mistake, James refused to complete the transaction. In spite of his mistake, an order of specific performance was granted against James. Objectively, the reasonable man would assume that the sale was made on the basis of the particulars (see also *Centrovincial Estates plc v Merchant Assurance Co Ltd* (1983); *Great Peace* (above)).

As the outcome of applying an objective test is uncertain, businesses should not make assumptions, but should clarify issues *before* contracting. Equally important is to ensure the contract specifically encompasses what is required.

6.2.3 Unilateral mistake

Here, **only one of the contracting parties is mistaken** as to the circumstances of the contract, and **the other party is aware of that fact**.

Most cases of unilateral mistake also involve misrepresentation (see 6.3 below), although this need not necessarily be so. It is important to distinguish between these two elements: whereas unilateral mistake makes a contract void and thus prevents the passing of title in any property acquired under it, misrepresentation merely makes a contract voidable and good title can be passed before the contract is avoided. This distinction will be seen in *Ingram v Little* (1960) and *Phillips v Brooks* (1919). A further important distinction relates to remedies available: damages are not available for mistake but, where there has been a misrepresentation, damages may be awarded.

Cases of unilateral mistake relate mainly to mistakes as to identity. To a businessman, *the identity* of the other contracting party is often of real importance, in relation to the ability to pay. However, creditworthiness is *not* the crucial issue in law; a contract will only be void for mistake where the seller *intended to contract with a different person* from the one with whom he actually contracted.

In *Cundy v Lindsay* (1878), a crook named Blenkarn ordered linen handkerchiefs from Lindsay & Co. His order, from 37 Wood Street, was signed to look as if it were from Blenkiron & Co, a reputable firm which was known to Lindsay and which carried on business at 123 Wood Street. The goods were sent to Blenkarn, who sold them to Cundy. Lindsay successfully sued Cundy in the tort of conversion. It was held that Lindsay intended only to deal with Blenkiron & Co, so the contract was void. Since there was no contract with Blenkarn, he received no title whatsoever to the goods and, therefore, could not pass title on to Cundy. The case is generally taken to indicate that, if **you do not deal face to face**, the **identity** of the other party is **fundamental**:

❖ KEY CASE *Shogun Finance Ltd v Hudson* (2001)

Facts:

The case confirmed that identity was fundamental if the parties did not deal face to face. This was despite the fact that the decision defeated the objective of s 27 of the Hire Purchase Act 1964, to protect the innocent third party purchaser of a hire purchase motor vehicle. A con man obtained a car on hire purchase, using the identity of Mr Patel, via a stolen driving licence. His contract was with the finance company, not the garage with whom he negotiated, so he did not deal face to face. The con man sold the car to Hudson and disappeared without paying the hire purchase instalments. The finance company sought damages in the tort of conversion from Hudson, on the basis that he had no title to the car. It should be noted that where goods are acquired on hire purchase, ownership does not pass until all instalments are paid, so that the con man had no title to pass to Hudson. However, s 27 gives title to the innocent third party purchaser of a motor vehicle from a 'debtor' who acquired it on hire purchase.

Decision:

The Court of Appeal held that, as the contract was not made face to face, the contracting party's identity was crucial, so the hire purchase contract was void for mistake. As it was void, there was no 'debtor' within the meaning of s 27; Hudson was not protected and was liable in conversion. An appeal to the House of Lords in 2003 was dismissed, confirming, by a bare majority, that s 27 did not operate to give good title to Mr Hudson. Also of interest were *dicta* relating to impersonation by telephone, videophone and by e-shopping.

Although *Kings Norton Metal Co v Eldridge, Merrit & Co* (1897) appears to be similar to *Cundy*, it was decided differently, on the ground that the crook had made use of a completely fictitious company to carry out his fraud. The mistake, therefore, was about the *attributes* of the company, rather than its identity.

Where the **parties enter into a contract face to face**, it is generally presumed that the seller intends to deal with the person before him; therefore, he cannot rely on unilateral mistake to avoid the contract; his concern is with the *attributes* (usually creditworthiness) of the other party *rather than his identity*. A shopkeeper will sell to you, no matter who you pretend to be, provided you pay.

In *Phillips v Brooks* (1919), a crook selected items in the plaintiff's jewellery shop, and proposed to pay by cheque. On being informed that the goods would have to be retained until the cheque was cleared, he told the jeweller that he was Sir George Bullough of St James's Square. On checking in a directory that such a person did indeed live at that address, the jeweller permitted him to take away a valuable ring. The crook pawned the ring to the defendant. Phillips then sued the defendant in conversion. It was decided that the contract between Phillips and the crook was not void for mistake. There had not been a mistake as to identity, but only as to the creditworthiness (that is, attributes) of the buyer. The contract had been voidable for misrepresentation, but the crook had passed title before Phillips took steps to avoid the contract.

A similar decision was reached by the Court of Appeal in *Lewis v Averay* (1971), in which a crook obtained possession of a car by misrepresenting his identity to the seller. The court declined to follow its earlier decision in *Ingram v Little* (1960), a very similar case. It is generally accepted that *Lewis v Averay* represents the more accurate statement of the law, and *Ingram* was said to be wrongly decided in *Shogun* (see also: *Citibank NA v Brown Shipley & Co Ltd; Midland Bank plc v Brown Shipley & Co Ltd* (1991)).

6.2.4 Mistake in respect of documents

Though businesses are advised to take particular care in drawing up and signing documents, there are two mechanisms for dealing with mistakes in written contracts:

- *Rectification*
  Where the written document fails to state the actual intentions of the parties, it may be altered under the equitable doctrine of rectification. In *Joscelyne v Nissen* (1970), the plaintiff agreed to transfer his car hire business to his daughter, in return for her agreeing to pay certain household expenses, although this was not stated in a later written contract. The father was entitled to have the agreement rectified to include the terms agreed.
- *Non est factum*
  Where a party signs a contract, they will usually be bound by its terms. It is assumed that the signatory has read, understood and agreed to the terms as stated, and the courts are generally reluctant to interfere in such circumstances. Where, however, someone signs a document under a misapprehension as to its true nature, the law may permit them to claim *non est factum*, that is, that the document is not their deed. Originally, the mistake relied on had to relate to the type of document signed, but it is now recognised that the defence is open to those who have made a *fundamental mistake as to the content of the document* they have signed. However, the person signing the document *must not have been careless* with regard to its content:

❖ KEY CASE *Saunders v Anglia Building Society* (1970)

Facts:
Mrs Gallie, an elderly widow, signed a document without reading it, as her glasses were broken. She had been told, by a person named Lee, that it was a deed of gift to her nephew, but it was in fact a deed of gift to Lee. Lee later mortgaged the property to the respondent building society. Mrs Gallie sought to repudiate the deed of gift on the basis of *non est factum*.

Decision:
Mrs Gaillie's action failed; she was **careless** in not waiting until her glasses were mended. Furthermore, the document was **not fundamentally different** from the one she had expected to sign. She thought that she signed a document transferring ownership and that *was* the effect of the document. The conditions laid down in *Saunders* for *non est factum* to apply were confirmed in *Avon Finance Co Ltd v Bridger* (1985).

Note: This decision can be contrasted with a later successful reliance on the defence in *Lloyds Bank plc v Waterhouse* (1990), where the illiterate defendant intended to sign a guarantee of his son's purchase of a farm. In fact, the document he signed was a guarantee of all his son's liabilities. The Court of Appeal decided that the father could rely on *non est factum*. He had not been careless – he had questioned the extent of his liability – and the document was fundamentally different from that which he had expected to sign.

Comment: In practice, it seems unlikely that a business would succeed in a plea of *non est factum*.

6.3 Misrepresentation

As already seen, a statement which induces a person to enter into a contract, but which does not become a term of the contract, is a representation. **A false statement of this kind is a misrepresentation** and renders the contract **voidable**. The innocent party may rescind the contract or, in some circumstances, claim damages. The overall situation, in relation to statements which induce a contract, can be seen overleaf.

Misrepresentation can be defined as **'a false statement of fact, made by one party before or at the time of the contract, which induces the other party to enter into the contract'**. Thus the necessary elements are:

6.3.1 There must be a false statement of fact

False

Usually it can be proved whether a statement is false, but some situations need consideration:

- Where the statement is a *half-truth*, it may be true but misleading because of facts not given; it will be treated as false. In *Dimmock v Hallett* (1866), it was truthfully stated that a farm being sold was rented to a tenant for £290 per annum. The failure to indicate that the tenant was in arrears, had left the farm, and a new tenant could not be found, rendered the statement false.
- Where the statement is true when made, but *becomes false* before conclusion of the contract, the change must be notified to avoid misrepresentation. In *With v O'Flanagan* (1936), the seller of a doctors' practice told the prospective buyer that it had an income of £2,000 per annum. When the contract was concluded, the income had fallen to £5 per week. The court held that the representation was of a continuing nature and, as it was false **when it induced the contract**, the buyer was entitled to rescind. The obligation to disclose such changes was affirmed by the Court of Appeal in *Spice Girls Ltd v Aprilia World Service BV* (2002).

A statement

There must be a written or oral statement. There is no general duty to disclose information, except in insurance contracts (and this may soon change); *silence is not generally misrepresentation*. In *Turner v Green* (1895), when negotiating a dispute settlement between T and G, T's solicitor failed to mention other legal proceedings he knew of which made the settlement to which G agreed a 'bad deal' – one he would not have made had he known. G was bound by the settlement; he was not induced by a misrepresentation, as silence is not misrepresentation. Thus, businesses might be advised to give full information or none at all. However, there have been cases where courts have found that there is a misrepresentation by conduct; for example, *Gordon v Selico* (1986) and, at first instance, *Spice Girls Ltd* (above).

A fact

The following statements will not amount to representations because they are not facts:

- *Mere sales puffs* – the statement must have some meaningful content. In *Dimmock* (above), it was held that a statement that land was fertile and improvable was not actionable as a misrepresentation. So a business advertising its product as 'mouth-watering', could escape liability for misrepresentation.
- *Statements of law* – in theory, everyone is presumed to know the law, so no one can be misled as to what the law is. **However**, some doubt exists on the issue, since *Kleinwort Benson Ltd v Lincoln City Council* (1999) where a mistake of law was actionable. In *Pankhania v Hackney London BC* (2002), the claimant sought damages for a misrepresentation in a sale catalogue, which induced him to buy property. The catalogue indicated that the current tenant of the property was a contractual licensee, who could be given notice to quit. In fact, the tenant was statutorily protected from eviction. The claim that the misrepresentation, being of *law*, was not actionable, was rejected. The judge concluded that, by analogy with *Kleinwort*, misrepresentations of law were actionable. However, one might argue that the catalogue did not misstate the law, but misstated the *fact* that the tenant was a licensee.
- *Statements of opinion* – are not actionable, because they are not statements of fact. In *Bisset v Wilkinson* (1927), the vendor of previously ungrazed land stated that it would be able to support 2,000 sheep. This turned out to be untrue, but the statement was only an expression of opinion and, as such, was not actionable; the purchaser knew that the vendor had no expertise. However, in *Smith v Land & House Property Corp* (1884), a statement that the tenant of a hotel was a 'desirable tenant' was a misrepresentation. Though descriptions like 'desirable' may seem to be subjective opinions, here there was *expert knowledge* that the tenant did not pay on time and was currently in arrears. That being so, the statement implied that there were facts on which it was based when there were not. So *businesses* making this type of statement could face liability.
- *Statements of intention* – do not give rise to a misrepresentation even if the intention subsequently changes, unless it can be shown that there was no such intention at the time it was stated (see *Edgington v Fitzmaurice* (1884)).

6.3.2 The statement must actually induce the contract

This means that:

- the statement must have been made by one contracting party to the other, and not by a third party;
- the statement must have been addressed to the person claiming to have been misled;
- the person claiming to have been misled must have been aware of the statement; and
- the person claiming to have been misled must have relied on the statement.

In *Horsfall v Thomas* (1962), Horsfall made and sold a gun to Thomas, having concealed a fault in it with a metal plug. Thomas did not examine the gun, which soon blew apart. Thomas claimed that he was misled, by the plug, into buying the gun. It was held that the plug could not have misled him, as he had not examined the gun at the time of purchase. In *Attwood v Small* (1838), a false statement as to the profitability of a mine was not a misrepresentation as the purchaser did not rely on it; he commissioned an independent survey of the mine. On the other hand, in *Redgrave v Hurd* (1881), where the purchaser of a business declined to examine accounts which would have revealed the falsity of the statement of the business's profitability, there was a misrepresentation.

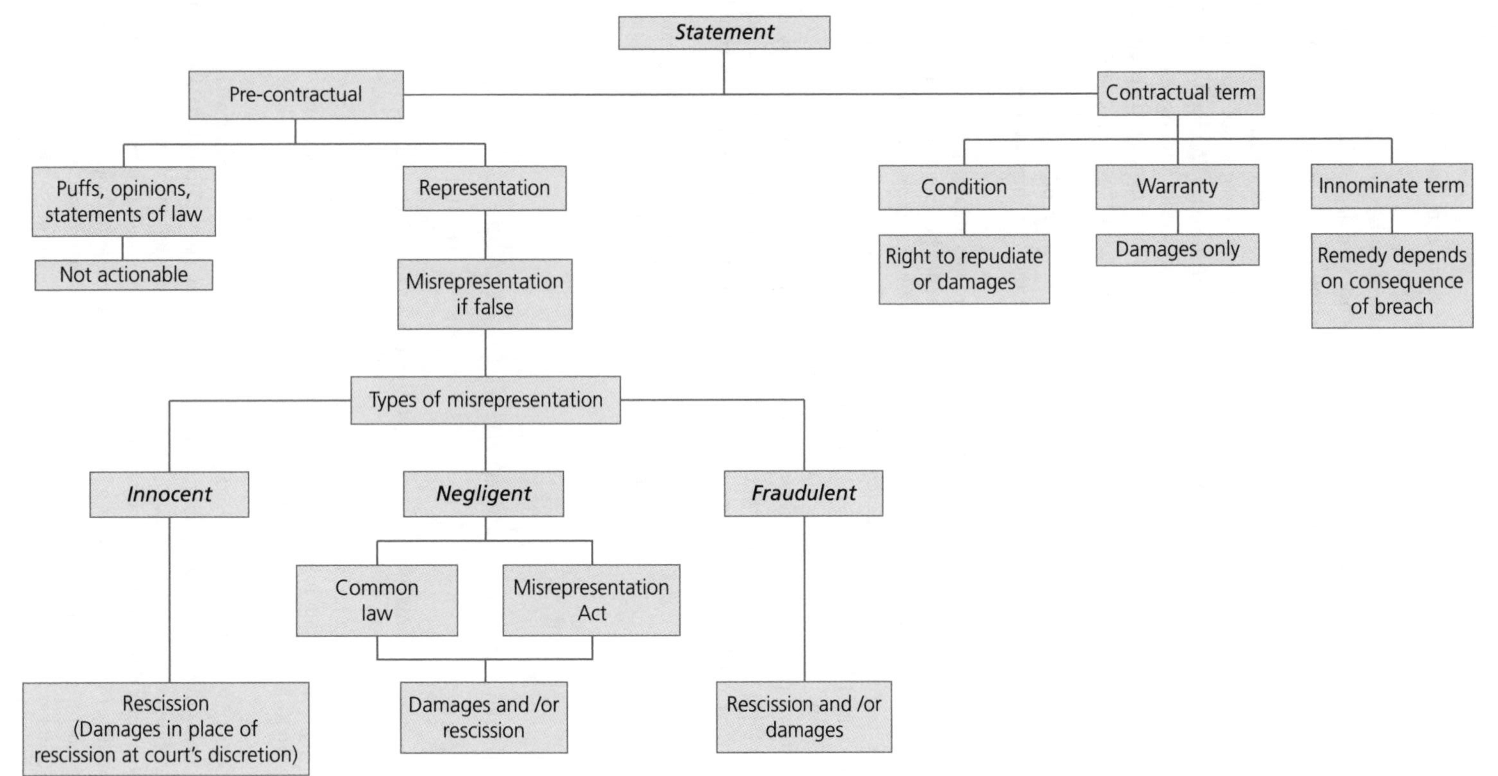
Statement
Pre-contractual
Contractual term
Puffs, opinions, statements of law
Not actionable
Representation
Misrepresentation if false
Types of misrepresentation
Innocent
Negligent
Fraudulent
Common law
Misrepresentation Act
Rescission (Damages in place of rescission at court's discretion)
Damages and /or rescission
Rescission and /or damages
Condition
Right to repudiate or damages
Warranty
Damages only
Innominate term
Remedy depends on consequence of breach

Figure 6.2

Because he declined to examine the accounts, he clearly relied on the statement of profitability; he had no obligation to check the truth of the statement.

Whether the reliance was reasonable or not is not material once the party claiming misrepresentation shows that they did, in fact, rely on the statement. See *Museprime Properties Ltd v Adhill Properties Ltd* (1990), where an inaccurate statement in auction particulars, repeated by the auctioneer, was held to constitute a misrepresentation, in spite of the claims that it was unreasonable for anyone to allow themselves to be influenced by the statement. This view was confirmed in *Indigo International Holdings Ltd & Another v The Owners and/or Demise Charterers of the Vessel 'Brave Challenger'; Ronastone Ltd & Another v Indigo International Holdings Ltd & Another* (2003). However, in *Barton v County Natwest Bank* (1999), the court indicated that an objective test would be applied to determine reliance. If, objectively, there was reliance, this was a presumption which was rebuttable.

6.3.3 Types of misrepresentation

There are three types of misrepresentation, each of which involves distinct procedures and provides different remedies:

Fraudulent misrepresentation

In this case, the statement is made **knowing it to be false, or believing it to be false, or recklessly careless as to whether it is true or false**. The difficulty with this type of misrepresentation is proving the necessary mental element; it is notoriously difficult to show the required *mens rea*, or guilty mind, to demonstrate fraud.

In *Derry v Peek* (1889), the directors of a company issued a prospectus, inviting the public to subscribe for shares. The prospectus stated that the company had the authority to run trams by steam power but, in fact, did not; it required the permission of the Board of Trade. The directors assumed that permission would be granted, but it was refused. When the company was wound up, the directors were sued for fraud. It was held that there was no fraud, since the directors honestly believed the statement in the prospectus. They may have been negligent, but they were not fraudulent.

Negligent misrepresentation

Here, the false statement is made **believing it is true, but without reasonable grounds for that belief** (so the directors in *Derry* would now be liable for negligent misrepresentation). There are two categories of negligent misrepresentation:

See Chapter 9

- *At common law* Prior to 1963, the law did not recognise a concept of negligent misrepresentation. The possibility of liability in negligence for misstatements arose from *Hedley Byrne & Co v Heller and Partners* (1964). There, however, the parties were not in a contractual or a pre-contractual relationship, so there could not have been an action for misrepresentation.
- *Under the Misrepresentation Act (MA) 1967* Although it might still be necessary, or beneficial, to sue at common law, it is more likely that such claims would be under the statute. This is because s 2(1) of the MA 1967 reverses the normal burden of proof. In a claim in negligence, the burden of proof is on the party claiming to show that the other party acted negligently. However, where a misrepresentation has been made, under s 2(1) of the MA 1967 it is for the party making the statement to show that they had reasonable grounds to believe it was true. In practice, a person making a statement in the course of his trade or profession might have difficulty providing such proof. In *Indigo Holdings* (1999) (see 6.2.2 above), the seller of a yacht could not escape liability for misrepresentation as he was unable to prove he had reasonable grounds to believe, and did believe, the facts he represented.

Innocent misrepresentation

This occurs where the false statement is made by a person who not only **believes it to be true**, but also has **reasonable grounds for that belief**.

6.3.4 Remedies for misrepresentation

At this point, it might be helpful to refer again to the diagram in 6.3.

For **fraudulent misrepresentation, the remedies are rescission and/or damages** for any loss sustained.

Rescission is an equitable remedy which is designed to return the parties to their original position. The action for damages is in the tort of deceit. In *Doyle v Olby (Ironmongers) Ltd* (1969), it was decided that where a contract was induced by a fraudulent misrepresentation, the measure of damages was not merely what was foreseeable, but all loss which directly resulted as a consequence of the aggrieved party having entered into the contract.

❖ KEY CASE *Smith and New Court Securities Ltd v Scrimgeour Vickers (Asset Management) Ltd* (1996)

Facts:

The plaintiffs were induced to buy 28 million shares in Ferranti plc by a fraudulent statement. They had been told falsely that two other companies had already bid for the package of shares; this led them to offer and pay 82.25p per share, in total £23,141,424. Without the false representation, they would not have offered more than 78p per share and, as the defendants would not have sold at that price, Smith New Court would not have acquired shares in Ferranti. When it transpired that Ferranti had been subject to a completely unrelated fraud, its share price fell and, although the plaintiffs managed to sell their shareholding at prices ranging from 30p–44p, they lost £11,353,220. The question to be decided was as to the amount that the defendants owed in damages. Was it the difference between the market value of the shares and the price actually paid at the time, a matter of 4.25p per share, or was it the full loss, which was considerably larger?

Decision:

The House of Lords awarded the latter, larger, amount. The total loss was the direct result of the share purchase, induced by the fraudulent statement; the defendants were liable for that amount under the foreseeability test in relation to negligence, as stated in *The Wagon Mound (No 1)* (1961), did not apply.

Note: The *Scrimgeour* test was applied in *Parabola Investments Ltd v Browallia Cal Ltd* (2010).

For negligent misrepresentation, the remedies are rescission and/or damages. The action for damages may be in the tort of negligence at common law, or under s 2(1) of the MA 1967. Under the statute, the measure of damages will still be determined as in a tort action (see: *Royscot Trust Ltd v Rogerson* (1991), where the Court of Appeal confirmed this approach).

See Chapter 9 →

For **innocent misrepresentation**, the common law remedy is **rescission**. Under s 2(2) of MA 1967, however, the court may award damages *instead* of rescission, where it is considered equitable to do so (see: *UCB Corporate Services Ltd v Thomason* (2005)).

With regard to s 2(2) of MA 1967, it was once thought that the court could only award damages, instead of rescission, where the remedy of rescission was itself available. The implication of that view was that, if the right to rescission was lost (for example, because the parties could not be restored to their original positions), then the right to damages under s 2(2) was also lost (*Atlantic Lines and Navigation Co Inc v Hallam* (1992)). However, in *Thomas Witter v TBP Industries* (below), Jacob J examined and rejected that suggestion. In his opinion, the right to damages under s 2(2) depended not upon the right to rescission still being available, but upon the fact that the plaintiff had had such a right in the past. Thus, even if the right to rescission was ultimately lost, the plaintiff could still be awarded damages. This was confirmed in *Zanzibar v British Aerospace Ltd* (2000).

The right to rescind can be lost:

- by affirmation, where the innocent party, with full knowledge of the misrepresentation, either expressly states that they intend to go on with the agreement or does some action from which it can be implied that they intend to go on with the agreement. Affirmation may be implied from lapse of time (see *Leaf v International Galleries* (1950));
- where the parties cannot be restored to their original positions; or
- where third parties have acquired rights in the subject matter of the contract (see *Phillips v Brooks*, below).

Section 3 of the MA 1967 (as amended by s 8 UCTA 1977), provides that any **exclusion of liability for misrepresentation** must comply with the **requirement of reasonableness**, a further matter considered in:

❖ KEY CASE — *Thomas Witter v TBP Industries* (1996)

Facts:

During pre-contractual negotiation for the sale of a business, the seller misrepresented its profitability, causing the purchaser to pay more than its real value. The subsequent written contract contained the following purported exclusion clause:

> This Agreement sets forth the entire agreement and understanding between the parties or any of them in connection with the business and the sale and purchase described herein. In particular, but without prejudice to the generality of the foregoing, the purchaser acknowledges that it has not been induced to enter into this agreement by any representation warranty other than the statements contained in or referred to in Schedule 6 [to the contract document].

Decision:

The court held the exclusion clause to be inoperative. In analysing the legal effect of the clause, Jacob J held that, on its own wording, it could not provide any exemption in relation to any pre-contractual misrepresentations that had been included as express warranties within the document. Moreover, he held that the clause was ineffective, even as regards those pre-contractual misrepresentations which had not been included expressly in the contract. His first ground for striking down the clause, and in spite of its apparently perfectly clear wording, was that it was not sufficiently clear to remove the purchaser's right to rely on the misrepresentation. Secondly, and as an alternative, he held that the clause did not meet with the requirement of reasonableness under s 3 of the MA 1967. The scope of the clause was held to be far too wide, in that it purported to cover 'any liability' for 'any misrepresentation'. In Jacob J's view, it could never be possible to exclude liability for fraudulent misrepresentation and, although it might be possible to exclude liability for negligent and innocent misrepresentation, any such exclusion had to pass the reasonableness test, which the clause in question had failed to do.

6.4 Duress

Duress is **physical or economic force**, which is used to override one party's freedom to choose whether or not to make a contract. Under such circumstances, the contract is voidable at the instance of the innocent party.

Its application used to be restricted to contracts entered into because of actual or threatened physical *violence to a person*. In *Barton v Armstrong* (1975), the defendant threatened Barton with death if he did not arrange for his company to buy Armstrong's shares in it. Barton sought to have the agreement set aside. It was found that threats had been made, but that Barton thought that the transaction was beneficial. Nonetheless, Barton succeeded because duress was present. The burden of proof was on Armstrong to show that the threats had played no part in Barton's decision. He failed to discharge this burden.

Subsequently, *threats to a person's property* were held to amount to duress, as in *Maskell v Horner* (1915). There, money paid for the return of unlawfully seized goods could be recovered.

In the business world, it is not unknown for a party to be pressurised into an agreement. In *D & C Builders v Rees* (1966), a firm in financial difficulty was pressurised into accepting part payment in full settlement of a debt. This case sowed the seeds for a doctrine of **economic duress**. Today, **the real issue is distinguishing between acceptable commercial pressure and unacceptable economic duress**; only the latter renders a contract voidable.

The distinction was made in *Occidental Worldwide Investment Corporation v Skibs A/S Avanti, The Sibeon and The Sibotre* (1976). Vessel charterers renegotiated charter rates with the shipowners, on the basis that otherwise they would become insolvent and not worth suing. The charterers also knew that it was unlikely the owners could find substitute charterers. Later the owners withdrew their vessels from the charterers service and were sued for breach of contract. The owners' defence was that the renegotiated contract resulted from economic duress, rather than legitimate commercial pressure. The defence failed, though Kerr J found there was great commercial pressure. Nevertheless, the judge recognised, in a limited way, that *economic* duress could allow rescission. Duress meant a party was **deprived of the intent to** consent to the contract; such coercion could be determined by two factors:

- a protest about the situation, by the coerced party; and
- an indication by the coerced party that they did not consider the matter closed.

North Ocean Shipping Co v Hyundai Construction (1979) concerned a contract to build a ship. The builders subsequently refused to complete construction unless the purchasers paid 10% extra. Without the ship, the buyers would lose a lucrative contract with a third party, which had already been made to charter the ship. The buyers paid the 10%, but later sued to recover it on the basis of, *inter alia*, economic duress. It was held that the threat to terminate the contract was economic duress, which rendered the contract voidable. However, the buyers' delay in suing was affirmation of the agreement, so they could not rescind.

Furthermore, rescission cannot be granted where '*restituto in integrum*' is impossible, as in *Halpern v Halpern* (2007) (see also: *Pao On v Lau Yiu Long* (1979)).

The existence of economic duress as a distinct principle of contract law finally received the approval of the House of Lords in:

❖ KEY CASE *Universe Tankships Inc v ITWF* (1982)

Facts:
The case concerned industrial action against the plaintiffs' ship by the defendant trade union, so that it could not leave the port. As part of negotiations to lift the action, the plaintiffs paid money into the union's benevolent fund.

Decision:
The plaintiffs successfully reclaimed the money, as it was paid under economic duress.

Comment: Lords Diplock and Scarman recognised the commercial reality that a business may reluctantly make a contract, bowing to the inevitable; though, perhaps, the party was not completely deprived of the intention to consent, such a suppression of the will to consent, would amount to economic duress. So, it appears that the economic duress concept has become less strict in its requirements.

It now seems that, in order to benefit from the doctrine of economic duress, claimants must show:

- that pressure, which resulted in an absence of real choice on their part, was brought to bear on them; and
- that pressure was of a nature considered to be illegitimate by the courts.

Only under such circumstances will the court permit rescission of an agreement, as can be seen in *Atlas Express v Kafco* (1990). The defendants had secured a highly profitable contract with Woolworths, and employed the plaintiffs as their carriers. After commencing performance of the contract, Atlas sought to increase their price. Although they protested, Kafco felt that they had no option but to agree to the demand, rather than break their contract with Woolworths, which would have proved economically disastrous for them. Atlas sued to recover the increased charges, but failed; the attempt to increase the charge was a clear case of economic duress. (This should be compared with the situation and outcome in *Williams v Roffey Bros* (1990), see 4.5.3 above.)

However, it must be said that, it is unclear how far a party's choice to consent must be interfered with. Furthermore, it will be for the court to decide whether any pressure exerted is legitimate or not.

6.5 Undue Influence

Transactions, either under contract or as gifts, may be avoided where they have been entered into because of undue influence by the beneficiary; delay may bar the right to avoid the agreement. The type of businesses likely to be in a position to exert undue influence are banks and professional advisors, such as solicitors. Undue influence may arise in two situations:

6.5.1 Special relationships

Where there is a special relationship between the parties, there is a **presumption** that the transaction results from undue influence. The burden of proof is on the person receiving the benefit to rebut the presumption. In *Re Craig* (1971), after the death of his wife Mr Craig, aged 84, employed

Mrs Middleton as his secretary-companion. During the six years she was employed, he gave her a total of £30,000. An action to have the gifts set aside succeeded. It was held that the circumstances raised the presumption of undue influence, which Mrs Middleton had failed to rebut.

Examples of special relationships are:

- parent and child, while the latter is still a minor;
- guardian and ward;
- religious adviser and follower;
- doctor and patient; and
- solicitor and client.

The list is not closed, however, and other relationships may be included within the scope of the special relationship, as in *Re Craig*.

Where a special relationship exists, then an important way to rebut the presumption of undue influence is to show that *independent advice* was taken by the other party, of *their own free will*.

Even where a special relationship exists, a transaction will not be set aside unless it is shown to be **manifestly disadvantageous**:

❖ KEY CASE *National Westminster Bank v Morgan* (1985)

Facts:

When a couple fell into financial difficulties, the plaintiff bank made financial arrangements which permitted them to remain in their house. The re-financing transaction secured against the house was arranged by a bank manager who had called at their home. Mrs Morgan had no independent legal advice. When the husband died, the bank obtained a possession order against the house in respect of outstanding debts. Mrs Morgan sought to have the refinancing arrangement set aside, on the ground of undue influence.

Decision:

The action failed, on the ground that the doctrine of undue influence had no place in agreements which did not involve any manifest disadvantage, and Mrs Morgan had actually benefited from the transaction by being able to remain in her home for a longer period.

Note: Recent cases are beginning to question whether this requirement of 'manifest disadvantage' is necessary before a contract can be avoided; for example, *Barclays Bank plc v Coleman* (2001).

Comment: The key element in deciding whether a relationship was a special one or not was whether one party was in a position of dominance over the other. In *Morgan*, the House of Lords indicated that the relationship of a bank, carrying out its normal activities with its customers was not a special relationship, where a presumption of undue influence arose. However, there may be circumstances where that relationship is treated as 'special' (see *Lloyds Bank Ltd v Bundy* (1975)).

6.5.2 No special relationship

Where no special relationship exists between the parties, the party claiming the protection of the undue influence doctrine has the burden proving **actual** undue influence.

The rule relating to **manifest disadvantage** (above), **does not apply where no special relationship exists**. In *CIBC Mortgages plc v Pitt* (1993), Mrs Pitt sought to set aside a mortgage which she had signed against her home in favour of the plaintiffs, on the basis that her husband had exerted undue influence over her. Whereas the Court of Appeal had rejected her plea on the ground that the agreement was not to her manifest disadvantage, the House of Lords declared that such a principle did not apply in cases where undue influence was actual, rather than presumed. They did, however, recognise the validity of the mortgage, on the ground that the creditor had no knowledge, either actual or constructive, of the exercise of undue influence in relation to the transaction. However, the House of Lords, in *Barclays Bank plc v O'Brien* (1993), referred to an **implied duty** on creditors in particular circumstances, which certainly included a marital relationship, to ensure that parties had not entered into agreements on the basis of misrepresentation or undue influence. The bank was held to have constructive notice of the undue influence wielded by the husband; that is, they *should* have known, whether they actually did or not. For that reason, the bank was not permitted to enforce the agreement made on the basis of that undue influence (see also: *Royal Bank of Scotland v Etridge (No 2)* (2001), which considered when influence was *undue*).

6.5.3 Inequality of bargaining power

It has been suggested that undue influence and duress are simply examples of a wider principle which is based on inequality of bargaining power. The existence of such a principle was suggested in a number of decisions involving Lord Denning (*Lloyd's Bank v Bundy* (1975) for example). It was intended to provide protection for those who suffered as a consequence of being forced into particular agreements due to their lack of bargaining power. This doctrine, however, was considered and firmly rejected by the House of Lords in *National Westminster Bank v Morgan*. It could be suggested that the very idea of inequality of bargaining power is incompatible with the reality of today's economic structure, which is dominated by large-scale, if not monopolistic, organisations. It should be recognised, however, that the idea of inequality of bargaining power has found a place in determining how the Unfair Contract Terms Act 1977 is to operate.

6.6 Contracts and Public Policy

It is evident that some agreements will tend to be contrary to public policy. The fact that some are considered to be more serious than others is reflected in the distinction drawn between those which are said to be illegal and those which are simply void.

6.6.1 Illegal contracts

A contract which breaks the law is illegal. No claim can be brought by a party to an illegal contract, though in some circumstances money or property transferred may be recovered. The contract may be either expressly prohibited by statute, or implicitly prohibited by the common law. Illegal contracts include:

- contracts to defraud the Inland Revenue;
- contracts involving the commission of a crime or a tort;
- contracts with a sexually immoral element, although contemporary attitudes may have changed in this respect (see *Armhouse Lee Ltd v Chappell* (1996));
- contracts against the interest of the UK or a friendly State;
- contracts leading to corruption in public life; and
- contracts which interfere with the course of justice.

6.6.2 Void contracts

Void contracts do not give rise to rights or obligations. The contract is void only in so far as it is contrary to public policy; the whole agreement may not be void. Severance is the procedure whereby the void part of a contract is excised, permitting the remainder to be enforced. Contracts may be void under statute (for example, price fixing agreements under the Competition Act 1998 and Enterprise Act 2002), or at common law. Those void at common law are:

- *Contracts to oust the jurisdiction of the court*
  Any contractual agreement which seeks to deny the parties the right to submit questions of law to the courts is void as being contrary to public policy. Agreements which provide for compulsory arbitration can be enforceable.
- *Contracts prejudicial to the status of marriage*
  It is a matter of public policy that the institution of marriage be maintained. Hence, any contract which seeks to restrain a person's freedom to marry, or undermines the institution of marriage in any way, will be considered void.

6.6.3 Contracts in restraint of trade

An area of particular importance to businesses, which is controlled by the common law, is contracts in restraint of trade. Under such an agreement, one party restricts their future freedom to engage in their trade, business or profession. As a general rule, such agreements are *prima facie* void, but they may be valid if they meet the following requirements:

- the person imposing the restrictions has a legitimate interest to protect;
- the restriction is reasonable as between the parties; and
- the restriction is not contrary to the public interest.

The doctrine of restraint of trade is flexible in its application and may be applied to new situations when they arise. However, it is usual to classify the branches of the doctrine as follows.

Restraints on employees

Employers cannot protect themselves against competition from an ex-employee, except where they have a *legitimate interest* to protect. The only legitimate interests recognised by the law are trade secrets and trade connections (such as confidential customer lists) and, the restraint must be of a *reasonable* nature. What constitutes reasonable in this context depends on the circumstances of the case.

In *Lamson Pneumatic Tube Co v Phillips* (1904), the plaintiffs manufactured specialised shop equipment. The defendant's employment contract stated that, on ceasing to work for the plaintiffs, he would not engage in a similar business for a period of five years, anywhere in the Eastern hemisphere. It was held that such a restriction was reasonable, bearing in mind the nature of the plaintiffs' business. However, in *Empire Meat Co Ltd v Patrick* (1939), Patrick had been employed as manager of the company's butchers business in Cambridge. The company sought to enforce the defendant's promise that he would not establish a rival business within five miles of their shop. In this situation, it was held that the restraint was too wide and could not be enforced, (see also: *GW Plowman & Son Ltd v Ash* (1964)).

The longer the period of time or the wider the geographical area covered by the restraint, the more likely it is to be struck down, but in *Fitch v Dewes* (1921), it was held that a lifelong restriction placed on a solicitor was valid.

Restraints on vendors of business

The interest to be protected here is the *goodwill* of the business, that is, its profitability. Restrictions may legitimately be placed on previous owners to prevent them from competing in the future with new owners. Again, the restraint should not be greater than is necessary to protect that interest.

In *British Reinforced Concrete Engineering Co Ltd v Schleff* (1921), the plaintiffs sought to enforce a promise given by the defendant, on the sale of his business to them, that he would not compete with them in the manufacturing of road reinforcements. It was held that, given the small size and restricted nature of the business sold, the restraint was too wide to be enforceable. However, in *Nordenfelt v Maxim Nordenfelt Guns and Ammunition Co* (1894), a worldwide restraint on competition was held to be enforceable, given the nature of the business sold.

Restraints on distributors/solus agreements

This category is usually concerned with *solus agreements* between petrol companies and garage proprietors, by which a petrol company seeks to prevent the retailer from selling its competitors' petrol. It is recognised that petrol companies have a *legitimate interest* to protect, and the outcome depends on whether the restraint is *reasonable*.

In *Esso Petroleum v Harper's Garage* (1968), the parties had entered into an agreement whereby Harper undertook to buy all of the petrol to be sold at his two garages from Esso, for four years and 21 years respectively. In return, Esso lent him £7,000, secured by way of a mortgage over one garage. When Harper broke his undertaking, Esso sued to enforce it. It was held that the agreements in respect of both garages were restraints of trade; however, the agreement which lasted for four years was reasonable, the one which lasted for 21 years was unreasonable and void.

Until fairly recently, it was thought that *Esso v Harper's* had set down a rule that any solus agreement involving a restriction of more than five years would be void as being in restraint of trade. In *Alec Lobb (Garages) Ltd v Total Oil Ltd* (1985), however, the Court of Appeal made it clear that the outcome of each case depended on its particular circumstances; in that case, it approved a solus agreement extending over a period of 21 years.

Exclusive service contracts

These are contracts specifically structured to *exploit* one of the parties by controlling and limiting their output, rather than assisting them. In *Schroeder Music Publishing Co v Macauley* (1974), an unknown songwriter, Macauley, entered into a five year agreement with Schroeder. Under it, he had to assign any music he wrote to them, but they had no obligation to publish it. The agreement provided for automatic extension of the agreement if it yielded £5,000 in royalties, but the publishers could terminate it at any time with one month's notice. It was decided that the agreement was so one-sided as to amount to an unreasonable restraint of trade and, hence, was void.

Summary

Contract (3): Vitiating Factors

Mistake

- Operative (fundamental) mistake renders a contract void.
- Equitable remedies may be available where mistakes are not fundamental.
- Operative common mistake usually involves *res sua* or *res extincta*.
- An objective test is applied to determine whether a mutual mistake is operative.
- Generally, unilateral mistake is not operative where the parties deal face to face.
- Where the mistake relates to a written contract, rectification or *non est factum* may be claimed.

Misrepresentation

- Misrepresentation can be defined as 'a false statement of fact, made by one party before or at the time of the contract, which induces the other party to contract'.
- Some statements will not amount to representations, for example, statements of opinion and law.
- Some pre-contract statements may be treated as terms of the contract. This gives rise to an alternative cause of action for breach of contract, which should be noted for examination purposes.
- Rescission and damages in the tort of deceit are available for *fraudulent misrepresentation*.
- Rescission and/or damages under s 2(1) of the Misrepresentation Act 1967 are available for *negligent misrepresentation*.
- Rescission or damages under s 2(2) of the Misrepresentation Act 1967 are available for *innocent misrepresentation*.

Duress

- A contract entered into in consequence of duress is voidable.
- Economic duress may render a contract voidable if there was illegitimate pressure, negating consent to the contract.

Undue influence

- Subject to delay, undue influence renders a contract voidable.
- Where there is a *special relationship* between the contracting parties, a rebuttable presumption of undue influence arises.
- Where there is *no special relationship* between the contracting parties, the party claiming undue influence has the burden of proof.

Contracts and public policy

- A contract rendered illegal by statute or common law cannot be the subject of legal action.
- Contracts rendered void as contrary to public policy (for example, contracts in restraint of trade) do not give rise to legal rights or obligations.

Further Reading

Dabbs, D, 'The risk of mistake in contract' (2002) NLJ 1654 (confirmation of importance of *Bell v Lever Bros* in the law of mistake)

Evans, R, 'Insurance overhaul' (2006) NLJ 1746 (misrepresentation and the duty of disclosure in insurance contracts)

Furmston, MP, *Cheshire, Fifoot and Furmston's Law of Contract*, 16th edn, 2012, Oxford: OUP

Malet, D, 'S 2(2) of the Misrepresentation Act 1967' [2001] LQR 524 (discussion of damages in lieu of rescission)

Peel, E, *Treitel on the Law of Contract*, 13th edn, 2011, London: Sweet & Maxwell

Poole, J, *Casebook on Contract Law*, 10th edn, 2010, Oxford: OUP

Richards, P, *The Law of Contract*, 11th edn, 2013, Harlow: Pearson Longman

Stone, R, 'Misrepresentation: answering problem questions' (1995) SLR (Summer) 20 (advice on problem solving)

Stone, R, 'Mistake: answering problem questions' (1993) SLR (Summer) 25 (advice on problem solving)

Stuart-Smith, J and de Chassiron, A, 'Recovery of damages after misrepresentation' (2000) NLJ 865 (damages under s 2(1) of Misrepresentation Act 1967)

Websites

www.statutelaw.gov.uk (for copy of Misrepresentation Act 1967)
www.lawreports.co.uk (daily summaries of new cases)

Chapter 7

Contract (4): Discharge of a Contract

Chapter Contents

Law in Context: Discharge of a Contract

Although contracts are made on the basis of consensual agreement, there are a number of ways in which they can be brought to an end. This is commonly referred to as 'discharge of a contract'. Where this occurs, each party to the agreement is effectively freed from their ongoing obligations under the contract. A contract may be discharged in a number of ways, namely, discharge by performance; repudiatory breach; by agreement; and finally, by frustration.

7.1 Introduction

When a contract is discharged, the parties to the agreement are freed from their contractual obligations.

Discharge of a Contract	
• **By agreement**	○ Executory contracts – both parties agree to discharge it ○ Contract executed by one party – new contract needed to discharge other party's obligations ○ Contract states method of discharge
• **By performance – both parties complete obligations FULLY**	○ Exceptions to full performance rule – ○ Divisible contracts ○ Substantial performance ○ Acceptance of a party's partial performance ○ Full performance prevented by other party
• **By frustration – contract becomes impossible to perform for reason beyond parties' control**	○ Destruction of contractual subject matter ○ Supervening illegality ○ Non-occurrence of event contract is based on ○ Commercial purpose of contract defeated ○ Illness/death in contract involving personal service
● **By breach**	○ Anticipatory breach – conduct/notice indicating party won't perform when performance becomes due ○ Actual breach – failure to perform on due date for performance

Figure 7.1

7.2 Discharge by Agreement

Emphasis has been placed on the consensual nature of contract law, and it follows that what was made by agreement can be ended by agreement. The contract itself may contain provision for its discharge by either the passage of a fixed period of time or the occurrence of a particular event.

Alternatively, it may provide, either expressly or by implication, that one or other of the parties can bring it to an end, for example, by notice in a contract of employment.

Where there is no provision in a contract, **another contract is required to cancel it** before all of the obligations have been met.

- Where the contract is **executory**, the mutual exchange of promises to release one another from future performance will be sufficient consideration.
- Where the contract is **executed**, that is, one party has performed, or partly performed, their obligations, the other party must provide consideration (that is, make a new contract) in order to be released from performing their part of the contract (unless the release is made under seal). The provision of this consideration discharges the original contract and there is said to be *accord and satisfaction*. This was found to have occurred in *Williams v Roffey Bros* (see 4.5.3 above).

7.3 Discharge by Performance

Performance is the normal way in which contracts are discharged; by the parties performing their contractual obligations. Normally, discharge requires **complete and exact performance** of the obligations in the contract.

In *Cutter v Powell* (1795), Cutter was employed on a ship sailing to Liverpool. It was agreed he would receive 30 guineas when the journey was completed. Before the ship reached Liverpool, Cutter died and his widow sued the ship's master, to recover a proportion of the wages due to her husband. It was held that she was not entitled to anything, as the contract required complete performance.

7.3.1 Exceptions to the complete performance rule

- *Where the contract is divisible*

  In a contract of employment, where payment is made periodically, the harshness of *Cutter v Powell* is avoided.

  In *Bolton v Mahadeva* (1972), the plaintiff had contracted to install central heating and supply a bathroom suite to the defendant. The heating system was defective and it cost £179 to remedy the defect. It was held that Bolton could not claim the installation cost, as he had failed to perform the contract. However, supply of the bathroom suite was divisible from the overall agreement, and had to be paid for.
- *Where the contract is capable of being fulfilled by substantial performance*

  This occurs where the essential element of an agreement has been performed but some minor part or fault remains to be done or remedied. The contract price can be claimed, but with a deduction for the work outstanding. In *Hoenig v Isaacs* (1952), Hoenig was employed by Isaacs to decorate his flat. The price was £750, to be paid as the work progressed. Isaacs paid £400, but refused to pay the remainder, objecting to the quality of the work carried out. Hoenig sued for the outstanding £350. It was held that Isaacs had to pay the outstanding money less the cost of remedying the defects. A similar issue arose in *Williams v Roffey Bros* (1990).

  This should be compared with *Bolton v Mahadeva* (above), where no payment was allowed for work done in a *totally* unsatisfactory manner.
- *Where performance has been prevented by the other party*

  Under such circumstances, as occurred in *Planche v Colburn* (1831), the party prevented from performance can sue either for breach of contract or on a *quantum meruit* basis (see 7.7.5 below).

- *Where partial performance has been accepted by the other party*
- Suppose A orders 12 bottles of wine from B, but B only delivers 10. A can reject the 10 bottles, but if the goods are accepted, a proportionate price must be paid for them. In *Sumpter v Hedges* (1898), however, the plaintiff failed to complete agreed building work, thereby obliging the defendant to complete it himself. The plaintiff could not claim payment for the proportion of work completed, because the defendant had *no choice* but to complete the buildings.

7.3.2 Tender of performance

This means an offer to perform the contractual obligations. So, if a buyer refuses to accept the goods offered (where there are no legal grounds to do so, for example, the goods are defective), but later sues for breach of contract, the seller can rely on the fact that they tendered performance as discharging their liability under the contract. The seller would also be entitled to claim for breach of contract.

In *Macdonald v Startup* (1843), Macdonald promised to deliver 10 tons of oil to the defendant within the last 14 days of March. He tried to deliver on Saturday 31 March at 8.30 pm, and Startup refused to accept the oil. It was held that the tender of performance was equivalent to actual performance, and Macdonald was entitled to claim damages for breach of contract.

Section 29(5) of the Sale of Goods Act (SoGA) 1979 now provides that tender is ineffectual unless made at a *reasonable hour*. It is unlikely that 8.30 pm on a Saturday evening would be considered reasonable.

7.4 Discharge by Frustration

Where it is impossible to perform an obligation from the outset, no contract can come into existence. Furthermore, subsequent impossibility was, originally, no excuse for non-performance. However, the doctrine of frustration was developed to permit a contracting party, in some circumstances, to be excused performance because of **impossibility arising after formation of the contract**.

A contract will be discharged by frustration in the following circumstances:

- *Where destruction of the subject matter of the contract has occurred*
  In *Taylor v Caldwell* (1863), Caldwell had agreed to let a hall to the plaintiff for several concerts. Before the first concert, the hall was destroyed by fire. Taylor sued for breach of contract. It was held that the destruction of the hall made performance impossible, so the defendant was not liable for breach.
- *Where government interference, or supervening illegality, prevents performance*
  Performance of a contract may become illegal by a change in the law. The outbreak of war, making the other party an enemy alien, has a similar effect. In *Re Shipton, Anderson & Co* (1915), a contract was made for the sale of wheat, which was stored in a warehouse. Before the seller could deliver, it was requisitioned by the Government under wartime emergency powers. It was held that the seller was excused from performance, as it was no longer possible to lawfully deliver the wheat.
- *Where a particular event, which is the sole reason for the contract, fails to take place*
  In *Krell v Henry* (1903), Krell let a room to the defendant for the purpose of viewing the coronation procession of Edward VII. When the procession was cancelled, due to the King's illness, Krell sued Henry for the due rent. It was held that the contract was discharged by frustration, since its purpose could no longer be achieved. This only applies **where the cancelled event was the sole purpose** of the contract. In *Herne Bay Steamboat Co v Hutton* (1903), a naval review, arranged for Edward VII's coronation celebrations, was cancelled due to the King's illness. Hutton had contracted to hire a boat from the plaintiffs to see the review. Hutton had to pay

the hire charge. The sole foundation of the contract was not lost, as the ship could still have been used to view the assembled fleet.

- *Where the commercial purpose of the contract is defeated*
  This applies where the circumstances have so changed that to hold a party to their promise would require them to do something which, although not impossible, **would be radically different from the original agreement**. In *Jackson v Union Marine Insurance Co* (1874), the plaintiff's ship was chartered to proceed to Newport to load a cargo but, on the way, it ran aground. It could not be refloated for over a month, and needed repairs. The charterers hired another ship and the plaintiff claimed under an insurance policy which he had taken out to cover the eventuality of his failure to carry out the contract. The insurance company denied responsibility, on the basis that the plaintiff could claim against the charterer for breach of contract. The court decided, however, that the delay had put an end to the **commercial sense** of the contract. Therefore, the charterers were released from their contractual obligations and were entitled to hire another ship.

❖ KEY CASE *CTI Group v Transclear SA* (2007)

The Court of Appeal judgment in this case highlights the difficulties that lie in the way of anyone seeking to make use of the doctrine of frustration to avoid potential contractual liability.

Facts:
The case related to a contract for the supply and purchase of a cargo of cement to be loaded onto a ship in Padang in Indonesia. The claimants, CTI Group, intended to import substantial quantities of cement into Mexico, thus undermining a cartel operated by a local Mexican company, Cemex. The sellers, Transclear SA, intended to obtain the cargo from a supplier they had used on a number of previous occasions, PT Semen Padang, who had proved reliable in the past. On that basis the two parties entered into a contract. However, the supplier at Padang declined to provide the cargo because of pressure brought to bear on it by Cemex, which had a commercial link with it.

Decision:
In a resultant action for damages for breach of contract an arbitration panel found that the failure of the Padang company to supply the cement as a result of the pressure put on it by Cemex had frustrated the contract between CTI and Transclear.

However on appeal, the High Court refused to recognise the frustration and awarded damages for breach of contract. In confirming the award in the Court of Appeal, Lord Justice Moore-Bick stated that:

> In my view it is impossible to hold that the contract in this case was frustrated. As the decided cases show, the fact that a supplier chooses not to make goods available for shipment, thus rendering performance by the seller impossible, is not of itself sufficient to frustrate a contract of this kind. In order to rely on the doctrine of frustration *it is necessary for there to have been a supervening event which renders the performance of the seller's obligations* ***impossible*** *or* ***fundamentally different*** *in nature from that which was envisaged when the contract was made.*

- *Where, in the case of a contract of personal service, the party dies or becomes otherwise incapacitated*
  In *Condor v Barron Knights* (1966), Condor contracted to be a pop group's drummer. After he became ill, he was medically advised that he could only play four nights per week, not every night as agreed. The contract was discharged because the plaintiff's health prevented him from performing his contractual duties; thus, any contractual obligations were unenforceable. In *Hare v Murphy Bros* (1974), a foreman's employment contract was frustrated when he was jailed for unlawful wounding. This was not self-induced frustration (see 7.4.1 below), though the foreman was at fault; he **did not have a choice** as to his availability for work.

7.4.1 Situations where the doctrine of frustration does not apply

Tsakiroglou & Co v Noblee and Thorl (1962), stated that frustration is a doctrine which is only too often invoked by a party to a contract who finds performance difficult or unprofitable, but it is very rarely relied on with success. It is, in fact, a kind of last resort, and is a conclusion which should be reached rarely and with reluctance.

A contract will not be discharged by frustration:

- *Where the parties made express provision in the contract for the event which has occurred*
  In this case, the contractual provision will be applied.
- *Where the frustrating event is self-induced*
  In *Maritime National Fish Ltd v Ocean Trawlers Ltd* (1935), Maritime chartered a ship equipped for otter trawling from the owners, Ocean Trawlers. Permits were required for otter trawling, and Maritime, which owned four ships of its own, applied for five permits. Only three permits were granted, and they assigned them to their own ships. They claimed that the contract was frustrated, as they could not lawfully use the ship. It was held that the frustrating event was a result of their action in assigning the permits to their own ships and, therefore, they could not rely on it as discharging their contractual obligations. Effectively, self-induced frustration amounts to breach of contract.
- *Where an alternative method of performance is still possible*
  In such a situation, the person performing the contract is expected to use an available alternative method. In *Tsakiroglou* (above), a 'cif' contract was made to supply 300 tons of groundnuts to Hamburg. It was intended that the cargo should go via the Suez Canal; the appellants refused to deliver the nuts when the canal was closed. It was argued that the contract was frustrated, as to use the Cape of Good Hope route would make the contract commercially and fundamentally different from that which was agreed. The court decided that the contract was not fundamentally altered by the closure of the canal; it was not discharged by frustration, despite the expense and delay of the longer route. Thus, the appellants were liable for breach of contract. Obviously, if the cargo had been perishable, performance may not have been possible.
- *Where the contract simply becomes more expensive to perform*
  Courts will not allow frustration to be used as a means of escaping from a bad bargain. In *Davis Contractors v Fareham UDC* (1956), the plaintiffs contracted to build 78 houses in eight months, for £94,000. Due to a shortage of labour, it took 22 months to build the houses and cost £115,000. The plaintiffs sought to have the contract set aside for frustration, and to claim on a *quantum meruit* basis. The court determined that the contract was not frustrated by the shortage of labour and the plaintiffs were, thus, bound by their contractual undertaking with regard to the price.

7.4.2 The effect of frustration

At common law, the effect of frustration **was to make the contract void from the time of the frustrating event, but not void** *ab initio*, that is, from the beginning. This meant that each party had to perform any obligation which became due before the frustrating event, and was only excused from obligations which would arise after that event. This could lead to injustice, as in *Krell v Henry* (above). The plaintiff could not claim the rent, as it was not due until after the coronation event was cancelled. However, in *Chandler v Webster* (1904), the plaintiff had already paid £100 of the total rent of £141 15s for a room from which to watch the coronation procession, before it was cancelled. It was decided that, not only could he not recover the £100, but he also had to pay the outstanding £41 15s, as the rent had **fallen due** for payment **before** the frustrating event had taken place.

7.4.3 Law Reform (Frustrated Contracts) Act 1943

The Law Reform (Frustrated Contracts) Act 1943 was introduced to remedy the potential injustices of common law. Now:

- any money paid is recoverable;
- any money due to be paid ceases to be payable;
- the parties may be permitted, at the discretion of the court, to retain expenses incurred from any money received; or to recover those expenses from money due to be paid before the frustrating event;
- if no money was paid, or was due to be paid, before the event, then nothing can be retained or recovered; and
- a party who has received valuable benefit from the other's performance before the frustrating event may have to pay for that benefit.

The Act does not apply to contracts of insurance, contracts for the carriage of goods by sea and contracts covered by s 7 of the SoGA 1979.

7.5 Discharge by Breach

Breach of a contract occurs where one of the parties to the agreement **fails to comply, either completely or satisfactorily, with their obligations** under it. Breach may occur in three ways:

- where a party, prior to the time of performance, indicates they will not fulfil their contractual obligation;
- where a party fails to perform their contractual obligation; or
- where a party performs their obligation in a defective manner.

7.5.1 Effect of breach

Any breach entitles the innocent party to sue for damages. Additionally, **some breaches permit the innocent party to treat the contract as discharged**. In this situation, they can refuse either to perform their part of the contract or to accept further performance from the party in breach. The right to treat a contract as discharged arises in the following instances:

See Chapter 8

- where the other party has repudiated the contract before performance is due, or before they have completed performance; and
- where the other party has committed a fundamental breach of contract. As previously discussed, there are two methods of determining whether a breach is fundamental or not: the first is by relying on the distinction between conditions and warranties; the other is by relying on the seriousness of the consequences that flow from the breach.

7.5.2 Anticipatory breach

Anticipatory breach arises where one party, prior to the due date of performance, demonstrates, expressly or impliedly, **an intention not to perform their contractual obligations**:

- *Express*
  This occurs where a party actually states that they will not perform their contractual obligations. In *Hochster v De La Tour* (1853), in April, De La Tour engaged Hochster to act as courier on his European tour, starting on 1 June. On 11 May, De La Tour wrote to Hochster, stating that he would no longer require his services. The plaintiff started proceedings for breach of contract on 22 May; the defendant claimed that there could be no cause of action until 1 June. It was held, however, that the plaintiff was entitled to start his action as soon as the anticipatory breach occurred, on May 11.
- *Implied*
  This occurs where a party's conduct makes performance impossible. In *Omnium D'Enterprises v Sutherland* (1919), the defendant agreed to hire a ship to the plaintiff. Prior to the actual time for performance, he sold the ship. The sale amounted to repudiation of the contract and the plaintiff could sue from that date.

So, in cases of anticipatory breach, the innocent party can sue for damages immediately, as in *Hochster v De La Tour*. **Alternatively, they can wait until the actual time for performance before taking action**, thus **giving the other party a chance to perform**. In the latter instance, they are entitled to make preparations for performance and claim for actual breach if the other party fails to perform on the due date, even though this apparently conflicts with the duty to mitigate losses (see 7.7.2 below).

In *White and Carter (Councils) v McGregor* (1961), McGregor contracted with the plaintiffs to have advertisements placed on litter bins which were supplied to local authorities. The defendant wrote to the plaintiffs, asking to cancel the contract. The plaintiffs refused to cancel, and produced and displayed the adverts required under the contract, and claimed payment. It was held that the plaintiffs were not obliged to accept the defendant's repudiation. They were entitled to perform the contract and claim the agreed price. Thus, the duty to mitigate loss did not place the plaintiffs under an obligation to accept anticipatory breach and stop their own performance; as they were allowing the defendants a 'second chance', the plaintiffs had to commence their performance in case the defendants did perform on the due date.

On the other hand, clearly there are instances where allowing a party to continue performance could be unfair. By such continuance, the losses ultimately claimed for actual breach may be increased considerably. Indeed, in *White and Carter*, Lord Reid thought that a party should only be allowed to affirm and continue with performance if there was a **legitimate interest** in so doing. This view has been accepted subsequently (see *Hounslow BC v Twickenham Garden Developments Ltd* (1971)), but may still leave a business with the difficulty of knowing whether they have a legitimate interest in continuing (see *Ocean Marine Navigation Ltd v Koch Carbon Inc* (2003), where the court considered circumstances where damages would be an adequate remedy for anticipatory breach and it would be unreasonable for a party to choose continued performance).

Furthermore, where the innocent party elects to wait for the time of performance, they take **the risk of the contract being discharged for some other reason**, such as frustration, and, thus, of losing their right to sue.

In *Avery v Bowden* (1856), Bowden chartered the plaintiff's ship in order to load grain at Odessa within a period of 45 days. Although Bowden later told the ship's captain that he no longer intended to load the grain, the ship stayed in Odessa in the hope that he would change his mind. Before the end of the 45 days, the Crimean War started, so the contract was frustrated. Avery then sued for breach of contract, but the action failed. There was anticipatory breach, but the captain had waived the right to discharge the contract on that basis. The contract continued and was brought to an end by frustration, not by breach.

A more recent case sheds some light on the operation and effect of anticipatory breach. In *Vitol SA v Norelf Ltd* (1996), on 11 February, the parties made a contract for the purchase of a cargo by the plaintiff. On 8 March, Vitol sent a telex to Norelf which purported to repudiate the agreement for alleged breach by Norelf. As the allegation of breach turned out to be unfounded, the telex of 8 March was an anticipatory breach of the contract by Vitol. Norelf did not communicate with Vitol and sold the cargo to another party on 15 March. In arbitration, it was decided that this sale effectively represented Norelf's acceptance of the anticipatory breach and left Vitol with no claim. The Court of Appeal, however, held that Norelf should have indicated their acceptance of the anticipatory breach in a clear and unequivocal manner, and that silence could not amount to such acceptance. Restoring the decision of the arbitrator, the House of Lords decided that the fact that Norelf had not taken the next step in the contract by delivering a bill of lading was sufficient notification that they had accepted Vitol's repudiatory breach. In so doing, they set out **three principles that govern the acceptance of repudiatory breach**:

- In the event of repudiatory breach, the other party has the right either to accept the repudiation or to affirm the contract.
- The aggrieved party does not have to inform the other party specifically of their acceptance of the anticipatory breach; conduct which clearly indicates that the injured party is treating the contract as at an end is sufficient (though, of course, each case must be considered on its specific facts).
- The aggrieved party need not personally notify the other of the decision to accept the repudiation; it is sufficient that they learn of it from some other party.

7.6 Remedies for Breach of Contract

The principal remedies are:

- damages;
- *quantum meruit*;
- specific performance;
- injunction;
- action for the agreed contract price; and
- repudiation.

Which remedy is available for a particular breach depends on issues such as whether the breach is of a condition or a warranty.

See Chapter 8

7.7 Damages

According to Lord Diplock in *Photo Productions Ltd v Securicor Transport Ltd* (1980):

> Every failure to perform a primary obligation is a breach of contract. The secondary obligation on the part of the contract breaker to which it gives rise by implication of the common law is to pay monetary compensation to the other party for the loss sustained by him in consequence of the breach.

Monetary compensation for breach of contract is referred to as 'damages'. A party may be claiming for expenses incurred in reliance on a contract being performed (**reliance loss**), or in respect of the benefits they expected to gain from performance of the contract, such as profit (**expectation loss**).

Reliance loss damages were awarded in *Anglia Television Ltd v Reed* (1972), to cover the expenses of preparing for a film production which had to be abandoned when the defendant withdrew from the contract. Expectation loss was not claimed as it was impossible to assess what profit might have been made had the film been produced.

Where **expectation loss** is claimed, the loss, unlike reliance loss, may not be easily quantifiable, but, nevertheless is awarded. In *Chaplin v Hicks* (1911), breach of contract, depriving the plaintiff of an opportunity to compete in a beauty contest final, entitled her to damages for the lost opportunity. Of course, some expectation loss claims, notably for lost profit, may be highly speculative but, as the Court of Appeal noted in *Parabola Investments Ltd v Browallia Cal Ltd* (2010), sensible limits are imposed by the principles of causation, remoteness and the duty to mitigate loss (see 7.7.1 and 7.7.2 below).

The estimation of what damages are to be paid by a party in breach can be divided into two parts.

7.7.1 Remoteness of damage

This involves consideration of causation and the remoteness of cause from effect, to determine how far down a chain of events a defendant is liable. **The rule** in *Hadley v Baxendale* (1854) states that damages will only be awarded for losses which arise naturally, that is, in the natural course of things; or which both parties may reasonably be supposed to have contemplated, when the contract was made, as a probable result of its breach.

❖ KEY CASE *Hadley v Baxendale* (1854)

Hadley, a miller in Gloucester, had engaged the defendant to take a broken mill-shaft to Greenwich so that it could be used as a pattern for a new one. The defendant delayed delivering the shaft, thus causing the mill to be out of action for longer than it would otherwise have been. Hadley sued for loss of profit during that period of additional delay. It was held that it was **not a natural consequence of the delay** in delivering the shaft that the mill should be out of action. The mill might, for example, have had a spare shaft. So, the first part of the rule stated above did not apply. Additionally, Baxendale was unaware the mill would be out of action during the delay, so the second part of the rule did not apply, either. Baxendale, therefore, although liable for breach of contract, was not liable for the loss of profit caused by the delay.

Note: Wessanen Foods Ltd v Jofson Ltd (2006), considered which losses came within the *Hadley* rule.

The effect of the first part of the rule in *Hadley v Baxendale* is that the party in breach is **deemed to expect** the normal consequences of the breach, whether they actually expected them or not. The House of Lords, in *Transfield Shipping Inc v Mercator Shipping Inc* (2008), re-examined the rule. They concluded that, *not only* should the loss be foreseeable, *but* that the parties, at the time of contracting, should be able to forsee the *type* of loss which could follow from breach.

Under the second part of the rule, however, the party in breach can only be **liable for abnormal consequences** where they **have actual knowledge** that the abnormal consequences might follow.

Thus, in *Victoria Laundry Ltd v Newham Industries Ltd* (1949), the defendants contracted to deliver a new boiler to the plaintiffs, but delayed in delivery. The plaintiffs claimed for normal loss of profit during the period of delay, and for the loss of abnormal profits from a highly lucrative contract which they could have undertaken had the boiler been delivered on time. It was decided that damages could be recovered in regard to the normal profits, as that loss was a natural consequence of the delay. The second claim failed, however, as the loss was not a normal one; it was a consequence of an especially lucrative contract, about which the defendant knew nothing.

The decision in *Victoria Laundry* was confirmed by the House of Lords in *Czarnikow v Koufos (The Heron II)* (1967), although the actual test for remoteness was reformulated in terms of whether the consequence should have been *within the reasonable contemplation of the parties at the time of the contract*.

In *The Heron II*, the defendants contracted to carry sugar from Constanza to Basra. They knew that the plaintiffs were sugar merchants, but did not know that they intended to sell the sugar as soon as it reached Basra. During a period in which the ship was delayed, the market price of sugar fell. The plaintiffs claimed damages for the loss from the defendants. It was held that the plaintiffs could recover. It was **common knowledge** that the market value of such commodities could fluctuate; therefore, the loss was within the reasonable contemplation of the parties (see also: *Bailey v HSS Alarms* (2000)).

In *John Grimes Partnership Ltd v Gubbins* (2013) the Court of Appeal held that a property developer could recover damages for losses suffered from a diminution in market value following the failure of a consulting engineer to perform tasks by the agreed date. In ruling that the developer could claim damages of up to £400,000 for the loss in value of the land in question the court held that the fall in property prices at the start of the recession was reasonably foreseeable.

As a consequence of the test for remoteness, a party may be liable for consequences which, although within the reasonable contemplation of the parties, are much **more serious in effect than would be expected**. In *H Parsons (Livestock) Ltd v Uttley Ingham & Co* (1978), the plaintiffs, who were pig farmers, bought a large food hopper from the defendants. While erecting it, the plaintiffs failed to unseal a ventilator on the top of the hopper. Because of a lack of ventilation, the pig food stored in the hopper became mouldy. The pigs that ate the mouldy food contracted a rare intestinal disease and died. It was held that the defendants were liable for the loss of the pigs. The food that was affected by bad storage caused the illness as a natural consequence of the breach, and the death from such illness was not too remote.

As the question of foreseeability is often fraught one, businesses may well find it efficacious to inform each other of matters such as further contracts dependent on the current one, at the time of contracting.

It should be noted that the foreseeability test in contract is **not** the same as that in the law of tort.

See Chapter ◀ 9

7.7.2 Measure of damages

The intention is to **compensate an injured party** for any financial loss sustained as a consequence of another party's breach. The object is not to punish the party in breach, so the amount of damages awarded can never be greater than the actual loss suffered; this principle was confirmed in *Omak Maritime Ltd v Mamola Challenger Shipping Co Ltd* (2010)(see below). The aim is to put the injured party in the same position they would have been in had the contract been properly performed. There are a number of procedures which seek to achieve this end:

- *The market rule*
  Where the breach relates to a contract for the sale of goods, damages are usually assessed in line with the market rule. This means that if goods are not delivered under a contract, the buyer is entitled to go into the market and buy similar goods, paying the market price prevailing at

the time. They can then claim the difference in price between what they paid and the original contract price as damages. Conversely, if a buyer refuses to accept goods under a contract, the seller can sell the goods in the market and accept the prevailing market price. Any difference, between the price they receive and the contract price, can be claimed in damages (see ss 50 and 51 of the SoGA 1979, below at 8.6).

- *The duty to mitigate losses*

  The injured party is **under a duty to take all reasonable steps to minimise their loss**. So, in the above examples, the buyer of goods which are not delivered has to buy the replacements as cheaply as possible, and the seller of goods which are not accepted has to try to get as good a price as they can when they sell them.

  In *Omak Maritime Ltd v Mamola Challenger Shipping Co* (2010) it was held that any money recovered by way of mitigation, following a breach of contract, must be taken into account when assessing the claimant's loss. The fundamental principle is that the claimant's actual position after mitigation must be compared to what it would have been had the contract been performed. In making such a comparison, any benefits received must be set off against the loss incurred from the original breach.

  In *Payzu v Saunders* (1919), the parties contracted for the sale of fabric, to be delivered and paid for in instalments. When Payzu failed to pay the first instalment on time, Saunders refused to make further deliveries unless Payzu agreed to pay cash on delivery. Payzu refused to accept this and sued for breach of contract. The court decided that the delay in payment had not given the defendant the right to repudiate the contract, so he had breached the contract by refusing further delivery. The buyer, however, should have mitigated his loss by agreeing to pay cash on delivery. His damages were restricted, therefore, to what he would have lost under those terms, namely, interest over the repayment period.

  Western Web Offset Printers Ltd v Independent Media Ltd (1995) highlights the problems which can arise in relation to the market rule and the mitigation rule. The parties made a contract under which the plaintiff would publish 48 issues of a weekly newspaper for the defendant. In the action which followed the defendant's repudiation of the contract, the issue in question was the extent of damages to be awarded. The plaintiff argued that damages should be decided on the basis of gross profits, merely subtracting direct expenses such as paper and ink, but not labour costs and other overheads; this would result in a total claim of some £177,000. The defendant argued that damages should be on the basis of net profits, with labour and other overheads being taken into account; this would result in a claim of some £38,000. Although the trial judge awarded the lesser sum, the Court of Appeal decided that he had drawn an incorrect analogy from cases involving sale of goods. It was not simply a matter of calculating the difference between cost price and selling price to reach a nominal profit. The plaintiff had been unable to replace the work, due to the economic recession, and, therefore, had not been able to mitigate the loss. Accordingly, the plaintiff was entitled to the full amount that would have been due, in order to allow it to defray the expenses that it would have had to pay during the period that the contract should have lasted.

- *Time of assessment*

  Though courts may exercise discretion, depending on particular circumstances, damages are usually assessed as at the **time of breach** (see *Golden Strait Corp v Nippon Yusen Kubishka (The Golden Victory)* (2007)).

- *Non-pecuniary loss*

  Originally, damages could not be recovered where the loss sustained through breach of contract was non-financial. Nowadays, non-pecuniary damages can be recovered, as in *Jarvis v Swan Tours Ltd* (1973). The defendant's brochure stated that various facilities were available at a particular ski resort. However, the facilities were much inferior to those advertised. The plaintiff sued for breach of contract. The Court of Appeal decided that Jarvis was entitled to recover not just the financial loss he suffered, which was not substantial, but also damages for loss of entertainment and enjoyment; damages could be recovered for mental distress in appropriate cases, and this was one of them. The scope of recovery of damages for 'distress and disappointment' was examined by the House of Lords in *Farley v Skinner* (2001).

Particular problems arise in relation to estimating damages in construction contracts. Where a builder has not carried out the agreed work, or has carried it out inadequately, there is breach of contract and the aggrieved party will be entitled to damages. The usual measure of such damages is the cost of carrying out the work or repairing the faulty work. However, this may not be the case where the costs of remedying the defects are **disproportionate** to the difference in value between what was supplied and what was ordered.

❖ KEY CASE *Ruxley Electronics and Construction Ltd v Forsyth* (1995)

The parties had made a contract for the construction of a swimming pool and buildings for £70,000. Although the contract required the pool to be 7 ft 6 in deep at one end, the constructed depth was 6 ft 9 in. Fixing the error would require a full reconstruction, costing £20,000. The trial judge decided that the measure of damages for the plaintiff's breach was the difference between the value of the pool actually provided and the value of the pool contracted for. He decided that the difference was nil, but awarded the defendant £2,500 for loss of amenity. The Court of Appeal overturned that award, holding that Forsyth was entitled to the full cost of reconstruction. However, the House of Lords reinstated the trial judge's decision. They considered that, in building contracts, there were two possible ways of determining damages: either the difference in value, as used by the trial judge; or the cost of reinstatement, as preferred by the Court of Appeal. As the costs of reinstatement would have been out of all proportion to the benefit gained, the House of Lords awarded the difference in value. According to Lord Jauncey, 'damages are designed to compensate for an established loss and not to provide a gratuity to the aggrieved party'. Lord Lloyd said that **the plaintiff could not, in all cases, 'obtain the monetary equivalent of specific performance'**.

Note: Evidentally, construction contracts are to be treated differently from sale of goods contracts: purchasers of goods can reject them under s 13 of the SoGA 1979 where they do not match their description, even if they are otherwise fit for the purpose for which they were bought (see 8.2 below).

7.7.3 Restitutionary damages

Though the avowed aim of damages is compensatory, not punitive, there are some exceptional circumstances where **a party will be deprived of the benefits of his breach of contract**:

❖ KEY CASE *HM Attorney General v Blake* (2000)

Blake, jailed for treason as a spy for the Soviet Union, escaped and then wrote his autobiography. This was alleged to be a breach of his contract of employment with the British Intelligence Service. The Attorney General sought an injunction to prevent publishers from paying Blake £90,000 royalties on his book. The Court of Appeal granted the injunction on the ground that it was against public policy for a criminal to profit from his crime. The House of Lords did not uphold the grant of the injunction, as they could find no statutory or common law authority for such grant; accordingly, the money could be paid to Blake. However, Blake's treachery made the case exceptional, allowing application of the principle of restitution to Blake's breach of contract. Therefore, the Attorney General recovered the royalties from Blake.

(See further *Experience Hendrix LLC v PPX Enterprises Inc* (2003).)

7.7.4 Liquidated damages and penalties

It is possible, and common in business contracts, for the parties to state in advance the amount of damages that will have to be paid in the event of any breach occurring. Damages under such a provision are known as **liquidated damages**. They will only be recognised by the court if they represent a **genuine pre-estimate of loss** and are not intended to operate as a penalty against the party in breach. Where the liquidated damages clause is upheld, the agreed damages are awarded, regardless of the actual loss. If the court considers the provision to be a penalty, it is ineffective and the court will assess the damages in the normal way, that is, award **unliquidated damages**.

In deciding the legality of such clauses, the courts consider the effect, rather than the form, of the clause, as can be seen in *Cellulose Acetate Silk Co Ltd v Widnes Foundry* (1925) *Ltd* (1933). There, the contract expressly stated that damages for late payment would be a *penalty* of £20 per week. In fact, the sum of £20 was in no way excessive and represented a reasonable estimate of the likely loss. On that basis, the House of Lords enforced the clause, in spite of its actual wording.

The Court of Appeal, in *Murray v LeisurePlay Ltd* (2005), indicated what factors should be examined in determining whether a clause was a penalty or not, namely:

- the breaches to which it applies;
- the amount payable for breach;
- the amount which would be payable as unliquidated damages; and
- whether the clause was a deterrent or a genuine pre-estimate of loss.

In *Duffen v FRA Bo SpA* (1998), it was held that a term in an agency contract which established so-called 'liquidated damages' for the dismissal of the agent at £100,000, was an unenforceable penalty clause. This was despite the agreement specifically stating that £100,000 was 'a reasonable pre-estimate of the loss and damage which the agent will suffer on the termination of the agreement'. The court held that, although the wording of the agreement was persuasive, it was outweighed by the fact that the damages did not alter in proportion to the time remaining to be served in the agreement. Consequently, the claimant could only claim normal damages, although these could be augmented under the Commercial Agents (Council Directive) Regulations 1993.

See Chapter 12 →

In *Azimut-Benetti SpA v Darrell Marcus Healey* (2010) the court upheld a very onerous liquidated damages clause which was triggered by termination of a shipbuilding contract. In that case the liquidated damages clause provided that, in the event of lawful termination, Azimut would be entitled to retain and/or recover an amount equal to 20% of the contract price of €38 million. When Shoreacres, a company wholly owned by the defendant who had personally guaranteed its debts under the contract, failed to pay the first instalment, Azimut terminated the contract, and sought summary judgment for €7·1 million plus the deposit of €500,000. The court held that, on the facts of the case, the provision was 'not even arguably' a penalty clause and, read as a whole, it represented a commercially justifiable balance between the parties' interests. Consequently the €7·1 million had to be paid and the deposit retained.

The whole question of penalty clauses is fraught. It is obviously advantageous, in a business context, for the parties to a contract to know with certainty what the financial consequences of any breach of the contract will be, so as to allow them to manage their risk properly. However, the possibility of the courts subsequently holding a damages clause to be punitive introduces the very uncertainty that such a clause was designed to avoid.

7.7.5 *Quantum meruit*

Quantum meruit means that **a party should be awarded as much as he has earned**, and the award can be contractual or quasi-contractual (see 7.12 below). If the contracting parties do not determine the reward for performance, then, in the event of dispute, the court will award a *reasonable sum*.

Payment may also be claimed *quantum meruit*, where a party has carried out work under a void contract and the other party has accepted that work. In *Craven-Ellis v Canons Ltd* (1936), the plaintiff had acted as the managing director of a company under a deed of contract. However, since he had not acquired any shares in the company, as required by its articles, his appointment was void. He sued to recover remuneration for the service he had provided prior to his removal. The court decided that, although he could not claim under contract, he was entitled to recover a reasonable sum on the basis of *quantum meruit*.

Furthermore, where the defendant prevents the claimant from completing performance, the claimant may be entitled to payment for work done so far. In *Planche v Colburn* (1831), the plaintiff contracted to write a book for the defendants, with payment to be made on completion of the manuscript. The defendants abandoned publication plans before the manuscript was completed; the plaintiff, having done some research and writing for the manuscript, could claim for that work done.

7.8 Specific Performance

It may suit a party to break a contract and pay damages; through an order for specific performance; however, the party in breach **may be instructed to complete their part of the contract**. The following rules govern this remedy:

- Specific performance will only be granted where the common law remedy of damages is inadequate. It is not usually applied to contracts concerning the sale of goods where replacements are readily available. It is most commonly granted in cases involving the sale of land and where the subject matter of the contract is unique (for example, a painting by Picasso).
- Specific performance will not be granted where the court cannot supervise its enforcement. For this reason, it will not be available in respect of contracts of employment or personal service.

  In *Co-operative Insurance Society Ltd v Argyll Stores (Holdings) Ltd* (1997), the House of Lords held that it would be inappropriate to enforce a covenant to trade entered into by the defendant company. The case concerned a shopping centre owned by the claimants, in which the defendant's Safeway supermarket was the largest attraction. Although it had contracted in its lease to keep its supermarket open during usual trading hours, the defendant company decided to close the shop, causing significant threat to the continued operation of the shopping centre. The plaintiff's action for specific performance to force Argyll to keep the store open was unsuccessful at first instance, although it was supported in the Court of Appeal. The House of Lords, however, restored the traditional approach by refusing to issue an order for specific performance as it would require constant supervision by the court. Damages were held to be the appropriate remedy.

- Specific performance is an equitable remedy which the court grants at its discretion. It will not be granted where the claimant has not acted properly; neither will it be granted where mutuality is lacking. Thus, a minor will not be granted specific performance, because no such order could be awarded against a minor.

7.9 Injunction

This is also an **equitable order of the court, which directs a person not to break their contract**. It can have the effect of indirectly enforcing contracts for personal service. Thus, an injunction could be used to prevent an employee breaching a confidentiality clause in an employment contract, but will not be granted where its effect would be to prevent a person from working. An injunction was refused in *Page One Records Ltd v Britton* (1968), because it would force the defendants to wind up their pop group, The Troggs, if they did not engage the plaintiffs as their agents/managers.

An injunction will only be granted to enforce negative covenants within the agreement and cannot be used to enforce positive obligations. In *Whitwood Chemical Co v Hardman* (1891), the defendant had contracted to give the whole of his time to the plaintiffs, his employers, but he occasionally worked for others. The plaintiffs applied for an injunction to prevent him working for anyone else. No injunction was granted. Hardman had said what he would do, not what he would not do; therefore, there was no negative promise to enforce.

7.10 Action for the Agreed Contract Price

In some circumstances, a party may sue for non-payment of the price rather than seeking damages for breach. For example, s 49 of the SoGA 1979 gives this right to the seller where either the buyer fails to pay on the agreed date, or ownership in the goods has been transferred to the buyer.

7.11 Repudiation

Where there is a breach of condition, the party not in breach has the option of treating the contract as repudiated, so that he need not perform his contractual obligations.

7.12 Quasi-contractual Remedies

Quasi-contractual remedies are based on the assumption that a person should not receive any undue advantage from the fact that there is no contractual remedy to force them to account for it. An important quasi-contractual remedy is an action for money paid and received. If no contract comes into existence by reason of a total failure of consideration, then, under this action, any goods or money received will have to be returned to the party who supplied them.

Summary

Contract (4): Discharge of a Contract

Discharge by agreement

- Executory contracts may be discharged by mutual exchange of promises to discharge.

- Where one party has executed the contract, the other is only released from the obligation to perform by providing new consideration.

Discharge by performance

- As a general rule, discharge by performance requires complete and exact performance of the obligations in the contract, except where the contract is divisible, is capable of being fulfilled by substantial performance, performance has been prevented by the other party or partial performance has been accepted by the other party.

Tender of performance

- Tender of performance (an offer to perform the contractual obligations) discharges liability under a contract.

Discharge by frustration

- Frustrating events, such as destruction of the subject matter of the contract, discharge the contract.
- A contract will not be frustrated where the contract expressly provides for the frustrating event, nor where the frustration is self-induced nor where an alternative method of performance is available.
- Contracts frustrated at common law are void from the time of frustration.
- Under the Law Reform (Frustrated Contracts) Act 1943, money paid before frustration is recoverable and money due is recoverable/not payable. In the court's discretion, claims may be made for expenses incurred prior to frustration.

Discharge by breach

- Breach may be anticipatory or by failure to perform/defective performance of the contract.
- Breach of a contract entitles the innocent party to damages. Additionally, a breach of condition entitles the innocent party to treat the contract as discharged.

Damages

- Damages may be *liquidated* or *unliquidated*.
- Assessment of unliquidated damages is determined by the rules of *remoteness* (reasonable forsee-ability) and *mitigation of loss*.
- Damages may be awarded for pecuniary and non-pecuniary loss.
- Restitutionary damages are only awarded exceptionally.

Quantum meruit

- Where the contract does not fix the price, a reasonable sum is payable.
- Where a person is prevented from completing performance by the other party, payment can be claimed for work done so far.
- Payment may be claimed for work done under a void contract which is accepted by the other party.

Specific performance

- A party in breach may be instructed to complete their part of the contract.
- An order of specific performance will only be granted in cases where the common law remedy of damages is inadequate and supervision of enforcement is not required.
- Specific performance is an equitable remedy, which the court grants at its discretion.

Injunction

- This is also an equitable order of the court, which directs a person not to break their contract.

Quasi-contractual remedies

- These are based on the assumption that a person should not receive any undue advantage from the fact that there is no contractual remedy to force them to account for it.

Further Reading

Atkinson, D, 'Value judgment' (2006) NLJ 1045 (*Quantum meruit* payments in the construction industry, when no contract was concluded)

Furmston, MP, *Cheshire, Fifoot and Furmston's Law of Contract*, 16th edn, 2012, Oxford: OUP

Kramer, A, 'Money isn't everything – contract damages for non-pecuniary loss' (2003) SLR 16 (views on cases dealing with the assessment of non-pecuniary loss)

Macdonald, E, 'Contractual damages for mental distress' [1994] Journal of Contract Law 134 (examination of when damages are recoverable for mental distress)

Peel, E, *Treitel on the Law of Contract*, 13th edn, 2011, London: Sweet & Maxwell

Phang, A, 'The Crumbling Edifice? The award of contractual damages for mental distress' [2003] Journal of Business Law 341 (examination of when such damages will be awarded)

Poole, J, *Casebook on Contract Law*, 109th edn, 2010, Oxford: OUP

Richards, P, *The Law of Contract*, 11th edn, 2013, Harlow: Pearson Longman

Stone, R, 'Damages – the forgotten topic' (1996) SLR (Summer) 15 (brief overview of rules relating to damages)

Websites

www.statutelaw.gov.uk (for text of Law Reform (Frustrated Contracts) Act 1943)

www.lawreports.co.uk (daily summaries of new cases)

Chapter 8

Sale of Goods and Supply of Services

Chapter Contents

Law in Context: Sale of Goods and Services – a Consumer's Charter?

The sale and supply of both goods and services can give rise to civil and criminal liability, the latter being of particular importance in relation to the protection of consumers. A detailed examination of all the laws relating to all transactions for the sale or supply of goods/services is outside the remit of this book; therefore, civil and criminal laws relating to the commonest of such transactions will be considered below.

One of the commonest transactions made by businesses is the contract for the sale of goods to other businesses or consumers. However, goods may be supplied under contracts other than sale, such as a hire contract. There, the owner of goods transfers possession for a fixed period but retains ownership; common examples are television rental, rental of office equipment and car hire.

A person may also be supplied with goods as a gift. Though the recipient has no contract, defects in the goods can, in some circumstances, give recourse against a business supplier.

8.1 The Sale of Goods Act 1979

This Act, which replaced previous legislation, regulates contracts for the sale of goods. Some of its provisions have been amended; in particular, note should be taken of the Sale and Supply of Goods to Consumers Regulations 2002 (2002 Regulations), which amend the Sale of Goods Act 1979, mainly where the buyer of goods is a consumer. The Regulations define a 'consumer' as a natural person who is acting for purposes which are outside his or her business. All references to the Sale of Goods Act 1979 (SoGA 1979) are to the provisions as amended.

8.1.1 Definition

Under s 2(1) SoGA 1979, a contract for the sale of goods is one 'by which the seller transfers or agrees to transfer the property in the goods to the buyer for a money consideration, called the price'.

Under this definition **property** means 'ownership', so the object of the contract is to transfer ownership in the goods to the buyer. The **buyer's consideration must be money**. Accordingly, an exchange of goods is not within the Act; following *Connell Estate Agents v Begej* (1993), however, it can be argued that part exchange contracts are within the Act, particularly where the value of the goods given in part exchange is apparent.

'Goods' (defined in s 61(1)) must be the subject matter of the contract. 'Goods' includes personal property of a moveable type (anything which can be physically possessed, and is not attached to the land). Thus, crops become goods on harvesting. Money becomes goods when antique or collectable (and no longer legal tender). The definition of 'goods' excludes real property (for example, land and buildings); and those in action (for example, debts, cheques and currency in circulation).

8.1.2 Form of the agreement

The rules for forming any contract, such as capacity to contract, must be met, but there are no requirements as to form: the contract can be oral, written or inferred from conduct, as might be the case in a supermarket sale, where the parties are unlikely to actually state that they wish to buy and sell the goods.

8.1.3 The price of the goods

As an essential element of the contract under s 2(1), the price is usually expressly agreed; for example, when buying goods in a shop, the buyer agrees to pay the marked price. Section 8(1) confirms that the price may be fixed by the contract, and indicates that the price can be determined by a course of dealing between the parties or in a manner agreed by the contract.

Thus, when re-ordering goods without reference to the price, the parties can be taken to agree that the price paid in a previous transaction applies to this contract. Equally, the parties might validly agree that an independent third party should determine the price payable. If that third party does not make, or is prevented from making, that determination of the price payable, s 9 applies:

(1) Where there is an agreement to sell goods on the terms that the price is to be fixed by the valuation of a third party, and he cannot or does not make the valuation, the agreement is avoided; but if the goods or any part of them have been delivered to and appropriated by the buyer, he must pay a reasonable price for them.

(2) Where the third party is prevented from making the valuation by the fault of the seller or buyer, the party not at fault may maintain an action for damages against the party at fault.

However, some problems arising from determination of the price are not specifically addressed by the Sale of Goods Act 1979. Though s 8(2) indicates that 'a reasonable price' is payable where the price has not been determined under s 8(1), it has been suggested that failure to agree a price or a manner of fixing it means that there is no contract concluded and s 8(2) cannot operate to make such an arrangement a contract.

In *May and Butcher v The King* (1934), an agreement for the purchase of government tentage provided that the price was to be agreed from time to time; effectively, they agreed to make later agreements as to the price. Had there been no mention of the price at all, then failure to actually agree a price would not mean that there was no contract: a 'reasonable price' would have been payable, under the SoGA 1893. However, as the parties expressly stated that the price was to be agreed later, it was held they were agreeing to agree and had not intended to make a binding contract.

In *Foley v Classique Coaches Ltd* (1934), the defendants agreed to purchase petrol from the plaintiffs, at a price 'to be agreed by the parties from time to time'. Failing agreement, the price was to be settled by arbitration. The Court of Appeal found that, by providing a method (arbitration) for fixing the price, the parties had shown an intention to make a legally binding agreement. Accordingly, it seems that *intention to be bound* is the key issue, and agreement as to price is merely a factor in determining such intention.

8.2 Seller's Implied Obligations

As well as performing express undertakings in the contract, the seller must also comply with certain terms implied into the contract by the SoGA 1979, regardless of whether the buyer is a consumer or a business. These implied terms are of particular importance to the consumer, who rarely negotiates and agrees express terms. In supermarket sales, for example, it is unlikely that there will be any discussion, let alone specific undertakings given, as to the quality and functions of the goods sold. Nevertheless, the implied terms place a seller under obligations as to matters such as quality and functions of the goods that he or she sells. The seller's obligations under the implied terms apply **even though the seller is not actually at fault**; liability is undertaken by the act of selling the goods. So, if goods do not function properly because of a manufacturing defect, the buyer may sue the seller for breach of contract. Of course, though the seller must take responsibility to his buyer, such loss could be recouped by suing the party who supplied him with the goods.

Finally, it should be realised that the implied terms of the SoGA 1979 are classified as conditions or warranties, which give rise to different remedies for breach (see below).

8.2.1 Title (s 12)

As already stated, the objective of a contract for the sale of goods is to buy ownership of goods; accordingly, **s 12(1) implies a condition into the contract that the seller has the 'right to sell' the goods**.

A seller who cannot transfer ownership, does not have the 'right to sell'. In *Rowland v Divall* (1923), the buyer of a car did not receive ownership, as the seller did not own it. There was a breach of s 12(1) and he could recover the full purchase price paid (s 54), despite having used the car for four months. Where ownership is not transferred, *there is a total failure of consideration*, as the buyer does not receive what he contracted to buy. Clearly, legal ownership is of paramount importance, so transferring use and possession of goods only is insufficient for performance of a sale of goods contract.

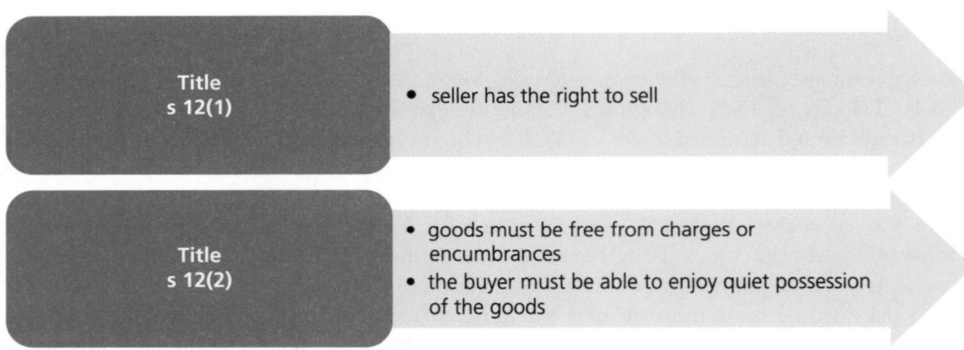

Figure 8.1 Sale of Goods Act 1979 (as amended) Implied Terms s 12

Section 12(2) implies into the contract warranties of quiet possession and freedom from encumbrances. Effectively, the seller undertakes that the buyer's title will not be interfered with or be subject to anyone else's rights, except in so far as such are known by or disclosed to the buyer before the contract is made.

In *Rubicon Computer Systems Ltd v United Paints Ltd* (2000), the supplier and installer of a computer system wrongfully attached a time-lock which prevented the owners accessing the system; this was a breach of s 12(2). In *Microbeads AC v Vinhurst Road Markings* (1975), the seller sold some road marking machines to the buyers. Unbeknown to the seller at the time of the sale, another firm was in the process of patenting this type of equipment, although rights to enforce the patent did not commence until after the contract between the seller and buyer was made. A patent action was subsequently brought against the buyer, who then claimed that the seller was in breach of s 12(1), as he had no right to sell, and was in breach of the warranty of quiet possession. It was held that, at the time of sale, the seller had every right to sell the goods, but breached the warranty for quiet possession, because that amounted to an undertaking as to the future – that he would be able to use the goods without disturbance. The patent owner's claim prevented use. However, the decision has been criticised as it could imply that the seller undertakes there will never be future interference with title. Such an interpretation would produce the untenable position that, for example, a subsequent government requisition of goods would be a breach of warranty by the seller. Perhaps that situation can be distinguished from the facts of the case, as the third party patent application had already been made at the time of the contract of sale.

8.2.2 Description (s 13(1))

There is an **implied condition that, where goods are sold by description, they must correspond with that description**.

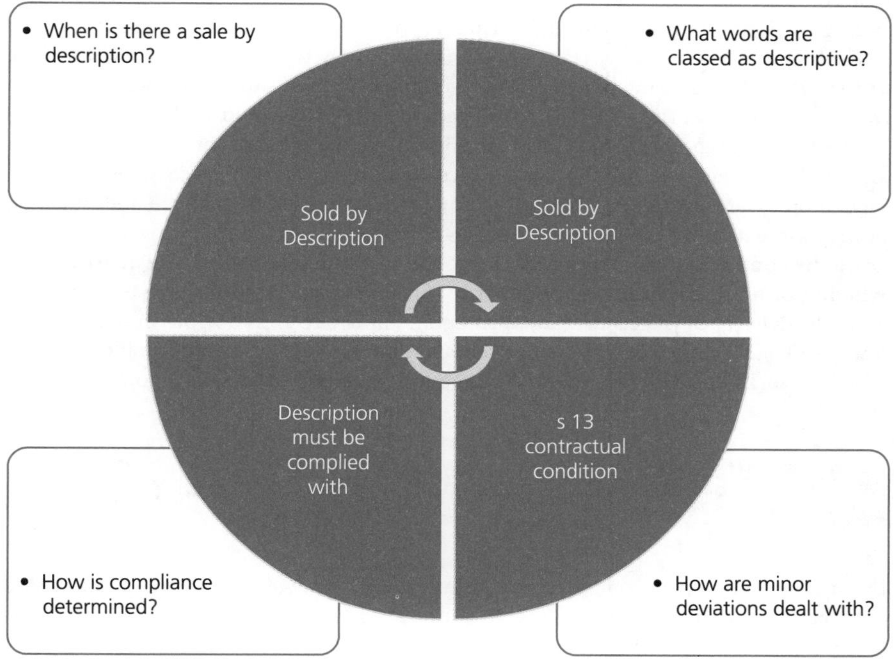

Figure 8.2 Sale of Goods Act 1979 and s 13

- **Goods are sold 'by description'** where the buyer does not see the goods but relies on a description of them, or where the buyer sees the goods but relies on terms describing features of the goods or a description on the goods themselves. So, descriptive words printed on packaging could form part of the description; for example, if someone purchased a packet labelled 'Cornflakes' they would rely on that word as indicating that the contents were cornflakes.

  Not all words used by the seller are part of the contract description (for example, it is a 'moot' point whether the ingredients list on the 'Cornflakes' packet is part of the contract description). *Reliance* on the words as *identifying* the goods being bought is the important issue (see *Harlingdon and Leinster Enterprises Ltd v Christopher Hull Fine Art Ltd* (1990)), and this was illustrated in *Beale v Taylor* (1967). The buyer answered an advertisement for the sale of a 'Herald Convertible 1961'. Having bought the car, he found it consisted of the back half of a 1961 model welded to the front half of an earlier model. The description in the advertisement was clearly relied on in buying the car and was, therefore, part of the contract description, which had not been complied with.

  The description may be very simple; in *Grant v Australian Knitting Mills* (1936), the buyer asked for 'underpants', which was the contract description, as that was how the buyer identified what he was purchasing. The court also indicated that retail sales, where goods were asked for over the counter or chosen from a display, were still sales by description. In other contracts, the description may be a very detailed one, such as a formula (see, for example, *Ashington Piggeries v Christopher Hill Ltd* (1972)) or design specifications. It is not always easy to determine which words used are part of the contract description. In *Re Moore & Co and Landauer & Co* (1921), the contract required tins of fruit to be packed in cases of 30. The correct quantity of tins was delivered, but some were in cases of 24 tins. The court decided that a stipulated method of packaging was part of the contract description, so there was a breach of s 13(1).

However, as later authority leans towards looking only to those words which the *buyer relies on as identifying the goods* being bought, the case might be decided differently today. Thus, in *Reardon Smith Line Ltd v Hansen Tangen* (1976), a contract stated a ship would be built at 'Yard 354'; in fact it was built at another yard in the same port. The yard was *not* part of the contract description as, on the evidence, it had no significance to the parties as a place with any particular reputation. Where *goods are 'sold as seen'*, this is an indication that the goods are not sold under any description within the meaning of s 13.

- **Once the contractual description of the goods has been established, the question arises of whether or not it has been complied with.** This may be easy to determine in some cases (for example, delivery of jackets instead of trousers), but is often less obvious. In *Arcos Ltd v Ronaasen & Son* (1933), a delivery of staves, some of which were nine-sixteenths of an inch thick instead of half an inch thick, as required by the contract, was a breach of description.

❖ KEY CASE *Ashington Piggeries v Christopher Hill* (1972)

Facts:

By written contract, the seller agreed to make up a formula specified by the buyer to produce a 'vitamin fortified' mink food to be called 'King Size'. One ingredient in the formula was herring meal, and that used by the seller was contaminated and harmful to mink. If 'mink food' was part of the contract description under s 13(1), there would be breach of condition, as a product which harmed mink could hardly be correctly described as 'mink food'.

Decision:

However, the House of Lords decided that the statement that the end product was to be a 'mink food' was not part of the contract description; the contract description was the specified formula which indicated what the end product was. Therefore, it was the words 'herring meal' in issue as regards compliance with the contract description. Despite the fact the contaminated herring meal was harmful to mink, and even potentially harmful to other animals, it was decided that the contract description was complied with, as the meal was still identifiable as 'herring meal'.

Comment: This finding has been criticised on the basis that 'herring meal' should be regarded as meaning 'a food which can be safely fed to animals'; if it cannot fulfil that function, it is not 'herring meal'.

Though strict compliance with the description was required in cases such as *Arcos*, where there was a breach even though the staves could still have been used as the buyer intended (to make barrels), the *de minimis* rule may allow minor deviations in certain situations. Where a description has acquired a meaning in the trade, goods which comply with that trade meaning will comply with s 13(1) even if they do not comply with the strict wording of the contract description. In *Peter Darlington Partners Ltd v Gosho Co Ltd* (1964), there was a contract for the purchase of canary seed on a 'pure basis'. The buyers refused to accept 98% pure seed, but, because 98% pure was the highest standard in the trade, there was no breach of description and the buyers were in breach themselves for wrongfully refusing the seed.

- Although s 13(1) is a condition of the contract, it **does not have the effect of making every descriptive word a condition**. The usual contractual principles concerning conditions, warranties and pre-contract representations apply.
- Section 13 also indicates that, **where goods are sold by sample and description**, there must be compliance with both sample and description. It is not sufficient that the goods comply with either description or sample. Sale by sample is the subject of s 15 (see below).
- Section 13(1) **does not require that the seller is undertaking a business transaction**, so the *private seller*, such as a person selling goods through a classified advertisement column, *has the obligation to supply goods complying with the contract description*. Section 13(1) is the only implied term of the Act binding on a private seller, so the buyer contracting with a private seller has much less protection than when goods are bought from a business.

8.2.3 Satisfactory quality (s 14(2))

The original implied condition of 'merchantable quality' was replaced by the Sale and Supply of Goods Act 1994 and s 14(2) now **implies a condition that the goods shall be of satisfactory quality**.

Section 14(2) does not apply to private sales; the **goods must be sold in the course of a business**. 'Sale in the course of a business' is not defined in the SoGA 1979, but in *Stevenson v Rogers* (1999), it was held that a fisherman 'acted in the course of business' when he sold his trawler. Although he did not deal in vessels, it was a *sale connected with his business*. (See also *R & B Customs Brokers Ltd v UDT* (1988), which discusses the meaning of 'in the course of business' in the context of s 12(1) of the UCTA 1977 (see above).) Thus, goods which come within s 14(2) include not only goods sold in the normal course of business, but also goods used in or connected with the business, for example, the sale of a van which has been used in a grocery business.

- The 'satisfactory quality' requirement applies to the **goods actually supplied under the contract**. In *Wilson v Rickett Cockerell* (1954), it was argued that explosives mixed in with a bag of Coalite did not amount to a breach of s 14(2), as the provision only applied to the goods *purchased*. The Court of Appeal rejected this argument.
- Goods **sold second hand** should be of satisfactory quality (see: *Business Appliances Specialists Ltd v Nationwide Credit Corp Ltd* (1988).
- **The meaning of 'satisfactory quality' must also be considered**. Section 14(2A) states that 'goods are of satisfactory quality if they meet the standard that a reasonable person would regard as satisfactory, taking account of any description of the goods, the price (if relevant) and all other relevant circumstances'.

❖ KEY CASE *Jewson Ltd v Boyhan* (2003)

Facts:

The buyer purchased heating boilers for the flats he was refurbishing for sale as low cost/energy efficient buildings. The boilers did not comply with low cost/energy efficient ratings but did provide adequate heating. At first instance, the boilers were found not to be of satisfactory quality under s 14(2A), because a reasonable person buying such a flat would expect it to be possible to show evidence of the low cost/energy efficient claim, that is, what a 'reasonable person' would expect had to be looked at in the context of the particular requirements of the contract.

Decision:
The Court of Appeal found there was no breach of s 14(2A); **the particular requirements of a buyer in the context of a particular contract were a matter for s 14(3) (see below), not s 14(2)**. Under s 14(2A), the factor to consider was the intrinsic quality of the goods; the court should determine what quality a reasonable person would expect from a heating boiler. The court decided a reasonable person would expect a boiler to heat adequately, which these boilers did; the expectations of a reasonable person in relation to these particular boilers (that they were low cost/energy efficient) should be decided under s 14(3).

Section 14(2A) must be read subject to s 14(2B), which states: '. . . the quality of the goods includes their state and condition and the following factors (among others) are in appropriate cases aspects of the quality of goods:

- fitness for all the purposes for which goods of the kind in question are commonly supplied;
- appearance and finish;
- freedom from minor defects;
- safety; and
- durability.'

This is considered to be a non-exhaustive list, and failure to comply with one of the factors will not necessarily result in goods being of unsatisfactory quality. As ss 14(2A) and (2B) resulted from decisions identifying shortcomings of previous legislation, earlier case law can be relevant in interpreting them. For example, the price of the goods may be extremely relevant in the case of second hand goods, but may not be of significance in relation to new goods sold at a reduced price in a sale (see *Business Appliances* (above)). In *Rogers v Parish (Scarborough) Ltd* (1987), the buyer bought a Range Rover for £16,000. It transpired that it had a defective engine, gearbox and bodywork, all of which were below the standard normally expected of a vehicle costing that much. It was held that the vehicle was not of merchantable quality. The fact that it was driveable and repairable was not enough; merchantable quality could only be judged by considering whether it was of a reasonable standard for a vehicle of its type. Accordingly, the buyer's rejection was valid and he could recover the purchase price and damages.

With regard to new cars, in *Bernstein v Pamson Motors (Golders Green) Ltd* (1987), the buyer purchased a new Nissan car for £8,000. He drove it for three weeks, covering some 140 miles. The engine then seized and had to undergo extensive repairs. The buyer rejected the car and refused to take it back after it had been repaired. The court felt that the **buyer of a new car was entitled to expect more than the buyer of a used car**, although how much more depended upon the nature of the defect, the length of time that it took to repair it and the price of the vehicle. The court distinguished between 'the merest cosmetic blemish on a new Rolls Royce which might render it unmerchantable, whereas on a humbler car it might not'. However, whilst the car was unmerchantable at the time of delivery, it was further held that a period of three weeks and 140 miles was a reasonable time to examine and try out the goods. The buyer was, therefore, deemed to have accepted the goods within the meaning of s 35 (see 8.7 below) and could only claim for breach of warranty.

It is unlikely that the decisions in *Rogers* and *Bernstein* in relation to breach of 'satisfactory quality' would have been different in the light of the new definition. Now, however, the **goods have to be**

suitable for all their common purposes under s 14(2B). As a result, *Aswan Engineering Establishment v Lupdine* (1987) (where containers which could fulfil some, though not all, of their normal uses (as now required by s 14(2B)), were of merchantable quality) may need to be reconsidered. However, the decision would probably stand in *Kendall (Henry) & Sons v William Lillico & Sons Ltd* (1968) (where groundnut extraction which harmed pheasants was still of merchantable quality, as it could be safely fed to other poultry, which was its normal use) and *Brown & Sons Ltd v Craiks Ltd* (1970) (where cloth which was suitable for its normal industrial use was of merchantable quality, though it was not fit for the buyer's intended purpose of dressmaking). Of course, the **real issue** for business sellers now, is what a court will determine **are** the normal uses of particular goods.

The 'factors' now specifically **include appearance and finish, as well as freedom from minor defects**. The former clearly refer to cosmetic defects which may or may not affect the quality of the goods by reference to the type of goods, price, etc. The same is true of minor defects. For example, a scratch on a Rolls Royce may affect quality, whereas a scratch on a second hand Ford Fiesta may not.

Safety is now a specific factor in assessing satisfactory quality, and it would appear that any matter which results in the goods being unsafe will fall within s 14(2).

Finally, **durability** of the goods falls to be considered, raising the contentious issue of the length of time for which a buyer can expect goods to remain of satisfactory quality. However, the test to be applied is that of the reasonable man, that is, *an objective test*. Again, an assessment of durability can only be made by reference to description, purpose, price, etc. Indeed, it would appear that it will only be in rare situations that these factors are considered in isolation from each other. Where the 2002 Regulations apply, the 'six month' rule will clarify the durability issue in some circumstances (see below). Note should be taken of s 14(2C), which provides for **exceptions to the 'satisfactory quality' requirement**. The implied condition of s 14(2) does not extend to **any 'matter'** making the quality of goods unsatisfactory:

(a) which is specifically drawn to the buyer's attention before the contract is made;
(b) which examination ought to reveal, where the buyer examines the goods before the contract is made; or
(c) which, in the case of a contract for sale by sample, would have been apparent on reasonable examination of the sample.

These exceptions are essentially the same as those in previous legislation; so, for example, if somebody buys a sweater labelled 'shop soiled', they cannot later argue that marks on the goods render them of unsatisfactory quality. Of course, if the sweater also has a hole in the sleeve which was not drawn to the buyer's attention, this defect could mean the sweater was not of satisfactory quality.

Nevertheless, it could be argued that the seller may now be able to invoke this exception not by actually specifying the defect (as was previously necessary), but by simply mentioning a 'matter' which could affect quality.

The relationship of s 14(2C) to goods 'sold as seen' was considered in *Bramhill and Bramhill v Edwards and Edwards* (2004). It should be remembered that the buyer is under no obligation to actually examine the goods before sale. If, however, the buyer chooses to undertake such an examination, then defects which that examination actually reveal, or ought to have revealed, will be excluded from s 14(2).

The 2002 Regulations add four new sub-sections to s 14(2), which apply where the buyer is a consumer, as defined in the 2002 Regulations. The effect of these additions is that, in determining whether goods are of 'satisfactory quality', the s 14(2B) factors that the court should consider will also include any 'public statements on the specific characteristics of the goods made about them by the seller, the producer or his representative, particularly in advertising or on labelling'. A 'producer' is not only the manufacturer but also a person who imports the goods into the EC or puts his name, sign or trademark on the goods. The English courts have already taken account of this factor but, as far as the retailer is concerned, having the obligation specifically stated in the 2002 Regulations will mean that more care must be taken to check advertisements and labelling of goods. Of course, many such statements will be taken to be 'sales puff', which will not affect the legal position; this was one of the arguments put forward by the company in *Carlill v Carbolic Smoke Ball Co*, as to why their advertisement was not an offer (see earlier chapters on formation of contracts).

It should be noted that this additional factor will not apply if the seller shows that he was not/could not have been aware of the statement, or it had been corrected at the time of contracting, or the buyer could not have been influenced to buy by the statement or the statement had been publicly withdrawn before sale. Though the additional factor, relating to advertising and labelling statements, only has to be considered by the courts where the buyer is a consumer, nevertheless, where the buyer is a business, the factor may be considered as a 'relevant circumstance' determining 'satisfactory quality' for the purposes of s 14(2A). Thus, those who sell to businesses (for example, manufacturers) may need to consider their advertising or labelling more carefully.

8.2.4 Reasonable fitness for purpose (s 14(3))

Under s 14(3), there is an **implied condition in a contract for the sale of goods that the goods supplied are reasonably fit for any purpose expressly or impliedly made known to the seller or credit-broker**.

A credit-broker is an intermediary; for instance, a furniture shop might allow a buyer to have goods under a credit sale. To achieve this, the goods are sold, 'on paper', to a finance company with whom the buyer then contracts to buy the goods and pay by instalments.

- **Where goods have a normal purpose, the law implies that they are bought for that purpose**, unless stated otherwise. In *Grant v Australian Knitting Mills* (1936), the purpose of 'underpants' was that they could be worn; in *Godley v Perry* (1960), in purchasing a toy catapult, the buyer did not have to state specifically the purpose for which the object was being bought. Note, also, *Kendall & Sons v Lillico & Sons Ltd* (1969), where *resale* was held to be a normal purpose of goods. It is for a court to determine what the normal purpose of goods is.
- **If the purpose is unusual or the goods have several normal but distinct uses**, for example, timber for paper or for furniture, then **the purpose must be made known expressly** – it must be spelt out clearly, either orally or in writing – to the seller before the buyer can rely on this section. So, in *Ashington Piggeries* (see above), for the purposes of s 14 (3), the buyers made it clear to the seller that the end product would be fed to mink, even though they supplied the formula. In fact, the court found the 'normal' purpose was 'feeding animals'. As the contaminated herring meal was harmful in varying degrees to all animals, it was not fit for its normal purpose. If the herring meal had not been harmful to *all* animals, the s 14(3) issue would have turned on the fact it was made known the meal would be fed to mink. However, in *Griffiths v Peter Conway Ltd* (1939), a woman who contracted dermatitis from a tweed coat did not indicate her sensitivity to the sellers, so the coat was only required to be fit for wearing by a 'normal' person.

❖ KEY CASE *Slater v Finning Ltd* [1997] AC 473

Facts:

A new camshaft in a ship caused problems resulting in a new engine being installed. The old engine was used in another vessel without any problems. It transpired that excessive torsional resonance in the ship had caused damage to the camshaft. The buyer argued that, as the seller knew the camshaft was for a particular ship, there was reliance on him to supply a camshaft suitable for that ship.

Decision:
It was held that there was no breach of condition where failure of goods to meet a particular purpose arose from an abnormal feature or idiosyncrasy of the buyer (or, as here, in the circumstances in which the buyer used the goods), and this was not made known to the seller. The camshaft was suitable for use in this type of ship and this was the extent of the buyer's reliance on the seller. It was only an unknown idiosyncrasy of this ship which made the usual type of camshaft unsuitable.

Note: It is interesting to compare this decision with *Manchester Liners Ltd v Rea* (1922).

- **Whether goods are reasonably fit for the purpose made known, is a question of fact**. In *Crowther v Shannon Motor Co* (1975), in determining whether a second hand car which needed a new engine after 2,300 miles was 'reasonably fit', the court said that the age, condition and make of the car should be considered in order to determine what could reasonably be expected of it. The fact that defects rendering the goods not reasonably fit are **not obvious** does not relieve the seller of liability (see: *Frost v Aylesbury Dairies* (1905)). **Poor instructions for use, or a failure to give warning of dangers** related to the use of the goods which are not generally known, can render the goods unfit for the buyer's purpose (see *Vacwell Engineering Co Ltd v BDH Chemicals Ltd* (1969) and *Wormell v RHM Agriculture (East) Ltd* (1986)). This may explain rather bizarre warnings in instruction booklets, such as advice not to dry underwear or newspapers in microwave ovens.
- **The condition does not apply where the buyer does not rely on the skill and judgment of the seller** or credit-broker; for example, where a brand other than that recommended by the seller is chosen, or where it is unreasonable for the buyer to have relied on that skill and judgment because the buyer had greater expertise. In *Teheran-Europe Corp v ST Belton Ltd* (1968), buyers ordered compressors for resale in Iran, where they traded. The sellers had not previously traded in Iran. For technical standards reasons, the compressors could not be sold in Iran. It was unreasonable for the buyers to rely on the seller that the goods could be resold in Iran; the buyers had specialised knowledge which the seller did not have, (see also *Jewson v Kelly* (2003)). However, even if the buyer selects the product (for example, from a supermarket shelf), there is still reliance on the seller that the product will fulfil its normal functions.
- **Reliance on the seller's skill and judgment may be partial**, as in *Ashington Piggeries* (see above), where it was held that the buyer, in supplying the formula, did not rely on the seller's skill and judgment that the end product would be suitable for mink (in the sense that he did not rely on the seller that the specified combination of ingredients was suitable for mink), but he did rely on the seller to use ingredients which were not defective. Accordingly, there was a breach of s 14(3).

8.2.5 Sale by sample (s 15)

The implied condition under s 15 is that **where goods are sold by sample**:

- The bulk must correspond with the sample;
- The buyer shall have a reasonable opportunity to compare the goods with the sample; and
- The goods will be free from any defect rendering them unsatisfactory which would not be apparent on reasonable examination of the sample.

This section applies only if a term of the contract indicates that it is a sale by sample. The mere act of showing a sample of the goods during negotiations does not make the sale one of sale by sample unless the parties agree to this. In *Drummond v Van Ingen* (1887), Lord MacNaughten examined the function of a sample, stating that '. . . the office of a sample is to present the real meaning and intention of the parties with regard to the subject matter of the contract, which, owing to the imperfection of language, it may be difficult or impossible to express in words. The sample speaks for itself'.

Everyday examples could be the purchase of carpets or wallpaper by reference to a sample book. It is no defence under s 15(2) to say that the bulk can easily be made to correspond with the sample. In *E & S Ruben Ltd v Faire Bros & Co Ltd* (1949), a material was sold which was crinkled, whereas the sample had been soft and smooth. The seller argued that, by a simple process of warming, the bulk could have been made as soft and smooth as the sample. Nevertheless, there was a breach of s 15(2).

A buyer may not be able to claim damages under s 15(2) of the SoGA 1979 for defects which he or she could reasonably have discovered upon examination of the goods. However, they may still have a claim under s 14(2) and (3).

8.3 Delivery and Payment Obligations

Under s 27 SoGA 1979, **the seller has an obligation to deliver the goods to the buyer, and the buyer has a duty to accept the goods and pay for them**. These obligations are not categorised as either conditions or warranties.

- *Seller's delivery obligation*

  Delivery means the voluntary transfer of possession (s 61), but, depending on the contractual agreement, delivery could be effected without the buyer having physical possession. Thus, if a third party storing the seller's goods in his warehouse informs the buyer he holds the goods for the buyer, delivery is effected (s 29(4)).

  The seller's obligation, under s 27, is to deliver the goods **at the right time and by the correct method**. Therefore, a stipulated time for delivery is considered by the courts to be 'of the essence' (a condition of the contract), as is a specified date of shipment of goods. Where the time of delivery is not complied with or, in the absence of an agreed time, a reasonable time has elapsed, the buyer may treat the contract as repudiated for breach of condition.

  Alternatively, late delivery can be accepted and damages claimed. Under s 29(1), the place of delivery may be expressly agreed or implied (for example, the usual place of delivery under previous contracts). Where there is no agreement, the place of delivery is determined by s 29(2); for example, the seller's place of business. If a method of delivery is agreed, it must be complied with.
- *Buyer's obligation to accept and pay for the goods*

  Unless the buyer has a right to repudiate the contract for the seller's breach (for example, due to delivery of defective goods), he or she must take and pay for the goods. Failure to do so means that the buyer is in breach of contract and the seller will be able to sue for the contract price or damages for non-acceptance (see below). The *time* of payment is not normally a condition of the contract, unless the parties have expressly agreed otherwise.

8.4 Seller's Personal Remedies

Where the buyer is in breach of contract, the seller may seek a remedy against the buyer **personally**:

- *Action for the price of the goods*
  Under s 49, the seller can sue for the contract price, where the buyer has failed to pay on the date fixed in the contract, or wrongfully fails to pay, the property in the goods having passed to the buyer (see 12.2.12 below). If neither of these conditions applies and the buyer wrongfully refuses to take and pay for the goods, the contract price cannot be claimed. If this were allowed, the seller would have both the money and the goods. Instead, the seller may sue for damages for non-acceptance.
  The Late Payment of Commercial Debts (Interest) Act 1998 provides for statutory interest to accrue on debts paid late in certain circumstances.
- *Damages for non-acceptance of the goods*
  This right is given by s 50(1) and, by ss (2), the measure of damages, as in *Hadley v Baxendale* (1854), is the loss arising naturally from the breach. However, in this context, note should be taken of ss (3), which imposes an obligation on sellers to mitigate their loss by reselling the goods that the buyer has refused to accept. Where there is an available market for the goods in question, the measure of damages is *prima facie* to be ascertained by the difference between the contract price and the market or current price at the time or times when the goods ought to have been accepted, or, if no time was fixed for acceptance, at the time of refusal to accept (see *WL Thompson Ltd v Robinson Gunmakers Ltd* (1955) and *Charter v Sullivan* (1957)). Currently, problems might arise in applying ss (3) because of constant 'price wars', which may make it difficult to determine the 'market' or 'current' price.

8.5 Seller's Real Remedies

A seller may be unable to pursue personal remedies against the buyer because, for example, the buyer has gone into liquidation. However, the seller may be able to use **'real' remedies by taking action against the goods**:

- **Lien (ss 41–44)**
  The seller has the right to retain possession of the goods, even though the property has passed to the buyer. The SoGA 1979 assumes that delivery and payment are normally concurrent events, except where sales are on credit. The lien, or right to keep the goods, is based on possession of the goods and is only available for the price of the goods, and not for other debts such as storage charges. It may be a useful remedy in times of economic stress where there are rumours of bankruptcies and liquidations. Unpaid sellers may be better off financially with the goods in their possession than if they simply become creditors in the bankruptcy. Delivery of part of the goods will not destroy the unpaid seller's lien unless the circumstances show an intention to waive the lien. The unpaid seller will lose the lien if the goods are delivered for carriage to the buyer and the seller has not reserved the right of disposal over them or if the buyer lawfully obtains possession of the goods.
- **Stoppage in transit (ss 44–46)**
  If the buyer becomes insolvent and the goods are still in transit to the buyer, the unpaid seller can stop the goods in transit and recover them from the carrier. The cost of re-delivery must be borne by the seller.
- **Right of resale**
  An unpaid seller can pass a good title to the goods to a second buyer after exercising a right of lien or stoppage in transit. The contract with the first buyer is automatically rescinded, so that the property in the goods reverts to the seller, who can keep any further profit made from the resale and any deposit put down by the buyer. If a loss is made on the resale, damages may be claimed from the original buyer. There is no requirement that the second purchaser

takes delivery or buys in good faith (that is, without knowledge of the first sale originally made).

- ***Reservation of title (s 19)***
  In contracts for the sale of specific goods, or where goods have been appropriated to the contract (see below), the seller can reserve the right to dispose of the goods. The seller can insert a clause in the contract under which the property in the goods does not pass to the buyer (even if the buyer has possession of the goods) until payment is made.
  This could protect an unpaid seller where the buyer is in liquidation. If the buyer owns the goods, the liquidator can sell them and the money raised goes towards paying all creditors. The seller would merely be a creditor for the purchase price and might only receive a small part of the price if there is insufficient to pay all creditors in full. Clearly, it is better for the seller to retain ownership, then resell the goods.
- ***The Romalpa clause***
  This arose from the case of *Aluminium Industrie Vassen BV v Romalpa Aluminium Ltd* (1976), which established that the manufacturer or supplier of goods had rights to retain some proprietary interest over the goods until paid for, even when the goods supplied had been processed or sold. Furthermore, proprietary rights could be maintained even after a sub-sale of the goods (sale by the buyer to another party), so that debts owed to the buyer could be transferred to the manufacturer or supplier if an appropriate *Romalpa* clause had been inserted.

8.6 Buyer's Remedies

8.6.1 Action for specific performance (s 52(1))

The court can order specific performance in contracts to deliver specific or ascertained goods; the order cannot be made for unascertained or future goods (see below). The seller is required to deliver the goods and is not given the option of paying damages instead. The courts will not make the order unless damages for non-delivery would not be adequate, for example, where the goods are in some way unique or rare.

8.6.2 Remedies for breach of condition

Where the seller is in *breach of condition*, the buyer can treat the contract as repudiated. Accordingly, the buyer can *reject* the goods, claim a *refund* of the price paid or refuse payment *and* claim *damages* for further loss suffered; however, where the seller is in *breach of warranty*, the buyer may only sue for damages for breach of contract.

From a practical point of view, the buyer who sues for breach of implied terms of the SoGA 1979 would be well advised to sue for breach of more than one implied term, in order to increase the chance of success. In *Godley v Perry* (1960) (see above), the injured child successfully pleaded breaches of s 14(2) and (3). There may appear to be an overlap of the provisions of the implied terms on the facts of some cases, but all the implied terms are needed to protect a buyer. For example, if one buys a new washing machine and it is delivered badly dented but in full working order, one could claim that it was not of satisfactory quality under s 14(2). However, as it worked properly, there would be no breach of s 13 or s 14(3).

- *Rejection* of goods means refusing to take delivery or informing the seller that they are rejected and returning the goods. A buyer in possession of rejected goods will often take them back to the seller, but is under no obligation to do so; the seller has the obligation to collect rejected goods from the buyer (s 36). The buyer does not have a lien over rejected goods and must hand them back, even if the purchase price paid has not been refunded.

Section 15A may now limit the right to reject goods for 'technical' breaches of condition. The courts may refuse to allow rejection of goods by a *business buyer* for breach of s 13, 14 or 15 where 'the breach is so slight that it would be unreasonable for him to reject them'. Instead, the buyer may sue for damages for breach of warranty, though it should be noted that the effect of s 15A can be circumvented by a 'contrary intention' in or be 'implied from' the contract. Whether the breach is 'slight' is a question of fact in each case. Section 15A recognises sensible business practice – a buyer who receives one faulty item in a batch of 100 will take the conforming items, rather than reject the whole batch – and prevents a business which changes its mind about contracting, from using a minor breach to escape liability.

Section 15A does not apply where the buyer is a consumer. Guidance on whether or not a person 'deals as consumer' can be found in UCTA 1977, under s 12(1), which was discussed previously (see 9.6.3). Section 12(1) has a wide remit and, since the burden is on the seller to prove that the buyer does not deal as consumer, the average sale of goods contract is unlikely to be affected. However, it should be noted that the 2002 Regulations omit the requirement that the goods are of a type 'ordinarily supplied for private use or consumption'.

Rejection of goods not conforming with the contract in *quantity* is covered by s 30. Where a lesser quantity is delivered, the buyer can reject or accept them, paying pro rata. Where a larger quantity is delivered, the buyer can reject the whole, or take the contract quantity and reject the excess, or accept the whole paying pro rata. However, s 30(2A), prohibits a *business buyer* from rejecting the whole, for an excess or shortfall in quantity which is so slight as to make rejection unreasonable.

Section 35A gives the buyer a right of *partial* rejection. In line with what many businesses would do in practice, the buyer may to choose to accept those goods which do *conform* with the contract and to reject those which do not. Acceptance of some of the goods, does not imply acceptance of all of them. (*Acceptance* is discussed below.) The provision also applies to delivery of goods by instalments. However, where each instalment is treated as a separate contract, whether breach in one instalment allows rejection of the future instalments, depends on the size of breach in relation to all the instalments contracted for and the likelihood of the breach being repeated (s 31(2)).

- A buyer claiming **a refund of the price paid**, can recover all payments made if the consideration has failed. This applies to non-delivery, and for a breach of condition of the sale. If the contract is severable (for example, where there are separate delivery times and instalments for different parts of the goods), the buyer can accept part and reject part of the goods and recover the price paid on the rejected goods.
- The buyer's **claim for damages** for non-delivery or for breach of condition.

  Where the claim is for non-delivery, damages are recoverable for losses arising naturally from the breach (s 51(2)), but this may not allow a buyer to claim the whole of the profit expected on resale of the undelivered goods. The buyer must mitigate that loss by purchasing replacement goods for resale, and the measure of damages which can be claimed is the difference between the contract price and the current or market price which would have to be paid for replacements, assuming that it is higher (s 51(3)).

Damages for breach of condition are assessed according to the usual contractual rules. Such claims may include a claim for loss of a sub-sale or for damages payable to a sub-buyer, if the seller knew or ought to have known of the possibility of a sub-sale. The whole issue of sub-sales was examined in *Louis Dreyfus Trading Ltd v Reliance Trading Ltd* (2004).

Damages for breach of warranty

Such damages may be claimed:

- where a warranty of the contract is breached; or
- s 11(4) applies. The buyer who **accepts** a breach of condition (see below), can only treat the breach as one of **warranty**.

The damages are assessed under s 53, which indicates the measure as *prima facie* the difference between the value of the goods at the time of delivery to the buyer and the value they would have had if they had fulfilled the warranty.

Additional remedies under the 2002 Regulations

The 2002 Regulations give additional remedies to the 'consumer' buyer of goods which do not conform with the contract of sale, by adding s 48(A)–(D) to the SoGA 1979. The additional remedies are **replacement, repair, reduction in price and rescission**. Whilst such remedies were previously given voluntarily by sellers, there was no legal obligation to do so. If the buyer chooses replacement or repair, he cannot reject for breach of condition until he has given the seller a reasonable time to carry out the chosen remedial action. The right to such remedies is further limited by reference to whether they are disproportionate in relation to other remedies available or are impossible. So, for example, if repair costs more than replacement, a claim for repair could not be enforced.

Under s 48(A)(3), if the goods do not conform with the contract of sale at any time within **six months** of the transfer of ownership to the buyer, it will be presumed that they did not conform at the time property was transferred. Thus, the buyer does not bear the burden of proving that non-conformity existed when the goods were supplied to him. However:

- as a presumption, it is rebuttable by evidence to the contrary; and
- the 'six month' rule only applies in relation to a claim for the additional remedies given by the Regulations.

8.7 Acceptance

Acceptance of a breach of condition deprives the buyer of the right to reject the goods and claim a refund or refuse payment. It does not remove all remedies; the buyer may still claim damages for breach of *warranty*. Under s 35, acceptance occurs when:

- the buyer states to the seller that the goods are acceptable, for example, where an acceptance note is signed; or
- the goods have been delivered to the buyer, who then does an act in relation to them which is inconsistent with the ownership of the seller; for example, selling or processing the goods.

These rules are subject to s 35(2):

> Where goods are delivered to the buyer, and he has not previously examined them, he is not deemed to have accepted them until he has had a reasonable opportunity of examining them for the purpose –
>
> (a) of ascertaining whether they are in conformity with the contract; and
> (b) in the case of a contract for sale by sample, of comparing the bulk with the sample. This right cannot be removed or excluded in consumer sales.

Section 34(1) has been repealed, but s 34 continues to provide that, subject to agreement, the seller is bound on request to afford the buyer a reasonable opportunity of examining the goods to ascertain whether they conform with the contract. Following s 35(2), acceptance cannot occur until this examination has been carried out.

- Section 35(4) provides that acceptance is also deemed to have taken place when the buyer retains the goods after a reasonable length of time without telling the seller they will be rejected. What amounts to a reasonable length of time has to be considered in conjunction with the reasonable opportunity to examine the goods. It is a question of fact in each case, as in *Bernstein* (see earlier), where the car was not of merchantable quality nor fit for the purpose, but the plaintiff had accepted the car under s 35, so could only treat the breach of condition as a warranty and claim damages. The court felt that 'reasonable time' meant a reasonable time to try out the goods, not a reasonable time to discover the defect. As a result of the new provisions, the decision in *Bernstein* would be different today.

❖ KEY CASE *Clegg v Andersson* (2003)

Facts:
A yacht did not comply with the manufacturer's specifications, as required by the contract of sale. The buyer asked the seller for information to enable him to decide whether to have repairs carried out. Whilst awaiting the information, the buyer registered and insured the yacht. After five months, the information was supplied, and three weeks later the buyer rejected the yacht.

Decision:
The Court of Appeal decided that registration and insurance of the vessel were not acts inconsistent with the seller's ownership and that the request for information was not an intimation of acceptance. Furthermore, the buyer had not retained the yacht for more than a reasonable time, given the circumstances, and *Bernstein* was no longer good law. Accordingly, the buyer had not accepted the yacht.

- Under s 35(6), a buyer is not deemed to have accepted the goods merely by requesting or agreeing to their repair (see: *J & H Ritchie v Lloyd Ltd* (2007)).

Whilst the 'traditional' remedies of rejection and refund are lost by acceptance, the 2002 Regulations make no correlation between acceptance and the new remedies. Therefore, it is arguable that the new remedies could be available for the six year limitation period for breach of contract claims.

8.8 Exclusion and Limitation of Liability

The rules relating to exclusion and limitation of liability for breach of contract have been discussed, but, in so far as they apply to sale of goods contracts, they can be summarised as follows:

- **Section 12** cannot be excluded in consumer or non-consumer sales (the distinction between consumer and non-consumer sales is covered by s 12(1) of UCTA 1977).
- **In consumer sales** (for example, where an individual buys goods from a shop), liability for breach of ss 13–15 cannot be excluded. Businesses should be aware that it is a criminal

offence to include a term in a contract, or to display a notice, which purports to exclude the statutory implied terms or restrict liability for their breach as against a person who deals as a consumer (by virtue of the Consumer Transactions (Restrictions on Statements) Order 1976, as amended by SI 1978/127). Accordingly, a notice in a shop which states 'No refunds' is a criminal offence, but one which states 'No refunds, except on faulty goods' does not contravene the Order, as there is no obligation to give refunds, except where the goods are faulty.

- **The 2002 Regulations** indicate that, for the purposes of ss 13–15, the definition of a consumer sale in s 12(1) of UCTA 1977 will not apply. Instead, there is a new definition:

  > . . . a party deals as a consumer where –
  >
  > (a) he is a natural person who makes the contract otherwise than in the course of a business; and
  >
  > (b) the other party does make the contract in the course of a business.

  Thus, the s 12(1) of UCTA 1977 requirement that the goods be of a type ordinarily supplied for private use and consumption is omitted. However, there will not be such a consumer sale if the buyer is an individual buying second hand goods at a public auction which consumers may attend in person; but there will be a consumer sale if new goods are bought at such an auction or the consumer may not attend the auction in person (for example, internet auctions).
- **In non-consumer sales**, it is possible to exclude liability for breach of ss 13–15 of the SoGA 1979, provided that the exclusion clause satisfies the test of 'reasonableness'. The requirement of reasonableness means that the exclusion clause 'shall be a fair and reasonable one to be included, having regard to the circumstances which were or ought to have been known to or in the contemplation of the parties when the contract was made'. UCTA 1977 provides that, **in determining 'reasonableness'**, regard shall be had in particular guidelines stated in Schedule 2.
- Any other liability for breach of contract can be excluded or restricted only to the extent that it is reasonable.
- Exclusion of liability for death and personal injury caused by negligence is prohibited. It is possible to exclude liability for other loss or damage arising from negligence or misrepresentation only to the extent that the clause is deemed to be reasonable.
- The Unfair Terms in Consumer Contracts Regulations 1999 provide further protection with respect to exclusion or other unfair terms in consumer contracts where the term has not been individually negotiated, such as may be found in a standard form contract. 'Consumer' in this context is confined to natural persons not acting in the course of business and is, therefore, currently narrower than UCTA 1977.

8.9 Guarantees

Many consumer goods are sold with a *voluntary guarantee* given by the seller or manufacturer, and often give the right to replacement or repair. However, these rights are not given *instead* of statutory rights under ss 13–15 of the SoGA 1979; they are *additional* rights which the consumer may choose to exercise against the guarantor.

The 2002 Regulations control these voluntary (or 'commercial') guarantees. The controls operate where a natural person who acts outside the course of a business is supplied with goods under contract and is also given a guarantee. The main provisions of the 2002 Regulations are as follows:

- The guarantee creates a contract between the consumer and the guarantor, subject to any conditions stated in the guarantee or associated advertising.
- The guarantee must be in plain, intelligible language, written in English where the goods are supplied within the UK, and must indicate how to claim under the guarantee, its duration and the name and address of the guarantor. The consumer may require that a copy of the guarantee, in writing or other durable medium, be made available to him or her within a reasonable time.
- Failure to comply with these provisions allows enforcement of an injunction against the guarantor.
- The Supply of Extended Warranties on Domestic Electrical Goods Order 2005 applies to retailers and manufacturers who supply directly to consumers. The Order is aimed at businesses who charge for the extended warranties they supply with domestic electrical goods, and requires retailers to show the price of extended warranties alongside the goods, in stores, catalogues, printed advertisements and on websites.
- Consumers must receive detailed information about their statutory rights in relation to the warranty and have the right to cancel the extended warranty agreement.

8.10 Transfer of Property and Risk

The main essential of the s 2 definition is the transfer of property (ownership) to the buyer. It is important to know when property is transferred because:

- if the property has passed, the unpaid seller can sue the buyer for the agreed contract price (see above); and
- usually, risk passes with property (s 20(1)), although this rule may be varied by agreement or custom. 'Risk' determines who bears the cost of accidental loss or damage; that is, loss or damage to the goods caused by reasons beyond the control of the seller, buyer or their employees. The 2002 Regulations add s 20(4) to the SoGA 1979, stating that s 20(1) does not apply where the buyer deals as a consumer; the goods remain at the seller's risk until they are delivered to the buyer. Section 20(4) also applies to s 20(2) (below).

The SoGA 1979 gives rules for determining when property is transferred and divides goods into four categories:

- *Specific goods* are goods which are identified and agreed upon at the time of contracting (for example, a contract to buy a particular second hand car). The term also includes a share in a specific bulk which has not been divided up at the time of contracting, expressed as a percentage or fraction (s 61); thus, 'sale of 50% of the seller's 100 tons of grain in the warehouse' would be a sale of specific goods, but 'sale of 50 tons of the 100 tons of grain in the seller's warehouse' would not be, as the goods are not expressed as a percentage or fraction of the 100 tons.
- *Unascertained goods* mean that the seller possesses goods of the type that the buyer (B) agrees to buy but, at the time of contracting, B does not know exactly which goods he or she will get. For example, B agrees to buy a sofa like the one displayed but, at the time of contracting, B does not know which of six such sofas in stock will be delivered. In this context, s 16, states: '. . . where there is a contract for the sale of unascertained goods, no property in the goods is transferred to the buyer unless and until the goods are ascertained.' However, s 16 must now be read subject to s 20A (below).
- *Ascertained goods* are goods identified after the contract is made. When B agrees to buy one of the six sofas that the shop has in stock, the goods are not ascertained until one of the sofas is labelled/set aside for B.

- *Future goods* are goods to be manufactured or acquired by the seller after the contract is made. Generally, future goods are unascertained.

Subject to s 16, **s 17 provides that the property passes when the parties intend it to pass** and, in determining this, regard should be had to the terms of the contract, the conduct of the parties and all other circumstances. A reservation of title clause (see above) is a common example of an expression of the parties' intention. Where the parties have not agreed on when property is to pass, s 18, rr 1–4 determine the time of transfer, as described below.

8.10.1 The passing of property in specific goods

- Rule 1 – The general rule for passing of property in specific goods is that, if a contract of sale is unconditional, **property passes to the buyer when the contract is made**, regardless of whether delivery and/or payment are postponed (see *Tarling v Baxter* (1827)). This is subject to the intention of the parties. In *Re Anchor Line (Henderson Bros Ltd)* (1937), a crane was sold to buyers, who agreed to pay annual sums for depreciation. As the buyers would not have paid depreciation on their own goods, the intention must be inferred that the property in the goods remained with the sellers until the price was fully paid.
- Rule 2 – If the contract is for the sale of specific goods, **but the seller is bound to do something to them to put them in a deliverable state**, ownership does not pass until that thing is done and the buyer has notice of such. Goods are in a 'deliverable state' when their state is such that the buyer is bound to take delivery of them (s 61 (5)). In *Underwood v Burgh Castle Brick and Cement Syndicate* (1922), the parties entered a contract for the sale of a 30 ton engine. When the contract was made, the engine was embedded in a concrete floor. Whilst it was being removed and loaded onto a truck, it was damaged. The seller claimed the price. As the engine was not in a deliverable state when the contract was made r 2 applied. Property would not pass until the engine was safely loaded on the truck; therefore, the seller bore the risk and could not claim the price.
- Rule 3 – If the goods are to be **weighed, tested or measured by the seller**, or are to be subjected to some other act or thing for the purpose of ascertaining the price, the property will not pass until the process is complete and the buyer is informed, unless there is a specific agreement to the contrary.
- Rule 4 – Where goods are supplied **on sale or return or on approval**, property passes to the buyer when:
    - the buyer signifies approval or acceptance to the seller (see *Kirkham v Attenborough* (1897)); or
    - the buyer does any other act adopting the transaction; or
    - the buyer, whilst not giving approval or acceptance, retains the goods beyond the agreed time or, if no time is agreed, beyond a reasonable time. In *Poole v Smith's Car Sales (Balham) Ltd* (1962), following several requests by the seller for return of his car (which had been left at a garage on a sale or return basis), it was returned damaged. As it had not been returned within a reasonable time, property had passed to the defendant, who would be liable for the price.

Section 18 rr 1–4 clearly apply where the specific goods are those identified and agreed upon at the time of sale, but the s 61 definition of specific goods also includes a share in a specific bulk which has not been divided up at the time of contracting and which is expressed as a percentage or fraction. Though such goods would be unascertained at the time of contracting, they are defined as 'specific goods'. Unfortunately, there is no statutory provision stating when the property is to pass.

8.10.2 The passing of property in unascertained goods

Under s 16, **property cannot pass in unascertained or future goods**, unless and until the goods become ascertained (see *McDougall v Aeromarine of Emsworth Ltd* (1958)). Under s 18 r 5:

> (1) . . . where there is a contract for the sale of unascertained or future goods by description, and goods of that description and in a deliverable state are unconditionally appropriated to the contract, either by the seller with the assent of the buyer or by the buyer with the assent of the seller, the property in the goods then passes to the buyer and the assent may be express or implied, and may be given either before or after the appropriation is made.

Carlos Federspiel & Co v Charles Twigg & Co Ltd (1957), held that goods are unconditionally appropriated to the contract if they have been 'irrevocably earmarked' for use in that contract.

> (2) Where the seller places the goods in the hands of a carrier for transmission to the buyer, there is deemed to be 'unconditional appropriation', unless the seller reserves the right to dispose of the goods.

In *Healy v Howlett* (1917), 190 boxes of fish were carried by rail. The buyer was to purchase 20 boxes and the seller directed the railway company to set aside 20 boxes; before this was done, the fish went rotten. The seller had sent the buyer an invoice, stating that the fish was carried at the buyer's sole risk. It was held that since the fish became rotten before the goods were ascertained, property could not pass to the buyer, who, therefore, could reject the goods. Obviously, the critical factor in this case was the failure on the part of the railway company to identify the 20 boxes by setting them aside for the buyer. It would have been untenable for future buyers if the courts had made the buyer 'bear the loss' in these circumstances.

Section 18, r 3 provides for ascertainment by exhaustion. This occurs where the goods are part of a designated bulk and the bulk is reduced to a quantity which is equal or less than the contract quantity. In these circumstances, the goods are deemed to be appropriated. Suppose a buyer agrees to buy 200 cases of wine from 500 in the seller's warehouse but the seller then sells and delivers 300 cases to another buyer. The remaining 200 cases are deemed to be appropriated to the contract and property passes to the buyer when the other 300 cases are removed from the warehouse.

Finally, **s 16 must be considered in the light of s 20A**, which provides that where the buyer purchases a specified quantity (for example, 100 tons, but not a quantity expressed as a percentage or fraction of the whole) from an identified bulk source, and has paid for some or all of the goods forming part of the bulk, the buyer becomes co-owner of the bulk. No specific provision is made for the passing of risk in such situations, but it has been suggested that if the bulk is partially destroyed before the shares of several buyers are divided, they bear the risk, and so suffer loss proportionate to the size of their undivided shares.

8.10.3 Exceptions to s 20(1)

The exceptions to the general rule that property and risk pass together are:

- Under s 20(2), 'where delivery has been delayed through the fault of either buyer or seller, the goods are at the risk of the party at fault as regards any loss which might not have occurred but for such fault'. The rule is subject to s 20(4) (above).
- The contract or trade custom may indicate that the passing of property and risk is separated. For example, in a 'cif' (cost, insurance and freight) contract, goods are sold abroad and carriage by sea is part of the contract. In such contracts, property passes to the buyer on loading for sea transit; risk does not pass until later, when the seller sends shipping documents to the buyer against payment.

8.10.4 Consequences of bearing the 'risk'

- If the buyer bears the risk at the time of loss or damage, the goods must be paid for and there is no claim allowed for breach of condition, where no goods or damaged goods are received.
- If the seller bears the risk at the time of loss or damage and the contract is for future or unascertained goods, a replacement must be delivered; otherwise, there is breach of condition by failure to deliver or by delivering damaged goods.
- Under s 7, where there is a contract for the sale of specific goods and they perish whilst at the seller's risk, the contract is frustrated (see 11.4 above). The rules of the Law Reform (Frustrated Contracts) Act 1943 do not apply to s 7 situations. However, frustration *is* possible in the sale of unascertained goods of a *specific origin* (see *CTI Group Inc v Transclear SA* (2008)).

8.11 Sale by a Person Who is Not the Owner

There is an implied condition in s 12 that the seller has a right to sell the goods (pass on a good title to them). The rule *nemo dat quod non habet* means that you cannot give what you have not got. The general rule is that where goods are sold by a person who is not the owner, the buyer acquires no better title than the seller (s 21). However, there are exceptions, and the law may have to choose between the rights of two innocent parties – the innocent purchaser and the real owner of the goods. Usually, the buyer must return the goods to the true owner, without any recompense. However, where the goods have been 'improved', the buyer may be entitled to some reimbursement.

If the innocent purchaser does not get good title, the seller is in breach of s 12(1). See *Rowland v Divall* (see above). The **exceptions to the *nemo dat* rule** are:

8.11.1 Estoppel

If the true owner, by his conduct, leads an innocent buyer to believe that the seller owns what he sells, the real owner is *estopped* (prevented) from claiming ownership. Thus, the innocent buyer is protected and gets ownership (see *Eastern Distributors Ltd v Goldring* (1957)). In order to make a successful claim, estoppel can only be raised against a person who had actual knowledge of the facts and actually agreed to them, knowing that a third party might rely on the 'apparent' authority.

8.11.2 Agency

If a principal appoints an agent to sell his goods to a third party, then sale by the agent, in accordance with the instructions given, will pass good title to the third party. If, however, the agent has disobeyed the instructions, then no title passes to the third party unless the agent had apparent authority.

8.11.3 Mercantile agency

A third party has an even stronger claim to the title of the goods where the agent is a mercantile agent. A mercantile agent is one 'having in the customary course of business as such agent, authority either to sell goods or to consign goods for the purposes of sale or to buy goods, or to raise money on the security of goods' (s 1(1) of the Factors Act 1889). Thus, if the third party, as a consumer, buys a car from an agent who is in the car trade, this provision may apply.

The Factors Act **binds the owner by the actions of a mercantile agent** in the following circumstances:

- The agent has possession of goods or documents of title, with the owner's consent, and makes any sale, pledge or other disposition of them in the ordinary course of business, whether or not the owner authorised it (s 2(1); *Folkes v King* (1923)). Third parties claiming against the owner in this situation must prove, *inter alia*, that, at the time of the sale, they had no notice of the agent's lack of authority. In *Pearson v Rose and Young* (1951), the owner of a car took it to a dealer and asked him to obtain offers. The owner did not intend to hand over the registration book, but left it with the dealer by mistake. The dealer sold the car with the book to an innocent buyer. The question of true ownership of the car was raised. The dealer had obtained the car 'with the consent of the owner' but not the registration book; hence, the sale had to be treated as a sale without registration book which was not in the ordinary course of business, and the buyer could not get a good title to the car.
- The mercantile agent pledges goods as security for a prior debt. The pledgee acquires no better right to the goods than the factor has against his or her principal at the time of the pledge (s 4).
- The mercantile agent pledges goods in consideration of either the delivery of the goods or a document of title to goods or a negotiable security. The pledgee acquires no right in the goods pledged beyond the value of the goods, documents or security when so delivered in exchange (s 5).
- The mercantile agent receives possession of goods from their owner for the purpose of consignment or sale and the consignee has no notice that the agent is not the owner. The consignee has a lien on the goods for any advances he or she has made to the agent (s 7).

8.11.4 Sales authorised by law

Sometimes title does not pass directly from the owner, because the sale is authorised by the court, for example, the sale of goods which are the subject matter of legal proceedings. Similarly, in common law or by statute, it is sometimes declared that a non-owner is entitled to sell goods, for example, an unpaid seller (see 12.2.7 above).

8.11.5 Sale in market overt (s 22)

This exception ceased in 1995.

8.11.6 Sale under a voidable title (s 23)

A buyer who obtains goods by fraud, acquires a voidable title in them and has title unless and until the seller avoids the contract, so that the title in the goods reverts to the seller. The seller may avoid the contract by telling the buyer or by, for example, informing the police. If the person who obtained the goods by fraud resells them before the original seller avoids the contract, the buyer in good faith (who did not know that the person who sold the goods had a defective title) acquires good title and keeps the goods. In *Car & Universal Finance Co v Caldwell* (1965), the buyer obtained a car by fraud, paying by a cheque, which was dishonoured. The seller told the police and then the buyer resold the car to a purchaser, who was later found by the court not to have acted in good faith. The original owner had good title and could recover the car, because he had avoided the buyer's title *before* resale *and* the person who subsequently purchased the car was not an innocent purchaser.

8.11.7 Disposition by a seller in possession (s 24)

A contract of sale can be complete and valid though the goods are still in the seller's possession, for example, when they are awaiting delivery. If, in this scenario, the seller sells the goods to a second buyer, that buyer will obtain a good title to those goods if delivery is taken. However, the second buyer must take in good faith and without notice of the original sale. The first buyer would have to sue the seller for breach of contract. In *Pacific Motor Auctions Ltd v Motor Credits (Hire Finance) Ltd* (1965), a car dealer sold vehicles to the plaintiffs under a 'display agreement', which allowed the seller to retain possession of the cars for display in their showroom. He was paid 90% of the purchase price and was authorised to sell the cars as agent for the plaintiff. The seller got into financial difficulties and the plaintiffs revoked the authority to sell the cars. However, the dealer sold them to the defendants, who took in good faith and without notice of the previous sale. Whilst the defendants knew about the 'display agreement', it was presumed that the dealer had the authority to sell the cars; as a result s 24 applied and, as the defendant had obtained a good title to the cars, the plaintiffs' claim for the return of the vehicles failed.

8.11.8 Disposition by a buyer in possession (s 25)

A buyer may possess the goods though the seller has retained property in them. If the buyer has the goods and any necessary documents of title with the seller's consent and transfers these to an innocent second buyer, that buyer obtains a good title to the goods; this is subject to the proviso that the second buyer takes in good faith and without notice of any lien or other claim on the goods by the original seller. In *Cahn v Pockett's Bristol Channel Co* (1899), it was held that possession of a bill of lading (a document of title) with the owner's consent was sufficient to pass a good title to a third party under s 25; in *Re Highway Foods International Ltd* (1995), it was held that, where there is a reservation of title clause the sub-purchaser may not be able to rely on s 25.

Newtons of Wembley Ltd v Williams [1965]

Facts:

A car was sold with an agreement that property would not pass until the price was paid. The payment cheque was dishonoured, so that no title passed because of the provisions of the contract. Therefore, the buyer was a buyer in possession without any title, when he sold the car in a London street market. The car was then sold to the defendant.

Decision:

It was held that, as the buyer took the car in good faith when it was resold in the market, he obtained a good title under s 25, which he then transferred by sale to the defendant.

Comment: It should be stressed, however, that s 25 only applies where the buyer in possession resells as if he were 'a mercantile agent'; in *Newtons*, this aspect was satisfied by sale in the street market. It is worth comparing *Newtons* with *Car & Universal Finance Co v Caldwell*; once the buyer's title was avoided in *Caldwell*, he became a buyer in possession within the meaning of s 25. However, s 25 could not have operated because the subsequent purchaser did *not* act in good faith.

8.11.9 Sale of motor vehicles which are subject to hire purchase agreements

The law changed in 1964 (by Pt III of Hire Purchase Act 1964 (re-enacted in the Consumer Credit Act 1974)) to protect 'private purchasers' of motor vehicles which were subject to hire purchase agreements. The original hirer will still have the same obligation to the finance company. The purchaser who takes the car in good faith, without notice of the hire purchase agreement, gets a good title thereto. However, it appears that the original hire purchase contract must be valid for the third party to be protected (see *Shogun Finance Ltd v Hudson* (2001), 6.2.3 above).

Finally, it should be noted that if none of the exceptions to the *nemo dat* rule applies, the original owner retains title and may sue, in the tort of conversion, anyone who does possess or has possessed the goods since they were obtained from the original owner.

8.12 The Supply of Goods and Services Act 1982

8.12.1 Implied terms

The SGSA 1982 provides protection in respect of agreements which do not fulfil the definition of the SoGA 1979. The Act has been amended in a similar way to the SoGA 1979; furthermore, the 2002 Regulations have amended the Act to give consumers the same additional rights and remedies as in contracts for the sale of goods. References to the SGSA 1982 will be to its provisions, *as amended*. The types of contracts covered by the Act are:

- A transfer of the property in goods, such as an exchange contract, where there is no money consideration.
- Hire of goods, such as car rental.
- Contracts to supply a service, such as dry cleaning.
- Contracts which combine some of the other types. Thus, a car service including a replacement part involves *service* and *transfer of goods*. Where there is *a transfer of property in goods*, the Act mirrors the SoGA 1979. In ss 2–5 there are implied conditions similar to ss 12–15 of the SoGA 1979 (title, description, quality and fitness for purpose, as well as sample).
- Contracts of hire.

Sections 6–10 imply terms similar to ss 12–15 of the SoGA 1979.

In relation to contracts for *the supply of services*, the Act protects the victims of poor quality workmanship, including the time it takes to provide services and the price for such services. It implies *terms*; accordingly, a court will have to determine, depending on the circumstances, whether the breach is of condition or warranty.

- Section 13 states that there is an implied term that where the supplier is *acting in the course of a business*, the supplier will carry out the service with *reasonable skill and care*.
- Section 14 states that where the supplier is *acting within the course of a business* and the time for the service to be carried out is not fixed by the contract or determined by a course of dealings between the parties, the supplier will carry out the service *within a reasonable time*.
- Section 15 states that, where the consideration is not determined by the contract or in a manner agreed in the contract or by the course of dealing between the parties, the party contracting with the supplier will pay a *reasonable price*.

Where contracts are '*hybrids*' (for example, a decorating contract could involve supply of goods (paint, wallpaper, etc) and supply of a service (the labour)), the provisions of ss 2–5, relating to the supply of goods, apply to the paint and wallpaper and the provisions of ss 13–15, relating to the supply of a service, apply to the labour.

8.12.2 Exclusion clauses

UCTA 1977 governs exclusion and limitation of liability under the Act.

- Title cannot be excluded and any attempt to exclude renders the clause void.
- In consumer contracts, any attempt to exclude the terms contained in ss 2–5 will render the clause void.

If the buyer does not deal as a consumer, any attempt to exclude these terms will be subject to the test of reasonableness. The 2002 Regulations make similar amendments to such rules as for sale of goods (see above). In a contract of hire, the terms as to title and quiet possession can be excluded or restricted by an exemption clause, subject to the test of reasonableness. Where an exclusion clause relates to s 13, it must satisfy the test of reasonableness. Liability for death or personal injury caused by negligence cannot be excluded.

8.13 The Consumer Protection (Distance Selling) Regulations 2000

8.13.1 Application

The Regulations apply to contracts for the supply of goods or services which are concluded solely by distance communication (no face to face meeting) where the supplier normally contracts in this way (not a one-off transaction). For example, they apply to press advertisements with order forms, catalogues, telephone sales, internet shopping, email, fax and letter. However, some contracts are specifically excluded; for example, financial services, vending machine sales, contracts concluded via payphone operator and internet auctions. Other contracts are only partially covered by the Regulations, for example, home delivery from a curry house.

8.13.2 Main provisions

Consumers must receive **clear information** about the goods/services *before* contracting; for example, the name of the supplier, the price, delivery arrangements and costs, the cost of using distance communication (for example, premium telephone rate) and (where it applies) of the right to cancel the contract. So, internet shopping channels should allow access to this information at the time people might order; catalogues should contain such information. The consumer must receive confirmation of this information in a 'durable medium' (for example, email, fax, letter) and the confirmation must contain further information, such as details of any guarantee and how to exercise the right to cancel. The confirmation must be received by the consumer, at the latest, on delivery of the goods or commencement of the supply of services.

The consumer can **withdraw from the contract** without liability, by exercising the right of cancellation up to seven working days (excluding weekends and bank holidays) from receipt of the confirmation of information. However, the right of cancellation is not available in some circumstances, for example, perishable goods (such as food shopping via the internet); sale of videos and software which the customer has 'unsealed'; supply of newspapers and magazines; goods made to order. If the consumer is not given prior notice of the right to cancel, the cancellation period is extended by three months. The consumer must give written notice of cancellation (by, for example, email, letter, fax), but cannot cancel where the goods have been used or damaged.

If the consumer who cancels already has possession of the goods, then (unless the details sent of the right to cancel state otherwise) the supplier must collect them within 21 days of cancellation, after giving the consumer notice of when they will be collected. Whilst awaiting collection, the consumer must take reasonable care of the goods. On cancellation, the consumer is entitled to a refund of money paid.

8.14 The Consumer Protection Act 1987, Part 1

8.14.1 Introduction

The Consumer Protection Act (CPA) 1987 provides a means of redress for a consumer against the 'producer' of a product, for injury or property damage caused by that product. Such redress is of particular importance to the non-buyer (for example, the recipient of a gift), but a buyer might pursue a claim under the CPA 1987 where, for example, it is not worth suing an insolvent seller. Although a consumer might have had a claim against the manufacturer in negligence (*Donoghue v Stevenson* (1932)); this would involve establishing fault; the CPA 1987 does not require such evidence in order to establish liability.

A consumer might also encounter problems in suing a manufacturer abroad; apart from the expense involved, English law may not be applied by a foreign court to determine the issue. The CPA 1987 solves this problem by providing the possibility of suing a person or body in this country. Accordingly, a business which does not manufacture the defective goods or sell them to the consumer may nevertheless find itself liable to compensate a consumer who suffers loss because of the defects in the goods, because it is a 'producer'.

Under the CPA 1987, **the claimant must show that:**

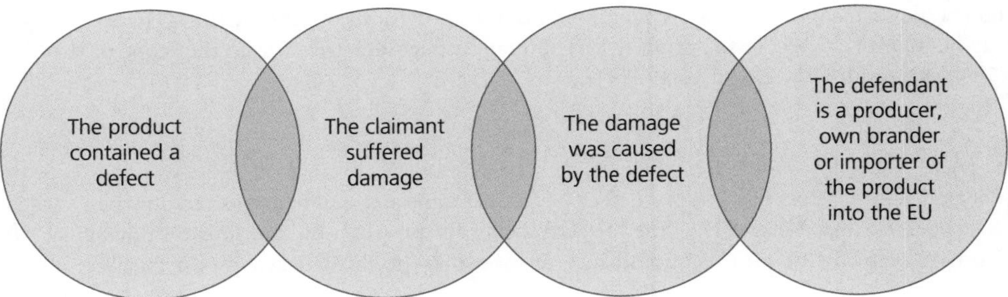

Figure 8.3

8.14.2 Meaning of 'producer' (s 2(2))

A '*producer*' of a product is defined as including the manufacturer of a finished product or of a component; any person who won or abstracted the product; or, where goods are not manufactured or abstracted, any person responsible for an industrial or other process to which any essential characteristic of the product is attributable, for example, a person who processes agricultural produce.

- Although *a supplier* of a defective product (for example a retail outlet) *does not have primary liability*, the supplier will be liable if he or she fails to identify the producer or importer when requested to do so.
- Businesses may be deemed to be 'producers' of a defective product if they claim to be producers *by putting their name or trademark on the product.*

8.14.3 'Defective' product (s 3)

A product will be **'defective'** if the safety of the product is not such as persons generally are entitled to expect (*see: Pollard v Tesco Stores Ltd* (2006)), taking all circumstances into account, including: the marketing of the product; the presentation of the product, including instructions and warnings; the use to which it might reasonably be expected to be put; and the time when it was supplied (that is, the state of the product at the time of supply).

For example, in *A & Others v National Blood Authority* (2001) claims were made under the CPA 1987 by people infected by hepatitis C through blood transfusions. At the time, doctors knew there could be such infection, but no warnings were given as there was then no test to detect the virus in blood. As no warnings of the risk were given, the public were found to have a legitimate expectation that no risk existed. Thus, the transfused blood was 'defective'. In *Worsley v Tambrands* (2000) a woman suffering toxic shock syndrome from tampon use alleged the tampons were not as safe as people were entitled to expect; though the risks of use were stated in the leaflet in the tampon box, the information was not printed on the box and regular users would not always read the leaflet. The court held that the warnings in the leaflet were sufficient to meet the expectations of users under s 3.

A **'product'** is 'any goods or electricity and . . . includes a product which is comprised in another product, whether by virtue of being a component part or raw materials or otherwise' (s 1). **'Goods'** includes substances (which can be natural or artificial, solid, liquid, gaseous or in the form of a vapour), things comprised in land by virtue of being attached to it (but not land itself), ships, aircraft and vehicles (s 45).

Thus, for example, all processed and manufactured goods supplied by a business are covered by the CPA 1987, as are raw materials and components incorporated into them. However, services such as advice are not included and agricultural produce and game which have not undergone an industrial process were specifically exempted from the provisions of the CPA 1987. However, probably because of the BSE crisis, primary agricultural products are now within the scope of the CPA 1987 (as a result of EC Directive 99/34).

8.14.4 Extent of liability (s 5)

A person suffering loss because of a defective product can claim, but damages can only be awarded for property damage over £275 (the property being for private use), and for death or injury. No claim can be made for 'pure' economic loss, or for damage to the defective product itself.

8.14.5 Exclusion of liability (s 7)

Liability cannot be excluded, though a claim for damages is subject to the defences of the CPA 1987 and the time limitations of the Limitation Act 1980.

8.14.6 Defences (s 4)

One of the following defences may be available:

- the defect is attributable to compliance with a domestic or EC enactment;
- the person was not at any time the supplier of the product;
- the supply was not in the course of business;
- the defect did not exist in the product at the time it was supplied;
- the state of scientific and technical knowledge at the relevant time was not such that the producer might be expected to have discovered the defect (the 'development risks' defence);
- the defect was in a product in which the product in question had been comprised and was wholly attributable to the design of the subsequent product;
- more than ten years has elapsed since the product was first supplied.

The **'development risks' defence** allows the producer to show that the defect was not discoverable at the time of supplying the product. What is required of a producer for this defence to operate is an area of contention, awaiting clarification by the courts. Should producers be aware of all available knowledge related to the product and then ensure that it is applied, or will it suffice to do limited research, bearing in mind the cost of development and the potentially small risk to the consumer?

❖ KEY CASE *Abouzaid v Mothercare (UK) Ltd* (2000)

Facts:

The 12-year-old plaintiff was helping his mother attach a 'Cosytoes' bag to a pushchair. Attachment was by elastic straps joined by a metal buckle. A stretched elastic strap flew back and the buckle hit the plaintiff in the eye; he suffered a detached retina and impaired eyesight.

The product was found to be defective because its design permitted the risk to arise and no warnings were given. It was irrelevant that no such accident had been reported in the ten years the product had been available; it *was* a design defect, otherwise the accident would not have happened. *The development risks defence* failed because a simple test of pulling back the elastic strap could have revealed the risk. The test could easily have been done and the public were entitled to expect better.

Under s 6(4), the defence of contributory negligence is available.

8.14.7 Limitations on claims

There is a three-year limitation period for claims, commencing from the date of injury or damage. Where the injury or damage is not apparent, the date runs from the time that the claimant knew or could reasonably have known of the claim.

8.15 Criminal Liability

8.15.1 Introduction

The businessman must be aware that, as well as seeking to protect buyers and consumers generally by providing remedies, the law also strives to prevent consumers being misled and defective products being supplied by imposing criminal liability. The conviction of a business could cause harm to its commercial reputation, apart from any other consequences, such as payment of a fine and seizure of dangerous goods.

8.15.2 The Consumer Protection Act 1987, Part II

This part of the Act **protects the public from unsafe consumer goods** by imposing criminal liability. It enables the Secretary of State to make safety regulations in respect of specific products. Safety regulations already exist in respect of a wide range of products, including children's nightdresses and the coverings and fillings of upholstered furniture.

- Section 13 empowers the Secretary of State to serve either a 'prohibition notice' on a supplier, prohibiting that supplier from supplying goods which are unsafe, or a 'notice to warn', which requires the supplier to publish warnings about the unsafe goods. Breach of such orders is a criminal offence.

- *Section 12* lists offences relating to *safety regulations*. These offences attract a maximum fine of £5,000 and six months imprisonment.
- *Enforcement* of safety regulations is by trading standards officers, who may:
  - Issue *suspension orders*, requiring a trader to stop supplying goods thought to breach safety regulations, for up to six months. It is a crime to breach such order.
  - Apply to court for forfeiture of goods breaching safety regulations.

A consumer may have a *civil claim for breach of statutory duty* against the supplier of unsafe goods under Part II of the CPA 1987.

8.15.3 The General Product Safety Regulations 2005

The General Product Safety Regulations (GPSR) 2005 can impose criminal liability for supplying *unsafe products* onto the market.

The GPSR 2005 implemented EC Directive 2001/95/EC; and the regulations supersede the GPSR 1994. Essentially, the GPSR 2005 give a 'blanket' safety rule where there are no specific safety regulations for a particular product, which is intended for/likely to be used by consumers.

Thus, reg 5 imposes an obligation on a *producer*, not to place/offer to place a consumer product on the market, unless it is a *safe product*. Terms used in the regulations are defined in reg 2. *Consumer products* are those goods, supplied in the course of commercial activity, which are intended for/likely to be used by consumers (those not acting in the course of commercial activities) for private use. Such goods can be second hand (other than antiques), or reconditioned, and it is irrelevant whether a consumer gave consideration for them. *Safe products* are those which, in normal/ reasonably foreseeable situations of use (including duration, putting into service, installation and maintenance requirements), do not present risks (or only minimal risks, compatible with use considered acceptable/consistent with high standards to protect health and safety). This definition recognises that *no product is absolutely safe* and adds factors to consider in determining whether a product is safe:

(a) the characteristics of the product, including its composition, packaging, instructions for assembly and maintenance;
(b) the effect on other products, where it is reasonably foreseeable that it will be used with other products;
(c) the presentation of the product, the labelling, any instructions for its use and disposal and any other indication or information provided by the producer; and
(d) the categories of consumers at risk when using the product, in particular children.

The producer can be an EU manufacturer or reconditioner (including an own-brander), or an importer into the EU. *Others in the supply chain*, whose activities can affect the safety of goods placed on the market are also included; for example, a distributor fitting replacement car tyres. The specific duties of distributors are stated in reg 8.

Where the producer or distributor is accused of an offence, the *due diligence defence* may be raised (reg 29); for example, see: *Rotherham MBC v Raysun (UK) Ltd* (1988); *P & M Supplies (Essex) Ltd v Devon CC* (1991); *Sutton LB v David Halsall plc* (1995); *Whirlpool (UK) Ltd & Magnet v Gloucester CC* (1995).

On conviction of an offence, the penalty may either be imprisonment up to 12 months and/or a fine up to £20,000 (reg 20). *Enforcement* is mainly through Local Authority Trading Standards and Environmental Health departments; suspension and withdrawal (previously prohibition) notices may be issued and forfeiture of goods can be ordered.

8.15.4 The Consumer Protection from Unfair Trading Regulations 2008

The Regulations (CPR) implement EC Directive 2005/29/EC and replace Pt III of the CPA 1987 and most of the Trade Descriptions Act 1968.

- The CPR apply to **business to consumer transactions** and **business to business transactions, which could affect consumers**; for example, purchase of goods by a retailer from a manufacturer could affect consumers when the retailer sells the goods. Advertisements, marketing, after sales service and debt collection are within the scope of CPR as they relate to the **transactions**.
- Regulation 3 prohibits **unfair commercial practices** (those which do not meet standards of professional diligence and can materially distort the economic behaviour of consumers in relation to products).

Commercial practices are acts, omissions, conduct, representations or commercial communication (such as advertising), which are directly linked to promotion, sale or supply of a product. *Products* means products, services, immovable property, rights and obligations. *Professional diligence* is measured by reference to the standard of skill and care a trader can be expected to exercise in relation to honest market practice and good faith in a particular field of activity. *Material distortion* of economic behaviour essentially means impairing the average consumer's ability to make an informed decision about whether to transact or not. Regulation 3(4) states that a **commercial practice is unfair** (and so prohibited), if it is a misleading action or omission or is aggressive, or is listed in Sched 1 to CPR. Regulation 5 defines *misleading actions* in terms of:

- giving false information to or deceiving consumers;
- creating confusion in relation to products (for example, with the trademark of a competitor), or failing to comply with a code of conduct the trader says he has signed up to;
- other matters listed in reg 5(4), which a consumer is likely to take into account in determining whether to transact (for example, the price or the way it is calculated).

Regulation 6 defines a *misleading omission* as omitting/hiding material information or presenting it in such a way as to make it misleading (for example, ambiguous statements), where the commercial practice is an invitation to buy. Regulation 6(4) lists the information which is considered material.

Regulation 7 encompasses *aggressive commercial practices*, which are practices likely to significantly impair consumers' choice through harassment, coercion or undue influence; for example, exploiting the misfortunes of a consumer.

Criminal offences covered by the CPR are given in reg 8 and can result in a maximum fine of £5,000 in a Magistrates' Court and an unlimited fine or two years' imprisonment in the Crown Court. The defences listed in reg 8 are due diligence and innocent publication of an advertisement. Additionally, there is a 'by-pass' provision, allowing prosecution of the person really responsible for the unfair commercial practice (such as the person responsible for the advertisement which another innocently published). Enforcement is undertaken by the Office of Fair Trading and Local Authority Trading Standards departments, who can investigate an alleged offence, make test purchases, enter premises, copy documents and seize/detain goods (regs 19–27).

8.15.5 The Cancellation of Contracts made in a Consumer's Home or Place of Work etc Regulations 2008

The Regulations (SI 2008/1816), are designed to protect consumers in relation to *doorstep selling*. Though there are some exceptions (Sched 3), they **apply where traders make written/oral**

contracts in the consumer's home, place of work, the home of another individual, or a place organised by the trader away from his business premises. The regulations list the type of traders to whom the regulations apply, for example, those providing home improvements, energy, mobility products. The consumer who makes such contracts (involving more than £35), has the *right to cancel* the agreement:

- The consumer must receive written notice of this right at the time the contract is made. The notice must give the consumer at least 7 days from receipt of the notice to cancel the agreement in writing.
- If the consumer has received the services/goods before expiry of the cancellation period, payment may have to be made for what was received up to the date of cancellation, and the goods must be returned.
- If the trader fails to comply with the regulations, the contract cannot be enforced and fines up to £5,000 can be imposed.

8.15.6 The Business Protection from Misleading Marketing Regulations 2008

The regulations aim to control advertising (any form of representation made in connection with a trade/business/craft/profession, to promote the supply or transfer of a product (reg 2(1)). In this context, *product* includes goods, services, immovable property, rights and obligations. Regulation 3 prohibits *misleading advertising*. Advertising is misleading where it deceives/is likely to deceive traders and is likely to affect their economic behaviour; or injures/is likely to injure a competitor. This refers to *comparative* advertising, such as comparing one supermarket chain's prices with those of another.

Regulation 3(3) lists factors to be taken into account in determining whether an advertisement is misleading, such as the characteristics of the product. Obviously, information about a product's characteristics could persuade a retailer to purchase from a manufacturer. Regulation 3(4) and (5) gives non-exhaustive lists of what such *characteristics* may be; for example, uses of the product, tests (and the results) carried out on a product.

Regulation 4 deals specifically with *comparative advertising*. Rather than directly prohibiting particular comparisons, it indicates what is allowed; for example, an advertisement may compare products if they meet the same needs or are intended for the same purposes. Regulation 5 specifically prohibits a code owner from promoting prohibited misleading or comparative advertising in a code of conduct. 'Code owners' are traders or bodies which formulate, revise and/or monitor codes of conduct. Such codes are common in particular trades.

- Under reg 6, engaging in misleading advertising is a criminal offence. This attracts a fine, not exceeding the statutory maximum, on summary conviction. Where conviction is on indictment, the penalty is a fine and/or imprisonment up to two years (reg 7). Prosecution for an offence is time limited (reg 10).
- The defences of *due diligence* (reg 11) and *innocent publication* (reg 12), are available in relation to the criminal offences.
- **Enforcement** of the regulations (regs 13–20) is undertaken by '*every enforcement authority*' (this includes local weights and measures authorities and the Office of Fair Trading). To enable such authorities to enforce the regulations, they are given certain powers by regs 21–24. The main powers are to require information and production of documents, make test purchases, inspect goods, enter premises, and seize goods and documents.

Summary

Sale of Goods and Supply of Services

A. Civil Liability

Sale of Goods Act 1979

- A contract for the sale of goods is one by which the seller agrees to transfer the property in goods to the buyer, for a money consideration called the price.
- The price may be expressly agreed by the parties, but otherwise a reasonable price is payable.
- The Act implies conditions into contracts for the sale of goods: the goods must correspond with the contract description, must be of satisfactory quality, must be reasonably fit for the purpose made known by the buyer and must correspond with any sample by reference to which the goods are sold. The Sale and Supply of Goods to Consumers Regulations 2002 make amendments to s 14(2).
- It is the duty of the seller to deliver the goods and of the buyer to accept and pay for them.
- Acceptance of a breach of condition deprives the buyer of the right to reject the goods and claim a refund; however, damages may be claimed for breach of warranty.
- The seller's remedies for breach of contract are an action for the price, damages for non-acceptance, lien, stoppage in transit and the right of resale.
- The buyer's remedies for breach of contract are specific performance, rejection of the goods, recovery of the price paid/refusal of payment and damages. Damages may be claimed for non-delivery, breach of condition and breach of warranty.
- Additional remedies are given by the Sale and Supply of Goods to Consumers Regulations 2002.
- Liability for loss caused by breach of the contract cannot be excluded in consumer sales. In non-consumer sales, liability for failure to transfer title cannot be excluded, but exclusion of liability for other implied conditions of the Act may be valid, subject to the requirement of reasonableness.
- Controls on voluntary guarantees are made by the Sale and Supply of Goods to Consumers Regulations 2002.
- The purpose of sale of goods contracts is the transfer of property (ownership). The time of such transfer is important because, once property has passed to the buyer, the risk of accidental loss is usually transferred and an unpaid seller can sue for the contract price. The time of transfer of property depends on whether the contract is for the sale of specific, ascertained or unascertained goods. Section 20 of the Sale of Goods Act 1979 is amended in relation to consumer buyers by the 2002 Regulations.
- The *nemo dat quod non habet* rule means that, generally, a person who does not own goods cannot transfer title in them by sale. There are several statutory exceptions to this rule, contained mainly in the Sale of Goods Act 1979.

The Supply of Goods and Services Act 1982

- Where goods are supplied, terms similar to those of ss 13–15 of the Sale of Goods Act 1979 are implied.
  The ability to exclude these terms is governed by the Unfair Contract Terms Act 1977. Amendments are made by the Sale and Supply of Goods to Consumers Regulations 2002.
- In relation to any service aspect of the contract, there are implied terms that the work will be carried out with reasonable skill and care, that the work will be carried out within a reasonable time (if no time is agreed) and that a reasonable price is payable where none was agreed.

The Consumer Protection (Distance Selling) Regulations 2000

- The Regulations control contracts for the supply of goods and services which are not made face to face, such as online shopping. Some such contracts are not covered, such as internet auctions.
- The Regulations cover information to be given to the consumer before contracting, require confirmation of orders by the supplier and give consumers the right to cancel the contract.

Part I of the Consumer Protection Act 1987

- The Act imposes strict liability on the 'producer' of 'defective' products in relation to a person suffering property loss over £275, death or injury.
- Liability cannot be excluded (s 7) but defences are available under the Act (ss 4 and 6(4)).
- To succeed in proceedings under the Act, the claimant must show that he or she suffered loss, that the product was defective and that it was the defective product which caused the loss.

B. Criminal Liability

Part II of the Consumer Protection Act 1987

- Breach of safety regulations made under the Act is a criminal offence.
- The Secretary of State may make safety regulations and issue prohibition notices and notices to warn.

General Product Safety Regulations 2005

- It is a criminal offence to supply unsafe goods to the market.
- The regulations can apply to new, second-hand and reconditioned goods.

The Consumer Protection from Unfair Trading Regulations 2008

- The Regulations apply to *business to business* and *business to consumer* transactions which could affect consumers.
- Unfair commercial practices are prohibited. A commercial practice is unfair if it is a misleading act or omission or is aggressive. Such practices amount to criminal offences.
- The defences of due diligence and innocent publication of an advertisement may be available.
- Enforcement is by the Office of Fair Trading and Trading Standards departments.

The Cancellation of Contracts made in a Consumer's Home or Place of Work etc Regulations 2008

- The Regulations create criminal offences to protect consumers in relation to *doorstep selling*.
- Notice of the right to cancel the agreement must be given.

The Business Protection from Misleading Marketing Regulations 2008

- The Regulations create the criminal offence of misleading traders by way of advertising.
- Code owners who promote misleading advertising in their codes of conduct, commit a criminal offence.
- The defences of due diligence and innocent publication may be available.
- Enforcement is by *every enforcement authority*; for example, the Office of Fair Trading.

Further Reading

Adams, JN and MacQueen, H, *Atiyah's Sale of Goods*, 12th edn, 2010, Harlow: Pearson Longman.
Dobson, P, 'Sale of Goods Forming Part of a Bulk' (1995) 16 SLR 11 (discussion of s 20A of the SoGA 1979)
Dobson, P, 'The General Product Safety Regulations 2005' (2006) SLR 9 (discussion of the regulations)
Hedley, S, 'Fitness for the buyer's peculiar purpose' [1996] 4 Web JCL1 (discussion of aspects of s 14(3) of the SoGA 1979)
Hodges, C, 'Liability for Old Products' (2001) NLJ 424 (discussion of *Abouzaid v Mothercare (UK) Ltd*)
McAdams, A, 'Product Liability Law and the Consumer – a new era?' (2001) NLJ 647 (discussion of *A & Others v National Blood Authority*)

Websites

www.lawreports.co.uk (daily summaries of new cases)
www.statutelaw.gov.uk (for texts of statutes and regulations referred to in Chapter 8. Use of the SLD facility gives updated versions of amended legislation)
www.oft.gov.uk (powers and work of the Office of Fair Trading)
www.tradingstandards.gov.uk (powers and work of Trading Standards departments)

Part 3

Business Liability

This part of the book examines the potential liability of a business in tort law as well as any liability which may arise as a result of the plethora of environmental regulations which now exist. In addition to contractual liability, a business may attract what is known as tortious liability via the civil law since tort law creates a number of civil obligations which are imposed by law on both individuals and businesses. Liability usually arises via a breach of duty or some other legal obligation and such obligations increasingly impact upon business. The vicarious liability of employers for the tortious acts of employees and the liability of an employer for injured employees can result in significant financial liabilities for business as well as an impact on reputation. A business may attract liability in tort in a number of ways and it is therefore extremely important for those in business to be aware of the wide range of circumstances in which tortious liability may arise so that managers can avoid such impositions.

Environmental law represents another area where liability may arise and increasingly impacts on the management of business liabilities. The rise of environmental legislation, including increased legal regulation to combat climate change, means businesses now have to manage risk and liability to avoid environmental claims and penalties for non-compliance. The value of business assets depends to a large extent upon whether a business is environmentally compliant and in certain instances, corporate individual liability can also arise. Chapter 11 introduces the nature of liability for environmental damage and a basic outline of environmental regulation.

Chapter 9

Negligence

Chapter Contents

Law in Context: Negligence and Compensation Claims

Before considering the legal requirements for negligence, it is useful to discuss two issues which have impacted on tort law in recent times. First, the emergence of what has been referred to as a 'compensation culture', and secondly, the findings of a review on civil litigation and costs (the Jackson Review). In relation to the former, in recent years it has been suggested that the UK is in the grip of a compensation culture in which claimants will sue for compensation at every possible opportunity and for any loss whatsoever. The media frequently report on cases being initiated for trips on village greens, black eyes from conkers, etc. The 'blame and claim' culture certainly impacts on the behaviour of businesses, which increasingly have to assess and manage risk as part of corporate strategy. It is argued that the development of such a culture encourages unwillingness on the part of individuals to take responsibility for their own actions and an increased burden on business to assess and manage risk. In 2004, the Better Regulation Task Force Report *Better Routes to Redress* (2004) played down the existence of a compensation culture. However, the report recognised that any 'belief' that all losses should be compensated created an expectation in individuals that they are somehow entitled to compensation. Accordingly, the fear of potential liability can lead people and organisations to avoid risk and be over-cautious, which can have a detrimental effect on business development and the management of risk. The implementation of the Compensation Act 2006 seeks to respond to such concerns and will be discussed during the section on breach of duty. In more recent times, a Review of Civil Litigation Costs (Jackson Review, 2010), led by Lord Justice Jackson, made a number of recommendations to reduce the costs of civil litigation. The recommendations of the report have sent shockwaves through the personal injury sector of legal services, with many arguing it will reduce access to civil justice as opposed to enhancing it. You will find further reading on the Jackson Review at the end of this chapter.

9.1 Introduction

Negligence is a tort. A tort is a wrongful act against an individual or body corporate and his, her or its property, which gives rise to a civil claim usually for damages, although other remedies are available (for example, injunctions). Liability arising in tort is not dependent upon the existence of a contractual relationship (see previous chapters) and obligations in tort are not agreed to voluntarily like many contractual terms, rather, obligations in tort are imposed by the law. Liability is generally based on fault, although there are exceptions to this, and it is the courts which develop the principles relating to standards of care and required conduct. The motive of the defendant in committing the tort is generally irrelevant.

There are several kinds of harm for which tort law affords potential protection, for example, trespass to land and person, defamation of character and nuisance. Negligence, however, is now the most important of all the torts, not only because an understanding of it is vital to the comprehension of other torts, such as employers' and occupiers' liability, but also because it is the one tort which is constantly developing in the light of social and economic change. This can be seen by reference to professional negligence and liability for economic loss, all of which were originally only compensated if there was in existence a valid contract; in other words, 'no contract, no claim'. After a period of continual development in the scope and application of negligence within these areas, more recent case law indicates that the courts are more cautious in the creation of new duties. The wider economic implications on the public and private sectors are taken into account by the

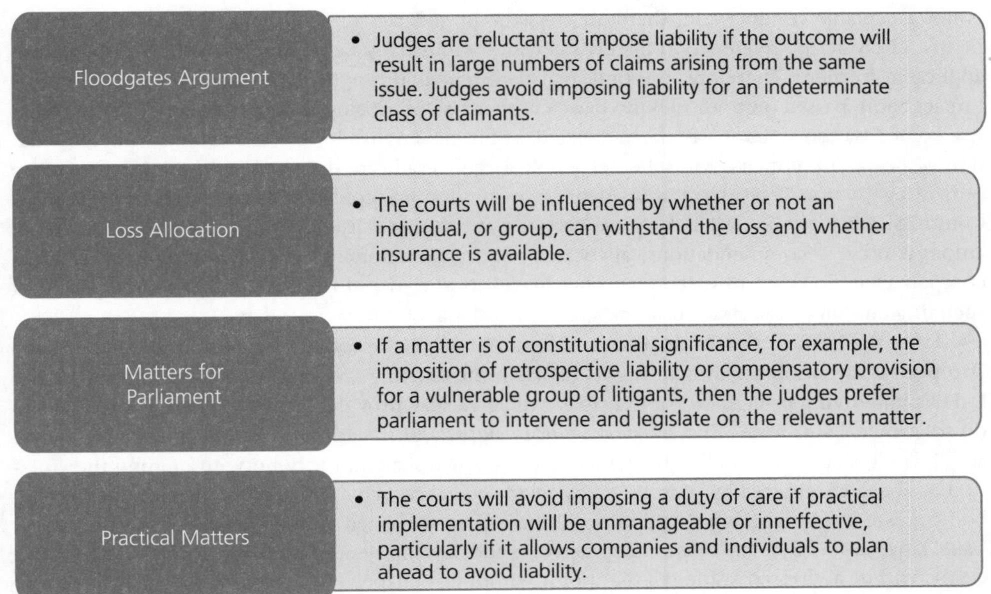

Figure 9.1 Examples of policy considerations in negligence

courts under what are referred to as 'policy considerations' and such considerations continue to influence the courts' decisions when deciding whether or not to extend the scope of actions in negligence. Whether this should be an issue for the courts is always open to debate, but if the courts are to be pragmatic, then they may have no choice but to be restrained in certain economic climates. Nonetheless, if justified, the courts will extend liability to new situations and have also recognised that a duty of care in tort can co-exist with contractual liability (see *Customs and Excise Commissioners v Barclays Bank plc* (2006)).

The tort of negligence has important implications for the business environment and for individuals seeking to enter business, or a related profession. It is vital to possess a basic understanding of the manner and form in which negligent liability can arise. Such knowledge allows the business manager, or professional, to screen business activities for practices which might attract liability. For example, a professional person, such as an auditor, accountant or lawyer may find themselves in a non-contractual relationship with another who will have little choice but to pursue a claim in negligence if they suffer loss as a result of professional malpractice. In order to cover potential claims in negligence and contract, many professional bodies require, as part of membership approval and the issue of practising certificates, that their members take out insurance cover to meet the cost of potential claims (usually, a minimum amount of cover is stipulated for an individual claim). This is known as professional indemnity insurance.

The primary objective of negligence is to provide compensation for the injured party, referred to as the claimant. The aim of compensatory damages within tort law is to attempt to place the claimant back in the position they would have been had the tort not been committed, referred to as *restitution in integrum* (see *Livingstone v Rawyards Coal Company* (1880)). In practical terms, this is not always possible since no amount of monetary compensation equates to good health where an individual has been seriously harmed by someone's negligence. It has also been suggested that liability in tort provides a deterrent and that negligence is no exception; that is, it helps to define what is or is not acceptable conduct and, therefore, sets the boundaries of such behaviour. In everyday life people rarely act by reference to the civil law and will usually be unaware of the civil obligations applicable to them. Therefore, the only real deterrent is through market forces – the economic impact being passed on to those who have a higher risk of causing injury. For many years, alternative compensation systems have been debated within the English legal system and the implementation of no-fault compensation schemes would largely eradicate the need for the injured party to pursue legal action. The subject of accident compensation was considered extensively in the Pearson Commission's *Report on Civil Liability and Compensation for Personal Injury* (Cmnd 7054, 1978) which, amongst other recommendations, advocated the introduction of a no-fault system of accident compensation. To date, no such system has been introduced and is unlikely to arise in a period of spending cuts and economic austerity.

Since the introduction of the Human Rights Act 1998, the courts have been implementing the European Convention on Human Rights (ECHR) into existing law so as to avoid conflict with the ECHR's underlying principles. For example, Article 13 may provide a remedy where UK law fails to do so. Article 13 provides that 'everyone whose rights and freedoms as set out in this convention are violated, shall have an effective remedy before a national authority notwithstanding the violation has been committed by persons acting in an official capacity'. As a result, there is an emerging body of case law in which public authorities have been subjected to negligence claims (see *Osman v United Kingdom* (1998)). The relationship between the development of negligence and human rights claims will be addressed at the relevant point within this chapter.

9.2 Elements of Negligence

There are specific elements of the tort of negligence which have to be established in the correct order if a claim by an injured party is to succeed. The burden of proof is on the claimant to show, on a balance of probabilities, that the defendant owed the claimant a duty of care, that the defendant breached the duty of care and that the defendant's breach of duty is causally linked to the claimant's loss. The three elements are usually referred to as duty of care, breach of duty and causation and remoteness of damage.

Figure 9.2 Elements of negligence

9.3 Duty of Care: Introduction

A person is not automatically liable for every negligent act that he or she commits. The need to establish duty of care sets a legal limit on who can bring a claim, as a duty is not owed to the world at large. The onus is on the claimant to establish that the defendant owes the claimant a duty of care. Unless this first hurdle is crossed, no liability can arise. The modern test for establishing whether a duty of care exists developed from the famous 'snail in the ginger beer bottle case' *Donoghue v Stevenson* (1932). Prior to this case, the duty of care was only owed in limited circumstances. Now, it is said that the categories of negligence are never closed, in that the law can change to take into account new circumstances and social or technical change. Therefore, where there is unintentional or careless damage, there is, potentially, a claim in negligence.

❖ KEY CASE *Donoghue v Stevenson* (1932)

Facts:

Donoghue went into a cafe with her friend, who bought her a bottle of ginger beer. After she had drunk half the bottle, she poured the remainder of the ginger beer into a glass. She then saw what she thought was the remains of a decomposed snail at the bottom. She alleged that she suffered nervous shock as a result of what she saw, and what she thought she had consumed. Donoghue sued the manufacturer, arguing the snail must have got into the bottle at the manufacturer's premises, since the bottle top was securely sealed when her friend bought it. At that time, she was unable to sue the cafe owner as she was not in a contractual relationship with them, her friend having purchased the drink. The case proceeded to the House of Lords and the Law Lords had to consider preliminary arguments as to whether the alleged facts could give rise to a claim in negligence. The manufacturer sought to argue that the facts did not fall into one of the established categories of 'exceptional circumstances' and therefore did not disclose a claim whereby duty of care was recognised. In terms of the outcome, the defendants actually settled the claim out of court and therefore it was never factually established at trial whether there had been a snail or not in the ginger beer (a fact omitted from many textbooks!). However, the case is extremely important for the preliminary ruling on whether a duty of care could be owed in such circumstances.

Decision:

It was held that a manufacturer owed a duty of care to the ultimate consumer of his or her products. He or she must therefore exercise reasonable care to prevent injury to the consumer. The fact that there is no contractual relationship between the manufacturer and the consumer is irrelevant to this action. This is sometimes referred to as the narrow rule in *Donoghue* because the wider implications were identified in what has come to be known as the **neighbour test**, also referred to as the foreseeability test, as laid down by Lord Atkin, who stated that:

> You must take reasonable care to avoid acts and omissions which you could reasonably foresee would be likely to injure your neighbour. Who, then, in law is my neighbour? . . . any person so closely and directly affected by my act that I ought reasonably to have them in contemplation as being so affected when I am directing my mind to the acts and omissions which are called in question.

Lord Atkin's formulation of a general principle of liability forms the basis of the modern law of negligence. The neighbour test formed the basis for deciding the existence of a duty, and today, still forms part of the current incremental test found in *Caparo Industries plc v Dickman* (1990). It follows that, if a duty of care is to exist, the question for the court is somewhat hypothetical, in that the court does not look at the reality (that is, 'did you contemplate the effect of your actions on the injured party?') but asks, 'should you have done so?'; that is, the question is objective, rather than subjective. This does not require specific identity of the injured person; it merely requires ascertainment of the identity of the class of person, for example, pedestrians, children, etc.

9.4 Development of Duty of Care

Before examining the modern law on duty of care in *Caparo Industries plc v Dickman* (1990) it is useful to examine the expansion and retraction of liability in negligence before the courts. Following the adoption of the neighbour test in *Donoghue v Stevenson*, the approach was eventually qualified in *Anns v Merton LBC* (1978). In *Anns* Lord Wilberforce introduced a two-stage test for establishing the existence of a duty, as follows:

(1) Is there a sufficient relationship of proximity, or neighbourhood, between the alleged wrong-doer and the person who has suffered damage such that, in the reasonable contemplation of the former, carelessness on his part may be likely to cause damage to the latter?
(2) If the first question is answered in the affirmative, are there then any considerations which ought to negate, reduce or limit the scope of the duty or the class of persons to whom it is owed or the damages to which a breach of duty may give rise?

The first question clearly corresponded with the 'neighbour test' as laid down in *Donoghue v Stevenson* (1932), although it was referred to as the 'proximity test'. The second question introduced the consideration of public policy issues (see earlier examples of policy considerations), which may have been grounds for limiting the situations where a duty of care could be found to exist. The impact of *Anns* led to the expansion of negligence, as the policy reasons acted only to limit liability once a duty had been found to exist, as opposed to limiting the existence of the duty itself. This was illustrated in the case of *Junior Books Ltd v Veitchi Co Ltd* (1983), in which the House of Lords extended the duty of care because of the close proximity between the parties, in that their relationship was quasi-contractual.

In *Junior Books Ltd*, the defendants were flooring specialists who were subcontracted by the claimants. The claimants alleged that the subcontractors had been negligent when they laid the factory floor and that as a result the floor was defective, although not dangerous. The normal route would have been to pursue a claim for breach of contract but this was unavailable between the claimants and the defendant subcontractors. As a result of the close proximity between the parties, in part due to the fact the claimants had specified which subcontractor was to carry out the work, the House of Lords held that a duty of care existed. The defendants in *Junior Books Ltd* were found to be liable for pure economic loss resulting from their negligent actions. It should be noted that the decision in *Junior Books Ltd* came to be regarded as a special case, providing a narrow exception to the rule that, in general, there can be no liability in negligence for pure economic loss. The decision in *Junior Books Ltd* is often described as the 'high water mark' of liability in the expansion of duty of care and after this decision a period of retraction commenced.

There was gradual criticism of, and retraction from, the approach taken by Lord Wilberforce in *Anns* during the 1980s and early 1990s. This can be evidenced in two cases: *Peabody Donation Fund v Sir Lindsay Parkinson & Co Ltd* (1984), in which the court stressed that the proximity test had to be satisfied before a duty of care could be found to exist; and *Leigh and Sullivan Ltd v Aliakmon Shipping Co Ltd* (1986) (known as *The Aliakmon*), in which Lord Brandon stated that when Lord Wilberforce laid down the two stage test in *Anns*, he was:

> . . . dealing with the approach to the questions of existence and scope of duty of care in a novel type of factual situation, which was not analogous to any factual situation in which the existence of such a duty had already been held to exist. He was not suggesting that the same approach should be adopted to the existence of a duty of care in a factual situation in which the existence of such a duty had repeatedly been held not to exist.

This further limitation was developed in *Yuen Kun Yeu v AG of Hong Kong* (1987), in which Lord Keith stated that Lord Wilberforce's approach 'had been elevated to a degree of importance greater than it merits and greater, perhaps, than its author intended'. Finally, the decision in *Anns* was overruled by *Murphy v Brentwood DC* (1990), where it was held that local authorities owed a duty of care to a building owner to avoid damage to the building which would create a danger to the health and safety of the occupants. The duty arose out of the local authority's powers to require compliance with building regulations. However, as the damage was held to be pure economic loss, it was deemed irrecoverable.

The retraction from *Anns* led to the courts seeking to keep the boundaries of negligence in check by developing what has been referred to as the incremental approach. This now forms the basis of the modern test for duty of care found in *Caparo Industries plc v Dickman* (1990). In many ways, negligence and duty of care appear to have gone full circle, although the judicial interpretation of the incremental approach in *Caparo* has allowed for the controlled expansion of negligence into some areas previously restricted.

9.5 *Caparo v Dickman*: The Modern Test

In *Caparo Industries plc v Dickman* (1990), the application of a three-stage test for establishing a duty of care was recommended. The test is referred to as the 'incremental approach' or 'tripartite test' and requires consideration of the following questions:

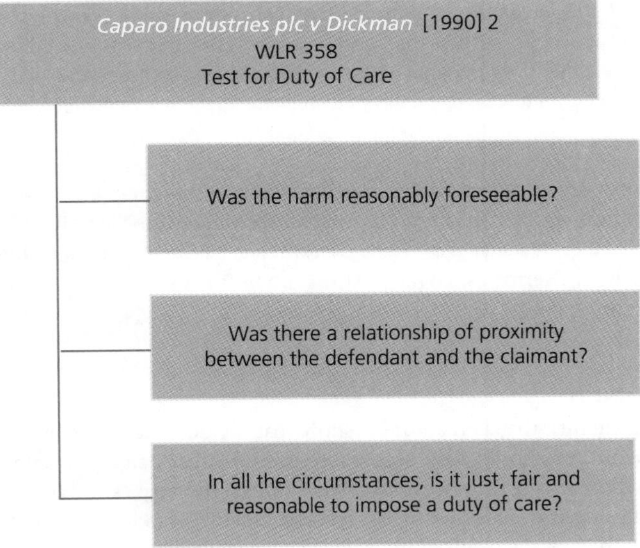

Figure 9.3 Elements of the *Caparo* test

This decision has since been followed in *Marc Rich Co AG v Bishop Rock Marine Co Ltd (The Nicholas H)* (1994). In practical terms, foreseeability of damage will determine proximity in the majority of personal injury cases. The courts will then, where appropriate, consider whether there is proximity and whether it is just and reasonable to impose a duty by considering whether there are any policy reasons for denying or limiting the existence of a duty, for example, the floodgates argument. The courts will not necessarily consider these in all cases, but proximity and the concept of just and reasonableness will have more significance in new or novel situations.

❖ **KEY CASE** *Caparo Industries plc v Dickman* (1990)

Facts:

The claimants owned shares in a company, Fidelity plc, whose annual accounts were audited by the defendants. As part of a takeover bid, the claimants relied on the information contained in the audited accounts prepared by the defendants, and purchased more shares. The accounts had shown a pre-tax profit of £1.2 million. Following the successful takeover bid, the claimants suffered a financial loss when it transpired the company had in fact suffered a loss of £400,000. The claimants argued that the auditors owed them a duty of care and that they had negligently breached this duty. The issue for the court was whether the defendant auditors owed the claimants a duty of care in negligence. The case presented the House of Lords with not only with an opportunity to restate the principles involved in determining liability for negligent economic loss, but also to revisit the general principles for determining duty of care in negligence. The economic loss aspects will be examined in the later section on negligent misstatement.

Decision:

The court held that in determining whether or not a duty of care is owed depends upon foreseeability of damage, proximity of relationship and whether it is just and reasonable to impose a duty of care in the circumstances. On the facts, the House of Lords held that only a limited duty is owed by company auditors to shareholders. This limited duty did not extend to individual members of the company in relation to decisions whether or not to invest further in the company and neither did it extend to members of the public who relied on the accounts to buy shares in a company.

Whilst the concepts are grouped under the incremental approach of Caparo, several judicial comments have indicated that they are no more than convenient labels which are not easily disentangled from each other. In *Customs and Excise Commissioners v Barclays Bank plc* (2006) Lord Hoffman warned against using the terms as 'slogans'. At this point it is useful to explore the three concepts in a little more depth.

9.5.1 Foreseeability

In respect of foreseeability, the claimant must show that the defendant foresaw that damage would occur to the claimant, or should have reasonably foreseen that damage would occur (*Donoghue v Stevenson* (1932)). If there is no foreseeability, there can be no duty (see *Bourhill v Young* (1943)). A more recent illustration can be found in *Topp v London Country Bus (South West) Ltd* (1993) where the claimant sued in respect of the death of his wife who was killed when a joy rider stole the defendant's bus and collided with her bicycle. The claimant was unable to establish that the defendant ought reasonably to have foreseen that a joy rider would have stolen a bus left unattended in a lay-by by the defendant's employee. Whilst the decision of this case may seem somewhat harsh, it illustrates where there is no foreseeability there can be no duty of care.

9.5.2 Proximity

The meaning of proximity is less clear. Proximity does not necessarily relate to the physical proximity of the parties. Rather, it is a term which describes if the circumstances of the legal relationship between the claimant and defendant is sufficient to give rise to a duty of care. What constitutes proximity will vary from case to case and will mean different things. In *Stovin v Wise* (1996), Lord Nicholls remarked:

> The Caparo tripartite test elevates proximity to the dignity of a separate heading. This formulation tends to suggest that proximity is a separate ingredient, distinct from fairness and reasonableness, and capable of being identified by some other criteria. This is not so. Proximity is a slippery word . . . Proximity is convenient shorthand for a relationship between two parties which makes it fair and reasonable that one should owe the other a duty of care.

Proximity is also difficult to separate from the concept of just and reasonableness. A clear example of this can be found in the case of *Hill v Chief Constable of West Yorkshire* (1989), to which we will turn next.

9.5.3 Just and reasonableness

Whether it is just and reasonable to impose a duty of care involves the courts considering a number of legal and policy matters and is often intertwined with the presence or absence of proximity. *Hill v Chief Constable of West Yorkshire* (1989) demonstrates circumstances in which a duty of care was denied on both grounds of proximity and policy. Mrs Hill's daughter was the last murder victim of Peter Sutcliffe, also known as the 'Yorkshire Ripper', a brutal serial killer. She alleged that the police had failed to take reasonable care in apprehending the murderer, as they had interviewed him but had not arrested him prior to her daughter's unlawful killing. Mrs Hill argued that if they had conducted the criminal investigation with more care, the police would have arrested Sutcliffe at an earlier stage and her daughter would still be alive. The House of Lords had to determine whether the police owed her a duty of care. After confirming the need to establish foresight and proximity, the court went on to state that there were policy reasons for not allowing the existence of a duty in this case, namely, that any other result might lead to police discretion being limited and exercised in a defensive frame of mind. This might, in turn, distract the police from their most important function – 'the suppression of crime'. Therefore, it was deemed that Mrs Hill was not in a relationship of proximity with the police and that policy reasons denied a duty of care being established.

9.5.4 Duty of Care and the Human Rights Act 1998

The impact of the Human Rights Act (HRA) 1998 and its relationship to negligence, and in particular, duty of care also needs to be considered. This may be particularly relevant where, for example, the duty of care is restricted on policy grounds. The decision in *Hill* (1989) subsequently came to be interpreted as imposing blanket immunity on the police on policy grounds. As a result of the decision in *Osman v United Kingdom* (2000), an individual may now be able to pursue a claim using the HRA 1998 as the basis of the claim. In the *Osman* case, the claim arose from the tragic shooting of a family member following a campaign of stalking carried out by a third party. The family alleged that the police had negligently handled their complaints and failed to protect the family. The claim against the police failed in the Court of Appeal on the basis of policy reasons and the court's decision appeared to impose what was regarded to be blanket immunity on the police, justified on the basis of the decision in *Hill*. The claimants were refused leave to appeal to the House of Lords. However, the claimants succeeded before the European Court of Human Rights on the basis of a breach of Article 6 of the European Convention on Human Rights (ECHR), which guarantees the right to a fair trial and access to justice. The decision was problematic for the UK courts and it has been argued that the European Court of Human Rights misinterpreted English tort law! (See Lord Browne-Wilkinson in *Barrett v Enfield London Borough Council* (1999).)

Since *Osman*, the courts have had to consider on numerous occasions the relationship between duty of care and the striking out procedure. The HRA 1998 has certainly bought a new perspective to the future development of the tort. Recent case law suggests that the courts are now more reluctant to dismiss claims on this basis and more inclined to hear the facts on merit, even if this results in duty being denied on policy grounds (for example, see *Z v UK* (2001); *D v East Berkshire Community Health Trust* (2003); *Smith v Chief Constable of Sussex* (2008); *Mitchell v Glasgow City Council* (2009)).

9.6 Duty of Care and Omissions

Whether the duty of care principle should extend to omissions to act has proved to be a difficult issue within negligence. Lord Atkin's statement in *Donoghue* refers to 'acts or omissions'; however, later judicial interpretations have limited it to situations where a pre-tort relationship gives rise to an obligation to take action. For example, a contractual relationship may create an obligation to act, or there may be a statutory requirement to take certain positive action. Outside such situations, there is a general exclusionary rule preventing a duty of care in the case of omissions (see *Smith v Littlewoods* (1987), *Stovin v Wise* (1996)). Three exceptions apply to this rule. First, a defendant may owe a duty of care because they exercise a high degree of control over the claimant and therefore should have responsibility for the claimant's safety. For example, prisoners in custody (see *Reeves v Commissioner of Police for the Metropolis* (2000)). Secondly, a duty of care can arise in situations where a defendant has assumed responsibility, for example an assumption of responsibility for the claimant's wellbeing. Assumption of responsibility most commonly arises in contractual or employment situations and therefore is of relevance to businesses. *Barrett v Ministry of Defence* (1995) provides an interesting application of this approach. In this case, a naval pilot stationed on a remote Norwegian base became very drunk and collapsed after a party. The officer in charge ordered that he was to be carried to his bed, and he was left to recover. He lapsed into unconsciousness and choked to death on his own vomit. In the claim that followed, the Court of Appeal took the view that a duty of care arose from the assumption of responsibility. The Court indicated that whilst the deceased was responsible for his own conduct and drunkenness, at the point the officer took control of the situation, he assumed responsibility and in the circumstances should have ensured someone watched over him until he recovered. Consider how this might apply to business events. Finally, a duty of care for an omission may also arise where the defendant is regarded to have created, or adopted, a risk (see *Capital & Counties plc v Hampshire County Council* (1997)). Many of the principles relating to omissions and duty of care have been developed in the context of omissions and public bodies. However, given that the dividing line between a public body and private enterprise is increasingly becoming blurred with new organisational approaches to the public sector, this is an area that business students should keep a keen eye on when developing knowledge of the law and management of risk.

9.7 Breach of Duty

Once a claimant has established that the defendant owes him, or her, a duty of care, he or she must then establish that the defendant is in breach of this duty. The test for establishing breach of duty was laid down in *Blyth v Birmingham Waterworks Co* (1856). A breach of duty occurs if the defendant:

> fails to do something which a reasonable man, guided upon those considerations which ordinarily regulate the conduct of human affairs, would do; or does something which a prudent and reasonable man would not do [*per* Alderson B].

The test is an objective test, judged through the eyes of the reasonable man. The fact that the defendant has acted less skilfully than the reasonable man would expect will usually result in breach being established. This is the case even where the defendant is inexperienced in his particular trade or profession. For example, a learner driver must drive in the manner of a driver of skill, experience and care (*Nettleship v Weston* (1971)). Children should be judged on whether they have the 'foresight and prudence of a normal child of that age' (see *Mullin v Richards* (1998)). The degree or standard of care to be exercised by such a person will vary, as there are factors, which may increase the standard of care to be exercised by the defendant. The test therefore possesses some flexibility (for an interesting example, see *Mansfield v Weetabix Ltd* (1997)).

9.8 Breach of Duty: Relevant Factors

When determining whether breach of duty has arisen, the courts can have regard to a number of factors.

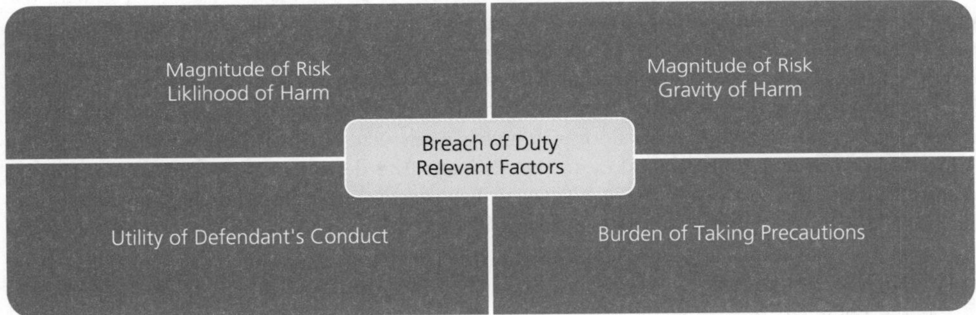

Figure 9.4 Relevant Factors

9.8.1 Magnitude of risk

In deciding whether the defendant has failed to act as the reasonable man would act, the degree of care must be balanced against the degree of risk involved. Consideration of this is comprised of two elements, firstly, the likelihood of injury and secondly, the gravity of the likely harm. The greater the risk of injury or the more likely it is to occur, the more the defendant will have to do to fulfil his duty and avoid liability. In *Bolton v Stone* (1951), a cricket ground was surrounded by a 17 ft high wall and the pitch was situated some way from the road. A batsman hit a ball exceptionally hard, driving it over the wall, where it struck the claimant, who was standing on the highway. It was held that the claimant could not succeed in his action, as the likelihood of such injury occurring was small, as was the risk involved, and therefore no breach of duty arose. The slight risk was outweighed by the height of the wall and the fact that a ball had been hit out of the ground only six times in 30 years (the defendants were able to produce records to prove this point).

This can be contrasted with *Hilder v Associated Portland Cement Manufacturers* (1961) a case in which the defendant had repeatedly allowed children to play football on waste ground which was situated next to a busy road. Balls frequently went onto the road and on one occasion a ball caused a motorcyclist to crash. The motorcyclist was killed. As a result of the frequency of the incidents, and the knowledge of this on the part of the defendant, the risk of accident was considered to be high and the defendant was held to be in breach of the duty of care.

The court may also consider the gravity of any potential harm. This is illustrated by *Haley v London Electricity Board* (1965), in which the defendants, in order to carry out repairs, had made a hole in the pavement. Haley, who was blind, often walked along this stretch of pavement. He was usually able to avoid obstacles by using his white stick. The precautions taken by the Electricity Board would have prevented a sighted person from injuring himself, but not a blind person. Haley fell into the hole, striking his head on the pavement, and became deaf as a consequence. It was held that the Electricity Board was in breach of its duty of care to pedestrians. It had failed to ensure that the excavation was safe for all pedestrians, not just sighted persons. It was clearly not reasonably safe for blind persons, yet it was foreseeable that they may use this pavement (see also *Gough v Thorne* (1966), concerning young children; *Daly v Liverpool Corp* (1939), concerning old people; and *Paris v Stepney BC* (1951), concerning existing conditions).

9.8.2 Burden of taking precautions against the risk

Another factor in deciding whether the defendant is in breach of his duty to the claimant is the cost and practicability of overcoming the risk. The foreseeable risk has to be balanced against the measures necessary to eliminate it. If the cost of these measures far outweighs the risk, the defendant will probably not be in breach of duty for failing to carry out these measures. This is illustrated by the case of *Latimer v AEC Ltd* (1952). A factory belonging to AEC became flooded after an abnormally heavy rainstorm. The rain mixed with oily deposits on the floor, making the floor very slippery. Sawdust was spread on the floor, but it was insufficient to cover the whole area. Latimer, an employee, slipped on a part of the floor to which sawdust had not been applied. It was held that AEC Ltd was not in breach of its duty to the claimant. The defendant's had taken all reasonable precautions and had eliminated the risk as far as they practicably could without going so far as to close the factory. There was no evidence to suggest that the reasonably prudent employer would have closed down the factory and, as far as the court was concerned, the cost of doing that far outweighed the risk to the employees.

If the defendant can show that what he or she has done is common practice, then this is evidence that a proper standard of care has been exercised. However, if the common practice is in itself negligent, then his or her actions in conforming to such a practice will be actionable, as can be seen in *Paris v Stepney BC* (1951). There, the common practice of not wearing safety glasses could not be condoned, as it was in itself inherently negligent.

9.8.3 Social utility

The degree of risk has to be balanced against the social utility and importance of the defendant's activity. If the activity is of particular importance to the community, then the taking of greater risks may be justified in the circumstances. In *Watt v Hertfordshire CC* (1954), the claimant, a fireman, was called out to rescue a woman trapped beneath a lorry. The lifting jack had to be carried on an ordinary lorry, as a suitable vehicle was unavailable. The jack slipped, injuring the claimant. It was held that the employer was not in breach of duty. The importance of the activity and the fact that it was an emergency were found to justify the risk involved in attempting to save a life. It should be noted that the courts would be unlikely to adopt such a position if the risk-taking conduct was part of a commercial venture.

9.9 Breach of Duty: Skilled Persons and Professionals

The standard of care to be exercised by people professing to have a particular skill is not judged on the basis of the reasonable man. The actions of a skilled person must be judged by what the ordinary skilled man in that job or profession would have done, for example, the reasonable doctor, accountant, engineer, electrician, etc. Such a person is judged on the standard of knowledge possessed by the profession at the time that the accident occurred. Obviously, there is an onus on the skilled person to keep himself abreast of changes and improvements in professional practice and technology.

❖ KEY CASE *Bolam v Friern Hospital Management Committee* (1957)

Facts:

The claimant sustained a fractured pelvis whilst undergoing electro-convulsive therapy (ECT) at the defendant's hospital. He alleged that the doctor had not warned him of the risks; he had not been given relaxant drugs prior to treatment; and had not been restrained during the treatment. At the time the injuries occurred there were two professional schools of thought on administration of this type of treatment. One advocated that relaxant drugs should be used whereas the other argued they should not.

Decision:

It was held that the doctor was not in breach of duty (and there was, therefore, no vicarious liability on the part of the hospital management committee), because this form of treatment was accepted at that time by a certain body of the medical profession. McNair, J stated: 'A doctor is not guilty of negligence if he has acted in accordance with a practice accepted as proper by a responsible body of medical men skilled in that particular art. Putting it another way round, a doctor is not negligent if he is acting in accordance with such a practice, merely because there is a body of opinion that takes a contrary view.'

The statement made by McNair, J was adopted by the House of Lords in later cases (see *Whitehouse v Jordan* (1981)). Although *Bolam* relates to a medical negligence claim, the rule extends to all claims for professional negligence when assessing breach of duty. The impact of the *Bolam* test is that doctors, and other professionals, will be able to demonstrate that they have not breached their duty of care, if they can produce expert witnesses to testify that the defendant's course of action falls within the ambit of accepted professional practice, even if other schools of thought and opinion exist. It is argued that the effect of the *Bolam* test disadvantages claimants in professional negligence claims.

The *Bolam* test has been qualified by the decision in *Bolitho v City and Hackney HA* (1998): in order to be accepted, expert opinion must be shown to be reasonable and responsible and to have a logical basis (*per* Lord Browne-Wilkinson). There is continued criticism of the decision in *Bolam*, particularly in so far as, in determining the standard of care, professionals are allowed to set their own standard which is not measured against that of the reasonable man. It can therefore be argued that professionals operate from a subjective standard determined by other professionals. As a result, they have a great degree of protection from allegations of negligence. However, if professionals are to push back the boundaries in their area of expertise, then it can also be argued that they should be given this leeway.

In considering breach of a professional duty of care, consideration will be given to the state of knowledge at the time the breach allegedly occurred. For example, in *Roe v Minister of Health* (1954), a patient was paralysed after being given a spinal injection. This occurred because the fluid being injected had become contaminated with the storage liquid, which had seeped through minute cracks in the phials. It was held that there was no breach of duty, since the doctor who administered the injection had no way of detecting the contamination at that time.

Trainee professionals must exercise the same high standard of care as those who are already proficient in that skill, and if in any doubt about the course of action to adopt, should immediately seek the advice of their professional supervisor or manager. There is evidence that professional negligence claims have risen sharply in recent years and the cost of professional indemnity insurance has risen accordingly.

9.10 Impact of the Compensation Act 2006

As discussed earlier in this chapter, there is a perception that compensation is too readily available in our legal system and the imposition of liability in all areas can have a detrimental effect in that it discourages individuals taking any sort of risk. The threat of potential claims may deter those involved in activities which are beneficial to society, for example, sporting activities, school trips, volunteering, etc. In an attempt to counteract this, the Compensation Act 2006 was introduced.

Section 1 of the Act provides that a court, when considering a claim in negligence or for breach of statutory duty, can take into account whether the steps required to meet the standard of care are likely to prevent a desirable activity taking place or discourage individuals from undertaking certain activities. The impact of the Compensation Act 2006 has been noted in cases (see *Perry v Harris* (2008), *Poppleton v Trustees of the Portsmouth Youth Activities Committee* (2008)). More recently, the point was considered in *Hopps v Mott McDonald Ltd* (2009), in which the claimant suffered severe personal injury when hit by an exploding IED in Iraq. The claimant was a civilian electrical engineer working for the MoD and the incident occurred when he was being transported in a civilian vehicle in an area known as 'bomb alley'. Although the judge acknowledged the claimant's contribution to improving the life of the people in the region, the claim was ultimately dismissed on the basis that there was only a very small risk of injury and it was therefore not unreasonable for a civilian to be transported in an unarmoured civilian vehicle.

9.11 Proof of Negligence and *Res Ipsa Loquitur*

The burden of proof in establishing breach of duty normally rests on the claimant. There are two circumstances when this may change. First, s 11 of the Civil Evidence Act 1968 provides that where a criminal conviction is found in relation to a matter also to be determined by the civil courts, for example, a road accident, the burden of proof shifts from the claimant to the defendant to demonstrate that he or she was not in fact negligent in the civil claim.

Secondly, in certain circumstances, the inference of negligence may be drawn from the facts. If this can be done, the claimant is relieved of the burden, which moves to the defendant to rebut the presumption of negligence. This is known as *res ipsa loquitur*, that is, the thing speaks for itself. It can only be relied upon where the sole explanation for what happened is the negligence of the defendant, yet the claimant has insufficient evidence to establish the defendant's negligence in the normal way (see *Scott v London and St Katherine Docks Co* (1865). If the defendant can rebut the presumption of negligence by giving a satisfactory explanation, it is open to the claimant to establish negligence in the normal way. In practice, he or she is unlikely to succeed because, if sufficient evidence were available in the first place, *res ipsa loquitur* would not have been pleaded. There are three criteria which must be satisfied for the rule to apply.

9.11.1 Exclusive control

It must be shown that the damage was caused by something under the sole management or control of the defendant, or by someone for whom he or she is responsible or whom he or she has a right to control (*Gee v Metropolitan Railway* (1873)).

9.11.2 The occurrence cannot have happened without negligence

This depends on the facts of each case. If there are other possible explanations as to how the incident occurred, *res ipsa loquitur* will fail. In *Mahon v Osborne* (1939), a patient died after a swab was left in her body after an operation. No one could explain how this had happened; therefore, *res ipsa loquitur* applied.

9.11.3 The cause of the occurrence is unknown

If the defendant can put forward a satisfactory explanation as to how the accident occurred which shows no negligence on his part, the maxim is inapplicable. In *Pearson v NW Gas Board* (1968), the claimant's husband was killed and her house destroyed when a gas main fractured. She pleaded *res ipsa loquitur*. However, the Gas Board put forward the explanation that the gas main could have fractured due to earth movement after a heavy frost. This explanation was plausible and, as it showed no negligence on the board's part, it was not liable.

9.12 Causation and Remoteness

To recap, for a claimant to succeed in negligence they must be able to prove that the defendant owed the claimant a duty of care in relation to the harm suffered; that the defendant breached the duty of care by failing to live up to the standard of care expected of him or her; and finally that the claimant suffered harm as a result of the breach of duty which is not regarded as being too remote a consequence of the defendant's activity. Causation and remoteness of damage are the shorthand names given to the final element of an action in negligence. They are referred to as 'causation in fact' and 'causation in law'. Although separate topics, together they demonstrate that the defendant should be legally responsible for the harm caused by the breach of duty of care. Policy has influenced many of the decisions in this area and the cases do not always present a coherent or consistent approach to the question of causation.

9.12.1 Causation in fact: The 'but for' test

The claimant must show that he or she has suffered some injury, but it does not necessarily have to be physical injury. Furthermore, he or she must show that this injury was caused by the defendant's negligence. This is known as causation in fact. The 'but for' test is used to establish whether the defendant's negligence was the cause of the injury to the claimant.

Barnett v Chelsea & Kensington Hospital Management Committee (1969)

Facts:

Mr Barnett attended the hospital casualty department complaining of vomiting and stomach pains. The doctor on duty failed to examine the patient and sent him home without treatment, informing him to attend his own doctor in the morning if there had been no improvement. Shortly afterwards, Mr. Barnett died from arsenic poisoning. The doctor owed the patient a duty of care and breached the duty by failing to attend. However, it was argued that the doctor was not negligent, the medical evidence indicated that the patient would have died anyway as the poisoning was advanced by the time the patient presented at the hospital.

Decision:

The doctor was not held to be liable for breach of duty. The evidence indicated that even if the doctor had examined the patient promptly, the patient would have died in any event. It could not be said that 'but for' the negligence the man would not have died.

Therefore, in order to satisfy the test, the claimant must show that, 'but for' the defendant's actions, the damage would not have occurred. If the damage would have occurred irrespective of a breach of duty on the part of the defendant, then the breach is not the cause. For example, in *Cutler v Vauxhall Motors Ltd* (1971), the claimant suffered a grazed ankle whilst at work, due to the defendant's negligence. The graze became ulcerated because of existing varicose veins and the claimant had to undergo an immediate operation to remove the veins. It was held that the claimant could not recover damages for the operation, because the evidence was that he would have had to undergo the operation within five years anyway, irrespective of the accident at work.

A problem arises with the *But For* test when there is more than one possible cause for the injury or loss, for example, a negligent and a natural cause. Multiple causes raise a number of difficulties in negligence. Where there are a number of potential causes the established rule is that the claimant must prove that the defendant's breach of duty 'materially contributed' to the risk of injury (*Bonnington Castings Ltd v Wardlow* (1956)). It has been suggested that a 'material increase in the risk' of injury is sufficient and equates to 'material contribution' (*McGhee v National Coal Board* (1973)) although such an approach has not proved popular with the courts (*Wilsher v Essex AHA* (1988)). A detailed examination of the case law within this area is complex and beyond the scope of this textbook. However, it is illustrative to examine the policy arguments in cases involving asbestos related injury since because of the nature of the disease, it can be extremely difficult to establish a sole cause, and therefore some flexibility in applying the legal principles is justifiable. A case which illustrates these complexities and the role of policy considerations is *Fairchild v Glenhaven Funeral Services Ltd* (2002).

❖ KEY CASE — *Fairchild v Glenhaven Funeral Services Ltd* (2002)

Facts:

The case involved a number of claimants who had developed mesothelioma after exposure to asbestos. Mesothelioma is a malignant disease which is caused by the single inhalation of an asbestos fibre, as opposed to cumulative exposure. All the claimants had been exposed to asbestos at work. The problem for the claimants was that it was evidentially impossible to prove which employer's exposure had resulted in the inhalation of the fibre. The case was complicated by the fact that many of the employers could not be traced or had gone out of business. The Court of Appeal applied the 'but for' test and held that because the claimants could not prove on a balance of probabilities which employer had caused the injury, the action failed.

Decision:

The House of Lords reversed the decision and held that a strict application of the 'but for' test resulted in injustice and an unfair result. The court recognised that in special circumstances the 'but for' test could be departed from and in this case relied upon the 'material increase in risk' approach in *McGhee*. On the facts, each of the defendants had materially increased the risk of the claimants contracting mesothelioma and therefore each defendant should be jointly and severally liable. *Fairchild* is an exceptional example and is clearly influenced by policy considerations. Lord Bingham commented that the injustice involved in imposing liability was outweighed by the injustice that would arise if redress was denied to the victims in the case.

The limits of *Fairchild* were considered in *Barker v Corus* (2006) and since then the implementation of the Compensation Act 2006, s 3, provides that where the conditions of *Fairchild* arise and it cannot be conclusively shown which of the employers actually, or most likely, caused the disease, the 'responsible person' will be liable for the full damages. *Sienkiewicz v Greif* (2011) considered the impact of the Compensation Act 2006 in greater detail. In *Sienkiewicz*, the claimant had worked at the defendant's factory for approximately 20 years during which time she had regularly entered areas of the factory that were contaminated with asbestos. Following a successful claim, the defendants appealed to both the Court of Appeal and the Supreme Court, which found in favour of the claimant, the Supreme Court clarifying that even though there was only one employer, the case fell within the *Fairchild* exception. Lord Phillips took the view that gaps in our knowledge of mesothelioma continue to justify the adoption of special causation rules and that even where liability of only one employer is considered, this falls within the ambit of s 3 of the Compensation Act 2006 and not the 'but for' test. What remains unclear is whether the exception will apply to other diseases whose aetiology is also uncertain.

9.12.2 Causation: loss of chance

Sometimes, the argument is put forward that the breach of duty caused loss through loss of opportunity or benefit and this is referred to as 'loss of chance'. It has been raised unsuccessfully in medical negligence cases. For example, in *Hotson v East Berkshire AHA* (1987) the court considered whether the defendant could be liable for loss of chance. Here, a boy fell from a tree and injured his hip. At the hospital, his injury was misdiagnosed and, by the time the mistake was discovered, he was left with a permanent disability. It was held that, as 75% of such cases were inoperable, there was no lost chance and, therefore, the claimant could not recover as he had not proved causation in fact. The argument was also unsuccessful in *Gregg v Scott* (2005) where a doctor failed to accurately diagnose a growth as cancerous and as a result the claimant's chance of survival decreased. The courts have indicated a willingness to take a slightly different approach in commercial cases of loss of chance (*Allied Maples Group Ltd v Simmons and Simmons* (1999); *Platform Home Loans v Oyston Shipways Ltd* (1999); and *Dixon v Clement Jones* (2004)).

9.12.3 Break in the chain of causation: *novus actus interveniens*

Where there is a break in the chain of causation, the defendant will not be liable for damage caused after the break. The issues are whether the whole sequence of events is the probable consequence of the defendant's actions and whether it is reasonably foreseeable that these events may happen (*Home Office v Dorset Yacht Co Ltd* (1970)). This break in the chain is caused by an intervening act and the law recognises that such acts fall into three categories, as follows.

A natural event

A natural event does not automatically break the chain of causation. If the defendant's breach has placed the claimant in a position where the natural event can add to that damage, the chain will not be broken unless the natural event was totally unforeseen. In *Carslogie Steamship Co Ltd v Royal Norwegian Government* (1952), a ship which was owned by Carslogie had been damaged in a collision caused by the defendant's negligence. The ship was sent for repair and, on this voyage, suffered extra damage, caused by the severe weather conditions. This resulted in the repairs taking 40 days longer than anticipated. It was held that the bad weather acted as a new intervening act, for which the defendant was not liable. The effect of the new act in this case prevented the claimant from recovering compensation for the time that it would have taken to repair the vessel in respect of the collision damage, as the ship would have been out of use in any case, due to the damage caused by the weather.

Act of a third party

Where the act of a third party following the breach of the defendant causes further damage to the claimant, such an act may be deemed to be a *novus actus*; the defendant will not then be liable for damage occurring after the third party's act. In *Lamb v Camden LBC* (1981), due to the defendant's negligence, a water main was damaged, causing the claimant's house to be damaged and the house to be vacated until it had been repaired. While the house was empty, squatters moved in and caused further damage to the property. It was held that the defendant was not liable for the squatters' damage. Although it was a reasonably foreseeable risk, it was not a likely event. Furthermore, it was not the duty of the council to keep the squatters out. The third party's act need not be negligent in itself in order to break the chain of causation, although the courts take the view that a negligent act is more likely to break the chain than one that is not negligent, as can be seen in *Knightley v Johns* (1982).

Act of the claimant

In *McKew v Holland, Hannen and Cubbitts (Scotland) Ltd* (1969), the claimant was injured at work. As a result, his leg sometimes gave way without warning. He was coming downstairs when his leg gave way, so he jumped in order to avoid falling head first and badly injured his ankle. It was held that the defendants were not liable for this additional injury. The claimant had not acted reasonably in attempting to negotiate the stairs without assistance and his actions amounted to a *novus actus interveniens*.

The case of *Reeves v Commissioner of Police* (2000) questioned whether an act of suicide amounted to a *novus actus*. In this case, D, apparently of sound mind, committed suicide in police custody. At first instance, the police were held to be in breach of their duty of care, but the court treated the deceased's behaviour as a totally voluntary act, which broke the chain of causation. The Court of Appeal initially allowed the Commissioner's appeal. However, the House of Lords found the police liable on the basis that they were under a specific duty to protect D from the risk of suicide and had failed to do so. The defence of voluntary assumption of risk was not compatible with this duty. The House of Lords allowed the appeal, reducing the amount of damages. A deliberate act of suicide was not a *novus actus interveniens* negating the casual connection between breach of duty and death. To hold as such would lead to the absurd result that the very act which the duty sought to prevent would be fatal to establishing a causative link. On the issue of causation, both the police, who had been negligent in leaving the door hatch open, and the deceased, who had responsibility for his own life, were the causes of his death. The deceased was held to be contributorily negligent and damages were reduced by 50%.

It can be seen from the above that whilst generally the 'but for' test can be used to establish causation, more complex circumstances require a different approach. However, even where causation in fact can be established, it does not mean that the defendant will be liable for all of the damage to the claimant. A *novus actus* may break the chain of causation and there must also be causation in law which is examined in the next section.

9.13 Causation in Law: Remoteness of Damage

It must be understood that, even where causation is established, the defendant will not necessarily be liable for all of the damage resulting from the breach. This was not always the case and the way in which the law has developed must be considered. In *Re Polemis and Furness, Withy & Co* (1921), the claimant's ship was destroyed by fire when one of the employees of the company to whom the ship had been chartered negligently knocked a plank into the hold. The hold was full of petrol vapour. The plank caused a spark as it struck the side and this ignited the vapour. It was held that the defendants were liable for the loss of the ship, even though the presence of petrol vapour and the causing of the spark were unforeseen. The fire was the direct result of the breach of duty and the defendant was liable for the full extent of the damage, even where the manner in which it took place was unforeseen.

The directness test and the case of *Re Polemis* is no longer regarded as the current test for remoteness of damage. The test currently used arose from the *The Wagon Mound* (No 1) (1961) case.

❖ KEY CASE *Overseas Tankship (UK) Ltd v Morts Docks Engineering Co Ltd (The Wagon Mound (No. 1))* (1961)

Facts:
The defendants negligently allowed furnace oil to spill from a ship into Sydney harbour. The oil spread and came to lie beneath a wharf, which was owned by the claimants. The claimants had been carrying out welding operations and, on seeing the oil, they stopped welding in order to ascertain whether it was safe. They were assured that the oil would not catch fire, and so resumed welding. Cotton waste, which had fallen into the oil, caught fire. This in turn ignited the oil and a fire spread to the claimant's wharf.

Decision:
It was held that the defendants were in breach of duty. However, they were only liable for the damage caused to the wharf and slipway through the fouling of the oil. They were not liable for the damage caused by fire because damage by fire was at that time unforeseeable. This particular oil had a high ignition point and it could not be foreseen that it would ignite on water. The court refused to apply the rule in *Re Polemis*.

The test of reasonable foresight arising out of *The Wagon Mound* (No. 1) clearly takes into account such things as scientific knowledge at the time of the negligent act. The question to be asked in determining the extent of liability is whether the damage is of such a kind as the reasonable man should have foreseen. This does not mean that the defendant should have foreseen precisely the sequence or nature of the events. This is illustrated in the case of *Hughes v Lord Advocate* (1963), where employees of the Post Office, who were working down a manhole, left it without a cover but with a tent over it and lamps around it. A child picked up a lamp and went into the tent. He tripped over the lamp, knocking it into the hole. An explosion occurred and the child was burned. The risk of the child being burned by the lamp was foreseeable. However, the vapourisation of the paraffin in the lamp and its ignition were not foreseeable. It was held that the defendants were liable for the injury to the claimant. It was foreseeable that the child might be burned and it was immaterial that neither the extent of his injury nor the precise chain of events leading to it was foreseeable.

The test of remoteness is not easy to apply. The cases themselves highlight the uncertainty of the courts. For example, in *Doughty v Turner Manufacturing Co Ltd* (1964), an asbestos cover was knocked into a bath of molten metal. This led to a chemical reaction, which was at that time unforeseeable.

The molten metal erupted and burned the claimant, who was standing nearby. It was held that only burning by splashing was foreseeable and that burning by an unforeseen chemical reaction was not a variant on this. It could be argued that the proper question in this case should have been 'was burning foreseeable?', as this was the question asked in *Hughes*. A similar issue surrounding the questions asked to establish whether the harm is foreseeable can be seen in *Tremain v Pike* (1969), in which a farmhand contracted a rare disease transmitted by rat's urine. It was foreseeable that the claimant might sustain injury from rat bites or from contaminated food, but not from the contraction of this disease. Once again, this case raises the issue of whether the correct question was asked (see also *Robinson v Post Office* (1974)).

In *Jolley v London Borough of Sutton* (2000), the House of Lords, overruling the Court of Appeal, decided that it was sufficient to satisfy the test of remoteness if some harm was foreseeable, even though the precise way in which the injuries occurred could not be foreseen. In this particular case, the Council failed to move an abandoned boat for two years. It was known to the Council that children were attracted to and played in the boat even though it was dangerous. A 14 year old boy was seriously injured when he and a friend tried to jack-up the boat to repair it.

The above sections have provided an overview of the general principles relating to negligence. For those involved in business, or the study of business and related professions, it is important to have a thorough grasp of the general principles so as to be able to understand their application in more complex and business specific circumstances. The remainder of this chapter will look at a range of specific issues relating to negligence and business.

9.14 Negligence and Economic Loss

There are two categories of economic loss which may form the basis of a claim in negligence. First, there is economic loss arising out of physical injury or damage to property; and, secondly, there is what is known as 'pure' economic loss, which is the sole loss sustained, unconnected with physical damage. Only the former is recoverable, unless the claimant can show that there was a 'special relationship' between him or her and the defendant, in which the defendant assumed responsibility for the claimant's economic welfare (see *Williams v Natural Life Health Foods Ltd* (1998)). In effect, the law has reverted to the decision in the following case for defining the extent of liability for pure economic loss.

In *Spartan Steel and Alloys Ltd v Martin & Co* (1973), the claimants manufactured steel alloys 24 hours a day which required continuous power. The defendant's employees damaged a power cable, which resulted in a lack of power for 14 hours. There was a danger of damage to the furnace, so this had to be shut down and the products in the process of manufacture removed, thereby reducing their value. The claimants also suffered loss of profits as a result of the interruption to manufacturing. It was held that the defendants were liable for the physical damage to the products in the furnace and the loss of profit arising out of this. There was, however, no liability for economic loss which was unconnected with the physical damage.

The rule that economic loss was only recoverable where it was directly the consequence of physical damage had been challenged in *Junior Books Ltd v Veitchi Ltd* (1983) (see earlier), in which a claim for pure economic loss was allowed on the basis of there being sufficiently close proximity between the claimants and the subcontractors who had carried out the work for the main contractor. However, following this case, there was a gradual retraction from recovery for pure economic loss. For example, in *Muirhead v Industrial Tank Specialties Ltd* (1986), it was held that there was insufficient proximity between the purchaser of goods and the manufacturer of the goods with respect to a claim for pure economic loss. This was reinforced in the cases of *Simaan General Contracting Co v Pilkington Glass Ltd (No 2)* (1988) and *Greater Nottingham Co-operative Society Ltd v Cementation Piling and Foundations Ltd* (1988), where the courts refused to find sufficient proximity in tripartite business relationships. The expansion of the law in this area had resulted from Lord Wilberforce's two stage test in *Anns v*

Merton LBC (1978). As the gradual withdrawal from that decision grew apace, it was inevitable that a final blow would be dealt to this test. In D and F Estates Ltd v Church Commissioners for England (1988), it was held that a builder was not liable in negligence to the owner for defects in quality, only for personal injury or damage to other property, thereby bringing back the distinction between actions in tort and contract. Additionally, it was held that pure economic loss could only be recovered in an action for negligent misstatement or where the circumstances fell within Junior Books. Finally, in Murphy v Brentwood DC (1990), the decision in Anns was overruled; it was made clear that liability for pure economic loss could only be sustained in an action for negligent misstatement based on Hedley Byrne & Co v Heller and Partners (1964).

9.15 Liability for Negligent Misstatements

Historically, there was only liability for negligent misstatements causing physical damage, intentionally dishonest or fraudulent statements, or where there was a fiduciary or contractual relationship between the parties (Derry v Peek (1889)). The development of duty of care in relation to negligent misstatements arose from the case of Hedley Byrne & Co Ltd v Heller and Partners (1964).

❖ KEY CASE — *Hedley Byrne & Co Ltd v Heller and Partners (1964)*

Facts:

Hedley Byrne was an advertising agency which had been asked, by a company called Easipower Ltd, to purchase them some advertising space. Hedley Byrne's bank contacted Easipower's bank, Heller (the defendants), to make inquiries into the financial position of Easipower. On two separate occasions, the defendants responded with a favourable reply about the client's financial position, adding the words 'without responsibility'. Hedley Byrne relied on this advice and lost a lot of money when their clients went into liquidation. However, they lost their action against the bank because of the exclusion clause, which at that time was held to be valid. The importance of the case is the *dictum* on negligent misstatements.

Decision:

It was held that a duty of care would exist where:

> . . . one party seeking information and advice was trusting the other to exercise such a degree of care as the circumstances required, where it was reasonable for him to do that, and where the other party gave the information or advice when he knew or ought to have known the enquirer was relying on him.

In Hedley Byrne liability for negligent misstatements is based on the existence of a 'special relationship'; that is, the defendant must hold himself out in some way as having specialised knowledge, knowing that any information that he or she gives will be relied upon by the claimant. Interestingly, it has been decided that there may be concurrent liability in tort and contract, so that the claimant may choose which cause of action provides him or her with the best remedy. This is illustrated in Henderson v Merrett Syndicates Ltd (1994), in which it was held that an assumption of responsibility by a person providing professional or quasi-professional services, coupled with reliance by the person for whom the services were provided, could give rise to tortious liability, irrespective of whether there was a contractual relationship between the parties. This decision finally laid to rest the decision in *Tai Hing Cotton Mill Ltd v Liu Chong Hing Bank Ltd* (1986), which excluded concurrent liability in contract and tort.

As the law has developed, some attempts to limit liability can be found in the case law. For example, in *Mutual Life and Citizens Assurance Co v Evatt* (1971), it was held that the defendant should be in the business of giving such advice, although the minority in this case required the claimant to make it clear to the defendant that he was seeking advice which he may then have relied on. There is, in general, no liability for information given on a purely social occasion, but advice from friends on other occasions may result in liability, as can be seen in *Chaudry v Prabhakar* (1988). Silence or inaction can rarely amount to misstatement, unless there was a duty on the defendant to disclose or take action. In *Legal and General Assurance Ltd v Kirk* (2002), the Court of Appeal held that for a claim based on negligent misstatement in respect of an employment reference, a statement must actually have been made to a third party. The fact that Mr Kirk had not applied for a reference in the knowledge that the contents of the reference would inevitably have led to his being rejected by a prospective employer was insufficient to establish liability on the part of the employer. In *Spring v Guardian Assurance* (1995) the court confirmed that a duty of care was owed to take care in providing accurate references. The courts have recognised that it is possible for there to be a voluntary assumption of responsibility by the defendant and reliance by the claimant on that assumption (*La Banque Financière de la Cité v Westgate Insurance Co Ltd* (1990)).

The House of Lords reviewed the principles relating to liability for negligent misstatement in *Caparo v Dickman* (1990) (see earlier). It was held that, when the accounts were prepared, a duty of care was owed to members of the company (that is, the shareholders), but only so far as to allow them to exercise proper control over the company. This duty did not extend to members as individuals and potential purchasers of shares. The onus was clearly on the appellants in these circumstances to make their own independent inquiries, as it was unreasonable to rely on the auditors. The House of Lords indicated that they preferred an incremental approach to establishing liability and laid down a number of guidelines as to the circumstances in which the *Hedley Byrne* duty will be owed, namely:

- the advice given must be required for a purpose,
- the purpose must be made known to the advisor at the time the advice is given,
- the advisor must know that the advice will be communicated to the advisee,
- it must be known the advice will be acted upon without independent advice or inquiry,
- the advice must be so acted upon to the detriment of the advisee.

The House of Lords indicated that the conditions were not conclusive or exclusive. Further guidance on the *Caparo* requirements was provided by the Court of Appeal in *James McNaughten Paper Group Ltd v Hicks Anderson & Co* (1991).

James McNaughten Paper Group Ltd v Hicks Anderson & Co (1991)

Facts:

The accountants were asked by the Chairman at very short notice to draw up the company accounts. The information was reviewed by the claimants who acquired the company as part of a takeover bid and subsequently suffered a loss. The Court of Appeal had to consider whether the defendant accountants owed the claimants a duty of care.

Decision:

The Court of Appeal held no duty of care to exist and identified that the following factors should be taken into account:

- the purpose for which the statement is made,
- the purpose for which the statement is communicated,
- the relationship between the person giving the advice, the person receiving the advice, and any relevant third party,
- the size of any class that the person receiving the advice belonged to,
- the degree of knowledge of the person giving the advice.

Reflecting on the development of liability for negligent misstatement, the scope of the duty of care has become narrower. This has important implications for those in business practice although liability can still be an issue.

❖ KEY CASE *Gorham v British Telecommunications* (2000)

Facts:

The defendant employer had advised their employee to switch pension schemes – he had opted out of the employer's pension scheme, which meant that upon his death, his widow could not be paid out benefits from the associated insurance scheme. His widow sued for economic loss.

Decision:

The Court of Appeal awarded damages and considered the defendants had 'assumed responsibility' for the risk of the advice. They drew an analogy with the 'wills' cases involving lawyers and clients (see below).

9.16 Professional Negligence and Misstatements

In considering whether a duty of care is owed by the defendant to the claimant, it is necessary to consider the particular position of the professional person who, through the nature of his or her job, will be giving advice or carrying out acts which may leave him or her open to a claim in negligence. It is useful to examine the case law as it applies to groups.

9.16.1 Accountants and auditors

While there may be a contractual relationship between an accountant and his client, on which the client can sue, the contentious legal area arises in respect of other people who may rely on reports made or advice given in a non-contractual capacity. Indeed, in many situations, the potential claimant may be unknown to the accountant. Whether there is liability appears to depend upon the purpose for which reports are made or accounts prepared.

In *JEB Fasteners v Marks Bloom & Co* (1983), the defendant accountants negligently overstated the value of stock in preparing accounts for their client. At the time of preparation, the accountants were aware that their client was in financial difficulties and was actively seeking financial assistance. After seeing the accounts, the claimant decided to take over the company. They then discovered the true financial position and sued the accountants for negligent misstatement. It was held that a duty of care was owed by the accountants, as it was foreseeable that someone contemplating a takeover might rely on the accuracy of the accounts; they were not liable, however, as their negligence had not caused the loss to the claimant. The evidence revealed that when they took over the company, they were interested not in the value of the stock but in acquiring the expertise of the directors. Thus, although they relied on the accounts, the accounts were not the cause of the loss, as they would have taken over the company in any event. This case is interesting from the perspective of the causation issues, although if similar facts arose today it is unlikely that a duty of care would be held to exist on the facts following *Caparo* and *James McNaughten*.

❖ KEY CASE *Law Society v KPMG Peat Marwick* (2000)

Facts:

The defendants, a firm of accountants, were hired by solicitors to prepare their annual accounts and were also found to owe a duty to the Law Society. The Law Society alleged that the negligent preparation of the accounts had failed to identify irregularities relating to fraud, for which the Law Society had compensated.

Decision:

The court held that it was reasonable that a duty of care should be owed and there was little difficulty in bringing this within the *Caparo* criteria. This was on the grounds that there was a statutory and professional duty on solicitors to produce annual accounts for the Law Society, and because the Law Society was also liable to solicitors' clients for mismanagement of solicitors' accounts, resulting in the possible payment of compensation by the Law Society.

Where express representations are made about the accounts and the financial state of a company by its directors or financial advisers, with the intention that the person interested in the takeover will rely on them, a duty of care may be owed (*Morgan Crucible Co plc v Hill Samuel Bank Ltd* (1991)).

For further examples of case law relating to accountants and auditors see *Coulthard v Neville Russell* (1998) and *RBS plc v Bannerman Johnstone Maclay (a firm)* (2003).

Finally, when assessing the potential liability of auditors, the courts are also likely to refer to the Fifth European Directive on Harmonisation of Company Law, which outlines the circumstances when a company's auditors owe a duty of care to third parties in respect of negligent acts.

9.16.2 Lawyers

Solicitors are usually in a contractual relationship with their client; however, there may be circumstances outside this relationship where they are liable in tort for negligent misstatements. The definitive position was stated in *Ross v Caunters* (1980), where the defendant solicitors prepared a will, under which the claimant was a beneficiary. The solicitors sent the will to the person instructing them, but failed to warn him that it should not be witnessed by the spouse of a beneficiary. When the will was returned to them, they failed to notice that one of the witnesses was the claimant's spouse. As a result, the claimant lost her benefit under the will. It was held that a solicitor may be liable in negligence to persons who are not his clients, either on the basis of the principle in *Hedley Byrne & Co v Heller and Partners* (1964) or under *Donoghue v Stevenson* (1932). The latter was specifically applied in this case, the claimant being someone so closely and directly affected by the solicitors' acts that it was reasonably foreseeable that they were likely to be injured by any act or omission.

The decision in *Ross v Caunters* was further supported by the decision of the House of Lords in *White v Jones* (1995).

❖ KEY CASE *White v Jones* (1995)

Facts:
In this case the claimant was cut out of his father's will. The father then instructed his solicitors to reinstate him. Unfortunately, the solicitors delayed some six weeks in carrying out the change and, in the meantime, the father died.

Decision:
It was held that the solicitors owed a duty of care to the son as a potential beneficiary. The loss to the claimant was reasonably foreseeable and the duty of care was broken by their omission to act promptly.

In *Esterhuizen v Allied Dunbar Assurance plc* (1998) the principle applied in *White* was held to also apply to other companies offering will-drafting services.

Barristers are in the position of not being in a contractual relationship with their 'client', that is, the person they are representing; neither are they liable in tort for the way in which they conduct a case in court. Traditionally, policy reasons were put forward for this, on the basis that the duty to the court is higher than the duty to a client and must come first (see *Rondel v Worsley* (1969)). In *Saif Ali v Sidney Mitchell* (1980), it was confirmed that a barrister was neither liable for conduct of the case in court, nor was he liable for pre-trial work connected with the conduct of the case in court. However, it was acknowledged that he would be liable in tort for negligent opinions, that is, written advice where there was no error on the part of the solicitor briefing him.

The issue of limits on immunity for solicitors was revisited in *Arthur JS Hall & Co v Simons* (2000), in which solicitors who were being sued for negligence in civil proceedings attempted to rely on *Rondel v Worsley*. The House of Lords held that public policy arguments in favour of such an exemption were no longer appropriate and *Rondel v Worsley* was disapproved. It was felt that the courts would be able to judge between errors of judgment which were an inevitable part of advocacy and true negligence and, as a result, the floodgates would not be opened. This has resulted in immunity being removed in both criminal and civil proceedings (see *Moy v Pettman Smith* (2005)).

Lawyers may also be liable for psychiatric injury resulting from negligence. In *McLoughlin v Jones* (2001), a person who was wrongly convicted and imprisoned as a result of his solicitor's negligence was able to claim psychiatric injury as a result of the trauma involved.

9.16.3 Surveyors

A duty of care is owed by surveyors, builders and architects, etc, to the client, with whom they are usually in a contractual relationship. The decision in *Murphy v Brentwood DC* (1990) has limited the potential liability of builders, architects and quantity surveyors in respect of claims arising out of defective buildings. Where the defect is discovered prior to any injury to person or health, or damage to property other than the defective premises itself, this is to be regarded as pure economic loss, not physical damage to property, and is not, therefore, recoverable in negligence.

However, there may also be liability in tort as a result of *Hedley Byrne & Co v Heller and Partners* (1964), although this hinges on the question of reasonable reliance by the third party and whether the defendant ought to have foreseen such reliance. The problem usually arises when a surveyor is asked to value a house on behalf of a bank or building society and their client, usually a purchaser, relies on the valuation when deciding whether or not to proceed with the house purchase.

In *Yianni v Edwin Evans & Sons* (1982), surveyors who were acting for the defendant building society valued a house at £15,000 and, as a result, the claimants were able to secure a mortgage of

£12,000. The house was, in fact, suffering from severe structural damage and repairs were estimated at £18,000. The basis of the claim was not only the surveyor's negligence, but also the fact that he ought reasonably to have contemplated that the statement would be passed on by the building society to the claimants and that they would rely on it, which they did. It was held that a duty of care was owed by the defendants. An important factor was that the price of the house indicated that the claimant was of modest means, would not be expected to obtain an independent valuation and would, in all probability, rely on the defendant's survey, which was communicated to them by the building society. The court was also confident that the defendants knew that the building society would pass the survey to the purchasers and that they would rely on it.

The decision in *Yianni* was approved in *Smith v Eric Bush* (1989) and *Harris v Wyre Forest DC* (1989). The facts of the former case are very similar to *Yianni*, in that the claimant was sent a copy of the surveyor's report by the defendant building society. This report stated that no essential repairs were necessary and, although it contained a recommendation on obtaining independent advice, the claimant chose to rely on the report. In fact, the property had defective chimneys. In *Harris*, the claimants did not see the surveyor's report, as it was stated on the mortgage application that the valuation was confidential and that no responsibility would be accepted for the valuation. However, the claimant paid the valuation fee and accepted the 95% mortgage on offer. When they attempted to sell the house three years later, structural defects were revealed and the property was deemed to be uninhabitable and unsaleable. It was held, in both cases, that there was sufficient proximity between the surveyor and the purchaser and that it was foreseeable that the purchaser was likely to suffer damage as a result of the negligent advice. It was felt that, in general, surveyors knew that 90% of purchasers relied on their valuation for the building society; it was, therefore, just and reasonable for a duty to be imposed. The limitation on this decision is that it does not extend protection to subsequent purchasers or where the property is of a high value (although this will need to be determined on the facts of each case). The attempt to exclude liability in this case was seen as an attempt to exclude the existence of a duty of care, which, it was felt, was not within the spirit of the Unfair Contract Terms Act 1977 and could not be permitted. In practice, what has happened is that purchasers are now offered a choice of surveys ranging from the Homebuyer's survey to a full structural report and valuation.

❖ KEY CASE — *Merrett v Babb* (2001)

Facts:

The defendant was held to have assumed personal responsibility to the buyers of a house he surveyed. This was despite the fact that he had not met the client, nor was the fee paid to him individually. However, he signed the valuation report personally and this report proved to be defective. The firm had gone bankrupt and the claimants pursued the individual surveyor.

Decision:

The defendant surveyor was held to owe a duty of care and was liable.

In *Francis v Barclays Bank* (2004) the court held that a surveyor was liable in negligence to a bank for failing to make proper enquiries about the status of a grant of planning permission relating to property held by the bank.

One issue to have arisen in the past and likely to resurrect itself in light of the recession is the question – what happens if a surveyor negligently overvalues a property for a lender? In *Banque Bruxelles Lambert SA v Eagle Star Insurance Co Ltd* (1995) the House of Lords held that a valuer was under a duty to take reasonable care to provide information on which a lender could decide on a course of action. Where a valuer had negligently overvalued a property on which the lender had secured a mortgage, the valuer was not responsible for all the consequences of that course of action. A valuer was only responsible for the foreseeable consequences of the information being wrong. This issue, and the distinction between information and advice has been examined in *Aneco Reinsurance Underwriting Ltd (In Liquidation) v Johnson & Higgins* (2002).

9.17 Psychiatric Injury

Psychiatric injury, or nervous shock as it used to be called, is a form of personal injury and may give rise to a claim for damages. Historically, this is an area in which the courts have been fearful of the 'floodgates' opening and have therefore tended to treat such claims with suspicion, restricting liability with special principles. The Law Commission Report, *Liability for Psychiatric Illness* (No 249, 1998) highlighted the continuing problem for the courts in determining the extent of liability for psychiatric injury. If damages are to be recoverable, psychiatric injury must take the form of a recognised mental illness; mental suffering, such as grief, is generally not recoverable (see *Vernon v Bosley (No 1)* (1997)), although no physical injury need be suffered.

The liability regime differs according to whether a claimant falls within the category of primary victim or secondary victim. A primary victim is someone who is physically endangered by the defendant's conduct and subsequently suffers psychiatric injury. It is well established that a claimant is able to recover damages for psychiatric injury stemming from actual physical injury or the reasonable fear or apprehension of danger to their safety (*Dulieu v White* (1901); *Page v Smith* (1996)).

A secondary victim is someone who is not personally at risk of physical injury but who suffers psychiatric injury as a result of witnessing someone else being harmed or endangered. In such cases, liability is limited by a range of policy-based controls. Historically, liability for this type of psychiatric injury depended upon whether the injury was reasonably foreseeable and whether there was sufficient proximity between the claimant and the defendant. In *Bourhill v Young* (1943), the claimant, a pregnant woman, heard a motor accident as she alighted from a tram. A little while later, she saw some blood on the road. She alleged that, as a result of seeing the aftermath of the accident, she suffered nervous shock, which led to a miscarriage. It was held that the claimant did not fall within the class of persons to whom it could be reasonably foreseen that harm might occur. Indeed, it was made clear in this case that one could expect passers-by to have the necessary 'phlegm and fortitude' not to suffer nervous shock as a result of seeing the aftermath of an accident. As a result, the abnormally sensitive claimant will not recover for nervous shock unless the person with normal phlegm and fortitude would have sustained shock in those circumstances (see *Jaensch v Coffey* (1984)).

The essential elements for establishing a duty in similar cases arose out of Lord Wilberforce's *dictum* in *McLoughlin*, which was that, in addition to foresight, the claimant must show that there was a close relationship between him or her and the person suffering injury; secondly, that there was sufficient proximity between the claimant and the accident in terms of time and space; and, finally, it was concluded that being told about the accident by a third party was outside the scope of the duty. In *McLoughlin v O'Brian* (1982), a mother was informed at home that her family had been injured in a road accident two miles away. As a result, she suffered psychiatric illness, caused by the shock of hearing this news and seeing her family in hospital, who were still in a particular bloody state because they had not yet received any treatment. One child had been killed. It was held that she should recover damages, as the shock was a foreseeable consequence of the defendant's negligence. The courts felt that the proximity of the mother to the accident was relevant. However, 'proximity' here meant closeness in time and space. Furthermore, the shock must be caused by the sight or hearing of the event or its immediate aftermath.

The application of Lord Wilberforce's *dictum* was considered in *Alcock & Others v Chief Constable of South Yorkshire* (1991).

Alcock & Others v Chief Constable of South Yorkshire (1991)

Facts:

This case arose out of the accident at Hillsborough stadium in Sheffield, involving Liverpool supporters who were crushed as a result of a surge of supporters being allowed into the ground by the police. The psychiatric injury claim was made by those friends and relatives who witnessed the scenes, as secondary victims, either first hand at the ground or saw or heard them on television or radio.

Decision:

The House of Lords repeated the requirements for establishing duty of care in cases of psychiatric injury. There should be:

- a close and loving relationship between the primary and secondary victim if reasonable foresight is to be established;
- proximity in time and space to the accident or its aftermath;
- and psychiatric injury resulting from seeing or hearing the accident or its immediate aftermath.

It is still open to debate whether viewing live television is equivalent to seeing the accident. It is generally considered not to be, because broadcasting guidelines prevent the showing of suffering by recognisable individuals.

Psychiatric injury may arise from a series of events which can be viewed holistically rather than as a single traumatising event. In *North Glamorgan NHS Trust v Walters* (2002), a mother, having been informed that her 10 month old baby, who was suffering from hepatitis, would survive, then witnessed the baby have a major fit. As a result, both mother and baby were immediately transferred to another hospital for the baby to undergo a liver transplant. However, in the interim, the baby had suffered severe brain damage. Within 36 hours the life support machine had to be switched off and the baby died in its mother's arms. As a result, the mother suffered a recognised psychiatric illness and successfully sued the hospital. It was held by the Court of Appeal that the chain of events should be viewed as having an immediate impact on the mother and could therefore be distinguished from cases involving psychiatric illness over a period of time.

Grieves v FT Everard & Sons (2007)

Facts:

The claimant developed what are known as 'pleural plaques', which on their own do not cause any illness. They are however, evidence that asbestos has entered the body and indicate that in the future a person might develop more serious asbestos-related diseases. The claimant worried so much about the risk that he developed serious clinical depression. The defendant attempted to argue that because of the foreseeable risk of personal injury, his psychiatric injury was also foreseeable and that he should be treated as a primary victim.

Decision:
The court rejected the claim and regarded his reaction to be unforeseeable on the grounds that whilst the pleural plaques might be anticipated to cause anxiety, there was no evidence to support the view that it would lead them to experience such a serious and extreme reaction as mental illness. The court also confirmed that primary victims should be confined to persons who suffered physical or psychiatric injury from involvement in an accident or its 'immediate aftermath'. In particular, Lord Hoffman felt that psychiatric injury in this context should not be extended to psychiatric illness caused by apprehension of an event which had not actually occurred.

9.17.1 Bystanders and rescuers

In *Dooley v Cammell Laird & Co* (1951), a faulty rope was being used on a crane to secure a load as it was hoisted into the hold of a ship. The rope broke, causing the load to fall into the hold, where people were working. The crane driver suffered shock arising out of a fear for the safety of his fellow employees. It was held that the crane driver could recover damages, as it was foreseeable that he was likely to be affected if the rope broke. It would appear that the decision in *Dooley* is confined to situations where the employee making the claim was directly involved in the incident, rather than a mere 'bystander'.

In *Robertson and Rough v Forth Road Bridge Joint Board* (1995), two employees claimed damages for psychiatric injury after witnessing another colleague, who was working alongside them on the Forth Road Bridge, fall to his death. It was held that their claim would fail, as they were in effect mere bystanders and their illness was not, therefore, reasonably foreseeable. This was confirmed in *Hegarty v EE Caledonia Ltd* (1996), in which the claimant, who was on one of the support vessels, witnessed at close range the Piper Alpha oil rig disaster, in which over 150 men died. He claimed he had suffered psychiatric damage but was found to be a person of normal fortitude who, as a 'mere bystander', was close to the danger but not actually in danger himself. However, it could now be argued that damages for psychiatric harm suffered by an employee who witnesses the event and is in danger himself may be recoverable, following the decision in *Young v Charles Church (Southern) Ltd* (1996), in which an employee working alongside a man who was electrocuted and killed was also held to be a 'primary victim'.

In *Chadwick v British Railways Board* (1967), Chadwick took part in the rescue operation after a train crash. He suffered a severe mental condition as a result of the horrific scenes. He had a previous history of mental illness. It was held that the British Railways Board was liable. It was reasonably foreseeable that, in the event of an accident, someone other than the defendant's employees would intervene and suffer injury. Injury to a rescuer in the form of shock was reasonably foreseeable, even if he suffered no physical injury. However, compare this to *White (formerly Frost) v CC of South Yorkshire* (1999), in which a number of policemen involved in the Hillsborough stadium disaster (in which 95 football supporters were crushed to death) brought claims for psychiatric damage attributable to witnessing the events. It was held by the Court of Appeal that the police who attended the scene in the immediate aftermath of the incident were rescuers and were entitled to recover on that basis. It was further held that a rescuer, whether a policeman or layperson, may recover against a defendant for physical or psychiatric injury sustained during a rescue. Among the factors to be considered in determining whether a particular person is a rescuer are: the character and extent of the initial incident caused by the defendant; whether that incident has finished or is continuing; whether there is any danger, continuing or otherwise, to the victim or to the claimant; the character of the claimant's conduct, both in itself and in relation to the victim; and how proximate, in time and place, the claimant's conduct is to the incident. However, the decision of the Court of Appeal was reversed by the House of Lords (*White v Chief Constable of South Yorkshire*

Police (1999)). The House of Lords concluded that the police officers who were present should not be treated as primary victims. They were secondary victims, like any person who witnesses injury to others but is not in danger himself or herself. As such a victim, the conditions laid down in *Alcock* (1991) must, therefore, be met. Furthermore, they were not to be treated as a special category of rescuer. To claim as 'rescuers', the police officers would still have to show that they met the criteria under which rescuers could recover as secondary victims.

It is certainly possible for the law to be extended in this area. For example, in *Attia v British Gas* (1987), the claimant was able to recover damages for nervous shock resulting from the sight of her house being burned down as a result of the defendant's negligence. An area where expansion has taken place is in relation to psychiatric injury arising from 'stress at work' claims. As the duty of care arises from employers' liability this area of psychiatric injury will be examined in depth in the next chapter.

9.18 Defences

The extent of the liability of the defendant may be reduced or limited by one of the defences commonly pleaded in negligence proceedings.

9.18.1 Contributory negligence

Where the claimant is found in some way to have contributed through his or her own fault to his or her injury, the amount awarded as damages will be reduced accordingly (under the Law Reform (Contributory Negligence) Act 1945). The onus is on the defendant to show that the claimant was at fault and that this contributed to his or her injury.

The court, if satisfied that the claimant is at fault, will reduce the amount of damages by an amount which is just and reasonable, depending on the claimant's share of the blame. For example, damages may be reduced by anything from 10% to 75%. However, a 100% reduction has been made, as can be seen in *Jayes v IMI (Kynoch) Ltd* (1985).

9.18.2 *Volenti non fit injuria*

Volenti, or consent, as it applies to negligent acts, is a defence to future conduct of the defendant which involves the risk of a tort being committed. *Volenti* may arise from the express agreement of the claimant and defendant, or it may be implied from the claimant's conduct.

In *ICI v Shatwell* (1965), the claimant and his brother ignored the safety precautions issued by their employer and breached the regulations in testing detonators. As a result, the claimant was injured in an explosion. The action against the employer was based on vicarious liability and breach of statutory duty on the part of the claimant's brother. It was held that the defence of *volenti* would succeed. The claimant not only consented to each act of negligence and breach of statute on the part of his brother, but also participated in them quite willingly. It must be stressed that this particular case highlights extreme circumstances where *volenti* is likely to succeed.

However, if the defence is to succeed, it must be shown that the claimant was fully informed of the risks when he or she gave his or her consent. In *Dann v Hamilton* (1939), a girl accepted a lift in the car of a driver whom she knew to be drunk. She could have used alternative transport. She was injured as a result of his negligent driving. It was held that, although she knew of the risk, this was insufficient to support the defence of *volenti*. It was necessary to show that she had consented to the risk, which could not be established. She therefore succeeded in her action against the driver. Following this case, it is unlikely that this defence will succeed where the implied consent is given before the negligent act occurs. In practice, the courts do not look favourably on this defence in respect of negligent actions and, therefore, it is not usually pleaded.

9.19 Limitation of Claims

Finally, there is a limitation period for commencing a claim in tort. The Limitation Act 1980 states that, generally, proceedings must be brought within six years from the date on which the negligent act occurred. If the claim is for personal injury, the period is three years from the date on which it occurred or the date of knowledge, that is, the date that the injury becomes attributable to another person's negligent actions, whichever is the later.

Summary

Negligence

The tort of negligence imposes a duty to take reasonable care to prevent harm or loss occurring from one's actions. The elements of the tort which must be established by the claimant are:

- duty of care;
- breach of duty; and
- causation and remoteness of damage.

Duty of care

Established by the application of the *Caparo v Dickman* (1990) test, which introduced a **three-stage test** for establishing the existence of a duty of care. This test applies to all situations, and is incremental, requiring consideration of:

- **foreseeability** (*Donoghue v Stevenson* (1932));
- **proximity** (*Stovin v Wise* (1996), *Hill v Chief Constable of West Yorkshire* (1989)) and;
- whether it is **just and reasonable** to impose a duty (*Hill v CC of West Yorkshire* (1989)).

It was approved in *Marc Rich & Co AG v Bishop Rock Marine Co Ltd (The Nicholas H)* (1996).

> When considering duty of care also consider the impact of the **Human Rights Act 1998** (see *Osman v United Kingdom* (1999), *Barrett v Enfield London Borough Council* (1999), *Z v UK (2001), D v East Berkshire Community Health Trust* (2003), *Smith v Chief Constable of Sussex* (2008)).

Breach of duty

Once the claimant has established a duty of care, breach of duty must be proven. The test for establishing breach of duty is whether the defendant has acted as a **reasonable person** in all the circumstances of the case (see *Blyth v Birmingham Waterworks Co* (1856)). The courts will take the following factors into account:

- likelihood of harm occurring (*Bolton v Stone* (1951));
- egg-shell skull rule (*Haley v London Electricity Board* (1965); *Paris v Stepney BC* (1951));
- cost and practicability of taking precautions (*Latimer v AEC* (1952));
- social utility of the act (*Watt v Hertfordshire CC* (1954)); and
- common practice (*Roe v Minister of Health* (1954)).

In certain circumstances, the claimant may rely on the maxim *res ipsa loquitur* in order to establish breach. However, it must be shown that:

- there was sole management or control on the part of the defendant;
- the occurrence could not have happened without negligence; and
- the cause of the occurrence is unknown.

Breach of duty in professional negligence is determined by the application of the **Bolam test** (*Bolam v Friern Hospital Management Committee* (1957)) which has been qualified to a limited extent by *Bolitho v City and Hackney HA* (1998).

Breach of Duty – also consider the impact of s 1 Compensation Act 2006.

Causation and remoteness of damage

Finally, the claimant must show that the breach of duty on the part of the defendant was the cause of his or her loss. The test for establishing causation in fact is the **'but for' test**:

- If there is another acceptable explanation for the injury, causation may not be proven (see *Barnett v Chelsea & Kensington Hospital Management Committee* (1969)).
- Where there is more than one possible cause for the injury or loss, the onus rests on the claimant to show that the defendant's breach was a **material contribution** (see *Bonnington Castings Ltd v Wardlaw* (1956), *Wilsher v Essex AHA* (1988); *Fairchild v Glenhaven Funeral Services Ltd* (2002)), unless exceptional circumstances justify departure from the rule.

A breach of duty can sometimes result in a lost opportunity, this is referred to as **'loss of chance'** (see *Hotson v East Berkshire AHA* (1987), *Allied Maples Group Ltd v Simmons and Simmons* (1995), *Platform Home Loans v Oyston Shipways Ltd* (1999)).

The extent of the defendant's liability may be limited by the rules for determining **remoteness of damage** and *novus actus interveniens*.

Where the cause and extent of the harm is unforeseen, the loss will not be recoverable. Only damage which is reasonably foreseeable will be recoverable as seen in *The Wagon Mound (No 1)* (1961).

As a general rule, it is not necessary to foresee the exact cause of the harm, as long as it is within the general range which any reasonable person might foresee:

- *Hughes v Lord Advocate* (1963);
- *Doughty v Turner Manufacturing Co Ltd* (1964);
- *Tremain v Pike* (1969);
- *Jolley v London Borough of Sutton* (2000).

There may be exceptional circumstances where for policy reasons, the normal legal rules may not be applied strictly:

- *Fairchild v Glenhaven Funeral Services Ltd* (2002).

Economic loss

Liability for economic loss arising out of physical injury or damage to property may be compensated in negligence. Liability for pure economic loss cannot, in general, be compensated see:

- *Spartan Steel & Alloys Ltd v Martin & Co* (1973);
- *Junior Books Ltd v Veitchi Ltd* (1983).

Liability for pure economic loss will generally only be upheld where negligent misstatement is proven (*Murphy v Brentwood DC* (1990)). Liability for **negligent misstatement requires proof of a special relationship** between the parties, see *Hedley Byrne & Co v Heller & Partners* (1964).

- *Mutual Life and Citizens Assurance Co v Evatt* (1971);
- *Caparo Industries plc v Dickman* (1990);
- *James McNaughten Paper Group Ltd v Hicks Anderson & Co* (1991);
- *Chaudry v Prabhakar* (1988).

However, the claimant will have to show that he or she actually **relied on the advice**:

- *JEB Fasteners v Marks Bloom & Co* (1983);
- *Caparo Industries plc v Dickman* (1990);
- *White v Jones* (1995);
- *Merrett v Babb* (2001);
- *Law Society v KPMG Peat Marwick* (2000);
- *Arthur JS Hall & Co v Simons* (2000).

Psychiatric injury

The tort of negligence also recognises liability for psychiatric injury sometimes known as post-traumatic stress disorder. The claimant must establish:

- a recognised medical condition which goes beyond grief and distress.

The courts clearly distinguish between primary victims and secondary victims. Where primary victims are involved, the claimant needs to establish that the three elements of the test for duty of care are present, namely, the existence of foreseeability, proximity and that it is just and reasonable to impose a duty, see:

- *Dulieu v White* (1901);
- *Page v Smith* (1996).

A contentious issue arises where the claimant is a **secondary victim**, namely, someone who witnesses the accident or its immediate aftermath. In these circumstances, the claimant must establish the criteria laid down in *Alcock & Others v Chief Constable of South Yorkshire* (1991):

- a close, loving relationship with the primary victim;
- proximity to the accident in terms of time and space;
- psychiatric injury resulting from seeing or hearing the accident, or its immediate aftermath.

See the following:

- *McLoughlin v O'Brian* (1982);
- *Alcock & Others v Chief Constable of South Yorkshire* (1991); and
- *North Glamorgan NHS Trust v Walters* (2002).

Rescuers are usually treated as a special case, particularly where they are not professional rescuers:

- *Chadwick v BRB* (1967); and
- *White v Chief Constable of South Yorkshire* (1998).

Mere 'bystanders' may not receive such favourable treatment by the courts.

- *Robertson and Rough v Forth Road Bridge Joint Board* (1995);
- *Hegarty v EE Caledonia Ltd* (1996).

Defences

Damages may be reduced by the claimant's negligence (Law Reform (Contributory Negligence) Act 1945).

The defence of *volenti* or consent may operate as a complete defence (*ICI v Shatwell* (1965); *Dann v Hamilton* (1939)).

Further Reading

There are a number of further reading materials which are useful if you wish to find out more about the general nature of tort law. The classic work, which can be found in most good law libraries, is:

Jones, MA, and Dugdale, AM (eds), *Clerk & Lindsell On Torts*, 20th edn, 2010, London: Sweet & Maxwell

For general textbooks on tort law, the following represent a good range:

Harpwood, VH, *Modern Tort Law*, 7th edn, 2008, London: Routledge-Cavendish
Horsey, K and Rackley, E, *Tort Law*, 2009, Oxford: OUP
Lunney, M and Oliphant, K, *Tort Law: Text and Materials*, 4th edn, 2010, Oxford: OUP
Murphy, J, *Street on Torts*, 12th edn, 2007, Oxford: OUP
Rogers, WVH (ed), *Winfield & Jolowicz on Tort*, 18th edn, 2010, London: Sweet & Maxwell
Steele, J, *Tort Law: Text, Cases and Materials*, 2nd edn, 2010, Oxford: OUP

A useful work which examines the manner in which accident compensation is dealt with in our legal system is:

Cane, P, *Atiyah's Accidents, Compensation and the Law*, 7th edn, 2006, Oxford: OUP

If you wish to examine more specific issues relating to the nature of negligent liability in tort then the following articles may be of use:

Bailey, S, 'Public Authority Liability in Negligence: The Continued Search for Coherence' (2006) 26(2) *Legal Studies* 155
Howarth, D, 'Many Duties of Care – Or a Duty of Care? Notes from the Underground' (2006) 26(3) *Oxford Journal of Legal Studies* 449
McBride, N, 'Duties of Care – Do They Really Exist?' (2004) 24(3) *Oxford Journal of Legal Studies* 417
Stanton, K, 'Professional Negligence: Duty of Care Methodology in the Twenty-first Century' (2006) *Professional Negligence* 134

For information on the Jackson Review, see: www.judiciary.gov.uk/publications-and-reports/review-of-civil-litigation-costs

Chapter 10

Vicarious and Employers' Liability

Chapter Contents

Law in Context: Managing Risk in Employment

An employer can be liable for injuries negligently caused by his or her employee and also for injuries negligently caused to his or her employee. The former arises out of vicarious liability and the latter from the duty of an employer to take reasonable care for the safety of his or her employees whilst they are at work. Both types of liability have important implications for business and both are areas where insurance is required to meet the cost of any claims arising. Employers' liability has developed largely through cases involving negligent accidents at work. Following developments in medical knowledge about the impact of work-related stress on health an emerging area in employers' liability is the issue of 'stress at work' claims. According to the Labour Force Survey during 2011/12, 10.4 million working days were lost due to stress-related absence, the average absence being 24 days – one of the highest rates in recognised health complaints (LFS). Whilst it could be argued that such cases are a branch of psychiatric injury within common law negligence, the basis of many such claims arises from arguments that the stress arose as a result of employees being subjected to unsafe systems of work, and hence the claims can be argued to fall within the ambit of employers' liability. This is an increasingly complex area for employers to negotiate and the liability issues often overlap with employment law areas such as constructive dismissal.

10.1 Vicarious Liability: An Introduction

An employer can become liable for the tort of an employee if it is committed during the course of employment. As a general rule, vicarious liability arises out of the employer/employee relationship, although it can be found in the principal/agent relationship and as an exceptional case in the employer/independent contractor relationship. Vicarious liability is dependent upon this type of relationship being established, and a claimant can sue both the employer vicariously and the employee personally, although in the majority of claims it is the employer who will be pursued due to the presence of compulsory insurance.

Vicarious liability, therefore, is not a tort; it is a concept used to impose strict liability on a person who does not have primary liability, that is, who is not at fault. Literally it means that one person is liable for the torts of another. The employer is, therefore, liable for the torts of his or her employee. In one sense the concept is at odds with the idea of fault-based loss redistribution since liability is strict and arises out of the existence of a set of circumstances. However, the concept has found favour with courts and claimants alike, because, realistically, the employer is likely to have the money to pay for any claim for damages, whereas the primary tortfeasor, the employee, will usually not.

Although the imposition of vicarious liability may seem harsh on the employer such an approach has been justified on the grounds of 'social convenience and rough justice' and this rationale was endorsed in *Majrowski v Guy's and St Thomas's NHS Trust* (2006). Vicarious liability does not mean that the employee will escape liability. The employer can insist that he or she is joined in any action or, if the employer is found to be vicariously liable, may insist on an indemnity from his or her employee. The effect of this is that the employee will have to pay towards the damages imposed on the employer (see the Civil Liability (Contribution) Act 1978, which provides for this).

For vicarious liability to arise three criteria must be established. Firstly, it must be established that there is an employer/employee relationship. Secondly, the tort depends on the primary liability of the employee being established; that is, the employee must have committed a tort and finally, the employee must have committed the tort during his or her 'course of employment'.

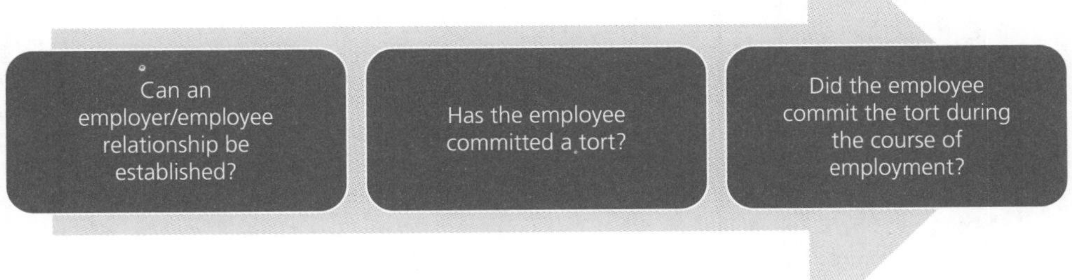

Figure 10.1 Conditions for vicarious liability

10.1.1 The employer/employee relationship

The claimant must establish that there is in existence an employer/employee relationship (or, in less common situations, a principal/agent relationship), that is, a contract of service as opposed to a contract for services. In the majority of cases, this may not be an issue, but just because the word 'employee' is used in the contract, it does not automatically follow that it is a contract of service (or employment). Likewise, a contract may specify that a person is an independent contractor, or that the contract is a contract for services, but it is for the court to ultimately decide the exact nature of the contractual terms.

Problems arise when attempting to establish the employer/employee relationship because employers may attempt to evade potential liability by classifying employees as independent contractors. The search for a comprehensive test has caused difficulties for the courts and various formulations have been used such as the control test and integration test. The modern approach has been to abandon any search, or creation of a single principle, and look at all the factors in the case. This position was adopted in *Ready Mixed Concrete (South East Ltd) v Minister of Pensions* (1968) in which the court held that there were a number of criteria for a contract of service, or employment, namely:

- that the employee has agreed, in return for a wage or other form of remuneration, to provide their skill and work for the employer;
- that the employee has agreed expressly, or impliedly, to be subject to their employer's control; and
- that the other contractual terms are consistent with a contract of employment.

The above factors are not exclusive, other facts will be examined by the courts (see *Lane v Shire Roofing Co (Oxford) Ltd* (1995)).

KEY CASE *Mersey Docks and Harbour Board v Coggins and Griffiths (Liverpool) Ltd* (1947)

Facts:

In this case, the court had to consider the loan of an employee. A crane driver was hired out by his employer, the harbour authority, to another business. Contractual terms provided that the crane driver was an employee of the business, but the harbour authority continued to pay the driver's wages and also retained the right to dismiss the driver if necessary. As a result of the crane driver's negligence a person was seriously injured and the House of Lords had to determine who constituted the employer for the purpose of vicarious liability.

Decision:
The court held that the harbour authority remained the employer. The House of Lords indicated that a contractual term was not to be regarded as decisive, and that when employees are loaned out, the burden of proof remains on the permanent employer to demonstrate that the other party has become the employer for vicarious liability purposes. On the facts the harbour board had failed to rebut the presumption. In *Viasystems (Tyneside) Ltd v Thermal Transfers (Northern) Ltd* (2006) the court held that dual vicarious liability could exist between the permanent and temporary employer, albeit in limited circumstances.

In recent years, determining who is an employer, has become more difficult because of the emergence of more varied, and flexible, working patterns. For example in *Hawley v Luminar Leisure Ltd* (2006) a bouncer seriously injured a claimant by assaulting them during the course of his employment. The defendants argued that they did not employ the bouncer but hired him from another company, ASE Security Services (who had in fact gone into liquidation). When considering who was to be treated as employer for the purpose of vicarious liability, the Court of Appeal addressed the question; who was entitled and therefore obliged to control the door steward's act so as to prevent it? In answering this question, the defendant nightclub owners were held vicariously liable on the basis that they were in the position to control his behaviour and prevent him behaving badly. The court also acknowledged that the bouncer was readily identifiable as an employee of the defendant by both his presence on the door over a period of time and the fact that he wore the uniform of the defendants.

The above decision highlights an increased acceptance of what has been described as 'atypical' workers and in certain instances the courts may classify a worker as an employee solely to ensure the loss distribution and compensatory function of the tort of vicarious liability. However, for a recent case where vicarious liability was denied, see *Poole v Wright (t/a Simon Wright Racing Development)* (2013).

10.1.2 Scope of vicarious liability – the requirement for primary liability

Once it is established that there is in existence a contract of service and that the employee has committed a tort, that is, that he or she has primary liability, the question of whether the employer should be vicariously liable can be considered. This stage is important because the employer will only be liable if the employee is 'acting within the course of his employment' when the tort is committed. It is therefore essential to consider what is meant legally by this term. If the employee is outside the scope of his or her employment, the injured person has no choice but to sue the employee, who may not be in a financial position to pay compensation.

10.1.3 Course of employment

The interpretation given by the courts is wide – in the past, they have favoured making the employer liable, if it is at all possible to do so. There is little consistency in the decisions and this is an area influenced by policy considerations, namely, the need to provide compensation and justice for the victim. The onus is on the claimant to show that the tortfeasor is an employee and that the tortious act was committed whilst he or she was going about his or her employer's business, in other words, whilst the employee was within the course of employment. Once this is established, the onus moves to the employer, who must show that the tortious act was one for which he or she was not responsible.

As a general rule, to be within the course of employment, one of the following must be established:

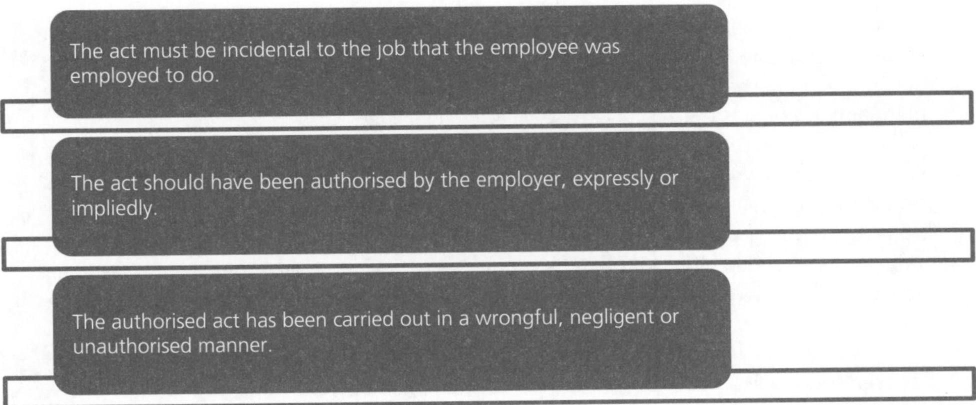

Figure 10.2 Conditions for 'within the course of employment'

The above can best be illustrated through the case law, which shows how far the courts are prepared to go in holding an employer vicariously liable. The following cases relate to situations where the employee was found to be 'within the course of his employment'.

In *Century Insurance Co Ltd v Northern Ireland Road Transport Board* (1942), Davison was employed as a tanker driver for the NIRTB. He was delivering petrol at a garage. Whilst the underground storage tank was being filled with petrol, Davison lit a cigarette and threw away the lighted match. The petrol vapour ignited, resulting in an explosion. The employer's insurance company claimed that the driver's actions regarding the cigarette were outside the course of his employment as being wholly unauthorised, thereby avoiding liability on the part of the employer and payment of compensation by the insurance company. It was held that the employer was vicariously liable for the negligent act of the employee. The lighting of the cigarette was an act of convenience on the part of the employee and, although it was not necessarily for the employer's benefit, it did not prevent him from being made liable. It was the time and place at which the employee struck the match that was negligent. The employee was seen to be carrying out the job he was employed to do in a negligent manner.

From this case, it can be seen that such acts as taking a tea break, having a cigarette, going to the washroom, etc, are all acts which are incidental to the main job, although it is still necessary to consider all the facts of the case at the time of the tortious act; of course, the question as to whether, in the present climate of no smoking policies, the smoking of a cigarette would be seen as incidental to one's employment is debatable. The next case is regarded as the leading authority with respect to actions which are specifically prohibited by the employer.

❖ KEY CASE *Rose v Plenty* (1976)

Facts:

Plenty was employed as a milkman by the Co-operative Dairy. A notice had been posted up in the depot which prohibited all milkmen from using young children to deliver milk and from giving lifts to them on the milk float. Plenty ignored this notice and engaged the assistance of Rose, a 13-year-old boy. Rose was injured whilst riding on the milk float through the negligent driving of Plenty.

Decision:

It was held that, applying the decision in *Limpus v London General Omnibus Co* (1862), since the prohibited act was being done for the purpose of the employer's business and not for the employee's own benefit or purpose, Plenty was within the course of his employment and, therefore, the employer was vicariously liable.

Where the employee carries out a prohibited act, all the circumstances will have to be considered to see if the employee remains within the course of his or her employment. However, the key to establishing vicarious liability in such cases is to ask the question: 'Who is the intended beneficiary of the prohibited action?' In *Rose v Plenty*, Lord Denning applied his own earlier judgment in *Young v Edward Box & Co Ltd* (1951), in which he said:

> In every case where it is sought to make the master liable for the conduct of his servant, the first question is to see whether the servant was liable. If the answer is yes, the second question is to see whether the employer must shoulder the servant's liability.

This approach gives little weight to the issue of the 'course of employment' by adopting the view that, generally, it is the employer who will have the money to pay the compensation because of insurance cover and, therefore, if it is at all possible to do so, the employer should be made responsible for an employee's tortious acts. It should not be forgotten that the concept of vicarious liability may also enable an employee who has been injured by a fellow employee to recover compensation, even though a claim for employers' liability would fail. In *Harrison v Michelin Tyre Co Ltd* (1985), Harrison was injured when a fellow employee, Smith, deliberately tipped up the duckboard on which he was standing to work at his machine. The employer contended that Smith, who caused the injury, was on a 'frolic of his own' when he caused the injury. However, the court held that, although it was an unauthorised act, Smith was going about his job when he committed the act, which was so closely connected with his employment that he remained within the course of his employment, thereby resulting in the employer being vicariously liable. Some doubt about the decision in *Harrison* was expressed in *Aldred v Nacanco* (1987).

Vicarious liability extends to acts which may be crimes as well as torts, for example, assault and fraud. Where the employee uses force or violence, the courts will look closely at the circumstances surrounding its use and question whether it was necessary or excessive. Early case law illustrates that the use of force may result in the employer being vicariously liable. In *Poland v Parr & Sons* (1927), an employee saw some boys who he believed to be stealing from his employer's wagon. He struck one of them, who fell and was run over. The employer was held to be vicariously liable, as the servant was legitimately protecting his employer's property. However, as the social climate has changed, so has the attitude of the courts. This is illustrated in *Keppel Bus Co Ltd v Sa'ad bin Ahmad* (1974), in which the employer was found not to be vicariously liable for an assault carried out by a bus conductor on a passenger. Whether the employee has an implied authority to use force in a given situation, such as protecting his employer's property, and why and how that force is used are key issues.

The employer of an off-duty police officer who assaulted a young man as he was attempting to steal the policeman's property was found to be vicariously liable. This was as a result of the police officer informing the young man at the time of the assault that he was a police officer; therefore, the young man was entitled to believe that he was being assaulted by a police officer (see *Weir v Chief*

Constable of Merseyside Police (2003)). Similarly, the employers of a ticket collector were held liable when the employee assaulted a customer after an argument (see *Fennelly v Connex South Eastern Ltd* (2001)).

The following cases consider the position where the employee is put in a position of trust and abuses that position so that a crime or tort is committed. In *Morris v Martin & Sons Ltd* (1966), Morris's mink stole was sent by her furrier to Martin to be cleaned. An employee of Martin, who had been entrusted with the cleaning of the fur, stole it (committing the tort of conversion). It was held that the employer was liable for the act of conversion of their employee. Martin were bailees for reward of the fur and were therefore under a duty to take reasonable care of it. It was then entrusted to an employee to do an act which was within the course of his employment, that is, clean it. What the employee did in stealing the fur was merely an abuse of his job. A critical element in this case was the fact that Martin had become bailees of the fur and would, therefore, probably have been liable for anything happening to it.

There is a further limitation on the application of the rule in *Morris v Martin & Sons*; it can only serve to make the employer vicariously liable where the goods come into the employee's possession as part of his or her job. If, for example, an employee who was not involved in the cleaning of the fur had stolen it, the employer would not have been vicariously liable. The courts have reinforced the limit on the application of the decision in the *Morris* case by requiring a nexus between the criminal act and the circumstances of the employment. In *Heasmans v Clarity Cleaning Co Ltd* (1987), an employee of a firm contracted to clean offices, whose job involved the cleaning of telephones, dishonestly made use of the telephones to make private calls. It was held that the telephone calls were outside the purpose for which the man was employed. For an employer to be liable for the criminal acts of his employees, there must be some nexus between the criminal act of the employee and the circumstances of his or her employment. In this case, the requirement to dust the telephones merely provided the employee with an opportunity to commit the crime – access to the premises was an insufficient nexus.

How far the question of nexus is becoming an issue in all cases of vicarious liability can be seen in *Irving v Post Office* (1987) and *Aldred v Nacanco* (1987). Where an employee is involved in a fraud, the fact that the employer has placed the employee in a position to perpetrate the fraud may result in the employer being vicariously liable.

Interestingly, in an older case, *Lloyd v Grace, Smith & Co* (1912), Lloyd went to the defendant solicitors to discuss some properties that she had for investment purposes. She saw their managing clerk, who persuaded her to sell the properties and to sign some documents, which, unbeknown to her, transferred the properties to him. He then disposed of them for his own benefit. It was held that the solicitors were liable for the fraudulent act of their employee, even though they did not benefit from the fraud. They had placed him in a position of responsibility, which enabled him to carry out the fraud. Also, as far as the general public was concerned, he was in a position of trust and appeared to have the authority for his actions. The facts of the *Lloyd* case are rather special and the decision is based on the special relationship between solicitor and client, which is one of trust. The court did not regard 'benefit to the employer' as an issue.

In reality, there can be no set formula for deciding whether an employer should be vicariously liable. The fact that in many of the cases it appears that justice was seen to be done probably justifies Lord Denning's stance in *Young v Edward Box and Co Ltd* (1951). It is pertinent to mention the case of *Lister v Hesley Hall Ltd* (2001), as it challenges the common law test for establishing vicarious liability.

❖ KEY CASE — *Lister v Hesley Hall Ltd* [2001]

Facts:

The case involved a warden, an employee of a boarding school for children with educational and behavioural problems. The warden sexually abused a number of children, aged between 12 and 15, who were boarders at the school. The school was owned and managed by the defendants. It was difficult to regard the sexual abuse as a wrongful mode of carrying out an authorised act since the conduct was not authorised and was intentional.

Decision:
The House of Lords held in determining whether an employee's wrongful act has been committed in the course of his employment so as to make the employers vicariously liable, the correct approach is to concentrate on the relative closeness of the connection between the nature of the employment and the employee's wrongdoing. The question is whether the employee's tort was so closely connected with his employment that it would be fair and just to hold the employers vicariously liable.

In the present case, the employee's position as warden and the close contact with the boys which that work involved created a sufficiently close connection between the acts of abuse which he committed and the work which he had been employed to do, so that it would be fair and just to hold the employers vicariously liable to the claimants for the injury and damage which they suffered at his hands. The sexual abuse was inextricably interwoven with the carrying out by the warden of his duties. The sexual assaults were committed in the employers' time and on their premises while the warden was also busy caring for the children. The fact that the warden performed his duties in a way which was an abuse of his position, and an abnegation of his duty, did not sever the connection with his employment.

The House of Lords went on to overrule the decision of the Court of Appeal in *Trotman v North Yorkshire CC* (1999). In effect, a purposive approach has been adopted in line with the interpretation of the statutory form of vicarious liability developed in equality legislation. Employers must realise that there will be situations where providing an opportunity to the employee to commit tortious acts will result in the employer being vicariously liable. This approach has subsequently been adopted in cases involving harassment and bullying at work. For example, in *Green v DB Group Services (UK) Ltd* (2006) the defendant employers were held liable for the bullying and harassment of an employee by fellow employees. In *Majrowski v Guy's and St Thomas's NHS Trust Hospital* (2006) an employer was held to be vicariously liable for harassment under s 3 of the Protection from Harassment Act 1997.

A similar approach was adopted in *Maga v Birmingham Roman Catholic Archdiocese Trustees* (2010), in which a Roman Catholic priest befriended a young boy and employed him to do odd jobs around the church. The priest went on to sexually abuse the boy on several occasions. Although the events took place in the 1970s, the court held that the action was not prevented from proceeding under the Limitation Act 1980. The key issue for the Court of Appeal to consider was whether the acts had been committed during 'the course of employment'. The court considered that Father Chris, as he had come to be known in the community, was in a similar position to a parent or carer. He had a special responsibility for youth work in the community and through abusing this position he had been in a position to develop a relationship with his victim. The trust the community placed in him arose from the nature of his employment. This resulted in a sufficiently close connection between the priest's employment and the abuse to make it fair, just and reasonable to make the employers vicariously liable. The circumstances of *Maga* are certainly wider than *Lister* and indicate how willing the courts are to stretch the course of employment to deliver justice to injured parties.

10.1.4 Outside the course of employment

In considering those cases in which the employee has been held to be outside the course of employment, a significant issue has been the employee's deviation from the job that he or she was employed to do. Once again, there are no set criteria for judging this issue; it remains a question of fact in each case, based on the nature of the job and the actions of the employee.

The standard is laid down in *Hilton v Thomas Burton (Rhodes) Ltd* (1961). Four workmen were allowed to use their employer's van, as they were working on a demolition site in the country. At lunchtime, they decided to go to a café some seven miles away. Before reaching the cafe, they changed their minds and set off to return to the site. On the return journey, one of them was killed through the negligent driving of the van driver. It was held that the employer was not vicariously liable. By travelling such a distance to take a break, they were no longer doing something incidental to their main employment, nor were they doing anything for the purpose of their employer's business. As far as the court was concerned, they were 'on a frolic of their own'.

Following this case, it is pertinent to ask how far the employee has deviated from his course of employment. This is a question of degree, which depends on the facts of each case. There are cases dealing with prohibited acts where it has been decided that the employee is outside the course of his or her employment. It should be noted that many of these decisions were made before *Rose v Plenty* (1976) (see above), which is seen as the watershed for such cases. It could, therefore, be argued that the decision in *Twine v Bean's Express Ltd* (1946), in which the employer was not liable for the injuries to a hitch-hiker who had been given a lift, contrary to the express instructions of the employer, would be different today, as the reasoning that no duty was owed because he was a trespasser is doubtful in the light of the decision in *Rose*. However, the problem of tortious acts which are also crimes has not been totally resolved, although it is possible to distinguish the case law on their facts.

In *Warren v Henly's Ltd* (1948), a petrol pump attendant employed by Henly's used verbal abuse when wrongly accusing Warren, a customer, of trying to drive away without paying for petrol. Warren called the police and told the attendant that he would be reported to his employer. This so enraged the attendant that he physically assaulted Warren. It was held that the employer was not liable. The act of violence was not connected in any way to the discharge of the pump attendant's duties. When he assaulted Warren, he was not doing what he was employed to do, but was acting in an unauthorised manner. The act was done in relation to a personal matter affecting his personal interests, not in respect of the protection of his employer's property, as was the case in *Poland v Parr* (1927).

Where an employee commits an act which takes him or her outside the course of his or her employment, in this case by committing a fraudulent act, the employer will be entitled to an indemnity from the employee should the employer be sued for vicarious liability – see *Padden v Arbuthnot Pensions and Investment Ltd* (2004).

10.2 Employers' Liability

If an employee is injured at work, he or she may be able to establish that the employer is in breach of the personal duty owed to him or her. This is an area which is interwoven with statutory provisions since there are many statutes which impose specific duties in relation to health and safety within the workplace (see chapter on Health & Safety). An employer's liability in tort for injury caused to their employees can take one of the following forms:

- the employer may be vicariously liable for a tort committed by another employee and which has injured the employee in question;
- the employer may be in breach of a specific statutory duty which has caused injury to the employee;
- the employer may be in breach of their personal 'non-delegable' duty of care to the employee which has resulted in injury.

Historically, it was not until the late 19th century that employees were able to proceed with such claims. The courts originally took the view that the doctrine of common employment precluded an action against the employer, where the employee had been injured by the actions of a fellow employee (*Priestley v Fowler* (1837)), the rationale for this being that the employee had impliedly agreed to accept any risks incidental to his contract of employment. There was also concern expressed for the possible financial burden placed on employers having to pay compensation for industrial accidents if such actions were allowed to proceed. In addition, the defences of *volenti* and contributory negligence removed any chance of success in such claims, as *volenti* in particular was freely available to the employer. Gradually, the doctrine of common employment was removed and limitations were placed on the use of *volenti* as a defence (*Smith v Baker & Sons* (1891)). During the 20th century, the tort of employers' liability was developed by the judges, who introduced the concept of 'non-delegable' duties.

Employers' liability is a negligence-based tort, in that it is a specialised form of negligence arising out of a duty imposed by the employer/employee relationship. It is, therefore, necessary to refer to the basic elements of that tort. It gives the employee the right to sue the employer when injured at work for negligent acts by the employer arising out of the course of his or her employment. In order to ensure that the employer can pay any award of damages, the Employers' Liability (Compulsory Insurance) Act 1969 imposes a duty on the employer to take out the necessary insurance cover.

10.2.1 Employers' liability: the nature of the duty of care

The employer's duty of care is owed to each individual employee and, as it is a personal duty, it cannot be delegated by the employer to anyone else. This was made quite clear in *Wilsons and Clyde Coal Co v English* (1938), where the day-to-day responsibility for a mine was delegated to a mine manager, as required by statute. However, the court concluded that the ultimate responsibility for health and safety remained with the employer (see also *McDermid v Nash Dredging and Reclamation Ltd* (1987) and *Morris v Breaveglen Ltd (t/a Anzac Construction Co)* (1993), which reaffirm this principle).

The duty is owed only whilst the employee is acting within the course of his or her employment; that is, doing something reasonably incidental to the employee's main job. For example, in *Davidson v Handley-Page Ltd* (1945), the claimant was washing his teacup in the sink at his place of work when he slipped and hurt his leg whilst standing on a duckboard. The duckboard had become slippery because water was constantly splashed upon it. It was held that the employer was in breach of his duty, because the employee was carrying out a task which was reasonably incidental to his job; tea breaks were an accepted part of working life.

As a general rule, employees are not acting within the course of their employment whilst travelling to and from work. The exception to this was recognised in *Smith v Stages and Darlington Insulation Co Ltd* (1989), which offers some protection to peripatetic workers or any employee who may have to work away from his or her main base. Where employees are paid their normal wage for this travelling time, they will be within the course of their employment.

As the duty is of a personal nature, the standard of care will vary with the individual needs of each employee. It follows, therefore, that special regard must be had for the old, young, inexperienced and less able bodied. The general nature of the duty can be expressed as follows: the employer must take reasonable care in the way he conducts his operations so as not to subject his employees to unnecessary risks (*Smith v Baker & Son* (1891)).

10.2.2 Scope of the employer's duty

This was outlined in *Wilsons and Clyde Coal Co v English* (1938). Following this case, the employer's duty has been determined as extending to the provision of:

- competent fellow employees;
- safe plant and appliances;
- a safe place of work; and
- a safe system of work.

However, it has been recognised that there is often an overlap between the duties owed at common law and the duties implied into the contract of employment, breach of which would allow the employee to pursue either course of action. An example of this can be seen in *Johnstone v Bloomsbury HA* (1991), where it was concluded that requiring junior hospital doctors to work excessive hours may be a breach of the employer's implied duty, although the implied contractual duty, to take reasonable care for the safety of employees, would have to be read subject to the express terms in the contract of employment. The issue of working hours has been superseded to some extent by the Working Time Regulations 1998 (SI 1998/1833).

The remit of the employer's duty is open to expansion through the case law. It does not, however, extend to the provision of insurance cover against special risks – *Reid v Rush and Tomkins Group plc* (1989). In *McFarlane v EE Caledonia* (1994), a claim was made that an employer owed a duty to prevent psychiatric injury. The Court of Appeal concluded that, as the claimant was not directly involved in the accident and did not fall within the recognised categories of claimants who can recover, as outlined in *Alcock v Chief Constable of South Yorkshire* (1991), the employer could not be liable.

It was originally held by the Court of Appeal in *Frost v Chief Constable of South Yorkshire* (1997) that an employer owed a duty of care to avoid exposing an employee to unnecessary risk of physical or psychiatric injury. However, on appeal (*White v Chief Constable of South Yorkshire* (1998)), the House of Lords reversed the Court of Appeal's decision. The House of Lords concluded that the police officers who attended the scene of the Hillsborough stadium disaster were secondary victims and, therefore, the criteria in *Alcock* must be met. However, the standard of care in discharging the duty will vary from case to case according to the nature of the job and the degree of fortitude to be expected of the employee. As a result, police officers who were at the ground in the course of duty, within the area of risk of physical and psychiatric injury, dealing with the dead and dying and who were thus exposed, by their employer's negligence, to the exceptionally horrific events which occurred, could recover damages. However, the risks from passive smoking may well be within the remit of the employer's duty. As a result, a reasonable employer would be expected to produce and implement a no smoking policy (*Bland v Stockport CC* (1993)).

10.2.3 Competent fellow employees

The employer must ensure that all his or her staff are competent to do the job which they have been employed to do. The employer must, therefore, make sure that they have the necessary experience and qualifications, and, where necessary, must be prepared to train them accordingly. If an employee is injured as a result of the incompetence of a fellow employee, then the employer may be liable. The word 'incompetence' covers a range of ineptitudes; many of the cases arise out of practical jokes. In this situation, whether the employer is liable will depend on the depth of knowledge about the incompetent employee. If, for example, the employer has been put on warning or given notice that the employee is capable of committing an incompetent act, such as a practical joke, the employer will be liable. If necessary, the duty extends to disciplining, or even dismissing, employees who fail to act on warnings about their conduct.

In *O'Reilly v National Rail and Tramway Appliances Ltd* (1966), O'Reilly was employed with three others to break up scrap from railways. His colleagues persuaded him to hit, with his sledgehammer, a shell case embedded between the railway sleepers. When he did this, the shell exploded. It was held that the employer was not in breach of his duty because he had no previous knowledge that these workmen played practical jokes or were capable of encouraging such an act. He had not, therefore, failed to employ competent fellow employees.

The previous conduct of the incompetent employee is, therefore, extremely relevant. Where the employer has been given notice, he should take suitable action to ensure that such conduct does not result in something more serious; failure to take action will leave the employer open to a claim in the event of an accident arising out of the employee's incompetence. If necessary, the duty extends to disciplining, or even dismissing, employees who fail to act on warnings about their conduct. In *Hudson v Ridge Manufacturing Co Ltd* (1957), Hudson was on his way to the sick room when a fellow employee tripped him up and broke his wrist. This employee was known as a practical joker and had been warned by his employer to stop fooling about. It was held that the employer was in breach of his duty because he was aware of his employee's tendency to fool around. He should have done more to curb this employee, even if this meant dismissal.

Interestingly, the employer will have primary liability in these circumstances for a deliberate and blatant act as well as the negligent act. However, an isolated incident will not incur liability, as can be seen in *Smith v Crossley Bros Ltd* (1951). A claim based on vicarious liability may be open to an injured employee where the employee is unable to show that the employer had breached this particular duty, for example, through lack of prior knowledge (see *Harrison v Michelin Tyre Co Ltd* (1985) below). However, the decision in *Waters v Commissioner of Police for the Metropolis* (2000) takes the issue one step further by placing a common law duty of care on the employer to protect his employees against victimisation and harassment by fellow employees, which may give rise to physical or psychiatric injury.

10.2.4 Safe plant and appliances

The employer must not only provide his employees with the necessary plant and equipment to do the job safely, he or she must also ensure that such plant and equipment is safe, that is, properly maintained. For example, guards must be provided on dangerous machinery to protect the employee from injury and these guards must be inspected regularly to ensure that they are securely in position and are not damaged in any way.

In *Bradford v Robinson Rentals Ltd* (1967), Bradford was employed as a driver. He was required to drive over 400 miles in extremely cold weather, in a van with a broken window and a heater that did not work. He suffered severe frostbite. It was held that the van was not safe and, therefore, the employer had failed in his duty to provide safe plant and equipment. Although the conditions were extreme, it was foreseeable that the employee would suffer some injury if sent out on a long journey in a van in that condition. A further illustration of this duty can be seen in *Taylor v Rover Car Co Ltd* (1966). Taylor was using a hammer and chisel when a piece of metal flew off the chisel and blinded him in one eye. This batch of chisels was in a defective state when supplied by the manufacturers. It was held that Taylor's employer was liable because a similar incident had occurred four weeks previously (without anyone being injured). This meant that the employer should have known of the likelihood of such an accident occurring. To avoid this, the chisels should have been taken out of use and returned to the manufacturer.

If the previous incident in the *Taylor* case had not occurred, Taylor's only remedy at that time would have been against the manufacturer. However, the Employers' Liability (Defective Equipment) Act 1969 provides that where an employee is injured at work as a consequence of defective equipment supplied by his employer and the defect is the fault of a third party, for example, the manufacturer, the employer will be deemed to be negligent and, therefore, responsible for the injury. This statute removes the need to establish foresight on the part of the employer in cases like *Taylor*.

In the earlier case of *Davie v New Merton Board Mills Ltd* (1959), the issue of whether an employer could be liable for a manufacturer's negligence where an employee was injured by a fragmented tool was considered. The conclusion was that the employer could not be responsible for a manufacturer's negligence. Obviously, the Employers' Liability (Defective Equipment) Act 1969 reverses this decision. This Act is potentially wide in scope: 'equipment' has been held to include a defective ship (*Coltman v Bibby Tankers Ltd* (1988)) and a flagstone (*Knowles v Liverpool CC* (1993)).

10.2.5 Safe place of work

The employer must ensure that his employees are not exposed to any dangers arising out of the place where the employee is expected to work. This covers any place under the control of the employer, including access and egress, and may extend to the premises of a third party, although, in the latter case, the employer may not reasonably be expected to go to the same lengths as he or she would on his own premises. However, as can be seen in *Wilson v Tyneside Window Cleaning Co* (1958), at the very least it may be necessary to warn the employee of the dangers when visiting/working on the premises of a third party (see *Wilson v Tyneside Window Cleaning Co* (1958)).

In *Smith v Vange Scaffolding and Engineering Co Ltd* (1970), Vange employed Smith on a building site. There were other contractors on site. As Smith returned to the changing hut at the end of the working day, he tripped over the cable of a welding machine, which had been left there by a contractor. Vange were aware of the obstructions on site which made access to and from the place of work difficult and dangerous, but they had not complained to the other contractors. It was held that the employer had failed in his duty to his employee because, being aware of the situation, he should have made the necessary complaints to the main contractor. It was foreseeable that such an accident might occur and reasonable precautions should have been taken. In *Rahman v Arearose Ltd* (2000), the employer was liable for failing to provide a safe place of work when his employee, a restaurant worker, was seriously assaulted by customers. The employer had failed in his duty because other members of staff had been assaulted previously and the employer, being aware of this, had failed to take precautionary measures.

The remit of this duty extends to consideration of the nature of the place and the potential risks involved, the work to be carried out, the experience of the employee and the degree of control or supervision which the employer can reasonably exercise. There may be situations where providing a safe place of work overlaps with the employer's duty to provide a safe system of work. Finally, the duty may apply where the employer sends employees overseas to work. However, whether there has been a breach of duty will depend on whether the employer acted reasonably in the circumstances of that particular case. In *Square D Ltd v Cook* (1992), an employee was sent to Saudi Arabia on a two month contract. His employer was satisfied that the site occupiers and the contractors were reliable companies and had a good health and safety record. In these circumstances, it was held that the employer could not be held to be responsible for the day to day running of the site, nor undertake safety inspections. However, the situation may be different where a number of employees were required to work there for long periods.

Providing a safe place of work extends to protecting staff from the risks of passive smoking. In *Waltons and Morse v Dorrington* (1997), it was stated that there is 'an implied term that the employer will provide and monitor for employees, so far as is reasonably practicable, a working environment which is reasonably suitable for the performance by them of their contractual duties. This extends to the right of an employee not to be required to sit in a smoke filled atmosphere'.

10.2.6 Safe system of work

The duty on the employer to provide a safe system of work extends to a consideration of the following by the employer: the physical layout of the job; safety notices; special procedures; protective clothing; training; and supervision.

In order to fulfil this duty, the employer must take into account all foreseeable eventualities, including the actions of any employees. Any system, to be safe, must reduce the risks to the employee to a minimum; it is accepted that not all risks can be eliminated. Furthermore, the employer must do more than introduce a safe system of work; he or she must ensure that it is observed by the employees. The case law highlights the breadth of this duty.

For example, it can extend to preventing staff being exposed to risk of violence if this is a foreseeable risk, as in *Charlton v Forrest Printing Ink Co Ltd* (1980). More recently, in *Lloyd v Ministry of Justice* (2007), a prison officer succeeded in claiming damages for injury following a violent attack by a prisoner. The claimant based his claim on the absence of a safe system of work arising from the fact that information about the prisoner's past violent conduct had not been passed on to him. The claimant argued that, had he been informed of the prisoner's violent history, he would have taken additional precautionary measures to protect his own safety. The essential information had not been transferred to the segregation unit of the prison and the computer system did not hold all relevant information. This amounted to a failure to provide a safe system of work on the part of the defendant (see also *Cook v Bradford Community NHS Trust* (2002)).

This aspect of the duty will also cover claims for compensation for work-related upper limb disorder, as in *Bettany v Royal Doulton (UK) Ltd* (1993). This was questioned as a result of the decision of the House of Lords in *Pickford v Imperial Chemical Industries plc* (1998). The House of Lords concluded that, in order to recover for work-related upper limb disorder, it must be organic in origin. In this particular case, whilst the claimant suffered from cramp of the hand, the question of whether it was due to repetitive movement and organic in origin was unresolved, due to inconclusive evidence. Furthermore, in *Alexander & Others v Midland Bank plc* (2000), the Court of Appeal concluded that where upper limb disorder is physical rather than psychogenic in origin and can be linked to an unsafe system of work, a personal injury claim will succeed.

Another contentious issue is instruction and supervision. Is it sufficient to order an employee to take safety precautions, or should they be supervised as well if the duty is to be satisfied? The answer depends on the degree of risk and the experience of the employee concerned, including how far the employee has been warned of the risks. It is, however, quite clear from the decision in *Pape v Cumbria CC* (1991) that merely providing protective clothing without warning of the risks may not be sufficient to discharge the duty.

In *Woods v Durable Suites Ltd* (1953), Woods worked in the veneer department at Durable Suites. He was an extremely experienced employee. As there was a risk of dermatitis from the synthetic glues, his employer posted up a notice specifying the precautions to be taken. Woods had also been instructed personally by the manager in the protective measures but had not observed them fully. As a result, he contracted dermatitis. It was held that the employer was not liable for failing to provide a safe system of work because he had taken all reasonable care in posting up notices and providing barrier cream, etc. He was under no obligation, given the age and experience of Woods, to provide someone to watch over him to make sure he followed the precautions.

Constant supervision is, on the whole, not necessary where the employees have the necessary experience and have been trained or instructed accordingly. However, the degree of supervision is commensurate to the severity of the risk. In *Bux v Slough Metals Ltd* (1974), Bux's job involved the removal of molten metal from a furnace and the pouring of this metal into a die-casting machine. Goggles were supplied and Bux was made aware of the risks. He refused to wear the safety goggles because they misted up and he complained to the supervisor, who informed him that no other goggles were available. He was injured when molten metal splashed into his eye. It was held that the employer was liable because, where the work was of a particularly hazardous nature, he must do more than merely provide safety equipment. He should constantly urge his employees to use or wear it.

Finally, in *King v Smith* (1995), King, a window cleaner employed by Smith, was seriously injured when he fell 35 ft from the exterior window sill on which he was standing to clean a window. The employers' rulebook contained an instruction that if a window could only be cleaned by standing on the sill, the employee must secure his safety belt to a structure which would support his weight in the event of a fall. Unfortunately, in this particular case there were no anchorages for the safety belt. King claimed that his employer had failed to provide a safe system of work. The Court of Appeal concluded that there had been a breach of this duty, as, given the inherent danger involved, the employer should have prohibited the act rather than issue an instruction.

10.3 Employers' Liability and Occupational Stress

In *Walker v Northumberland CC* (1995), the scope of the duty to provide a safe system of work was extended to include the requirement to provide working conditions which do not cause undue stress to employees. Walker was employed as an area social services officer with responsibility for four teams of field workers. As the volume of work increased, Walker wrote reports and memoranda regarding the increased workload and the need for urgency in redistributing staff to assist. Nothing was done about this and, one year later, Walker suffered a nervous breakdown. Before returning to work, Walker's superior agreed to provide him with assistance. However, one month after he returned to work, assistance was withdrawn and, in September 1987, he suffered a second nervous breakdown. In 1988, he was dismissed on grounds of permanent ill health. It was held that the defendants were in breach of the duty of care owed to the claimant in respect of the second nervous breakdown which he suffered as a result of stress and anxiety occasioned by his job.

In *Lancaster v Birmingham CC* (1999), the county court awarded damages of £67,000 for mental injury as a result of work-related stress. Whilst this case did not break legal ground, it was the first time an employer had admitted liability. The employee in this case was able to establish each element of the negligence claim against her employer and show that she had a recognised illness, which was caused by work-related stress. As she had also persistently asked for training and administrative support, which had not been forthcoming, she was able to show that her injury was foreseeable (see also *Young v Post Office* (2002)).

Following *Walker* there has been a significant increase in claims involving alleged stress at work. In *Sutherland v Hatton* (2002) the Court of Appeal took the opportunity to introduce some guidelines for determining an employer's liability for psychiatric illness caused by stress at work. The appeal involved appeals by four separate employers who had been found liable for stress at work claims in different county courts. The appellants argued that negligence had not been established against them. The Court of Appeal indicated that the key factors are whether such harm is reasonably foreseeable and 'whether the employer failed to take the steps which are reasonable in the circumstances bearing in mind the magnitude of the risk of harm occurring, the gravity of the harm which may occur, the costs and practicability of preventing it and the justification for running the risk'. An employer was entitled to assume that an employee could withstand the normal pressures of a job unless they were aware of a particular problem or vulnerability.

The court indicated it was necessary to distinguish such claims from general psychiatric injury claims and apply ordinary principles of employers' liability. The Court of Appeal applied the decision in *Hatton* in *Bonser v RJW Mining (UK Ltd)* (2003) stressing the importance of establishing foreseeability in work-related stress cases. The external evidence that the employee, in this case, was not coping was a public display of tears a year before she was forced to give up work due to a stress-related psychiatric illness. The Court of Appeal felt that this was insufficient and did not provide adequate notice of foreseeability of work-related stress.

One of the unsuccessful claimants in *Hatton* appealed against the decision by the Court of Appeal and this appeal was allowed by the House of Lords in *Barber v Somerset* (2004).

❖ KEY CASE *Barber v Somerset* (2004)

Facts:

The claimant was a local authority-employed teacher. Following restructuring of the school at which he taught, the claimant was informed that, in order to maintain his salary and grade, he would be required to take on additional duties. Following the implementation of the additional duties it became common for the claimant to work 60-70 hours per week, including evenings and weekends. After around six months, the claimant complained about 'work overload' to his deputy head teacher and consulted his GP. The claimant also made enquiries about early retirement. He was certified sick on the grounds of stress and depression for a three week period and upon returning to work informed his managers that he could not cope with his workload. His employers took no steps to help or support the claimant, neither did they reduce his workload. As a consequence of the pressure, the claimant became seriously ill and following an altercation with a pupil left the school and ceased to work altogether. The claimant sued his employers for breach of duty.

Decision:

The House of Lords allowed the claimant's appeal and found that the school management committee had breached their duty of care. They held that the test of an employers' duty of care was that of the conduct of the reasonable and prudent employer, taking positive thought for the safety of his employees in the light of what he knew or ought to have known. The defendants, through the school management team, had known of the claimant's problems from around June/July, 1996 when he first raised his concerns with members of the team. Their failure to respond to the concerns amounted to a continuing breach of their duty of care. The House of Lords relied on the judgment of Hale LJ in *Hatton v Sutherland* who had remarked:

> But in every case it is necessary to consider what the employer not only could but should have done. We are not here concerned with such comparatively simple things as gloves, goggles, earmuffs or non-slip flooring. Many steps might be suggested: giving the employee a sabbatical; transferring him to other work; redistributing the work; giving him some extra help for a while; arranging treatment or counselling; providing buddying or mentoring schemes to encourage confidence; and much more. But in all of these suggestions it will be necessary to consider how reasonable it is to expect the employer to do this, either in general or in the particular . . .

Since *Hatton* and *Barber*, the principles and guidelines have been applied in a number of cases. In *Hartman v South Essex Mental Health and Community Care NHS Trust* (2005) the claimant had provided information about a previous breakdown and her vulnerability to stress in a confidential medical questionnaire to the occupational health department. The Court of Appeal, applying *Hatton* held that it was not reasonably foreseeable to her employers that she would suffer psychiatric injury and they were not in breach of duty.

In *Daw v Intel Corporation* (2007) the claimant, described as a 'highly efficient, conscientious and loyal employee', suffered psychiatric injury as a result of work overload. Despite the fact that the employer had provided counselling services, the employer was still held to have breached their duty of care by failing to take steps to alleviate the problem of 'overload' once they had become aware of the problem. The claimant, a long-standing payroll analyst, had complained about work load on 14 separate occasions, and having broken down in tears at work, set out problems in a detailed email. The claimant was promised help, but this never materialised. In reaching the decision, the court identified two issues which contributed to her breakdown. Firstly, the blurred lines of managerial responsibility (she was answerable to three individuals, who often conflicted) and secondly, that there had been insufficient assistance with an increased and heavy workload. The appellants accepted that the claimant was suffering from psychiatric harm caused by chronic stress but appealed the finding of the trial judge that such harm became foreseeable at the point of email communication. However, the court took the view that Mrs Daw's email of March 2011 should have been read with care, particularly as it referred to previous incidents of breakdown (unrelated to work). Urgent action should have followed the communication and her workload should have been immediately reduced. Of interest was the fact that the court considered that an organisation the size of Intel were in a position to engage assistance immediately and in fact upon commencement of Mrs Daw's breakdown, it had covered the work without difficulty.

In *Dickins v O2* (2008) the claimant had progressed successfully at work to become a manager, but subsequently asked for help with workload and none was provided. During March 2002, the claimant indicated that she felt 'exhausted', and asked to be moved to a less stressful job. Her manager told her to 'hold on' but, after three months and no intervention, the claimant asked for time off without pay. Subsequently she told her manager she was at the 'end of her tether' and was advised to see Occupational Health, but was not provided with urgent appointment. Following this she was diagnosed as unfit for work due to anxiety and depression, and following a period of sick leave her employment terminated in 2003. The Court of Appeal rejected the defendant's argument that the employee's psychiatric injury was not foreseeable and also held that the provision of a counselling service was not sufficient to avoid liability where the claimant had openly admitted the problem was due to management of workload.

To conclude, of interest, is the fact that both *Daw* and *Dickins* involved large private sector organisations and the courts seem willing to take a more robust approach to stress at work claims, particularly where such organisations have resources to cope with work overload.

10.4 Breach of Duty

Once duty is established, the remaining essentials are judged on the same basis as any action in negligence. The burden is on the employee to show that the employer is in breach of his or her duty. The employee must prove fault on the part of the employer, that is, has the employer failed to act as a reasonable employer? Alternatively, can *res ipsa loquitur* be established? If the employer has taken all reasonable precautions, considering all the circumstances of the case, then he or she will not be liable (see *Latimer v AEC Ltd* (1953)).

The standard of care will vary with respect to the individual needs of each employee. The employer must have special regard for the old, young, inexperienced and employees with special disabilities; that is, the standard of care will be increased. For example, in *Paris v Stepney DC* (1951), Paris worked for the council in one of their garages. One of his jobs, which he did frequently, was to chip out rust from under buses and other vehicles owned by the council. At that time, it was not customary to provide safety goggles for such work. Paris was already blind in one eye. One day, as he was chipping out rust, a fragment of rust entered his good eye and he was rendered totally blind. It was held that the employer had failed to exercise the necessary standard of care. It was foreseeable that there was an increased risk of greater injury to this particular employee because of the nature of his existing disability. He should, therefore, have been provided with safety goggles, which at the very least would have reduced the risk.

This case illustrates the basic rule that 'you must take your victim as you find him'. In applying this rule, whether there has been a breach will be a question of fact in each case, as illustrated in

James v Hepworth and Grandage Ltd (1968), in which the employer erected large notices in their foundry, informing their employees that they should wear spats (a form of leg protection). Unbeknown to the employer, the plaintiff could not read; he was injured when molten metal hit his leg and ran into his shoe. He failed in his claim for damages, as it was held that he had observed the other workmen wearing spats and his failure to make enquiries indicated that, even if he had been informed about the notice, he would not have worn them.

The standard of care is increased in potentially high risk occupations where an employee may be illiterate or may not comprehend English. This can be seen in *Hawkins v Ian Ross (Castings) Ltd* (1970). The employer employed a large number of Asians as labourers. Hawkins was carrying a ladle of molten metal with the assistance of one such labourer. When he shouted to him to stop, the labourer did not understand and carried on walking. Hawkins overbalanced and was injured by the molten metal spilling over his leg. It was held that the employer had failed in his duty because, where he chooses to employ labourers or, indeed, any staff who may not have a good understanding of the English language, the standard of care is increased. Furthermore, this increase is not confined to the particular employee; it is extended to his or her workmates, as there is a foreseeable increase in the risk to them of having to work with people who do not understand instructions.

10.5 Causation and Damage

Having established duty and breach, the employee must show that injury has been suffered as a result of the employer's breach of duty. Injury is not confined to physical injury; it includes damage to personal property, loss of earnings, etc. The test for establishing liability is the one used in negligence: the 'but for' test (see previous chapter). The question which has to be answered by the court is, therefore, but for the employer's breach of duty, would the employee have been injured? If the answer is no, causation is established.

In *McWilliams v Arrol Ltd* (1962), a steel erector employed by Arrol fell from the scaffolding that he was working on and was killed. The employer had provided safety harnesses in the past but, since they had not been worn, they had been removed to another site. It was held that, although the employer was in breach of his duty, he was not liable because it could not be proved that McWilliams would have worn the harness, even if it had been available. The 'but for' test was not satisfied.

Even after causation has been established, the employer is not necessarily liable for all the damage to his or her employee. The employer will only be liable for foreseeable damage. This does not mean that the precise nature or extent of the injury has to be foreseen, only that some harm will result from the breach of duty. However, there is a legal limit to the extent of liability imposed by *The Wagon Mound (No 1)* (1961) (see above). Applying this rule, the employer will only be liable for the foreseeable consequences of his breach, that is, he will not be liable for the unexpected. In *Doughty v Turner Manufacturing* (1964), a lid made of asbestos and cement, covering a bath of sulphuric acid, was knocked accidentally into the acid. A chemical reaction took place between the cover and the acid. In the eruption which followed, Doughty was severely burned. It was held that the employer was not liable because the only harm which could be foreseen from the incident was splashing. A chemical reaction of this type resulting in an eruption was at the time unknown and, therefore, unforeseeable. This is regarded as a rather harsh decision, since it demands a degree of foresight as to the way in which the injury occurred.

The decision is doubtful in the light of such cases as *Hughes v Lord Advocate* (1963) and *Smith v Leech Brain & Co* (1962). In the latter, Smith's lip was splashed with molten metal. At the time, unknown to anyone, his lip contained cancerous tissue, which became malignant as a result of the burn. He subsequently died of cancer. It was held that the employer was liable for his death from cancer because the risk of being splashed with molten metal was foreseeable. Smith's death was, therefore, merely an extension of the foreseeable injury, which was a burn. This latter case is a much more sympathetic interpretation of the rule in *The Wagon Mound* (No 1).

10.6 Remedies and Defences

The main remedy available for employers' liability is compensation for personal injury, the object being to put the claimant in the position he or she would have been in if the accident had never occurred. The limitation period for bringing such an action is three years from the date on which the cause of action arose or the date of knowledge, whichever is the later (Limitation Act 1980).

There are no defences unique to this particular tort. In general, the main ones pleaded are contributory negligence and *volenti*: the former may result in a reduction in the amount of damages payable; the latter is rarely accepted by the courts in actions founded in employers' liability.

10.7 Principal and Agent

The rules relating to the vicarious liability of a principal for the tortious acts of his or her agent operate in the same way as those for the employer/employee relationship. However, the key to the principal's liability will be based on whether the agent has exceeded the authority. As was seen in an earlier chapter, an agent's authority can be extremely wide, in that it can be express, implied, ostensible or usual. There is, therefore, more scope for making the principal vicariously liable, even though in *Lloyd v Grace, Smith & Co Ltd* (1912), the employee had only intended to benefit himself.

10.8 Employer and Independent Contractor

Generally, an employer will not be liable for the torts of any independent contractor whom he or she chooses to employ. However, he or she may be made a joint tortfeasor with the independent contractor where he or she has: ratified or authorised the tortious act; contributed to the commission of the tort by the independent contractor, either by the way in which the work was directed or by interfering with the work; or been negligent in the selection of his or her independent contractor.

In *Balfour v Barty-King* (1957), Barty-King's water pipes were frozen. She asked two men at a nearby building site to help to defrost them. They did this by using a blowlamp, rather than a heated brick, on the lagged pipes in her loft. The lagging caught fire and the fire spread to the adjoining premises. It was held that Barty-King was jointly liable for the negligence of the contractor. She had chosen them, invited them onto her premises and then left them to do the job. She should have exercised more care, not only in her selection, but also in overseeing their work.

In *Salsbury v Woodland* (1970), the independent contractor was contracted to fell a tree in his client's garden, which was close to the highway. He was an experienced tree feller but was negligent in felling the tree. Telephone lines were brought down and the claimant, whilst attempting to move the wires from the highway, was struck by a car. It was held that the person employing the independent contractor was not liable. The work was not being carried out on the highway, and *near* to the highway is not the same thing as *on* the highway. Furthermore, this work would only be regarded as extra hazardous if it had been carried out on the highway. The independent contractor had to bear sole responsibility.

The criteria for judging whether work is particularly hazardous involves looking at where the work is to be carried out, whether members of the public are at risk and what the dangers are (see *Honeywell and Stein Ltd v Larkin Bros Ltd* (1934)).

Summary

Vicarious and Employers' Liability

Vicarious liability

An employer may be liable for torts committed by his or her employees providing they are acting within the course of their employment. For an employer to be liable, the following must apply:

- There must be in existence an employer/employee relationship (*Ready Mixed Concrete (South East Ltd) v Minister of Pensions* (1968) and *Hawley v Luminar Leisure Ltd* (2006)).
- The employee must be acting within the course of his or her employment, that is, they must be doing something incidental to his or her job or carrying out an authorised act in a wrongful, negligent or unauthorised manner. See further:
    - *Century Insurance Co Ltd v Northern Ireland Road Transport Board* (1942);
    - *Rose v Plenty* (1976);
    - *Harrison v Michelin Tyre Co Ltd* (1985);
    - *Poland v Parr & Sons* (1927);
    - *Morris v Martin & Sons Ltd* (1966);
    - *Lister v Hesley Hall Ltd* (2001).
- For examples of circumstances falling 'outside the course of employment' see:
    - *Hilton v Thomas Burton (Rhodes) Ltd* (1961);
    - *Warren v Henly's Ltd* (1948);
    - *Aldred v Nacanco* (1987);
    - *Heasmans v Clarity Cleaning Co Ltd* (1987);
    - *Irving v Post Office* (1987);
    - *Padden v Arbuthnot Pensions & Investment Ltd* (2004).

The concept of vicarious liability arises where there is in existence a 'special relationship'. It can, therefore, also arise between principal and agent and, in limited circumstances, between employer and independent contractor (see *Balfour v Barty-King* (1957), *Salsbury v Woodland* (1970) and *Honeywell and Stein Ltd v Larkin Bros Ltd* (1934).

Employers' liability

An employer is under a duty to take reasonable care in respect of the health and safety of his or her employees.

An employers' duty is personal, in that it is owed to each individual employee and cannot be delegated. The scope and nature of the duty was originally defined in *Wilsons and Clyde Coal Co v English* (1938).The duty is owed whilst the employee is acting within the course of his or her employment. The course of employment extends to the carrying out of tasks reasonably incidental to one's job:

- *Davidson v Handley-Page Ltd* (1945);
- *Smith v Stages and Darlington Insulation Co Ltd* (1989).

The scope of the duty is fourfold:

- To provide competent fellow employees:
    - *O'Reilly v National Rail and Tramway Appliances Ltd* (1966);
    - *Hudson v Ridge Manufacturing Co Ltd* (1957).

- To provide safe plant and appliances:
  - *Bradford v Robinson Rentals* (1967);
  - Employers' Liability (Defective Equipment) Act 1969 – *Taylor v Rover Car Co Ltd* (1966);
  - *Coltman v Bibby Tankers Ltd* (1988);
  - *Knowles v Liverpool CC* (1993).

- To provide a safe place of work:
  - *Smith v Vange Scaffolding and Engineering Co Ltd* (1970);
  - *Rahman v Arearose Ltd* (2000).

- To provide a safe system of work:
  - *Charlton v Forrest Printing Co Ltd* (1980);
  - *Bettany v Royal Doulton (UK) Ltd* (1993);
  - *Walker v Northumberland CC* (1995);
  - *Pickford v Imperial Chemical Industries plc* (1998);
  - *Barber v Somerset* (2004);
  - *Sutherland v Hatton* (2002);
  - *Bonser v RJW Mining (UK) Ltd* (2003);
  - *Daw v Intel Corporation* (2007).

Employers' liability and breach of duty

The claimant must establish a breach of duty on the part of the employer. The standard of care is that of the reasonable employer. The courts will generally consider the same factors as discussed in the earlier chapter on negligence:

- *Barker v Saint Gobain Pipelines plc* (2004);
- *Latimer v AEC Ltd* (1953);
- *Paris v Stepney DC* (1951);
- *Hawkins v Ian Ross (Castings) Ltd* (1970);
- *James v Hepworth and Grandage Ltd* (1968).

Causation and resultant damage

The next stage is for the claimant to establish causation. The claimant must show that 'but for' the defendant's breach of duty, the injury would not have occurred and that harm was foreseeable:

- *McWilliams v Arrol Ltd* (1962);
- *Doughty v Turner Manufacturing* (1964);
- *Smith v Leech Brain & Co* (1962).

Further Reading

There are a number of further reading materials which are useful if you wish to find out more about vicarious and employers' liability. The classic work on employers' liability is:

Cotter, B, and Bennett, D, *Munkman on Employer's Liability*, 15th edn, 2009, London: Lexis-Nexis

There are a number of general textbooks on tort law which contain excellent chapters on vicarious and employers' liability:

Harpwood, VH, *Modern Tort Law*, 7th edn, 2008, London: Routledge-Cavendish

Horsey, K, and Rackley, E, *Tort Law*, 2009, Oxford: OUP
Lunney, M, and Oliphant, K, *Tort Law: Text and Materials*, 4th edn, 2010, Oxford: OUP
Murphy, J, *Street on Torts*, 12th edn, 2007, Oxford: OUP
Rogers, WVH (ed), *Winfield & Jolowicz on Tort*, 18th edn, 2010, London: Sweet & Maxwell
Steele, J, *Tort Law: Text, Cases and Materials*, 2nd edn, 2010, Oxford: OUP

If you wish to examine more specific issues relating to the nature of either vicarious or employers' liability then the following represent a balanced selection of articles:

Case, P, 'Developments in Vicarious Liability: Shifting Sands and Slippery Slopes' (2006) 22(3) *Professional Negligence* 161
Doran, C, and Lee, V, 'Employers on Suicide Watch' (2008) *New Law Journal* 537
McIvor, C, 'The Use and Abuse of the Doctrine of Vicarious Liability' (2006) 35 *Common Law World Review* 268
Stevens, R, 'Vicarious Liability or Vicarious Actions' (2007) 123 *Law Quarterly Review* 30
Weekes, R, 'Vicarious Liability for Violent Employees' (2004) 63(1) *Cambridge Law Journal* 53

Chapter 11

Liability for Land and Environmental Damage

Chapter Contents

Law in Context: Business Liability for Environmental Harm

As we have seen, an employer can become liable for injuries negligently caused by his or her employee and also for injuries negligently caused to his or her employee via both vicarious and employers' liability. An employer, particularly a business employer, is also likely to occupy or manage land and premises which form part of the business. Tort Law and Environmental Law provide the potential for both civil and criminal liability to arise from damage arising from the state of premises and also for harm and pollution to the environment. This chapter examines the key framework of controls that directly impact on business. Environmental law is an important and burgeoning area with potentially expensive compliance and liability costs for business and industry. Increasing concerns about climate change, sustainable use of natural resources and protection of energy resources have placed environmental protection at the top of the international and domestic political agenda. It is therefore important for students of business law to acquire an understanding of the framework of environmental controls regulating business and industry. Environmental liability can be expensive both in terms of compliance costs and failure to comply, which may result in criminal prosecution or a civil claim. A CBI Report published in 2010, *The Shape of Business: the next 10 Years,* highlighted the increased impact that sustainable development and the transfer to a low-carbon economy will have on business development over the next decade. It is therefore important that business students comprehend the framework of controls which exist in relation to environmental law.

11.1 Introduction

Whilst areas such as water pollution, waste management and integrated pollution control clearly fall within the ambit of environmental law, there are many other spheres of legal regulation and activity that do not, and yet they may have a significant environmental impact or cause loss or injury. For present purposes, this chapter will examine the key framework of controls that directly impact on businesses. Certain failures to regulate the state of premises may also attract civil liability if they also cause loss or injury to an individual. The most likely area where a claim may arise is via tortious liability, and an action may lie in negligence (see earlier chapters), occupiers' liability and nuisance. We will start by examining the potential for liability in occupiers' liability.

11.2 Occupiers' Liability

A business can expect many different people to enter premises they own, occupy or have control over. Some will have been invited to carry out certain tasks or provide services, others may enter to make enquiries and some may indeed be trespassing on the premises in question. Occupiers' liability is therefore concerned with the liability of an occupier for damage done to visitors on the premises. The concept of premises is widely defined and extends to ships, trains, scaffolding, etc. For example, a derelict boat left on a council estate was held to fall within the ambit of occupiers' liability (see *Jolley v Sutton London Borough Council* (2000)). The law within this area is negligence-based, and is contained within two key statutes, the Occupiers' Liability Act 1957 which regulates an occupier's liability to visitors and the Occupiers' Liability Act 1984 which regulates any liability potentially owned to trespassers.

11.2.1 Who constitutes an occupier?

The legislation gives no definition, so the test is to be found within common law principles by way of the Occupational Control Test. This test establishes that *where a person has a sufficient degree of control over the premises, then they will owe a duty of care to those lawfully on the premises.*

So, for example, in *Wheat v Lacon & Co Ltd* (1966) the defendants owned a public house, although the day-to-day running of the pub was conducted by a manager. The defendants granted the manager a licence to use the first floor of the property as private accommodation, but the defendants retained a right to repair. They also allowed the manager to take paying guests in part of the accommodation. One such guest fell down the unlit stairs of the private part and was killed as result of the fall. In determining who could be an occupier for the purposes of liability, the House of Lords held that there could be more than one occupier, so both the brewery and the manager could have been liable. However, on the facts, a light bulb from the stairs had been removed by an unidentifiable third party and the defendants were not therefore held to be in breach of the duty owed. It has also been established that an occupier does not have to be in actual physical occupation of premises for them to have a sufficient degree of control (see *Harris v Birkenhead Corporation* (1976)).

11.2.2 Who constitutes a visitor?

Section 1(2) of the Occupiers' Liability Act 1957 provides that visitors may be said to be '. . . the persons who would at common law be treated as . . . invitees or licensees'. It is important to distinguish visitors from non-visitors as if a claimant is regarded to be a trespasser, liability for any harm to them will be determined by the Occupiers' Liability Act 1984.

There are several ways in which a claimant can become a visitor for the purposes of the legislation. Additionally, if you enter by virtue of a contractual right, the 'common duty of care' is implied into the contract. The term visitor does not include users of public or private rights of way (any duty would need to be established under the ordinary principles of negligence).

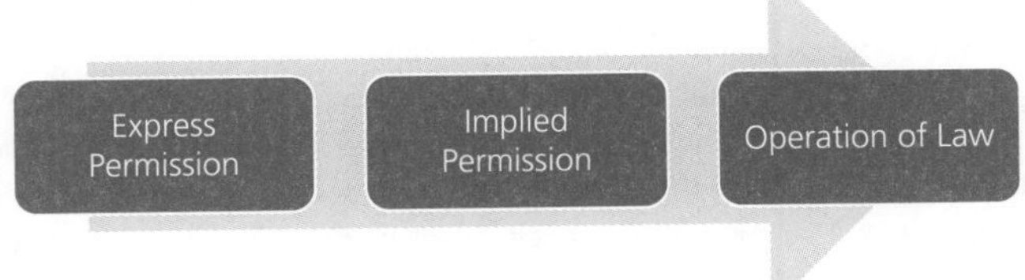

Figure 11.1 Types of visitor

Anyone who enters by way of invitation, or contractual licence, will be deemed to have entered by express permission. All entrants have implied permission to enter premises and state their purpose (unless of course this has been revoked in the case of an individual). If revoking the implied permission, an occupier must give the visitor reasonable time to exit the premises safely. Individuals exercising statutory powers of entry such as the Police or emergency workers will be classed as visitors by operation of law unless they abuse or exceed their powers of entry.

Occupiers can set limits on visitors on the premises as to time and length of stay and the purpose of the visit. Access to certain parts of the premises can also be restricted. If permission is abused then this may amount to a trespass. It is also possible to be a visitor for some purposes but not for others. In *Anderson v Coutts* (1984) the owner of land had erected railings near to the edge of a cliff and had also placed a notice warning of the danger of going near to the edge of the cliff. Despite such warnings a man fell over the edge. By entering the restricted area he had been warned not to enter, he had become a trespasser.

11.2.3 Nature of the duty of care

The Occupiers' Act 1957 states that the Act is designed to 'regulate the duty which an occupier of premises owes to his visitors in respect of dangers due the state of the premises or to things done or omitted to be done on them' (s 1(1)) and covers both damage to both person and property. Section 2(2) imposes a 'common duty of care' upon occupiers 'to take such care as in all the circumstances of the case is reasonable to see that the visitor will be reasonably safe in using the premises for which he is invited or permitted by the occupier to be there'. This is interpreted to mean that it is visitors whom must be made reasonably safe, and not the premises.

In light of this, the duty and standard of care may vary according to the type of visitor. For example, s 2(3)(a) of the 1957 Act provides that 'an occupier must be prepared for children to be less careful than adults'. The law recognises that children may not be able to appreciate danger, and whilst the danger of some things will be obvious to an adult, they could be 'fatal and fascinating' to a child (see *Latham v R Johnson & Nephew Ltd* (1913)). In *Glasgow Corporation v Taylor* (1922) a small child, aged seven, died after consuming poisonous berries. The claimant had entered the botanical gardens and seen a shrub with berries that resembled cherries. Although the defendants knew the berries to be poisonous, they had not fenced off the shrub or provided any warning. The defendants were held liable, as the berries were held to constitute an 'allurement' which had proved to be fatal and fascinating to the child.

As far as young children are concerned, even innocent items can become dangerous. In determining liability an occupier is allowed to take into account what 'prudent parents' would do in a situation (see *Phipps v Rochester Corporation* (1955)). The courts are usually sympathetic to wandering children, especially if an occupier has acquiesced in allowing children to be present. The court may find that such children have implied permission to be on premises, or as an alternative, be generous in the interpretation of the s 1(3) duty principles under the 1984 Act.

❖ KEY CASE *Jolley v Sutton LBC* (2000)

Facts:

A boat, left in a rotten and dangerous condition was abandoned on ground owned by the defendants. As the boat was dangerous, the council placed a notice on the boat warning people not to touch the boat and that if the owner did not claim the boat within seven days it would be taken away. The council never removed the boat. Two teenage boys decided to renovate the boat. The boys had been working on the boat and jacked the boat up to carry out repairs. The boat fell on one of them and caused severe spinal injuries, resulting in paraplegia. The claimant brought an action for damages for the personal injuries sustained. The trial judge found for the claimant. The Court of Appeal reversed the decision, holding that whilst it was foreseeable that younger children might play on the boat and suffer an injury by falling through the rotten wood, it was not foreseeable that older boys would try to do the boat up. The claimant appealed.

Decision:

The House of Lord allowed the claimant's appeal. The risk was that children would 'meddle with the boat at the risk of some physical injury'. The actual injury fell within the foreseeable range of that description.

In addition, s 2(3)(b) of the 1957 Act provides 'an occupier may expect that a person, in the exercise of his calling, will appreciate and guard against any special risks ordinarily incident to it, so far as the occupier leaves him free to do so'. In *Roles v Natham* (1963) two chimney sweeps were asked to enter the defendant's property to clean the flue of a boiler. Although they were warned not to work while the boiler was still lit, they proceeded to do so and as a result they died from carbon monoxide poisoning. The court held the defendant not to be liable as the claimants should have heeded the warnings and in any event the risk was incidental to the nature of the work.

An occupier may discharge their common duty of care by using an effective warning sign (see s 2(4)(a) 1957 Act). However, the warning must make the visitor reasonably safe by alerting them to the nature of the danger and any special measures needed to remain safe. In any litigation, the judge will decide on the evidence whether a warning was sufficient to make the visitor reasonably safe. Any attempt to exclude liability must be in line with the Unfair Contract Terms Act 1977.

UCTA 1977 applies to business premises, which are widely defined and include professions, government and local authorities. In particular, s 2(1) UCTA 1977 provides that any attempt to exclude liability for death or personal injuries caused by negligence, including breach of the common duty of care, will be void.

11.2.4 The common duty of care and independent contractors

Section 2(4)(b) of the 1957 Act provides that the general rule is that occupiers will not be liable for the negligence of independent contractors. In *Haseldine v CA Daw & Son* (1941) the contractors were lift maintenance engineers. The occupier of the premises was not held liable for the negligence of the contractors in maintaining a lift in a block of flats. The occupier had discharged his duty of care – he had hired whom he thought were competent contractors, and as it was a specialist job he had checked as far as he was able to see that the work had been carried out.

This can be contrasted to the decision in *Woodward v Mayor of Hastings* (1945), when a school cleaner cleaned some steps at a school and negligently left them in an icy condition. As a result a pupil slipped and injured themself on the steps. The court held the defendant to be liable in this case, holding that the occupier could have checked to see if the job had been carried out properly.

To avoid liability, businesses need to ensure therefore that they have engaged competent independent contractors, or where the work is of a simpler nature, checked to see that any work has been carried out properly.

11.2.5 The Occupiers' Liability Act 1984

The 1984 Act replaces the common law duty of care owed to trespassers, sometimes referred to as a 'humanitarian duty' and covers personal injuries arising out of the state of the premises, or things done, or omitted to be done, by the occupier. Unlike the Occupiers' Liability Act 1957, the 1984 Act does not cover damage to property. The term 'occupier' is defined as the person who owes the common duty of care under the Occupiers' Liability Act 1957, and the 1984 Act relates to those who are not visitors.

Under s 1(3) of the 1984 Act, an occupier will only owe a duty of care to trespassers if (a) he is aware of the danger, or should reasonably have known it existed, on his premises; and (b) he knows, or has reasonable grounds to believe, the trespasser is in the vicinity of the danger, or is likely to come into the vicinity; and (c) the risk is one which, considering all the facts, he could reasonably be expected to offer some protection against.

The question whether an occupier is liable to a trespasser depends whether a conscientious humane man with his knowledge, skill and resources could reasonably have been expected to have done something which could have avoided an accident or injury, and s 1(4) of the 1984 Act provides that the duty is to 'take such care as is reasonable in all the circumstances of the case to see that [the trespasser] does not suffer injury on the premises by result of the danger concerned'.

Under the 1984 Act, the occupier should also be able to discharge his duty by putting up notices, etc, warning of the dangers on his premises. Such notices will be subject to the same rules as those applying under the Occupiers' Liability Act 1957. The defence of *volenti non fit injuria* is also available under the 1984 Act, along with contributory negligence (see *Ratcliff v McConnell* (1999)).

❖ KEY CASE *Tomlinson v Congleton Borough Council* (2004)

Facts:

The claimant hit his head on the bottom of a lake after diving into shallow water, and as a result was paralysed from the neck down. The incident occurred in a public park managed by the defendants, who had placed prominent notices stating 'Dangerous Water: No Swimming'. The defendants had also employed rangers to warn people not to swim in the water. Despite the defendants' attempts to prevent swimming, people had continued to ignore them and several accidents had occurred. The claimant sued under the 1984 Act, as although he had entered the park as a visitor, his status as a lawful visitor ended when he entered the water against the occupier's express instructions.

Decision:

The House of Lords rejected the claim, holding the requirements for a claim under s 1(3) of the 1984 Act had not been met. Even though the occupiers were aware of the danger and had reasonable grounds to believe people were in the vicinity of it, the risk was not one that the occupier could be reasonably expected to offer protection against. Emphasis was placed on the fact that the claimant, Tomlinson, was a person of full capacity and had voluntarily chosen to engage in an activity which had inherent risk. The reasoning of the decision of the House of Lords placed a great deal of emphasis on the principle of 'individual responsibility'.

11.3 Nuisance

The tort of nuisance is concerned with protecting a person's interest in their use or enjoyment of property. In the past, unlawful interference with land has arisen because of offensive smells, toxic chemicals, noxious fumes, traffic jams, flooding, fires, etc. The essential element to this tort is that liability of the defendant arises from unreasonable interference with another's use and enjoyment of property. There are four different types of nuisance, public nuisance, statutory nuisance, private nuisance and the rule in *Rylands v Fletcher*.

11.3.1 Public nuisance

Public nuisance is concerned with interference with recognised public rights, the classic example being obstruction of a highway. The leading case in this area is *AG v PYA Quarries* (1957) in which Lord Justice Denning described public nuisance as '. . . a nuisance which is so widespread in its range or so indiscriminate in its effect that it would not be reasonable to expect one person to take proceedings on his own responsibility of the community at large'.

Whilst public nuisance is generally treated as a crime, business users of premises should note that an individual may bring a civil action in if they can establish that they have suffered special damage over and above that of the community at large, for example damage to property or loss of profits (see *Halsey v Esso Petroleum Company Ltd* (1961)).

11.3.2 Statutory nuisance

Members of the public can also initiate a statutory nuisance complaint which is a procedure arising from Part III of the Environmental Protection Act 1990. This allows individuals to complain about noise and smells to their local Environmental Health Department and by virtue of s 79 Environmental Protection Act 1990, local authorities come under a duty to inspect their areas for the existence of statutory nuisances. Section 80 Environmental Protection Act 1990 provides that where a local authority has identified the existence of a statutory nuisance, they are under a mandatory duty to serve an Abatement Notice on the person responsible for the nuisance and this extends to serving them on businesses which are deemed to have created a statutory nuisance.

Local authorities will investigate complaints and consider the nature and location of the nuisance, the duration of the nuisance and the utility of the activity. If one is found, an abatement notice will be served on the 'person responsible' and the notice will set out the measures necessary to abate the nuisance, and the timescale for doing so. It is a criminal offence to fail to comply with an abatement notice, or any requirement or prohibition imposed by the notice, without reasonable excuse (see s 80 EPA 1990). There are several potential defences provided for in s 80(7) EPA 1990, namely reasonable excuse, best practicable means and a range of special defences. For present purposes, the most relevant for businesses is the best practicable means defence which means that it is a defence for a business to show they have used the best practicable means in carrying out operations which may amount to a nuisance.

11.3.3 Private nuisance

The traditional definition of a private nuisance is '. . . an unlawful interference with a person's use or enjoyment of land, or some right over, or in connection with it' (*Read v Lyons* (1947)). The tort of private nuisance is primarily concerned with protecting interests in property and can arise in a number of ways, for example, by way of encroachment upon the claimant's land (eg tree roots), actual physical damage to the claimant's property (eg noxious fumes) and also interference with the claimant's comfort or convenience (eg smells).

An action in private nuisance is only available to an owner or occupier with a recognised legal interest in land (confirmed in *Hunter v Canary Wharf Ltd* (1997)). There are three potential defendants to sue in an action for private nuisance, namely, the creator of a nuisance; the occupier of the land; and in limited circumstances, the occupier's landlord. Therefore, a business can attract liability for private nuisance in a number of ways. It is also important to distinguish between actual physical damage to property and interference with the enjoyment of property as where the latter is concerned then proof of a substantial level of interference is required by the courts (see *St Helen's Smelting Co v Tipping* (1865)).

11.3.4 Factors taken into account

In deciding whether or not an actionable private nuisance has arisen, the courts will take into account a number of factors. These are locality, utility of the conduct, duration of the nuisance, any abnormal sensitivity on the part of the claimant, any malice involved and, if damage to property is concerned, whether such damage is foreseeable.

The locality in which the private nuisance arises is important. If the area is residential, the claimant will be expected to tolerate lesser interference than if the nuisance is occurring in an industrialised environment. A grant of planning permission may have an impact on the nature of

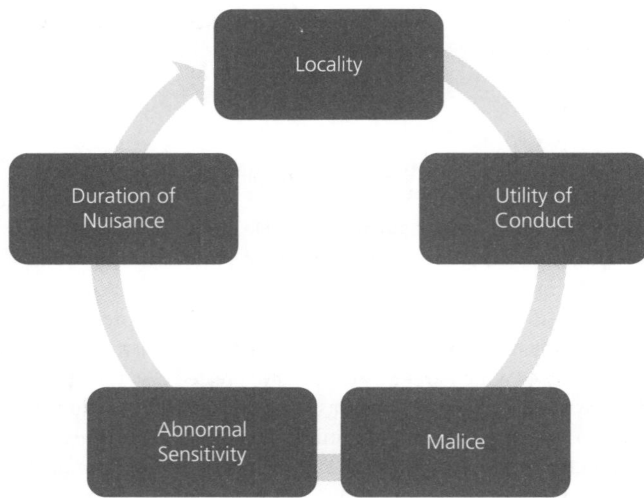

Figure 11.2 Factors taken into account when assessing private nuisance

the locality (see *Gillingham BC v Medway (Chatham) Dock Co Ltd* (1993) and *Wheeler v Saunders* (1996)). The courts will also take into account the duration of the nuisance and a private nuisance is usually associated with a continuing state of affairs.

In *Harrison v Southwark & Vauxhall Water Co* (1891) noise and disruption associated with building work carried out by the defendants was not held to be a nuisance, on the basis it was temporary and therefore not unreasonable. This can be contrasted with the decision in *De Keyser's Royal Hotel Ltd v Spicer Bros Ltd* (1914), when building work occurring through both the day and night was held by the court to constitute a nuisance on the grounds it disrupted the sleep of the residents of the claimant's hotel business.

The courts will not take into account any abnormal sensitivity in determining whether or not a nuisance has occurred in relation to either person or property. In *Heath v Mayor of Brighton* (1908) a vicar failed to establish liability for nuisance after complaining of noise nuisance from a nearby power sub-station. The alleged 'humming' from the station had not impacted on any of his congregation and the court treated the vicar as an abnormally sensitive claimant. It is worthwhile noting that activities on property may also be regarded to be 'sensitive', for example the storing of brown paper as opposed to ordinary paper (see *Robinson v Kilvert* (1889)).

In ascertaining whether an actionable nuisance exists, the purpose and conduct of a defendant's activity will also be considered. Any activities involving an element of malice will not be regarded as reasonable. For example, in *Christie v Davey* (1893), the claimant was a music teacher who worked from home. The defendant wrote the claimant a letter complaining about the noise from the music lessons, to which the claimant did not respond. Following the letter, the defendant set about interrupting the lessons by banging on the party wall, banging metal trays together and whistling/shouting each time he heard a lesson. The claimant sued successfully, the court holding that the defendant had acted 'only for the purpose of annoyance'.

11.3.5 Foreseeability of harm

Where actual damage to property occurs, there should be foreseeability of the kind of damage suffered. The leading case in this area is *Cambridge Water Co Ltd v Eastern Counties Leather plc* (1994).

❖ **KEY CASE** *Cambridge Water Co Ltd v Eastern Counties Leather plc* (1994)

Facts:
The defendants owned and operated a tannery. During the tanning process, the defendants used a number of solvents to degrease the skins. Up until around 1976, frequent spillages on the concrete floor of the tannery premises occurred. The contamination seeped through the concrete and ground and eventually entered the underground water supply. The claimants had constructed a borehole to pump drinking water for the benefit of the city of Cambridge. Once they became aware of the pollution in the water they had to relocate the borehole, at a cost of more than £1 million. The claimants brought an action alleging negligence, private nuisance and the rule in *Rylands v Fletcher*.

Decision:
On appeal to the House of Lords all three arguments were dismissed on the grounds that there was no foreseeability of the relevant type of harm occurring. At the time the spillages had occurred it would not have been foreseen by the defendants, or the reasonable person, that such spillages would cause the harm complained of. This outcome was greeted with much relief by the business world, who had been concerned that any liability created would in effect impose liability for historic pollution. Shortly afterwards, Parliament introduced legislation on liability for contaminated land (see later).

11.3.6 The rule in *Rylands v Fletcher*

The rule in *Rylands v Fletcher* has been described as a hybrid form of nuisance which imposes liability where something is brought onto land, or collected there, and subsequently escapes, causing damage. In this sense, the environmental implications of the rule are clear. Many potential pollutants consist of materials or substances that are brought onto land, and in the past, the rule has been invoked in relation to water, fire, gases, oil etc.

❖ **KEY CASE** *Rylands v Fletcher* (1865)

Facts:
The case involved the construction of a reservoir upon land rented by the defendant. Below the reservoir existed old mine workings that communicated with those of the claimant and a third party; the defendant's contractors failed to block off the mine shafts. The reservoir burst, and water flooded the mine belonging to the claimant. The defendant did not know of the existence of the mine workings until the incident.

Decision:
Although negligence could not be established on the part of the defendant, the court nevertheless held the defendant liable for the claimant's loss. Mr Justice Blackburn formulated the following famous principle:

> The person who, for his own purposes, brings onto his land and collects and keeps there something likely to do mischief if it escapes, must keep it in at his peril, and if he does not do so he is prima facie liable for all the damage which is the natural consequence of its escape.

The case went to the House of Lords, who affirmed the decision and the approach of Blackburn J, Lord Cairns LC emphasising that for the rule to apply, the use of the land must be 'non-natural'. As will be seen, it is this particular qualification that has proved to be one of the major limitations in subsequent interpretations of the *Rylands v Fletcher* rule.

As the rule developed, the most limiting aspect became the interpretation of non-natural use of land. This concept has been equated with 'extraordinary' or 'abnormal use', and the courts will generally take into account the degree of risk created by the defendant's use and the prevailing standards of the era. Since *Cambridge Water Company Ltd v Eastern Counties Leather* (1994) there is also the requirement to establish foreseeability of harm.

In *Transco plc v Stockport MC* (2003) the defendants owned a block of flats that were situated close to a railway embankment. A leaking pipe within the building caused a large amount of water to saturate the embankment (also owned by the defendants), which eventually led to it collapsing and damaging the claimant's gas pipeline. Transco were forced to carry out major repairs to prevent the pipe fracturing. Transco were unable to recover damages, on the basis that no escape had occurred (the water had remained on the defendant's land).

11.3.7 Defences and remedies

There are a number of defences which can be pleaded in private nuisance and the rule in *Rylands v Fletcher*. The two main defences that can be pleaded in an action for private nuisance are prescription and statutory authority. Other defences include act of God, consent and the unforeseeable act of a third party.

The continuance of a nuisance for 20 years in principle entitles the defendant to claim a prescriptive right to commit private nuisance (this defence is not available for public nuisance). However, it is difficult to establish that the interference constituted an actionable nuisance for the entire 20-year period (see *Sturges v Bridgman* (1879)). Equally, a defendant will not be liable for interferences that are the inevitable result of the authority of a statute. Statutory authority can be express or implied.

11.4 Environmental Harm and Liability

Environmental law is an area with potentially expensive compliance and liability costs for business and industry. Increasing concerns about climate change, sustainable use of natural resources and the prevention of pollution protection have placed environmental protection at the top of the international and domestic political agenda. It is therefore important for students of business law to acquire an understanding of the framework of environmental controls regulating business and industry.

Modern environmental law has now developed to such an extent that it has a coherent basis of theory and principles. Why has it developed so? Environmental issues are very important; this is clearly evidenced by the fact of climate change and the position this now occupies on the international political agenda. Environmental liability is also very expensive both in terms of compliance costs and failure to comply, which may result in criminal prosecution or a civil claim.

There are a diverse range of sources of environmental law, ranging from international treaties, conventions and protocols to European Union environmental policy and law, which are then translated into UK primary and secondary legislation. In turn this law will be interpreted with the assistance of relevant case law, government department policy notes, circulars and codes of practice.

Quite often, the task for the environmental lawyer is to decide which area of law, or rule, provides the most appropriate and cost effective way in which to resolve an environmental dispute. For the manager or professional, the task is more likely to involve a consideration of what action is necessary to ensure compliance with the myriad of environmental controls.

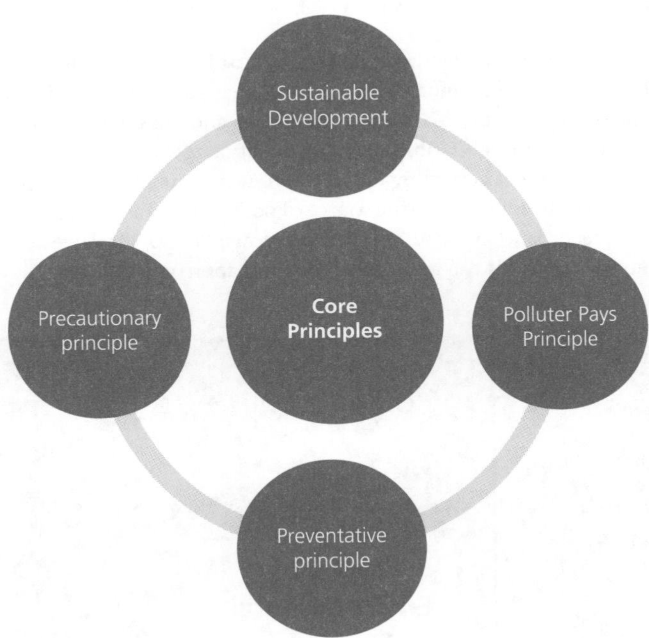

Figure 11.3 Key principles of environmental law

11.4.1 Who is responsible for regulating and enforcing environmental law in the UK?

One of the prime tools of environmental protection within the UK is regulation by public bodies such as the Environment Agency. Enforcement of environmental controls within the UK is carried out largely by the Environment Agency and local authorities. Private prosecutions and the use of civil law play a minimal role. The enforcement of regulatory controls is not limited to the use of criminal sanctions, but rather is based around an array of administrative controls such as the power to prohibit an activity, modify or revoke an authorisation, issue a warning etc.

However, it is important to note that the Agency does not have exclusive control over the enforcement of environmental law. The Agency is primarily concerned with the regulation and enforcement of pollution controls, and many areas of regulation remain with local authorities, for example, the implementation and enforcement of planning controls, monitoring and enforcement of statutory nuisance controls and less serious forms of contaminated land.

As far as criminal enforcement is concerned, environmental pollution offences are mainly of strict liability, that is, there is no need to prove a state of mind, simply the existence of a chain of causation. In theory, every breach amounts to an offence, since no element of fault is necessary on the part of the defendant. In practice, the severity of strict liability is mitigated by the high level of discretion in relation to enforcement policy. More recently, there have been calls for reform and greater flexibility when punishing polluters. The Regulatory Enforcement and Sanctions

Act 2008 authorises greater flexibility and Part 3 of the Act provides a varied range of penalties and sanctions.

In relation to regulation of environmental controls, the UK system revolves around a system of licensing controls which the Environment Agency, or other relevant regulator, will implement, monitor and enforce where necessary. The licensing system for pollution control is based around a range of licensing costs and fees, and constitutes a significant source of income for the Environment Agency and others.

In relation to environmental standards, EU membership has facilitated a move towards an increased reliance on centrally set standards and the tendency for detail to be incorporated in legislation and formal policy documents. Many environmental standards are now imposed via European Directives, for example water quality objectives, air quality targets, etc. Within regulatory systems standards are normally set either according to the target environment which is being protected (eg air, water, river, habitat) or by reference to the source of pollution (eg air emission, water, discharge). Standards are set in accordance with thresholds set down in EU directives aimed at pollution control. Environmental Standards can adopt the following approaches:

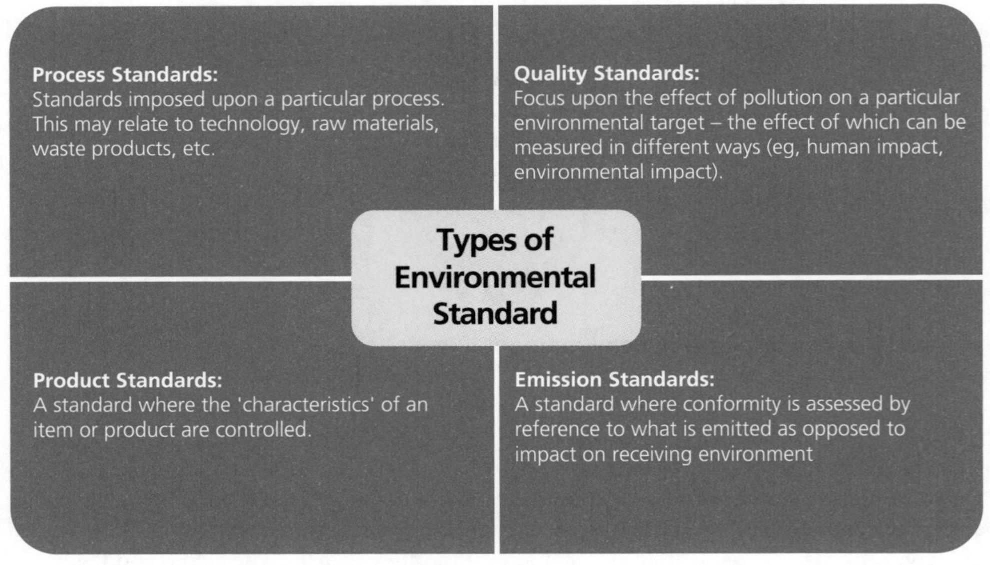

Figure 11.4 Types of Environmental Standard

The role of central government should also be mentioned. There are three government departments which have a significant impact on environmental matters. DEFRA, the Department for Environment, Food and Rural Affairs, has primary responsibility for environmental matters. DECC, the Department for Energy and Climate Change, as the name suggests, governs matters relating to energy and tackling climate change. Finally, the Department for Communities and Local Government should be noted, since this central government department occupies a significant role in the development of sustainable communities and has primary responsibility for planning matters. All three departments regularly draft legislation as well as policy documents which often request consultation comments from business and the public. Between them, these government departments are responsible for the drafting, consultation and development of new policy and legislation relating to environmental protection and climate change initiatives.

11.5 Pollution Control and Environmental Permitting

Historically, Part I of the Environmental Protection Act 1990 introduced a complicated system of integrated pollution control (IPC), which aimed to control some 5,000 major industrial processes. Control was exercised by the requirement of prior authorisation with specific conditions attached. The system of control under Part I EPA 1990 was replaced by a new system called Integrated Pollution Prevention Control (IPPC) which was phased in over a period of eight years from 2000 to 2008/09. New 'installations' were automatically covered by the new system and old IPC authorisations have been transferred over to the new IPPC system during the last eight years on a sector-to-sector basis.

IPPC proved to be much wider in scope, and as well as controlling installations it also included examination of environmental impact such as energy efficiency, waste minimisation, noise, accident prevention and clean-up after a site has been closed. From 2008 onwards, a more streamlined licensing system for IPPC and other environmental licences was introduced in the UK, which was revised in 2010 and 2012. The Environmental Permitting (England & Wales) Regulations 2010 creates a stand-alone system of environmental 'permits' for 'regulated facilities' (as updated by the 2012 Regulations).

11.5.1 When does environmental permitting apply?

Environmental permitting requires certain types of business, such as those carrying out power generation, manufacturing and other industrial activities such as waste management to obtain an environmental permit before commencing operations. The industrial activities covered by the IPPC element of the Environmental Permitting Regulations are very wide-ranging and cover installations in the following sectors:

- Energy industries
- Production and processing of metals
- Mineral industries
- Chemical industries
- Waste management
- Other activities

Other activities incorporated include paper manufacturing, carbon activities, tar and bitumen activities, coating, printing and textile treatments, dye manufacturing, timber activities, animal by-products, food industries and intensive farming. An activity which is 'regulated' requires a permit under the Environmental Permitting (England & Wales) Regulations 2010. A single permit can cover more than one regulated facility and one site with more than one installation, thereby avoiding the need for multiple permits/licences.

11.5.2 Compliance with environmental permitting for IPPC

If an operator is carrying out an activity which falls within the remit of IPPC, the operator must obtain an environmental permit from the Environment Agency. In relation to non-compliance, there are a number of offences contained in the Environmental Permitting (England & Wales) Regulations 2010. In particular, reg 38 provides that it is an offence for a person to contravene, or knowingly cause or knowingly permit, the following:

- fail to comply with, or to contravene, an environmental permit condition
- fail to comply with the requirements of an enforcement notice, a suspension notice or a landfill closure notice

- fail to comply with a notice requiring the provision of information, without reasonable excuse.

It is also an offence to make a statement known to be false or misleading, or recklessly to make a statement which is false or misleading, where the statement is made in purported compliance with a requirement to provide information imposed by, or under a provision, of the 2010 Regulations. An offence is also committed if false entries are made during record-keeping.

In relation to penalties, persons found guilty are liable on summary conviction to a fine not exceeding £50,000 or imprisonment for a term not exceeding 12 months, or to both; or on conviction on indictment to a fine or imprisonment for a term not exceeding five years, or to both. There are a limited range of defences available (see reg 40).

Offences committed by failing to possess the correct environmental permit for integrated pollution, prevention and control activities can be very costly for business ventures. It is also important for students of business law to understand that compliance or non-compliance with such environmental regulations can impact considerably on the value of a business or company.

11.6 Liability for Water Pollution

Water pollution can arise from a number of direct sources, but the most obvious 'pathway' for water pollution is the direct discharging/pumping of harmful substances into the aquatic environment. A common problem is the identification of water pollution which has emanated from indirect and diffuse sources such as landfill sites, agriculture and other contaminated areas of land, hence the implications of water pollution controls are extremely important.

The legal controls in the UK represent one of the most sophisticated and coherent spheres of regulatory activity within domestic environmental law. This is largely due to the historical development of water law and the impact of EU environmental policy. Whilst there are a number of international instruments which deal with water pollution, this chapter focuses on the regulatory controls under which a business could potentially become liable.

The Environment Agency inherited the responsibilities which previously fell under the remit of the NRA and essentially exercises control over water via the regulation of abstraction licences, pollution control, criminal enforcement of pollution controls, clean-up operations and flood defence. The remit of the Environment Agency in relation to water pollution extends to all inland and coastal waters that fall within the category of 'controlled waters' (s 104 Water Resources Act 1991).

11.6.1 Environmental permits and water pollution

The law relating to the licensing system for discharge consents was contained in Sched 10 Water Resources Act 1991 (as amended by Sched 10 to the Environment Act 1995). A discharge consent was required from the Environment Agency for any discharge, or trade, or sewage effluent into controlled waters, any discharge of trade, or sewage, effluent through a pipe from land into the sea outside the limit of controlled waters and finally, any discharge where a prohibition is in force.

The relevant law is now contained in the Environmental Permitting (England & Wales) Regulations 2010 which, as seen in the IPPC section above, have streamlined the permit application process. An applicant will, however, still need to state the place of the discharge activity, the content, the quantity and rate of flow and temperature. In administering the permit system, the Environment Agency operates a fee system and can attach such conditions 'as it may think fit' on environmental permits.

11.6.2 Criminal liability for water pollution

There are a number of ways in which liability can arise for breach of water pollution controls. The main water pollution offences are now contained in the Environmental Permitting (England and Wales) Regulations 2010 (see regs 38(1) and 12(1)). Although very new legislation, the offences are similar to the offences that used to be set out in s 85(1) of the Water Resources Act 1991. Under the 2010 Regulations, it is an offence to cause or knowingly permit a 'water discharge activity' unless the discharge activity complies with an environmental permit or exemption. Water discharge activities are listed in Sched 21 to the 2010 Regulations to include:

- discharging poisonous, noxious or polluting matter or solid waste matter into inland freshwater, coastal waters and relevant territorial waters;
- discharging trade or sewage effluent into inland freshwater, coastal waters and relevant territorial waters;
- cutting or uprooting substantial amounts of vegetation in any inland freshwaters, without taking reasonable steps to remove it.

The old s 85(1) Water Resources Act 1991 created a general pollution offence which provided that it was an offence 'to cause or knowingly permit any poisonous, noxious or polluting matter or any solid waste to enter controlled waters'. It should be noted that s 85(1) in effect created two separate offences: one of 'causing' pollution to enter controlled waters, and one of 'knowingly permitting' pollution to enter controlled waters (see *McLeod v Buchanan* (1940)). Section 85 also contained a number of specific offences relating to trade/sewage effluent (trade effluent defined in s 221 WRA 1991). There was also an offence relating to any matter whatsoever entering controlled waters and impeding proper flow of water and s 85(6) made it an offence to contravene the conditions of a discharge consent (see *R v Ettrick Trout Co Ltd* (1994) and *R v Wicks* (1998)).

At this point it is necessary to examine the general pollution offence in a little more depth since some of the key phrases still carry the same meaning in the 2010 Regulations. Whilst there is no statutory definition of 'poisonous, noxious or polluting' contained in the Act, the courts have indicated a willingness to provide guidance. In *NRA v Egger (UK) Ltd* (1992), the Crown Court interpreted 'polluting matter' to include matter/substances which are 'capable of causing harm in that it may damage a river's potential usefulness'. The court clarified that in relation to the s 85 offence, 'damage' related to harm to animal, vegetable or other life in a river, and/or aesthetic damage. Indeed, the court appreciated that aesthetic damage alone was sufficient to find a prosecution under s 85 (for example, discolouration). In *R v Dovermoss* (1995), the Court of Appeal considered the meaning of 'poisonous, noxious and polluting matter' and concluded that the phrase required only a likelihood, or capability of causing harm, to animals, plants or those who utilised the water. This suggests that proof of actual physical harm is not necessary.

All the offences have a common factor, that is, they are committed when a person 'causes' or 'knowingly permits' pollution to enter controlled waters. The offences fall into the classic model of the regulatory criminal offence of strict liability since no proof of negligence or fault is required. Again, there is no statutory definition of the terms contained in either the old WRA 1991 or the 2010 Regulations, but the courts have provided guidance on a number of previous occasions under the old law, most notably in the leading case of *Alphacell v Woodward* (1972).

❖ KEY CASE *Alphacell v Woodward* (1972)

Facts:

The defendants operated a paper factory. A pollution incident occurred when settling tanks became blocked by leaves and brambles. Pumps had been installed to prevent an overflow, and normally treated water was pumped back into the factory for reuse in paper production. Due to the blockage, the pumps failed to activate and the untreated water overflowed into a channel leading directly into the River Irwell, causing a serious pollution incident. The level of the polluting matter far exceeded the discharge consent possessed by the defendants. The defendants attempted to argue that they had not caused the pollution accident, but rather, the vegetation was the primary source of the incident. At the time the offence related to s 2(1)(a) of the Rivers (Prevention of Pollution) Act 1951, but the wording of the section referred to 'cause or knowingly permit'.

Decision:

The House of Lords upheld the conviction on the grounds that the offence did not require any proof of intention to cause the pollution. Lord Salmon explained that whilst the defendants may not have intended to cause the pollution, they did intend the acts which led to the pollution, namely the construction of the settling tank.

The fact of pollution taking place is sufficient to result in criminal liability and the approach of *Alphacell* was been adopted by many subsequent cases (see *Wrothwell Ltd v Yorkshire Water Authority* (1984) and *Southern Water Authority v Pegram* (1989)). *Alphacell* was expressly approved of in *Attorney General's Reference (No 1 of 1994)* (1995). The matter of what constitutes 'knowingly permit' has come before the courts less often than the first element of 'causing'. It has been suggested that the offence involves a failure to prevent pollution occurring with actual knowledge of that failure. It would appear to apply where a person allows polluting matter to pass over their land into a watercourse and doing nothing to prevent it.

11.6.3 Criminal liability and intervening acts

A problem can arise when a third party carries out an intervening act. Since positive causation is required under the first limb of the offences then the intervening act of a third party can arguably amount to a defence and a break in the chain of criminal responsibility.

In relation to s 85 WRA 1991, in *Empress Car Co (Abertillery) Ltd v NRA* (1998), the House of Lords considered the question of intervening acts and held that the intervening act of a third party would not be regarded as breaking the chain of causation unless it arose from extraordinary circumstances. The implications of the *Empress* decision are that liability will extend to defendants who fail to take steps to guard against the actions of trespassers, other third parties, equipment failure and natural events. The circumstances in which a defendant could successfully argue that such an incident breaks the chain of causation are extremely narrow.

In *NRA v Alfred McAlpine Homes East Limited* (1994) the defendant company was held liable when employees contravened s 85(1). The court indicated that it was unnecessary for those who were the controlling mind of the company to play a direct part in the events that gave rise to the polluting incident. Providing that the employees were acting within the course of their employment liability could arise.

11.6.4 Defences and penalties

It is a defence for the defendant to show that the entry/discharge was made in an emergency to avoid danger to life or health. A defendant must demonstrate that they took steps to notify the Environment Agency as soon as practicably possible and take reasonable steps to minimise any pollution (see *Express Dairies Distribution v Environment Agency* (2004)).

In relation to penalties, persons found guilty are liable on summary conviction to a fine not exceeding £50,000, or imprisonment for a term not exceeding 12 months, or to both; or on conviction on indictment to a fine or imprisonment for a term not exceeding five years, or to both. In relation to penalties, upon summary conviction there is a maximum fine of £20,000.

The Environment Agency possesses wide powers to prevent pollution incidents and to remediate afterwards.

11.7 Waste Management

Businesses and individuals involved in the production, collection, transport and disposal of regulated waste need to ensure that they are complying with any necessary permit requirements and duty of care requirements to avoid criminal liability. Only waste known as directive or hazardous waste is subject to the regulation of the Environment Agency and licensing procedures are now also codified in the Environmental Permitting (England & Wales) Regulations 2010.

In general, in order to keep, treat or dispose of waste in or on land a business must generally possess a valid environmental permit. An environmental permit is a legal document, issued under the Environmental Permitting Regulations 2010.

Following the implementation of the amended Framework Directive on Waste (75/442/EEC as amended by Directive 91/156/EEC) waste was referred to as 'Directive Waste'. It is important to understand that if something is classified as waste in legal terms it means that the producer, keeper, carrier and ultimate disposer will be subject to a variety of legal controls carrying penalties for non-compliance. Many businesses fall foul of the law in this area because they do not realise that they are dealing with waste in the legal sense of the word. The definition of Directive Waste essentially covers household, industrial and commercial waste, but also extends to include substances and materials that a holder may not consider to be waste in the ordinary sense of the word.

The Framework Directive on Waste was amended to provide a common definition of waste throughout EC member states, and Article 3(1) of the Directive 2008/98/EC now provides that 'Directive waste' means: 'any substance or object which the holder discards or intends or is required to discard'.

In UK law, reg 2 of the Environmental Permitting (England & Wales) Regulations 2010 defines waste as anything that: (a) is waste within the meaning of Art 3(1) of the Waste Framework Directive; and (b) is not excluded from the scope of that directive by Art 2(1), (2) or (3).

The List of Wastes (England) Regulations 2005 (SI 2005/895 as amended) provides a detailed list of the categories of substances/objects classified as waste. They include production or consumption residues, rejects, products whose 'sell-by' date has expired, damaged/contaminated materials, unusable parts and products for which the holder has no further use. There is also a catch-all category which includes 'any materials, substances or products which are not contained in the above categories'.

11.7.1 Exemptions from environmental permitting

The definition of waste is potentially very wide. Therefore, exemptions from the need for a permit for certain waste recovery activities and disposal activities at the place of production are allowed. The exemptions system is less onerous on industry than environmental permitting in terms of what is needed when registering. Activities currently exempt are listed in the Environmental Permitting (England & Wales) Regulations 2010. Rather than obtain a full environmental permit, the waste holder is required to register the exemption with the Environment Agency.

The UK recently reviewed the exemptions from environmental permitting. Many exemptions have been in place with little amendment since 1994. Some have become increasingly complex and there was also a need to develop new exemptions that take account of technical innovations and clarification of the definition of waste following European case law. Following the review, in April, 2010, new regulations came into force and anyone registering a new exempt waste operation on, or after, 6 April 2010 now registers under the new system. Existing registered exemptions will transfer over to the new system. The new regulations introduce over 60 new exemptions and apply immediately to new activities.

The main exempt activities include temporary storage of waste at the place of production pending disposal or recovery (this would cover contracted skip hire for commercial waste), activities related to recovery and reuse such as shredding and baling, storage or deposit of demolition waste for construction-related use and a wide range of recycling activities.

11.7.2 Waste management and the Duty of Care

A duty of care requirement is set out in s 34 of the Environmental Protection Act 1990 and associated regulations and applies to anyone who is the holder of Directive waste. Persons concerned with Directive waste must ensure that the waste is managed properly, recovered or disposed of safely, and not cause harm to human health or pollution of the environment. The waste must be transferred to someone who is permitted to receive it. The duty applies to any person who 'produces, imports, carries, keeps, treats or disposes of Directive waste or as a broker has control of such waste'. Breach of the Duty of Care is an offence with a penalty of up to £5,000 on summary conviction or an unlimited fine on conviction on indictment.

Parties transferring waste are required to complete and retain a 'transfer note', containing a written description of that waste. DEFRA has provided statutory guidance on the completion of the duty of care transfer notes and waste needs to be described on the transfer note by reference to the European Waste Catalogue (EWC) and its appropriate code number.

The Waste (Household Waste) Duty of Care (England & Wales) Regulations 2005 introduced a new duty on householders on 21 November 2005. Under this duty, householders are required to take reasonable measures to ensure that household waste produced on their property is passed on to an authorised person. There is not a requirement for the householder to complete and retain a written description of the waste (the 'transfer note'). This measure was implemented to facilitate better waste management and reduce illegal waste activity such as fly-tipping. If fly-tipped waste is traced back to a particular household, the householders can be fined up to £5,000.

11.7.3 Broker and carrier registration

Consultants, establishments or undertakings that arrange for the disposal, or recovery of, waste on behalf of others are required to be registered. It is an offence for any establishment to arrange for the disposal of waste on behalf of a third party unless they are registered as a waste broker.

Businesses often employ the services of others to remove and dispose of waste from their place of business. It is important to remember that where directive or hazardous waste is transported by a third party, that party needs a valid registration from the Environment Agency which covers the party's principal place of business. There is also a requirement on carriers to re-register every three years. Carrier registration can be refused or revoked by the Environment Agency if a carrier has been convicted of an environmental crime, or the Agency believes it is undesirable for the registration to continue.

Businesses intending to engage the services of a waste carrier should therefore check upon the status of the company they are proposing to use. The Environment Agency maintains a public register of authorised carriers. Carrying waste without a relevant registration is an offence. Those found guilty on summary conviction are subject to a fine not exceeding £5,000.

11.7.4 Hazardous waste

The Hazardous Waste (England and Wales) Regulations 2005 supplemented by the List of Waste (England) Regulations 2005 replaced the scheme for 'special' waste in the UK. The new regulations were introduced to enable the UK to comply with reforms made by the European Commission in relation to the regulation of hazardous wastes throughout member states. Many businesses will find themselves having to deal with hazardous waste regulation for the first time.

An important aspect of the new regime is the requirement for most producers of hazardous waste to notify their premises to the Environment Agency. The Environment Agency currently operates a notification process which can be accessed via their web pages. The new legislation has increased the number of wastes now treated as hazardous and in accordance with the new regulations some hazardous wastes are now classified as 'absolute' entries and thereby caught by the regulations, whereas other hazardous wastes are classified as 'mirror' entries. The latter require further assessment to evaluate whether they are hazardous in legal terms.

In January 2002, the EU updated the list of hazardous wastes and approximately 180 new substances were incorporated, many of which had not previously been regulated as hazardous waste, for example, televisions, computer monitors and fluorescent lights. Detailed technical guidance on assessing whether something constitutes hazardous waste or not can be found in the Environment Agency's Technical Guidance WM2 (listing hazardous waste types identified in the European Waste Catalogue).

Hazardous waste must be correctly consigned when it leaves the producer's premises and incorporate a special identification code. Recipients of hazardous waste are now legally obliged to submit quarterly returns to the Environment Agency. The new regulations implement more stringent record keeping and tighter controls in relation to hazardous waste.

11.7.5 Criminal offences for non-compliance

The relevant law is contained in s 33(1) EPA 1990, which operates in conjunction with reg 38 of the EPR 2010, and provides that it is also a criminal offence to:

> (1)(a) *deposit controlled (directive) waste, or knowingly cause or knowingly permit controlled (directive) waste to be deposited in or on any land, unless a waste management licence authorising the deposit is in force and the deposit is in accordance with the licence;*
>
> (b) *treat, keep or dispose of controlled (directive) waste, or knowingly cause or knowingly permit controlled (directive) waste to be treated, kept or disposed of:*
>
> *(i) in or on any land; or,*
> *(ii) by means of any mobile plant,*
> *(iii) except under and in accordance with a waste management licence;*

The main offences represent a classic command and control approach to criminal liability and waste. Section 33(1)(a) applies to all deposits whether temporary or permanent and s 33(1)(b) applies where permit conditions have been breached or there has been a failure to acquire the correct type of permit.

Section 33(1)(c) is much wider since it covers treating, keeping or disposing of directive waste in a manner likely to cause pollution of the environment or harm to human health. This applies irrespective of the need for an environmental permit. In other words exempted activities are within the remit of this offence.

It is important to remember that in addition to s 33 offences it is also an offence for a business to breach the s 34 duty of care. In order to fully understand how these offences can be committed it is necessary to understand the meaning of 'knowingly causing' and 'knowingly permitting' as well as 'deposit'. In addition it is a criminal offence to contravene any environmental permit. Conditions may extend to the management of the site and issues such as record keeping and site safety. There are powers available to enable the Agency to carry out the necessary remediation and recover costs.

The phrases 'knowingly cause' and 'knowingly permit' apply to s 33(1)(a) and s 33(1)(b). Knowingly cause suggests a knowledge of the deposit or other act involving the waste, but not knowledge to the extent that the deposit is outside or not in accordance with the terms of a licence or permit.

For example in *Shanks & McEwan (Teesside) Ltd v Environment Agency* (1997) a waste manager received waste that the company was licensed to take, but then transferred it to different storage. The manager failed to complete a new waste disposal form and the company was prosecuted for knowingly permitting the deposit of Directive waste in contravention of licensing conditions. The defendant company appealed, on the basis that although they knew waste had been deposited, they were unaware that they had breached their licence conditions. On appeal, the court held that knowledge of the deposit was sufficient to establish liability and that it was not necessary for the prosecution to prove that the defendant knew the deposit would breach the conditions of its operating licence.

Knowledge of a deposit may be inferred (see the case of *Kent CC v Beaney* (1993)). Indeed, the fact that a defendant operates a waste disposal facility will be interpreted by the courts as constructive knowledge that deposits are taking place.

Deposit includes tipping and burying waste at a landfill site, and will extend to both temporary and permanent deposits of waste. The courts have established that 'deposit' will extend to cover continuing activities on a waste site (see *R v Metropolitan Stipendiary Magistrate ex p London Waste Regulation Authority* (1993)).

In defence, a defendant may be able to argue that they have taken all reasonable precautions and exercised due diligence (which has been equated to an obligation to exercise reasonable care) to avoid the commission of an offence. A defendant may also attempt to argue that they acted under employer's instructions, and neither knew or had reason to believe, that his actions amounted to an offence. It can also be argued in defence that the alleged acts were committed in an emergency to avoid danger to the public and full particulars were furnished with the Environment Agency as soon as possible.

11.7.6 Defences and penalties

In defence, a defendant may be able to argue that they have taken all reasonable precautions and exercised due diligence (which has been equated to an obligation to exercise reasonable care) to avoid the commission of an offence. A defendant may also attempt to argue that they acted under employer's instructions, and neither knew or had reason to believe that his actions amounted to an offence. It can also be argued in defence that the alleged acts were committed in an emergency to avoid danger to the public and full particulars were furnished with the Environment Agency as soon as possible.

In respect of penalties, waste offences are punishable upon summary conviction with a fine of up to £50,000 and up to 12 months' imprisonment, and upon conviction on indictment an unlimited fine and up to three years' imprisonment. If the offence is identified to relate to hazardous waste then the prison sentence can be up to five years.

11.8 Contaminated Land

Contaminated land arises when there are polluting substances in, on or under the land. The contamination may arise from historic pollution when polluting matter has been left in buildings or on land or buried in the ground. Under Part IIA of the Environmental Protection Act 1990 every local authority is required to identify all contaminated sites within their area. If contamination is found to be significant, the local authority must take steps to remediate the pollution or reduce the risk to people and the environment. In serious cases of contaminated land the Environment Agency will intervene.

The key issue with contaminated land is whether the polluting matter on the land has a 'pathway' to enable the pollution to reach a target area. This is referred to as a 'pollution linkage'. For example, if someone left leaking chemical drums on land and the chemicals seeped through the ground and contaminated a water supply. Another example would be if dangerous substances were dormant in the ground but following development of a site they were released into the atmosphere.

Under the legislation, the presence of a pollution linkage can result in the land being designated as a contaminated site. Designation will depend upon whether:

- significant harm is being caused;
- there is a significant possibility of this type of significant harm being caused;
- pollution of controlled waters is being caused or likely to be caused.

11.8.1 Who bears responsibility for contaminated land?

This is a very complicated area and can result in liability for the unsuspecting purchaser or vendor of land. Part IIA of the EPA 1990 categorises responsible parties as 'appropriate persons'. Appropriate persons are divided into Class A and Class B persons. A Class A person is someone who caused or knowingly permitted the polluting substances to be in, on or under the land. The second category, Class B persons, is made up of current owners or occupiers of the contaminated land site.

Owners or occupiers only become 'appropriate persons' where no Class A person can be found. These owners and occupiers have neither caused nor permitted the pollution to be present on the land, but the law takes the view that someone should be responsible for the site. This approach to establishing liability for identified contaminated land can result in significant liability for the unsuspecting land owner.

In relation to liability, a business should exercise extreme care when either purchasing or selling land if contamination is suspected. If purchasing property, environmental surveys and checks need to be made to determine whether contamination is present, and if so, a remediation strategy needs to be created. In practice, this is usually dealt with via the planning system and the inclusion of indemnities into the contract of sale. If selling land, particularly if a lower price has been accepted as a result of the identification of contamination, then again, care needs to be taken to ensure appropriate indemnity from liability is drafted into the documentation.

11.9 Personal Liability for Corporate Crime

When sentencing a guilty business or company for environmental crime, the courts are limited to financial penalties as corporate bodies cannot be sent to prison or carry out community service. However, reg 41 of the Environmental Permitting Regulations 2010 permits corporate individual liability where it can be established than an offence has been committed by a company and that an officer of the company has consented, connived or being negligent in allowing the offence to be committed. For the purposes of the regulations an officer will include a director, member of the board, chief executive, manager, secretary or other similar officer purporting to act in such a capacity.

Summary

Liability for Land and Environmental Damage

An employer, particularly a business employer, is likely to occupy or manage land and premises which form part of the business. Tort Law and Environmental Law provide the potential for both civil and criminal liability to arise from damage arising from the state of premises and also for harm and pollution to the environment.

Areas such as water pollution, waste management and integrated pollution control clearly fall within the ambit of environmental law, there are many other spheres of legal regulation and activity that do not and yet they may have a significant environmental impact or cause loss or injury.

Environmental can be expensive both in terms of compliance costs and failure to comply, which may result in criminal prosecution or a civil claim.

Occupiers' liability – 1957 Act

The law within this area is negligence-based, and is contained within two key statutes:

- the Occupiers' Liability Act 1957, which regulates an occupier's liability to visitors; and
- the Occupiers' Liability Act 1984, which regulates any liability potentially owned to trespassers.

Who constitutes an occupier?

The test is to be found within common law principles by way of the Occupational Control Test. This test establishes that *where a person has a sufficient degree of control over the premises then they will owe a duty of care to those lawfully on the premises* (*Wheat v Lacon & Co Ltd* (1966) and *Harris v Birkenhead Corporation* (1976)).

Who constitutes a visitor?

Section 1(2) of the Occupiers' Liability Act 1957 provides that visitors are said to be '. . . the persons who would at common law be treated as . . . invitees or licensees'. The status of visitor can arise by way of:

- express permission;
- implied permission;
- operation of law.

Occupiers can set limits on visitors on the premises as to time and length of stay and the purpose of the visit.

Nature of the 1957 Act duty of care

The Occupiers' Act 1957 states that the Act is designed to 'regulate the duty which an occupier of premises owes to his visitors in respect of dangers due the state of the premises or to things done or omitted to be done on them' (see s 1(1)) and covers both damage to both person and property.

Therefore, the duty and standard of care may vary according to the type of visitor:

- children (s 2(3)(a) 1957 Act) (see *Latham v R Johnson & Nephew Ltd* (1913) and *Glasgow Corporation v Taylor* (1922));
- skilled visitors (s 2(3)(b) 1957 Act) (see *Roles v Natham* (1963)).

Warning signs and exclusion of liability

An occupier may discharge their common duty of care by using an effective warning sign (see s 2(4)(a) 1957 Act). However, any signs must be considered against UCTA 1977 provisions.

The common duty of care and independent contractors

The 1957 Act provides that the general rule is that occupiers will not be liable for the negligence of independent contractors (see s 2(4)(b)) and *Haseldine v CA Daw & Son* (1941)).

Occupiers' liability – 1984 Act

Under **s 1(3) of the 1984 Act**, an occupier will only owe a duty of care to trespassers if:

(a) he is aware of the danger, or should reasonably have known it existed, on his premises; and
(b) he knows, or has reasonable grounds to believe, the trespasser is in the vicinity of the danger, or is likely to come into the vicinity; and
(c) the risk is one which considering all the facts he could reasonably be expected to offer some protection against.

See further: *Tomlinson v Congleton BC* [2004] HL.

Nuisance

Public nuisance

> *. . . .a nuisance which is so widespread in its range or so indiscriminate in its effect that it would not be reasonable to expect one person to take proceedings on his own responsibility of the community at large.*

(See *AG v PYA Quarries* (1957).)

Public nuisance is concerned with interference with recognised public rights, the classic example being obstruction of a highway.

Statutory nuisance

Part III of the Environmental Protection Act 1990.

Individuals complain about noise and smells to their local Environmental Health Department and by virtue of s 79 Environmental Protection Act 1990, local authorities come under a duty to inspect their areas for the existence of statutory nuisances.

Section 80 Environmental Protection Act 1990 provides that where a local authority has identified the existence of a statutory nuisance, they are under a mandatory duty to serve an Abatement Notice on the person responsible for the nuisance.

Private nuisance

Private nuisance is 'an unlawful interference with a person's use or enjoyment of land, or some right over, or in connection with it' (*Read v Lyons* (1947)).

Private nuisance is primarily concerned with protecting interests in property. An action in private nuisance is only available to an owner or occupier with a recognised legal interest in land (confirmed in *Hunter v Canary Wharf Ltd* (1997)).

You must distinguish between actual physical damage to property and interference with the enjoyment of property as where the latter is concerned then proof of a substantial level of interference is required by the courts (see *St Helen's Smelting Co v Tipping* (1865)).

In deciding whether or not an actionable private nuisance has arisen, the courts will take into account a number of factors. These are:

- locality;
- utility of the conduct;
- duration of the nuisance;
- abnormal sensitivity on the part of the claimant;
- any malice involved; and
- if damage to property is concerned, whether such damage is foreseeable.

Where actual damage to property occurs, there should be foreseeability of the kind of damage suffered. The leading case in this area is *Cambridge Water Co Ltd v Eastern Counties Leather plc* (1994).

Rylands v Fletcher rule

The rule in *Rylands v Fletcher* is a hybrid form of nuisance which imposes liability where something is brought onto land, or collected there, and subsequently escapes causing damage.

Environmental law and liability

International environmental law and policy has a significant impact upon the development of national environmental policy and it is also important to remember the impact of EU membership.

There are a number of principles which guide the development of international environmental law:

- the principle of state sovereignty over, and environmental responsibility for, the use of natural resources;
- the principle of good neighbourliness and cooperation;
- the principle of preventative action;
- the precautionary principle;
- the polluter pays principle;
- the principle of common but differentiated responsibility;
- the principle of sustainable development.

The majority of European environmental legislation is created in the form of directives. Directives are binding on EU Member States but allow some discretion as to the manner and form of implementation.

Who is responsible for the enforcement of environmental law?

Enforcement of environmental controls within the UK is carried out largely by the Environment Agency and local authorities. Private prosecutions and the use of civil law play a minimal role.

The Environment Agency possesses wide-ranging powers to facilitate environmental regulation and the preference is to achieve compliance without resorting to criminal prosecution.

As far as criminal enforcement is concerned, environmental pollution offences are mainly of strict liability, that is, there is no need to prove a state of mind, simply the existence of a chain of causation. In practice, the severity of strict liability is mitigated by the high level of discretion in relation to enforcement policy.

Environmental controls and environmental permitting

Environmental permitting requires certain types of business, such as those carrying out power generation, manufacturing and other industrial activities such as waste management to obtain an environmental permit before commencing operations.

An activity which is 'regulated' requires a permit under the Environmental Permitting (England & Wales) Regulations 2010.

In relation to non-compliance, there are a number of offences contained in the Environmental Permitting (England & Wales) Regulations 2010 (see reg 38).

Water pollution

The relevant law is now contained in the Environmental Permitting (England & Wales) Regulations 2010 which have streamlined the permit application process.

An applicant will, however, still need to state the place of the discharge activity, the content, the quantity and rate of flow and temperature. In administering the permit system, the Environment

Agency operates a fee system and can attach such conditions 'as it may think fit' on environmental permits.

Water discharge activities are listed in Sched 21 to the 2010 Regulations to include:

- discharging poisonous, noxious or polluting matter or solid waste matter into inland freshwater, coastal waters and relevant territorial waters;
- discharging trade or sewage effluent into inland freshwater, coastal waters and relevant territorial waters;
- cutting or uprooting substantial amounts of vegetation in any inland freshwaters, without taking reasonable steps to remove it.

Refer to case law:

- *McLeod v Buchanan* (1940);
- *R v Ettrick Trout Co Ltd* (1994) and *R v Wicks* (1998);
- *NRA v Egger (UK) Ltd* (1992);
- *R v Dovermoss* (1995);
- *Alphacell v Woodward* (1972);
- *Wrothwell Limited v Yorkshire Water Authority* (1984);
- *Southern Water Authority v Pegram* (1989);
- *Attorney General's Reference (No 1 of 1994)* (1995).

Waste management

Businesses and individuals involved in the production, collection, transport and disposal of regulated waste need to ensure that they are complying with any necessary permit requirements and duty of care requirements to avoid criminal liability.

Only waste known as directive or hazardous waste is subject to the regulation of the Environment Agency and licensing procedures are now codified in the Environmental Permitting (England & Wales) Regulations 2010.

In general, in order to 'keep, treat or dispose of waste in or on land, or by means of a mobile plant', a business must generally possess a valid environmental permit.

An environmental permit is a legal document, issued under the Environmental Permitting Regulations 2010. Environmental Permits are issued by the Environment Agency.

A duty of care is imposed by s 34 of the Environmental Protection Act 1990 and associated regulations and applies to anyone who is the holder of directive waste. Persons concerned with directive waste must ensure that the waste is managed properly, recovered or disposed of safely, and not cause harm to human health or pollution of the environment.

Both waste carriers and waste brokers need to be registered.

There are a number of criminal offences contained in s 33 Environmental Protection Act 1990.

Contaminated land

Under Part IIA of the Environmental Protection Act 1990 every local authority is required to identify all contaminated sites within their area. If contamination is found to be significant, the local authority must take steps to remediate the pollution or reduce the risk to people and the environment. In serious cases of contaminated land the Environment Agency will intervene.

Under the legislation, the presence of a pollution linkage can result in the land being designated as a contaminated site. Designation will depend upon whether:

- significant harm is being caused;
- there is a significant possibility of this type of significant harm being caused;
- pollution of controlled waters is being caused or likely to be caused.

Who is responsible for remediation of contaminated land?

- A Class A person is someone who caused or knowingly permitted the polluting substances to be in, on or under the land.
- The second category, Class B persons, is made up of current owners or occupiers of the contaminated land site.

Further Reading

If you wish to find out more about environmental law there are three excellent textbooks:

Bell, S, and McGillivray, D, *Environmental Law*, 7th edn, 2008, Oxford: OUP
McEldowney, J, and S, *Environmental Law*, 2010, Harlow: Pearson
Wolf, S, and Stanley, N, *Environmental Law*, 5th edn, 2010, Abingdon: Routledge

In relation to articles, the following represent a useful introduction to the subject and have significance for students of business:

Baldwin, R, and Black, J, 'Really responsive regulation' (2008) 71 *Modern Law Review* 59
Gunningham, N, 'Environment law, regulation and governance: shifting architectures' (2009) *Journal of Environmental Law* 179
Hollingsworth, K, 'Environmental monitoring of government – the case of an environmental auditor' (2000) 20 *Legal Studies* 241
Lawrence, D, and Lee, R, 'Permitting uncertainty: owners, occupiers and responsibility for remediation' (2003) 66 *Modern Law Review* 261
Ross, A, and Nash, H, 'European Union environmental law – who legislates for whom in a devolved Great Britain' (2009) *Public Law* 564
Stallworthy, M 'Legislating against climate change: a UK perspective on a Sisyphean challenge' (2009) 73(3) *Modern Law Review* 412

Reports:

R MacRory, *Regulatory Justice: Making Sanctions Effective,* 2006, London: Cabinet Office
Sir Nicholas Stern, *The Economics of Climate Change*, 2006, London: HM Treasury, Stationery Office

Websites:

Royal Commission on Environmental Pollution at:
www.rcep.org.uk

Environment Agency at:
www.environment-agency.gov.uk

European Union environmental matters at:
www.europa.eu.int/eur-lex/en/index/html

Defra can be found at: www.defra.gov.uk

Environmental Law Foundation at:
www.elflaw.org

Part 4

Business Organisation

This section of the book turns the focus to the legal forms that businesses can adopt in order to carry out their business activities. Given that the main contemporary business form is the registered limited company, most attention, two chapters, is paid to that form, but the other forms of the partnership and indeed the sole trader are also considered.

Chapter 12 examines the operation of the law of agency. Whilst it is a relatively brief treatment of the topic, it is essential to emphasise its importance, as an understanding of the principles of agency is fundamental to understanding the later forms of partnership law and company law.

Chapter 13 introduces one of the oldest, and still very common, business forms – the partnership. However, even that venerable form has been updated by the introduction of the possibility of members limiting their personal liability by registering as LLPs, limited liability partnerships. That fairly new form is dealt with in some detail in the chapter.

Chapter 14, entitled The Nature and Formation of Companies, examines the most common and most important of contemporary business forms, the registered company, although it also considers other types of company in passing. The chapter looks to differentiate between partnerships and companies and locates the private limited company as an intermediate form: as a business assuming the legal form of a company while retaining the economic form of a partnership. The chapter also explains the concept of separate legal personality and the situations in which the law will ignore that doctrine. It goes on to explain the process of registering a company and the constitutional documents of any such company. It concludes with an examination of the various meanings of, and rules relating to, 'capital' as applied in company law.

Chapter 15 then goes on to deal with the issues involved in the day-to-day running of companies within the general context of corporate governance. It pays particular attention to the role of company directors but also considers the functions of other company officers such as company secretaries and auditors. The role of the company meeting is critically examined and the chapter concludes with a consideration of companies in difficulty, by examining corporate winding up and administration.

Chapter 12

Agency

Chapter Contents

Law in Context: Agency

This chapter focuses on the role of the agent, and the interrelationships between the agent and the business. A business may use an agent to undertake specialist work which the principal does not have the time or specialist skills to undertake. The use of agents can be very helpful to a growing business, but the principal must be absolutely clear about the contractual and payment arrangements in advance. The relationship between the principal and the agent can become complicated if the agent acts inappropriately in relation to the contract. If the contract is approved, this ratifies the relationship between the principal and the agent, including the actions of the agent (which the principal can then be liable for). Writing out the agreement can help define the relationship between an agent and a principal. However, the principal must ensure that the agreement is written clearly and is unambiguous, otherwise there can be more problems in the future. Termination dates are particularly important for both parties, including the actions included within the termination date. See *Claramoda Ltd v Zoomphase Ltd* (2009). A key area of consideration is how and when the agent can act on behalf of the business – their right to do this and the legal nature of any agreements made in relation to the business. Complexities can arise for a business if the agent only has actual authority in a few areas. Implied authority may be construed in other areas as well, and this is when the arrangements, and who has authority to agree them, can become blurred. Principals and agents should be clear about the level of authority in place, and how areas where the agent does not have authority will be dealt with. For example, if the agent is providing a service on behalf of the company, does the agent have the right and the skills to perform that service? As you read through the chapter, think about the contract implications of using an agent, and how these may apply in different circumstances.

12.1 Introduction

The principles of agency law provide the basis for an understanding of many issues relating to partnerships and some of those relating to registered companies. The general assumption is that individuals engaging in business activity carry on that business by themselves, and on their own behalf, either individually or collectively. It is not uncommon, however, for such individuals to engage others to represent them and negotiate business deals on their behalf. Indeed, the role of the 'middleman' is a commonplace one in business and commerce. The legal relationship between such a representative, or middleman, and the business person making use of them is governed by the law of agency. Agency principles also apply in relation to companies registered under the companies legislation and the directors and other officers of such companies.

12.2 Definition of 'Agency'

An agent is a person who is empowered to represent another legal party, called the principal, and brings the principal into a legal relationship with a third party. It should be emphasised that the contract entered into is between the principal and the third party. In the normal course of events, the agent has no personal rights or liabilities in relation to the contract. This outcome represents an accepted exception to the usual operation of the doctrine of privity in contract law.

See Chapter 4 →

Since the agent is not actually entering into contractual relations with the third party, there is no requirement that the agent has contractual capacity, although, based on the same reasoning, it is essential that the principal has full contractual capacity. Thus, it is possible for a principal to use a minor as an agent, even though the minor might not have contractual capacity to enter into the contract on their own behalf.

There are numerous examples of agency relationships. For example, as their names imply, estate agents and travel agents are expressly appointed to facilitate particular transactions. Additionally, employees may act as agents of their employers in certain circumstances; or friends may act as agents for one another.

Some forms of agency merit particular consideration, as follows:

- A general agent, as the title indicates, has the power to act for a principal generally in relation to a particular area of business, whereas a special agent only has the authority to act in one particular transaction.
- A *del credere* agent is one who, in return for an additional commission by way of payment, guarantees to the principal that, in the event of a third party's failure to pay for goods received, the agent will make good the loss.
- A commission agent is a hybrid form which lies midway between a full principal/agent relationship and the relationship of an independent trader and client. In essence, the agent stands between the principal and the third party and establishes no contract between those two parties. The effect is that, although the commission agent owes the duties of an agent to his or her principal, he or she contracts with the third party as a principal in his or her own right. The effectiveness of this procedure is undermined by the normal operation of the agency law relating to an undisclosed principal (see 12.6.2 below).
- The position of a mercantile agent/factor is defined in the Factors Act 1889 as an agent:

  > . . . having in the customary course of his business as such agent authority either to sell goods, or to consign goods for the purpose of sale, or to buy goods, or to raise money on the security of goods.

However, of perhaps more contemporary importance are marketing agents, distribution agents and the question of franchising.

- Marketing agents have only limited authority. They can only introduce potential customers to their principals and do not have the authority either to negotiate or to enter into contracts on behalf of their principals.
- Distribution agents are appointed by suppliers to arrange the distribution of their products within a particular area. The distributors ordinarily cannot bind the supplier, except where they have expressly been given the authority to do so.
- Franchising arrangements arise where the original developer of a business decides, for whatever reason, to allow others to use their goodwill to conduct an independent business, using the original name of the business. Two prominent examples of franchises are McDonalds and The Body Shop, although there are many others. It is essential to emphasise that any such relationship does not arise from, or give rise to, a relationship of principal and agent. Indeed, it is commonplace, if not universal, that franchise agreements include an express clause to the effect that no such relationship is to be established.
- Commercial agents are specifically covered by the Commercial Agents (Council Directive) Regulations 1993, which were enacted in order to comply with EC Directive 86/653. The Regulations define a commercial agent as a self-employed intermediary who has continuing authority to negotiate the sale or purchase of goods on behalf of another person, or to negotiate and conclude such transactions on behalf of that person. Although intended to harmonise the operation and effect of agency law within the European Union, the regulations do not

introduce any major substantive change into UK agency law. The effect of the Regulations will be considered in more detail at 12.5.3 below.

- A power of attorney arises where an agency is specifically created by way of a deed.

12.3 Creation of Agency

No one can act as an agent without the consent of the principal, although consent need not be expressly stated.

❖ KEY CASE *White v Lucas* (1887)

Facts:

A firm of estate agents claimed to act on behalf of the owner of a particular property, though that person had denied them permission to act on his behalf. When the owner sold the property to a third party, who was introduced through the estate agents, they claimed their commission.

Decision:

It was held that the estate agents had no entitlement to commission, as the property owner had not agreed to their acting as his agent.

The principal/agent relationship can be created in a number of ways. It may arise as the outcome of a distinct contract, which may be made either orally or in writing, or it may be established purely gratuitously, where some person simply agrees to act for another. The relationship may also arise from the actions of the parties.

It is usual to consider the creation of the principal/agency relationship under five distinct categories.

12.3.1 Express appointment

This is the most common manner in which a principal/agent relationship comes into existence. In this situation, the agent is specifically appointed by the principal to carry out a particular task or to undertake some general function. In most situations, the appointment of the agent will itself involve the establishment of a contractual relationship between the principal and the agent, but need not necessarily depend upon a contract between those parties.

For the most part, there are no formal requirements for the appointment of an agent, although, where the agent is to be given the power to execute deeds in the principal's name, they must themselves be appointed by way of a deed (that is, they are given power of attorney).

12.3.2 Ratification

An agency is created by ratification when a person who has no authority purports to contract with a third party on behalf of a principal. Ratification is the express acceptance of the contract by the principal. Where the principal elects to ratify the contract, it gives retrospective validity to the action of the purported agent. There are, however, certain conditions which have to be fully complied with before the principal can effectively adopt the contract, as follows:

- *The principal must have been in existence at the time that the agent entered into the contract*

❖ **KEY CASE** *Kelner v Baxter* (1866)

Facts:
Promoters attempted to enter into a contract to purchase stock on behalf of an as yet unformed company.

Decision:
It was held that the company could not ratify the contract after it was created and that the promoters, as agents, were personally liable on the contract. (This is now given statutory effect under s 51 of the Companies Act 2006.)

- *The principal must have had legal capacity to enter into the contract when it was made*
  When the capacity of companies to enter into a business transaction was limited by the operation of the doctrine of *ultra vires*, it was clearly established that they could not ratify any such *ultra vires* contracts. Similarly, it is not possible for minors to ratify a contract, even though it was made in their name.
- *An undisclosed principal cannot ratify a contract*
  The agent must have declared that he or she was acting for the principal. If the agent appeared to be acting on his or her own account, then the principal cannot later adopt the contact (see *Keighley, Maxted & Co v Durant* (1901)).
- *The principal must adopt the whole of the contract*
  It is not open to the principal to pick and choose which parts of the contract to adopt; they must accept all of its terms.
- *Ratification must take place within a reasonable time*
  It is not possible to state with certainty what will be considered as a reasonable time in any particular case. Where, however, the third party with whom the agent contracted becomes aware that the agent has acted without authority, a time limit can be set, within which the principal must indicate their adoption of the contract for it to be effective.

12.3.3 Implication

This form of agency arises from the relationship that exists between the principal and the agent and from which it is assumed that the principal has given authority to the other person to act as his or her agent. Thus, it is implied from the particular position held by individuals that they have the authority to enter into contractual relations on behalf of their principal. So, whether an employee has the actual authority to contract on behalf of his or her employer depends on the position held by the employee.

Panorama Developments v Fidelis Furnishing Fabrics Ltd (1971)

Facts:
A company secretary hired cars in his company's name for his own private use.

Decision:
It was held that a company secretary had the implied authority to make contracts in the company's name relating to the day-to-day running of the company. The company was therefore liable on the contract.

Problems most often occur in relation to the implied extent of a person's authority, rather than their actual appointment (but see *Hely-Hutchinson v Brayhead Ltd* (1967) as an example of the latter).

12.3.4 Necessity

Agency by necessity occurs under circumstances where, although there is no agreement between the parties, an emergency requires that an agent take particular action in order to protect the interests of the principal. The usual situation which gives rise to agency by necessity occurs where the agent is in possession of the principal's property and, due to some unforeseen emergency, the agent has to take action to safeguard that property:

- *In order for agency by necessity to arise, there needs to be a genuine emergency*

❖ KEY CASE *Great Northern Railway Co v Swaffield* (1874)

Facts:
A railway company transported the defendant's horse and, when no one arrived to collect it at its destination, it was placed in a livery stable.

Decision:
It was held that the company was entitled to recover the cost of stabling, as necessity had forced them to act as they had done as the defendant's agents.

- *There must also be no practical way of obtaining further instructions from the principal*

❖ KEY CASE *Springer v Great Western Railway Co* (1921)

Facts:
A consignment of tomatoes arrived at port after a delayed journey due to storms. A railway strike would have caused further delay in getting the tomatoes to their destination, so the railway company decided to sell the tomatoes locally.

Decision:
It was held that the railway company was responsible to the plaintiff for the difference between the price achieved and the market price in London. The defence of agency of necessity was not available, as the railway company could have contacted the plaintiff to seek his further instructions.

This particular requirement means that agency by necessity is extremely unlikely, given modern means of communication.

- *The person seeking to establish the agency by necessity must have acted bona fide in the interests of the principal (see Sachs v Miklos (1948))*

12.3.5 Estoppel

This form of agency is also known as 'agency by holding out' and arises where the principal has led other parties to believe that a person has the authority to represent him or her. (The authority possessed by the agent is referred to as 'apparent authority' – see 12.4.2 below.) In such circumstances, even though no principal/agency relationship actually exists in fact, the principal is prevented (estopped) from denying the existence of the agency relationship and is bound by the action of his or her purported agent as regards any third party who acted in the belief of its existence:

- *To rely on agency by estoppel, the principal must have made a representation as to the authority of the agent*

❖ KEY CASE *Freeman and Lockyer v Buckhurst Park Properties Ltd* (1964)

Facts:

A property company had four directors, but one director effectively controlled the company and made contracts as if he were the managing director, even though he had never actually been appointed to that position and, therefore, as an individual, had no authority to bind the company. The other directors, however, were aware of this activity and acquiesced in it. The company was sued in relation to one of the contracts entered into by the unauthorised director.

Decision:

It was held that the company was liable, as the board, which had the actual authority to bind the company, had held out the individual director as having the necessary authority to enter such contracts. It was, therefore, a case of agency by *estoppel*.

- *As with estoppel generally, the party seeking to use it must have relied on the representation*
  In *Overbrooke Estates Ltd v Glencombe Properties Ltd* (1974), a notice which expressly denied the authority of an auctioneer to make such statements as actually turned out to be false was successfully relied on as a defence by the auctioneer's employers.

12.4 The Authority of an Agent

In order to bind a principal, any contract entered into must be within the limits of the authority extended to the agent. The authority of an agent can be either actual or apparent.

12.4.1 Actual authority

Actual authority can arise in two ways:

- *Express actual authority*
  This is explicitly granted by the principal to the agent. The agent is instructed as to what particular tasks are required to perform and is informed of the precise powers given in order to fulfil those tasks.
- *Implied actual authority*
  This refers to the way in which the scope of express authority may be increased. Third parties are entitled to assume that agents holding a particular position have all the powers that are

usually provided to such an agent. Without actual knowledge to the contrary, they may safely assume that the agent has the usual authority that goes with their position. (This has been referred to above in relation to implied agency.)

❖ **KEY CASE** *Watteau v Fenwick* (1893)

Facts:
The new owners of an hotel continued to employ the previous owner as its manager. They expressly forbade him to buy certain articles, including cigars. The manager, however, bought cigars from a third party, who later sued the owners for payment as the manager's principal.

Decision:
It was held that the purchase of cigars was within the usual authority of a manager of such an establishment and that for a limitation on such usual authority to be effective, it must be communicated to any third party.

12.4.2 Apparent authority

Apparent authority is an aspect of agency by estoppel considered at 12.3.5 above. It can arise in two distinct ways:

- *Where a person makes a representation to third parties that a particular person has the authority to act as their agent without actually appointing the agent*
In such a case, the person making the representation is bound by the actions of the apparent agent (see *Freeman and Lockyer v Buckhurst Park Properties Ltd* (1964)). The principal is also liable for the actions of the agent where it is known that the agent claims to be his or her agent and yet does nothing to correct that impression.
- *Where a principal has previously represented to a third party that an agent has the authority to act on their behalf*
Even if the principal has subsequently revoked the agent's authority, he or she may still be liable for the actions of the former agent, unless he or she has informed third parties who had previously dealt with the agent about the new situation (see *Willis Faber & Co Ltd v Joyce* (1911)).

12.4.3 Warrant of authority

If a person claims to act as agent, but without the authority to do so, the supposed principal will not be bound by any agreement entered into. Neither is there a contract between the supposed agent and the third party, for the reason that the third party intended to deal not with the purported agent but with the supposed principal. However, the supposed agent may lay themselves open to an action for breach of warrant of authority.

If an agent contracts with a third party on behalf of a principal, the agent impliedly guarantees that the principal exists and has contractual capacity. The agent also implies that he or she has the authority to make contracts on behalf of that principal. If any of these implied warranties prove to be untrue, then the third party may sue the agent in quasi-contract for breach of warrant of authority. Such an action may arise even though the agent was genuinely unaware of any lack of authority.

❖ KEY CASE *Yonge v Toynbee* (1910)

Facts:
A firm of solicitors was instructed to institute proceedings against a third party. Without their knowledge, their client was certified insane, and although this automatically ended the agency relationship, they continued with the proceedings.

Decision:
The third party successfully recovered damages for breach of warrant of authority, since the solicitors were no longer acting for their former client.

12.5 The Relationship of Principal and Agent

The following considers the reciprocal rights and duties that principal and agent owe to each other.

12.5.1 The duties of agent to principal

The agent owes a number of duties, both express and implied, to the principal. These duties are as follows:

- *To perform the agreed undertaking according to the instructions of the principal*
  A failure to carry out instructions will leave the agent open to an action for breach of contract. This, of course, does not apply in the case of gratuitous agencies, where there is no obligation whatsoever on the agent to perform the agreed task. See *Turpin v Bilton* (1843), where an agent was held liable for the loss sustained by his failure to insure his principal's ship prior to its sinking.
- *To exercise due care and skill*
  An agent will owe a duty to act with reasonable care and skill, regardless of whether the agency relationship is contractual or gratuitous. The level of skill to be exercised, however, should be that appropriate to the agent's professional capacity and this may introduce a distinction in the levels expected of different agents. For example, a solicitor would be expected to show the level of care and skill that would be expected of a competent member of that profession, whereas a layperson acting in a gratuitous capacity would only be expected to perform with such degree of care and skill as a reasonable person would exercise in the conduct of their own affairs. See *Keppel v Wheeler* (1927), where the defendant estate agents were held liable for failing to secure the maximum possible price for a property.
- *To carry out instructions personally*
  Unless expressly or impliedly authorised to delegate the work, an agent owes a duty to the principal to act personally in the completion of the task. The right to delegate may be agreed expressly by the principal, or it may be implied from customary practice or arise as a matter of necessity. In any such case, the agent remains liable to the principal for the proper performance of the agreed contract.
- *To account*
  There is an implied duty that the agent keep proper accounts of all transactions entered into on behalf of the principal. The agent is required to account for all money and other property received on the principal's behalf and should keep his or her own property separate from that of the principal.

In addition to these contractual duties, there are general equitable duties which flow from the fact that the agency relationship is a fiduciary one, that is, one based on trust. These general fiduciary duties are as follows:

- *Not to permit a conflict of interest to arise*
  An agent must not allow the possibility of personal interest to conflict with the interests of his or her principal without disclosing that possibility to the principal. Upon full disclosure, it is up to the principal to decide whether or not to proceed with the particular transaction. If there is a breach of this duty, the principal may set aside the contract so affected and claim any profit which might have been made by the agent.

❖ KEY CASE *McPherson v Watt* (1877)

Facts:

A solicitor used his brother as a nominee to purchase property which he was engaged to sell.

Decision:

It was held that since the solicitor had allowed a conflict of interest to arise, the sale could be set aside. It was immaterial that a fair price was offered for the property.

The corollary to the above case is that the agent must not sell his or her own property to the principal without fully disclosing the fact (see *Harrods v Lemon* (1931)). This leads into the next duty.

- *Not to make a secret profit or misuse confidential information*
- An agent who uses his or her position as an agent to secure financial advantage for him or herself, without full disclosure to his principal, is in breach of fiduciary duty. Upon disclosure, the principal may authorise the agent's profit, but full disclosure is a necessary precondition (see *Hippisley v Knee Bros* (1905) for a clear-cut case). An example of the strictness with which this principle is enforced may be seen in the case of *Boardman v Phipps* (1967) in which an agent was held to account for profits made from information which he had gained from his position as agent, even though his action also benefited the parties for whom he was acting.

❖ KEY CASE *Boardman v Phipps* (1967)

Facts:

A solicitor was requested by trustees to advise on the affairs of a particular private company in which the trust had a substantial minority holding. In the course of advising the trust the solicitor purchased a number of shares in the company and became its managing director. This was done with the knowledge of some but not all of the trustees. After Boardman had successfully turned the company round, and in the process making a considerable profit for himself as well as the trust, one of the beneficiaries of the trust brought an action against him to recover Boardman's personal profit.

Decision:

It was held that Boardman had only acquired the possibility of making the profit through his position as solicitor for the trust. Consequently he was liable to the trust for any profit he had made.

- *Not to take a bribe*
  This duty may be seen as merely a particular aspect of the general duty not to make a secret profit, but it goes so much to the root of the agency relationship that it is usually treated as a distinct heading in its own right. Again, for clear-cut cases, see *Boston Deep Sea Fishing & Ice Co Ltd v Ansell* (1888), in which the managing director of the company was held to have breached his fiduciary duties as an agent by accepting a bribe in return for orders. See also *Mahesan v Malaysian Government Officers Co-operative Housing Society* (1978), where the plaintiff received a bribe to permit a third party to profit at his principal's expense.
  Where it is found that an agent has taken a bribe, the following civil remedies are open to the principal:
  - to repudiate the contract with the third party;
  - to dismiss the agent without notice;
  - to refuse to pay any money owed to the agent or to recover such money already paid;
  - to claim the amount of the bribe; and
  - to claim damages in the tort of deceit for any loss sustained as a result of the payment of the bribe.

  The payment of the bribe may also have constituted a breach of criminal law.

12.5.2 The rights of an agent

It is a simple matter of fact that the common law does not generally provide agents with as many rights in relation to the number of duties that it imposes on them. The agent, however, does benefit from the clear establishment of three general rights. These rights are as follows:

- *To claim remuneration for services performed*
  It is usual in agency agreements for the amount of payment to be stated, either in the form of wages or commission or, indeed, both. Where a commercial agreement is silent on the matter of payment, the court will imply a term into the agreement, requiring the payment of a reasonable remuneration. Such a term will not be implied in contradiction of the express terms of the agreement. See *Re Richmond Gate Property Co Ltd* (1965), where it was held that no remuneration could be claimed where an agreement stated that payment would be determined by the directors of the company, but they had not actually decided on any payment.
- *To claim indemnity against the principal for all expenses legitimately incurred in the performance of services*
  Both contractual and non-contractual agents are entitled to recover money spent in the course of performing their agreed task. In the case of the former, the remedy is based on an implied contractual term; in the case of a gratuitous agent, it is based on the remedy of restitution. Money can, of course, only be claimed where the agent has been acting within his or her actual authority.
- *To exercise a lien over property owned by the principal*
  This is a right to retain the principal's goods, where they have lawfully come into the agent's possession, and hold them against any debts outstanding to him or her as a result of the agency agreement. The nature of the lien is usually a particular one relating to specific goods which are subject to the agreement, not a general one which entitles the agent to retain any of the principal's goods, even where no money is owed in relation to those specific goods. The general lien is only recognised on the basis of an express term in the contract, or as a result of judicially recognised custom, as in the area of banking.

12.5.3 Commercial Agents (Council Directive) Regulations 1993

These Regulations implement Council Directive 86/653/EEC on the Co-ordination of the Laws of Member States relating to Self-Employed Commercial Agents, and came into force at the beginning of 1994. Regulations 3–5 set out the rights and obligations as between commercial agents and their principals; regs 6–12 deal with remuneration; and regs 13–16 deal with the conclusion and termination of the agency contract. Regulations 17–19 contain provisions relating to the indemnity or compensation payable to a commercial agent on termination of his agency contract, and reg 20 relates to the validity of restraint of trade clauses.

Considering the provisions in more detail:

- reg 3 provides that agents must act dutifully and in good faith in the interests of their principal. The agents must negotiate in a proper manner, execute the contracts they are contracted to undertake, communicate all necessary information to, and comply with all reasonable instructions from, their principal;
- reg 4 relates to principals' duties and requires that they provide their agents with the necessary documentation relating to the goods concerned, obtain information necessary for the performance of the agency contract and, in particular, notify the commercial agent within a reasonable period once they anticipate that the volume of commercial transactions will be significantly lower than that which the commercial agent could normally have expected. Additionally, a principal shall inform the commercial agent, within a reasonable period, of their acceptance or refusal of a commercial transaction which the commercial agent has procured for them;
- reg 14 provides that agents are entitled to notice of termination of their situation;
- reg 17 states that commercial agents are entitled to indemnity or compensation on termination of the agency agreement; and
- reg 20 states that any agreements in restraint of trade in agency contracts are only effective if they are in writing. Such restraints must relate solely to the type of goods dealt with under the agency agreement and must be limited to the geographical area, or the particular customer group, allocated to the agent. In any case, such restraints may only be valid for a maximum period of two years (c.f. general contracts in restraint of trade at 6.6.3).

The relationship of the Commercial Agents (Council Directive) Regulations 1993 (SI 1993/3053) and the common law was considered in *Duffen v FRA Bo SpA* (1998), in which it was held that although a dismissed agent could not enforce a 'liquidated damages' clause in his contract because it was really a penalty clause, he might not be restricted to merely claiming common law damages, as the Regulations allowed him to claim 'compensation' which might well involve a premium over the level of ordinary damages (see further, 7.7.4).

Recently, however, controversy, not to say confusion, has arisen over the way in which the level of compensation provided for in reg 17 should be calculated. As has been stated, the regulation itself simply provides that, in the event of a principal terminating a relationship with a commercial agent, the latter is entitled to compensation. The Regulations do not, however, state precisely how such compensation should be calculated, and it this lack of detail that has led to the confusion, as follows:

- In *Douglas King v T Tunnock Ltd* (2000), the Inner House of the Scottish Court of Session determined that, as the EC Directive was based on French law, it would be appropriate to operate the system for the calculation of compensation on the same basis as was adopted by the French courts. On that basis, the Inner House held that the agent should receive compensation equal to the gross commission paid during the previous two years of the agency. Alternatively, the court held that a multiple of twice the average commission earned during the last three years could be used.
- In *Barrett McKenzie & Co Ltd v Escada (UK) Ltd* (2001), the High Court reached a different conclusion as to the way in which compensation should be calculated. It did so on the basis that the aim of the original Directive was simply to establish a general right to an entitlement and that the particular method of assessing the value of that entitlement was to be left to the individual member states

to decide upon. The Court, therefore, thought it inappropriate simply to follow the method of calculation operated by the French courts. Following *Duffen v FRA Bo SpA*, the High Court, contrary to general common law principles, held that, under the Regulations, an independent agency had a value, which was akin to the value of the goodwill in a business. Any assessment of that value, at or just before termination, required consideration of various factors, including the agent's expenditure incurred in earning the commission, the duration and history of the agreement, provision for notice, etc, and was not susceptible to the application of a simple formula.

- In *Ingmar GB Ltd v Eaton Leonard Inc (formerly Eaton Leonard Technologies Inc)* (2001), whilst Morland J felt himself bound to recognise the hierarchical superiority of the Scottish Court of Session decision as stated in *Douglas King v T Tunnock Ltd* in relation to a piece of British legislation, he nonetheless felt more in sympathy with the approach adopted by the High Court in *Barrett McKenzie & Co Ltd v Escada (UK) Ltd*. His mechanism for achieving both ends was to decide that the Scottish court had laid down 'not a principle of law but a guideline that in many cases . . . may be appropriate'. However, in the present case, he found it not appropriate and thus he could effectively avoid following the Court of Session's decision. This 'English' approach was followed in *Tigana Ltd v Decoro Ltd* (2003).

The situation as to the precise way in which reg 17 compensation payments are to be calculated remains uncertain. Although much academic work supports the approach of the English High Court, it remains for the final resolution to be determined by the House of Lords, either in that form or as the Privy Council in relation to Scottish cases.

12.6 Relationships with Third Parties

In the words of Wright J in *Montgomerie v UK Mutual Steamship Association* (1891), once an agent creates a contract between the principal and a third party, *prima facie* at common law, 'the only person who can sue is the principal and the only person who can be sued is the principal'. In other words, the agent has no further responsibility. This general rule is, however, subject to the following particular exceptions, which in turn tend to depend upon whether or not the agent has actually disclosed the existence of the principal.

12.6.1 Where the principal's existence is disclosed

Although the actual identity of the principal need not be mentioned, where the agent indicates that he is acting as an agent, the general rule is as stated above; only the principal and the third party have rights and obligations under the contract.

Exceptionally, however, the agent may be held liable as a party to the contract. This can occur in the following ways:

- *At third party insistence*
  Where the agent has expressly accepted liability with the principal in order to induce the third party to enter the contract, he or she will attract liability.
- *By implication*
  Where the agent has signed the contractual agreement in his or her own name, without clearly stating that he or she is merely acting as a representative of the principal, he or she will most likely be liable on it.
- *In relation to bills of exchange*
  As in the previous situation, where an agent signs a bill of exchange without sufficiently indicating that he or she is merely acting as the agent of a named principal, he or she will become personally liable on it.

- *In relation to the execution of a deed*
  Where the agent signs the deed other than under a power of attorney, he or she will be personally liable on it.
- *Where the agent acts for a non-existent principal*
  In such circumstances, the other party to the agreement can take action against the purported agent.

12.6.2 Where the principal's existence is not disclosed

Even in the case of an undisclosed principal, where the agent has authority but has failed to disclose that he or she is acting for a principal, the general rule is still that a contract exists between the principal and the third party, which can be enforced by either of them. The following, however, are some modifications to this general rule:

- The third party is entitled to enforce the contract against the agent and, in turn, the agent can enforce the contract against the third party. In both cases, the principal can intervene to enforce or defend the action on his or her own behalf.
- As stated previously, an undisclosed principal cannot ratify any contract made outside of the agent's actual authority.
- Where the third party had a special reason to contract with the agent, the principal may be excluded from the contract. This will certainly apply in relation to personal contracts, such as contracts of employment and, possibly, on the authority of *Greer v Downs Supply Co* (1927), where the third party has a right to set off debts against the agent.
- Authority exists in *Said v Butt* (1920), where a theatre critic employed someone to get him a ticket for a performance he would not have been allowed into, for claiming that an undisclosed principal will not be permitted to enforce a contract where particular reasons exist as to why the third party would not wish to deal with him or her. This decision appears to run contrary to normal commercial practice and is of doubtful merit.

12.6.3 Payment by means of an agent

Payment by means of an agent can take two forms:

- *Payment by the third party to the agent to pass on to the principal*
  In this situation, if the principal is undisclosed, then the third party has discharged liability on the contract and is not responsible if the agent absconds with the money. However, if the principal is disclosed, then any payment to the agent only discharges the third party's responsibility if it can be shown that the agent had authority, either express or implied, to receive money.
- *Payment by the principal to the agent to pass on to the third party*
  In this situation, the general rule is that if the agent does not pay the third party, the principal remains liable. This remains the case with an undisclosed principal (see *Irvine & Co v Watson & Sons* (1880)).

12.6.4 Breach of warrant of authority

As has been stated above (12.4.3), where an agent purports to act for a principal without actually having the necessary authority, the agent is said to have breached his or her warrant of authority. In such circumstances, the third party may take action against the purported agent.

12.6.5 Liability in tort

An agent is liable to be sued in tort for any damages thus caused. However, the agent's right to indemnity extends to tortious acts done in the performance of his or her actual authority. In addition, the principal may have action taken against him or her directly, on the basis of vicarious liability.

12.7 Termination of Agency

The principal/agent relationship can come to end in two distinct ways: either by the acts of the parties themselves, either jointly or unilaterally; or as an effect of the operation of law.

12.7.1 Termination by the parties

There are a number of ways in which the parties can bring an agency agreement to an end, as follows:

- *By mutual agreement*
  Where the agency agreement is a continuing one, the parties may simply agree to bring the agency relationship to an end on such terms as they wish. Where the agency was established for a particular purpose, then it will automatically come to an end when that purpose has been achieved. Equally, where the agency was only intended to last for a definite period of time, then the end of that period will bring the agency to an end.
- *By the unilateral action of one of the parties*
  Because of the essentially consensual nature of the principal/agency relationship, it is possible for either of the parties to bring it to an end simply by giving notice of termination of the agreement. Although the agency relationship will be ended by such unilateral action, in situations where the principal has formed a contractual relationship with the agent, such unilateral termination may leave the principal open to an action for damages in breach of contract.
- *Irrevocable agreements*
  In some circumstances, it is not possible to revoke an agency agreement. This situation arises where the agent has authority coupled with an interest. Such an irrevocable agency might arise where a principal owes money to the agent and the payment of the debt was the reason for the formation of the agency relationship. For example, where, in order to raise the money to pay off his debt, the principal appoints his creditor as his agent to sell some particular piece of property, the principal may not be at liberty to bring the agency to an end until the sale has taken place and the debt has been paid off.

12.7.2 Termination by operation of law

This refers to the fact that an agency relationship will be brought to an end by any of the following:

- *Frustration*
  Contracts of agency are subject to discharge by frustration in the same way that ordinary contracts are (see 7.4 above for the general operation of the doctrine of frustration).
- *The death of either party*
  Death of the agent clearly brings the agreement to an end, as does the death of the principal. The latter situation may, however, give rise to problems where the agent is unaware of the death and continues to act in the capacity of agent. In such circumstances, the agent will be in breach of his or her warrant of authority and will be personally liable to third parties.

- *Insanity of either party*
  As in the previous situation, the insanity of either party will bring the agency to an end; similarly, agents will have to be careful not to breach their warrant of authority by continuing to act after the principal has become insane (see *Yonge v Toynbee* (1910), 12.4.3 above).
- *Bankruptcy*
  Generally, the bankruptcy of the principal will end the agency agreement, but the bankruptcy of the agent will only bring it to an end where it renders him or her unfit to continue to act as an agent.

Summary

Agency

Definition

An agent is a person who is empowered to represent another legal party, called the principal, and brings the principal into a legal relationship with a third party.

Agency agreements may be either contractual or gratuitous.

Commercial agents are specifically covered by the Commercial Agents (Council Directive) Regulations 1993.

Creation of agency

Agency may arise:

- expressly;
- by ratification;
- by implication;
- by necessity; or
- by estoppel.

Nature of agent's authority

Actual authority may be divided into:

- express actual authority; and
- implied actual authority.

Apparent authority is based on estoppel and operates in such a way as to make the principal responsible for their action or inaction as regards someone who claims to be their agent.

Warrant of authority

If an agent contracts with a third party on behalf of a principal, the agent impliedly guarantees that the principal exists and has contractual capacity and that he or she has that person's authority to act as his or her agent. If this is not the case, the agent is personally liable to third parties for breach of warrant of authority.

The duties of agent to principal

The duties of the agent to the principal are:

- to perform the undertaking according to instructions;
- to exercise due care and skill;

- to carry out instructions personally;
- to account;
- not to permit a conflict of interest to arise;
- not to make a secret profit or misuse confidential information; and
- not to take a bribe.

The rights of an agent

The rights of an agent are:

- to claim remuneration for services performed;
- to claim indemnity for all expenses legitimately incurred in the performance of services; and
- to exercise a lien over property owned by the principal.

Commercial Agents (Council Directive) Regulations 1993

- Regulations 3–5 set out the rights and obligations as between commercial agents and their principals.
- Regulations 6–12 deal with remuneration.
- Regulations 13–16 deal with the conclusion and termination of the agency contract.
- Regulations 17–19 contain provisions relating to the indemnity or compensation payable to a commercial agent on termination of his agency contract.
- Regulation 20 relates to the validity of restraint of trade clauses.

Relations with third parties

Where the agent indicates that he or she is acting as an agent, the general rule is that only the principal and the third party have rights and obligations under the contract.

There are exceptions to this:

- at the insistence of the third party;
- by implication;
- in relation to bills of exchange; and
- in relation to deeds.

Where the principal's existence is not disclosed:

- the agent can enforce the contract against the third party;
- the principal can enforce the contract against the third party;
- the third party can choose to enforce the contract against the agent or the principal; or
- an undisclosed principal cannot ratify any contract made outside of the agent's actual authority.

Where the third party had a special reason to contract with the agent, the principal may be excluded from the contract. Where the agent misrepresents the identity of the principal, the third party may not be bound by the contract.

Payment by means of an agent

- If the agent does not pay the third party, the principal remains liable.
- If the agent absconds with money paid by the third party, then, if the principal is undisclosed, he or she sustains the loss. If, however, the principal is disclosed, the agent must have had authority to accept money, or else the third party is liable.

Termination of agency

Agreements may end:

- by mutual agreement;
- by the unilateral action of one of the parties;
- through frustration; or
- due to the death, insanity or bankruptcy of either party.

Further Reading

Munday, R, *Agency: Law and Principles*, 2010, Oxford: OUP

Chapter 13

Partnership Law

Chapter Contents

Law in Context: Partnership Law

This chapter will take you through the concept of partnerships as a type of business structure, the forms that partnerships can take and the importance of the partnership agreement. It is central to note that a partnership has no separate legal personality, other than its members. Therefore, if company A were to sue company B (a partnership), company A would sue the individual partners of company B, rather than the company in its own right. Partnerships are similar to sole traders in the sense that they will be responsible for any debts that the business runs up, and partners will be liable for debts of the business. The role of the partners is particularly important, and for some companies which specialise in a particular business type, the partners would be expected to be experts within their fields, such as a partnership of doctors or solicitors. The relationships between the partners will be key and can lead to potentially complex scenarios, such as if one partnership buys another. Or, if a partner in company A is also a partner in company B, and there is the potential for the companies to compete for business. Even if there is not the potential to compete, being on the board of both companies can bring about its own difficulties. Similarly, the relationship between partners and outside bodies is important. For example, if Clare signs a contract with ABC stationery suppliers to be the sole supplier of stationery to the partnership, this would effectively bind the other partners to the contract and they would need to abide by its terms. This chapter will also consider how partnerships can end. Most end amicably, but a partnership may also end if a court decrees that is should be dissolved. This could be due to capability, a breach of contract, or the business being undertaken at a loss. Usually such matters would be set out in the partnership agreement, and this would enable to dissolution to take place in a measured and planned manner.

13.1 Introduction

The partnership is a fundamental form of business/commercial organisation. Historically, the partnership predated the registered limited company as a means for uniting the capital of separate individuals, and it was of the utmost importance in financing the Industrial Revolution in the UK in the 18th and 19th centuries.

As an economic form, the partnership is still important. However, since the last quarter of the 19th century, as unlimited partnerships have transformed themselves into private limited companies, partnership law has given way to the control of company law as a form of legal regulation. It could be argued that, nowadays, the important partnership cases take place in the Companies Court. The continued relevance of partnership law should not be underestimated, however, since it remains the essential form of organisation within the sphere of such professional activities as the law, accountancy and medicine, where there is no wish, or need, for limited liability. However, even in these areas the possibility of securing limited liability through the use of the limited liability partnership under the Limited Liability Partnership Act 2000 has increasingly been taken advantage of.

13.2 The Partnership Acts

There are a number of statutes designed to provide specific rules for the various types of partnership that may be used by businesses. These partnership forms and their regulatory controls will be considered below.

13.2.1 Standard partnerships

The legal regulation of standard partnerships is mainly to be found in the Partnership Act (PA) 1890. The PA 1890 recognised the existing business and commercial practice and at least some of the previous decisions of common law and equity as they affected partnerships.

In line with the consensual nature of partnership undertakings, the PA 1890 did not seek to achieve a complete codification of the law; it merely sought to establish a basic framework, whilst leaving open the possibility of partners establishing their own terms. The limited nature of the PA 1890 means that reference has to be made to cases decided by the courts both before and after the PA 1890 in order to understand the full scope of partnership law (s 46 expressly maintains all the rules of the common law and equity, except where they are inconsistent with the provisions of the PA 1890).

13.2.2 Limited partnerships

A key attribute of the standard partnership is the fact that its members are liable to the full extent of their personal wealth for the debts of the business. The Limited Partnership Act 1907, however, allows for the formation of limited partnerships. In order for members of a partnership to gain the benefit of limited liability under this legislation, the following rules apply:

- Limited partners are not liable for partnership debts beyond the extent of their capital contribution but, in the ordinary course of events, they are not permitted to remove their capital.
- One or more of the partners must retain full, that is, unlimited, liability for the debts of the partnership.
- A partner with limited liability is not permitted to take part in the management of the business enterprise and cannot usually bind the partnership in any transaction (contravention of this rule will result in the loss of limited liability).
- The partnership must be registered with the Companies Registry.

In practice, the Limited Partnerships Act 1907 has had little effect and has been seldom used. The simple reason for such a situation is the emergence, legal recognition and development of the private limited company as an alternative form of organisation. At least to the extent that it affords the protection of limited liability, limited small businesses have seen the private company as the better and preferred form. The famous company law case of *Salomon v Salomon & Co* (1897) recognised the legal validity of the private limited company and predestined the failure of the Limited Partnerships Act 1907 (see, further 14.2.2 below).

13.2.3 Limited liability partnerships

The Limited Liability Partnership Act (LLPA) 2000 provided for a new form of business entity, the limited liability partnership (LLP). Although stated to be a partnership, the limited liability partnership is a corporation, with a distinct legal existence apart from its members. It has perpetual succession and, consequently, alterations in its membership do not have any effect on its existence. Most importantly, however, the creation of a separate legal entity will allow all of its members to benefit from limited liability, in that they will not be liable for more than the amount they have agreed to contribute to its capital.

This last advantage is significantly different from the previous limitation on liability available under the Limited Partnership Act 1907, which, as has been seen, required at least one general partner to remain fully liable for partnership debts. The provisions of the LLPA 2000 will be considered in detail at 13.9 below, and what follows before then will relate to the ordinary standard partnership.

13.3 Definition of 'Partnership'

Section 1 of the PA 1890 states that partnership is the relationship which subsists between persons carrying on a business in common with a view to profit.

In relation to this definition, the following points should be noted:

- *Membership numbers*
  There must be a minimum of two members. Section 716 of the Companies Act 1985 provided a maximum of 20 members in a partnership, except for some professional partnerships, but that provision was repealed in 2002, so now there is no maximum number of partners.
  See Chapter 14.2.2 →
- *Registered companies*
  Section 1 of the PA 1890 expressly excludes companies registered under the companies legislation from being treated as partnerships. However, as legal persons such companies can be members of partnerships.
- *The nature of the relationship is a contractual one*
  Partners enter into the agreement on the terms that they themselves have negotiated and acceded to. As a consequence, they are contractually bound by those terms, as long as they do not conflict with the express provisions of the PA 1890, and they may be enforced by the law in the same way as other contractual terms.
- *It is a requirement that a business be carried on*
  The term 'business' includes any trade, occupation or profession. The mere fact that individuals jointly own property does not necessarily mean that they are partners, if the property is not being used by them to pursue some collective business activity. See also *Britton v Commissioners of Customs & Excise* (1986), where it was held that the fact that a wife received a share of the profits of her husband's business did not make her a partner in the business, since this was a purely domestic arrangement.
- *Any business must be carried out in common*
  Partnerships are by definition collective organisations. Under English law, however, they are no more than a collection of individuals and do not enjoy the benefits of separate personality (see 13.4 below).
- *Partnerships may be created for the purposes of a single venture*
  It is usually the case that partnerships continue over an extended period of time, but this is not necessarily the case.
- *The business must be carried on with a view to profit*
  An immediate result of this provision is that neither charitable nor mutual benefit schemes are to be considered as partnerships. It used to be the case that the mere receipt of a share of profit was enough to make a person a partner and responsible for partnership debts (see *Waugh v Carver* (1793)). Nowadays, although the receipt of a share of profits may be *prima facie* evidence of a partnership relationship, it is not conclusive (see *Britton v Commissioners of Customs and Excise* above).

Section 2(2) of the PA 1890 expressly states that the sharing of gross returns does not in itself indicate the existence of a partnership agreement, since such an arrangement may simply represent a form of payment for the individual concerned. Thus, by way of example, the authors of this book will receive a percentage of the total sales value of the book. That, however, does not make them partners of the publishers so, if publication of the book results in massive losses for the publishers, third parties cannot look to the authors for any money owed.

❖ KEY CASE *Cox v Coulson* (1916)

Facts:
The defendant, who owned a theatre, agreed with another party, Mill, that he (Mill) could use the premises to put on a play. Coulson was to receive 60% of gross profits by way of payment. During a performance, the plaintiff was shot and she sued Coulson as Mill's partner for compensation for her injuries.

Decision:
Her action failed as the mere sharing of gross profits did not in itself create partnership relations.

Even receiving a share of net profits does not necessarily indicate a partnership. For example, a person would not be treated as a partner where they received payment of a debt by instalments made from business profits; or where they received wages in the form of a share of profit; or where they received interest on a loan to a business, the rate of which varied in relation to the level of the business profits.

❖ KEY CASE *Strathearn Gordon Associates Ltd v Commissioners of Customs & Excise* (1985)

Facts:
The company acted as management consultant to seven separate enterprises, receiving a share of their individual profits as part of its payment. The company argued that the consultancy was part of seven separate partnership agreements and, therefore, did not accrue value added tax (VAT), as would be the case if it were merely supplying its services to the various enterprises.

Decision:
The VAT tribunal found against the company, on the basis that merely receiving a share of profit was not sufficient to establish a partnership relationship. (See also *Britton v Commissioners of Customs & Excise*.)

13.3.1 Types of partners

It is sometimes thought to be necessary to distinguish between different types of partners but, in reality, such a division is of most use in pointing out particular dangers inherent in a failure to adopt an active, if only supervisory, role in a partnership enterprise. Thus, a general partner is the typical member of a partnership. The term is actually used in the Limited Partnership Act 1907 to distinguish that usual type from the unusual limited partner. The general partner is one who is actively engaged in the day to day running of the business enterprise, whereas the limited partner is actually precluded from participating in the management of the enterprise.

Section 24(5) of the PA 1890 provides that every partner is entitled to take part in the management of the partnership business. The partnership agreement may place limitations on the actual authority of any such person but, unless an outsider is aware of the limitation, the partnership is responsible for any business transaction entered into by a partner within his or her usual authority. (For further consideration of these types of authority, see 13.7.1 below.)

A dormant or 'sleeping' partner is a person who merely invests money in a partnership enterprise but, apart from receiving a return on capital invested, takes no active part in the day-to-day running of the business. The limited partner in a limited partnership may be seen as a dormant partner. The term is used more generally, however, to refer to people who simply put money into partnership enterprises without taking an active part in the business and yet do not comply with the formalities required for establishing a limited partnership. The essential point that has to be emphasised in this regard is that, in so doing, such people place themselves at great risk. The law will consider them as general partners in the enterprise and will hold them personally and fully liable for the debts of the partnership to the extent of their ability to pay. By remaining outside the day-to-day operation of the business, such people merely surrender their personal unlimited liability into the control of the active parties in the partnership.

The term 'salaried partner' applies in professional partnerships to someone who, although appropriately qualified, is not a partner in the full sense of the word. They will be recognised as partners and will have the satisfaction of having their name on the partnership's letterhead, but they will not fully participate in the business profits as the other, ordinary partners do – they will merely receive a salary. They might also be restricted in their participation in partnership meetings. Nonetheless, such partners are liable for partnership debts in the same way, and to the same extent, as the ordinary partners.

In *Tiffin v Lester Aldridge LLP* (2012) the Court of Appeal considered the employment status of a fixed share equity partner. Tiffin's cause of action was that despite being a fixed share equity partner, he was in reality no more than an employee of the firm. However, the court rejected his argument, accepting that a person can still be a partner, even if they have little, or even no, right to share in the firm's profits, had not made a significant, or indeed any, contribution, to its capital and exercised only limited, or no, voting rights.

13.4 The Legal Status of a Partnership

The standard partnership is an organisation established by individuals to pursue some business activity. Although the law is permissive in relation to the establishment of such enterprises, there are particular ways in which the law impinges on and controls not just the operation of partnerships, but their very formation and existence.

13.4.1 Legal personality

The definition of a partnership expressly states that it is a relationship between persons. The corollary of this is that the partnership has no existence outside of, or apart from, that relationship. In other words, the partnership has no separate legal personality apart from its members, unlike a joint stock company.

Although Scots law does grant corporate personality to the partnership without the benefit of limited liability, in English law a partnership is no more than a group of individuals collectively involved in a business activity. Section 4 of the PA 1890, however, does recognise an element of unity within the partnership organisation, to the extent that it permits the partnership to be known collectively as a firm and permits the business to be carried out under the firm's name. In addition, the procedural Rules of the Supreme Court, Ord 81, as stated in the Civil Procedure Rules 1998, provides that legal action may be taken by, and against, the partners in the firm's name, although any award against the partnership may be executed against any of the individual partners.

LLPs formed under the LLPA 2000 are incorporated and, as such, have a distinct legal personality apart from their members. (See 13.9 below for LLPs and 6.2 below for an analysis of corporations.)

In November 2003, the Law Commission and the Scottish Law Commission produced a joint proposal for the major alteration of partnership law under which partnerships would be extended the privilege of full legal personality. In relation to liability, the proposal was for the partnership, as a legal person, to assume primary liability for debts but for the members to retain secondary liability for any debts beyond the assets of the partnership.

It follows from the current lack of separate personality in the standard partnership that the partners are self-employed. The partnership can, of course, employ others. However, an interesting juxtaposition of the requirement to carry out a business collectively in the pursuit of profit and the requirements of employment law may be found in *Rennison & Sons v Minister of Social Security* (1970). It is essential for the purposes of employment law to distinguish between those who are self-employed (or in contracts for services) and those who are employees (in contracts of service), as different rights appertain to the different categories. In deciding any question, the courts will look at the reality of the situation, rather than the mere title that someone bears.

❖ KEY CASE *Rennison & Sons v Minister of Social Security* (1970)

Facts:

A firm of solicitors had purported to enter into contracts of service with their clerical staff and, subsequently, all of the staff had entered into a partnership agreement, under which the profits and losses were to be divided on terms to be agreed. In fact, the clerical staff continued to work as they had done before and continued to be paid at exactly the same hourly rate that they had previously been paid. The only difference was that the wages were paid in a lump sum to one of them who was responsible for dividing it out amongst the rest. The issue of responsibility for payment of national insurance was raised, as was required in relation to employees but not the self-employed.

See Chapter 10 above, for more detailed treatment of the employment law issues.

Decision:

It was held that neither of the devices successfully removed the reality that the staff concerned were employees. Simply calling them 'self-employed' did not alter their status as employees, nor did calling them 'partners'. In reality, the agreement simply affected the way in which they were paid, rather than their employment status.

13.4.2 Illegal partnerships

A partnership is illegal if it is formed to carry out an illegal purpose, or to carry out a legal purpose in an illegal manner. In such circumstances, the courts will not recognise any partnership rights between the persons involved, but will permit innocent third parties who have no knowledge of any illegality to recover against them.

13.4.3 Capacity

There are two distinct aspects relating to capacity, as follows:

- *Capacity of individuals to join a partnership*
  The general common law rules relating to capacity to enter into contracts apply in the particular case of the membership of a partnership. Thus, any partnership agreement entered

into by a minor is voidable during that person's minority and for a reasonable time after they have reached the age of majority. If the former minor does not repudiate the partnership agreement within a reasonable time of reaching the age of majority, then they will be liable for any debts as a *de facto* partner. Third parties cannot recover against partners who are minors, but they can recover against any other adult partners. Mental incapacity does not necessarily prevent someone from entering into a partnership, but subsequent mental incapacity of a partner may be grounds for the dissolution of a partnership.

- *Capacity of the partnership*
  A particular consequence of the fact that the partnership is, at least in the perception of the law, no more than a relationship between individuals is that there are no specific rules controlling the contractual capacity of partnerships, other than those general rules which constrain individuals' capacity to enter into contracts. This point was of more significance when companies were more strictly constrained by the operation of the *ultra vires* doctrine but, as will be seen at 14.5.1 below, that particular company law doctrine has been much relaxed. Section 5 of the PA 1890 provides that each partner is the agent of the firm and the other partners for the purpose of the business of the partnership but, as that purpose is determined by the members, and as it is not fixed by law, it can be changed by the unanimous agreement of those members. (See 13.5.2 below, on the alteration of the partnership agreement.)

13.5 Formation of a Partnership

There are no specific legal requirements governing the formation of a partnership. Partnerships arise from the agreement of the parties involved and are governed by the general principles of contract law. An agreement to enter into a partnership, therefore, may be made by deed, in writing or by word of mouth. Such agreement may even be implied from the conduct of the parties.

13.5.1 The partnership agreement

It is usual for the terms of the partnership to be set out in written form. The document produced is known as the 'articles of partnership'. The parties involved, no doubt after some negotiation, decide what they wish to be specifically included in the articles. Any gaps in the articles will be filled in by reference to the PA 1890 or the existing common law and equitable rules relating to partnerships, but it is necessary for the future partners to provide for any unusual or specialised terms to be included in the articles.

The detailed provisions in articles of partnership usually refer to such matters as the nature of the business to be transacted, the name of the firm, the capital contributions to be made by the individual partners, the drawing up of the business accounts, the method of determining and sharing profits and the dissolution of the partnership. It is also usual for there to be a provision for disputes between partners to be referred to arbitration for solution.

The partnership agreement is an internal document and, although it has effect between the partners, it does not necessarily affect the rights of third parties. Thus, where the agreement seeks to place limitations on the usual authority of a partner, it is effective with regard to the internal relations of the partners but does not have any effect as regards an outsider who deals with the partner without knowledge of the limitation.

❖ KEY CASE *Mercantile Credit v Garrod* (1962)

Facts:
Parkin and Garrod were partners in a garage business, which was mainly concerned with letting garages and repairing cars. The partnership agreement expressly excluded the sale of cars. After Parkin had sold a car, to which he had no title, to the plaintiffs, they claimed back the money they had paid from Garrod.

Decision:
It was held that since selling cars was within the usual scope of a garage business, it was within the usual authority of a partner in such a business. Parkin, therefore, had acted within his implied authority and the partnership was responsible for his actions. The plaintiffs had no knowledge of the limitation contained within the articles and could not be subject to it.

13.5.2 Alteration of the partnership agreement

Just as the consensual nature of the partnership relationship allows the parties to make the agreement in such terms as they wish, so are they equally free to alter those terms at a later date. Section 19 of the PA 1890, however, enacts the common law rule that any decision to alter the terms of partnership articles must be made unanimously. Consent does not have to be expressed but may be inferred from the conduct of the partners.

❖ KEY CASE *Pilling v Pilling* (1887)

Facts:
The articles of partnership entered into between a father and his two sons stated that the business was to be financed by the father's capital and that such capital was to remain his personal property and was not to be treated as the partnership property. The articles also stated that the father should receive interest on his capital. In practice, however, the sons, as well as the father, received interest on the partnership capital.

Decision:
It was held that the capital originally provided by the father was partnership property and that the conduct of the parties in treating it as such had amounted to a valid alteration of the written agreement.

13.5.3 The firm's name

Partnerships may use the words 'and Company', or its alternative form 'and Co', in their name; for example, a firm of solicitors may call itself 'Brown, Smith and Co'. This merely indicates that the names of all the partners are not included in the firm's name. As has been seen above, it in no way indicates that the partnership has any existence apart from its constituent members, or that those members have the benefit of limited liability. Even in the case of limited partnerships, someone must accept full liability for partnership debts. The Company and Business Names (Miscellaneous Provisions) Regulations 2009 prohibits any business, including a partnership, from using the 'Limited' (or the abbreviation 'Ltd') in its name.

A partnership may trade under the names of the individual partners or it may trade under a collective name. For the time being any name must comply with both the Business Names Act (BNA) 1985 and the common law provisions relating to the tort of passing off. The provisions in Pt 41 of the Companies Act 2006, which will replace the BNA, have as yet not been brought into effect.

13.5.4 Business names

Part 41, chapter 2, of the Companies Act 2006, restating the previous provisions of the Business Names Act 1985 which it repealed, was brought into effect in October 2009 by the Companies Act 2006 (Commencement No 8, Transitional Provisions and Savings) Order 2008.

Sections 1200–1204 require that where a partnership does not trade under the names of all of its members, the names of individuals must be displayed on the business premises and on the firm's letters and business documents. Where the partnership is a large one with more than 20 members, the individual names do not have to be listed on business documents, but a list of all partners must be available for inspection at the firm's principal place of business. Any failure to comply with the foregoing requirements is a criminal offence (s 1205) and, in addition, may result in the person in breach not being able to enforce a claim against another party who was disadvantaged by the breach (s 1206).

There is no longer any requirement that business names be registered as such, but the Companies Act 2006, part 41 chapter 1, requires the approval of the Secretary of State for Trade and Industry before certain names can be used. Such names may imply that the business is related in some way to the Crown, the Government, local authorities or other official bodies.

13.5.5 Passing off

The Companies Act 2006 does not prevent one business from using the same, or a very similar, name as another business. However, the tort of passing off prevents one person from using any name which is likely to divert business their way by suggesting that the business is actually that of some other person or is connected in any way with that other business. It thus enables people to protect the goodwill they have built up in relation to their business activity. See *Ewing v Buttercup Margarine Co Ltd* (1917), where the plaintiff successfully prevented the defendants from using a name that suggested a link with his existing dairy company. For a more up to date and less serious case, see *Stringfellow v McCain Foods GB Ltd* (1984), in which the owner of the famous Stringfellow's nightclub failed to prevent a manufacturer of long, thin oven chips from calling their product by the same name.

❖ KEY CASE *Ewing v Buttercup Margarine Co Ltd* (1917)

Facts:

Ewing conducted a retail business under the name the Buttercup Dairy Company. As its name implied it sold dairy products including butter, as well as margarine and tea and so on. The shops were mainly in Scotland but also spread into the North of England (the counter of one of the shops is actually displayed in the Glasgow People's Palace museum). The defendant company was registered in 1916 to carry on the business of supplying margarine wholesale. Ewing brought an action for an injunction to prevent the company trading under its registered name on the grounds that the general public might reasonably believe that there was a link between the two businesses.

Decision:
The injunction was granted. Although the defendants were wholesalers, the objects clause of its memorandum gave it power to enter the retail market, which it might exercise in future. Additionally, as the plaintiff intended to expand his business into the South of England, confusion was a real possibility.

13.5.6 Arbitration clauses

The consensual nature of the relationship on which any partnership is based has been repeatedly emphasised. It should always be remembered, however, that even the best of friends can fall out; when they are engaged in a joint business venture, any such conflict may be disastrous for the business. In an attempt to forestall such an eventuality, and to avoid the cost, delay and publicity involved in court procedure, it is standard practice for partnership articles to contain a clause referring disputes to arbitration for solution.

See Chapter 3

The actual procedure of arbitration has been considered above, but it should be recognised that arbitration, although relatively cheaper than the court system, is not cheap in absolute terms. Nor can it deal with situations where the partners have reached the stage where their continued conflict prevents the effective operation of the business. In such circumstances, it is probably wiser if the partnership is wound up on just and equitable grounds under s 35 of the PA 1890. (See 13.8.1 below and see also *Re Yenidje Tobacco Co Ltd* (1916) as an example of the partnership principle being extended to a quasi-partnership company.)

13.6 The Relationship Between Partners

The partnership agreement is contractual in nature. The partnership also involves a principal/agency relationship, but is complicated by the fact that partners are, at one and the same time, both agents of the firm and their fellow partners, and principals as regards those other partners. Partners are equally subject to the equitable rights and duties that derive from their being in a fiduciary position in relation to another. Thus, the legal nature of the partnership involves a complicated mixture of elements of contract, agency and equity.

Section 24(8) of the PA 1890 provides that, subject of course to any agreement to the contrary, any differences arising as to the ordinary matters connected with the partnership business are to be decided by a majority of the partners, although they must not impose their views without actually consulting the minority (see *Const v Harris* (1824)). Thus, the day-to- day business is conducted in line with the wishes of the majority. However, s 24(8) also states that the nature of that business cannot be changed without the unanimous agreement of the partners.

13.6.1 Duties of partners

The fiduciary nature of the partnership relationship imports the usual duties that derive from such a relationship, which can be summed up under the general heading of a duty to act in good faith. In addition to these general fiduciary duties, ss 28–30 of the PA 1890 lay down specific duties as follows:

- *The duty of disclosure*
  Section 28 provides that partners must render true accounts and full information in relation to all things affecting the partnership to the other partners or their legal representatives.

❖ KEY CASE *Law v Law* (1905)

Facts:
One partner accepted an offer from the other to buy his share of the firm. He later discovered that certain partnership assets had not been disclosed to him and sought to have the contract set aside.

Decision:
The court decided that, as the purchasing partner had breached the duty of disclosure, the agreement could have been set aside. In actual fact, the parties had come to an arrangement, so it was not necessary for such an order to be granted.

- *The duty to account*
  Section 29 of the PA 1890 provides that partners must account to the firm for any benefit obtained, without consent, from any transaction concerning the partnership; its property, including information derived from membership of the partnership; its name; or its business connection. As with fiduciary duties generally, such profit is only open to challenge where it is undisclosed. Full disclosure is necessary and sufficient to justify the making of an individual profit from a partnership position.

❖ KEY CASE *Bentley v Craven* (1853)

Facts:
Craven was in partnership with the plaintiff in a sugar refinery business. He bought sugar on his own account and later sold it to the partnership at a profit, without declaring his interest to the other partners.

Decision:
It was held that the partnership was entitled to recover the profit from the defendant.

- *The duty not to compete*
  Section 30 provides that where a partner competes with the partnership business, without the consent of the other partners, then that person shall be liable to account to the partnership for any profits made in the course of that business.

❖ KEY CASE *Glassington v Thwaites* (1823)

Facts:
A member of a partnership, which produced a morning paper, was also involved in the publishing an evening paper. It was argued that this latter activity was in competition with the partnership business.

Decision:

The argument was sustained and the partner was held to account for the profit he made from publishing the evening paper.

Once again, it is essential to note that full disclosure is necessary to validate any such profits made in competition with the partnership. (See *Trimble v Goldberg* (1906), where the court declined to recognise competition in relation to a partnership; but the likely severity of the courts' approach can be surmised from the company law case of *Industrial Development Consultants v Cooley* (1972).)

13.6.2 Rights of partners

Subject to express provision to the contrary in the partnership agreement, and it should be remembered that the consensual nature of the partnership allows the parties to avoid the provisions of the Act, s 24 of the PA 1890 sets out the rights of partners. Amongst the most important of these are the following rights:

- *To share equally in the capital and profits of the business*
  Even where the partnership agreement is silent on the matter, s 24 does not mean that someone who has contributed all, or the greater part, of the capital of a firm must share it equally with the other partners. In such circumstances, it would most likely be decided that the facts of the case provided evidence of such contrary intention as to rebut the statement in the PA 1890. What the section does mean is that, even in the same circumstances, the partners will share profits equally, although it is not unusual to find clauses in agreements which recognise differences in capital input by providing for profits to be shared on an unequal basis. The same effect can be achieved by permitting interest to be paid on capital before profits are determined. Where partners advance additional capital to the firm by way of a loan, they are entitled to interest at 5% unless there is an agreement to the contrary.

  The corollary of this right is the duty to contribute equally to any losses of capital, even where no capital was originally brought into the business. For example, if A and B enter into a partnership, with A providing all of the capital of £10,000 but A and B sharing the profits equally, and, upon winding up, the business has accrued a loss of £2,000, then both parties are required to contribute to the loss. In effect, B will have to contribute £1,000 and A will only receive a return of £9,000.
- *To be indemnified by the firm for any liabilities incurred or payments made in the course of the firm's business*
  This may be seen as merely an express declaration of the usual right of an agent to indemnity. The right of an agent to act outside their authority in the case of necessity is also expressly set out in s 24.
- *To take part in the management of the business*
  The unlimited nature of the ordinary partnership means that involvement in such a business brings with it the risk to one's personal wealth. It is essential under such circumstances, therefore, that partners are able to protect their interests by taking an active part in the operation of the business in order to assess and control the level of their risk. It is for this reason that the right to take part in the management of the business is stated expressly. In the case of quasi-partnership companies, the courts will imply such a right. A partner is generally not entitled to receive any salary for acting in the partnership business, but it is not unusual for the agreement effectively to provide for the payment of a salary to particular partners before the determination of net profit.
- *To have access to the firm's books*
  This right follows from, and is based on, the same reasoning as the previous provision. The books are normally kept at the firm's principal place of business.

- *To prevent the admission of a new partner or prevent any change in the nature of the partnership business*
  As has been seen, the majority can decide any differences relating to the partnership business, but unanimity is required to change the nature of the business. Again, this reflects the need for individual partners to accept risk voluntarily. They have only accepted existing business risks and cannot be forced to alter or increase that risk.
  Similarly, as principals, they have agreed to give their authority to bind them and make them liable for partnership debts to particular individuals. They cannot be forced to extend that authority against their wishes.
  In addition to the above rights, s 25 of the PA 1980 provides that no majority can expel another partner, unless such power is contained in the partnership agreement. Even where such a power is included, it must be exercised in good faith. See *Blisset v Daniel* (1853), where the majority attempted to expel a partner in order to acquire his share of the business cheaply; and *Green v Howell* (1910), where a partner was properly expelled for a flagrant breach of his duties. For somewhat more recent cases, see *Kerr v Morris* (1987) and *Walters v Bingham* (1988).

13.6.3 Partnership property

Property may be owned collectively by all of the partners and may thus amount to partnership property. Alternatively, it is possible for property to be used by the partnership as a whole and yet remain the personal property of only one of the partners.

Section 20 of the PA 1890 states that partnership property consists of all property brought into the partnership stock or acquired on account for the purposes of the firm. Section 21 further states that any property bought with money belonging to the firm is deemed to have been bought on account of the firm.

Whether or not any particular item of property belongs to the firm is always a matter of fact, to be determined in relation to the particular circumstances of any case. If there is no express agreement that property is to be brought into the firm as partnership property, the court will only imply such a term to the extent required to make the partnership agreement effective.

❖ KEY CASE *Miles v Clarke* (1953)

Facts:

Clarke had carried on a photography business for some time before taking Miles into partnership. The partnership agreement merely provided that the profits should be divided equally. When the partners fell out, a dispute arose as to who owned the assets used by the partnership.

Decision:

It was held that only the consumable stock-in-trade could be considered as partnership property. The leases of the business premises and other plant and equipment remained the personal property of the partner who introduced them into the business.

It is important to distinguish between partnership property and personal property for the following reasons:

- *Partnership property must be used exclusively for partnership purposes (s 20 of the PA 1980)*
  This may been seen as a statement of the general duty not to make a personal profit from a fiduciary position without full disclosure. Thus, partners are not supposed to use partnership

property for their own personal benefit or gain, and if they were to do so they would be liable to account to the partnership for any profit made.

It is also made clear that partners do not own the firm's assets directly. All they have, under s 30, is the partnership lien over those assets, which entitles them, on dissolution, to participate in any surplus after their realised value has been used to pay off partnership debts.

- *Any increase in the value of partnership property belongs to the partnership*
  As a consequence, the increased value when realised will be divided amongst all the partners.
- *Any increase in the value of personal property belongs to the person who owns the property*
  Consequently, the increased value will not have to be shared with the other partners.
- *On the dissolution of the firm, partnership property is used to pay debts before personal property*
  This is clearly stated in s 39, which has been considered above in relation to the nature of the partnership lien.
- *Partnership and personal property are treated differently in the satisfaction of claims made by partnership creditors, as opposed to personal creditors*
  Under s 23, a writ of execution can only be issued against partnership property in respect of a judgment against the partnership. A personal creditor of a partner may not, therefore, take action against partnership property. They can, however, apply for a charging order against that partner's share in the partnership, which would entitle them to receive the partner's share of profits, or assets on dissolution, to the extent of the debt and interest. The other partners may redeem the charge at any time by paying off the debt, in which case the charge becomes vested in them.
- *On the death of a partner, any interest in partnership land will pass as personalty, whereas land owned personally will pass as realty*
  In effect, this means that the interest may pass to different people, depending on whether or not the party has made an appropriate will. Specifically in relation to land, s 22 enacts the equitable doctrine of conversion by providing that any such partnership property is to be treated as personal property.

13.6.4 Assignment of a share in a partnership

Unless the partnership agreement states otherwise, partners are at liberty to mortgage or assign absolutely their shares in partnerships to outsiders. The assignee is, however, only entitled to the share of profits due to the partner assigning the shares or, on dissolution, to the appropriate share of partnership assets. Section 31 makes it clear that any such assignee does not become a partner and has no right whatsoever to become involved in the management of the business.

❖ KEY CASE *Garwood v Paynter* (1903)

Facts:

Garwood charged his shares to a trust, of which his wife was one of the beneficiaries. When the other partners began to pay themselves salaries, Mrs Garwood objected on the ground that such payment reduced the net profit of the firm and, hence, indirectly, the income to the trust.

Decision:

It was held that the payment of salaries was an internal management matter and, therefore, the trustees, who were assignees, by virtue of s 31 could not interfere in the absence of fraud.

The assignee does not take over responsibility for partnership debts. These remain the liability of the assignor. Where, however, the assignment is absolute, the assignee must indemnify the assignor in respect of future liabilities arising from the business.

13.7 The Relationship Between Partners and Outsiders

Of equal importance to the internal relationships of the partnership is the relationship of the members of the partnership to outsiders who deal with the partnership and, in particular, the extent to which the partnership and, hence, the partners are liable for the actions of the individual partners.

13.7.1 The authority of partners to bind the firm

As stated in s 5 of the PA 1890, every partner is an agent of the firm and of the other partners. Each partner, therefore, has the power to bind co-partners and make them liable on business transactions. The partnership agreement may, however, expressly seek to limit the powers of particular members. The effect of such limitations depends on the circumstances of each case. They do not apply where the other partners have effectively countermanded the restriction. This can occur in two ways:

- If the other partners give their prior approval for a partner to exceed his actual authority, then the partner in question has express actual authority and the firm is bound by his action.
- If the other partners give their approval after the event, then they have ratified the transaction and the partnership is again liable.

The firm may be liable even where the other partners have not expressly approved the action in excess of authority, as long as the partner has acted within his or her implied powers, that is, within the usual scope of a partner's powers in the particular business concerned (see *Mercantile Credit v Garrod* (1962), 13.5.1 above). If, however, the outsider had actual knowledge of the partner's lack of authority, then the partnership is not bound by the transaction.

Every partner other than a limited partner is presumed to have the implied authority to enter into transactions:

- to sell the firm's goods;
- to buy goods of a kind normally required by the firm;
- to engage employees;
- to receive payment of debts due to the partnership;
- to pay debts owed by the partnership and to draw cheques for that purpose; and
- to employ a solicitor to act for the firm in defence of an action or in pursuit of a debt.

The above implied powers apply equally to trading and non-trading partnerships. Partners in trading firms, that is, those which essentially buy and sell goods, have additional implied powers:

- to accept, draw, issue or endorse bills of exchange or other negotiable instruments on behalf of the firm;
- to borrow money on the credit of the firm; and
- to pledge the firm's goods as security for borrowed money.

13.7.2 The nature of partners' liability

Every partner is responsible for the full amount of the firm's liability. Outsiders have the choice of taking action either against the firm collectively or against the individual partners. Where damages are recovered from one partner only, the other partners are under a duty to contribute equally to the amount paid, as follows:

- *Liability on debts and contracts*

  Under s 9 of the PA 1890, the liability of partners as regards debts or contracts is joint. The effect of joint liability used to be that, although the partners were collectively responsible, a person who took action against one of the partners could take no further action against the other partners, even if they had not recovered all that was owing to them.

  That situation was remedied by the Civil Liability (Contributions) Act 1978, which effectively provided that a judgment against one partner *does not* bar a subsequent action against the other partners.
- *Liability for torts*

  Under s 10 of the PA 1890, the liability of partners with regard to torts or other wrongs committed in the ordinary course of the partnership business is joint and several. In such a situation, there is no bar on taking successive actions against partners in order to recover all that is due. It should be emphasised that, in order for the partnership to be responsible, the wrong sued on must have been committed in the ordinary course of partnership business or with the express approval of all the partners. If a tort is committed outside this scope, then the partner responsible is personally liable.

❖ KEY CASE *Hamlyn v Houston & Co* (1905)

Facts:

One of the partners in the defendant company bribed a clerk employed by the plaintiff, in order to get information about their rival's business. Hamlyn sued the defendant partnership to recover the loss he claimed to have suffered as a consequence.

Decision:

It was held that the defendant firm was liable for the wrongful act of the individual partner, as he had acted within the usual scope of his authority, although he had used illegal methods in doing so.

However, see *Arbuckle v Taylor* (1815), where the partnership was not liable because the individual partner had gone beyond the general scope of the partnership business.

As was stated in 13.4.1, partners may be sued in the firm's name, although they remain individually liable for any awards made as a consequence of any such claim.

13.7.3 The liability of incoming and outgoing partners

A person who is admitted into an existing firm is not liable to creditors of the firm for anything done before they became a partner (see s 17 of the PA 1890). The new partner can, however, assume such responsibility by way of a device known as novation. This is the process whereby a retiring partner is discharged from existing liability and the newly constituted partnership takes the liability on themselves. Novation is essentially a tripartite contract involving the retiring partner, the new firm and the existing creditors. As creditors effectively give up rights against the retiring partner, their approval is required. Such approval may be express, or it may be implied from the course of dealing between the creditor and the firm.

❖ KEY CASE *Thompson v Percival* (1834)

Facts:
Charles Thompson and James Percival had been in partnership until Thompson retired. The plaintiff creditors, on applying for payment, were informed that Percival alone would be responsible for payment, as Thompson had retired. As a consequence, they drew a bill for payment against Percival alone.

Decision:
It was held that there was no longer a right of action against Thompson, since the action of the creditors showed that they had accepted his discharge from liability.

Creditors do not have to accept a novation. A creditor may still hold the retired partner responsible for any debts due at the time of retirement. The newly constituted firm may, however, agree to indemnify the retiring partner against any such claims.

Apart from novation, a retired partner remains liable for any debts or obligations incurred by the partnership prior to retirement. The date of any contract determines responsibility: if the person was a partner when the contract was entered into, then they are responsible, even if the goods under the contract are delivered after they have left the firm. The estate of a deceased person is only liable for those debts or obligations arising before death.

Where someone deals with a partnership after a change in membership, they are entitled to treat all of the apparent members of the old firm as still being members, until they receive notice of any change in membership. In order to avoid liability for future contracts, a retiring partner must:

- ensure that individual notice is given to existing customers of the partnership; and
- advertise the retirement in the *London Gazette*. This serves as general notice to people who were not customers of the firm prior to the partner's retirement but who knew that that person had been a partner in the business. Such an advert is effective whether or not it comes to the attention of third parties.

A retired partner owes no responsibility to someone who had neither dealings with the partnership nor previous knowledge of his or her membership.

❖ KEY CASE *Tower Cabinet Co Ltd v Ingram* (1949)

Facts:
Ingram and Christmas had been partners in a firm known as Merry's. After it was dissolved by mutual agreement, Christmas carried on trading under the firm's name. Notice was given to those dealing with the firm that Ingram was no longer connected with the business, but no notice was placed in the *London Gazette*. New notepaper was printed without Ingram's name. However, the plaintiffs, who had had no previous dealings with the

partnership, received an order on old notepaper, on which Ingram's name was included. Tower Cabinet sought to enforce a judgment against Ingram.

Decision:
It was held that he was not liable, since he had not represented himself as being a partner, nor had the plaintiffs been aware of his membership prior to dissolution.

13.7.4 Partnership by estoppel

Failure to give notice of retirement is one way in which liability arises on the basis of estoppel or holding out. Alternatively, anyone who represents themselves, or knowingly permits themselves to be represented, as a partner is liable to any person who gives the partnership credit on the basis of that representation. Although they may become liable for partnership debts, they are not, however, partners in any other sense. (In *Tower Cabinet Co Ltd v Ingram* (1949) (see 13.7.3 above), the defendant was not affected by partnership by estoppel, since he was never actually aware that he had been represented as being a partner.)

13.8 Dissolution and Winding Up of the Partnership

There are a number of possible reasons for bringing a partnership to an end. It may have been established for a particular purpose and that purpose has been achieved, or one of the partners might wish to retire from the business, or the good relationship between the members, which is essential to the operation of a partnership, may have broken down. In all such cases, the existing partnership is dissolved, although, in the second case, a new partnership may be established to take over the old business.

13.8.1 Grounds for dissolution

As has been repeatedly emphasised, the partnership is based on agreement. It is created by agreement and it may be brought to an end in the same way. However, subject to any provision to the contrary in the partnership agreement, the PA 1890 provides for the automatic dissolution of a partnership on the following grounds:

- *The expiry of a fixed term or the completion of a specified enterprise* (s 32(*a*) *and* (*b*))
  If the partnership continues after the pre-set limit, it is known as a 'partnership at will' and it can be ended at any time thereafter at the wish of any of the partners.
- *The giving of notice* (s 32(*c*))
  If the partnership is of indefinite duration, it can be brought to an end by any one of the partners giving notice of an intention to dissolve the partnership.
- *The death or bankruptcy of any partner* (s 33(1))
  Although the occurrence of either of these events will bring the partnership to an end, it is usual for partnership agreements to provide for the continuation of the business under the control of the remaining/solvent partners. The dead partner's interest will be valued and paid to his or her personal representative, and the bankrupt's interest will be paid to his or her trustee in bankruptcy.
- *Where a partner's share becomes subject to a charge under* s 23 (s 33(2))
  Under such circumstances, dissolution is not automatic; it is open to the other partners to dissolve the partnership.

- *Illegality* (s 34)
  The occurrence of events making the continuation of the partnership illegal will bring it to an end. An obvious case would be where the continuation of the partnership would result in trading with the enemy (see *R v Kupfer* (1915)). The principle applied equally, however, in the more recent and perhaps more relevant case of *Hudgell, Yeates & Co v Watson* (1978).

❖ KEY CASE *Hudgell, Yeates & Co v Watson* (1978)

Facts:

Practising solicitors are legally required to have a practice certificate. However, one of the members of a three-person partnership forgot to renew his practice certificate and, thus, was not legally entitled to act as a solicitor.

Decision:

It was held that the failure to renew the practice certificate brought the partnership to an end, although a new partnership continued between the other two members of the old partnership.

In addition to the provisions listed above, the court may, mainly by virtue of s 35 of the PA 1890, order the dissolution of the partnership in the following circumstances:

- *Where a partner becomes a patient under the Mental Health Act 1983*
  The procedure is no longer taken under s 35 of the PA 1890 but, where the person is no longer able to manage their affairs because of mental incapacity, the Court of Protection may dissolve a partnership at the request of the person's receiver or the other partners.
- *Where a partner suffers some other permanent incapacity*
  This provision is analogous to the previous one. It should be noted that it is for the other partners to apply for dissolution and that the incapacity alleged as the basis of dissolution must be permanent. It is not unusual for partnerships to include specific clauses in their agreement in order to permit dissolution on the basis of extended absence from the business (see *Peyton v Mindham* (1971), where a clause in a partnership covering medical practice provided for termination after nine months' continuous absence or a total of 300 days in any period of 24 months).
- *Where a partner engages in an activity prejudicial to the business*
  Such activity may be directly related to the business, such as the misappropriation of funds. Alternatively, it may take place outside the business but operate to its detriment; an example of this might be a criminal conviction for fraud.
- *Where a partner persistently breaches the partnership agreement*
  This provision also relates to conduct which makes it unreasonable for the other partners to carry on in business with the party at fault.
- *Where the business can only be carried on at a loss*
  This provision is a corollary of the very first section of the PA 1890, in which the pursuit of profit is part of the definition of the partnership form. If such profit cannot be achieved, then the partners are entitled to avoid loss by bringing the partnership to an end.
- *Where it is just and equitable to do so*
  The courts have wide discretion in relation to the implementation of this power. A similar provision operates within company legislation and the two provisions come together in the

cases involving quasi-partnerships. On occasion, courts have wound up companies on the ground that they would have been wound up had the business assumed the legal form of a partnership. For examples of this approach, see *Re Yenidje Tobacco Co Ltd* (1916) and *Ebrahimi v Westbourne Galleries Ltd* (1973).

After dissolution, the authority of each partner to bind the firm continues so far as is necessary to wind up the firm's affairs and complete transactions that have begun but are unfinished at the time of dissolution (s 38 of the PA 1980). Partners cannot, however, enter into new contracts.

13.8.2 Dissolution and winding up

Since the introduction of the Insolvency Act (IA) 1986, partnerships as such are not subject to bankruptcy, although the individual partners may be open to such procedure. Partnerships may be wound up as unregistered companies under Pt V of the IA 1986 where they are unable to pay their debts.

13.8.3 Treatment of assets on dissolution

Upon dissolution, the value of the partnership property is realised and the proceeds are applied in the following order:

- in paying debts to outsiders;
- in paying to the partners any advance made to the firm beyond their capital contribution; and
- in paying the capital contribution of the individual partners.

Any residue is divided between the partners in the same proportion as they shared in profits (s 44 of the PA 1890).

If the assets are insufficient to meet debts, partners' advances and capital repayments, then the deficiency has to be made good out of any profits held back from previous years, or out of partners' capital, or by the partners individually in the proportion to which they were entitled to share in profits.

An example will clarify this procedure. Partners A, B and C contribute £5,000, £3,000 and £1,000 respectively. In addition, A makes an advance to the firm of £1,000. Upon dissolution, the assets realise £8,000, and the firm has outstanding debts amounting to £2,500. The procedure is as follows:

> First, the creditors are paid what is due to them from the realised value of the assets. Thus, £8,000 − £2,500 = £5,500.
> Secondly, an advance of £1,000 is paid back, leaving £4,500.

Assuming that there was no agreement to the contrary, profits and losses will be shared equally. The actual loss is determined as follows:

Original capital:	£9,000
Minus money left:	<u>£4,500</u>
	£4,500

This loss of £4,500 has to be shared equally in this case. Each partner has to provide £1,500 in order to make good the shortfall in capital. In the case of A and B, this is a paper transaction, as the payment due is simply subtracted from their original capital contribution. C, however, actually has to make a contribution of £500 from his personal wealth, as his due payment exceeds his original capital. The outcome is as follows:

- A's share of net assets: £5,000 – £1,500 = £3,500
- B's share of net assets: £3,000 – £1,500 = £1,500
- C's share of net assets: £1,000 – £1,500 = £ –500

A provision in the partnership agreement for profits to be shared in proportion to capital contribution, that is, in the ratio 5:3:1, would have the following effect:

- A would contribute five-ninths of the £4,500 loss, that is, £2,500
- B would contribute three-ninths of the £4,500 loss, that is, £1,500
- C would contribute one-ninth of the £4,500 loss, that is, £500

Their shares in net assets would, therefore, be as follows:

- A: (£5,000 – £2,500) = £2,500
- B: (£3,000 – £1,500) = £1,500
- C: (£1,000 – £500) = £500

13.8.4 Bankruptcy of partners

Where a partner is bankrupt on the dissolution of a firm, the partnership assets are still used to pay partnership debts. It is only after the payment of partnership debts that any surplus due to that partner is made available for the payment of the partner's personal debts.

Where one partner is insolvent and there is a deficiency of partnership assets to repay the firm's creditors and any advances, the burden of making good the shortfall has to be borne by the solvent partners in proportion to their share in profits. If, however, the shortfall only relates to capital, then the situation is governed by the rule in *Garner v Murray* (1904). This rule means that, in any such situation, the solvent partners are not required to make good the capital deficiency due to the insolvency of their co-partner. However, as a consequence, there will be a shortfall in the capital fund, which has to be borne by the solvent partners in proportion to their capitals.

To return to the original example, the net assets were £4,500 and the capital deficiency was £4,500. All three partners were to contribute £1,500. In effect, C was the only one who actually had to pay out any money, since A and B merely suffered an abatement in the capital returned to them. However, if it is now assumed that C is insolvent and can make no contribution, the situation is as follows:

C loses his right of repayment, so this reduces the capital fund required to pay back partners' contributions to £8,000.

As previously, A and B contribute their portion of the total loss, taking the available capital fund up to £7,500 (that is, £4,500 + (2 × £1,500)).

There still remains a shortfall of £500. This is borne by A and B in proportion to their capital contribution. Thus, A suffers a loss of five-eighths of £500; and B suffers a loss of three-eighths of £500.

So, from the capital fund of £7,500 they receive the following:

- A: £5,000 – (5/8 × £500) = £4,687.50 (in reality, he or she simply receives £3,187.50);
- B: £3,000 – (3/8 × £500) = £2,812.50 (in reality, he or she simply receives £1,312.50).

13.9 Limited Liability Partnerships

As has already been seen, the main shortcoming with regard to the standard partnership is the lack of limited liability for its members: members have joint and several liability for the debts of their partnership to the full extent of their personal wealth. The risk of such unlimited liability is increased by the fact that, due to the nature of the partnership, all members can enter into contracts on behalf of the partnership, and is further compounded when the membership of the partnership is extensive, as it is in the case of many professional partnerships. The dangers inherent in such partnerships were revealed in the US in the early 1990s, with the collapse of the savings and loans system. Many firms of accountants and lawyers who had advised on such schemes found themselves being sued for negligence and the partners in those firms found themselves personally liable for extremely large amounts of debt, even though they had had absolutely nothing to do with the transaction in question. Whilst such firms of professionals were reluctant to incorporate and turn themselves into limited liability companies, they clearly saw the benefit of limiting the liability of the individual partners in relation to the misbehaviour of one of their fellow members. The LLP was the device for achieving the desired end of limiting claims for such vicarious liability (for a consideration of vicarious liability, see Chapter 14 below). It should be noted, however, that although the LLP was introduced to offer protection to the large scale professional firms, it is not in any way limited to them, and it is open to any type of partnership, no matter how small, no matter what their business, to register as an LLP.

The possibility of registering as an LLP was introduced into the UK in 2000 with the passage of the LLPA 2000, although the Act did not come into effect until April 2001. The Act itself was a remarkable example of enabling legislation, merely providing a general framework and leaving the details to be supplied by the Limited Liability Partnership Regulations (LLPR) 2001 (SI 2001/1090). Section 1 of the LLPA 2000 states quite clearly that the LLP is a new form of legal entity, but before going on to consider the LLP in detail, it has to be stated at the outset that the LLP is something of a hybrid legal form, seeking, as will be seen, to amalgamate the advantages of the company's corporate form with the flexibility of the partnership form. However, s 1(5) states categorically that:

> . . . except as far as otherwise provided by this Act . . . the law relating to partnerships does not apply to a limited liability partnership.

13.9.1 Legal personality and limited liability

Although called a partnership, the LLP is a corporation with a distinct legal existence apart from its members. As such, it has the ability to:

- hold property in its own right;
- create floating charges over its property;
- enter into contracts in its own name; and
- sue and be sued in its own name.

It also has perpetual succession and, consequently, alterations in its membership will not have any effect on its existence. Similarly, the death or personal insolvency of a member will not affect the existence of the LLP. Most importantly, however, the new legal entity allows its members to benefit from limited liability, in that they are not liable for more than the amount they have agreed to contribute to its capital. There is no minimum amount for such agreed capital contribution. (For a further consideration of these attributes of incorporation, see 14.2 below.)

13.9.2 Creation

In order to form an LLP, the appropriate form must be registered with the Registrar of Companies. The form must contain:

- the signatures of at least two persons who are associated for the purposes of carrying on a lawful business with a view to profit;
- the name of the LLP, which must end with the words 'Limited Liability Partnership' or the abbreviation 'LLP';
- the location of the LLP's registered office in England and Wales or in Scotland;
- the address of the registered office of the LLP;
- the names and addresses of those persons who will be members on the incorporation of the LLP and a statement whether some or all of them are to be designated members (see below); and
- a statement of compliance.

On registration of the company, the Registrar will issue a certificate of incorporation.

13.9.3 Membership

There must be a minimum of two members of the LLP. If the membership should fall below two for a period of six months, then the remaining member will lose their limited liability and will assume personal liability for any liabilities incurred during that period that the LLP cannot meet.

There is no maximum limit on membership. This is clearly indicative of the fact that LLPs were initially designed to offer limited liability to large-scale professional firms, at a time when ordinary trading partnerships were limited to 20 members. As has been stated previously the removal of the maximum limit was extended to all partnerships in 2002. However, as has been seen, the LLP form is in fact open to any partnership. Membership is not limited to individuals, and other incorporated bodies can be members of an LLP, as can other LLPs.

Within the LLP, there is a special type of membership, known as *designated membership*. As will be seen, such members are responsible for ensuring that the LLP conforms with its duty to file its accounts with the Registrar of Companies.

Becoming a member

Section 4(1) states that the original subscribers to the incorporation document are automatically members of the LLP. Other members may join with the agreement of the existing members (s 4(2)).

Ceasing to be a member

Under s 4(3), membership ceases on the occurrence of any of the following eventualities:

- death;
- dissolution (if the member is a corporation);
- on gaining the agreement of the other members; or
- after the giving of reasonable notice.

13.9.4 Disclosure requirements

Just as with limited companies, members of LLPs get the benefit of limited liability; equally, however, as with limited companies, such a benefit has to be paid for in the form of publicity and disclosure. People dealing with limited business are put on notice of that fact by the need to indicate their limited status in the names of the LLPs; this applies to both companies and LLPs. In addition, both are required to submit their accounts and some of their affairs to public scrutiny by filing them with the Registrar of Companies. In respect of LLPs, the essential filing requirements relate to:

- accounts;
- annual returns;
- changes in membership generally;
- changes in designated membership; and
- change to the registered office.

Accounts

The provisions that apply to limited companies with regard to auditing apply equally to LLPs, and therefore they will be required to submit properly audited accounts which give a true and fair view of the affairs of the LLP. However, the exemptions open to small and medium sized companies also apply to LLPs.

13.9.5 Relationship between members and the limited liability partnership

Section 6(1) provides that every member of the LLP is an agent of the LLP and, consequently, they will bind the LLP to any agreement entered into within the scope of their actual or apparent authority. However, the LLP will not be liable where the third party is aware of the lack of authority or does not know, or believe, that the other party is a member of the LLP. The LLP is also liable to the same extent as the member for any wrongful acts or omissions of individual members.

13.9.6 Relationship between members

Section 5 makes clear the intention to retain the flexible and consensual nature of the internal regulation of standard partnerships by providing that the mutual rights and duties of the members shall be governed 'by agreement between the members'. It is expected that LLPs will draw up specific agreements but, in the absence of any agreement, the default provisions of the LLPR 2001 will apply, which in turn are generally based on the previous rules set out in the PA 1890.

13.9.7 Relationship between members and third parties

As the LLP is a distinct legal person in its own right with full contractual capacity, it follows that there is usually no relationship between a member as agent and third parties who contract with the LLP as principal. However, it is possible that, as stated previously, the member may be personally liable for any wrongful act or omission, in which case he or she will consequently make the LLP equally liable.

13.9.8 Creditor protection

Members' liability is limited to the amount of capital introduced into the partnership. However, unlike limited companies, there are no controls on the withdrawal of capital by members, so creditors are not protected by the doctrine of capital maintenance. Creditors, however, are protected by the following general mechanisms:

- the requirement for LLPs to file audited accounts;
- the rules relating to fraud or misconduct under the IA 1986;

- actions to recover money from members in relation to misfeasance, fraudulent and wrongful trading and other potential compensatory provisions under the IA 1986 (see further 13.9.10 below); and
- the power to disqualify members.

13.9.9 Taxation

Although the LLP enjoys corporate status, it is not taxed as a separate entity from its members. Section 10 of the LLPA 2000 expressly provides that where a LLP carries on business with a view to profit, the members will be treated for the purposes of income tax, corporation tax and capital gains tax as if they were partners in a standard partnership. Thus, members of LLPs gain the benefits of limited liability whilst retaining the tax advantages of a partnership.

13.9.10 Insolvency and winding up

The LLPR 2001 extend the provisions relating to the insolvency and winding up of registered companies to LLPs. Thus, the relevant sections of the CA 1985, the IA 1986, the Company Directors Disqualification Act 1986 and the Financial Services and Markets Act 2000 have been appropriately modified to apply to LLPs.

Of particular interest are two alterations to the IA 1986. Section 1(4) of the LLPA 2000 merely stated that members of LLPs should have liability to contribute to its assets in the event of its winding up as 'is provided for by virtue of this Act'. The actual extent of that liability is established by a new s 74, introduced into the IA 1986 under the LLPR 2001.

The new section provides that:

> . . . when a limited liability partnership is wound up every present and past member of the limited liability partnership who has agreed with the other members or with the limited liability partnership that he will, in circumstances which have arisen, be liable to contribute to the assets of the limited liability partnership in the event that the limited liability partnership goes into liquidation is liable, to the extent that he has so agreed, to contribute to its assets to any amount sufficient for payment of its debts and liabilities, and the expenses of the winding up, and for the adjustment of the rights of the contributories among themselves.

Thus, it is a matter for the members to agree the level of their potential liability, which may be set at a nominal level, as there is no minimum level established in the section. Indeed, there is no compulsion for the members to agree to pay any debts of the LLP.

As has been stated previously, members of LLPs are subject to the usual controls exerted over company members in relation to their conduct in relation to their insolvent companies, such as actions for misfeasance, fraudulent trading and wrongful trading (see further 13.7 above). In addition to these, however, the LLPR 2001 introduce a new s 214A into the IA 1986, which allows a liquidator to recover assets from members who have previously withdrawn property from their LLP. This measure strengthens the degree of creditor protection and is necessary in the light of the lack of the capital maintenance provisions which apply to companies. Section 214A applies in the following circumstances:

- A member withdrew property from the LLP in the two years prior to the start of its winding up. The property may be in the form of a share of profits, salary, repayment or payment of interest on a loan to the limited liability partnership, or any other withdrawal of property.
- It can be shown that, at the time of the withdrawal, the member knew or had reasonable grounds to believe that the LLP:

a. was unable to pay its debts; or
b. became unable to pay its debts as a result of the withdrawal.

In deciding whether a person had reasonable grounds to believe in the continued solvency of the LLP, the court will apply a minimum objective test, based on what they ought to have known in their position, as well as a potentially more onerous subjective test – what they ought to have known, given their personal attributes.

Under s 214A, the court may declare that the person who made the withdrawal is liable to make such contribution (if any) to the LLP's assets as it thinks proper. However, the court cannot make a declaration which exceeds the aggregate of the amounts of all the withdrawals made by that person within the period of two years previously referred to.

Summary

Partnership Law

Definition of 'partnership'

- Section 1 of the Partnership Act 1890 states that partnership is the relation which subsists between persons carrying on a business in common with a view to profit.

The legal status of a partnership

- A partnership, unlike a joint stock company, has no separate legal personality apart from its members, although the limited liability partnership formed under the Limited Liability Partnership Regulations 2000 does have separate legal personality.
- Partnerships are generally limited to 20 members; however, certain professional partnerships are exempt from this maximum limit.

Formation of a partnership

- There are no specific legal requirements governing the formation of ordinary, no-limit partnerships. Partnerships arise from the agreement of the parties involved and are governed by the general principles of contract law.

Duties of partners

- General fiduciary duties.
- Sections 28–30 of the PA 1890 lay down the specific duties:
    - of disclosure;
    - to account; and
    - not to compete.

Rights of partners

Subject to express provision to the contrary in the partnership agreement, s 24 of the PA 1890 sets out the rights of partners. Among the most important of these are the rights:

- to share equally in the capital and profits of the business;
- to be indemnified by the firm for any liabilities incurred or payments made in the course of the firm's business;

- to take part in the management of the business;
- to have access to the firm's books;
- to prevent the admission of a new partner; and
- to prevent any change in the nature of the partnership business.

Partnership property

It is important to distinguish between partnership property and personal property for the following reasons:

- partnership property must be used exclusively for partnership purposes;
- any increase in the value of partnership property belongs to the partnership;
- any increase in the value of personal property belongs to the person who owns the property;
- on the dissolution of the firm, partnership property is used to pay debts before personal property;
- partnership and personal property are treated differently in the satisfaction of claims made by partnership creditors, as opposed to personal creditors; and
- on the death of a partner, any interest in partnership land will pass as personalty, whereas land owned personally will pass as realty.

The authority of partners to bind the firm

Authority can be actual or implied on the basis of the usual authority possessed by a partner in the particular line of business carried out by the firm.

Partners' liability on debts

Every partner is responsible for the full amount of the firm's liability. Outsiders have the choice of taking action against:

- the firm collectively; or
- against the individual partners.

Where damages are recovered from one partner only, the other partners are under a duty to contribute equally to the amount paid.

Partnership by estoppel

Failure to give notice of retirement is one way in which liability arises on the basis of estoppel or holding out. Alternatively, anyone who represents themselves, or knowingly permits themselves to be represented, as a partner is liable to any person who gives the partnership credit on the basis of that representation.

Dissolution

Grounds for dissolution are:

- the expiry of a fixed term or the completion of a specified enterprise;
- the giving of notice;
- the death or bankruptcy of any partner;
- where a partner's share becomes subject to a charge;
- illegality;
- where a partner becomes a patient under the Mental Health Act 1983;
- where a partner suffers some other permanent incapacity;
- where a partner engages in activity prejudicial to the business;

- where a partner persistently breaches the partnership agreement;
- where the business can only be carried on at a loss; and
- where it is just and equitable to do so.

Winding up

Since the introduction of the Insolvency Act 1986, partnerships as such are not subject to bankruptcy. Partnerships may be wound up as unregistered companies under Pt V of the Insolvency Act 1986.

Treatment of assets on dissolution

On dissolution, the value of the partnership property is applied in the following order:

- in paying debts to outsiders;
- in paying to the partners any advance made to the firm beyond their capital contribution;
- in paying the capital contribution of the individual partners; and
- any residue is divided between the partners in the same proportion as they shared in profits.

Limited liability partnerships

The Limited Liability Partnership Act 2000, together with the Limited Liability Partnership Regulations 2001, provides for a new form of business entity, the limited liability partnership. Although stated to be a partnership, the new form is a corporation, with a distinct legal existence apart from its members. As such, it will have the ability:

- to hold property in its own right; and
- to sue and be sued in its own name.

It will have perpetual succession and, consequently, alterations in its membership will not have any effect on its existence.

Most importantly, however, the new legal entity will allow its members to benefit from limited liability, in that they will not be liable for more than the amount they have agreed to contribute to its capital.

Formation

To form a limited liability partnership:

- two or more persons must subscribe to an incorporation document;
- the incorporation document must be delivered to the Companies' Registry; and
- a statement of compliance must be completed by a solicitor or subscriber to the incorporation document.

The incorporation document must include:

- the name of the limited liability partnership (subject to restrictions);
- the address of the registered office;
- the names and addresses of those who will be members on incorporation of the limited liability partnership; and
- the names of at least two designated members whose duty it is to ensure that the administrative and filing duties of the LLP are complied with. If no such members are designated, then all members will be assumed to be designated members.

Regulation between members

The rights and duties of members will be governed by any agreement entered into. In the absence of any agreement, the default provisions of the Limited Liability Partnership Regulations 2001 will apply. These default rules are based on the previous rules set out in the Partnership Act 1890.

Section 6 of the Limited Liability Partnership Act 2000 provides that every member of the limited liability partnership is an agent of the limited liability partnership rather than a principal, and agent of the other members, as in an ordinary partnership. The extent of such authority is subject to the usual agency rules.

Liability and creditor protection

Members' liability is limited to the amount of capital introduced into the partnership. However, unlike limited companies, there are no controls on the withdrawal of capital by members, so creditors are not protected by the doctrine of capital maintenance. Creditors are protected by the following general mechanisms:

- the requirement for limited liability partnerships to file audited accounts; and
- the rules relating to fraud or misconduct under the Insolvency Act 1986.

Insolvency and winding up

The Limited Liability Partnership Regulations 2001 extended the provisions relating to the insolvency and winding up of registered companies to limited liability partnerships. Subsequently, the relevant sections of the Companies Act 2006, the Insolvency Act 1986, the Company Directors Disqualification Act 1986 and the Financial Services and Markets Act 2000 have been appropriately modified to apply to limited liability partnerships.

Further Reading

Banks, R, *Lindley and Banks on Partnership*, 19th edn, 2010, London: Sweet & Maxwell

Berry, E, *Partnership and LLP Law*, 2010, London: Wildy, Simmonds and Hill Publishing

Morse, G, *Partnership Law*, 7th edn, 2010, Oxford: OUP

Chapter 14

Company Law (1): The Nature and Formation of Companies

Chapter Contents

Law in Context: The Nature and Formation of Companies

This chapter focuses on registered companies, with the key difference between a partnership and a constituted company being that the constituted company has its own legal personality. This raises the importance of shareholders, and ensures that shareholders are genuine, for example by limiting all shareholders to the amount of investment made. As you read through, you will understand the benefits and limitations of incorporation, and how these support the continuation of the business. There are different types of businesses – public, private, limited and unlimited, even charitable incorporated organisations, and each is considered, with their differences explored. For example, the difference between private and public companies is that if a private company is limited by shares, then it cannot offer its shares to the public (such as through the stock exchange), shareholding usually being confined to a limited number of people. Only public companies can offer their shares to the public, and these companies are listed on the stock exchange. There may be occasions when the structure and ownership of the company need to be understood in greater detail, referred to as 'lifting the veil of incorporation'. This 'lifting' enables a judge to examine the structure and ownership in greater detail, to determine the company and its members. This is a restricted practice, and is only undertaken as part of a legal process. Towards the end of the chapter is an overview of the Nuttall Review 2013. The Nuttall Review made a set of recommendations based around employee ownership, and how employees can play a bigger role in the company's management. This has led to a number of government proposals on greater consultations and opportunities for employees to purchase shares as part of their employment package. As you progress through the chapter, think about companies which you know, and apply the principles you read about.

14.1 Introduction

This chapter deals with the formation and regulation of the most common alternative form of business association to the partnership, namely, the registered company. The flexibility of the company form of organisation is shown by the fact that it is used by businesses of widely different sizes and needs, from the one-person business to the transnational corporation. In fact, the register of all companies shows that the overwhelming number (now more than 99%) are, in fact, private companies which may be seen as sole traders, or partnerships which have assumed the legal form of the registered company (see 14.3.2 below).

As yet, it is too early to estimate the final impact of the availability of the limited liability partnership (LLP) form (see 13.9 above), but in spite of the growth in the number of LLPs, there are currently just over 50,000 in the UK, it is evident that the private company form remains overwhelmingly the most popular business form. This popularity has no doubt been increased by the overt intention of the previous Government to reduce the legal regulation of such businesses, an intention manifested in the major relaxation of control over private companies introduced by the Companies Act 2006.

The Companies Act (CA) 2006 is the major general legislation governing company law, although chapter 14 of the Companies Act 1985, covering company investigations, is still in force (see 15.11.3). There are, however, other Acts that govern specific aspects of company law, such as the Insolvency Act (IA) 1986, the Company Directors Disqualification Act (CDDA) 1986, the Criminal Justice Act (CJA) 1993, which covers insider dealing and the Corporate Manslaughter and Corporate Homicide Act 2007. There are also numerous regulations that apply to corporate control as well as non-statutory regulations such as the code on corporate governance, which have to be referred to. In this chapter, if no reference is made to any specific Act, then it can be assumed that reference is to the CA 2006. All other Acts or regulations will be specifically named.

14.2 Corporations and their Legal Characteristics

Partnerships may trade as, for example, 'J Smith and Co', but the use of the term 'company' in this instance does not mean that such a business is to be understood, or treated in the same way, as a company registered under the companies legislation. In terms of legal form, companies differ from partnerships, in that they are bodies corporate or corporations. In other words, they have a legal existence in their own right, apart from, and independent of, their members. Such is not the case with respect to ordinary partnerships, although limited liability partnerships have been granted the privilege of incorporation.

14.2.1 Types of corporation

Corporations can be created in one of four ways, which are as follows:

- *By grant of royal charter*
  Such corporations are governed mainly by the common law. The very earliest trading companies were created by royal charter, but this was essentially in order to secure monopoly privileges from the Crown, which could not be given to individuals. Nowadays, this method of incorporation tends to be restricted to professional, educational and charitable institutions and is not used in relation to business enterprises. It should be noted that the regime for the regulation of the press, following the Leveson inquiry, is proposed to be established by way of royal charter.
- *By special Act of Parliament*
  Such bodies are known as statutory corporations, although this method of incorporation was the only alternative to charters before the introduction of registration and was common during the 19th century. This was particularly true in relation to railway and public utility companies, which usually required powers of compulsory purchase of land. It is not greatly used nowadays, and certainly not by ordinary trading companies.
- *By registration under the Companies Acts*
  Since 1844, companies have been permitted to acquire the status of a corporation simply by complying with the requirements for registration set out in general Acts of Parliament. This is the method by which the great majority of trading enterprises are incorporated. The current legislation is the CA 2006.
- *By registration under the Limited Liability Partnership Act* (LLPA) 2000
  As has already been seen at 13.9 above, LLPs are granted the privilege of incorporation on registration with the Companies' Registry.

14.2.2 The doctrine of separate personality

English law, unlike continental or Scots law, treats the ordinary partnership simply as a group of individuals trading collectively. The effect of incorporation, however, is that a company, once formed, has its own distinct legal personality, separate from its members.

The doctrine of separate, or corporate, personality is an ancient one and may be found in Roman law. An early example of its application in relation to English business law can be seen in *Salmon v The Hamborough Co* (1671). That being said, the usual case cited in relation to separate personality is *Salomon v Salomon & Co* (1897).

❖ KEY CASE *Salomon v Salomon & Co* (1897)

Facts:

Salomon had been in the boot and leather trade for some time. Together with other members of his family, he formed a limited company and sold his previous business to it. Payment was in the form of cash, shares and debentures (the latter is loan stock which gives the holder priority over unsecured creditors if the company is wound up; see 14.6.7 below). When the company was eventually wound up, it was argued that Salomon and the company were the same and, as he could not be his own creditor, Salomon's debentures should have no effect.

Decision:

Although previous courts had decided against Salomon, the House of Lords held that, under the circumstances, in the absence of fraud, his debentures were valid. The company had been properly constituted and, consequently, it was, in law, a distinct legal person, completely separate from Salomon.

It is important to note that, contrary to what some, if not most, textbooks state, the *Salomon* case did not establish the doctrine of separate personality. It merely permitted its application to one-man and private companies (see 14.3.2 below).

Following the European Community's 12th Directive on Company Law (89/667), which was enacted in the UK in the form of the Companies (Single Member Private Limited Companies) Regulations 1992 (SI 1992/1699), provision was made for the establishment of true one-person companies. Those Regulations permitted the incorporation of private limited companies by one person and with only one member and, subsequently, the CA 2006 removed the general requirement for there to be at least two members to form a company. The specific requirements relating to one-person companies are set out in s 123. As a matter of interest, it should be noted that the LLPA 2000 does not permit individuals to register as an LLP as, by definition, a partnership involves more than one person.

14.2.3 The effects of incorporation

A number of consequences flow from the fact that corporations are treated as having legal personality in their own right, separate from their members, as follows:

- *Limited liability*

  No one is responsible for anyone else's debts unless they agree to accept such responsibility. Similarly, at common law, members of a corporation are not responsible for its debts without agreement. However, registered companies, that is, those formed under the various Companies Acts, are not permitted unless the shareholders agree to accept liability for their company's debts. In return for this agreement, the extent of their liability is normally set at a fixed amount. In the case of a company limited by shares, the level of liability is the amount remaining unpaid on the nominal value of the shares held. In the case of a company limited by guarantee, it is the amount that shareholders have agreed to pay in the event of the company being wound up. It is possible for companies to register as unlimited, in which case the shareholders are liable for the full extent for the debts of the company. In such instances the unlimited company is exempted, under s 448, from the duty of filing annual accounts with the registry.
- *Perpetual succession*

  As the corporation exists in its own right, changes in its membership have no effect on its status or existence. In contrast to the partnership, members of companies may die or be declared bankrupt or insane without any effect on the company. More importantly, however, members may transfer their shares to a third party without having any effect on the continuation of the business. In public limited companies, and certainly those listed on the stock exchange, freedom to transfer shares is unrestricted, although it is common for some restrictions to be placed on the transferability of shares in private companies (this is merely one of the many legal differences between the two forms of company, which reflects their essential difference as economic forms; see 14.3.2 below). As an abstract legal person, the company cannot die, although its existence can be brought to an end through the winding up procedure (see 15.7 below).

- *Business property is owned by the company*
  The company itself, not the shareholders, owns any business assets. This is normally a major advantage, in that the company's assets are not subject to claims based on the ownership rights of its members. It can, however, cause unforeseen problems.

❖ KEY CASE *Macaura v Northern Assurance* (1925)

Facts:
The plaintiff owned a timber estate. He later formed a one-man company and transferred the estate to it. He continued to insure the estate in his own name. When the timber was lost in a fire Macaura claimed against his insurance policy.

Decision:
It was held that Macaura could not claim on the insurance, since he had no personal interest in the timber, which belonged to the company.

What the member owns is a number of shares in the company. The precise nature of the share will be considered below (see 14.6.1 below).

- *The company has contractual capacity in its own right and can sue and be sued in its own name*
  The nature and extent of a company's contractual capacity will be considered in detail later (see 14.5.1 below). For the moment, it should be noted that contracts are entered into in the company's name and it is liable on any such contracts. The extent of the company's liability, as opposed to the members' liability, is unlimited, and all of its assets may be used to pay off debts. As a corollary of this, the members of the board of directors are the agents of the company. Members as such are not agents of the company; they have no right to be involved in the day-to-day operation of the business and they cannot bind the company in any way. This lack of power on the part of the members is one of the key differences between the registered company and the partnership, as partners have the express power to bind the partnership (s 5 of the Partnership Act 1890). However, members of private, quasi-partnership companies may have a legitimate expectation to be involved in the management of their company and may take action under s 994 of the CA 2006 to remedy any exclusion from the management.
- *Liability in crime and tort*
  Certain offences can be committed without regard to the mental element (*mens rea*) normally required for the commission of a crime, that is, guilty intention. Companies may be liable in relation to such strict liability offences. The situation, however, is less clear in relation to the potential liability of companies in relation to offences, which normally do require the presence of the necessary degree of *mens rea*. It is immediately obvious that, as an artificial, rather than a real legal, person, a company cannot have any *mens rea*. However, in certain circumstances, the

mens rea of the company's servants or agents may be ascribed to the company in order to make it liable for a particular criminal offence. In *Tesco Supermarkets v Nattrass* (1971), it was held that the *mens rea* of minor employees or agents could not normally be imputed to the company, and that to make the company liable the *mens rea* had to be presented by someone, such as a director, who could be said to be the embodiment of the company. This requirement made it particularly difficult for successful cases of manslaughter to be brought against large companies (*R v P& O European Ferries (Dover) Ltd* (1990)), although such a charge was successfully used in relation to a small private company, where the director was directly involved in the day-to-day operation of the business (*R v Kite and OLL Ltd* (1994)). In response to this perceived failure, the Corporate Manslaughter and Corporate Homicide Act 2007 was, belatedly, introduced and came into force in April 2008. The Act introduced the new offence of corporate killing, where the behaviour of the company causing the death is a result of failure in its management or organisation.

See Chapter 10 →

Companies, like other employers, are vicariously liable for the torts of their employees.

- *The rule in Foss v Harbottle* (1843)
  This states that where a company suffers an injury, it is for the company, acting through the majority of the members, to take the appropriate remedial action. Perhaps of more importance is the corollary of the rule, which is that an individual cannot raise an action in response to a wrong suffered by the company (exceptions to the rule in *Foss v Harbottle*, both at common law and under statute, will be considered in detail at 15.6 below).

Contemporary company lawyers explain the foregoing attributes as being the consequence of, and see them as following from, the doctrine of separate personality. It is possible, however, to reverse the causality contained in such conventional approaches. As a result, it may be suggested that the doctrine of separate personality, as we now know it, is itself the product, rather than the cause, of these various attributes, which were recognised and developed independently by the courts.

14.2.4 Lifting the veil of incorporation

There are a number of occasions, both statutory and at common law, when the doctrine of separate personality will not be followed. On these occasions, it is said that the veil of incorporation, which separates the company from its members, is pierced, lifted or drawn aside, and the members are revealed and made responsible for the actions of the company.

Such situations arise in the following circumstances:

- *Under the companies legislation*
  Section 399 CA 2006 requires consolidated accounts to be prepared by a group of related companies. In relation to the name of companies, officers may be personally liable if they fail to use their company's full name or fail to make any other required disclosures as required by regulations made by the Secretary of State (ss 82–85 CA 2006). Section 213 of the IA 1986 provides for personal liability in relation to fraudulent trading. Section 214 does the same in relation to wrongful trading (see 14.7.6 below). And, as has already been seen, the new s 214A, introduced into the IA 1986 by the LLPR 2001, operates in a similar way with regard to LLPs.
- *At common law*
  As in most areas of law that are based on the application of policy decisions, it is difficult to predict with any certainty when the courts will ignore separate personality. What is certain is that the courts will not permit the corporate form to be used for a clearly fraudulent purpose or to evade a legal duty. In such instances, the courts tend to refer to the company using terms

such as sham, cloak and mask, and ignore it in order to fix ultimate responsibility on the person who tries to hide behind it.

❖ KEY CASE *Gilford Motor Co Ltd v Horne* (1933)

Facts:
An employee had entered into a contractual agreement not to solicit his former employers' customers. After he left their employment, he formed a company to solicit those customers.

Decision:
It was held that the company was a sham and the court would not permit it to be used to avoid the prior contract.

As would be expected, the courts are prepared to ignore separate personality in times of war to defeat the activity of shareholders who might be enemy aliens. See *Daimler Co Ltd v Continental Tyre and Rubber Co (GB) Ltd* (1917).

Where groups of companies have been set up for particular business ends, the courts will not usually ignore the separate existence of the various companies, unless they are being used for fraud. *Adams v Cape Industries plc* (1990) is a particularly strong example of this approach. In that case, it was held that an award made in relation to asbestos-related injuries against a company in the US could not be enforced against the UK parent company. The basis for the decision was the doctrine of separate personality, even though it might have appeared that the company structure had been deliberately set up to avoid such a claim. Such ingenuity was not fraud.

There is authority for treating separate companies as a single group, as in *DHN Food Distributors Ltd v Borough of Tower Hamlets* (1976), but later authorities have cast extreme doubt on this decision and, although it has never been overruled, it is probably true to say that it is no longer an accurate statement of the law (see *Woolfson v Strathclyde Regional Council* (1978); *National Dock Labour Board v Pinn and Wheeler Ltd* (1989); and *Adams v Cape Industries plc*).

However, the single entity doctrine may be seen still to apply as regards breaches of European Union competition law. In *Cooper Tire & Rubber Company Europe Ltd & Ors v Dow Deutschland Inc & Ors* (2010) the Court of appeal held that, once the European Commission had found that an *undertaking*, made up of perhaps many individual constituent companies, had been found to be engaging in anti-competitive practices, the undertaking as a whole, or the parent company in the group undertaking were liable for such practices. Thus in such circumstances the doctrine of separate personality could not be relied upon to avoid the consequences of a decision of anti-competitive activity being visited on other members of the undertaking. As Longmore LJ explained:

> In English domestic law, which proceeds on the basis that corporate bodies are all separate legal personalities, one cannot say that the act of one company in a group of companies, all controlled by a holding company, is automatically the act of any other company in that group. The position in EU law is, however, different at least in the area of competition law and alleged breaches of Article 81 of the EC Treaty. What concerns EU law is the activity of 'undertakings' which may comprise a number of separate corporate entities. The question under Article 81 is whether an 'undertaking' has participated in anti-competitive practices and it will not avail the undertaking to say that because a corporate entity which is part of the undertaking is a party to anti-competitive practices, either the undertaking as a whole or a parent company in the group did not participate in those practices. Otherwise evasion of Article 81 would be too easy. Since,

> however, the Commission, in deciding whether to exact penalties for anti-competitive behaviour, has to find corporate entities on which to impose such fines, liability has to be imposed on a particular entity in the undertaking. As the Commission wants to identify an entity with an ability to pay, it will normally wish to fine a parent company in addition to any relevant subsidiaries and the European Court has evolved a concept of what may be called presumptive decisive influence if a subsidiary company is effectively controlled by a parent company.

At one time, it appeared that the courts were increasingly willing to use and extend their essential discretionary power in such a way as to achieve results they considered right. However, in *Ord v Bellhaven Pubs Ltd* (1998), Hobhouse LJ expressed what appears to be the contemporary reluctance of the courts to ignore separate personality simply to achieve what might be considered a subjectively fair decision. In overturning the decision at first instance, and at the same time overruling *Creasey v Breachwood Motors* (1993), he stated that:

> The approach of the judge in the present case was simply to look at the economic unit, to disregard the distinction between the legal entities that were involved and then to say: since the company cannot pay, the shareholders who are the people financially interested should be made to pay instead. That, of course, is radically at odds with the whole concept of corporate personality and limited liability and [from] the decision of the House of Lords in *Salomon v Salomon and Co Ltd* it is clear that . . . there must be some impropriety before the corporate veil can be pierced.

This more restrictive use of the court's power to pierce the corporate veil was continued by the Supreme Court in *VTB Capital Plc v Nutritek International Corp* (2012), where it rejected an invitation to extend the practice. As Lord Neuberger explained:

> On the assumption that the court can pierce the corporate veil on appropriate facts, VTB's case involves an extension to the circumstances where it has traditionally been held that the corporate veil can be pierced . . . This extension would mean that the person controlling the company could be held liable as if he had been a co-contracting party with the company concerned to a contract where the company was a party but he was not, and where neither he nor any of the contracting parties intended him to be.

The court agreed that such an extension would be contrary to authority and contrary to principle. In reaching that decision Lord Neuberger cast doubt on the earlier decision in *Kensington International Ltd v Republic of Congo* (2005).

The Supreme Court further considered the doctrine of separate personality in *Prest v Petrodel Resources Ltd* (2013). The proceedings related to financial remedies following a divorce. In her application against her former husband, Mrs Prest joined five companies that she claimed were merely devices for concealing her husband's assets. At first instance it was held that the corporate veil separating Prest from his companies could not be pierced at common law but was capable of being pierced by statute, viz s 24(1)(a) Matrimonial Causes Act (MCA) 1973.

The Court of Appeal subsequently overturned the order; the majority holding that s 24 MCA could not be used to make an order in respect of company property unless there were legitimate grounds to pierce the corporate veil, which was not the case in this instance. In the view of Patten LJ, the Family Division had developed 'an approach to company owned assets in ancillary relief applications which amounts almost to a separate system of legal rules unaffected by the relevant principles of English property and company law'. He maintained that it was not open to the judiciary to lift the veil where 'justice requires', and that such behaviour should cease.

The leading judgment in the Supreme Court was delivered by Lord Sumption, although it cannot be said that his analysis met with the unanimous approval of the other justices. In any event, it was held that the courts could not disregard the corporate veil by using s 24(1)(a) MCA 1973. However, on the facts of the case, it was held that the assets of Petrodel were held by the company on a resulting trust for the husband. As a result they were available to satisfy any financial provision ordered against the husband in favour of the wife.

In the course of his judgment, Lord Sumption rejected the previous 'façade' or 'sham' test for ignoring the separate personality of a company, in favour of a two-pronged analysis. Thus he distinguished the *concealment principle*, which involves the interposition of one or more companies to conceal the identity of real actors. In such circumstances, the court simply looks behind the company and will find the controller liable. In the view of Lord Sumption this does not involve piercing the corporate veil; rather it is more appropriate to describe it as 'lifting' the veil.

However in the second instance, engaging what he referred to as the *evasion principle*, where a legal right or liability exists against a person, and that individual looks to hide behind a company to avoid the application of that right or the enforcement of the liability. In such circumstance the court will hold the company liable, and only action such as this can accurately be referred to as piercing the corporate veil. Thus it can be seen that the essential feature of Sumption's evasion principle is that the liability being avoided has to arise independently of the company.

Following this line of reasoning Mrs Prest's claim had to fail, as the corporate structure had been set up before the marriage breakdown and the corporate ownership of the assets had been established for genuine business reasons and had not been used simply to avoid his liability to her.

In conclusion it should be pointed out that, according to Lord Sumption, in most cases the facts necessary to establish circumstances for piercing the veil will also be sufficient to establish a legal relationship between the company and its controller such as to establish equitable rights of the controller over the company's property, thus making it unnecessary to pierce the veil in any case. However, rather than eradicating the concept of piercing the corporate veil, Lord Sumption preferred to maintain its restricted sphere of application for that small minority of special cases in which an appropriate remedy could only be provided by ignoring the separate personality of the company concerned. Given the other judgments in *Prest*, whether Lord Sumption's analysis is accepted, applied and developed in the future remains to be seen. For the moment, all that can be stressed is the reluctance of the courts to ignore the rules of separate personality.

14.3 Types of Companies

Although the distinction between public and private companies is probably the most important, there are a number of ways in which companies can be classified.

14.3.1 Limited and unlimited companies

One of the major advantages of forming a company is limited liability, but companies can be formed without limited liability. Such companies receive all the benefits that flow from incorporation, except limited liability, but, in return, they do not have to submit their accounts or make them available for public inspection.

The great majority of companies, however, are limited liability companies. This means, as explained above, that the maximum liability of shareholders is fixed and cannot be increased without their agreement. There are two ways of establishing limited liability:

- *By shares*
  This is the most common procedure. It limits liability to the amount remaining unpaid on shares held. If the shareholder has paid the full nominal value of the shares, plus any premium

that might be due to the company, then that is the end of their responsibility with regard to company debts. So, even if the company goes into insolvent liquidation with insufficient assets to pay its creditors, the individual shareholder cannot be required to make any further contribution to its funds.

- *By guarantee*
  This type of limited liability is usually restricted to non-trading enterprises such as charities and professional and educational bodies. It limits liability to an agreed amount, which is only called on if the company cannot pay its debts on being wound up. In reality, the sum guaranteed is usually a nominal sum, so no real risk is involved on the part of the guarantor.

14.3.2 Public and private companies

Rather oddly, previous legislation defined the public company in relation to the private company. The current legislation, however, makes the public limited company (PLC) the essential form, with the private company as the exceptional form. Thus, s 4 CA 2006 defines a private company as any company which is not a public company and a public company as essentially a company:

(a) whose certificate of incorporation states that it is a public company; and
(b) in relation to which the appropriate registration requirements have been complied with.

The essential difference between these two forms is an economic one, although different legal rules have been developed to apply to each of them, as follows:

- *Private companies*
  Private companies tend to be small-scale enterprises, owned and operated by a small number of individuals who are actively involved in the day-to-day running of the enterprise. Outsiders do not invest in such companies and, indeed, private companies are precluded from offering their shares to the public at large. Their shares are not quoted on any share market, and in practice tend not to be freely transferable, with restrictions being placed on them in the company's articles of association. Many such companies – and they make up the vast majority of registered companies – are sole traders or partnerships which have registered as companies in order to take advantage of limited liability. When limited liability was made available to registered companies in 1855 and under the later CA 1862, it was clearly not intended that it should be open to partnerships or individuals. Nonetheless, it became apparent that such businesses could acquire the benefit of limited liability by simply complying with the formal procedures of the CA 1862, and a great many businesses converted to limited companies. The legal validity of such private companies was clearly established only in the House of Lords' decision in *Salomon v Salomon & Co* (1897), but since then the courts and the legislature have developed specific rules governing their operation.

  As the White Paper that preceded the enactment of the Companies Act 2006 stated, one of its four objectives was better regulation through 'a think small first approach', it is hardly surprising that the Act heralded a regime of even less rigorous control for the private company regime than had operated previously. The details of these changes will be considered in detail throughout the remainder of this and the following chapter.
- *Public limited companies*
  Public companies, on the other hand, tend to be large and are controlled by directors and managers rather than the shareholders. This division is sometimes referred to as the separation of ownership and control. These public companies are essentially a source of investment for their shareholders and have freely transferable shares which may be quoted on the stock exchange.

As a consequence of the difference with regard to ownership and control, many of the provisions of the companies' legislation, which are designed to protect the interests of shareholders in public companies, are not applicable, or indeed appropriate, to private companies.

It may also be suggested that, in cases involving private limited companies, which the courts view as quasi-partnerships, other general company law principles are applied less rigorously, or not at all. See, for example, *Ebrahimi v Westbourne Galleries Ltd* (1973) (otherwise known as *Re Westbourne Galleries*), where the court seemed to play down the effect of separate personality in such instances. Consider also *Clemens v Clemens Bros Ltd* (1976), over which much ink has been spilled in trying to establish a general rule concerning the duties owed by majority to minority shareholders. The reality is that there was no general principle that could be applied: the case merely reflects the courts' willingness to treat what they see as quasi-partnerships in an equitable manner. What is certain about the *Clemens* case is that it would find no application in public limited companies.

As a consequence of the difference with regard to ownership and control, many of the provisions of the companies' legislation, which are designed to protect the interests of shareholders in public companies, are not applicable to private companies. Previously, the inappropriateness of rules designed to regulate public companies being applied to private companies was dealt with by exempting private companies from the strict application of those rules and permitting private companies effectively to operate an elective system, by giving them the power to decide to apply rules or to opt out of them. However, as a result of the deregulatory approach to private companies effected by the Companies Act 2006, many of the rules simply do not apply to them. Consequently the previous elective regime has become the default for private companies.

The previous edition of this book cited a large number of specific exemptions available to private companies; the Companies Act 2006 has simply removed the majority of these although Pt 20 of the Act emphasises two essential distinctions; that:

- private companies cannot offer their shares to the public (s 755);
- public companies cannot start business without a trading certificate (s 761).

However, a few of the previous distinctions still operate, even if they do so as rules only applying to public companies rather than as rules applying to companies generally, with potential exemptions to private companies. Thus:

- Public companies must have at least two directors, whereas private companies need only have one.
- Public companies are required to appoint a company secretary, whereas private companies are no longer required to appoint one.
- Public companies must have a minimum issued capital of £50,000, which must be paid up to the extent of 25%. There is no such requirement in relation to private companies (see further at 14.6 below).
- The requirement to keep accounting records is shorter for private companies – three years, as opposed to six years for public companies.
- Private companies may also dispense with the need to appoint auditors annually, and to lay accounts before a general meeting.
- The controls over distribution of dividend payments are relaxed in relation to private companies.
- Private companies may purchase their own shares out of capital, whereas public companies are strictly forbidden from doing so.
- Private companies can provide financial assistance for the purchase of their own shares where public companies cannot.

- There are fewer and looser controls over directors in private companies with regard to their financial dealings with their companies than there are in public companies.
- Private companies are not required to call specific Annual General meetings (AGMs), although this remains a requirement of PLCs (s 336 CA 2006).

Many of the above issues will be dealt with in more detail below but, for the moment, it might be pointed out that there is much to be said for the suggestion that private limited companies should be removed from the ambit of the general companies' legislation and be given their own particular legislation. It is apparent that they are not the same as public companies and cannot be expected to submit to the same regulatory regime as applies to the latter. In practice, the law recognises this, but only in a roundabout way, by treating them as exceptions to the general law relating to public companies. The argument, however, is that they are not exceptions; they are completely different, and this difference should be clearly recognised by treating them as a legal form *sui generis*. The Companies Act 2006 has effectively recognised this distinction, but without actually separating the legislation dealing with either form of business of enterprise.

14.3.3 Community interest companies

Part 2 of the Companies (Audit, Investigations and Community Enterprise) Act 2004 introduced the possibility of establishment of a new corporate vehicle, the 'community interest company' (CIC). As is evident in the title, the new form was intended to make it simpler and more convenient to establish a business whose profits and assets are to be used for the benefit of the community. There is a statutory 'lock' on the profits and financial assets of CICs and, where a CIC is limited by shares, power to impose a 'cap' on any dividend. Companies wishing to become a CIC are required to pass a community interest test and to produce an annual report showing that they have contributed to community interest aims. An independent regulator is responsible for approving the registration of CICs and ensuring they comply with their legal requirements. The regulator has powers to obtain information from CICs, to appoint, suspend or remove CIC directors, to make orders in respect of the property of CICs, to apply to the court for a CIC to be wound up and to set the dividend cap. The CIC is specifically recognised in s 4 CA 2006.

14.3.4 The charitable incorporated organisation

The possibility of this form of incorporated organisation was established in Charities Act 2006 and given effect towards the end of 2012 (SI 2012/3012). The Charitable Incorporated Organisation (CIO) is similar to a company limited by guarantee, the form previously most frequently used by charities. As such it is a legal entity in its own right and allows its members to benefit from the protection of limited liability. However, unlike the private company limited by guarantee, the CIO is not subject to the administrative control of Companies House, but is created by registering with the Charity Commission, to which body it files its accounts and documents. As a result the previous need for dual registration and filing is avoided.

14.3.5 Parent and subsidiary companies

This description of companies relates to the way in which large business enterprises tend to operate through a linked structure of distinct companies. Each of these companies exists as a separate corporate entity in its own right but, nonetheless, the group is required to be treated as a single entity in relation to the group accounting provisions under s 399 CA 2006.

Section 1159 CA 2006 states that one company, S, is a subsidiary of another company, H, its holding company, in any of the following circumstances:

- where H holds a majority of voting rights in S;
- where H is a member of S and has a right to appoint or remove a majority of its board of directors;
- where H is a member of S and controls a majority of the voting rights in it; or
- where S is a subsidiary of a company which is in turn a subsidiary of H.

Section 1162, which relates to the relationship of parent and subsidiary companies, defines the relationship in a similar way but introduces the additional idea of the parent exercising a dominant influence over the subsidiary company.

14.3.6 Small, medium and large companies

Companies can be categorised in relation to their size. Small and medium sized companies are subjected to relaxation in relation to the submission of accounts under ss 444 and 445 CA 2006. Which category a company fits into depends on its turnover, balance sheet valuation and number of employees.

A small company must satisfy two of the following requirements:

- Turnover not more than £6.5 million.
- Balance sheet not more than £3.26 million.
- Employees not more than 50.

A medium sized company must satisfy two of the following requirements:

- Turnover not more than £25.9 million.
- Balance sheet not more than £12.9 million.
- Employees not more than 250.

It should be remembered that, as discussed at 14.2.2 above, it is now open to individuals to form companies, and the companies' legislation will apply, subject to appropriate alterations.

14.3.7 Overseas companies

Part 34 of the CA 2006 relates to what are known as overseas companies, and these are defined in s 1044 as companies incorporated elsewhere than in the United Kingdom but which have a place of business in this country. Such companies are required to maintain an address within the jurisdiction, at which all official communications can be served. Overseas companies are also required to register copies of their constitutional documents and to submit their accounts in the same way as domestic companies.

14.4 Formation of Companies

The CA 2006 establishes a strict procedure with which companies have to comply before they can operate legally. Those responsible for, or who actually undertake, the process of formation are called promoters.

14.4.1 Promoters

There is no general statutory definition of a promoter in company law and the courts have not given a comprehensive judicial definition. In *Twycross v Grant* (1877) Cockburn CJ defined a promoter as

'. . . one who undertakes to form a company with reference to a given project and to see it going, and who takes the necessary steps to accomplish that purpose'. In *Whaley Bridge Calico Printing Co v Green* (1880) Bowen L described the term promoter as 'a term not of law but of business, usefully summing up in a single word a number of business operations, familiar to the commercial world, by which a company is generally brought into existence'.

The consequence of the above two statements is that the answer to the question of whether a person is a promoter or not is a question of fact and the determining factor is whether the individual in question will be a person who exercises some control over the affairs of the company both before and after it is formed up until the process of formation is completed. The following are typical acts which promoters perform – taking the procedural steps necessary to form a company, inviting other persons to become directors and issuing a prospectus. A person is not to be treated as a promoter of a company simply on the basis that they act in a professional capacity with respect to the establishment of a company. Thus solicitors and accountants employed purely in their professional capacity in order to establish a company will not be considered to be promoters.

As with directors, so promoters are said to be in a fiduciary relationship with the company they are establishing. This is a position akin to that of a trustee and the most important consequence that flows from it is that the promoter is not entitled to make a profit from establishing the company, without full disclosure of that profit to either an independent board of directors, or to the existing and prospective shareholders in the company. Such a situation usually arises in situations where the promoters sell assets to the company they are in the process of forming. Failure to make such a disclosure will enable the company to: rescind the contract; claim damages or hold the promoter liable to account for any profit made (*Erlanger v New Sombrero Phosphate Co* (1878), *Gluckstein v Barnes* (1900); *Re Leeds & Hanley Theatres of Varieties* (1902)).

❖ KEY CASE *Erlanger v New Sombrero Phosphate Co* (1878)

Facts:

A syndicate bought a mine for £55,000 then formed a company to which they sold the mine (through a nominee) for £100,000. The syndicate failed to disclose their interest in the contract. Subsequently, when the company's operations ran into difficulty, the shareholders dismissed the original directors and sought to rescind the original contract of sale.

Decision:

It was held that as the promoters had not declared their interest to an independent board of directors the company could avoid the contract, as long as it was still possible to restore the parties to their original positions (what was known as *restitutio integrum*).

Although problems in relation to the promotion of companies have been greatly diminished by the introduction of rigorous rules relating to the provision of information in company prospectuses, nevertheless the Company Directors Disqualification Act 1986 also provides for the disqualification of anyone who has been convicted of an indictable offence in relation to the promotion or formation of a company.

14.4.2 Pre-incorporation contracts

A pre-incorporation contract is a contract which promoters enter into, naming the company as a party, prior to the date of the certificate of incorporation and hence prior to its existence as a separate legal person. The legal difficulty, of course, is that the company cannot enter into a binding contract until it has become incorporated, and it is not bound by any contract made on its behalf prior to incorporation. The legal consequences of the above propositions are that the company, when formed, is not bound by the contract even if it has taken some benefit under the contract. In *Kelner v Baxter* (1866) a contract was entered into supposedly on behalf of a company, but before it was actually registered. Although goods were supplied to the company under the contract, it was held that it could not be held liable under the contract, as it had not been in existence at the time the contract had been entered into. The parties who had purported to act as its agents were liable on the contract but the company itself could not be held responsible.

Similarly the company cannot ratify the agreement even after it has become incorporated.

One of the main consequences of the principles outlined above is that someone who contracts on behalf of a company in respect of a pre-incorporation contract is treated as if they had contracted on their own behalf. Such was the consequence of ordinary agency law as stated in *Kelner v Baxter* above, but that position has been bolstered by statutory authority. Thus, s 51 CA 2006 provides that 'a contract which purports to be made by or on behalf of a company, has effect, at a time when the company has not been formed, subject to any agreement to the contrary, as one made with the person purporting to act for the company or as agent for it, and he is personally liable under the contract accordingly'. It can be seen from the wording of s 51 that liability of the agent is contractual, but it should be noted that this liability arises whether the promoter contracts as agent or not.

❖ KEY CASE *Phonogram Ltd v Lane* (1982)

Facts:

Lane proposed to form a company, FM Ltd, to run a pop group. Lane entered into a contract with Phonogram Ltd 'for and on behalf of FM Ltd'. However, FM Ltd was never actually incorporated. Phonogram Ltd claimed the return of their money from Lane personally.

Decision:

It was held that Lane was personally liable for the money advanced to FM Ltd by the Phonogram Ltd. The Court of Appeal held that the fact that Lane had signed 'for and on behalf of FM' made no difference to his personal liability.

To give effect to the words 'subject to any agreement to the contrary' the words used would need to amount to an express exclusion of liability. Promoters can avoid liability for pre-incorporation contracts in a number of ways. For example it is possible to avoid entering the contract until the company has actually been incorporated. Alternatively, the promoter may enter into an agreement 'subject to contract' with the effect that there is no binding agreement until the company itself enters into one. As the promoters are usually the first directors of the company, they can assure that the company does in fact enter into the pre-arranged contract. Finally, the promoters can expressly provide that they will bear no responsibility for any pre-incorporation contracts as permitted under s 51 of the Companies Act 2006.

14.4.3 Registration

There are two Companies Registries in the UK, one in Cardiff, which deals with companies registered within England and Wales, and one in Edinburgh, which deals with Scottish companies. A registered company is incorporated when particular documents are delivered to the Registrar of Companies.

Section 7 of the Companies Act 2006 sets out the method for forming a company, which is that one or more persons must subscribe their name to a memorandum of association and comply with the requirements of the provisions of the Act as to registration. It should be noted that the Act allows a single person to form any type of company, either public or private. Sub-section (2) simply restates the requirement that a company may not be formed for an unlawful purpose.

Under s 9, two documents must be delivered to the registrar: the memorandum of association and the application for registration.

- *The memorandum of association*
  Although the 2006 Act retains the previous requirement for individuals wishing to form a company to subscribe their names to a memorandum of association, it nonetheless significantly reduces the importance of the memorandum and as a consequence it will not be possible to amend or update the memorandum of a company formed under the 2006 Act. Nonetheless, the memorandum of association, which must be in the prescribed form, remains an important document to the extent that, as required by s 8, it evidences the intention of the subscribers to the memorandum to form a company and become members of that company on formation. Also in relation to a company limited by shares, the memorandum also provides evidence of the members' agreement to take at least one share each in the company. Under s 28, provisions in the memorandums of existing companies will be treated as provisions in the articles if they are of a type that will not in be in the memoranda of companies formed under the 2006 Act.
- *Application for registration*
  Section 9 sets out the information or 'documents' that must be delivered to the registrar when an application for registration is made.
  In all cases the application for registration must state:
  - the company's proposed name;
  - whether the company's registered office is to be situated in England and Wales (or Wales), in Scotland or in Northern Ireland;
  - a statement of the intended address of the company's registered office (that is, its postal address as opposed to the preceding statement confirming the jurisdiction in which the company's registered office is to be situated);
  - whether the liability of the company's members is to be limited and if so whether it is to be limited by shares or by guarantee;
  - whether the company is to be a private or a public company;
  - a copy of any proposed articles to the extent that the company does not intend to use the model articles (this issue will be dealt with in more detail below).

The application must also contain the following additional documents:

- *A statement of capital and initial shareholdings or a statement of guarantee*
  This statement essentially provides a 'snapshot' of a company's share capital at the point of registration. For public companies, this requirement is linked to the abolition of authorised share capital (for further consideration of this see below). As set out in s 10, the statement of capital and initial shareholdings must state the following information:
  - the total number of shares of the company to be taken on formation by the subscribers to the memorandum;
  - the aggregate nominal value of those shares;
  - for each class of shares:

    (a) prescribed particulars of the rights attached to those shares,
    (b) the total number of shares of that class, and
    (c) the aggregate nominal value of shares of that class; and

- *the amount to be paid up and the amount (if any) to be unpaid on each share* (whether on account of the nominal value of the shares or by way of premium).
- such information as may be prescribed for the purpose of identifying the subscribers to the memorandum of association. With respect to each subscriber to the memorandum it must state—

  (i) the number, nominal value (of each share) and class of shares to be taken by him on formation, and
  (ii) the amount to be paid up and the amount (if any) to be unpaid on each share (whether on account of the nominal value of the share or by way of premium).

Where a subscriber to the memorandum is to take shares of more than one class, the information required under sub-section (4)(a) is required for each class.

Section 11 sets out the contents of the statement of guarantee that must accompany the application for registration where it is proposed that a company will be limited by guarantee on formation. The statement of guarantee must contain the information necessary to identify the subscribers to the memorandum.

- *a statement of the company's proposed officers*
  Section 12 requires the submission of particulars relating to:

  - person/persons who are, to be the first director or directors of the company. The details are set out in ss 163 to 166. The main change is that a service address must be provided for each director who is a natural person, in addition to the requirement for the usual residential address;
  - the person/s who is/are to be the first secretary. As private companies are no longer required to appoint company secretaries (see s 270(1)), details are only required where the company actually appoints someone to that role.
  - *a statement of compliance*
  - Section 13 requires a statement of compliance. Such a statement does not need to be witnessed and may be made in either paper or electronic form. Under s 1068, the registrar is authorised to specify the rules relating to, and who may make, such a statement. Section 1112 makes it a criminal offence to make a false statement of compliance, as is the case in relation to all documents delivered to, or statements made to, the Registrar.

If the Registrar is satisfied that the above requirements have been complied with, a certificate of incorporation will be issued. The registration certificate must state:

(i) the name and registered number of the company,
(ii) the date of its incorporation,
(iii) whether it is a limited or unlimited company, and if it is limited whether it is limited by shares or limited by guarantee,
(iv) whether it is a private or a public company, and
(v) whether the company's registered office is situated in England and Wales (or in Wales), in Scotland or in Northern Ireland.

Once issued the certificate is conclusive evidence that the requirements of the Act have been complied with and that the company is duly registered and properly incorporated (see *Jubilee Cotton Mills v Lewis* (1924)).

The Registrar can refuse to register a company if he or she considers it to have been formed for some unlawful purpose. Such a refusal can be challenged under judicial review (*R v Registrar of Joint Stock Companies ex p Moore* (1931)), as can the improper registration of a company formed for unlawful purposes (*R v Registrar of Companies ex p AG* (1991), where the company had been formed for the purposes of conducting prostitution).

In reality what appears to be a complex process can be achieved quite simply by downloading and filling in the appropriate forms from the Companies House website (www.companieshouse.gov.uk/). Pro forma memoranda and model articles of association can also be downloaded.

14.4.4 Commencement of business

A company exists from the date of its registration, and a private company may start its business and use its borrowing powers as soon as the certificate of registration is issued. A public company, however, cannot start a business or borrow money until it has obtained an additional certificate from the registrar under s 761 CA 2006. In relation to public companies, there is a requirement that they have a minimum allotted share capital, at present £50,000 (s 763 CA 2006), and, under s 586, they must not allot shares unless they have been paid up at least as to one-quarter of their nominal value (it follows that the statutory minimum issued and paid up capital for a public company is £12,500). The s 761 certificate confirms that the company has met these requirements.

14.4.5 Re-registration

A company may initially register as one type of company, only to decide at a later date that a different form is more appropriate. The CA 2006 makes the following provisions for such alterations:

- *Re-registration of a private company as public*
  This procedure, set out in ss 90–96 of the CA 2006, requires the passing of a special resolution (75% and 21 days' notice). The company must comply with the requirements as to minimum issued and paid up capital and all other requirements applicable to public companies, such as changing its name and appointing a company secretary.
- *Re-registration of a public company as private*
  This procedure, set out in ss 97–101 CA 2006, also requires a special resolution and the appropriate alteration to the company's name. Under s 98, a minimum of 50 members, or holders of 5% or more of the voting share capital of the company, may seek to have the resolution to re-register as a private company overturned by the courts. Where a public company's issued share capital is reduced to below the authorised minimum, the company is required to re-register as a private company (s 650 CA 2006).
- *Re-registration of a limited company as unlimited*
  This form of re-registration, as provided for under ss 102–104 of the CA 2006, requires the agreement of *all* members as well as the required alteration to the company's documentation. As public companies cannot be unlimited, a public limited company seeking to re-register as unlimited would first of all have to re-register as a private company before changing its status in terms of liability.
- *Re-registration of an unlimited company as limited*
  This procedure, under ss 105–107, requires a special resolution of the company together with the appropriate alteration of the company's documents.

  Since there is the danger that members of an insolvent unlimited company might seek to avoid liability for the company's debts by converting it into a limited company, s 77 of the IA 1986 provides that if the company goes into liquidation within three years of its conversion to limited liability status, any person who was a member at the time of the conversion continues to have unlimited liability in regard to any outstanding debts incurred while the company was unlimited.

14.5 The Constitution of the Company

Amongst the significant changes introduced in the Companies Act 2006 was a major alteration in relation to what are to be considered as the constitutional documents of a registered company. Previously, the most important document had been the memorandum of association, which established the company's relationship with the outside world. However, as has already been mentioned above, the memorandum no longer bears such significance and has been reduced in status to a document merely indicating that someone wishes to form a company. Thus, s 17 of the Companies Act 2006 specifically states that references in the Companies Acts to a company's constitution include the company's articles, resolutions and agreements, and makes no mention of the memorandum of association. As a result of these changes, the emphasis has shifted from the memorandum as the prime document, to the application for registration to establish the company and to the articles of association for its operation after its establishment.

14.5.1 Company name, registered office and objects

Many of the provisions that were formerly contained in the memorandum of association are now required to be stated in either the application for registration or the articles of association. However, the rules relating to these formerly constitutional requirements still apply and have to be complied with, so it is pertinent to deal with them at this juncture.

- *Company names*

  The rules relating to company names are to be found in Pt 5 of the Companies Act 2006. Except in relation to specifically exempted companies such as those involved in charitable work, companies are required to indicate that they are operating on the basis of limited liability. Thus, private companies are required to end their names either with the word 'limited' or the abbreviation 'ltd', and public companies must end their names with the words 'public limited company' or the abbreviation 'plc'. Welsh companies may use the Welsh language equivalents (ss 58 and 59).

  A further aspect of this requirement for publicity is that companies display their names outside their business premises, on business documents and on their seal. In addition to committing a criminal offence, any person who fails to use a company's full name on any document will be personally liable for any default. See *Penrose v Martyr* (1858), where a company secretary was held personally liable when he failed to indicate that the company against which he had drawn a bill of exchange was in fact a limited company.

  A company's name must not be the same as any that are already registered, nor should it constitute a criminal offence or be offensive (s 53).

  Any suggestion of connection with the Government or any local authority in a company's name requires the approval of the Secretary of State (s 54), as does the use of any of the many words listed in the Company, Limited Liability Partnership and Business Names (Sensitive Words and Expressions) Regulations (SI 2009/2615)(s 55). Among the words in the Regulations are such as imply connection with royalty, such as 'king', 'queen', 'prince', 'princess', 'royal', etc. Other controlled words in titles include abortion, benevolent and co-operative, through to stock exchange, trade union and university. The Company and Business Names (Miscellaneous Provisions) Regulations (SI 2009/1085) set out further specific requirements and prohibitions on company names, including the use of punctuation marks. They also provide for exemptions from the requirement for a private company's name to conclude in 'limited' and ensure that indicators of legal status, such as Ltd and plc may only be used by bodies entiled to use such indicators.

- *Similar company names: passing off and the names adjudication scheme*
Where company names are not the same but sufficiently similar to confuse those dealing with the companies involved, an action in the tort of passing off may be taken against a company which has registered with a name likely to mislead potential customers in to believing they are dealing with a different company (see 5.5.5 above, in relation to partnership law). However, under ss 69–74 of CA 2006 a new procedure has been introduced to cover situations where a company has been registered with a name

  (i) that is the same as a name associated with the applicant in which he has goodwill, or
  (ii) that is sufficiently similar to such a name that its use in the United Kingdom would be likely to mislead by suggesting a connection between the company and the applicant (s 69).

  Section 69 can be used not just by other companies, but by any person to object to a company names adjudicator if a company's name is similar to a name in which the applicant has goodwill. There is list of circumstances raising a presumption that a name was adopted legitimately, however even then, if the objector can show that the name was registered either to obtain money from them, or to prevent them from using the name, then they will be entitled to an order to require the company to change its name.

  Under s 70 the Secretary of State is given the power to appoint company names adjudicators and their staff and to finance their activities, with one person being appointed Chief Adjudicator.

  Section 71 provides the Secretary of State with power to make rules for the proceedings before a company names adjudicator.

  Section 72 provides that the decision of an adjudicator and the reasons for it, are to be published within 90 days of the decision.

  Section 73 provides that if an objection is upheld, then the adjudicator is to direct the company with the offending name to change its name to one that does not similarly offend. A deadline must be set for the change. If the offending name is not changed, then *the adjudicator will decide* a new name for the company.

  Under s 74 either party may appeal to a court against the decision of the company names adjudicator. The court can either uphold or reverse the adjudicator's decision, and may make any order that the adjudicator might have made.

  The name of a company can be changed by a special resolution of the company (s 77).
- *The registered office clause*
This is the company's legal address. It is the place where legal documents such as writs or summonses can be served on the company. It is also the place where particular documents and statutory registers such as the register of members (s 114), the register of directors' interests in shares (s 809), the register of debenture holders (s 190) and the register of charges held against the company's property (s 876) are required to be kept available for inspection. The memorandum does not state the actual address of the registered office, but only the country within which the company is registered, be it Scotland or England and Wales. The precise location of the registered office, however, has to be stated on all business correspondence (s 82). It is not necessary that the registered office be the company's main place of business and, indeed, it is not unusual for a company's registered office to be the address of its accountant or lawyer.
- *The objects clause*
Companies registered under the various Companies Acts are not corporations in the same way as common law corporations are. It was established in *Ashbury Railway Carriage and Iron Co Ltd v Riche* (1875) that such companies were established only to pursue particular purposes. Those purposes were stated in the objects clause of the company's memorandum of association and any attempt to contract outside of that limited authority was said to be *ultra vires* and, as a consequence, was void. It was felt for a long time that the operation of the *ultra vires* doctrine operated unfairly on outsiders and various attempts were made to reduce the scope of its application.

Since the introduction of the CA 1989, it has fortunately not been necessary to enter into a detailed consideration of the history and operation of the complexities of the doctrine of *ultra vires*. The CA 1989 effectively reduced *ultra vires* to an internal matter that did not affect outsiders; even as a means of limiting the actions of directors the concept of *ultra vires* was considerably weakened. This reduction in the consequences of the *ultra vires* doctrine has been confirmed in the 2006 Companies Act (see ss 39–41).

Whereas in the past companies used to register extended objects clauses to provide for unforeseen eventualities, s 31 CA 2006 expressly states that, unless a company's articles specifically restrict the objects of the company, then its objects are unrestricted and it is free to engage in any commercial activity it wishes to pursue.

Where its articles do place a restriction on a company's objects it is essentially an internal restriction and outsiders are not bound by any such restriction and can enforce *ultra vires* contracts entered into in contradiction of the company's objects. As an internal regulation, members can get an injunction to prevent any *ultra vires* transactions, but as has been stated they cannot challenge them once they have actually have been entered into.

14.5.2 The articles of association

The articles of association are the main element of a company's constitution and in effect they are the rules which govern a company's internal affairs, and all the company's key internal rules on matters such as the allocation of powers between the members of a company and its directors will be set out in the articles. Companies are free to make such rules about their internal affairs as they think appropriate, subject to the proviso than any such rules must not contain anything that is either contrary to:

- the general law, or
- the specific provisions of the Companies Act.

As previously, the articles of association form a statutory contract between the company and its members, and between each of the members in their capacity as members (s 33 CA 2006) and the previous common law will continue to be applied as appropriate (see below).

Section 18 requires all registered companies to have articles of association, and they have to be contained in a single document and must be divided into consecutively numbered paragraphs (s 18(3)).

Section 19 gives the Secretary of State the power to prescribe 'default' model articles for the different types of company. Such model articles apply to companies where they have not registered any articles of their own, or have not specifically excluded the operation of the model article in question. Whereas under the previous legislation the Secretary of State was only able to prescribe 'default' model articles for companies limited by shares, both private and public. Under s 19, private companies limited by guarantee, for the first time, could also be provided with model articles for their regulation. Model articles were provided for in the Companies (Model Articles) Regulations 2008 (SI 2008/3229).

Model articles for public companies

These model articles take the following form:

Part 1 is introductory:

- Article 1 merely sets out the definitions and interpretation to be applied in the articles.
- Article 2 sets out the potential liability of each member as '*the amount, if any, unpaid on the shares held by them.*'

Part 2 deals with directors thus:

- Articles 3–6 deal with directors' powers;
- Articles 7–19 relate to decision-making by directors;
- Articles 20–24 deal with the appointment of directors, and their remuneration and their removal;
- Articles 25–27 deal with alternate directors.

Part 3 relates to decision-making by members, general and class meetings thus;

- Articles 28–33 deal with the organisation of general meetings;
- Articles 34–42 deal with voting at general meetings.

Part 4 deals with share issue and distributions thus:

- Articles 43–62 deal with the issue of shares;
- Articles 63–68 deal with the transfer and transmission of shares;
- Articles 70–77 deal with distributions;
- Article 78 deals with the authority to capitalise profits.

Part 5 deals with miscellaneous provisions thus:

- Articles 79–80 deal with communications;
- Articles 81–84 deal with administrative arrangements;
- Articles 85–86 deal with directors' indemnity and insurance.

Alteration of articles

Articles can be altered by the passing of a special resolution (s 2(1) of the CA 2006). Any such alteration has to be made *bona fide in the interest of the company as a whole*, but the exact meaning of this phrase is not altogether clear. It is evident that it involves a subjective element in that those deciding the alteration must actually believe they are acting in the interest of the company. There is additionally, however, an objective element. In *Greenhalgh v Arderne Cinemas Ltd* (1951), it was stated that any alteration had to be in the interests of the 'individual hypothetical member'; thus, the alteration that took a pre-emption right from a particular member was held to be to the advantage of such a hypothetical member, although it severely reduced the rights of a real member. Such differentiation between concrete and hypothetical benefits is a matter of fine distinction, although it can be justified. In any case, persons suffering from substantive injustice are now at liberty to make an application under s 994 for an order to remedy any unfairly prejudicial conduct (see 15.6 below).

The following two cases may demonstrate the difference between the legitimate use and the abuse of the provision for altering articles; each of them relates to circumstances where existing shareholders' rights were removed.

❖ KEY CASE *Brown v British Abrasive Wheel Co* (1919)

Facts:

An alteration to the articles of the company was proposed, to give the majority shareholders the right to buy the shares of the minority.

Decision:
It was held, under the circumstances of the case, that the alteration was invalid, since it would benefit the majority shareholders rather than the company as a whole.

❖ KEY CASE *Sidebottom v Kershaw Leese & Co* (1920)

Facts:
In this case the alteration to the articles gave the directors the power to require any shareholder who entered into competition with the company to transfer their shares to nominees of the directors at a fair price.

Decision:
It was held that, under these circumstances, the alteration permitting the expropriation of members' interests was valid, since it would benefit the company as a whole.

As the power to alter their articles is a statutory provision, companies cannot be prevented from using that power, even if the consequence of so doing results in a breach of contract. Thus, in *Southern Foundries Ltd v Shirlaw* (1940), it was held that the company could not be prevented from altering its articles in such a way that eventually would lead to the breach of the managing director's contract of employment. Shirlaw was, of course, entitled to damages for the breach.

Effect of alteration of articles on company's members

Section 25 maintains the general principle that members of a company are not bound by any alteration to the articles requiring them, either:

- to increase their liability to the company; or
- to take more shares in the company.

A member may, however, give his written consent to such an alteration and where they do, they will be bound by it.

Where a company alters its articles s 26 requires a copy of the articles as altered to be sent to the Registrar not later than 15 days after the alteration takes effect. Should a copy fail to comply with this requirement the company and every officer of the company who is in default commits an offence. In addition, where the Registrar becomes aware of a failure to comply with s 26 then under s 27 he/she may give notice to the company requiring it to rectify the breach within 28 days. If the company complies with the notice, it will avoid prosecution for its initial failure to comply. However, if the company does not comply, it will be liable to a civil penalty of £200, recoverable by the Registrar as a debt, in addition to any criminal penalty that may be imposed.

Entrenchment of articles

Previous legislation allowed companies to entrench certain elements of their constitution by putting them in their memorandum and providing that they could not be altered. Section 22 of the 2006 Act replaces that practice but allows its effective continuation by permitting companies' articles to provide that certain provisions may be amended or repealed only if certain conditions are met and those conditions are more restrictive than would apply in the case of a special resolution.

Such a provision, referred to as a 'provision for entrenchment' may only be made:

- in the company's articles on formation, or
- by an amendment of the company's articles agreed to by all the members of the company.

However, any such provision for entrenchment does not prevent alteration of the company's articles:

- by agreement of all the members of the company, or
- by order of a court or other authority having power to alter the company's articles.

As a result of the above provisions, companies will not be permitted to provide in their articles that an entrenched provision can never be repealed or amended.

Section 23 introduces a new requirement for a 'statement of compliance' which is a notice of the existence of any entrenchment to be made known to the companies' Registrar. Similarly, notice is also required where the company alters its articles so as to remove a provision for entrenchment or where the articles are altered by order of a court or other authority so as to remove a provision for entrenchment or any other restriction on the power of the company to amend its articles.

The declared purpose of ss 23 and 24 is to ensure that the Registrar, and any person searching the public register, is made aware that the articles contain entrenching provisions and that special rules therefore apply to the company's articles.

Companies registered under previous legislation

Existing companies registered under previous legislation will continue to be subject to the version of the model articles in force when they were originally registered, although there changes have had to be made to the previous model articles to reflect the changed provisions of the Companies Act 2006. (For alterations consequent upon changes to resolutions, meetings and electronic communications see the Companies (Tables A to F) (Amendment) Regulations 2007 (SI 2007/2541).) However, existing companies will be free to adopt, wholly or in part, the new model articles established under the 2006 Act.

Also as the memoranda of pre-2006 companies will contain constitutional information of a type, which will in future be set out in the articles, s 28 provides that such material is to be treated for the future as part of the company's articles. Also, where the memorandum of a pre-2006 company contains a provision for entrenchment then s 28 states that the provision will be deemed to be in the company's articles.

Resolutions and agreements

It should be remembered that s 17 specifically includes resolutions and agreements in a company's constitution and s 29 sets out their exact nature; essentially special resolutions and unanimous shareholder agreements that effectively bind shareholders generally or members of specific classes of share membership. Section 30 requires copies of any such resolutions or agreements to be forwarded to the companies' registry. Resolution will be considered in the next chapter at 15.5.5.

14.5.3 Effect of company's constitution

Section 33 of the CA 2006 provides that:

> The provisions of a company's constitution bind the company and its members to the same extent as if there were covenants on the part of the company and each member to observe those provisions.

Thus, the articles, resolutions and agreements constitute a statutory contract. The effect of this is that:

- the constitutional documents establish a contract between each member and the company and bind each member to the terms of that contract. Thus, in *Hickman v Kent or Romney Marsh Sheep Breeders Association* (1915), the company was able to insist that a member complied with an article which provided that disputes between the company and any member should go to arbitration;
- the company is contractually bound to each member to abide by the terms of the documents. Thus, in *Pender v Lushington* (1877), a member was able to enforce his constitutional right in the face of the company's refusal to permit him to vote at a company meeting; and
- the members are bound *inter se*, that is, to each other. Authority for this was provided by *Rayfield v Hands* (1960), in which the directors of a company were required to abide by the articles of association, which required them to buy the shares of any members who wished to transfer their shares.

It is essential to note, however, that the constitutional document only creates a contractual relationship in respect of membership rights. Consequently, although members can enforce such rights, non-members, or any member suing in some other capacity than that of a member, cannot enforce the provisions contained in those documents. In *Eley v Positive Government Life Assurance* (1876), the company's articles stated that the plaintiff was to be appointed as its solicitor. It was held, however, that Eley could not use the article to establish a contract between himself and the company. The articles only created a contract between the company and its members, and although Eley was a member of the company, he was not suing in that capacity but in a different capacity, namely, as the company's solicitor.

14.5.4 Class rights

A company might only issue one class of shares giving the holders the same rights. However, it is possible, and quite common, for companies to issue shares with different rights. Thus, preference shares may have priority rights over ordinary shares with respect to dividends or the repayment of capital. Nor is it uncommon for shares to carry different voting rights. Each of these instances is an example of class rights and the holders of shares which provide such rights constitute distinct classes within the generality of shareholders. It is usual for class rights to attach to particular shares and to be provided in the articles of association. It is now recognised, however, that such class rights may be created by external agreements and may be conferred upon a person in the capacity of shareholder of a company, although not attached to any particular shares.

Cumbrian Newspapers Group Ltd v Cumberland and Westmorland Herald Newspaper and Printing Co Ltd (1986)

Facts:

Following a merger between the plaintiff and defendant companies, the defendant's articles were altered so as to give the plaintiff certain rights of pre-emption and also the right to appoint a director, so long as it held at least 10% of the defendant's ordinary shares.

Decision:

Scott J held that these rights were in the nature of class rights and could not be altered without going through the procedure for altering such rights.

As the *Cumbrian Newspapers* case demonstrates, class rights become an issue when the company looks to alter them. When it is realised that class rights usually provide their holders with some distinct advantage or benefit not enjoyed by the holders of ordinary shares, and that the class members are usually in a minority within the company, it can be appreciated that the procedure for varying such rights requires some sensitivity towards the class members.

Alteration of class rights

The procedure for altering class rights is set out in ss 630–633 of the CA 2006. Section 630 states that rights attached to a class of a company's shares may only be varied in the following ways:

- where the original articles set out a procedure for varying class rights, then that procedure should be followed (s 630(2)).
- where the company's articles contain no provision for altering the class rights then the holders of shares of that class must agree to the variation and any such consent must be either
  - (i) in writing from the holders of at least three-quarters in nominal value of the issued shares of that class; or
  - (ii) as a result of a special resolution passed at a separate general meeting of the holders of that class (s 630(4)).

Any resolution to amend an existing provision contained in a company's articles for the variation of class rights, or the insertion of a new provision into the articles, is itself to be treated as a variation of those rights (s 630 (5)).

It should also be noted that the *cancellation* of existing class rights is to be treated as, and dealt with in the same way, as an alteration of those rights (s 630(6)).

Any alteration of class rights under s 630 is subject to challenge in the courts. To raise such a challenge, any objectors must:

- hold no less than 15% of the issued shares in the class in question (s 633(2));
- not have voted in favour of the alteration (s 633(2)); and
- apply to the court within 21 days of the consent being given to the alteration (s 633(3)).

The court has the power to either confirm the alteration or cancel it as unfairly prejudicial (s 634(5)).

In *Greenhalgh v Arderne Cinemas* (1946), it was held that the sub-division of 50p shares, which had previously carried one vote each, into five 10p shares, which each carried one vote, did not vary the rights of another class of shares. Note that although, strictly speaking, such an alteration did not affect the rights held by the other shares, it did alter their real voting power. However, it should be noted that s 630(6) effectively overrules the decision in *House of Fraser plc v ACGE Investments Ltd* (1987), where it was held that the return of all the capital held in the form of preference shares amounted to a total extinction of right rather than a variation of those rights. Consequently the variation procedure did not have to be followed. Now such an extinction of class rights is expressly covered by the variation procedure.

14.6 Capital

There are many different definitions of 'capital'. For the purposes of this chapter, attention will be focused on the way in which companies raise such money as they need to finance their operation. The essential distinction in company law is between share capital and loan capital.

14.6.1 Share capital

It is essential at the outset of any consideration of capital and shares to distinguish two measures of share value:

- *The nominal value of shares*
  Section 542 requires all shares in limited companies to have a fixed nominal value in monetary terms. Indeed it is a criminal offence to allot shares that do not carry a nominal value (s 542(4)). Once established, the nominal value of the share remains fixed and does not change in the normal course of events.
- *The market value of shares*
  Shares in public limited companies quoted on the Stock Exchange are traded in large volumes daily. The value of those shares in the stock market are subject to daily fluctuation depending on a number of interrelated factors, such as the profitability of the company, the prevailing rate of interest or prospective take over bids. Thus the market value of a share of £1 nominal value may be as much as £5 or higher, or as low as 1 penny depending on the interplay of those circumstances.

Company law and company lawyers have been extremely hesitant in offering any precise definition of the share, being content to deal with shares in a pragmatic rather than a theoretical manner. The most generally accepted definition of the share states that it is:

> . . . the interest of the shareholder in the company measured by a sum of money, for the purposes of liability in the first place and of interest in the second, but also consisting of a series of mutual covenants entered into by all the shareholders [*Borland's Trustees v Steel* (1901)].

This definition can be divided into three elements, as follows:

- *Liability*
  The nominal value of the share normally fixes the amount which the shareholder is required to contribute to the assets of the company. Shareholders must pay at least the full nominal value of any shares issued to them (that is, shares must not be issued at a discount (s 580)), but where, as is quite common, the company issues shares at a premium, that is, at more than the nominal value of the shares, then the holders of those shares will be liable to pay the amount owed over and above the nominal value. The excess will form part of the company's capital and be included in the share premium account (s 610).
- *Interest*
  Legal definitions usually state that the share is a form of property, representing a proportionate interest in the business of the company, but tend to be much less certain as to the precise nature of such an interest. What is clear is that, as a consequence of separate personality, the share does not represent, in any other than a very contingent way, a claim against the assets owned by the company. What shareholders possess is not a right to own and control the capital assets operated by their company but, rather, a right to receive a part of the profit generated by the use of those assets. As McPherson put it: The market value of a modern corporation consists not of its plant and stocks of material but its presumed ability to produce a revenue for itself and its shareholders by its organisation of skills and its manipulation of the markets. Its value as a property is its ability to produce a revenue. The property of its shareholders have is the right to a revenue from that ability ['Capitalism and the changing concept of property', in Kamenka, E and Neale, RS (eds), *Feudalism, Capitalism and Beyond*, 1975]. It also has to be recognised that even this right is contingent upon the company making a profit and the directors of the company recommending the declaration of a dividend.

- *Mutual covenants*
  The effect of s 14 of the CA 1985 has already been considered at 14.5.3 above.

Section 541 of the CA 2006 provides that shares are personal property and are transferable in the manner provided for in the company's articles of association. Although the articles of private limited companies tend to restrict the transfer of shares within a close group of people, it is an essential aspect of shares in public limited companies that the investment they represent is open to immediate realisation; to that end, they are made freely transferable, subject to the appropriate procedure being followed.

14.6.2 Types of share capital

The word 'capital' is used in a number of different ways in relation to shares:

- *Statement of capital and initial shareholdings*
  Under the provisions of the Companies Act 1985 the memorandum of a limited company with a share capital was required to state the amount of the share capital with which the company proposed to be registered and the nominal amount of each of its shares. This was known as the 'authorised share capital' and set a limit on the amount of capital which the company could issue, subject to increase by ordinary resolution. Section 9 of the CA 2006 removes the concept of 'authorised capital' and replaces it with the requirement to submit a statement of capital and initial shareholdings to the registrar in the application to register the company.
  The statement of capital and initial shareholdings is essentially a 'snapshot' of a company's share capital at the point of registration.
  Section 10 CA 2006 requires the statement of capital and initial shareholdings to contain the following information:
  - the total number of shares of the company to be taken on formation by the subscribers to the memorandum;
  - the aggregate nominal value of those shares;
  - for each class of shares: prescribed particulars of the rights attached to those shares, the total number of shares of that class and the aggregate nominal value of shares of that class; and
  - the amount to be paid up and the amount (if any) to be unpaid on each share (whether on account of the nominal value of the shares or by way of premium).

  The statement must contain such information as may be required to identify the subscribers to the memorandum of association. And with regard to such subscribers it must state:
  - the number, nominal value (of each share) and class of shares to be taken by them on formation, and
  - the amount to be paid up and the amount (if any) to be unpaid on each share.

  Where a subscriber takes shares of more than one class of share, the above information is required for each class.
- *Issued capital*
  This represents the nominal value of the shares actually issued by the company and public companies must have a minimum issued capital of £50,000 or the prescribed euro equivalent (s 763 CA 2006).
- *Called/paid up capital.*
  This is the proportion of the nominal value of the issued capital actually paid by the shareholder (s 547 CA 2006). It may be the full nominal value, in which case it fulfils the

shareholder's responsibility to outsiders; or it can be a mere part payment, in which case the company has an outstanding claim against the shareholder. Shares in public companies must be paid up to the extent of at least a quarter of their nominal value (s 586 CA 2006).

- *Called and uncalled capital*
  Where a company has issued shares as not fully paid up, it can at a later time make a call on those shares. This means that the shareholders are required to provide more capital, up to the amount remaining unpaid on the nominal value of their shares. Called capital should equal paid up capital; uncalled capital is the amount remaining unpaid on issued capital.
- *Reserve capital*
  This arises where a company passes a resolution that it will not make a call on any unpaid capital. The unpaid capital then becomes a reserve, only to be called upon if the company cannot pay its debts from existing assets in the event of its liquidation.

14.6.3 Types of shares

Companies can issue shares of different value, and with different rights attached to them. Such classes of shares can be distinguished and categorised as follows:

- *Ordinary shares*
  These shares are sometimes referred to as 'equity in the company'. Of all the various types of shares, they carry the greatest risk, but in recompense receive the greatest return. The nominal value of shares is fixed but the exchange value of the shares in the stock market fluctuates in relation to the performance of the company and the perception of those dealing in the stock exchange. It is perhaps a matter of regret that the typical shareholder – and that includes the institutional investor – relates more to the performance of their shares in the market than to the actual performance of their company in productive terms. Ownership of ordinary shares entitles the holder to attend and vote at general meetings, although, once again, it is a matter of regret that very few shareholders actually exercise these rights.
- *Preference shares*
  These shares involve less of a risk than ordinary shares. They may have priority over ordinary shares in two respects: dividends and repayment. They carry a fixed rate of dividend which has to be paid before any payment can be made to ordinary shareholders. Such rights are cumulative unless otherwise provided. This means that a failure to pay a dividend in any one year has to be made good in subsequent years.

  As regards repayment of capital, preference shares do not have priority unless, as is usually the case, this is specifically provided for. Also, without specific provision, preference shares have the same rights as ordinary shares, but it is usual for their voting rights to be restricted. Preference shareholders are entitled to vote at class meetings convened to consider any alteration to their particular rights but, apart from that, they are usually restricted to voting in general meetings when their dividends are in arrears.
- *Deferred shares*
  This type of share postpones the rights of its holder to dividends until after the ordinary shareholders have received a fixed return. In effect, the ordinary shares are treated as preference shares and the deferred shares as ordinary shares. It is no longer a common form of organisation.
- *Redeemable shares*
  These are shares issued on the understanding that they may be bought back by the company (s 684). Redemption may be at the option of either the company or the shareholder, depending on the terms of issue. Companies, in any case, now have the right, subject to conditions, to purchase their own shares and, therefore, are no longer restricted to buying redeemable shares (s 690).

- *Treasury shares*
  Normally when a company buys back its shares, it is required to cancel them.
  However in the case of treasury shares companies are permitted not to cancel any of their own shares purchased, but may keep them in 'treasury'. Any shares held in treasury may be subsequently sold, with the money going to the company. The advantage of treasury shares is that they allow companies to raise capital quickly, as the directors do not have to seek prior approval from the company's members before selling the treasury shares.
  Sections 724–732 (as amended) of the CA 2006 deal with treasury shares and provide that:
  - they must be paid for from distributable profits (s 724((1)(a));
  - the company must not exercise any rights in relation to the shares held.

14.6.4 Allotment and issue of shares

Although the terms allotment and issue tend to be used interchangeably, they are different. Although reference to the tautological definition in s 546 of the CA 2006 is not particularly helpful, s 558 is more useful in that it refers to allotment as the time 'when a person acquires the unconditional right to be included in the company's register of members in respect of the shares'. Thus it can be seen that allotment is the contractual right to have shares allocated, while issue is the actual process of issuing those shares.

Directors generally are not allowed to allot shares without the authority of the members. In practice, however, it is usual for them to be granted general authority to issue the company's shares as they see fit, as long as that authority does not extend beyond a period of five years (ss 549 and 551). The directors must not use their power to issue shares for an improper purpose. Thus, it was held in *Hogg v Cramphorn* (1967) that the issue of shares as a way of defeating a takeover bid was an improper use of the directors' power. Conversely, in *Howard Smith v Ampol Petroleum* (1974), issuing shares in order to facilitate a takeover bid was also unlawful.

It should be noted that any such breach of directors' powers can be ratified by a subsequent vote of the members in a general meeting (*Bamford v Bamford* (1970)).

Company membership

Section 112 CA provides that the members of a company are:

(i) the subscribers of the company's memorandum who are deemed to have agreed to become members of the company;
(ii) every other person who agrees to become a member of the company, **and whose name is entered in its register of members**.

Thus s 111(2) makes appearing on the register of members a condition precedent of membership, with the corollary that if a person's name does not appear on that register, they are not a member. Consequently anyone who only has a merely beneficial or a purely economic interest in a share is not a member of the company. This is important due to the fact that many shares are held on trust, or through nominee accounts, for their ultimate owners. The effect of s 111 is that only the person whose name appears on the register, the owner in law, can exercise the rights attached to the shares, which may be crucially important when the actual owners look to prevent action being taken by the company which they do not approve of (*Eckerle v Wickeder Westfalenstahl GmbH* (2013)).

Pre-emption rights

Section 561 CA 2006 gives existing shareholders rights of pre-emption, i.e. the right to be offered new issues of shares in proportion to their existing shareholdings. This provision is to prevent their stakes in their companies from being watered down. Any issue of shares in contradiction of the pre-emption provisions will lead to the directors being required to compensate any shareholders for any loss suffered (s 568(4)). However, both private and public companies may disapply the pre-emption rules, for up to a maximum period of five years, by either a clause in their articles of association or the passing of a special resolution to that effect. In addition, directors of private companies may be given an unrestricted authority to allot shares, if such is provided in its articles or approved by a special resolution.

14.6.5 Payment for shares

Under s 582 of the CA 2006, shares are only treated as paid up to the extent that the company has received money or money's worth. Any shortfall in payment will have to be made up in the future, and this is especially true if the company goes into insolvent liquidation.

Issuing shares at a discount

This responsibility to make good any difference between consideration provided and the nominal value of the shares received is re-emphasised in s 580, which expressly prohibits the issuing of shares at a discount. The strictness of the rule may be seen in *Ooregeum Gold Mining Co of India Ltd v Roper* (1892).

❖ KEY CASE *Ooregeum Gold Mining Co of India Ltd v Roper* (1892)

Facts:

The £1 shares of the company were trading at only 12.5p and, in an attempt to refinance it, new £1 preference shares were issued and credited with 75p already paid. However, the company did not recover and on winding up the liquidator sought to recover the full value of the new share issued.

Decision:

It was held that the preference shares were required to be paid for at their full value and, therefore, the shareholders had to subscribe a further 75p.

The court has the power to grant relief from such payment in appropriate circumstances (s 589). Section 590 extends criminal liability to both the company and any officer of the company who has breached the rules relating to issuing shares at a discount.

Issuing shares at a premium

It is possible, and indeed quite common, for companies to issue their shares at a premium, that is, to charge those who take the shares more than their nominal value. In such circumstances, any additional payment received must be transferred into a share premium account, which may only be used for specific limited purposes, such as paying any premium due on the redemption of preference shares or paying for previously unissued shares to be issued to the existing members. As a capital reserve, the share premium account certainly cannot be used to finance dividend payments.

It was held in *Henry Head v Ropner Holdings* (1952), and subsequently confirmed in *Shearer v Bercain* (1980), that the requirement to create a share premium account applied to situations where non-cash assets were transferred to pay for shares. The perceived inequity of this decision led to the provision of specific relief relating to mergers where assets are transferred in consideration of shares between formerly distinct companies (ss 611 and 612 of the CA 2006).

Where public companies accept non-cash consideration for the issue of shares, they are required to have the value of the consideration provided independently reported on by some person who is qualified to act as a company auditor (ss 593 and 1150). Such reports must be filed with the Companies Registry (s 597).

Bonus issues and rights issues

It should be recognised that although both of these procedures operate to the benefit of the existing shareholders, they are not contrary to the above rules relating to payment for shares. In relation to bonus issues, the company rather than the individual shareholders pays fully for the shares issued. Such payment can come from retained profits, or from the company's share premium account or capital redemption reserve fund, but it must never be funded from the company's ordinary capital.

Rights issues offer existing shareholders additional shares in the company in proportion to their existing shareholding. The inducement in such a procedure is that the offer price is usually less than the prevailing market price of the shares and so includes an element of potential profit for the shareholders.

14.6.6 Capital maintenance

The immediately preceding section focused on the way in which the law insists on companies receiving the full capital value for the shares they issue. Once the company has received the capital, there are equally as important rules controlling what can be done with it, or, more accurately, controlling what cannot be done with it.

Thus, in *Flitcroft's Case* (1882), Jessel MR stated:

> The creditor has no debtor but the impalpable thing is the corporation, which has no property except the assets of the business. The creditor, therefore, I may say, gives credit to that capital, gives credit to the company on the faith of the implied representation that the capital shall be applied only for the purposes of the business, and he has therefore a right to say that the corporation shall keep its capital and not return it to the shareholders . . .

This quotation highlights two aspects of the doctrine of capital maintenance: first, that creditors have a right to see that the capital is not dissipated unlawfully; and, secondly, that members must not have the capital returned to them surreptitiously. These two aspects of the single doctrine of capital maintenance are governed by the rules relating to capital reduction and company distributions.

Capital reduction

The procedures under which companies can reduce the amount of their issued share capital are set out in ss 641–653 of the CA 2006. Section 641states that a company limited by shares may reduce its capital in any way, but sets out three particular ways in which such capital can be reduced, which are as follows:

- removing or reducing liability for any capital remaining as yet unpaid, that is, deciding that the company will not need to make any call on that unpaid capital in the future;
- cancelling any paid up share capital which has been lost through trading and is unrepresented in the current assets of the company, that is, bringing the balance sheet into balance at a lower level by reducing the capital liabilities in acknowledgment of the loss of assets; or

- paying off any already paid up share capital that is in excess of the company's requirement, either now or in the future, that is, giving the shareholders back some of the capital that they have invested in the company.

Section 641 sets out distinct procedures for private and public companies, thus

- *private companies* may reduce their capital by passing a special resolution supported by a solvency statement. In line with s 643, a solvency statement confirms that each of the directors is of the opinion that the company is not only currently able to pay its debts, but that it will remain able to pay its debts in the coming 12 months. In forming their opinions, the directors must take into account all of the company's liabilities and if the directors make a solvency statement without having reasonable grounds for the opinions expressed in it, and the statement is delivered to the Registrar, an offence is committed by every director who is in default;
- *public limited companies* are not only required to pass a special resolution, but that resolution must be confirmed by the court (s 645), on such terms as it thinks fit (s 648). For example, it is possible that the court will require the company to add the words 'and reduced' after its name, in order to warn the general public that the company has undergone such an alteration to its capital structure. In considering any capital reduction scheme, the court will take into account the interests not just of the members and creditors of the company, but of the general public as well.

It should be noted that the process of capital reduction is distinct from, and treated more restrictively than, the process of capital alteration, which is governed by s 617 and is an essentially internal affair, which does not affect the interests of creditors. However, it should be noted that the alteration procedure allows for the re-denomination of shares, which refers to the changing of the nominal values of the shares from one currency to another (s 622). In the process of re-denomination, it is possible that the total share value might be reduced by up to a maximum of 10%, but in such an eventuality a re-denomination reserve will have to be created to maintain the previous capital structure (s 628).

Amongst the alterations governed by s 617 is the procedure for increasing a company's capital through the allocation of new shares. The procedure of allocation, by the directors of the company, is governed by ss 549–559 (see above). Clearly, outside creditors have no say in relation to any such decision to increase the company's capital, as it would actually increase their security. Of equal importance is the fact that existing members cannot be required to subscribe for any of the increased capital.

Distribution/dividend law

As has been seen, it is a fundamental rule of company law that capital must be maintained and that any reduction in capital is strictly controlled by the courts. This doctrine of capital maintenance led to two statements of a general rule with respect to the payment of dividends, which are that:

- dividends may only be paid out of profits; and
- dividends may not be paid out of capital.

However, just as with capital, there are a number of different, not to say contradictory, ways to determine profit. The lack of certainty in this regard led to an extremely lax regulation of the manner in which dividends could be paid out to shareholders, which was only remedied by the introduction of clear and stricter rules under the CA 1980. The current rules about what may be distributed to shareholders are to be found in Pt 23 of the CA 2006 and, once again, the rules relating to public limited companies are more restrictive than those governing private companies.

Section 830 of the CA 2006 imposes restrictions on companies generally and sets out the basic requirement that any distribution of a company's assets to its members must come from 'profits available for that purpose'. This latter phrase is then defined as 'accumulated realised profits (which have not been distributed or capitalised) less accumulated realised losses (which have not been written off in a reduction of capital)'. Any such profits may be either revenue or capital in origin, the key requirement being that they are realised, that is, that they are not merely paper profits.

Public companies are subject to the additional controls of s 831, which imposes a balance sheet approach to the determination of profits by requiring that:

- net assets at the time of distribution must exceed the total of called up capital plus undistributable reserves; and
- the distribution must not reduce the value of the net assets below the aggregate of the total called up capital plus undistributable reserves.

The undistributable reserves include the share premium account, capital redemption reserve fund, and the excess of accumulated unrealised profits. There are special and distinct rules relating to investment companies.

At common law, directors who knowingly paid dividends out of capital were liable to the company to replace any money so paid out, although they could seek to be indemnified by shareholders who knowingly received the payments. Section 847 of the CA 2006 additionally provides that shareholders who receive payments, with reasonable grounds to know that they are made in breach of the rules, shall be liable to repay the amount received to the company.

Purchase of own shares

It was once an extremely strict rule of company law that companies were not allowed to buy their own shares. Any such purchase was treated as a major contravention of the capital maintenance rules (*Trevor v Whitworth* (1887)). Subsequently, companies were granted the power to issue specifically redeemable shares and such a power still finds expression in s 684 of the CA 2006, although there are strict controls over how any such redemption has to be financed (s 687). However, in a Green Paper in 1980, the leading academic company lawyer, Professor Gower, recommended that the right to buy back should be extended to cover all, rather than just redeemable, shares. Professor Gower's recommendations were accepted and are currently enacted in ss 690–736 of the CA 2006.

The Act provides for three distinct ways in which companies can buy their own shares:

- through a market purchase, conducted under the rules of recognised investment exchange (ss 693 and 701);
- through an off-market purchase, which effectively relates to any other method of purchase (ss 693–694); or
- through a contingent purchase contract, which essentially relates to options to buy shares (s 694(3)).

The rules for financing the purchase by a company of its own shares are the same as those that apply to the redemption of redeemable shares, and are to be found in s 692 of the CA 2006. The most essential rule is that no purchase or redemption is to be financed from the company's capital, and can only be paid from profits properly available for distribution to the company's members or from the product of a fresh issue of shares.

However, as in most areas of company law, there are relaxations of the strict rules in relation to private limited companies. Thus, in ss 709–723, private companies are permitted to use the company's capital to finance the purchase of their own shares, although even here the controls established are extremely rigorous. Thus, any payment out of capital will not be lawful unless:

- the company has passed a special resolution approving the procedure;
- the directors of the company have made a statutory declaration to the effect that the company is solvent and will remain so for the following year;
- the directors' declaration is supported by auditors; or
- the company, within a week of the resolution to that end, advertises its proposed conduct.

Further:

- the procedure cannot be implemented less than five weeks or more than seven weeks after the resolution;
- any member who did not vote in favour, or any creditor of the company, can apply to the courts for the cancellation of the resolution;
- s 175 of the CA 2006 provides that any director who made the statutory declaration without reasonable grounds for so doing is guilty of a criminal offence;
- s 76 of the IA 1986 provides that directors who signed the statutory declaration, together with those former shareholders from whom shares were purchased, are liable to make any shortfall in assets up to the level of the payment from capital if the company goes into insolvent liquidation within 12 months of the capital repayment.

The Nuttall Review

In April 2013, following a review conducted by Graeme Nuttall, the Government announced changes to the statutory regime for share buy-backs. The changes were designed to encourage employee share ownership in private companies, by stimulating the operation of internal share markets. However, the final six specific measures went wider than that and were not restricted to buy-backs in connection with an employees' share scheme or indeed private companies.

The six changes can be split into three categories, as follows:

Authorising a share buy-back

- Off-market share buy-backs can be authorised by an ordinary, rather than special, resolution of the shareholders;
- a single ordinary resolution may be used to authorise multiple share buy-backs for the purposes of or pursuant to an employees' share scheme (subject to certain financial and time limits).

Financing a share buy-back

- A private company can agree with a selling shareholder to pay in instalments for shares that are being bought back for the purposes of or pursuant to an employees' share scheme;
- a private company is permitted to buy back shares each financial year up to a limit of either £15,000 or the cash equivalent of 5% of its share capital (whichever is lower) without having to identify whether this is funded from capital or distributable profits;
- a private company buying back shares out of capital for the purposes of or pursuant to an employees' share scheme may do so using a special resolution and directors' solvency statement only.

Disposal of repurchased shares

- Shares of **all** limited companies can be held as treasury shares following a buy-back, and subsequently be reissued to new shareholders. This provision applies equally to public companies whose shares did not previously qualify.

Financial assistance for the purchase of the company's own shares

Section 678 of the CA 2006 makes it illegal for a public limited company to provide financial assistance to any person to enable them to buy shares in the company. The company, and any officer, in breach of the section is liable to criminal sanctions. The section applies to both direct and indirect assistance, no matter whether it is given before or after the share purchase. Thus, it covers gifts, loans and any other transactions that allow the purchaser of the shares to use the company's assets to pay for those shares (s 677).

Section 682, however, provides for general exceptions to the application of s 678. Thus, lending in the ordinary course of business is not covered, nor is assistance provided for employees' share schemes. The most significant exception, however, is that provided under s 678(4) which allows the company to finance share purchases as long as it is done:

(i) in good faith, *and*
(ii) in the pursuit of some larger purpose.

The precise extent of this relaxation is uncertain and was not helped by the refusal to consider it in the *Guinness* trials or the House of Lords' confused, and confusing, decision in *Brady v Brady* (1989). It is even more disappointing that the opportunity was not taken to clarify the situation in the 2006 legislation.

What the 2006 Act did do, was to take private companies completely out of this sphere of regulation. Perhaps this was in recognition that the previous 'whitewash' procedure used to change public companies into private concerns to allow them to use the previous exemptions open to private companies completely undermined the whole regulatory regime (those interested in football and company regulation might like to consider the recent takeovers of both Manchester United and Liverpool football clubs using the whitewash procedure).

14.6.7 Loan capital

Companies usually acquire the capital they need to engage in their particular business through the issue of shares. It is, however, also common practice for companies to borrow additional money to finance their operation. It is usual for the memorandum of association of companies to contain an express power allowing the company to borrow money but, in any event, such power is implied as incidental to the conduct of the business of any trading company. Nonetheless, it should be remembered that public limited companies are prohibited from using their borrowing powers until they have been issued with a trading certificate under s 761of the CA 2006. It is also possible for the articles of association to attempt to limit the borrowing powers of the directors, to whom the general power to borrow is delegated. Again, it should be remembered that, as a consequence of s 39 any such purported limitation remains an internal issue and is not effective as against an outsider.

Even where the lender is given such security, it is essential to realise that borrowing, even when it is secured, does not give the lender any interest in the company but represents a claim against the company. The relationship between the company and the provider of loan capital is the ordinary relationship of debtor/creditor, even where specific mechanisms exist to facilitate the borrowing of companies and to secure the interests of their creditors.

Debentures

In strict legal terms, a debenture is a document which acknowledges the fact that a company has borrowed money and does not refer to any security that may have been given in relation to the loan. In business practice, however, the use of the term 'debenture' is extended to cover the loan itself and usually designates a secured loan, as opposed to an unsecured one. Debentures may be issued in a variety of ways:

- *Single debentures*
  A debenture may be issued to a single creditor, for example, a bank or other financial institution or, indeed, an individual. The debenture document will set out the terms of the loan: interest, repayment and security.
- *Debentures issued in series*
  Alternatively, the company may raise the specific capital that it requires from a number of different lenders. In this case, the global sum of the loan is made up from all of the individual loans. In such a situation, the intention is that each of the participant lenders should rank equally (*pari passu*) in terms of rights and security.
  Thus, although each lender receives a debenture, they are all identified as being part of a series and consequently have equality of rights.
- *Debenture stock*
  This third method is the way in which companies raise loans from the public at large. The global sum of the loan is once again raised from a large number of people, each of whom holds a proportional part of the total loan stock. The individual lender receives a debenture stock certificate, which in some ways is similar to a share certificate, at least to the extent that such debenture stock is freely transferable and may be dealt with on the Stock Exchange. The loan and the rights appertaining to it are set out in a deed of trust, and a trustee for the debenture stockholders is appointed to represent and pursue the interests of the individual stockholders. In law, it is the trustee, rather than the individual lender, who is the creditor of the company, and the individual debenture stockholders have no direct relationship with the company. In this way, the individuals are relieved of the need to pursue their own causes and the company is relieved of the need to deal with a multiplicity of lenders. Of course, if the trustee fails to pursue the interests of the beneficiaries, they can have recourse to the courts to instruct him to pursue his duties. The content of the trust deed sets out the terms relating to the loan, and in particular it will detail any security and the powers of the trustee to act on behalf of the lenders to enforce that security.

Debentures may be issued as redeemable or irredeemable under s 739 of the CA 2006. In addition, they may carry the right to convert into ordinary shares at some later time. Just as with shares, debentures may be transferred from the current holder to another party, subject to the proper procedure under s 770 of the CA 2006.

However, debentures differ from shares in the following respects:

- Debenture holders are creditors of the company; they are not members, as shareholders are and as a result are not entitled to attend or vote at company meetings.
- As creditors, they receive interest on their loans; they do not receive dividends, as shareholders do.
- They are entitled to receive interest, whether the company is profitable or not, even if the payment is made out of the company's capital; shareholders' dividends must not be paid out of capital.
- Debentures may be issued at a discount, that is, at less than their nominal value; shares must not be issued at a discount and the company must receive the equivalent to the shares' nominal value.

Company charges

As has been stated previously, it is usual for debentures to provide security for the amount loaned. 'Security' means that, in the event of the company being wound up, the creditor with a secured debt will have priority as regards repayment over any unsecured creditor. There are two types of security for company loans, which are as follows:

- *Fixed charge*
  In this case, a specific asset of the company is made subject to a charge in order to secure a debt. The company cannot thereafter dispose of the property without the consent of the debenture holders. If the company fails to honour its commitments, then the debenture holders can sell the asset to recover the money owed. The asset most commonly subject to fixed charges is land, although any other long term capital asset may also be charged, as may such intangible assets as book debts. It would not be appropriate, however, to place a fixed charge against stock in trade, as the company would be prevented from freely dealing with it without the prior approval of the debenture holders. This would obviously frustrate the business purpose of the enterprise.
- *Floating charge*
  This category of charge does not attach to any specific property of the company until it crystallises through the company committing some act or default in relation to the loan. On the occurrence of such a crystallising event, the floating charge becomes a fixed equitable charge over the assets detailed, the value of which may be realised in order to pay the debt owed to the floating charge holder. It is usual for the document creating the floating charge to include a list of events which will effect crystallisation of the floating charge. Examples of such occurrences are typically that the company is in a position where it is unable to pay its debts or some other holder of a charge appoints a receiver; or it ceases business or goes into liquidation. The floating charge is most commonly made in relation to the undertaking and assets of a company. In such a situation, the security is provided by all the property owned by the company, some of which may be continuously changing, such as stock in trade. The use of the floating charge permits the company to deal with its property without the need to seek the approval of the debenture holders.

Registration of charges

The previous regime governing the registration of company charges was altered significantly in April 2013 when the Companies Act 2006 (Amendment of Part 25) Regulations 2013 (SI 2013/40) came into effect. The new regulations repealed chapters 1 and 2 of Part 25 and replaced those provisions with a new s 859, which details all of the changes.

All charges, including both fixed and floating charges, have to be registered with the Companies Registry within 21 days of their creation (s 859A CA 2006). If they are not registered, then the charge is void, that is, ineffective, against any other creditor or the liquidator of the company, but it is still valid against the company (s 859H CA 2006). This means that the charge holder loses priority as against other creditors.

Under s 859F of the CA 2006, the court has the power to permit late registration, that is, at some time after the initial 21-day period. In allowing any late registration, the court can impose such terms and conditions 'as seem to the court to be just and expedient'. Where the court accedes to a request for late registration, as a matter of custom, it does so with the proviso that any rights acquired as a consequence of the late registration are deemed to be without prejudice to the rights of any parties acquired before the time of actual registration. Thus, parties who lent money to the company and received security for their loans will be protected and will not lose out to the rights given under the late registration.

Although companies are no longer required to maintain a register of all their charges, ss 859P and 859Q do require them to keep, and make available for inspection, copies of the instruments creating the charges.

Among the principal changes to be effected by the new regulations may be cited:

(1) the introduction of a single UK-wide system of registration of security;
(2) the introduction of electronic filing to simplify the security registration process;

(3) the removal of criminal sanctions for failing to register (as mentioned previously, however, sanctions will remain in that such a security may be invalid against a liquidator, administrator or creditor of the security provider);

(4) the introduction of the assumption that all security can be registered, including security created under the law of Scotland;

(5) the improvement of access to information available on the public register at Companies House and ensuring security providers allow access to copies of their security;

(6) the abolition of the need for UK companies and LLPs to keep their own registers of security;

(7) provision is made for the notification of a negative pledge (s 859O).

Priority of charges

In relation to properly registered charges of the same type, charges take priority according to their date of creation. Thus, although it is perfectly open for a company to create a second fixed or floating charge over assets that are already subject to such pre-existing charges, it is not possible for the company to give the later charge equality with, let alone priority over, the charge already in existence.

However, with regard to charges of different types, a fixed charge takes priority over a floating charge even though it was created after it. Generally, there is nothing to prevent the creation of a fixed charge after the issuing of a floating charge and, as a legal charge against specific property, that fixed charge will still take priority over the earlier floating charge. The reason for this apparent anomaly lies in the whole purpose of the floating charge.

As has been seen, the floating charge was designed specifically to allow companies to continue to deal with their assets in the ordinary course of their business, without being subject to the interference of the holder of the floating charge. Consequently, the courts have held that this freedom extended to the ability to create fixed charges over the assets in order to secure later borrowings in the course of the business (*Wheatley v Silkstone and Haigh Moor Coal Co* (1885)). It is possible, however, for the debenture creating the original floating charge to include a provision preventing the creation of a later fixed charge taking priority over that floating charge. The question then is whether the registration of that restriction has any effect on subsequent debenture holders. The current position is that, for such a restrictive provision to be effective, it is necessary that the holder of the subsequent charge should have knowledge of the specific restriction in the original debenture. As registration has been held only to give constructive notice of the existence of a debenture, and not its contents, it is likely that the courts will maintain the position that subsequent charge holders are not subject to limitations contained in previous debentures, unless they actually have knowledge of the existence of such restrictions.

Summary

Company Law (1): The Nature and Formation of Companies

The effects of incorporation

- *Separate personality* is where the company exists as a legal person in its own right, completely distinct from the members who own shares in it.
- *Limited liability* refers to the fact that the potential liability of shareholders is fixed at a maximum level, equal to the nominal value of the shares held.
- *Perpetual succession* refers to the fact that the company continues to exist, irrespective of any change in its membership. The company only ceases to exist when it is formally wound up.

- The company owns the business property in its own right. Shareholders own shares; they do not own the assets of the business in which they have invested.
- The company has contractual capacity in its own right and can sue and be sued in its own name. Members, as such, are not able to bind the company.

Lifting the veil of incorporation

The courts will, on occasion, ignore separate personality. Examples include:

- statutory provisions; and
- the use of the company form as a mechanism for perpetrating fraud.

It is difficult, however, to provide a general rule to predict when the courts will lift the veil of incorporation.

Public and private companies

This is an essential distinction which causes/explains the need for different legal provisions to be applied to the two forms. The essential difference is to be found in the fact that the private company is really an economic partnership seeking the protection of limited liability.

The company's documents

- The memorandum of association is no longer as important as it was previously and merely indicates that particular individuals wish to form a company.
- The articles of association, resolutions and agreements of the company provide its constitution.
- The articles of association regulate the internal working of the company.

Share capital

A 'share' has been defined as 'the interest of the shareholder in the company measured by a sum of money, for the purposes of liability in the first place and of interest the second, but also consisting of a series of mutual covenants entered into by all the shareholders' (*Borland's Trustees v Steel* (1901)).

The main ways of categorising shares are in terms of:

- nominal capital;
- issued or allotted capital;
- paid up and unpaid capital; and
- called and uncalled capital.

Types of shares

Shares can be divided into:

- ordinary;
- preference;
- deferred;
- redeemable shares, and
- treasury shares.

Loan capital

The term 'debenture' refers to the document which acknowledges the fact that a company has borrowed money, and also refers to the actual debt:

- A fixed charge is a claim against a specific asset of the company.
- A floating charge does not attach to any specific property of the company until it crystallises through the company committing some act or default.
- All charges, both fixed and floating, have to be registered with the Companies Registry within 21 days of their creation.
- A fixed charge takes priority over a floating charge, even though it was created after the floating charge.
- Similar charges take priority according to their date of creation.

Further Reading

Bourne, N, *Bourne on Company Law*, 5th edn, 2010, London: Routledge
Davies, P, *Introduction to Company* Law, 2nd edn, 2010, Oxford: Clarendon Press
Dignam, A and Lowry, J, *Core Text Series: Company Law*, 7th edn, 2012, Oxford: OUP
Kershaw, D, *Company Law in Context:Text and Materials*, 2nd edn, 2012, Oxford: OUP
Wild, C and Weinstein, S, *Smith and Keenan's Company Law*, 15th edn, 2011, London: Pearson Education

Websites

www.bis.gov.uk/ – Department of Business Innovations and Skills
www.fsa.gov.uk/ – Financial Services Authority
www.companieshouse.gov.uk/index.shtml – registration of companies
www.ipo.gov.uk/cna – companies' names tribunal
www.frc.org.uk/corporate/ukcgcode.cfm – Financial Reporting Council, see for corporate governance
www.legislation.gov.uk/ukpga/2006/46/contents – On-line Companies Act 2006
www.legislation.gov.uk/uksi/2008/3229/contents/made – On-line Model Articles of Association

Chapter 15

Company Law (2): The Management and Operation of Companies

Chapter Contents

Law in Context: The Management and Operation of Companies

This chapter deals with the management of the company, from its initial inception through to winding up, and stresses the important role of key people involved in the company, primarily the directors, the company secretary and the auditors. Different types of directors can be involved in companies, appointed and removed, and there may also be shadow directors who can influence or control the company directors directly. For example, a parent company may control the financial decisions of the other company. But be careful not to confuse a shadow director with a professional advisor, such as an accountant or solicitor. These professionals are paid for their advice, and would not constitute the role of a director. Directors have duties towards the company, and the Companies Act 2006 set out these duties. This Act applies to all companies – both private and public – and to all directors. No director is immune from the Act, and every director has a responsibility to ensure that they individually and the company are acting in accordance with their duties. For example, if a director is overseeing the sale of an asset on behalf of the company, the director should act responsibly and ensure that the best possible outcome is reached for the company, and not to the benefit of individuals. Directors may also be removed from a company and even disqualified under the Company Directors Disqualification Act 1986, either voluntarily or as a result of a legal process. As you read the chapter, think about who would be involved in each action/requirement and why, the role of the Directors and how this plays out in terms of management practices.

15.1 Introduction

Shareholders in public limited companies typically remain external to the actual operation of the enterprise in which they have invested. They also tend to assess the performance of their investment in relation to the level of dividend payment and the related short-term movement of share prices on the Stock Exchange rather than in relation to any long-term business strategy. These factors have led to the emergence of what is known as the separation of ownership and control. As it suggests, this idea refers to the fact that those who provide a company's capital are not actually concerned in determining how that capital is used within the specific business enterprise. In effect, the day-to-day operation of the business enterprise is left in the hands of a small number of company directors, whilst the large majority of shareholders remain powerless to participate in the actual business from which they derive their dividend payments.

In theory, the shareholders exercise ultimate control over the directors through the mechanism of the general meeting. The separation of ownership and control, however, has resulted in the concentration of power in the hands of the directors and has given rise to the possibility that directors might operate as a self-perpetuating oligarchy which seeks to run the company in its own interests, rather than in the interests of the majority of shareholders. In light of the lack of fit between theory and practice, both non-statutory rules and statute law have intervened to place a number of specific controls on the way in which directors act.

15.1.1 Corporate governance

Corporate governance refers to the way in which companies are run and operated with the stated aim that they are run effectively and properly and are not subject to mismanagement, as has unfortunately been the case in regard to some notorious instances in the fairly recent past. Corporate governance has been defined as the system through which business corporations are directed and controlled. The corporate governance structure relates to the distribution of rights and responsibilities among different participants in the organisation, such as, the board, managers, shareholders and other stakeholders, and lays down the procedures for decision-making in relation to corporate affairs. Corporate governance also provides, not only the structure through which the company objectives are set, but also the means through which those objectives are achieved and the process of monitoring the company's performance in the pursuit of those objectives.

In order to ensure the effective corporate governance framework necessary to promote confidence in corporate reporting and governance, it has been deemed necessary to set out defined rules and regulations, including voluntary codes. One such code is the UK Corporate Governance Code, which was initially issued in May 2009 and replaced the Combined Code On Corporate Governance. The most recent version of the Code was issued in September 2012. The Corporate Governance Code is produced and overseen by the Financial Reporting Council (FRC), an independent regulator charged with that duty.

All companies incorporated in the United Kingdom that are listed on the main market of the London Stock Exchange must comply with its Listing Rules, which require them to account for the application of the Corporate Governance Code.

The code adopts a principled approach in that it sets out what are considered best practices for running companies rather than imposing strict rules that must be adhered to. As a consequence it establishes what is known as the 'comply or explain' approach and companies that are subject to its operation must comply with its rules and general principles, or explain why they have not complied with them. Whilst listed companies are expected to comply with the Code's provisions most of the time, it is recognised that departure from its provisions may be justified in particular circumstances. Every company must review each provision carefully and give a considered explanation if it departs from the Code provisions.

The Code establishes principles of corporate governance under five broad areas, and also establishes principles and guidelines for each area.

- leadership;
- effectiveness;
- accountability;
- remuneration;
- relations with shareholders.

It also focuses attention on the role of institutional investors, whose passivity has been much criticised in the past.

15.2 Directors

It is a feature of the companies' legislation that it tends to define terms in a tautological way, using the term to be defined as part of the definition. Thus, s 250 of the CA 2006 defines the term 'director' to include any person occupying the position of director, by whatever name that person is called. The point of this definition is that it emphasises the fact that it is the function that people perform, rather than the title given to them, that determines whether they are directors or not. Section 251 introduces the concept of the shadow director. This is a person who, *although not actually appointed to the board*, instructs the directors of a company as to how to act. A person is not to be treated as a shadow director if the advice is given in a purely professional capacity. Thus, a business consultant or a company doctor would not be liable as a shadow director for the advice they might give to their client company.

A distinction is sometimes drawn between *de facto* directors who hold themselves out to be directors without actually being formally appointed, and shadow directors who deny being directors (see *Re Hydrodan (Corby) Ltd* (1994)). However, as was pointed out by the Court of Appeal in *Secretary of State for Trade and Industry v Deverell* (2001), in most cases the distinction is irrelevant, and in any event both categories are covered by s 250. The point is that such a person is subject to all the controls and liabilities to which the ordinary directors are subject.

In *Holland v HMRC Commissioners* (2010), the issue before the court was whether or not the director of a company, which in turn acted as the corporate director of 42 other companies, was a *de facto* director of those 42 companies. At first instance the High Court had held that the director was a *de facto* director, but that decision was reversed by the Court of Appeal. The Supreme Court confirmed the judgment of the Court of Appeal by a majority of 3 to 2.

The actual position of a director may be described in a number of ways:

- They are officers of the company (s 1173 CA 2006).
- The board of directors is the agent of the company with Art 3 of the Model Articles for Public Companies 2008 (SI 2008/3229) expressly providing that the directors are 'responsible for the management of the company's business for which purpose they may exercise all the powers of the company. This general authority is subject to the reserve power of the membership to direct the directors to take, or refrain from taking, specified action. Such control is to be exercised through the passing of a special resolution at a company meeting. However, even the passage of such a resolution cannot invalidate anything done by the directors before it was passed. Given that special resolutions require a 75% vote and the fact that, as will be seen subsequently, the board of directors effectively control the conduct of meetings, such residual power in the hands of shareholders is not as potentially threatening to directors' control as some have suggested. It should be noted that directors are not the agents of the shareholders (see below in relation to the powers of directors).

  Under Art 5, the board may delegate any of the powers, which are conferred on them under the articles, to such person or committee as they think fit and any such act of delegation may authorise further delegation of the directors' powers by any person to whom they are delegated. In this way, the board may appoint one or more managing directors or chief executives who have the authority to exercise all the powers of the company and to further delegate those powers as they see fit. Article 5 also makes provision for the board of directors to revoke any delegation in whole or in part, or alter the terms and conditions under which it may be operated.
- Directors are in a fiduciary relationship with their company. This means that they are in a similar position to trustees. The importance of this lies in the nature of the duties that it imposes on directors, although those duties have now been given statutory effect (see 15.2.5 below).
- Directors are not employees of their companies *per se*. They may, however, be employed by the company, in which case they will usually have a distinct service contract detailing their duties and remuneration. Apart from service contracts, the articles usually provide for the remuneration of directors in the exercise of their general duties.

15.2.1 Appointment of directors

A public company must have at least two directors, whilst a private company can operate with only one director (s 154). A company must have at least one director who is a natural person (s 155). Thus an ordinary corporation cannot be a sole director, although, paradoxically, a corporation sole is allowed to be a single director (s 155(2)).

The first directors are usually appointed by the subscribers to the memorandum of the company on its initial application for registration. As has been seen previously s 12 requires a statement of the company's officers to be submitted to the Companies Registry prior to the incorporation of a company. This requires the inclusion of the names and signatures of those individuals who agree to be the first directors of the company. These initial directors are required to resign at the company's first annual general meeting, but can stand for re-election (Art 21). Subsequent directors are appointed under the procedure stated in the articles. Thus Art 20 of the model articles provides for directors to be elected by an ordinary resolution of the company in a general meeting. However, Art 20 also allows for casual vacancies to be filled by the board of directors co-opting someone to act as director. That person then serves until the next AGM, when they must stand for election in the usual manner.

It used to be the case that essentially anyone could be a director of a company as long as they were not disqualified from so acting (see 15.2.3 below). However, s 157 CA 2006 introduced a minimum age for the first time, so that now directors must be at least 16. There is no maximum age for directors.

As a distinct legal person, one company can be a director of a second company. There is no minimum qualification to act as a director; neither is there a requirement for a director to be a member of the company. However, the articles of some companies do require the directors to hold shares in them. If the director does not acquire such qualifying shares within a two-month period of being appointed, or subsequently disposes of those shares, then they will be required to resign their position. Even where the director does not comply with this provision, their acts are nonetheless binding on the company.

Companies are required to keep a register of their directors (s 162) containing, amongst other things, their names, ages, nationalities, business occupations and *service* addresses (s 163). This register is open to members free of charge, and to the public on the payment of the appropriate fee. A second register containing directors' *residential* addresses must also be kept (s 165), but this register is not open to inspection.

15.2.2 Removal of directors

There are a number of ways in which a person may be obliged to give up their position as a director:

- *Rotation*
  Model Article 21, as has already been said, requires the initial directors to retire at the first AGM. Article 21 also provides that any directors who have been appointed by the directors since the last annual general meeting, or who were not appointed or reappointed at one of the preceding two annual general meetings, must retire from office but may offer themselves for reappointment. Effectively this will maintain the old rule of requiring one third of the board to stand for re-election at each AGM.
- *Retirement*
  Directors of public companies are no longer required to retire at the age of 70, but they may retire at any time.
- *Removal*
  It is not unusual for a company's Articles of Association to provide for the removal of individual directors by a majority vote of the board of directors. Additionally, however, the Companies Act 2006 provides a statutory procedure to allow shareholders to remove a director by passing an ordinary resolution at a general meeting of the company.

  Thus a director can be removed at any time by the passing of an ordinary resolution of the company (s 168 CA 2006). The company must be given special notice (28 days) of the intention to propose such a resolution. The power to remove a director under s 168 cannot be taken away or restricted by any provision in the company's documents or any external contract (see *Southern Foundries v Shirlaw* (1940), at 14.5.2 above).

It is possible, however, for the effect of the section to be avoided in private companies by the use of weighted voting rights.

❖ KEY CASE *Bushell v Faith* (1969)

Facts:
The articles of association of a company, which had three equal shareholders, each of whom was a director, provided that, on a vote to remove a director, that person's shares would carry three votes as against its usual one. The effect of this was that a s 168 resolution could never be passed.

Decision:
The House of Lords held that such a procedure was legitimate, although it has to be recognised that it is unlikely that such a decision would be extended to public limited companies.

As regards private/quasi-partnership companies, it has been held, in *Re Bird Precision Bellows Ltd* (1984), that exclusion from the right to participate in management provides a ground for an action for a court order to remedy unfairly prejudicial conduct under s 994 of the CA 2006 (see 15.11.2 below).

- *Disqualification*
  The articles of association usually provide for the disqualification of directors on the occurrence of certain circumstances: bankruptcy; mental or physical illness (Model Article 22). In addition, there are statutory controls over directors, other officers and promoters of companies.

15.2.3 Company Directors Disqualification Act 1986

Individuals can be disqualified from acting as directors for up to a maximum period of 15 years under the CDDA 1986. The Act was introduced in an attempt to prevent the misuse of the company form. One of its specific aims was the control of what are described as 'phoenix companies'. These are companies which trade until they get into financial trouble and accrue extensive debts. Upon this eventuality, the company ceases trading, only for the person behind the company to set up another company to carry on essentially the same business, but with no liability to the creditors of the former company. Such behaviour is reprehensible and is clearly an abuse of limited liability. The CDDA 1986 seeks to remedy this practice by preventing certain individuals from acting as company directors, but the ambit of the Act's control is much wider than this one instance.

The CDDA 1986 identifies three distinct categories of conduct which may, and in some circumstances must, lead the court to disqualify certain persons from being involved in the management of companies:

- *General misconduct in connection with companies*
  This first category involves the following:
  - A conviction for an indictable offence in connection with the promotion, formation, management or liquidation of a company or with the receivership or management of a company's property (s 2 of the CDDA 1986). The maximum period for disqualification

under s 2 is five years where the order is made by a court of summary jurisdiction, and 15 years in any other case.

- Persistent breaches of companies legislation in relation to provisions which require any return, account or other document to be filed with, or notice of any matter to be given to, the Registrar (s 3 of the CDDA 1986). Section 3 provides that a person is conclusively proved to be persistently in default where it is shown that, in the five years ending with the date of the application, he has been adjudged guilty of three or more defaults (s 3(2) of the CDDA 1986). This is without prejudice to proof of persistent default in any other manner. The maximum period of disqualification under this section is five years.
- Fraud in connection with winding up (s 4 of the CDDA 1986). A court may make a disqualification order if, in the course of the winding up of a company, it appears that a person:

  a. has been guilty of an offence for which he is liable under s 458 of the CA 1985, that is, that he has knowingly been a party to the carrying on of the business of the company either with the intention of defrauding the company's creditors or any other person or for any other fraudulent purpose; or
  b. has otherwise been guilty, while an officer or liquidator of the company or receiver or manager of the property of the company, of any fraud in relation to the company or of any breach of his duty as such officer, liquidator, receiver or manager (s 4(1)(b) of the CDDA 1986).

  The maximum period of disqualification under this category is 15 years.

- *Disqualification for unfitness*

  The second category covers:

  - disqualification of directors of companies which have become insolvent, who are found by the court to be unfit to be directors (s 6 of the CDDA 1986). Under s 6, the minimum period of disqualification is two years, up to a maximum of 15 years; and
  - disqualification after investigation of a company under Pt XIV of the CA 1985 (s 8 of the CDDA 1986).

A disqualification order may be made as the result of an investigation of a company under the companies' legislation. Under s 8 of the CDDA 1986, the Secretary of State may apply to the court for a disqualification order to be made against a person who has been a director or shadow director of any company, if it appears from a report made by an inspector under s 437 of the CA or s 94 or 177 of the Financial Services Act 1986 that 'it is expedient in the public interest' that such a disqualification order should be made. Once again, the maximum period of disqualification is 15 years.

The CDDA 1986 sets out certain particulars to which the court is to have regard where it has to determine whether a person's conduct as a director makes them unfit to be concerned in the management of a company (s 9). The detailed list of matters to be considered is set out in Sched 1 to the Act.

In addition, the courts have given indications as to what sort of behaviour will render a person liable to be considered unfit to act as a company director. Thus, in *Re Lo-Line Electric Motors Ltd* (1988), it was stated that:

> Ordinary commercial misjudgment is in itself not sufficient to justify disqualification. In the normal case, the conduct complained of must display a lack of commercial probity, although . . . in an extreme case of gross negligence or total incompetence, disqualification could be appropriate.

A 'lack of commercial probity', therefore, will certainly render a director unfit, but, as Vinelott J stated in *Re Stanford Services Ltd* (1987):

> . . . the public is entitled to be protected, not only against the activities of those guilty of the more obvious breaches of commercial morality, but also against someone who has shown in his conduct of a company a failure to appreciate or observe the duties attendant on the privilege of conducting business with the protection of limited liability.

Consequently, even where there is no dishonesty, incompetence may render a director unfit. Thus, in *Re Sevenoaks Stationers (Retail) Ltd* (1990), the Court of Appeal held that a director was unfit to be concerned in the management of a company on the basis that:

> His trouble is not dishonesty, but incompetence or negligence in a very marked degree, and that is enough to render him unfit; I do not think it is necessary for incompetence to be 'total' to render a director unfit to take part in the management of a company.

- *Other cases for disqualification*
  This third category relates to:
  - participation in fraudulent or wrongful trading under s 213 of the IA 1986 (s 10 of the CDDA 1986);
  - undischarged bankrupts acting as directors (s 11 of the CDDA 1986); and
  - failure to pay under a county court administration order (s 12 of the CDDA 1986).

Disqualification orders

For the purposes of most of the CDDA 1986, the court has discretion to make a disqualification order. Where, however, a person has been found to be an unfit director of an insolvent company, the court has a duty to make a disqualification order (s 6 of the CDDA 1986).

The precise nature of any such order is set out in s 1, under which the court may make an order preventing any person (without leave of the court) from being:

- a director of a company;
- a liquidator or administrator of a company;
- a receiver or manager of a company's property; or
- in any way, whether directly or indirectly, concerned with or taking part in the promotion, formation or management of a company.

However, a disqualification order may be made:

- with leave to continue to act as a director for a short period of time, in order to enable the disqualified director to arrange his business affairs (*Re Ipcon Fashions Ltd* (1989));
- with leave to continue as a director of a named company, subject to conditions (*Re Lo-Line Electric Motors Ltd* (1988)); or
- with leave to act in some other managerial capacity but not as director (*Re Cargo Agency Ltd* (1992)).

Period of disqualification

With regard to the period of disqualification, in *Re Sevenoaks Stationers (Retail) Ltd* (1990), Dillon LJ in the Court of Appeal divided the potential maximum 15 year period of disqualification into three distinct brackets:

- over 10 years for particularly serious cases (for example, where a director has been disqualified previously);

- two to five years for 'relatively not very serious' cases; and
- a middle bracket of between six and 10 years for serious cases not meriting the top bracket.

Penalty for breach of a disqualification order

Anyone who acts in contravention of a disqualification order is liable to:

- imprisonment for up to two years and/or a fine, on conviction on indictment; or
- imprisonment for up to six months and/or a fine not exceeding the statutory maximum, on conviction summarily (s 13 of the CDDA 1986).

Under s 14, where a company is guilty of an offence under s 13, then any person who consented or contributed to its so doing will also be guilty of an offence. In addition, s 15 imposes personal liability for company debts arising during a period when a person acts as a director whilst disqualified, either under an order or whilst personally bankrupt. The Secretary of State is required to maintain a register of disqualification orders which is open to public inspection (s 18).

Disqualification undertakings

In April 2001 an alternative form of disqualification was introduced (s 1A CDDA 1986). Individuals can now voluntarily disqualify themselves by making such undertakings. Disqualification undertakings, administered by the Insolvency Service on the part of the Secretary of State, have the same effect as a disqualification order, but without the need to involve court proceedings. The disqualification undertaking will normally include a schedule setting out the basis on which it has been accepted by the Secretary of State and is a public document in the same way as a court order.

Under s 18 of CDDA 1986 the Secretary of State maintains a register of disqualified directors, available for inspection at Companies House at: http://wck2.companieshouse.gov.uk//dirsec.

In 2011/2012, 1,151 directors were disqualified wither by means of court orders or voluntary undertakings: http://www.bis.gov.uk/insolvency/search?keywords=number+of+disqualified+directors&type=all.

Case study: *Re Uno* (2004)

The operation of the CDDA 1986 was considered extensively in *Re Uno, Secretary of State for Trade and Industry v Gill* (2004). This case related to a group of two furniture companies which, although in severe financial difficulties, continued to trade whilst the directors investigated possible ways of saving the businesses. During this period, one of the companies, Uno, continued to raise its working capital from deposits taken from customers to secure orders that were never to be met, when the company eventually went into liquidation. Although the directors were advised that they could have safeguarded the deposits by placing the money in a trust account for the customers, they decided not to do so, as they needed the money to keep the business going in the short term. An application from the Department for Business Innovation and Skills for the disqualification of the directors on the basis of this behaviour was unsuccessful. In refusing the application, the court emphasised the fact that in order to justify disqualification there had to be behaviour that was either dishonest or lacking in commercial probity. Moreover, that behaviour had to be such as to make the person concerned unfit to be involved in the management of a company. In the circumstances of the case, the court found that the directors had pursued realistic opportunities to save the businesses and consequently were blameless for the eventual failure of the businesses and the loss to the customers.

15.2.4 Directors' powers

In considering the topic of directors' powers, it is necessary to distinguish between the power of the directors as a board and the powers of individual directors.

The power of directors as a board

As has been seen, Art 2 of the Model Articles provides that the directors of a company may exercise all the powers of the company. It is important to note that this power is given to the board as a whole and not to individual directors, although Art 5 does allow for the delegation of the board's powers to one or more directors or committees.

Article 2 gives the board of directors general power, but the Articles may seek to restrict the authority of the board within limits expressly stated in those Articles. Such restrictions may be introduced by either setting limits on what the company can do, i.e. by introducing a restricted objects clause into the Articles, or alternatively by introducing an article to specifically limit the powers of the directors, rather than the company. In either event the effectiveness of such restrictions is limited to internal effect by virtue of ss 39 and 40 of the CA 2006. Section 39 provides that no action of the company's can be challenged on the ground that it is beyond the company's capacity, or indeed based on any other provision of its constitution. Section 40 extends this to cover third parties dealing with companies in good faith, even where a transaction entered into is beyond the directors' actual powers as stated in the company's constitution. Section 40(2)(b)(ii) provides that simple knowledge of the fact that the transaction is beyond the directors' powers is not in itself evidence of bad faith.

The power of individual directors

There are three ways in which the power of the board of directors may be extended to individual directors. These ways are, however, simply particular applications of the general law of agency, considered above (see 12.3):

- *Express actual authority*
  This category is unproblematic, in that it arises from the express conferral by the board of a particular authority onto an individual director. For example, it is possible for the board to specifically authorise an individual director to negotiate and bind the company to a particular transaction.
- *Implied actual authority*
  In this situation, the person's authority flows from their position. Model Art 5 provides for the board of to appoint and delegate its powers to a managing director/chief executive, or indeed any other specific officer. The board of directors may confer any of their powers on that person as they see fit. In the case of a managing director the mere fact of appointment, however, will mean that the person so appointed will have the implied authority to bind the company in the same way as the board, whose delegate they are. Outsiders, therefore, can safely assume that a person appointed as managing director or chief executive has all the powers usually exercised by a person acting as a managing director or chief executive.

❖ KEY CASE *Hely-Hutchinson v Brayhead Ltd* (1968)

Facts:

Although the chairman and chief executive of a company acted as its *de facto* managing director, he had never been formally appointed to that position. Nevertheless, he purported to bind the company to a particular transaction. When the other party to the agreement sought to enforce it, the company claimed that the chairman had no authority to bind it.

Decision:

It was held that although the director derived no authority from his position as chairman of the board, he did acquire such authority from his position as chief executive; thus, the company was bound by the contract he had entered into on its behalf.

- *Apparent or ostensible authority/agency by estoppel*

  This arises where an individual director has neither express nor implied authority. Nonetheless, the director is held out by the other members of the board of directors as having the authority to bind the company. If a third party acts on such a representation, then the company will be estopped from denying its truth. Problems tend to arise where someone acts as a managing director without having been properly appointed to that position. In such a situation, although the individual concerned may not have the actual authority to bind the company, they may still have apparent authority and the company may be estopped from denying their power to bind it to particular transactions.

❖ **KEY CASE** *Freeman and Lockyer v Buckhurst Park Properties (Mangal) Ltd* (1964)

Facts:

Although a particular director had never been appointed as managing director, he acted as such with the clear knowledge of the other directors and entered into a contract with the plaintiffs on behalf of the company. The plaintiffs sought to recover fees due to them under that contract.

Decision:

It was held that the company was liable: a properly appointed managing director would have been able to enter into such a contract and the third party was entitled to rely on the representation of the other directors that the person in question had been properly appointed to that position.

15.2.5 Directors' duties

One of the most significant changes introduced by the Companies Act 2006 was the codification of directors' duties restating those previously common law duties in statutory form. Part 10 of the Act deals with 'A Company's Directors' and Chapter 2 refers to the General Duties of directors and ss 170–177 sets out the exact nature of duties.

Section 170 addresses the scope and nature of the duties owed by company directors and makes two essential points:

- *Directors owe their duties to the company as a separate legal person*

  This is clearly stated in s 170(1). As a consequence not only do they not owe their duties to the shareholders of the company but nor do they owe them to any other stakeholder who might have an interest in the company's affairs. This will become important when the exact nature of the individual duties is considered later.
- *The statutory general duties are a reworking of the previous common law rules*

  Section 170(3) states that the new statement has effect in place of 'certain common law rules and equitable principles as they apply to directors'. As a result the previous common law rules are displaced by the new statutory provisions. However, sub-section 170(4) says that the duties set out in statutory form are to be 'interpreted and applied in the same way as common law rules or equitable principles and regard shall be had to the corresponding common law principles and equitable principles in interpreting and applying the general duties'.

The pre-2006 regime of directors' duties

At common law, the duties owed by directors to their company and the shareholders, employees and creditors of that company were at worst non-existent or at best notoriously lax. Statute has, by necessity, been forced to intervene to increase such duties in order to provide a measure of protection for those concerned. As the CA 2006 specifically retains the previous common law and equitable rules it remains apposite to consider the previous approach to directors' duties in order to understand those rules as they still apply, but equally to understand why those rules had to be reworked to make them more appropriate for the demands of contemporary companies.

Fiduciary duties

As fiduciaries, directors/owe the following duties to their company:

- *The duty to act bona fide in the interests of the company*
  In effect, this meant that directors are under an obligation to act in what they genuinely believe to be the interests of the company.
- *The duty not to act for any collateral purpose*
  This may be seen as a corollary of the preceding duty, in that directors cannot be said to be acting *bona fide* if they use their powers for some ulterior or collateral purpose. For example, directors should not issue shares to particular individuals in order merely to facilitate, or indeed prevent, a prospective takeover bid (see *Howard Smith v Ampol Petroleum* (1974) and *Hogg v Cramphorn* (1967)). The breach of such a fiduciary duty is, however, subject to *post hoc* ratification (see *Bamford v Bamford* (1970)).
- *The duty not to permit a conflict of interest and duty to arise*
  This equitable rule is strictly applied by the courts and the effect of its operations may be seen in *Regal (Hastings) v Gulliver* (1942), where the directors of a company which owned one cinema provided money for the creation of a subsidiary company to purchase two other cinemas. After the parent and subsidiary companies had been sold at a later date, the directors were required to repay the profit they had made on the sale of their shares in the subsidiary company on the ground that they had only been in the situation to make that profit because of their positions as directors of the parent company. (The profits made went back to the parent company, which was by then in the hands of the person who had paid the money to the directors in the first place.) One obvious area where directors place themselves in a position involving a conflict of interest is where they have an interest in a contract with the company. The common law position was that in the event of any such situation arising, any contract involved was voidable at the instance of the company (*Aberdeen Railway Co v Blaikie* (1854)). However, Art 85 of Table A specifically excluded the no-conflict rule where the director in question had declared the nature and extent of his interest. Section 317 of the CA 1985 also placed a duty on directors to declare any interest, direct or indirect, in any contracts with their companies, and provided for a fine if they failed in this regard. A director's disclosure could take the form of a general declaration of interest in a particular company, which was considered sufficient to put the other directors on notice for the future. Any declaration of interest had to be made at the board meeting that first considered the contract, or, if the director became interested in the contract after that, at the first meeting thereafter. Article 94 of Table A generally prohibited directors from voting in regard to contracts in which they had an interest. Failure to disclose any interest

rendered the contract voidable at the instance of the company and the director might be liable to account to the company for any profit made in relation to it.

Duty of care and skill

Common law did not place any great burden on directors as regards their duty of care to their companies or the level of skill or diligence that was expected of them. Damages could be recovered against directors for losses caused by their negligence but the level of such negligence was high. As was stated in *Lagunas Nitrate Co v Lagunas Syndicate* (1989), it must, in a business sense, be culpable or gross. The classic statement is to be found in *Re City Equitable Fire Assurance Co* (1925), which established three points:

- First, in determining the degree of skill to be expected, the common law applied a *subjective* test and established no minimum standard. A director was expected to show the degree of skill, which might reasonably be expected of a person of their knowledge and experience. As a result, if they were particularly experienced and skilled in the affairs of their business, then they would be expected to exercise such skill in the performance of their functions. On the other hand, however, if the director was a complete incompetent, they would only be expected to perform to the level of a complete incompetent. The reasoning behind this seemed to be that the courts left it to the shareholders to elect and control the directors as their representatives. If the shareholders elected incompetents, then that was a matter for them and the courts would not interfere.
- Secondly, the duties of directors were held to be of an intermittent nature and, consequently, directors were not required to give continuous attention to the affairs of their company. In *Re Cardiff Savings Bank* (the *Marquis of Bute's* case) (1892), it emerged that the Marquis had inherited his position as president of the bank at the age of six months and, in the course of 38 years, he had only ever attended one board meeting.
- Thirdly, in the absence of any grounds for suspicion, directors were entitled to leave the day-to-day operation of the company's business in the hands of managers and to trust them to perform their tasks honestly.

This very relaxed attitude to what was expected of company directors was subject to change through both statute and at common law, especially the introduction of wrongful trading in s 214 of the Insolvency Act (IA) 1986, which established a minimum standard by applying an *objective* test which requires directors to have the general knowledge, skill and experience which may reasonably be expected of a person carrying out the same functions as are carried out by that director in relation to the company. Interestingly, the common law approach to directors' duty of care has recently been extended to accommodate the requirements of s 214 (*Re D'Jan of London Ltd* (1993), *Re Barings plc (No 5)* (2000) and *Dorchester Finance Co Ltd v Stebbing* (1989)).

This shift to a minimum objective standard has been continued in the provision of s 174 of the Companies Act (CA) 2006, which will be considered in some detail below.

The post-2006 Companies Act regime of director's duties

- *Section 171 Duty to act within their powers*

  Section 171 replaces the similar common law duties and requires directors to act in accordance with the company's constitution. Section 17 of the Act provides that a company's constitution includes not only the company's articles of association but the resolutions and agreements specified in s 29, which includes special resolutions passed by the company and any resolutions or agreements that have been agreed to, or which otherwise bind classes of shareholders.

Directors are also required to use powers only for the purposes for which they were conferred. This is a restatement of the long-standing 'proper purposes doctrine'.

- *Section 172 Duty to promote the success of the company for the benefit of members as a whole*
  This provision replaces the previous common law duty on directors to act in good faith in the best interests of the company. In the course of making their decisions directors are now required to have regard to each of the following list of matters:

  - the likely consequences of any decision in the long-term,
  - the interests of the company's employees,
  - the need to foster the company's business relationships with suppliers, customers and others,
  - the impact of the company's operations on the community and the environment,
  - the desirability of the company maintaining a reputation for high standards of business conduct, and
  - the need to act fairly as between members of the company.

  The above list is non-exhaustive and directors must also have regard to other non-specific matters. Sub-section (3) makes specific reference to the need to consider the interests of the company's creditors under straightened circumstances where such rights should be protected.

  This section is based on the concept of 'enlightened shareholder value' but, nonetheless, it clearly privileges the rights of the shareholders over the other interests mentioned. This is especially apparent when it is remembered that, as emphasised in s 17, all duties are owed, not to the various interested stakeholders mentioned, but to the company itself. As a result, there is likely to be no little difficulty in any disgruntled stakeholder taking action where the directors have not taken any of the above aspects into consideration in making some decision. This will especially be the case where the board have considered the particular issue, only to dismiss it as not being 'for the benefit of the members as a whole'.
- *Section 173 Duty to exercise independent judgment*
  This duty reflects the previous rule prohibiting directors from fettering their discretion unless acting in accordance with an agreement duly approved by the company.
- *Section 174 Duty to exercise reasonable skill, care and diligence*
  This section codifies and replaces the previous common law duty but in a way that reflects the recent tightening of control over directors in line with the standard set out in relation to wrongful trading in the Insolvency Act 1986, s 214.

  Section 174 requires that a director must exercise 'reasonable' care, skill and diligence and adds that, the requirement means the care, skill and diligence that would be exercised by a reasonably diligent person with:

  (a) the general knowledge, skill and experience that may reasonably be expected of a person carrying out the functions carried out by the director in relation to the company and
  (b) the general knowledge, skill and experience that the director has.

  Although the overall standard required is not set at a punitive level and only requires a reasonable standard of activity and skill, it is important to note the relationship between the two elements of the test. The first, an objective test, sets a basic standard that must be complied with in all circumstances. It will be expected that all directors who are performing either specific or general functions perform to a standard appropriate to those functions. Directors who actually lack the knowledge or skills to fulfil particular roles or perform particular functions will not be allowed to rely on their lack of competency as an excuse for not showing a required measure of skill or diligence.

Under the second, subjective, element of the test, a director's particular professional or business skills will have a bearing on whether they have met the standard of skill and diligence expected of them. However, this element can only increase that basic standard. For example, a qualified lawyer or accountant would be expected to know more about certain issues than a non-specialist director and would be expected to bring their particular skill to bear on company issues in the area of their particular expertise.

- *Section 175 Duty to avoid conflicts of interest*
  This section restates the common law rule that directors must respect the trust placed in them and should do nothing to undermine or abuse their position as fiduciaries. It merely gives statutory form to the equitable rules considered above. However, it should be recalled that conflicts of interest are not inherently bad, but any such conflict of interest must be declared and authorised by the members of the company, or by an alternative procedure provided for in the company's articles of association.
- *Section 176 Duty not to accept benefits from third parties*
  A director must not accept a benefit from a third party, which is conferred by reason of

  (a) his being a director,
  or
  (b) his doing (or not doing) anything as director.

  This duty is an aspect of the previous general duty to avoid conflicts of interest, but it has been stated separately in order to ensure that the obtaining of a benefit from a third party by a director can only be authorised by members of the company rather than by the board. However s 176(4) provides that no breach of duty takes place if the acceptance of the benefit by the director 'cannot reasonably be regarded as likely to give rise to a conflict of interest'. As a result, it is likely that 'inconsequential' benefits or those 'totally unrelated' to the affairs of the company will be permissible. The question arises as to how and who decides the nature of these gratuities.
- *Section 177 Duty to declare to the company's other directors any interest a director has in a proposed transaction or arrangement with the company*
  Under this provision a director must declare to the other directors any situation in which they are in any way, directly or indirectly, interested in a proposed transaction or arrangement with the company. Again this is a further emphasising of the duty to avoid a conflict of interest by ensuring that directors are transparent about personal interests, which might be seen as affecting their judgment. The actual provisions for making such a declaration, and the criminal consequences of any failure so to do, are set out in ss 182–187.

15.3 Company Secretary

Section 1173 of the CA 2006 includes the company secretary among the officers of a company. Every public limited company must have a company secretary (s 271) but that is no longer the case for private companies, which may operate without the need to appoint a company secretary. Section 273 of the CA 2006 requires that the directors of a public company must ensure that the company secretary has the requisite knowledge and experience to discharge their functions. Section 273(2) sets out the necessary qualifications, that are:

- having been a company secretary of a public company for three out of the previous five years before appointment;
- membership of a designated professional body;
- being a barrister, advocate or solicitor.

Section 273(3) sets out a list of professional bodies, including the ICA, ACCA, ICMA and ICSA, membership of which enables a person to act as a company secretary.

15.3.1 Duties of company secretaries

The duties of company secretaries are set by the board of directors, and therefore vary from company to company but, as an officer of the company, the secretary will be responsible for ensuring that the company complies with its statutory obligations. Some of the most important duties undertaken by company secretaries are to:

- ensure that the necessary registers required to be kept by the Companies Acts are established and properly maintained;
- ensure that all returns required to be lodged with the Companies Registry are prepared and filed within the appropriate time limits;
- organise and attend meetings of the shareholders and directors;
- ensure that the company's books of accounts are kept in accordance with the Companies Acts and that the annual accounts and reports are prepared in the form and at the time required by the Acts;
- be aware of all the statutory requirements placed on the company's activities and to ensure that the company complies with them; and
- sign such documents as require signature under the Companies Acts.

15.3.2 Powers of company secretaries

Although old authorities, such as *Houghton & Co v Northard Lowe and Wills* (1928), suggest that company secretaries have extremely limited authority to bind their company, later cases have recognised the reality of the contemporary situation and have extended to company secretaries potentially significant powers to bind their companies. As an example, consider *Panorama Developments Ltd v Fidelis Furnishing Fabrics Ltd* (1971), in which a company secretary hired cars for his own use, although he signed the documents as 'company secretary'. His company was held liable to pay for the hire of the cars. In the Court of Appeal, Lord Denning stated that a company secretary was entitled:

> . . . to sign contracts connected with the administrative side of a company's affairs, such as employing staff and ordering cars and so forth. All such matters now come within the ostensible authority of a company's secretary.

Although Lord Denning dealt with the secretary's authority on the basis of ostensible authority, it would be more accurate to define it as an example of implied actual authority (see 12.4.1 above).

15.4 Company Auditor

As usual in the Companies Act 2006 different provisions have been made for private and public limited companies. Sections 485–488 state the rules relating to private companies and ss 489–494 set out the rules relating to plcs.

The fall-back position is that a company must appoint an auditor, the only possible exception being for those small private companies where the directors resolve that audited accounts are unlikely to be required (s 485(1)).

The auditor's duty is to report to the company's members as to whether or not the company's accounts have been properly prepared and to consider whether the directors' report is consistent with those accounts.

In the case of a newly registered company, the first auditors are appointed by the directors until the first general meeting, at which they may be reappointed by the members of the company. Thereafter, auditors are appointed annually at general meetings at which accounts are laid (s 489 CA 2006). The Secretary of State has the power to appoint an auditor where the company has not appointed one (s 486 for private companies and s 490 for plcs).

A person cannot be appointed as auditor where they are an officer or employee of the company in question.

Auditors are appointed to ensure that the company is being run on a proper basis. They represent the interests of the shareholders and report to them. They are, however, employed by the company and owe their contractual duty to the company rather than the shareholders. Auditors are required to make a report on all annual accounts laid before the company in a general meeting during their tenure of office (s 475(1)). The report must state the names of the auditors and must be signed by them (s 503).

The auditors are required to report (s 495) whether the accounts have been properly prepared in accordance with the CA 2006, and whether the individual and group accounts show a true and fair view of the profit or loss and state of affairs of the company and of the group, so far as concerns the members of the company.

Auditors are required to make the necessary investigations and consider the following, which need only be reported on if there are deficiencies:

- whether the company has kept proper accounting records and obtained proper accounting returns from branches;
- whether the accounts are in agreement with the records;
- whether they have obtained all the information and explanations that they considered necessary (all of the above under s 498);
- whether the requirements concerning disclosure of information about directors and officers remuneration, loans and other transactions, have been met; and whether the information in the directors' report is consistent with the accounts (s 496).

Where the company circulates a summary financial statement, the auditors are required to give a report on whether the summary statement is consistent with the company's annual accounts and directors' report, and whether it complies with the requirements of the CA 2006 and regulations in relation to this statement s 427(4)(d).

If the auditors' report does not state that, in their unqualified opinion, the accounts have been properly prepared in accordance with the relevant legislation governing the relevant undertakings' accounts (s 495(4)) then the accounts are said to be qualified.

Auditors have the right of access at all times to the company's books and accounts, and officers of the company are required to provide such information and explanations as the auditors consider necessary (s 499). It is a criminal offence to make false or reckless statements to auditors (s 501). Auditors are entitled to receive notices and other documents in connection with all general meetings, to attend such meetings and to speak when the business affects their role as auditors (s 502).

An auditor may be removed at any time by ordinary resolution of the company (s 510). This does, however, require special notice. Any auditor who is to be removed or not reappointed is entitled to make written representations and require these to be circulated or have them read out at the meeting (s 511).

An auditor may resign at any time (s 516). Notice of resignation must be accompanied by a statement of any circumstances that the auditor believes ought to be brought to the attention of members and creditors, or, alternatively, a statement that there are no such circumstances (s 519). The company is required to file a copy of the notice with the Registrar of companies within 14 days (s 520). Where the auditor's resignation statement states that there are circumstances that should be brought to the attention of members, then he may require the company to call a meeting to allow an explanation of those circumstances to the members of the company (s 518).

The tortious liability of auditors is considered at 9.15.1 above.

15.5 Company Meetings

In theory, the ultimate control over a company's business lies with the members in general meeting. In practice, however, the residual powers of the membership are restricted to their ultimate control over the company's constitution, together with their control over the composition of the board of directors. The reality of such limited theoretical powers are further constrained by the practicalities involved with the operation of company meetings, as will be seen in what follows.

In line with this approach, some powers are specifically reserved to the members by statute, such as the right to petition for voluntary winding up and Model Art 4 provides that the shareholders, by passing a special resolution, can instruct the directors to act in a particular way. In reality, the ideal typical shareholder tends either not to be bothered to take an active part in the conduct of company meetings or to use their votes in a way directed by the board of directors, so the underlying idea of a participative democratic structure is no little undermined.

The consequences of the deregulatory approach of the Companies Act 2006, in relation to private companies, has been mentioned repeatedly, but there is no clearer example of this difference of approach than in relation to company meetings. In effect, private companies are permitted to operate without the need for meetings, simply making use of the written resolution process. Whereas this possibility was open to private companies previously by electing to opt out of the general requirements relating to meetings, now it is the default position and such companies now have to opt in to the meeting procedures for them to apply.

15.5.1 Types of meetings

One would obviously conclude that a meeting involved more than one person and, indeed, there is authority to that effect in *Sharp v Dawes* (1876). In that case, a meeting between a lone member and the company secretary was held not to be validly constituted. It is possible, however, for a meeting of only one person to take place in the following circumstances:

- in the case of a meeting of a particular class of shareholders and all the shares of that class are owned by the one member; or
- by virtue of s 306 of the CA 2006, the court may order the holding of a general meeting, at which the quorum is to be one member. This eventuality might arise in a quasi-partnership where a recalcitrant member of a two-person company refused to attend any meetings, thus preventing the continuation of the enterprise.

There are three types of meeting:

- *Annual General Meeting*
  By virtue of s 336 of the CA 2006, every *public* company must hold a specifically designated Annual General Meeting in each period of 6 months beginning with the day following its accounting reference date. This is in addition to any other meetings held during that period. If the company fails to comply an offence is committed by every officer of the company who is in default. As can be seen this requirement does not apply to private companies.
- *General meeting*
  General meetings are any meeting that is not designated an Annual General Meeting. They are usually called by the directors, although members holding 5% of the voting shares may

requisition such a meeting (ss 302 and 303, see below). Under previous legislation such meetings were called Extraordinary General Meetings (EGM), however, the Companies Act 2006 only refers to general meetings and AGMs so this category as a distinct meeting has gone, but reference to it will still be found in some texts and cases.

- *Class meeting*
  This refers to the meeting of a particular class of shareholder, that is, those who hold a type of share providing particular rights, such as preference shares (considered at 9.6.3 above).

15.5.2 Calling meetings

Meetings may be convened in a number of ways by various people:

- *the directors* of the company under s 302. Apart from this usual power, directors of public limited companies are required, under s 656, to call meetings where there has been a serious loss of capital, defined as the assets falling to half or less than the nominal value of the called up share capital;
- *the members* using the power to requisition a meeting under s 303. To require the convening of a company meeting, any shareholders must hold at least 5% of the share capital carrying voting rights. The minimum threshold was reduced from 10% by the Companies (Shareholders' Rights) Regulations 2009 (SI 2009/1633). If the directors fail to convene a meeting as required within 21 days of the deposit of the requisition, although the actual date of the meeting may be within eight weeks of the date of requisition, then the requisitionists may themselves convene a meeting and recover any expenses from the company (ss 304 and 305).

  Model Art 28 allows two or more members of a public limited company to call a general meeting where there are fewer than two directors of the company;
- *the auditor* of a company under s 518, which provides for a resigning auditor to require the directors to convene a meeting in order to explain the reason for the auditor's resignation;
- *the court* may order a meeting under s 306 where it is otherwise impracticable to call a meeting, as considered above.

15.5.3 Notice of meetings

Proper and adequate notice must be sent to all those who are entitled to attend any meeting. Details of the following must be given:

- *Time*
  This is set out in s 307. As regards *public limited companies* the minimum period of notice is:

  - 21 clear days for an AGM; and
  - 14 clear days for all other meetings.

  The notice period may be extended in the company's articles. However, shorter notice is only permissible as follows:

  - in the case of an AGM, where all the members entitled to attend agree; and
  - in the case of any other meeting, where holders of 95% of the nominal value of the voting shares agree.

  The extremely high levels of approval required, unanimity in relation to the AGM, effectively means that these provisions are unlikely to be used in anything other than extremely small plcs.

As has been stated above, private companies can operate without the need to call meetings, but where they do elect to call meetings the rules are significantly less rigorous than those applied to public companies. Thus the minimum period of notice is 14 days and the minimum percentage required to approve shorter notice is 90%.

A resolution to remove a director under s 168 requires special notice of 28 days, but in that case the notice is given *to* the company by the person proposing the resolution and not *from* the company to the members (s 312).

- *Content*

  Adequate notice of the content of any resolution must be sent to members, so that they can decide whether to attend the meeting or to appoint a proxy to vote in line with their instructions. In respect of anything other than standard business, it is desirable that the full text of any resolution to be put to the meeting be circulated to all of the members entitled to vote on it.

15.5.4 Agenda

It is usually the prerogative of the directors to decide which motions will be put to the company in the general meeting. Members, however, may present a resolution for the agenda where they have requisitioned a meeting under the procedure established in s 303 (see 15.5.2 above). They can also require the circulation of a statement of no more than 1,000 words in support of the resolution, the costs of which they will have to bear, unless the meeting votes to take on the costs (ss 314–315). This latter procedure can also be used to require the circulation of statements about any resolutions to be considered at company meetings.

In relation to an AGM, s 338 provides a procedure whereby a minority of members, amounting to 5% of the total voting rights or 100 members holding an average of £100 worth of shares, may have a motion considered. This mechanism is complicated and expensive, and the difficulties involved in putting it into practice, especially in large public companies, mean that it is not often used.

The difficulties involved in ordinary members getting issues onto the agenda also extend to resolutions to remove directors. Although s 168 provides for the removal of directors on the passing of an ordinary resolution, it was held in *Pedley v Inland Waterways Association Ltd* (1977) that a disgruntled member could only get such a resolution onto the agenda if he satisfied the requirements of what is now s 303.

15.5.5 Types of resolutions

Since the enactment of the Companies Act 2006 there are now essentially three types of resolution (the concept of extraordinary resolutions no longer exits):

- *Ordinary resolution*

  Section 282 CA 2006 defines an ordinary resolution of the members generally, or a class of members of a company, as a resolution that is passed by a simple majority.

  If the resolution is to be voted on a show of hands the majority is determined on the basis of those who vote in person or as duly appointed proxies. Where a poll vote is called the majority is determined in relation to the total voting rights of members who vote in person or by proxy.

  Members who do not attend or appoint a proxy, or who attend but do not vote, are disregarded.

- *Special resolution*

  A special resolution of the members (or of a class of members) of a company means a resolution passed by a majority of not less than 75% determined in the same way as for an ordinary resolution (s 283). If a resolution is proposed as a special resolution, it must be indicated as such, either in the written resolution text or in the meeting notice. Where a resolution is proposed as a special resolution, it can only be passed as such although anything that may be done as an ordinary resolution may be passed as a special resolution (s 282(5)). There is no longer a requirement for 21 days' notice where a special resolution is to be passed at a meeting.

Where a provision of the Companies Acts requires a resolution, but does not specify what kind of resolution is required, the default provision is for an ordinary resolution. However the company's articles may require a higher majority, or indeed may require a unanimous vote to pass the resolution. The articles cannot alter the requisite majority where the Companies Acts actually state the required majority, so if the Act provides for an ordinary resolution the articles cannot require a higher majority.

The companies' legislation requires special resolutions to be passed in so many situations that they cannot all be listed here. Amongst those in the CA 2006 are the following examples:

- alteration of articles (s 21);
- change of company name (s 77);
- re-registration of a private company as a public company (s 90) and vice versa (s 97);
- reduction of capital (s 641).

Written resolutions

As has been stated repeatedly above, private limited companies are no longer required to hold meetings and can take decisions by way of written resolutions (s 281). The 2006 Companies Act removed the previous requirement for unanimity to pass a written resolution. It now merely requires the appropriate majority of total voting rights, a simple majority for an ordinary resolution (s 282(2)) and a 75% majority of the total voting rights for a special resolution (s 283(2)).

By virtue of s 288(5), anything which in the case of a private company might be done by resolution in a general meeting, or by a meeting of a class of members of the company, may be done by written resolution with only 2 exceptions:

- the removal a director; and
- the removal of an auditor.

Both of these procedures still require the calling of a general meeting of shareholders.

A written resolution may be proposed by the directors or the members of the private company (s 288(3)). Under s 291 in the case of a written resolution proposed by the directors, the company must send or submit a copy of the resolution to every eligible member. This may be done as follows:

- either by sending *copies* to all eligible members in hard copy form, in electronic form or by means of a website;
- by submitting *the same copy* to each eligible member in turn (or different copies to each of a number of eligible members in turn);
- by a mixture of the above processes.

The copy of the resolution must be accompanied by a statement informing the members both how to signify agreement to the resolution and the date by which the resolution must be passed if it is not to lapse (s 291(4)). It is a criminal offence not to comply with the above procedure, although the validity of any resolution passed is not affected.

The members of a private company may require the company to circulate a resolution if they control 5% of the voting rights (or a lower percentage if specified in the company's articles). They can also require a statement of not more than 1,000 words to be circulated with the resolution (s 292). However, the members requiring the circulation of the resolution will be required to pay any expenses involved, unless the company resolves otherwise.

Agreement to a proposed written resolution occurs when the company receives an authenticated document, in either hard copy form or in electronic form, identifying the resolution and indicating agreement to it. Once submitted, agreement cannot be revoked.

The resolution and accompanying documents must be sent to all members who are entitled to vote on the circulation date of the resolution. The company's auditor should also receive such documentation, although they do not have to approve the resolution (s 502 CA 2006).

15.5.6 Quorum

This is the minimum number of persons whose presence is required for the transaction of business at any meeting. The precise details are set out in the articles of association, although s 318 sets the default minimum at two, although the articles may increase that number and, of course in a single person company the quorum is one.

15.5.7 Votes

A resolution is decided upon initially by a show of hands, unless a poll is demanded. On a show of hands, every member has one vote. In a poll, it is usual for each share to carry a vote and, thus, for the outcome of the poll to reflect concentration of interest in the company (for exceptions to this, see *Bushell v Faith* (1969), 14.2.2 above).

Generally the procedures for calling for a poll vote are left to the articles of association, but s 321 prohibits the exclusion of the right to demand a poll except in relation to:

- the election of the chairman of the meeting, or
- the adjournment of the meeting.

Nor can the articles require more than five members to require a poll.

In fact Model Art 36 provides that a poll on a resolution may be demanded by:

- the chairman of the meeting;
- the directors;
- two or more persons having the right to vote on the resolution; or
- a person or persons representing not less than one tenth of the total voting rights of all the members.

15.5.8 Proxies

Section 324 of the CA 2006 provides that any member of a company who is entitled to attend and vote at a meeting may appoint another person as their proxy, that is, to act as their agent in exercising the member's voting right. Every notice of a meeting must state the member's right to appoint a proxy and, although the articles may require notice of the appointment of a proxy to be given to the company, they may not require more than 48 hours' notice. Proxies need not be members of the company. They have no right to speak at meetings of public companies but may speak in private companies. They are not allowed to vote on a show of hands, but only in regard to a poll vote.

Section 324A, introduced by the Companies (Shareholders' Rights) Regulations 2009, makes it expressly clear that proxies are required to vote on the instructions of the person appointing them.

15.5.9 Chairman

Although s 319 provides that any member may act as chair, this is subject to the provision of the articles and Model Art 31states that if the directors have appointed a chairman, the chairman shall chair general meetings. If the directors have not appointed a chairman, or if the chairman is unwilling to chair the meeting then (a) the directors present, or (b) (if no directors are present), the meeting, must appoint a director or member to chair the meeting, and the appointment of the chairman of the meeting must be the first business of the meeting.

The chairman conducts the meeting and must preserve order and ensure that it complies with the provisions of the companies' legislation and the company's articles. He or she may adjourn it with the consent of, or where instructed to do so by, the meeting. The chairman has a casting vote in the case of equality. He or she is under a general duty at all times to act *bona fide* in the interests of the company as a whole, and thus must use his or her vote appropriately.

15.5.10 Minutes

Section 358 requires that copies of all resolutions passed and the minutes of all general meetings must be kept for at least 10 years and are regarded as evidence of the proceedings when signed by the chairman. Similar records have to be kept relating to directors' meetings under s 248.

15.6 Majority Rule and Minority Protection

It has been seen how the day-to-day operation of a company's business is left in the hands of its directors and managers, with shareholders having no direct input into business decisions. Even when the members convene in general meetings, the individual shareholder is subject to the wishes of the majority, as expressed in the passing of appropriate resolutions. In normal circumstances, the minority has no grounds to complain, even though the effect of majority rule may place them in a situation with which they do not agree. Even where the minority shareholders suspect that some wrong has been done to the company, it is not normally open to them to take action. This situation is encapsulated in what is known as the rule in *Foss v Harbottle* (1843) (see 14.2.3 above), where individual members were not permitted to institute proceedings against the directors of their company. It was held that if any wrong had been committed, it had been committed against the company, and it was for the company, acting through the majority, to decide to institute proceedings. A more recent example of the operation of this rule may be seen in *Stein v Blake* (1998), in which the court refused to allow an individual shareholder to pursue an action against a sole director for his alleged misappropriation of the company's property. Although the shareholder did suffer a loss as a consequence of the fall of value in his shares, that loss was a reflection of the loss sustained by the company; consequently, it was for the company, and not the shareholder, to take any action against the director.

It is important to distinguish the various ways in which one or more minority shareholders may take action against the company, the directors or the majority shareholders. The possible cases of action are:

- *A personal action*
  In a personal action, shareholders sue in their own name to enforce personal rights. An example might be where the individuals' voting rights are denied, as in *Pender v Lushington* (1877).
- *A representative action*
  A representative action is a collective action taken where the rights of other shareholders have been affected by the alleged wrongdoing. Once again, if the rights in question are membership rights, the rule in *Foss v Harbottle* does not apply.

- *A derivative action*

  A derivative action is the usual form of action, where minority shareholders sue under the fraud on the minority exception to the rule in *Foss v Harbottle*. The claimants sue in their own name, usually in representative form on behalf of themselves and all the other shareholders, except those who are named as defendants. The defendants in the action are, first, the alleged wrongdoers and, secondly, the company itself. As the claimant shareholders are seeking to redress a corporate wrong, they are actually seeking a remedy on the company's behalf. As a result, if the action is successful, the judgment takes the form of an order against the first defendants and in favour of the company as second defendant. With regard to the costs of such an action, it was held in *Wallersteiner v Moir (No 2)* (1975) that where the minority shareholder has reasonable grounds for bringing the action, the company itself should be liable, on the basis that the individual was acting not for himself but for the company.

  Particular problems may arise where those in effective control of a company use their power in such a way as either to benefit themselves or cause a detriment to the minority shareholders. In the light of such a possibility, the law has intervened to offer protection to minority shareholders. The source of the protection may be considered in three areas.

  Part 11 of the Companies Act 2006, ss 260–269, has codified the previous common law rules relating to derivative actions and in doing so it has replaced the previous procedures, while at the same time maintaining their essential purpose and effect.

  Section 260 defines a derivative action as one in respect of which the actual cause of action is vested in the company, but the action is brought by a member of the company who seeks relief on behalf of the company.

  Sub-section 260(2) provides that a derivative claim may only be brought either:

  - under the Pt 11 procedure; or
  - the unfair prejudice procedure under s 994.

  The grounds for pursuing a derivative claim, under Pt 11, are restricted to an actual or proposed act or omission by a director of the company involving one of the following grounds:

  - negligence;
  - default;
  - breach of duty; or
  - breach of trust.

  The cause of action may be against the director or another person (or both).

  Section 261 essentially restates the common law procedure relating to derivative actions. Thus, and most importantly, the member of a company who looks to bring a derivative claim must apply to the court for permission to continue it.

  On hearing the application, the court may:

  - give permission (or leave) to continue the claim on such terms as it thinks fit;
  - refuse permission (or leave) and dismiss the claim; or
  - adjourn the proceedings on the application and give such directions as it thinks fit.

  The standard that must be reached in order to pursue the action is the common law one, that there must be a *prima facie* case on the merits to justify the action. If the evidence filed by the applicant does not disclose a *prima facie* case, then the court:

  - must dismiss the application, and
  - may make any consequential order it considers appropriate.

Section 263 also provides a list of factors to be considered by the court in determining whether to accede to the application to pursue the derivative action. Foremost amongst these is the rather unusual requirement to consider whether a person acting in accordance with the s 172 duty (ie the duty to promote the success of the company) would pursue the proceedings. Further aspects to be taken into consideration by the court are:

- whether or not the member bringing the action is acting in good faith;
- the likelihood that the company may ratify any act or omission on which the action is based;
- whether the company has decided not to pursue the claim;
- whether the member bringing the action could pursue a personal action instead.

In order to further protect minority shareholders, s 262 allows an action in a company's name to be transferred into a derivative action where the company may not be pursuing the action with sufficient vigour, with the implication that its action is a stratagem to prevent the raising of a derivative action.

15.6.1 Common law – fraud on the minority

The immediately preceding paragraphs have considered the codification of derivative actions, which will determine the way in which such actions are dealt with in the future, but it remains to examine in more detail the grounds for such actions.

At common law, it has long been established that those controlling the majority of shares are not to be allowed to use their position of control to perpetrate what is known as a fraud on the minority. In such circumstances, the individual shareholder will be able to take legal action in order to remedy their situation.

❖ KEY CASE *Menier v Hooper's Telegraph Works* (1874)

Facts:
The plaintiff, who was the majority shareholder in the company, had entered into a contract with it to lay a submarine telegraph cable. However, he was approached by another party, with a more lucrative offer, to lay a cable for them. As a result, he used his majority power to cause his company to abandon its contract, allowing him to pursue the other one.

Decision:
It was held that, in the face of such an abuse of power amounting to fraud, a minority shareholder could pursue a derivative action, the result of which required the majority shareholder to account to the company for any profits made on the second contract.

❖ KEY CASE *Cook v Deeks* (1916)

Facts:
Directors who were also the majority shareholders of a company negotiated a contract on its behalf. They then took the contract for themselves and used their majority voting power to pass a resolution declaring that the company had no interest in the contract. The

minority shareholder in the company sought action against the majority for their abuse of power.

Decision:
It was held that the majority could not use their votes to ratify what was a fraud on the minority. The contract belonged to the company in equity and the directors had to account to the company for the profits they made on it. Thus, the minority shareholder was not excluded from benefiting from the contract.

Fraud

The foregoing cases provide clear-cut examples of fraudulent activity, but there are less clear-cut situations relating to the issue of fraud. What is certain is that mere negligence, in the absence of any more serious allegation of fraud, will not permit a derivative action. Thus, in *Pavlides v Jensen* (1956), a company sold an asbestos mine for £182,000, although a minority shareholder claimed that it was worth £1 million. An action by the minority shareholder failed, on the basis that the directors had done nothing unlawful and, in the absence of any assertion of fraud on their part, any negligence they had shown could have been ratified by the majority of shareholders. The case, therefore, clearly fell within the scope of the rule in *Foss v Harbottle* (1843). However, the meaning of fraud, with specific reference to fraud on the minority, was extended in *Daniels v Daniels* (1977). In this case, a married couple were the directors and majority shareholders in the company. The company bought land for £4,250 and later sold it, at the same price, to the female director. She subsequently sold it for £120,000. A minority shareholder's action was successful, in spite of *Pavlides v Jensen* and the fact that no allegation of fraud was raised against the majority shareholders. In the view of Templeman J:

> If a minority shareholder can sue if there is fraud, I see no reason why they cannot sue where the action of the majority, and the directors, though without fraud, confers some benefit on those directors or majority shareholders.

Minority

In normal circumstances, control is the correlation of holding the majority of the voting shares in a company. However, the meaning of 'control' has also been extended by the courts in relation to fraud on the minority. In *Prudential Assurance Co Ltd v Newman Industries Ltd (No 2)* (1980), the chair and vice chair of a public company controlled a substantial, but nonetheless minority, shareholding in that company through another company. They proposed that the public company should buy the share capital of the second company, on the basis of the latter's supposed asset value. It was subsequently alleged that the information provided by the chair and vice chair to the general meeting which approved the purchase was incomplete and misleading. Prudential, which was a minority shareholder in the company, sought to pursue a derivative action on the basis of the common law exceptions to the rule in *Foss v Harbottle*. At first instance, it was held that the action could proceed as, although the chair and vice chair did not constitute majority shareholders, they did control the flow of information to the company's board, its advisers and the general meeting. On that basis, they could be said to control the company. Although the directors' appeal on the substance of the allegation was upheld in the Court of Appeal, the above point was not overruled, and so remains effective.

In relation to voting rights, it was stated in *Greenhalgh v Arderne Cinemas Ltd* (1950) that shareholders were entitled to pursue their own interests when voting. However, there is judicial authority for the suggestion that special restrictions apply to the way in which majority shareholders are permitted to use their voting powers. Thus, in *Clemens v Clemens Bros Ltd* (1976), a majority shareholder was prevented from using her voting power in such a way as would affect the rights of a minority shareholder. Much time has been spent trying to explain, and justify, the decision in *Clemens*, but it should be recognised that the case involved a private, family-run company and its application should be restricted to such a case. It certainly will not be applied in regard to public companies (*Re Astec (BSR) plc* (1998)).

15.6.2 Statutory protection

In circumstances where the minority shareholders disagree with the actions of the majority, but without that action amounting to fraud on the minority, one remedy is simply to leave the company. In a listed public limited company, this procedure is easily achieved by selling the shares held, but things are more difficult in the case of small, private companies. In these quasi-partnership cases, an alternative to bringing a derivative action in the name of the company is to petition to have the company wound up, or to apply to the court for an order to remedy any unfairly prejudicial conduct.

Just and equitable winding up

Section 122(g) of the IA 1986 gives the court the power to wind up a company if it considers it just and equitable to do so. Such an order may be applied for where there is evidence of a lack of probity on the part of some of the members. It may also be used in small private companies to provide a remedy where either there is deadlock on the board or a member is removed from the board altogether or refused a part in the management of the business.

❖ KEY CASE *Re Yenidje Tobacco Co Ltd* (1916)

Facts:

The company only had two shareholders, who also acted as its directors. After quarrelling, the two directors refused to communicate with one another, except through the company secretary. One of the members sought to have the company wound up.

Decision:

It was held that the company was essentially a partnership and that, as a partnership would have been wound up in this eventuality, the company should be wound up as well.

❖ KEY CASE *Re Westbourne Galleries* (1973)

Facts:

A business which two parties had previously carried on as a partnership was transformed into a private limited company. After a time, one of the two original partners was removed from the board of directors of the company.

Decision:

It was held that the removal from the board and the consequential loss of the right to participate in the management of the business were grounds for winding up the company.

In reaching his decision in *Re Westbourne Galleries*, Lord Wilberforce made the following observations, which go a long way to explain *Clemens v Clemens Bros Ltd* (1976) and have important implications for the operation of actions for unfairly prejudicial conduct under s 94 of the CA 2006 (see below):

> The words ['just and equitable'] are a recognition of the fact that a limited company is more than a mere judicial entity, with a personality in law of its own; that there is room in company law for recognition of the fact that behind it, or amongst it; there are individuals, with rights, expectations and obligations *inter se* which are not necessarily submerged in the company structure . . . The 'just and equitable' provision does not, as the respondents suggest, entitle one party to disregard the obligation he assumed by entering a company, nor the court to dispense him from it. It does, as equity always does, enable the court to subject the exercise of legal rights to equitable considerations; considerations, that is, of a personal character arising between one individual and another, which may make it unjust, or inequitable, to insist on legal rights or to exercise them in a particular way.
>
> It would be impossible, and wholly undesirable, to define the circumstances in which these considerations may arise. Certainly, the fact that a company is a small one, or a private company, is not enough. There are very many of these where the association is a purely commercial one, of which it can safely be said that the basis of association is adequately and exhaustively laid down in the articles. The superimposition of equitable considerations requires something more, which typically may include one, or probably more, of the following elements: (a) an association formed or continued on the basis of a personal relationship, involving mutual confidence – this element will often be found where a pre-existing partnership has been converted into a limited company; (b) an agreement, or understanding, that all, or some (for there may be 'sleeping' members), of the shareholders shall participate in the conduct of the business; (c) restriction on the transfer of the members' interest in the company so that, if confidence is lost, or one member is removed from management, he cannot take out his stake and go elsewhere.

Unfairly prejudicial conduct

Use of the procedure under s 122 of the IA 1986 is likely to have extremely serious consequences for a business. Indeed, the fact that the company has to be wound up will probably result in losses for all the parties concerned. It is much better if some less mutually destructive process can be used to resolve disputes between members of private companies.

Under s 994 of the CA 2006, any member may petition the court for an order on the ground that the affairs of the company are being conducted in a way that is unfairly prejudicial to the interests of some of the members or the members generally. Section 996 gives the court general discretion as to the precise nature and content of any order it makes to remedy the situation. The following case demonstrates the operation and scope of the procedure.

❖ KEY CASE — *Re London School of Electronics* (1986)

Facts:

The petitioner held 25% of the shares in the company LSE. The remaining 75% were held by another company, CTC. Two directors of LSE, who were also directors and the principal shareholders in CTC, diverted students from LSE to CTC. The petitioner claimed that such action deprived him of his share in the potential profit to be derived from those students.

Decision:
It was held that the action was unfairly prejudicial and the court instructed CTC to purchase the petitioner's shares in LSE at a value which was to be calculated as if the students had never been transferred.

In *Re Ringtower Holdings plc* (1989), Gibson J made the following four points in relation to the operation of s 994:

(1) the relevant conduct (of commission or omission) must relate to the affairs of the company of which the petitioners are members;
(2) the conduct must be both prejudicial (in the sense of causing prejudice or harm) to the relevant interests and also unfairly so: conduct may be unfair without being prejudicial or prejudicial without being unfair and in neither case would the section be satisfied;
(3) the test is of unfair prejudice, not of unlawfulness, and conduct may be lawful but unfairly prejudicial;
(4) the relevant interests are the interests of members (including the petitioners) as members, but such interests are not necessarily limited to strict legal rights under the company's constitution, and the court may take into account wider equitable considerations such as any legitimate expectation which a member has which go beyond his legal rights.

The s 994 procedure has also been used in cases where a member has been excluded from exercising a 'legitimate expectation' of participating in the management of a company business (see *Re Bird Precision Bellows Ltd* (1984)). And, in *Re Sam Weller & Sons Ltd* (1990), the court decided that a failure to pay dividends may amount to unfairly prejudicial conduct.

In *Re Elgindata Ltd* (1991), it was held that, depending on the circumstances of the case, serious mismanagement could constitute unfairly prejudicial conduct, although the court would normally be reluctant to make such a finding. On the facts of that case, evidence of mismanagement was found, together with a lack of managerial purposefulness, but it was not sufficient to amount to unfairly prejudicial conduct. However, in *Re Macro (Ipswich) Ltd* (1994), the court found that mismanagement in relation to two companies had been so bad as to warrant the requirement that the majority shareholder and sole director in both companies should buy out the minority. The order was made to the effect that the price to be paid should ignore the current value of the shares and value them as if the mismanagement had not taken place.

Although s 994 is referred to, and tends to be thought of, as a minority shareholders' remedy, it has been held that it is equally open to the majority shareholders to use it under appropriate circumstances (*Re Legal Costs Negotiators Ltd* (1998)).

As stated previously, the powers of the court under s 996 are extremely wide and extend to making 'such orders as it thinks fit for giving relief in respect of the matters complained of'. Section 996(2) provides examples of such orders but expressly states that any such are 'without prejudice to the generality of sub-s (1)'. The examples cited in the section are powers to:

- regulate the conduct of the company's affairs in the future;
- require the company to refrain from doing or continuing an act complained of by the petitioner or to do an act which the petitioner has complained that it omitted to do;
- authorise civil proceedings to be brought in the name and on behalf of the company, by such person or persons and on such terms as the court may direct; and
- provide for the purchase of the shares of any members of the company by other members or by the company itself, and, in the case of a purchase by the company itself, the reduction of the company's capital accordingly.

The ambit of judicial discretion extends to not providing a remedy, even where there has been unfairly prejudicial conduct (*Re Full Cup International Trading Ltd* (1998)).

It should be noted, however, that when the House of Lords came to consider the ambit of s 994 in *O'Neill v Phillips* (1999), it adopted a restraining role in the extent to which the term 'legitimate expectation' should be interpreted in order to permit access to the remedies available under s 994. As Lord Hoffmann put it, the term should not be allowed to 'lead a life of its own' as a way of justifying judicial intervention in business relationships. On the facts of the case, the House of Lords declined to award a remedy under s 994 simply on the basis of a breakdown of a previous relationship of trust and confidence. Rather, it required that prejudicial conduct should be clearly demonstrated, which was not the situation in the immediate case.

Section 994 is an extremely active area of company law and has replaced s 122 of the IA 1986 as the most appropriate mechanism for alleviating the distress suffered by minority shareholders. It is essential, however, to note that the cases considered above all involved economic partnerships, which had merely assumed the company legal form as a matter of internal and external convenience. The same outcomes would not be forthcoming in relation to public limited companies. The statutory protections still apply in the case of public companies but it is extremely unlikely that they would be used as freely or as widely as they are in quasi-partnership cases. As evidence of this claim, see *Re A Company* 003843 (1986), in which the exclusion of a party from management was held not to be unfairly prejudicial, as the business had not been established on a quasi-partnership basis (see also *Re Astec (BSR) plc* (1998)). *Boughtwood v Oak Investment Partnership XII, Ltd Partnership* (2010) is a more recent example of how the courts will deal with quasi-partnership cases. In following *O'Neill v Phillips*, the Court of Appeal ordered one party to buy out the other on the basis of a fair valuation carried out by an expert independent valuer.

15.6.3 Investigations

In order for minority shareholders to complain, they must know what is going on in their company. It is part of their situation as minority shareholders, however, that they do not have access to all the information that is available to the directors of the company. As a possible means of remedying this lack of information and, thus, as a means of supporting minority protection, the Department for Business, Innovation and Skills (BIS), formerly the Department of Trade and Industry, has been given extremely wide powers to conduct investigations into the general affairs of companies, their membership and their dealings in their securities. Such powers are framed extremely widely and the courts have accepted the need for such wide powers. As Lord Denning stated in *Norwest Holst Ltd v Secretary of State for Trade* (1978):

> It is because companies are beyond the reach of ordinary individuals that this legislation has been passed so as to enable the Department of Trade to appoint inspectors to investigate the affairs of a company.

Bearing in mind the foregoing caveat, the Secretary of State has the power under s 431 of the CA 1985 (this part of that Act remains in force) to appoint inspectors to investigate the affairs of a company on application by:

- the company itself, after passing an ordinary resolution;
- members holding 10% of the company's issued share capital; or
- 200 or more members.

However, s 431(3) requires that any such application must be supported by such evidence as the Secretary of State may require for the purpose of showing that the applicant has good reason for requiring the investigation. This at least somewhat undermines the whole purpose of the exercise.

Shareholders may want an investigation because, although they might suspect that something untoward is going on, they do not know exactly what is happening in their company. Yet, before they can get such an investigation, they have to supply evidence that something is going on, which is exactly the reason why they want the investigation in the first place.

The Secretary of State may also require the applicant to give security of up to £5,000 before appointing inspectors (s 431(4)).

Under s 432 of the CA 1985, the Secretary of State may order such an investigation where:

- the court orders that such an investigation should be made;
- the company's affairs have been conducted with intent to defraud creditors, or for an unlawful or fraudulent purpose;
- the company's affairs have been conducted in a manner which is unfairly prejudicial to some of the members;
- the promoters or managers have been found guilty of fraud; or
- the shareholders have not been supplied with proper information.

Once appointed, the investigators have very wide powers. Thus, inspectors appointed under s 431 or s 432 of the CA 1985 may also investigate the affairs of any other body corporate which is or has been in the same group, if they consider it necessary (s 433).

The inspectors also have extensive powers to require production of company documents, that is, any information recorded in any form. Information which is not in legible form can be required to be produced in legible form. All officers and agents of the company being investigated and of any related company that is being investigated are required:

- to produce for the inspectors all documents concerning the company or related company which are in their custody or power;
- to attend before the inspectors when required to do so; and
- otherwise to give the inspectors all assistance in connection with the investigation which they are reasonably able to give (s 434(1) of the CA 1985).

The inspectors' powers extend to any person who is or may be in possession of information relating to a matter which the inspectors believe may be relevant to the investigation (s 434(2) of the CA 1985); so, for example, banks may be required to provide information about any clients who are under investigation.

Failure to comply with these requirements renders an individual liable for contempt of court (s 436 of the CA 1985).

Both during and at the end of an investigation, inspectors are required to report to the Secretary of State (s 437 of the CA 1985). Inspectors may or, if the Secretary of State so directs, must inform the Secretary of State of any matters coming to their knowledge as a result of their investigations (s 437).

The Secretary of State may, if he thinks fit, cause the report to be printed and published (s 437(3)(c)). The Secretary of State has a discretion as to whether to publish the report (*R v Secretary of State for Trade and Industry ex p Lonrho plc* (1989)).

Where the investigation has been carried out on the order of the court under s 432 of the CA 1985, the Secretary of State must provide a copy of any report to the court.

Under s 439 of the CA 1985, the expenses of an investigation are met in the first instance by the Secretary of State. The following persons, however, may be liable to reimburse the Secretary:

- any person who is convicted on a prosecution as a result of the investigation or who is ordered to pay damages or restore property may, in the same proceedings, be ordered to pay the expenses or part of them;

- any company in whose name proceedings are brought is liable to the amount or value or any sums or property recovered as a result of the proceedings;
- any company dealt with by the report where the inspector was not appointed at the Secretary of State's initiative, unless the company was the applicant for the investigation and the Secretary of State directs otherwise; and
- the applicants for the investigation, where the inspector was appointed under s 431 or s 442, to the extent that the Secretary of State directs.

In an investigation, individuals cannot only be required to attend; they must answer any questions that are put to them. There is no privilege against self-incrimination and all the evidence given may be used in subsequent proceedings. Section 441 renders the report admissible evidence of the inspectors' opinion in any legal proceedings. In contrast, where a disqualification order is sought under s 8 of the CDDA 1986, it may be treated as 'evidence of any fact stated therein'.

In *R v Seelig* (1991), the Court of Appeal rejected an argument that answers given under s 434 should be inadmissible in criminal proceedings as being oppressive under s 76(2) of the Police and Criminal Evidence Act 1984 (see also *Re London United Investments plc* (1992)).

However, the European Court of Human Rights (ECtHR) has decided that the use in criminal proceedings of evidence obtained by inspectors under their compulsory powers is an infringement of Art 6(1) of the European Convention on Human Rights (*Saunders v United Kingdom* (1996)). Even before the Human Rights Act 1998 was introduced, the Secretary of State had made it clear that, in light of the *Saunders* decision in the ECtHR, the prosecution would no longer rely on evidence compelled from the accused under the mandatory powers conferred on company inspectors. However, it has been decided subsequently that evidence acquired through the use of such powers of compulsion can still be used in actions taken in relation to the CDDA 1986. The reason for such a conclusion, and the means of distinguishing *Saunders*, was that such actions are not criminal in nature (*R v Secretary of State for Trade and Industry ex p McCormick* (1998)). It remains to be seen whether such a fine distinction can survive the increased emphasis on human rights ushered in by the Human Rights Act 1998.

On receipt of the final report of the investigation, the Secretary of State may:

- institute criminal proceedings against any person believed to be guilty of offences;
- petition to have the company wound up under s 124 of the IA 1986;
- petition for an order under s 994 CA 2006;
- bring a civil action in the name of the company against any party; or
- apply to the courts to have any director disqualified from acting as a director in future, under s 8 of the CDDA 1986.

In addition to the above investigation into the affairs of a company, the Secretary of State has the power, under s 442, to appoint inspectors to investigate the ownership and control of companies. In this regard, the general powers of the inspector are the same as those relating to an investigation into the affairs of the company (s 443). Additionally, however, an inspector may require documents and evidence from all persons who are or have been, or whom the inspector has reasonable cause to believe to be or to have been financially interested in, the success or failure of the company or related company. This provision also applies to those able to control or materially to influence the policy of the company or related company (s 444).

Where there is difficulty in finding out the relevant facts about the ownership of particular shares, the court may impose restrictions on those shares (s 454). These restrictions, commonly known as 'freezing orders', provide that:

- any transfer of the securities or, in the case of unissued securities, any transfer of the right to be issued with securities, and any issue of them, will be void;

- voting rights may not be exercised in respect of those securities;
- no further securities shall be issued in right of those securities or in pursuance of any offer made to the holder of them;
- except in a liquidation, no payment shall be made of any sums due from the company on the securities.

The foregoing has focused on full-scale investigation, but it has to be recognised that such investigations can be not only extremely time consuming, but also extremely expensive, not to mention potentially very damaging to the company that is the object of the investigation. In the light of these patent disadvantages of a full investigation, a possible alternative, and perhaps a precursor to a full investigation, exists in the investigation of a company's documents, supported by the power to require an explanation of such documents, where necessary. These investigations are carried out by officials of the Department for Business, Innovation and Skills.

Thus, under s 447 of the CA 1985, the Secretary of State may require a company, or any person who is in possession of them, to produce specified documents. Section 447 also empowers the Secretary of State to take copies of the documents and to require the person who produces them, or any other person who is a present or past officer or employee of the company, to provide an explanation of them.

The Secretary of State may obtain a search warrant, enabling the police to enter and search premises and take possession of documents (s 448 of the CA 1985). Any information obtained under s 447 of the CA 1985 may not be published or disclosed, except for specified purposes set out in s 449 of that Act, including criminal proceedings and proceedings for a disqualification order under the CDDA 1986. Any company officer who destroys, mutilates or falsifies a document relating to the company's property or affairs is guilty of an offence (s 450 of the CA 1985), and any person who makes a materially false statement in relation to a requirement under s 447, whether recklessly or deliberately, is also liable to a criminal charge.

Given the extent of the powers possessed by the Secretary of State and the investigators appointed by him, it is a little ironic, if not symptomatic of the failures in the system of company investigations, that some of the most famous cases of the early 1970s, that is, *Re Pergamon Press Ltd* (1971) and *Maxwell v Department of Trade and Industry* (1974), involved the late, and generally unlamented, publishing mogul, Robert Maxwell. Maxwell's death in 1991 revealed the corruption and criminal illegality on which his business empire was based and had been sustained. The blameworthy part of the Maxwell saga was, however, that his corrupt behaviour was an open secret that should have been investigated before it reached its inevitably disastrous conclusion. The manner in which Maxwell used the threat of libel actions to ensure his immunity from criticism is also to be regretted, but is a matter beyond the scope of this book.

15.7 Winding Up and Administration Orders

Winding up and administrative orders are alternative mechanisms for dealing with companies whose business activity is in a state of potentially terminal decline.

15.7.1 Winding up

Winding up, or liquidation, is the process whereby the life of the company is terminated. It is the formal and strictly regulated procedure whereby the business is brought to an end and the company's assets are realised and distributed to its creditors and members. The procedure is governed by the Insolvency Act (IA) 1986 and may be divided into three distinct categories, which are as follows:

- *Members' voluntary winding up*
  This takes place when the directors of a company are of the opinion that the company is solvent, that is, capable of paying off its creditors. The directors are required to make a statutory declaration to that effect and the actual liquidation process is initiated by a special resolution of the company. Section 89 of the IA 1986 requires that the directors of the company which wishes to go into voluntary winding up must make a declaration that the company will be able to pay its debts within 12 months from the date of the commencement of the winding up. If the directors make a false declaration, they may be criminally liable under s 89(4).
  A company may be wound up voluntarily in the following ways:
  - where an event takes place which the articles provide should bring about the liquidation of the company, then the members need only pass an ordinary resolution;
  - where the company is to be wound up for any other reason, a special resolution is required except:
    On the appointment of a liquidator, all directors' powers cease, although the liquidator may continue to employ them (s 91). On appointment, the liquidator proceeds to wind up the affairs of the company. When this is achieved, the liquidator calls a final meeting of the members and presents a report to members of how the procedure has been carried out. The liquidator must also send a copy of the report and a notice that the final meeting has been held to the Registrar of Companies (s 94).

  Three months after registration, the company is deemed to be dissolved and no longer exists.
  If at any time during the winding up process the liquidator forms the opinion that the company will not be able to pay its debts in full, then a meeting of the company's creditors must be called and the winding up will proceed as a creditors' winding up (ss 95 and 96).
- *Creditors' voluntary winding up*
  This occurs when the directors of the company do not believe that it will be able to pay off its debts and thus do not make the necessary declaration required for a members' voluntary winding up. Within 14 days of the passing of the special resolution to wind up the company voluntarily, a meeting of its creditors has to be called (s 98), at which the directors are required to present a full statement of the company's affairs together with a list of its creditors and an estimation of how much is owed to them (s 99). The creditors' meeting may require the formation of a committee of inspection, consisting of representatives of the creditors and the members (s 101). The purpose of the committee is to assist the liquidator and it does away with the need to call full creditors' meetings to get approval for particular actions. In the event of any disagreement as to who should act as liquidator, the nomination of the creditors prevails over that of the members. As in a members' voluntary winding up, once appointed, the liquidator proceeds to wind the company up and on completion of that task calls meetings of both the members and creditors to account for his actions in so doing (s 106).
  Once again, a copy of the account has to be sent to the registrar of companies and, three months after registration, the company is deemed to be dissolved.
- *Compulsory winding up*
  This is a winding up ordered by the court under s 122 of the IA 1986. Although there are seven distinct grounds for such a winding up, one of which, depending upon just and equitable grounds, has already been considered (see 13.11.2 above), the most common reason for the winding up of a company is its inability to pay its debts. Section 123 provides that if a company with a debt exceeding £750 fails to pay it within three weeks of receiving a written demand, then it is deemed unable to pay its debts.
  Section 124A provides for the Secretary of State to petition to have a company wound up on public interest grounds following an investigation of the company's affairs under the powers considered at 15.6.3 above.

On the presentation of a petition to wind up a company compulsorily, the court will normally appoint the Official Receiver to be the company's provisional liquidator.

Consequences of an order for compulsory winding up are as follows:

- the winding up is deemed to have started on the date the petition was presented;
- any disposition of the company's property and any transfer of its shares after that date is void;
- the company's property may not be seized by creditors;
- no action can be taken against the company or its property without leave of the court;
- the directors are dismissed;
- the employees are also dismissed automatically.

The Official Receiver will require the present or past officers, or indeed employees of the company, to prepare a statement of the company's affairs. This statement must reveal:

- particulars of the company's assets and liabilities;
- names and addresses of its creditors;
- any securities held by the creditors (fixed or floating charges) and the dates on which they were granted; and
- any other information which the Official Receiver may require.

After his appointment, the Official Receiver calls meetings of the company's members and creditors in order to select a liquidator to replace him and to select a liquidation committee if required. Once again, in the event of disagreement, the choice of the creditors prevails. Section 143 of the IA 1986 states that the functions of the liquidator are 'to secure that the assets of the company are got, realised and distributed to the company's creditors and, if there is a surplus, to the persons entitled to it'. Once the liquidator has performed these functions, he must call a final meeting of the creditors, at which he gives an account of the liquidation and secures his release from the creditors. Notice of the final meeting has to be submitted to the Registrar of Companies and, three months after that date, the company is deemed to be dissolved.

15.7.2 Order of payment of company debts

The assets of a company being wound up are to be applied in the following order:

- *Secured creditors holding fixed charges*
  This category of creditor is entitled to have their debt met from the assets before any other payment is made. If, however, the security is insufficient to meet the full amount owed, then the creditor ranks merely as an unsecured creditor for the balance.
- *Expenses incurred in the winding up*
  Thus, liquidators are entitled to recover their remuneration plus the costs of the winding up.
- *Preferential creditors who all rank equally*
  Section 175 of, and Sched 6 to, the IA 1986 set out what are to be treated as preferred payments and these are essentially wages of employees together with all accrued holiday pay (£800 maximum).

  The Enterprise Act 2002 removed the previous Crown preference in relation to moneys owed in relation to national insurance, income tax and VAT. These now lose their priority and stand as unsecured debts.
- *Expenses incurred in the winding up*
  There has been some controversy around this topic in the recent past. Liquidators, as a matter of course, are entitled to recover their remuneration plus the costs of the winding up and prior

to *Buchler v Talbot* (2004) they were permitted to claim all expenses *before* payment to holders of floating charges. In the latter case, the House of Lords confirmed that preferential debts were to be paid out of the property covered by a floating charge so far as the non-charged assets were insufficient to discharge those debts. However, it held that there was nothing to suggest that, additionally, liquidation expenses as such were to be discharged out of the charged property. Nor was there any reason for implying such an additional incursion into the debenture holder's rights. The costs incurred by liquidators in realising charged assets were payable ahead of the debenture holder's claims (*Re Regents Canal Ironworks Co* (1875) approved) and if there were no uncharged assets, the administrative costs of liquidators identifying and paying preferential creditors pursuant to the statutory obligation would be payable ahead of the debenture holder. However that did not have the effect of subjecting the charged assets to the payment of the costs and expenses of the liquidation as a whole (*Re Barleycorn Enterprises Ltd* (1970) overruled).

Subsequently, the decision of the House of Lords in Buchler has been expressly overruled by statutory intervention, the Companies Act 2006 introducing the interestingly numbered s 176ZA into the Insolvency Act to that effect. So the position is now that winding up expenses come before floating charge howlers' claims.

- *Creditors secured by a floating charge*
  See 14.6.7 above.
  In removing Crown preference, it would appear that the Enterprise Act 2002 ensured that more potential assets would be made available to holders of floating charges who stand next in terms of priority. However, in order to improve the position of unsecured creditors, the Act also introduced the concept of ring-fencing some of a company's assets for the exclusive use of unsecured creditors. Under the new regime, s 176A of the IA 1986, which applies to floating charges created after 15 September 2003, a liquidator, administrator or receiver is required to make a prescribed part of the company's net assets available for the satisfaction of unsecured debts before any money can be paid in satisfaction of a floating charge. Currently, the procedure does not apply if the company's assets are less than £10,000; thereafter, the prescribed amount is set at 50% of the first £10,000 and 20% of any assets above that value up to a maximum of £600,000.
- *Ordinary unsecured creditors*
  This category is the one that stands to lose most. It comprises the customers and trade creditors of the company. As creditors, they rank equally but, as is likely, if the company cannot fully pay its debts, they will receive an equal proportion of what is available.
- *The deferred debts of the company*
  These are debts owed to the members as members, for example, dividends declared but not paid.
- *Members' capital*
  After the debts of the company are paid, the members are entitled to the return of their capital, depending on, and in proportion to, the provisions of the articles of association.

Any remaining surplus is distributed amongst the members, subject to the rights given in the articles of association or other documents.

Fraudulent and wrongful trading

It is appropriate to consider these two related concepts at this juncture as they both may come into play on the winding up of a company.

Fraudulent trading: civil and criminal liability

It should be noted that there has long been civil liability for any activity amounting to fraudulent trading. Thus, s 213 of the IA 1986 governs situations where, in the course of a winding up, it appears that the business of a company has been carried on with intent to defraud creditors, or for any fraudulent purpose. In such cases, the court, on the application of the liquidator, may declare that any persons who were knowingly parties to such carrying on of the business are liable to make such contributions (if any) to the company's assets as the court thinks proper. There is a major problem in making use of s 213, however, and that lies in meeting the very high burden of proof involved in proving dishonesty on the part of the person against whom it is alleged. It should be noted that there is also a criminal offence of fraudulent trading under s 993 of the CA 2006, which applies to anyone who has been party to the carrying on of the business of a company with intent to defraud creditors or any other person, or for any other fraudulent purpose.

Wrongful trading: civil liability

Wrongful trading does not involve dishonesty but, nonetheless, it still makes particular individuals potentially liable for the debts of their companies. Section 214 applies where a company is being wound up and it appears that, at some time before the start of the winding up, a director knew, or ought to have known, that there was no reasonable chance of the company avoiding insolvent liquidation. In such circumstances, then, unless the directors took every reasonable step to minimise the potential loss to the company's creditors, they may be liable to contribute such money to the assets of the company as the court thinks proper. In deciding what directors ought to have known, the court will apply an objective test, as well as a subjective one. As in common law, if the director is particularly well qualified, they will be expected to perform in line with those standards. Additionally, however, s 214 of the IA 1986 establishes a minimum standard by applying an objective test which requires directors to have the general knowledge, skill and experience which may reasonably be expected of a person carrying out the same functions as are carried out by that director in relation to the company.

The manner in which incompetent directors will become liable to contribute the assets of their companies was shown in *Re Produce Marketing Consortium Ltd* (1989), in which two directors were held liable to pay compensation from the time that they ought to have known that their company could not avoid insolvent liquidation, rather than the later time when they actually realised that fact. In that case, the two directors were ordered to contribute £75,000 to the company's assets. In reaching that decision, Knox J stated that:

> In my judgment, the jurisdiction under s 214 is primarily compensatory rather than penal. *Prima facie*, the appropriate amount that a director is declared to be liable to contribute is the amount by which the company's assets can be discerned to have been depleted by the director's conduct which caused the discretion under s 214(1) to arise . . . The fact that there was no fraudulent intent is not of itself a reason for fixing the amount at a nominal or low figure, for that would amount to frustrating what I discern as Parliament's intention in adding s 214 to s 213 in the Insolvency Act 1986 . . .
>
> It should also be recalled, as considered previously, that directors may be disqualified from holding office for a period of up to 15 years under the provisions of the CDDA 1986 if they are found liable for either fraudulent or wrongful trading [see 15.2.3 above].

Interestingly, the common law approach to directors' duty of care was extended to accommodate the requirements of s 214. Thus, in *Re D'Jan of London Ltd* (1993), Hoffmann LJ, as he then was, held that the common law duty of care owed by a director to his company was stated in s 214 of the IA 1986, and contained both objective and subjective tests. In that particular case, the managing director of a small company had signed a proposal for fire insurance which had been filled in by his insurance broker and which contained inaccurate answers to some questions. When the insurers subsequently declined liability for a fire which destroyed the company's premises and stock,

Hoffmann LJ held that the director was liable to the company for breaching his duty of care (see 15.2.5 above for a consideration of directors' duties).

15.7.3 Administration orders

Administration, as a means of safeguarding the continued existence of business enterprises in financial difficulties, was first introduced in the IA 1986. The aim of the administration order is to save the company, or at least the business, as a going concern by taking control of the company out of the hands of its directors and placing it in the hands of an administrator. Alternatively, the procedure is aimed at maximising the realised value of the business assets.

Once an administration order had been issued, it was no longer possible to commence winding up proceedings against the company, or enforce charges, retention of title clauses or even hire-purchase agreements against the company. This major advantage was in no small way undermined by the fact that, under the previous regime, an administration order could not be made after a company had begun the liquidation process. Since companies are required to inform any person who is entitled to appoint a receiver of the fact that the company is applying for an administration order, it was open to any secured creditor to enforce their rights and to forestall the administration procedure. This would cause the secured creditor no harm, since their debt would more than likely be covered by the security, but it could well lead to the end of the company as a going concern.

The Enterprise Act 2002 introduced a new scheme, which limited the powers of floating charge holders to appoint administrative receivers, whose function had been essentially to secure the interest of the floating charge holders who had appointed them rather than the interests of the general creditors. By virtue of the Enterprise Act 2002, which amends the previous provisions of the IA 1986, floating charge holders no longer have the right to appoint administrative receivers, but must now make use of the administration procedure as provided in that Act. As compensation for this loss of power, the holders of floating charges are given the right to appoint the administrator of their choice.

The function of the administrator is to:

- rescue the company as a going concern;
- achieve a better result for the company's creditors *as a whole* than would be likely if the company were to be wound up; or
- realise the value of the property in order to make a distribution to the secured or preferential creditors.

The administrator is only permitted to pursue the third option where:

- he or she thinks it is not reasonably practicable to rescue the company as a going concern;
- he or she thinks that he or she cannot achieve a better result for the creditors as a whole than would be likely if the company were to be wound up; and
- he or she does not unnecessarily harm the interests of the creditors of the company as a whole.

Appointment of administrator under a court order

The original operation of administration required an application to the court for an administration order, which could be made by the company, the directors of the company, or any of its creditors.

Out of court appointments of administrator

Administrators may also be appointed without the need for prior court approval. This way of putting companies into administration was introduced in the Enterprise Act 2002, which repealed the existing rules and procedures and instituted new ones contained in the Sched B1 to the Insolvency Act 1986.

Such 'out of court' applications can be made by the company or its directors, but may also be made by any floating charge holder.

The company, or its directors, will be permitted to appoint an administrator only where:

- the company has not been in administration in the previous 12 months;
- the company either cannot, or is likely to become unable to, pay its debts;
- there is no existing application for either winding up or the administration of the company and the company is not in the process of liquidation; or
- no administrative receiver has already been appointed.

Floating charge holders may appoint the administrator of their choice subject to the following conditions:

- they have a qualifying floating charge over the whole or substantially the whole of the company's property;
- the floating charge is enforceable, that is, the circumstances are such that the creditor is in a position to seek to enforce their security;
- the floating charge holder has notified other such charge holders who may have priority over their own claim. This allows the prior chargee to appoint their own preferred administrator;
- the company is not in the process of liquidation; or
- neither a receiver nor an administrator is already in position.

The consequences of administration are that:

- winding up orders are either suspended (if the administrator is appointed by a floating charge holder) or dismissed (if the appointment is by order of the court);
- no further procedures to have the company wound up may be pursued whilst the administration is in effect;
- creditors are prevented from taking action to recover debts without the approval of the administrator; and
- all company documents must state that the company is in the process of administration.

The process of administration requires the administrator to:

- notify the Registrar of Companies and all creditors of his or her appointment;
- require a statement of the company's affairs to be produced by the company's officers and employees, giving details of the company's assets, liabilities, details of creditors and any security they might hold;
- produce, within eight weeks, a statement of proposed actions to be delivered to the Registrar and all creditors of the company; and
- arrange a meeting of creditors to consider the proposals of the administrator. The meeting may modify the proposals only with the consent of the administrator.

During the administration process, the administrator has the powers to: do anything necessary for the management of the company;

- remove or appoint directors;
- pay out moneys to secured or preferential creditors without the need to seek the approval of the court;

- pay out moneys to unsecured creditors *with the approval of the court*;
- take custody of all property belonging to the company; and
- dispose of company property. This power includes property which is subject to both fixed and floating charges, which may be disposed of without the consent of the charge holders, although they retain first call against any money realised by such a sale.

The administration period is usually 12 months, although this may be extended by six months with the approval of the creditors, or longer with the approval of the court. When the administrator concludes that the purpose of his or her appointment has been achieved, a notice to this effect is sent to the creditors, the court and the Companies Registry. Such a notice terminates the administrator's appointment. If the administrator forms the opinion that none of the purposes of the administration can be achieved, the court should be informed, and it will consider ending the appointment. Creditors can always challenge the actions of the administrator through the courts.

15.8 Insider Dealing

It is essential to distinguish between the nominal value of a share and its market value, that is, what it is actually worth. Whilst the former is fixed, the latter is free to fluctuate with demand. The fluctuation in the exchange value of shares in listed public limited companies is readily apparent in the constantly changing value of shares on the Stock Exchange. It is, of course, the fact that share prices do fluctuate in this way that provides the possibility of individuals making large profits, or losses, in speculating in shares. Speculation, which is not unlike gambling, refers to the purchase of shares in the hope of a quick capital gain and should be distinguished from investment, which refers to the purchase of shares as a longer-term basis for income as well as capital gain. The Stock Exchange is insistent on its role as a mechanism for facilitating investment rather than speculation but, nonetheless, that does not prevent it from being a mechanism for a huge amount of such short-term speculation. The question remains to be asked, however, as to what actually causes the fluctuation in share prices. The obvious answer, that it is the result of the working out of the law of supply and demand, merely begs the question and prompts the further question as to why particular shares should be in more demand than others. A more fundamental answer to the original question may be located in the nature of the share itself.

It will be recalled that one of the essential attributes of the share is the right it provides to participate in the profits generated by the company. At least at a very basic level, the value of shares may be seen as a reflection of the underlying profitability of the company: the more profitable the company, the greater its potential to pay dividends and the higher the value of its shares. In such a simplified model, the function of the market is to act in a rational way to ascribe a fitting capital value to the business undertaking of the company. However, it will be appreciated that the accuracy of any such valuation relies on the information provided intermittently in the company's published accounts. Once the actual performance of a company is revealed in its accounts and statements, the market value of its share capital will be adjusted in the market to reflect its true worth: either upwards, if it has done better than expected; or downwards, if it has done worse than was expected. It will be seen, therefore, that the accuracy of any current valuation is always uncertain in the face of a shortage of accurate information relating to the company's current performance, which itself may fluctuate considerably over time.

The market's valuation of the company's performance and, consequently, the market value of the individual share in that company can never be completely accurate. Speculators, in particular, look to make large capital gains by capitalising on large disparities between performance and share value through buying shares that are currently undervalued and selling them at a profit when the market adjusts the share value in line with performance. It has actually been claimed that the distorting effect of speculation is so strong that it undermines the rational operation of the market. Consequently, share prices are described as assuming a 'random walk' pattern; that is, there is no way of accurately predicting which direction they will go in, rather like a drunk man staggering back from the pub. It might be thought that the short term success of many internet '.com' companies before their ultimate collapse undermined the forgoing analysis, in that very few of them had generated any profit to sustain the value of the many millions of pounds they had been valued at. The answer to this apparent anomaly is that, in those cases, individuals were investing in the prospects of future large scale profits, not to mention the immediate short-term capital gains to be made as interest in such shares intensified.

Substantial capital gains can also be made as a result of a takeover bid, for it is usual for the predator company to pay a premium, over and above the market value of the shares in the company it has targeted for takeover. Once again, speculators may buy shares in companies which they think will be likely targets of a takeover bid, in the hope of receiving such premium payoffs.

To reiterate, it can be seen that share valuation depends upon accurate information as to a company's performance or its prospects. To that extent, knowledge is money, but such price sensitive/affected information is usually only available to the individual share purchaser on a *post hoc* basis, that is, after the company has issued its information to the public. If, however, the share buyer could gain prior access to such information, then they would be in the position to predict the way in which share prices would be likely to move and, consequently, to make substantial profits. Such dealing in shares, on the basis of access to unpublished price sensitive information, provides the basis for what is referred to as 'insider dealing' and is governed by Pt V of the CJA 1993.

15.8.1 The Criminal Justice Act 1993

Section 52 of the CJA 1993 sets out the three distinct offences of insider dealing:

- An individual is guilty of insider dealing if they have information as an insider and deal in price-affected securities on the basis of that information.
- An individual who has information as an insider will also be guilty of insider dealing if they encourage another person to deal in price-affected securities in relation to that information.
- An individual who has information as an insider will also be guilty of insider dealing if they disclose it to anyone other than in the proper performance of their employment, office or profession.

It should be noted that s 52(3) of the CJA 1993 makes it clear that any dealing must be carried out on a regulated market or through a professional intermediary.

The CJA 1993 goes on to explain the meaning of some of the above terms. Thus, s 54 defines which securities are covered by the legislation. These are set out in the second Schedule to the Act and specifically include: shares; debt securities, for example, debentures; warrants; options; futures; and contracts for differences (the last do not involve the exchange of the security but merely require one party to pay or receive any change in value of the security in question).

'Dealing' is defined in s 55 as, amongst other things, acquiring or disposing of securities, whether as a principal or agent, or agreeing to acquire securities.

Who are insiders and what amounts to insider information are clearly crucial questions, and s 56 defines 'inside information' as:

- relating to particular securities;
- being specific or precise;
- not having been made public; and

- being likely to have a significant effect on the price of the securities (this latter definition applies the meaning of 'price sensitive' and 'price affected').

Section 57 of the CJA 1993 goes on to provide that a person has information as an insider only if they know that it is inside information and they have it from an inside source. The section then considers what might be described as primary and secondary insiders. The first category of primary insiders covers those who get the inside information directly, through either:

- being a director, employee or shareholder of an issuer of securities; or
- having access to the information by virtue of their employment, office or profession.

Significantly, the term 'insider' is extended to the secondary category of anyone who receives, either directly or indirectly, any inside information from anyone who is a primary insider. Thus, anyone receiving information from an insider, even second or third hand, is to be treated as an insider. It is important to note that if the primary insider merely recommends that the second party should buy shares, without passing on information, then, although the tipper has committed an offence under s 52(2) in recommending the shares, the tippee does not commit any offence under the CJA 1993 because they have not received any specific information, as required by s 56.

The requirement that information must not have been made public is dealt with in s 58 of the CJA 1993, although not exhaustively. Of interest is the fact that information is treated as public even if it can only be acquired through the exercise of skill or expertise.

Schedule 1 to the CJA 1993 sets out special defences for those who act in good faith in the course of their jobs as market makers, but perhaps of more importance are the general defences set out in s 53 of the Act. These require the individual concerned to show one of three things:

- that they did not expect the dealing to result in a profit attributable to the price sensitive information; or
- that they reasonably believed that the information had been previously disclosed widely enough to ensure that those taking part in the dealing would be prejudiced by not having the information; or
- that they would have done what they did even if they did not have the information.

Remembering that the legislation applies to individuals who are seeking to avoid losses, as well as to those seeking to make gains, an example of the last defence listed above would be where an individual who had access to inside information nonetheless had to sell shares in order to realise money to pay a pressing debt because they had no other funds to pay it.

The seriousness of the offence is highlighted by penalties available to the courts in the event of a conviction for insider dealing. Thus, on summary conviction, an individual who is found guilty of insider dealing is liable to a fine not exceeding the current statutory maximum and/or maximum of six months' imprisonment. On indictment, the penalty is an unlimited fine and/or a maximum of seven years' imprisonment.

15.8.2 The reality of insider dealing

From the forgoing exposition of the CJA 1993, it can be seen that insider dealing is viewed as a very serious offence, with severe penalties for those found guilty of engaging in it. However, doubts have to be expressed about how the law actually operates in practice in order to control the activities of insiders. The fact that insider dealing continues to be carried out is reflected in the 'spike' that quite often appears in the graph of share prices just before a takeover bid is announced. This spike reflects a sudden, and otherwise inexplicable, rise in market value of the shares in question and suggests, if it cannot categorically prove, that some people have been trading on the basis of inside information about the takeover.

When legislation against insider dealing was first introduced in the CA 1980, there was no provision for any independent investigation of suspected dealing. This shortcoming was remedied, at least to a degree, by the provision of s 177 of the Financial Services Act 1986, which gives the Secretary of State for Trade and Industry power to appoint inspectors to carry out investigations into suspected insider dealing. The powers of any such inspectors appointed are considerable (see 9.11.3 above).

It has been claimed that insider dealing is a 'victimless crime', to the extent that no one is forced to sell or buy shares that they would not have bought or sold in any case. Take, for example, a company that is the target of a takeover bid. The insider knows about the bid and, equally, knows that if they buy shares before the bid becomes public knowledge, they will stand to make a considerable profit on any shares bought. It is quite clear that the possessor of inside information will benefit from that knowledge, but the question is as to who actually loses in the share dealing. One argument is that the sellers of the shares are in no way coerced into selling at the prevailing price, so they get what they want and, therefore, have no grounds for complaint. From this perspective, the only shareholder who could complain about losing would be the one who was mistakenly persuaded to sell by the market activity generated by the insider dealing. Some have even gone as far as to suggest that the profits derived from insider dealing are a legitimate perk of those in the know, and that they cut down the need to pay such people even higher salaries than those that they already enjoy.

There is, however, an overpowering argument against the practice of insider dealing, and not just in the fact that it unjustly rewards particular individuals. Perhaps more importantly, in so doing, it undermines the faith in, and the integrity of, the whole investment mechanism. In a system designed to encourage the concept of shareholder democracy, how can ordinary individuals be persuaded to invest in shares if they are faced with the reality of insider dealing?

15.8.3 Market abuse

Given the practical difficulties in using the insider dealing legislation effectively, it is hardly surprising that a change of approach was implemented by the introduction of the 'civil offence' of market abuse under s 118 of the Financial Services and Markets Act (FSMA) 2000. Under the various provisions of the Act, the Financial Services Authority has the power of regulating financial activity and 'market abuse' is merely one of those areas of regulation. Market abuse can be seen to encompass insider dealing, but is a wider ranging concept and one that is decided on the basis of the civil law burden of proof, on the balance probabilities rather than the criminal burden of beyond all reasonable doubt.

For the purposes of the FSMA, market abuse is behaviour, by one or more persons which;

- occurs in relation to qualifying investments;
- is likely to be regarded by a regular user of the market as failing to observe the standard of behaviour reasonably expected of a person in their position.

Section 118(2) goes on to explain that behaviour amounting market abuse may be:

- *based on information which is not generally available* to those using the market but which, if available to a regular user of the market, would or would be likely to be regarded by him as relevant when deciding the terms on which transactions in investments of the kind in question should be effected;
- behaviour *likely to give a regular user of the market a false or misleading impression* as to the supply of, or demand for, or as to the price or value of, investments of the kind in question;

- a regular user of the market would, or would be likely to, regard the behaviour as behaviour which would, or would be *likely to, distort the market in investments* of the kind in question.

Summary

Company Law (2): The Management and Operation of Companies

Corporate Governance

Corporate governance refers to the way in which companies are run and operated with the stated aim that they are run effectively and properly and are not subject to mismanagement.

Directors

The board of directors is the agent of the company and may exercise all the powers of the company.

- Individual directors may be described as being in a fiduciary relationship with their companies.
- A director can be removed at any time by the passing of an ordinary resolution of the company (s 168 CA 2006).
- Individuals can be disqualified from acting as directors up to a maximum period of 15 years under the Company Directors Disqualification Act 1986.

Directors traditionally owed the following fiduciary duties to their company:

- to act *bona fide* in the interests of the company;
- not to act for a collateral purpose; and
- not to permit a conflict of interest to arise.

Directors now owe the following statutory duties to their company:

- Duty to act within their powers (s 171);
- Duty to promote the success of the company for the benefit of members as a whole (s 172);
- Duty to exercise independent judgment (s 173);
- Duty to exercise reasonable skill, care and diligence (s 174);
- Duty to avoid conflicts of interest (s 175);
- Duty not to accept benefits from third parties (s 176);
- Duty to declare to the company's other directors any interest a director has in a proposed transaction or arrangement with the company (s 177).

Meetings

In theory, the ultimate control over a company's business lies with the members in a general meeting. In practice, however, the residual powers of the membership are extremely limited.

There are three types of meeting:

- Annual General Meeting;
- general meeting; and
- class meeting.

Proper and adequate notice must be sent to all those who are entitled to attend any meeting, although the precise nature of the notice is governed by the articles of association.

There are three types of resolutions:

- ordinary resolutions;
- special resolutions;
- written resolution (these only apply to private companies).

Voting is by a show of hands or according to the shareholding on a poll. Proxies may exercise voting rights if properly appointed.

Majority rule and minority protection

The majority usually dictate the action of a company and the minority is usually bound by the decisions of the majority. Problems may arise where those in effective control of a company use their power in such a way as to benefit themselves or to cause a detriment to the minority shareholders.

Three remedies are available to minority shareholders, which are as follows:

- The minority may seek court action to prevent the majority from committing a fraud on the minority.
- An order to have the company wound up on just and equitable grounds may be applied for where there is evidence of a lack of probity on the part of some of the members. It may also be used in small private companies to provide a remedy where there is either deadlock on the board or a member is removed from the board altogether or refused a part in the management of the business.
- Under s 994 of the Companies Act 2006, any member may petition the court for an order, on the ground that the affairs of the company are being conducted in a way that is unfairly prejudicial to the interests of some of the members.

In addition to the above remedies, the Secretary of State has the power under s 431 of the Companies Act 1985 to appoint inspectors to investigate the affairs of a company.

Winding up

Liquidation is the process whereby the life of the company is brought to an end.

There are three possible procedures:

- compulsory winding up;
- a members' voluntary winding up; and
- a creditors' voluntary winding up.

Administration

This is a relatively new procedure, aimed at saving the business as a going concern by taking control of the company out of the hands of its directors and placing it in the hands of an administrator. Alternatively, the procedure is aimed at maximising the realised value of the business assets. The Enterprise Act 2002 introduced a new scheme which reduced the powers of floating charge holders to appoint administrative receivers to the potential detriment of the company.

Insider dealing

Insider dealing is governed by Pt V of the Criminal Justice Act 1993:

- Section 52 of the Criminal Justice Act 1993 states that an individual who has information as an insider is guilty of insider dealing if they deal in securities that are price affected securities in relation to the information.
- They are also guilty of an offence if they encourage others to deal in securities that are linked with this information, or if they disclose the information otherwise than in the proper performance of their employment, office or profession.

- Section 56 makes it clear that securities are price affected in relation to inside information if the information, made public, would be likely to have a significant effect on the price of those securities.
- Section 57 defines an insider as a person who knows that they have inside information and knows that they have the information from an inside source. 'Inside source' refers to information acquired through:
    - being a director, employee or shareholder of an issuer of securities; or
    - having access to information by virtue of their employment.

  It also applies to those who acquire their information from primary insiders previously mentioned.
- Section 53 makes it clear that no person can be so charged if they did not expect the dealing to result in any profit or the avoidance of any loss.
- On summary conviction, an individual found guilty of insider dealing is liable to a fine not exceeding the statutory maximum and/or a maximum of six months' imprisonment.
- On indictment, the penalty is an unlimited fine and/or a maximum of seven years' imprisonment.

Market abuse

This is an alternative to insider dealing introduced by s 118 of the Financial Services and Markets Act 2000.

Further Reading

Bourne, N, *Bourne on Company Law*, 5th edn, 2010, London: Routledge
Davies, P, *Introduction to Company* Law, 2nd edn, 2010, Oxford: Clarendon Press
Dignam, A and Lowry, J, *Core Text Series: Company Law*, 7th edn, 2012, Oxford: OUP
Kershaw, D, *Company Law in Context:Text and Materials*, 2nd edn, 2012, Oxford: OUP
Wild, C and Weinstein, S, *Smith and Keenan's Company Law*, 15th edn, 2011, London: Pearson Education

Websites

www.bis.gov.uk/ – Department of Business Innovations and Skills
www.fsa.gov.uk/ – Financial Services Authority
www.companieshouse.gov.uk/index.shtml – registration of companies
www.bis.gov.uk/insolvency – Insolvency Service
www.ipo.gov.uk/cna – companies' names tribunal
www.frc.org.uk/corporate/ukcgcode.cfm – Financial Reporting Council, see for corporate governance
www.legislation.gov.uk/ukpga/2006/46/contents – On-line Companies Act 2006
www.legislation.gov.uk/uksi/2008/3229/contents/made – On-line Model Articles of Association

Part 5

Employment Law and Health and Safety

Employment law relies on voluntary codes and on legal duty. Businesses need to be aware of conduct that could hold them liable and obligations they must fulfil for their role as an employer. Employment law also crosses boundaries with health and safety. With a duty to provide a safe working environment, businesses need to be able to understand their duties to their employees as well as to the public at large (on and off business premises). As health and safety can come under civil and criminal liability it is of the upmost importance that businesses understand how to provide safe working practices and safe working environments.

Accordingly, Part 5 will examine the general legal principles of employment law, and specific rules relating to contracts of employment, discrimination and equality as well as termination. Health and safety law will be examined, from the introduction of health and safety as a legal duty through to the recent changes in corporate manslaughter. The European dimension and the implications on UK employers will also be explored.

Chapter 16

Individual Employment Rights (1): The Contract of Employment

Chapter Contents

Law in Context: The Contract of Employment

Studying the contract of employment may at first consideration appear procedural and tiresome. However the contract of employment underpins the relationship between the employee and employer, setting out the rights and responsibilities of both parties, and is usually the first document referred to in a dispute. Thus, the contract of employment becomes one of the most important documents a business can produce. The type of contract offered can vary, and guides the work practices of the employee, such as the number of hours worked, location, rights and benefits. The employer would also need to consider which type of contract is most suitable to the type of work, such as a zero hours contract, a full-time or part-time employment contract. So for both parties, being clear about expectations at the outset can help to avoid uncertainties. The contract of employment can also distinguish between employed and self-employed, identifying, for example, who pays tax and National Insurance, and establishing employment rights and protection for the employee. Recent years have seen variations on the traditional employment contract emerging, such as the increasing use of zero hours contracts. It could be argued that these more flexible contracts suit businesses during difficult economic times and enable businesses to continue to trade, but their impact and the employment rights of the employee are not clear-cut. In the event of an issue arising, there is an expectation that the employer and employee would refer back to the contract of employment, and try to work through the issue informally. There is an expectation that the employer would act reasonably, and seek to reach an agreement. You will see how important the contract of employment can be to a business as you read through this chapter, and how it can shape working relationships on a practical level.

16.1 Introduction

Prior to the 1970s, the traditional approach in the UK to industrial relations and employment law was non-interventionist. A change to this legal abstentionism came about during the office of the Labour Government 1974–79, which resulted in the enactment of a statutory floor of employment rights as part of the 'Social Contract', for example, the Employment Protection (Consolidation) Act 1978, the Sex Discrimination Act 1975, the Race Relations Act 1976 and the Health and Safety at Work etc Act 1974.

The law relating to individual employment rights has undergone numerous changes over the past three decades, either in the form of statutory regulation or through the interpretation of the law by the employment tribunals (formerly industrial tribunals) or courts. In the past few decades, the policy has been one of deregulation, which has led to some abuse of individual employment rights by employers, clearly illustrated by the reduction in State support for collective bargaining and trade union rights. However, the impact of EC law has halted the deregulation progress, particularly in the fields of discrimination and maternity rights and transfer of undertakings. A further halt was called for in the Labour Government's White Paper on *Fairness at Work* (Cm No 3968, 1998), in which the Prime Minister stated that the White Paper:

> . . . steers a way between the absence of minimum standards of protection at the workplace and a return to the laws of the past. It is based on the rights of the individual, whether exercised on their own or with others, as a matter of their choice. It matches rights and responsibilities. It seeks to draw a line under the issue of industrial relations law.

The Prime Minister went on to make it clear that there would be no return to the days of strikes without ballots, mass picketing or closed shops. The three main elements of the *Fairness at Work* framework are:

- provisions for the basic fair treatment of employees;
- new procedures for collective representation at work; and
- policies that enhance family life, while making it easier for people – both men and women – to go to work.

A notable feature of the *Fairness at Work* legislation was that it leaves a substantial amount of the detail to regulations. In practical terms, this means that consultation is made in the lead-up to specific regulations being passed. It also allows for such regulations to be further developed and amended swiftly. There has been some criticism of the *Fairness at Work* White Paper as being too cautious and extremely qualified (see Simpson, 'Review of the Department of Trade and Industry: fairness at work' (1998) 27 ILJ 245), although many of the proposals have been implemented by the Employment Relations Act 1999 and the Employment Act 2002. The Employment Relations Act 2004 provides further protection for collective employment rights.

When considering individual employment rights, it must be borne in mind that the legislation was originally drafted to protect full time, rather than part time, employees. As a result, thousands of workers did not qualify for employment protection on the basis that they were either self-employed or worked part time, even though the trend in working patterns shows that there has been an increase in these groups of workers.

For example, a recent report from the Office of National Statistics showed that

> The number of people working part-time hours rose by 143,000 in the three months to August [2010] to reach 7.96m, the highest figure since comparable records began in 1992. Part-time working accounted for 27.3pc of total employment, with the number of people in work rising by 178,000 on the quarter to 29.16m.
>
> A record 1.14m employees and self-employed people were working part-time because they could not find a full job, up 65,000 on the quarter, the ONS said. (*Daily Telegraph*, 13 October 2010)

These changes have come about because of changes in the labour market. The recession had an enormous impact on the loss of full-time jobs. Part-time jobs are rising to try and compensate for this loss and to kick-start the economy as businesses slowly emerge from the recession.

However, the Part-Time Workers Directive (97/81 EC) provided for 'the removal of discrimination against part time workers and to improve the quality of part time work and to facilitate the development of part time work'. Section 19 of the Employment Relations Act 1999 gave the Secretary of State the power to make regulations to implement the Directive, which resulted in the Part-Time Workers (Prevention of Less Favourable Treatment) Regulations 2000 (SI 2000/1551), these were amended in 2002.

16.2 Contract of Employment

The relationship between employee and employer is governed by the contract of employment, which forms the basis of the employee's employment rights. The distinction between contracts of employment and those of self-employment is of fundamental importance, because only 'employees' qualify for employment rights such as unfair dismissal, redundancy payments, minimum notice on termination, etc. Wider protection is provided under the discrimination and equal pay legislation, which applies to both a contract of service and a contract 'personally to execute any work or labour', which in effect includes some self-employed relationships. The Health and Safety at Work etc Act 1974 is also broader in scope, as it protects employees, the self-employed and, indeed, the general public (see health and safety chapter). It is, therefore, important to understand the meaning of the term 'employee'. Employees are employed under a contract of employment or contract of service, whereas self-employed persons, that is, independent contractors, are employed under a contract for services. A worker's employment status is not a matter of choice, ie whether they are considered to be employed or self-employed. It all depends on the terms and conditions of the relevant engagement. Distinguishing whether there is a contract of service or contract for services is simply not a case of tallying the number of factors that satisfy the requirements for an employee and comparing this against the number satisfied for an independent contractor. The courts have purposely stayed away from using this approach and instead attempt to evaluate the overall effect, as not all the requirements are of the same significance and the importance of each may differ from case to case. If it is unclear as to whether a contract of services or a contract for services exists, then it may be necessary to look back at the original intention of the parties. The following example assists in distinguishing between employees and independent contractors.

If A employs a plumber to install his washing machine, A does not become an employer, as the plumber is an independent contractor, although a firm of plumbers may employ him or her.

Over the past decade or so there has been a huge growth in freelance, casual, homeworking and teleworking types of employment. With technology growing at an incredible rate this has allowed a number of individuals to carry out work in a different way. The difficulty that arises is whether these individuals are classified within employment, as workers or whether they are self-employed.

There is very limited guidance in the legislation as to what is meant by the term 'employee'. However, s 230 of the Employment Rights Act (ERA) 1996 offers the following definition:

> (1) In this Act, 'employee' means an individual who has entered into or works under (or, where the employment has ceased, worked under) a contract of employment.
>
> (2) In this Act, 'contract of employment' means a contract of service or apprenticeship, whether express or implied, and (if it is express) whether oral or in writing.

However this definition is not satisfactory, and as a result tests have been developed through the case law for determining whether a person is an employee and, therefore, employed under a contract of service or employment, or whether he or she is self-employed and engaged under a contract for services. (See *Lee Ting Sang v Chung Chi-Keung* (1990), in which Lord Griffith argued that the question of employee status was largely one of fact.) These enable the courts to distinguish between the two types of contract and, clearly, s 230 should be read in the light of those tests. Although, for the majority of people at work, there is no problem in deciding whether they are employees or independent contractors, there may be occasions on which the distinction is not clear-cut. These tests will be considered in chronological order since, although the early tests are still of relevance, the multiple test and the mutuality of obligations test are now at the forefront, should the question of employment status arise.

16.2.1 Control test

In applying the control test, the question to be asked is does the person who is to be regarded as the employer control the employee or servant? Control extends to not just what the employee does, but how it is done. If the answer is in the affirmative, there is an employer/employee relationship.

The reasoning behind this question was that an independent contractor might be told what to do, but probably had discretion as to how to do the work. However, in the modern workplace, this question has become a little unreal and, therefore, has fallen into decline as the sole test applied by the courts, although it is still a vital element in the multiple test.

In *Walker v Crystal Palace Football Club* (1910), Walker was employed as a professional footballer with the defendant club. It became necessary to decide whether he was employed under a contract of service or a contract for services. It was held that he was employed under a contract of service (or employment) because he was subject to the control of his master in the form of training, discipline and method of play.

One problem in applying the control test was that, if interpreted strictly, it resulted in skilled and professional people being categorised as independent contractors, which, at a time when there were limited employment rights, was not a problem for them, but proved to be a problem for persons injured as a result of their negligence at work, as such a person would be unable to rely on the principle of vicarious liability to claim against the employer. As a result, the courts saw fit to develop another test which would reflect this development in the workplace by recognising that skilled and professional people could also be employees.

16.2.2 Integration test

This test was developed to counter the deficiencies of the control test. In applying the integration test, the question to be asked is how far is the servant/employee integrated into the employer's business? If it can be shown that the employee is fully integrated into the employer's business, then there is in existence a contract of employment. It is clear that an independent contractor does not become part of the employer's business. The use of this test was confirmed in *Stevenson Jordan and Harrison Ltd v MacDonald and Evans* (1952), in which Lord Denning expressed the following view:

> One feature which seems to run through the instances is that, under a contract of service, a man is employed as part of the business and his work is done as an integral part of the business; whereas, under a contract for services, his work, although done for the business, is not integrated into it but is only accessory to it.

In *Whittaker v Minister of Pensions and National Insurance* (1967), Whittaker was employed as a trapeze artist in a circus. She claimed industrial injury benefit as a result of an accident sustained at work. Initially, this was refused, on the basis that she was not an employee of the circus. She was, however, able to show that, for at least half of her working day, she was expected to undertake general duties other than trapeze work, such as acting as usherette and working in the ticket office. It was held that her general duties showed that she was an integral part of the business of running a circus and was, therefore, employed under a contract of employment.

Although this test developed due to the impracticalities of the control test, it never gained popularity with the courts. It was successfully used in cases such as *Cassidy v Ministry of Health* (1951) to establish that highly skilled workers, such as doctors and engineers, can be employed under a contract of employment, and may even have a type of dual employment, where in some circumstances they are to be regarded as employees and in others they are seen as self-employed. The control test was clearly inapplicable to these situations. The need to develop a test which would suit all circumstances became of paramount importance. Employers were able to avoid various aspects of the statutory provisions by categorising employees as self-employed when, in reality, this was not necessarily the case, but at that time there was no test to cover these situations. For example, an employer could avoid tax and national insurance provisions, as well as liability for accidents caused by these persons whilst going about their jobs. As a result, the following test was developed.

16.2.3 Multiple test

The multiple test is, by definition, much wider than either the control test or the integration test. It requires numerous factors to be taken into account in deciding whether a person is employed under a contract of service or a contract for services. It arose out of the case of *Ready Mixed Concrete (South East) Ltd v Minister of Pensions and National Insurance* (1968). RMC previously employed a number of lorry drivers under a contract of employment. The company then decided to dismiss the drivers as employees. However, it allowed them to purchase their vehicles, which had to be painted in RMC's colours. The contract between the drivers and the company stated that the drivers were independent contractors. The Minister of Pensions, who believed that the drivers were employees and, therefore, that RMC was liable for national insurance contributions, disputed this. There were a number of stipulations under the contract. The drivers had to wear the company's uniform and the company could require repairs to be carried out to the vehicles at the drivers' expense. The vehicle could only be used for carrying RMC's products for a fixed period and the drivers were told where and when to deliver their loads, although, if a driver was ill, a substitute driver could be used. It was held by MacKenna J that a contract of service exists if the following three conditions are fulfilled:

- The servant agrees that, in consideration of a wage or other remuneration, he or she will provide his or her own work and skill in the performance of some service for his or her master.
- He or she agrees, expressly or impliedly, that, in the performance of that service, he or she will be subject to the other's control in a sufficient degree to make that other master.
- The other provisions of the contract are consistent with its being a contract of service.

In this case, it was decided that the drivers were independent contractors, as there were factors which were inconsistent with the existence of a contract of employment, for example, the ability to provide a replacement driver if the need arose.

This test has proved to be most adaptable, in that it only requires evaluation of the factors which are inconsistent with the existence of a contract of employment. It is important to appreciate that there is no exhaustive list of inconsistent factors. The courts will ask questions such as: who pays the wages? Who pays income tax and national insurance? Is the person employed entitled to holiday pay?

They will treat as irrelevant the fact that there is a contract in which someone is termed 'independent contractor' when the other factors point to him or her being an employee. This is illustrated in *Market Investigations Ltd v Minister of Social Security* (1969), in which Market Investigations employed Mrs Irving as an interviewer on an occasional basis. If she was selected from the pool of interviewers maintained by the firm, she was not obliged to accept the work. However, if she accepted, she would be given precise instructions of the methods to be used in carrying out the market research and the time in which the work had to be completed. However, she could choose the hours she wanted to work and do other work at the same time, as long as she met Market Investigations' deadlines. It was held that she was an employee of the company every time she decided to undertake work for them. It was felt that the question to be asked is, 'is the person who has engaged himself to perform these services performing them as a person in business on his own account?'. If the answer is yes, then there is a contract for services; if the answer is no, there is a contract of service. Cooke J in that case stated that no exhaustive list could be compiled of the considerations which are relevant to this question, nor could strict rules be laid down as to the relevant weight which the various considerations should carry in particular cases. The most that could be said is that control will always have to be considered, although it will not be the sole determining factor. Whilst this multifactorial test found approval in *Lee Ting Sang v Chung Chi-Keung* (1990), the Court of Appeal in *Hall*

(HM Inspector of Taxes) v Lorimer (1994) warned against adopting a mechanistic application of Cooke J's checklist.

A further illustration of the problem of defining status and the implications for the individual can be seen in *Lane v Shire Roofing Co (Oxford) Ltd* (1995). The plaintiff was a roofer who traded as a one-man firm and was categorised as self-employed for tax purposes. In 1986, he was hired by the defendants, a newly established roofing business, which had not wanted to take on direct labour and so had taken on the plaintiff on a 'payment by job' basis. While re-roofing a porch of a house, he fell off a ladder, sustaining serious injuries. It was held initially that the defendants did not owe the plaintiff a duty of care, as he was not an employee. However, on appeal, the Court of Appeal found for the plaintiff. They concluded, in recognition of greater flexibility in employment patterns, that many factors had to be taken into account in determining status. First, control and provision of materials were relevant but were not decisive factors; secondly, the question may have to be broadened to 'whose business was it?'; finally, these questions must be asked in the context of who is responsible for the overall safety of the men doing the work in question. There were clear policy grounds for adopting this interpretation, the safety of the individual being of paramount importance. Whether such an interpretation would have been adopted in an unfair dismissal case is open to debate.

Obviously, as was seen in the *Ready Mixed Concrete* case, there are other factors which may have to be taken into account, even though there may be some reluctance on the part of the courts to articulate what these other factors might be, with the exception of control. It is important that the multiple test continues to be flexible, so that it can adapt with changes in the labour environment. Unfortunately, these tests have tended to result in the atypical worker, that is, those with irregular working patterns, being categorised as self-employed. This is particularly true of casual or seasonal workers, even though, in practical terms, they may see themselves tied to a particular firm and, therefore, have an obligation to that business. There have, however, been some developments in this area which provide possible redress for such workers.

The test which has developed is known as the 'mutuality of obligation' test. This arose out of the case of *O'Kelly v Trusthouse Forte plc* (1983). O'Kelly and his fellow appellants worked on a casual basis as wine waiters at the Grosvenor House Hotel. They were regarded as regular casuals, in that they were given preference in the work rota over other casual staff. They had no other employment. They sought to be classified as employees, so that they could pursue an action for unfair dismissal. They argued that if they were to be classified as employees, then each independent period of work for the defendant could be added together and the qualifying period of employment under the Employment Protection (Consolidation) Act 1978 would be met. It was held that the regular casuals in this case were self-employed, as there was no mutuality of obligation on the part of either party, in that Trusthouse Forte was not obliged to offer work, nor were O'Kelly and his colleagues obliged to accept it when it was offered. The preferential rota system was not a contractual promise.

The court made it clear that an important factor in determining whether there is a contract of service in this type of situation is the custom and practice of the particular industry. The case of *Wickens v Champion Employment* (1984) supports the decision in *O'Kelly*. In *Wickens*, 'temps' engaged by a private employment agency were not accorded employment status because of the lack of binding obligation on the part of the agency to make bookings for work and the absence of any obligation on the worker to accept them. Such an approach by the courts is obviously disadvantageous to atypical workers. However, a more liberal approach was taken in *Nethermore (St Neots) v Gardiner and Taverna* (1984), in which home workers who were making clothes on a piecework basis were accorded employee status, on the basis that a mutuality of obligation arose out of an irreducible minimum obligation to work for that company 'by the regular giving and taking of work over periods of a year or more'.

❖ KEY CASE *Autoclenz v Belcher* (2011)

Facts:

Car Valeters were paid by piecework. All contractual documentation labelled them as self-employed contractors and not employees of the company. They had to pay their own tax and national insurance. There was no obligation to provide work. The workers were allowed to send a substitute, but never did. They were paid by piecework but the invoices were prepared by Autoclenz. Equipment and materials were provided by Autoclenz as were two sets of overalls.

Decision:

The Supreme Court held that there was a mutuality of obligation upon Autoclenz to provide work, and for the valeters to accept it. It was found that there was a large degree of control over the work undertaken and that the contracts were in fact a sham and that in looking at the facts of the case and the parties' actual working relationship they were employees rather than self-employed contractors.

In *Express and Echo Publications Ltd v Tanton* (1999), Mr Tanton worked for the claimants as an employee until he was made redundant. He was then re-engaged as a driver, ostensibly on a self-employed basis. One clause in his contract stated that if he was unable or unwilling to perform the services personally, he should, at his own expense, find another suitable person. Mr Tanton found the agreement unacceptable and refused to sign it. He did, however, continue to work in accordance with its terms and, on occasions, utilised a substitute driver. He then brought a claim to an employment tribunal that he had not been provided with written particulars – thereby confirming his employee status. The employment tribunal found in Mr Tanton's favour on the basis of what had actually occurred, particularly the element of control exercised by the company. It was also concluded by the employment tribunal, and then on appeal by the Employment Appeal Tribunal (EAT), that the substitution clause was not fatal to the existence of a contract of employment. However, the Court of Appeal ruled that the right to provide a substitute driver was 'inherently inconsistent' with employment status, as a contract of employment must necessarily contain an obligation on the part of the employee to provide services personally.

There has been some criticism of this judgment (see Rubenstein, M, 'Highlights' [1999] IRLR 337), as it may allow unscrupulous employers to:

> . . . draft contracts which will negate employment status for certain workers by including a substitution clause in their contracts. Clearly, the whole issue of employment status needs clarification. The position of atypical workers or those on zero hours contracts is particularly vulnerable until this issue is resolved.

The approach taken in *Express* was also followed in *Staffordshire Sentinel Newspapers Ltd v Potter* [2004]. However, a return to the *Wickens* approach is again in evidence in *Montgomery v Johnson Underwood Ltd* (2001). Mrs Montgomery was registered with an agency and was sent to work as a receptionist for the same client company for more than two years. Following her dismissal, she named both the agency and the client as respondents. The employment tribunal and the EAT both held that she was an employee of the agency, but this view was rejected by the Court of Appeal. Buckley J stated that 'mutuality of obligation' and 'control' are the 'irreducible minimum legal requirement for a contract of employment to exist'. According to Buckley J, 'a contractual relationship concerning work to be carried out in which one party has no control over the other could not possibly be called a contract of employment'. In Mrs Montgomery's case, there may have been sufficient mutuality, but a finding of fact that there was no control by the agency was fatal to the argument that she was an employee of the agency.

Although some confusion relating to the status of agency work was introduced by the decision of the Scottish EAT in *Motorola v Davidson and Melville Craig* (2001), this has been largely solved by the introduction of the Agency Workers Regulations (2010). Davidson worked for Motorola as a mobile telephone repairer. His contract was with Melville Craig, who assigned him to work for Motorola. Motorola paid Melville Craig for his services, and Melville Craig paid Davidson. Davidson was largely subject to Motorola's control. They gave him instructions, provided tools, and he arranged holidays with them. He wore their uniform and badges, and obeyed their rules. If Davidson chose not to work for Motorola, that might have breached his contract with Melville Craig, but not a contract with Motorola. The agreement between Motorola and Melville Craig gave Motorola the right to return Davidson to them if they found him 'unacceptable'. His assignment was terminated by Motorola following a disciplinary hearing held by one of their managers. Mr Davidson claimed unfair dismissal against Motorola, who maintained that he was an employee of Melville Craig. However, the employment tribunal concluded that there was sufficient control to make Motorola the employer and the EAT agreed. In the view of the EAT, in determining whether there is a sufficient degree of control to establish a relationship of employer and employee, there is no good reason to ignore practical aspects of control that fall short of legal rights. Nor is it a necessary component of the type of control exercised by an employer over an employee that it should be exercised only directly between them and not by way of a third party acting upon the directions, or at the request of the third party.

In the case of *Carmichael v National Power plc* (1998), where a tourist guide employed on a casual basis was initially found to be an employee, the Court of Appeal held that there was the requisite mutuality of obligations between the parties, because there was an implied term in the contract that the applicants would take on a reasonable amount of work and that the employers would take on a reasonable share of such guiding work as it became available. However the case went on appeal to the House of Lords (*Carmichael v National Power plc* (2000)). It was held that the relationship, on its facts, did not have the mutuality of obligation necessary to create an employment relationship. However, in determining the terms of the contract of employment, the House of Lords concluded that where the parties intended all of the terms of the contract to be contained in documents, the terms should be determined solely by reference to these documents. In other situations, the court can look beyond the written documentation to the evidence of the parties in relation to what they understand their respective obligations to be, and to their subsequent conduct as evidence of the terms of the contract. It is argued that this approach, while it did not assist Carmichael, would assist many other marginal workers.

A number of wider implications flow from *Carmichael*. The decision has erected significant obstacles in the way of any attempts to extend employment status to casual workers. Furthermore, it could be used by employers to try to question the employment status of other workers on the margins of employment protection, for example, agency workers and homeworkers. Finally, 'highly evolved' human resource practitioners have always faced an uphill struggle in trying to convince line managers that it was not sufficient to label a worker as 'casual' and then assume that they possessed no employment rights. The *Carmichael* decision does not aid the HR manager's cause (see Leighton, P and Painter, RW, 'Casual workers: still marginal after all these years' (2001) 23(1/2) Employee Relations 75).

Finally, in *Stevedoring & Haulage Services Ltd v Fuller & Others* (2001), workers who voluntarily accepted redundancy were then re-employed as casual workers. A letter from the company offering employment made it clear that they were not employees and that there was no obligation on either the part of the company to provide work or on the applicants to accept it. However, they worked for the company on more days than not and did not work for any other employer. After three years, they applied to an employment tribunal for written particulars of their employment under s 1 of the ERA 1996. The employment tribunal and EAT concluded that the applicants were employed because there was an 'overarching contract of employment', evidenced by the implied mutuality of obligation which reflected the reality of the agreement. However, the company successfully appealed to the Court of Appeal on the basis that the implied term and express terms contained in the documents could not be reconciled.

This case therefore opens up the possibility that employers will be able to avoid legal responsibilities by including express terms denying 'employee' status to their workers. In effect, an express term will be able to override statutory employment rights. However, *Autoclenz v Belcher* demonstrates a change in attitude by the Supreme Court who looked to see of the contract was in fact a 'sham'.

The introduction of a new third employment status, that of the 'worker', has enabled some people who fall short of being an employee to have some limited employment rights. Workers were created by the National Minimum Wage Act 1998 and the Working Time Regulations 1998. Both provide basic protection on both rates of pay and working hours to all workers. They do not have protection against unfair dismissal or other full employment rights that employees have, but have greater rights than self-employed contractors.

It is still open to the Government to ensure that legislation is extended to provide cover to such workers. Section 23 of the Employment Relations Act 1999 provides the Secretary of State with such a power, and the broadening of the scope of legislative provisions can be seen in the Working Time Regulations 1998 and the National Minimum Wage Act 1998, both of which extend protection to 'workers' (see Painter, RW, Puttick, K and Holmes, AEM, *The Gateway to Employment Rights, Employment Rights*, 2nd edn, 1998, Chapter 1).

'Zero hour contracts' are a different style of contract and are growing in popularity by employers, with the Office for National Statistics suggesting that thousands of workers are on zero hour contracts. A zero hour contract is given to a worker, but the worker is not guaranteed any work. However, the worker is expected to stay available and ready for work, so when the employer offers work they are ready to accept. The worker is only paid for the work they undertake – not for being available for work. This means the contracts are flexible and useful for the employer, as they need only offer work when it is available. However, this style of contract has been heavily criticised by trade unions, because they expect the worker to be ready to work yet not be paid for this, and because the contracts mean that the worker is not regarded as an employee, so is not entitled to employment rights.

The full impact of these contracts will be tested over the coming years, and the full implications of the rights is expected to be confirmed through case law.

The Growth and Infrastructure Act 2013 has introduced a new type of contract, called an 'Employee-Owner Contract'. In this new type of contract, the employee is offered shares in the company, in exchange for sacrificing some fundamental employment rights such as protection against unfair dismissal, right to a redundancy payment and family-friendly working rights such as the right to request flexible working.

Summary of the rights and duties of an employee and an independent contractor

Employee	Independent Contractor
• Employed under a contract of employment or contract **of** service	• Employed under a contract **for** services
• Definition in s 230 (1) of the Employment Rights Act (ERA) 1996	• Definition in s 230 (2) of the Employment Rights Act (ERA) 1996
• Fulfils the control test – the engager must have a right of control over the employee	• Does not fulfil the control test – more likely to be an expert and have the freedom to do work when and where he/she wants
• Fulfils the integration test – the employee is fully part and parcel of the employer's business	• Does not fulfil the integration test – does not become part of the employer's business
• Fulfils the various requirements of the multiple test	• Does not fulfil the multiple test
• Absence of a right of substitution – it is a necessary condition of a contract of services that the worker is required to provide his/her services personally	• Fulfils the right of substitution – both the worker and his/her engager understand that a suitably qualified or skilled person can (or must) be put forward by that worker in his/her absence
• A mutuality of obligation exists	• A mutuality of obligation does not exist
• Length of engagement – more likely to have an open-ended contract	• More likely to take on a number of short term engagements
• The individual has employee-type benefits	• Absence of employee-type benefits
• The individual has a right to terminate the contract	• A contract for services usually ends on completion of the given task

Agency workers

Under the Agency Workers Regulations 2010 all agency workers who work in the same job for 12 weeks or more must be given equal treatment in respect of pay and basic working conditions. They also acquire 'day 1' rights to access employer facilities such as childcare, canteens and access to information about internal as well as job vacancies. The regulations were implemented on 1 October 2011, and mark a significant change in the rights of agency workers and also in how companies use them. Most companies will seek to avoid the 12-week period taking effect by asking for a new agency worker before they reach 12 weeks.

Wrongful dismissal

A claim for wrongful dismissal is essentially a claim for breach of contract, in this case the employment contract. If an employee has not been paid the notice due under their contract of employment or has been unjustifiably dismissed they may bring a claim. This is different to a claim for unfair dismissal which is concerned with the statutory protection contained in the Employment Rights Act 1996 against dismissal for an unfair reason. A claim for breach of the employment contract may be commenced in the employment tribunal, subject to an upper award limit of £25,000. Compensation in the form of wages and damages can, in general, only be awarded for the notice period and will be subject to the calculation of damages in contract. This has been confirmed by the decision in *Johnson v Unisys Ltd* (2001), where the applicant argued that his claim for dismissal should include compensation for breach of various implied terms which led to his mental breakdown. It was held that, if wrongful dismissal is the only cause of action, nothing can be recovered for mental distress or damage to reputation. Please see the next chapter for a more detailed discussion on wrongful dismissal.

Unfair dismissal

There are certain eligibility requirements before a claim for unfair dismissal may be commenced. The claimant must be an employee, workers and contractors do not have any protection. The employee must if employed after 6 April 2012 have 2 years continuous employment. Anyone employed prior to 6th April 2012 need only have one year's continuity of employment. The employees cannot be in an excluded category such as crown employees and share fishermen and must have been dismissed. They have a time limit of three months in which to pursue their claim. Employees who qualify for protection under the ERA 1996 have the right not to be unfairly dismissed; that is, the employer must show that the reason for the dismissal was reasonable. The ERA 1996 provides greater protection and a wider range of remedies for the unfairly dismissed employee and, in this respect, is a much needed provision in the light of the inadequacies of the common law. Further procedural protection is provided by the ACAS Code of Practice on Disciplinary and Grievance procedures. Whilst a failure to follow the procedure does not render a dismissal unfair, a failure to do may lead to an increase in the compensatory award to which an employee may be entitled. All employers should have written dismissal, disciplinary and grievance procedures in line with the ACAS model. Please see the next chapter for a more detailed discussion on unfair dismissal.

16.2.4 Part-time workers

Part-time workers as well as casuals have also found themselves to be in a vulnerable position in the labour market (see Dickens, L, *Whose Flexibility? Discrimination and Equality Issues in Atypical Work*, 1992). The Part-Time Workers Directive (EC 97/81), which the UK Government had originally opposed on the ground that it would have a negative employment effect, has finally been adopted in the Part-Time Workers (Prevention of Less Favourable Treatment) Regulations 2000. The main thrust of the Regulations is to ensure that part-time employees will be treated no less favourably than comparable full-time employees in relation to a variety of matters, including pay, leave, training and pensions. A part-time employee is defined under the Regulations as 'one who is not identifiable as a full-time employee'. Comparison will be made with a full-time employee 'who is engaged in the same or broadly similar work as a part-time employee . . . [and] works at the same establishment or, where no full-time employee working at the establishment meets the preceding criteria, works at a different establishment and satisfies those requirements'. This means that part-time employees are entitled to:

- the same hourly rate of pay;
- the same access to company pension schemes;
- the same entitlement to annual leave and maternity/parental leave on a pro rata basis;
- the same entitlement to contractual sick pay; and
- no less favourable treatment in access to training.

It has been recognised by the Department of Trade and Industry (DTI) in its regular impact assessment that the Regulations are likely to have a limited effect. Although there are over 6 million part-time employees in Great Britain, less than 17% of all part-time workers work alongside a potential full-time comparator, and less than 7% stand directly to benefit through an increase in pay and long term wage benefits. The right of part-timers not to be treated less favourably than a comparable full-timer applies only if the treatment is not justified on objective grounds within reg 5(4). Regulation 5(4) allows the employer to justify his action if it is to achieve a legitimate objective, for example, a genuine business objective, and it is necessary to achieve that objective, and it is an appropriate way to achieve the objective. (See Jeffery, M, 'Not really going to work? Of the Directive on part time work, atypical work and attempts to regulate it' (1998) 27 ILJ 193.)

Despite the broadening of the coverage of the 2000 Regulations to 'workers' as opposed to 'employees', the Regulations retain the potential to disenfranchise many economically dependent workers from the scope of their protection. This is because comparisons under the Regulations can only be employed under the Regulations between an actual comparator (Equality Act 2010) employed under the same contract. Thus, for example, a part-time worker employed as a fixed term contract worker cannot compare his or her treatment with that of a full-time worker employed on a permanent contract. Similarly, workers employed under contracts for services ('workers') cannot compare their treatment with full-time workers employed under contracts of employment ('employees') – see reg 2(3). In other words, the *Carmichael v National Power plc* (2000) problem is not resolved. The only cases in which a claim may be made without reference to an actual full-time comparator are set out in the Regulations. Broadly, these exceptions cover (a) a full-time worker who becomes part-time (reg 3), and (b) full-time workers returning to work part-time for the same employer within a period of 12 months (reg 4). In the past, the threshold qualifying hours also imposed a barrier for part-time and casual workers in qualifying for employment protection rights, for example, the requirement that a worker had worked 16 hours per week for a minimum of two years in order to qualify for unfair dismissal or redundancy payments. However, this was changed by the decision in *R v Secretary for Employment ex p Equal Opportunities Commission* (1995). As a result of this, the Employment Protection (Part-Time Employees) Regulations 1995 (SI 1995/31) were introduced, which removed the 16 hours per week qualification. The decision of the European Court of Justice in *R v Secretary of State for Employment ex p Seymour-Smith* (1999) went one step further, in concluding that the two-year qualifying period discriminated against part-time employees, who are predominantly female. Such a qualifying period may, therefore, contravene Art 141 of the EC Treaty. However, in *R v Secretary of State for Employment ex p Seymour-Smith and Perez* (2000), the House of Lords concluded that although the qualifying period was discriminatory, it was justified on the basis that, when it was introduced, there was evidence that a shorter qualifying period might inhibit employers recruiting employees. The Employment Relations Act 1999, in which the qualifying period for unfair dismissal was reduced to one year, has overtaken the decision in the *Seymour-Smith* case. The situation regarding unlawful dismissal and the period of employment has changed, and is considered in more detail later.

The Part-Time Workers (Prevention of Less Favourable Treatment) Regulations (Amendment) Regulations 2002 (SI 2002/2035) attempt to address the issue of the comparator by recognising that fixed term and permanent workers may be regarded as 'employed under the same contract'. The two year time limit on remedies has also been removed.

16.3 Loaning or Hiring Out Employees

One area of contention involves the loaning or hiring out of an employee; the issue is, whose is the employee? This is particularly important in respect of who should be vicariously liable for the employee's torts. As can be seen in *Mersey Docks and Harbour Board v Coggins and Griffiths (Liverpool) Ltd* (1947), there is a rebuttable presumption that, when an employee is loaned out, he or she remains the employee of the first/original employer. In *Mersey Docks*, a crane and its driver were hired out to C and G to assist in the loading of a ship. C and G paid the driver's wages. While the crane driver was doing this work, he negligently injured an employee of the stevedores, C and G. The issue to be decided by the courts was whether the harbour board or C and G were vicariously liable for the crane driver's negligence. It was held that the harbour board remained the employer of the crane driver. He was under their ultimate control in respect of the work he should do, even though he was under the temporary direction of the stevedores; that is, the original employer retained the right to hire, dismiss and decide on his work, even though day to day control passed to the stevedores.

The courts are reluctant to find that there has been a transfer of employment where employees are loaned or hired out, unless there is consent on the part of the employee or there is an agreement which clearly states the position in the event of liability accruing. There may, however, be exceptional circumstances where the courts may declare that, *pro hac vice* (for that one occasion), a loaned or hired employee has become the employee of the 'second' employer, as in *Sime v Sutcliffe Catering* (1990).

16.4 Continuity: Periods Away from Work

In order to acquire employment protection rights, there should normally be continuity of employment. It is, therefore, necessary to consider the impact of weeks away from work. Section 212 of the ERA 1996 is the main legislative provision. The key point is that any week or part of a week in which the employee's relations with his employer are governed by a contract of employment must count in computing the employee's period of employment. The section also reinforces the point that absence through pregnancy or childbirth, sickness or injury, temporary cessation of work or custom or practise will generally count in computing the period of employment. Any such custom or practise must be established before or at the time that the absence commences. Even where employers engage employees on a series of short term contracts, they may find that these will be added together for the purpose of computing the period of employment – *Ford v Warwickshire CC* (1983). This mathematical approach may be used where the gaps in employment are regular, whereas where the pattern is irregular, the courts should be flexible and adopt a 'broad brush' approach – *Flack v Kodak Ltd* (1986). This approach is of benefit to many workers, such as part time or temporary teachers, and makes it more difficult for employers to avoid the employment protection laws by offering a succession of fixed term contracts. However, where patterns of employment are more irregular, it may not be appropriate to consider continuity in this way. Indeed, in *Flack v Kodak Ltd* (1986), where the periods of employment were particularly irregular, a broad brush approach was adopted, whereby the whole of the employment period was deemed to be relevant; to do otherwise would have led to a most misleading comparison being drawn. Section 212(3)(c) provides for any absence counting towards continuity where it is recognised by 'arrangement or custom'.

In *Curr v Marks & Spencer plc* (2003), the Court of Appeal considered the question of continuity of employment whilst on a career break. The court, in applying the ERA 1996, s 212(3)(c), decided that, if an ex-employee was to fall within s 212(3)(c), he or she must, by arrangement or custom, be 'regarded' by each of the parties as continuing in the employment of the employer for any purpose during that period. There must be *mutual recognition* through the arrangement that the ex-employee, though absent from work, nevertheless continues in the employment of the employer. Without there being a meeting of minds in respect of this arrangement, s 212(3)(c) will not be satisfied.

Booth v United States of America (1999) is a prime example of the vulnerability of workers on fixed term contracts. The case concerned a US airbase in the UK, where maintenance workers were employed under a series of fixed term contracts for a total period in excess of two years but with a gap of about two weeks between each contract. Despite the fact that the aim of this arrangement was to evade the employment protection legislation, the EAT declined to adopt a purposive approach and to find continuity. As Morrison J put it:

> Whilst it is generally desirable that employees should enjoy statutory protection during their employment, Parliament has laid down the conditions under which that protection is afforded. If, by so arranging their affairs, an employer is lawfully able to employ people in such a manner

> that the employees cannot complain of unfair dismissal or seek a redundancy payment, that is a matter for him. The courts simply try and apply the law as it stands. It is for the legislators to close any loopholes that might be perceived to exist.

The position of such workers is improved by the implementation of the EC Fixed Term Work Directive in the Fixed-Term Employees (Prevention of Less Favourable Treatment) Regulations 2002 (SI 2002/2034). The key aim of the Directive and Regulations is to ensure that fixed term employees are not, without justification, treated less favourably than comparable permanent staff. The Directive does not cover pay or pensions and so, without further legislation or evidence of sex/race/disability discrimination, it is lawful to continue to pay a fixed term worker less than a member of the permanent staff. Fixed term employees can compare their conditions to employees who are not on fixed term contracts and are employed by the same employer to do the same or broadly similar work. Where relevant, the comparator should have similar skills and qualifications to the fixed term employee. If there is no comparator in the establishment, a comparison can be made with a similar permanent employee working for the same employer in a different establishment.

The key question employers must ask themselves is, 'is there a reason for treating this employee less favourably?'. Employers should give due regard to the needs and rights of the individual employee and try to balance those against business objectives.

Less favourable treatment will be justified on objective grounds if it can be shown that the less favourable treatment is to achieve a legitimate and necessary business objective and is an appropriate way to achieve that objective. Objective justification is a matter of degree; employers should therefore consider whether it is possible to offer fixed term employees certain benefits, such as annual subscriptions, loans, clothing allowances and insurance policies, on a pro-rata basis, depending on the length of the fixed term contract. A comparison may be made either on a term-by-term basis, or on a package basis.

A fixed term employee has the right to ask their employer for a written statement setting out the reasons for less favourable treatment if they believe this may have occurred. The employer must provide this statement within 21 days (reg 5).

The use of successive fixed term contracts will be limited to four years, unless the use of further fixed term contracts is justified on objective grounds. If a fixed term contract is renewed after the four year period, it will be treated as a contract for an indefinite period unless the use of a fixed term contract is objectively justified (reg 8).

16.5 Industrial Disputes

Any week in which an employee takes part in a strike does not count towards continuity (s 212 of the ERA 1996) but, at the same time, continuity is not broken. The same is true of absences due to lock-outs by the employer.

16.6 Formation of the Contract of Employment

In general terms, there are no formalities involved in the formation of a contract of employment. The contract itself may be oral or in writing, with the exception of apprenticeship deeds and articles for merchant seamen, which obviously, by their nature, have to be in writing. Therefore, it follows that, within reason, the parties to the contract, that is, the employer and employee, can decide on whatever terms they wish. This, however, raises the issue of the respective bargaining position of the parties, as the employer will always be in the strongest position. In industries which have traditionally had strong trade union representation, a collective agreement may form the basis of the employment terms, where it is expressly agreed that such agreements should be incorporated into the contract. The contract may also be subject to implied terms, which will be considered subsequently.

16.6.1 Written statement of terms

Although the contract of employment itself need not be in writing, the employee must be given written particulars of the main terms. This is required by s1 of the ERA 1996 and they are generally known as s1 statements. These written particulars must be supplied within two months of the date on which employment commenced. The particulars must contain:

- the names of the parties and the date on which the employment commenced; if there is a change of employer, resulting in continuity of employment, the date on which continuity commences must be specified;
- the rate of pay or the method of calculating it;
- the intervals at which wages are to be paid, for example, weekly or monthly;
- terms and conditions relating to hours of work;
- terms and conditions relating to holidays and holiday pay;
- the length of notice which the employee must give and the amount that he or she is entitled to receive on termination of his or her employment; and
- job title and description.

The Trade Union Reform and Employment Rights Act (TURERA) 1993 made further changes, so that the statement must also include:

- where the employment is non-permanent, the period for which it is expected to continue;
- either the place of work or, where the employee is required or permitted to work at various places, an indication of that fact, plus the address of the employer;
- any collective agreement which directly affects the terms and conditions of employment, including, where the employer is not a party, the persons by whom they were made; and
- where an employee is required to work outside the UK for more than a month, the period of such work, the currency of remuneration, any additional remuneration or benefit by reason of the requirement to work outside the UK and any terms and conditions relating to his or her return to the UK.

These form the basis of the written particulars and the employer must provide this information in one document (s 2 of the ERA 1996; see Figure 16.1 below). In addition, the employer must specify (s 3):

- any disciplinary rules which apply to the employee, or reference to the document containing them;
- any procedure applicable to the taking of disciplinary decisions relating to the employee or to a decision to dismiss the employee, or referring the employee to the provisions of a document specifying a procedure which is reasonably accessible to the employee;
- the person to whom the employee can apply if he or she is dissatisfied with any disciplinary decision relating to him or her;
- the grievance procedure, including the person to whom he or she can apply if he or she has a grievance relating to his or her employment; and
- the document containing rights to sick pay and pension schemes.

The following statement of written particulars is provided in accordance with the ERA 1996. It is not intended to be a comprehensive statement of the terms and conditions of your employment.

The parties:

Employer: (name and address)

Employee: (name and address)

Job title and description: (as flexible as possible)

Place of work:

Date of commencement:

Remuneration: (for example, rate x hours) payable weekly/monthly

Hours of work: (for example, 8.45 am to 5.15 pm Mondays to Fridays inclusive, plus one Saturday in four)

Holiday entitlement: (for example, whether paid leave and when it can be taken; statutory holidays)

Notice: (period to be given by the employer and employee in order to terminate the contract of employment subject to the statutory periods)

The terms and conditions relating to pensions, sick leave and pay; the grievance and disciplinary procedures; the works rules; and the safety policy are set out in reference documents. Copies can be seen on the main notice board and are contained in the staff handbook or are available from the Human Resources Office.

You will be notified in writing of any changes to your terms and conditions within one month of the date of such change.

Acknowledgment: I have received and read a copy of the terms and conditions of employment, which are correct and which I accept.

Figure 16.1 Specimen statement of terms of employment

At the very least, the employee must have reasonable access to this information. Any agreed changes must be communicated to the employee in writing within one month of the change. It is permissible for the employer to refer the employee to additional terms contained in a document, such as a collective agreement, as long as it is reasonably accessible. The written statement, whilst not being a contract, is *prima facie* evidence of what is agreed between the employee and the employer. (See *Gascol Conversions Ltd v Mercer* (1974) and *Systems Floors (UK) Ltd v Daniel* (1982) for consideration of the distinction between signing an acknowledgment and signing a statement described as a 'contract'.) If the employer fails to provide a statement, or if there is a disagreement with respect to its contents, or if a change has not been properly notified, the employee may apply to an employment tribunal in order to determine which particulars ought to be included in the statement (s 11 of the ERA 1996) (see *Mears v Safecar Security Ltd* (1982)). In such cases, applications must be brought within three months of termination of the contract of employment.

Following amendments implemented by TURERA 1993 and the Employment Protection (Part-Time Employees) Regulations 1995, the eight hour threshold has been removed and the right to receive a written statement has been extended to all part-time employees, as well as full-time employees whose contract subsists for one month. However, certain categories of employee are still excluded, including Crown employees, registered dock workers and those employees who work wholly or mainly outside Great Britain.

If there is a change to any of the terms about which particulars must be provided or referred to in the document, the employer must notify employees individually in writing. If an employer fails to provide a s 1 statement within two months of the commencement of employment, the employee may make an application to the Employment Tribunal for a declaration of their terms of employment, and between two and four weeks' pay as compensation.

16.6.2 Terms

Terms may be incorporated into the contract of employment from a variety of sources. Such terms may be express or implied. Section 179 of the Trade Union and Labour Relations (Consolidation) Act (TULR(C)A) 1992 provides that a written collective agreement which states that the parties intend all or part of it to be legally enforceable is then expressly incorporated into the contract.

The express terms are those agreed upon by the employer and employee on entering into the contract of employment. They may be oral or in writing and will cover such things as the point on the salary scale at which the employee will commence employment. However, oral terms may be open to dispute and it is in the interests of both parties to have such terms in writing; for example, a restraint of trade clause is unlikely to be enforceable unless it is in writing. Disputes about oral terms may result in the employee pursuing an action for clarification before an employment tribunal. A breach of an express term of the contract may result in the dismissal of the employee and, if it is a breach by the employer, may enable the employee to resign and bring an action for constructive dismissal. As we have seen, a collective agreement made between the employer or his association and a trade union may be expressly incorporated into the contract of employment (s 179 of TULR(C)A 1992). Such agreements usually provide a comprehensive set of terms and conditions for particular types of employees. In such cases, the trade union usually has equal bargaining power to the employer. Where they are expressly incorporated under s 1 of the ERA 1996, they will bind both employer and employee. However, as Kerr LJ stated in *Robertson v British Gas Corp* (1983):

> . . . it is only if and when those terms are varied collectively by agreement that the individual contracts of employment will also be varied. If the collective scheme is not varied by agreement, but by some unilateral abrogation or withdrawal or variation to which the other side does not agree, then it seems to me that the individual contracts of employment remain unaffected.

There may be a subtle distinction between a 'collective agreement', which is legally binding, and a 'local arrangement', which is not (*Cadoux v Central Regional Council* (1986); see also Napier, B, 'Incorporation of collective agreements' (1986) 15 ILJ 52). It is possible, in the absence of express agreement, for terms to be incorporated by conduct, for example, where collectively bargained terms and conditions are uniformly observed for a group of workers of which the employer is a member. Another issue which may arise relates to the validity of all the terms of the agreement. Some terms may be deemed to be inappropriate for incorporation, as they relate to the individual, as opposed to collective, relationship. In *Alexander v Standard Telephone and Cables Ltd (No 2)* (1991), a redundancy agreement written into a collective agreement was held to be unenforceable as being inappropriate for incorporation. Part of the reasoning in this case was that the redundancy provisions were to be found in a part of the agreement containing other provisions incapable of incorporation, that is, statements of policy. (See Rubenstein, M, 'Highlights' [1991] IRLR 282 for a critique of this decision.) In the case of *Kaur v MG Rover* (2005), the Court of Appeal held that a statement of collective aspiration in a collective agreement was not incorporated into individual contracts of employment.

❖ KEY CASE *Kaur v MG Rover* (2005)

Facts:
In 2003, Kaur, along with 100 other employees, was faced with the threat of compulsory redundancy. She maintained that, in line with the terms of collective agreements which were expressly incorporated into her contract of employment, her employer was not entitled to declare employees of her category and grade compulsorily redundant. The agreements in question were 'Rover Tomorrow – The New Deal', which included a job-security provision, and second, 'The Way Ahead', which stated that: 'There will be no compulsory redundancy'. Her contract also gave her the option to give notice to terminate her employment for any reason. Kaur applied to the court for a declaration that both the collective agreements were incorporated into her contract of employment, with the effect that she had a contractual right not to be made compulsorily redundant.

Decision:
In the High Court, the judge held that the provision relating to job-security in the 'New Deal' agreement was no more than an expression of an aim or expectation and so was not incorporated into the individual employee contracts. However, the judge agreed that 'The Way Ahead' agreement was incorporated, and had the effect that no compulsory redundancy was the aim of the agreement and it prevailed over the employers' right to terminate on notice. Kaur, therefore, had a contractual right not to be made compulsorily redundant. The employer went to the Court of Appeal. Kaur cross-appealed, on the grounds that the job security provision of 'The New Deal' was not incorporated in her contract of employment. The Court of Appeal allowed the appeal and dismissed the cross-appeal.

Termination of a contract

A contract of employment may be ended by mutual agreement or by the employer or employee giving the required notice of termination. Thus either party to a contract of employment – (as long as the employer has a lawful reason and follows a fair procedure) can terminate the contract by giving notice. An employment contract will usually set out how much notice one must give the other before an employee leaves. In some cases this may be more generous than the minimum notice period required to be given by law. An employment contract cannot provide that an individual get less than the legal minimum notice. The majority of contracts will contain an express term detailing the notice which must be given on either side, although employee's also have statutory rights to minimum notice and protection against unfair dismissal. If an employment contract does not specify a notice period, a 'reasonable' period of notice must be given – what is reasonable will depend on various factors including your seniority within the business and your length of service. It could also be determined by your pay period: if you are paid weekly, you could argue that a week's notice is reasonable; and if you are paid monthly, you could argue that a month is reasonable.

A dismissal takes place when:

- the employer terminates the employment, with or without notice (a dismissal without notice is a 'summary dismissal' due to, for example, gross misconduct);
- a fixed-term contract expires and is not renewed; or
- the employer's behaviour counts as such a fundamental breach of the contract of employment that the employee is entitled to respond by resigning – a constructive dismissal.

A termination of contract may also arise by mutual agreement between the employee and employer, regardless of the fact that the employment contract is concluded with or without the definite period of time. In reality, this method is frequently used as an alternative to termination of notice.

Disciplinary, grievance and dismissal procedures

The Employment Act 2008 changed the way in which employers are required to handle disciplinary, grievance and dismissal procedures. The ACAS Code of Practice 1, which is essentially a simplified version of the old one, requires that employers will need to follow certain steps when investigating an allegation of misconduct or steps when considering a disciplinary procedure or a grievance is raised. For example, when starting disciplinary proceedings, an employer should:

- write to the employee setting out the reasons for the disciplinary meeting;
- give the employee a right to be accompanied by a work colleague or a trade union official;
- confirm the reasons for the disciplinary warning in writing; and
- give the employee a right of appeal against the decision.

The code advises employers to take prompt action when dealing with issues of conduct, and to have a consistent approach when disciplining members of staff. The procedures that employers have to follow are now more strict, where a formal investigation process must be adhered to. If an employer faces a claim and the Tribunal considers that it was unreasonable that the employer had not followed the ACAS Code of Practice, the Tribunal can increase any award by 25%. Conversely, if the employee did not comply with the code, (for example by failing to attend disciplinary meetings) the award made to an employee could be decreased by 25%.

16.6.3 National minimum wage

Before considering the terms which may be implied into a contract of employment, it is pertinent, in the light of the more interventionist approach taken by the Government, to consider the national minimum wage. It is anticipated that the statutory requirement to pay a minimum wage will impact not only on the nature of the labour market, but also on equality, as it relates to pay.

The statutory provisions are to be found in the National Minimum Wage Act (NMWA) 1998. With effect from 1 April 1999, all relevant workers are entitled to the national minimum wage. The current minimum wage is set at £6.31 per hour for persons aged 22 and over, and £5.03 for those aged between 18 and 21. All workers aged 18 years and over are entitled to the minimum wage – this is defined in s 54 of the National Minimum Wage Act 1998. A national minimum wage of £3.72 per hour has been introduced for 16 and 17 year olds. The National Minimum Wage for an Apprentice is £2.68. These figures have been set as of 1 October 2013.

The national minimum wage applies to all workers, whether they are paid hourly, monthly, etc. The Low Pay Commission was set up to advise the Secretary of State for Employment in respect of the key issues relating to the minimum wage. The Low Pay Commission monitors the level at which the rate is set and makes recommendations for change on an annual basis. The Commission also reviews the working of the NMWA 1998 with a view to correcting anomalies, closing loopholes, etc – see Low Pay Commission, *Second Report*, 2000, The Stationery Office. For example, the number of exempted categories of worker has been increased – National Minimum Wage (Amendment) Regulations 2000 (SI 2000/1989).

The First Annual Report on the national minimum wage showed that over £2 million had been won back by enforcement officers – see *National Minimum Wage Annual Report*, 1999–2000, available from the DTI.

The enforcement officers are appointed by the Inland Revenue.

As part of the requirements under the NMWA 1998, employers are required to keep adequate records to show that the wage has been paid and must produce such records on request (by workers, the enforcement agency, tribunals and courts). In proceedings, the onus is generally on the employer to show that the wage has been paid correctly. It is a criminal offence to refuse to pay the minimum wage or to fail to keep proper records. There is no provision for employers or workers to 'opt out' of the requirements.

The right to a national minimum wage is given to 'workers'. A 'worker' is defined in s 54 of the NMWA 1998 as an individual who has entered into or works under:

(a) a contract of employment; or
(b) any other contract, whether express or implied and (if it is express) whether oral or in writing, whereby the individual undertakes to do or perform personally any work or services for another party to the contract whose status is not by virtue of the contract that of a client or customer of any profession or business undertaking carried on by the individual; and any reference to a worker's contract shall be construed accordingly.

This wide definition is intended as an anti-avoidance measure. It seeks to exclude only the genuinely self-employed from its ambit and makes it extremely difficult for an employer to restructure its working relationships in order to avoid paying the national minimum wage and gaining an unfair competitive advantage in relation to market rivals. Agency and home workers are effectively also included by virtue of ss 34 and 35 of the NMWA 1998 respectively.

There are, however, specific exclusions, for example, share fishermen, voluntary workers, prisoners and people living and working within the family, such as nannies and au pairs; also, they do not apply to family members who work in the family business (National Minimum Wage Regulations 1999 (SI 1999/584) and the National Minimum Wage (Amendment) Regulations 2009). It has already been decided that pupil barristers are not 'workers' within the meaning of the Act (*Lawson & Others v Edmonds* (2000)).

Employers should express the minimum wage as an hourly rate. However, the minimum wage need only be paid over the worker's 'pay reference period'. This is defined as a calendar month or, where the worker is paid by reference to a shorter period, that period (reg 10(1) of the National Minimum Wage Regulations 1999 (SI 1999/584)).

In determining whether the national minimum wage is being complied with, it is necessary to exclude certain items from gross pay and include others. The following are not included:

- loans or advances to workers;
- pension payments, lump sums on retirement and compensation for losing one's job;
- court or tribunal awards;
- redundancy payments;
- awards under suggestion schemes;
- payments during absences from work (for example, sick pay and maternity pay);
- benefits in kind, except living accommodation, for which there is a maximum permitted offset;
- the monetary value of vouchers, etc, which can be exchanged for money, goods or services;
- premium payments for overtime and shift work;
- unsociable hours payments and standby payments;
- service charges, tips and gratuities;
- payments made to reimburse the worker, for example, travel expenses; and
- deductions made in respect of worker's expenditure, for example, cost of uniforms, tools, etc.

Where a worker has reasonable grounds for believing that he or she has been, or is being, paid less than the national minimum wage during the pay reference period, he or she may require his or her employer to produce any relevant records. The worker must supply the employer with a 'production notice'. The employer must then produce the records within 14 days following the date of receipt of the notice. A worker may complain to the tribunal where the employer either fails to produce the records or does not produce the relevant records.

The Low Pay Commission Report 2010 highlighted that in October 2009, the adult minimum wage had increased by 61% in comparison with April of 1999 when it first started. The rise for October 2009 was the smallest increase to date (1.2%). This is likely to have necessitated from the fact of the downturn in the economy.

16.6.4 Implied terms

Implied terms may arise out of the custom and practice of a particular industry; for example, deductions from wages for bad workmanship were accepted as a term of contracts in the cotton industry. The courts may be the final arbiters as to whether an implied term is incorporated into the contract and, as can be seen in *Quinn v Calder Industrial Materials* (1996), such claims are not always successful.

In the case of *Henry v London General Transport Services Ltd* (2001), the EAT confirmed that there were four requirements in establishing implied terms by custom and practice, as follows:

- In relation to the incorporation into a contract of employment of a term by way of a custom and practice, the custom and practice so relied on must be reasonable, certain and notorious.
- Where what is shown in relation to the custom and practice, the term thus supported is incorporated on the assumption that it represents the wishes of the parties.
- Strict proof is required of the custom and practice and the burden of such proof is upon the party seeking to rely upon the consequential incorporation of the term into the contract.
- There is some relevant distinction generally to be made between custom and practice, enabling changes to be made, and one enabling 'fundamental' changes to be made in a man's terms and conditions of employment.

See Chapter 17 →

Implied terms generally have to be read subject to any express terms, which may be to the contrary. The courts have moved towards a more objective test for determining incorporation based on 'necessity' or 'business efficacy', that is, is the term a 'necessary condition of the relationship?'. However, where the implied term is necessary to give efficacy to the contract, the implied term will take precedence over the express term. This is illustrated in *Johnstone v Bloomsbury HA* (1991).

A hospital doctor was obliged to work a stipulated number of hours under his contract, plus additional hours if required. As a result, the doctor found himself working, on average, over 80 hours per week and, as a result, became ill. It was held that the express term regarding the additional hours had to be read subject to the implied term of care and safety. The implied term in this case was necessary to give efficacy to the contract.

A reasonableness test is also appropriate when determining whether implied terms are incorporated. This is particularly so where one of the parties is relying on custom and practice as the basis for incorporation (see Smith, I, 'The creation of the contract of employment', in *Employment Law Guide*, 2nd edn, 1996, p 15). An employee must know of the custom and practice if it is to be accepted as incorporated into the contract. In *Sagar v Ridehalgh & Sons Ltd* (1931), it was common practice in the defendant's mill to make deductions for bad work. This practice had operated for at least 30 years and all weavers had been treated the same. The plaintiff weaver challenged its validity. The court held that the matter of whether the plaintiff knew of its actual existence was immaterial in this case, as he had accepted employment on the same terms and conditions as the other workers at the mill. However, it is clear that a worker should have either express or constructive knowledge of such 'terms' if they are to be valid and enforceable (see *Meek v Port of London* (1913) and *Quinn v Calder Industrial Materials Ltd* (1996)).

A number of 'standard' implied terms have developed in respect of the employer/employee relationship. These take the form of duties imposed on the respective parties. A breach by the employee may result in disciplinary action or even dismissal; a breach by the employer may result in legal proceedings before a tribunal.

16.6.5 Duties imposed on the employer

The duties imposed on the employer are to provide work; to pay wages; to indemnify the employee; and to treat with mutual respect and provide for the care and safety of the employee.

To provide work

An employer will not be in breach of the implied duty to provide work as long as he or she continues to pay his or her employees, even though there may be no work available. However, in certain situations, the employer may be liable for failing to provide work, for example, if a reduction in the employee's earnings occurs. This is most likely to affect those employees on piecework commission or where the employee's professional reputation is dependent upon working, for example, actors. For example, in *Devonald v Rosser & Sons* (1906), Devonald's employers found that they could no longer run the works at a profit, so they gave Devonald, a pieceworker, one month's notice but closed the factory immediately. Devonald claimed damages for the wages he lost during this period, arguing that there was an implied term that he would be provided with work during the notice period. It was held that the necessary implication from the contract was that the master would find a reasonable amount of work up to the expiration of the notice. Furthermore, if the employee needs to work in order to maintain particular skills, then to deny him or her this right may also be a breach of this duty.

In *Collier v Sunday Referee Publishing Co Ltd* (1940), Collier was employed as a sub-editor with the defendant's newspaper. The defendant sold the newspaper and continued to pay the plaintiff, although he was not provided with any work. Collier claimed that the company was under a duty to supply work. It was held that there was a breach of the duty to provide work in this case, as the plaintiff had been appointed to a particular job, which had been destroyed on the sale of the newspaper, thereby denying him the right to maintain his skills as a sub-editor. However, Asquith J stated:

> It is true that a contract of employment does not necessarily, or perhaps normally, oblige the master to provide the servant with work. Provided I pay my cook her wages regularly, she cannot complain if I choose to eat all my meals out.

Interestingly, the courts took this duty one step further in *Langston v Amalgamated Union of Engineering Workers* (1974), in which Langston refused to join the trade union. As a result of union pressure, his employers were forced to suspend him from work on full pay. It was said (*obiter*) that where a person employs a skilled employee who needs practice to maintain or develop those skills, there may be an obligation to provide a reasonable amount of work.

In *William Hill Organisation Ltd v Tucker* (1998), the Court of Appeal, in considering whether, where work is available and an employee is not only appointed to do that work but is ready and willing to do it, the employer must permit him to do it, concluded that the contract of employment gave rise to such an obligation.

As a result, unless there is an express provision on garden leave contained in the contract, the employer may be in breach of contract.

To pay wages

As a general rule, the employer must pay his or her employees their wages even if there is no work available. In relation to pieceworkers, this means that they should be given the opportunity to earn their pay. However, it is possible for the employer to exclude or vary this implied term by providing that there will be no pay where there is no work available. Zero hours contracts become relevant here, see 16.2.3

However, where an employee offers only partial performance of his or her contract, for example, where he or she is on a 'go-slow', the employer need not accept partial performance, in which case the employer need not pay for the employee's services, even on a *quantum meruit* basis (see *Miles v Wakefield MDC* (1987)). However, where the employer accepts this part performance, he or she will be required to pay the full wage. In determining whether the employer had accepted part performance, a restrictive interpretation was given in *Wiluszynski v Tower Hamlets LBC* (1989), in which employees were allowed into work, even though the employer had made it clear that it would not accept partial performance of their duties. Allowing the employees onto the premises was not found to be inconsistent with the employer's initial statement in respect of part performance and did not amount to the employer resiling from its original position. As a result, the employer in this case did not have to pay for the services received.

Whilst the employer is under a duty to pay wages, deductions from wages are regulated by Pt II of the ERA 1996, formerly the Wages Act 1986. First, the mode of payment is as agreed between the employer and employee (for example, directly into a bank account). Every employee is entitled to an itemised pay statement showing gross salary or wages, deductions, net salary or wages, variable deductions and fixed deductions and the purpose for which they are made (see Figure 16.2 below). Failure to provide this may result in a reference to an employment tribunal.

Furthermore, there is a general rule that no deductions can be made unless the deduction falls within one of the following:

- it is required or authorised by statute, such as PAYE;
- it is authorised by a provision in the employee's contract, for example, contributions to occupational pension schemes; or
- the employee has agreed in advance in writing to the deduction being made.

There are exceptions which allow for deductions in respect of overpayment of wages, etc. There are also specific provisions relating to the retail industry, which provide that it is permissible to make deductions in respect of cash shortages and stock deficiencies. However, the right to deduct must be included in the contract of employment and any deductions should not exceed 10% of the gross wages payable on the day in question.

Employer:		Employee:
NI No:		Internal Code No:
Tax Code:		
Pay Date + Period:		
Tax Period:		
Pay + Allowances:	Deductions:	Balances:
Description:	Rate x Hours:	
Amount		
DES:		Gross Tax:
Tax:		DES:
NI:		Tax:
Others:		NI:
Gross:		
	Deductions:	NET:

Figure 16.2 Itemised pay statement

Any contravention allows the employee to complain to an employment tribunal within three months of the deduction being made.

To indemnify the employee

Where the employee, in the course of his or her employment, necessarily incurs expenses on behalf of the employer, the employee is entitled to be reimbursed. This extends to such things as postage, parking fees, damage to property, etc.

To treat with mutual respect

The employer is under a duty to treat any employee with respect. The basis of the employment relationship is mutuality of respect, trust and confidence. In deciding whether there has been a breach of this term, the actions of the employer are of great importance.

In *Donovan v Invicta Airways Ltd* (1970), Donovan, an airline pilot, was subjected to abusive conduct by his employer and asked to fly the plane in circumstances he considered unsafe. As a result, Donovan resigned. It was held on appeal that that had been asked to take unjustified risks and that his employer's conduct and criticism of his professional judgment meant his continued employment was impossible. Where there has been a breach of the implied term of trust and confidence by the employer, the employee is not entitled to withhold performance of his contractual obligations – see *Macari v Celtic Football and Athletic Co Ltd* (1999). It is also clear that there is now a duty under which all of the parties to the contract of employment must treat each other with due consideration and courtesy. In *Isle of Wight Tourist Board v Coombes* (1976), a director was heard to describe his personal secretary as 'an intolerable bitch on a Monday morning'. This was held to be a breach of the duty of mutual respect and was conduct that entitled her to resign. In *Malik v BCCI SA (In Liq)* (1997), it was stated that the employer should not conduct itself in a manner likely to destroy or seriously damage the relationship of confidence and trust between employer and employee. Failure to exercise a discretion in good faith may also amount to a breach of the implied terms of trust and confidence – *Horkulak v Cantor Fitzgerald International* (2004).

❖ KEY CASE *Horkulak v Cantor Fitzgerald International* (2004)

Facts:

Mr Horkulak was a broker who resigned with two years left to run on a fixed term contract of employment. The contract stated that 'the company may in its discretion, pay you an annual bonus'. Having successfully brought claims for unfair and wrongful dismissal against Cantor Fitzgerald, Mr Horkulak claimed an entitlement to the bonus that he would have expected to receive had he remained working for the company for the full term of the contract. Cantor Fitzgerald naturally resisted this claim, arguing that, as the bonus was discretionary, they would have been under no obligation to pay any bonus and that Mr Horkulak should only be able to recover those sums to which he was contractually entitled.

Decision:

The Court of Appeal in *Horkulak* approved the decision in *Clark v Nomura* and developed the law by stating that Mr Horkulak was entitled to a 'bona fide and rational' exercise of discretion by Cantor Fitzgerald in relation to the bonus scheme. In reaching this decision, the Court of Appeal relied on the fact that the relevant clause was set out in Mr Horkulak's contract of employment and that it related to a high earning and competitive activity in which the payment of discretionary bonuses was part of the company's remuneration structure. The Court of Appeal thought it clear from the wording and the purpose of the clause that it was intended to be read as a contractual benefit to the employee, as opposed to merely a declaration of the employer's right to pay a bonus if it wished.

Failure to investigate grievances in certain specific instances has, in the past, been regarded as a breach of the obligation of trust and confidence on the part of the employer. This is illustrated in *Bracebridge Engineering v Darby* (1990), where a complaint of sexual harassment against a manager was not investigated. In *Reed v Stedman* (1999), it was held that an act of sexual harassment may also amount to a breach of the implied term of trust and confidence. More recently, the EAT has held in *WA Goold (Pearmak) Ltd v McConnell & Another* (1995) that there is a general implied term that employers will reasonably and promptly afford a reasonable opportunity to their employees to obtain redress of any grievance they may have.

See Chapter 11 →

There is generally no requirement that the employer provide a reference for an outgoing or former employee. However, in certain circumstances, failure to provide a reference may leave the employer open to a claim of victimisation under Art 6 of EC Directive 76/207 and the discrimination legislation – *Coote v Granada Hospitality Ltd* (1998) and *Chief Constable of West Yorkshire Police v Khan* (2001). Also, if a reference is provided, the employer must ensure that the reference is a fair and accurate reflection of the employee's capabilities, etc. Following the decision in *Spring v Guardian Assurance plc* (1995), the employer may be liable in defamation, subject to the defence of qualified privilege and/or negligent misstatement, where he provides an inaccurate or misleading reference. The House of Lords in *Spring* held that an employer who supplies a reference is under a duty to take reasonable care in compiling it. Following the case of *TSB Bank plc v Harris* (2000), to provide a reference containing details of several complaints made about the employee, of which she was unaware, constitutes a breach of the implied term of trust and confidence by the employer. This case further supports the view that references should be balanced and fair.

In *Cox v Sun Alliance Life Ltd* (2001), the Court of Appeal found employers liable in negligence for failing to take reasonable care to be accurate and fair when they provided a reference which suggested that they had a reasonable basis for dismissing the claimant on the ground of dishonesty amounting to corruption. In fact, the charges of dishonesty had never been put to him, had not been made the subject of proper investigation and were shelved pending negotiation of an agreed resignation settlement.

According to Mummery LJ, discharge of the duty of care to provide an accurate and fair reference will usually involve making a reasonable inquiry into the factual basis of the statement in the reference. A similar approach to that set out in *British Home Stores Ltd v Burchell* (1978) in relation to dismissal on grounds of misconduct is appropriate. In order to take reasonable care to give a fair and accurate reference, an employer should confine unfavourable statements about the employee to those matters into which they had made reasonable investigation and had reasonable grounds for believing to be true. However, in order to discharge the duty of care, an employer is not obliged to carry on with an inquiry into an employee's conduct after the employee has resigned. If an investigation is discontinued, unfavourable comments should be confined to matters which had been investigated before the investigation.

In a helpful *obiter dictum*, Mummery LJ advised that where the terms of an agreed resignation or the compromise of an unfair dismissal claim make provision for the supply of a reference, the parties should ensure, as far as possible, that the exact wording of a fair and accurate reference is fully discussed, clearly agreed and carefully recorded in writing in a settlement agreement or if negotiated via ACAS then on the COT3 (form used for ACAS negotiated settlements) at the same time as other severance terms.

To provide for the care and safety of the employee

This duty is based on the law of negligence and health and safety. Suffice it to say here that the common law requires the employer to take reasonable care for the safety of his or her employees and this duty extends to the provision of competent fellow employees, a safe plant and equipment, a safe place of work and a safe system of work.

See Chapters 17 and 18

16.6.6 Duties imposed on the employee

There are a number of duties imposed on the employee, many of which are tied to the idea of trust and confidence, underpinned by the concept that the employee owes a degree of loyalty to the employer.

To obey lawful and reasonable orders

If an order given by the employer is reasonable and lawful, it must be obeyed. Indeed, failure to obey may give the employer the right to dismiss the employee. Whether an order is lawful and reasonable is a question of fact in each case, depending upon the nature of the job.

In *Pepper v Webb* (1969), an employer instructed his gardener to carry out certain planting work in the garden. The gardener swore at his employer and indicated that he was not prepared to obey the instructions. It was held that the employee was in breach of his implied duty, as the orders were not only lawful, but also reasonable in the circumstances. A change in working practices may also be a reasonable order. In *Cresswell v IRB* (1984), the introduction of a computerised system which tax officers were expected to operate was found to be a reasonable order, given their grading and their job descriptions.

Any dismissal for failing to follow an illegal order, that is, failing to commit a criminal offence, is unlawful and the employee will be able to pursue an action for either unfair or wrongful dismissal (see *Morrish v Henlys (Folkestone) Ltd* (1973), where a refusal to falsify the accounts did not amount to a breach of contract on the part of the employee). Further protection is provided by TURERA 1993 in respect of dismissals in connection with health and safety if an employee has refused to work where there is a serious and imminent danger; such dismissals are automatically unfair.

To act with good faith or fidelity

This duty is fundamental to the relationship of employer and employee. The employee's first loyalty must be to the employer. The duty encompasses such things as confidentiality, not competing with the employer, etc.

In *Faccenda Chicken Ltd v Fowler* (1986), Faccenda employed Fowler as a sales manager. He resigned with a number of other employees and set up a chicken selling company in competition with his previous employer. Although there was no restraint of trade clause in the contract, the plaintiff alleged that the duty of confidentiality had been broken, as information such as lists of customers had been copied and used by the defendant. It was held that, as the scope of the duty to act faithfully varied according to the nature of the contract of employment, it was necessary to consider all the circumstances of the case, particularly the nature of the employment and the information obtained and used; that is, was the information of such a nature as to be a trade secret and, therefore, highly confidential? It was held that the employer's claim would be rejected, as the information was not so confidential that it could be covered by an implied prohibition on its use.

This case limits the protection afforded to the employer with respect to confidential information. The only information which will be protected is that which could be legitimately protected by a restraint of trade clause and does not appear to cover information 'recalled' by the employee, as opposed to information which is copied or memorised.

Working for another employer whilst still in the employ of the original employer may also be a breach of the duty to act faithfully. Generally, this will only amount to a breach where the second employer is in competition with the first employer, where the nature of the contract is one of exclusivity or where there is a conflict of interest. In all other circumstances, the courts will not seek to curb an employee's legitimate 'spare time' activities. If, for example, an employee was a car mechanic by day and worked in a public house at night, there would be no breach (see *Nova Plastics Ltd v Froggatt* (1982), in which it was held that, even where an employee worked for a competitor in his spare time, there had to be some evidence of potential harm).

In *Hivac Ltd v Park Royal Scientific Instruments Ltd* (1946), employees of the plaintiff company were found to be working in their spare time for a company which was in direct competition with their employer. The employees concerned were doing the same job at both establishments. It was held that the employees were under a duty not to work for a competitor of their employer where this work would conflict with their duty of fidelity and may inflict harm on their employer's business. The duty to act faithfully was found to have been breached in *Adamson v B and L Cleaning Services Ltd* (1995), where an employee put in a tender for the future business of his employer's customers.

The employer may prevent his or her employees either working for rival firms or setting up a business in competition with him or her after they have left their employment by including in the contract of employment an express term which restricts the employee's future employment in some way. Such clauses are known as *covenants in restraint of trade*. Many professional people, such as solicitors and accountants, will have this type of clause in their contracts. Restraint of trade clauses are only valid if they protect a legitimate business interest and are reasonable in all the circumstances of the case; that is, the protection afforded the employer must not be excessive. For example, in a fast paced international industry a covenant may not have an excessive duration as the information may have limited value after a few months but may need a wide geographical restriction. You would need to consider the role of the employee as part of the consideration, a marketing director would have greater restrictions than a junior salesperson. Furthermore, the interests of the public must be considered; this is particularly relevant with respect to trade secrets, inventions, etc. Such clauses will also be subject to rules of construction and severance, which may result in part of a clause being struck out.

In *Home Counties Dairies Ltd v Skilton* (1970), Skilton was a milkman. His contract of employment contained a clause which provided that, for a period of one year after the termination of his contract with the plaintiff dairy, he would not sell milk or dairy produce to any person who had been a customer of the dairy for the last six months of his contract and whom he had served. Soon after leaving his employment, he set up his own milk round in the same area as the one in which he had worked for the dairy company. It was held that the former employer should be awarded an injunction to prevent Skilton from working this area. The clause in his contract was valid, as the time limit was reasonable in order to protect the interests of the dairy.

Restraint of trade clauses may not be found to be reasonable where the area of protection is unacceptably large. For example, in *Greer v Sketchley Ltd* (1979), a restraint of trade clause prevented Greer from working anywhere in the UK in a related business, even though his actual job covered only the Midlands. The Court of Appeal found that the restraint was invalid, as Sketchley did not currently operate over the whole of the UK and the likelihood of them expanding the business into other areas was too uncertain. Restraint of trade clauses may also be struck out if they are contrary to public policy, for example, depriving a community of a particular service – see *Bull v Pitney-Bowes* (1966).

Under the requirement of fidelity, the employee must not disclose confidential information which has been acquired in the course of his or her employment. The duty extends to trade secrets, financial state of the company, new designs, etc.

In *Cranleigh Precision Engineering Co Ltd v Bryant* (1965), Bryant was the managing director of a firm which designed swimming pools. He left the company and started his own business, using information which he had gained from his previous employment. It was held that Bryant was in breach of the implied term in his contract of employment, as he could only have gained this information from his previous employment. He had made improper use of information gained in confidence to the detriment of his former employer.

Over recent years, there has been an increase in litigation trying to enforce restrictive covenants. In particular, many employers have through the use of IT been able to trace the theft by former employees of information such as client lists or sensitive pricing information, and have made substantial claims for loss of profit against their former employees, as well as seeking injunctions to freeze their new business activities.

To use skill and care

The employee is under a duty to use reasonable skill and care in the performance of the job. If he or she does so and incurs loss or damage, the employer will indemnify him or her. However, should the employee be grossly incompetent, the employer may have grounds to dismiss him or her. The duty extends to taking proper care of the employer's property, as is illustrated by the decision in *Superlux v Plaisted* (1958), in which an employee was held liable for allowing his employer's goods to be stolen whilst in his care.

In *Lister v Romford Ice and Cold Storage Co Ltd* (1957), Lister, a lorry driver employed by the defendant company, negligently reversed his lorry, seriously injuring a fellow employee. The company claimed an indemnity from Lister, on the grounds that he had broken the implied term of skill and care in his contract of employment. It was held that the employer was entitled to an indemnity because the employee had failed to use reasonable skill and care, as required by the implied terms. Lister was therefore liable for the damages awarded to his fellow employee.

See also *Janata Bank v Ahmed* (1981), in which a bank manager who failed to check customers' creditworthiness adequately before giving them loans and arranging credit was held to be personally responsible for failing to use sufficient skill and care.

Not to take bribes or make a secret profit

While this duty is part and parcel of the general duty of fidelity, it extends to accounting for any monies or gifts received which may compromise an employee. A breach of this duty by an employee is an abuse of position and may result in a fair dismissal. This is illustrated in *Sinclair v Neighbour* (1967), in which a clerk in a betting shop took £15 from the till without the permission of his employer, whom he knew would refuse to let him do so. The clerk intended to replace it the next day. However, in the interim, the employer discovered what the clerk had done and dismissed him. It was held that the clerk had not acted honestly in attempting to deceive his employer and, therefore, the employer was entitled to dismiss him.

In *Reading v AG* (1951), Reading, who was a sergeant in the British Army based in Egypt, used his position to accompany lorries containing illicit spirits, so that they would not be stopped by the police. Over a period of time, Reading received £20,000 for his 'services'. When his role was finally discovered, he was arrested and the army authorities confiscated his money. When he was released from prison, he brought an action for the return of the money. It was held that Reading was in breach of the implied duty not to take bribes or make secret profits. He had misused his position of trust and had, therefore, to account for those 'profits' to his employer. He was not entitled to have any of the money returned to him.

In *British Syphon Co Ltd v Homewood* (1956), Homewood was employed as chief technician by the plaintiff company in the design and development department. During his employment, he designed a new type of soda syphon. He did not disclose his invention to his employers. He then left his employment and applied for letters patent in respect of his invention. It was held that the invention and the profits from it belonged to his employer. The invention was clearly related to his employer's business and they were therefore entitled to the benefits from it.

The common law position regarding employees' inventions has been qualified by ss 39–41 of the Patents Act 1977 and s 11 of the Copyright Designs and Patents Act 1988. In such cases, the invention or design will belong to the employer only if:

- it is made in the course of normal duties or duties specifically assigned and the invention could reasonably be expected to derive from that work; or
- it is made in the normal course of duties and, at the time of the invention, there is a special obligation to further the employer's business interests.

One solution is to have an express clause in the contract of employment which addresses this issue and makes it clear any inventions created during the course of their employment belong to the employer.

Summary

Individual Employment Rights (1): The Contract of Employment

An employee is employed under a contract of employment (or contract of service), whereas an independent contractor is employed under a contract for services. The distinction is important because many employment rights only accrue in an employer/employee relationship:

- An express term in a document which defines status will override an implied term where there is conflict between them – *Stevedoring & Haulage Services Ltd v Fuller & Others* (2001).

The tests which have developed for establishing the employer/employee relationship are:

- the *control test*, which extends not just to what the employee does, but how it is done. As a single definitive test, the use of control is now rather limited;
- the *integration test*, which considers how far or to what extent the employee is integrated into the employer's business. This has not proved to be a popular test, but, as with the control test, may be used as part of the multiple test;
- the *multiple test*, which was developed in the case of *Ready Mixed Concrete (South East) Ltd v Minister of Pensions and National Insurance* (1968). The key factors are:
    - the provision of own work or labour in return for remuneration;
    - a degree of control; and
    - all other terms being consistent with the existence of a contract of service – *Lane v Shire Roofing Co (Oxford) Ltd* (1995); and
- the *mutuality of obligations test*, which was developed to overcome the problems faced by the 'regular, casual' worker, who could not be deemed to be an employee using the other tests and, as a result, had to forgo any employment rights:
    - *O'Kelly v Trusthouse Forte plc* (1983);
    - *Autoclenz v Belcher* (2011);
    - *Carmichael v National Power plc* (2000);
    - *Montgomery v Johnson & Underwood Ltd* (2001);
    - *Motorola v Davidson and Melville Craig* (2001).
    - Part-time and fixed term employees have the right not to be treated less favourably than full-time employees in respect of pay and conditions: the Part-Time Workers (Prevention of Less Favourable Treatment) Regulations 2000 and the amendment Regulations 2002 and the Fixed-Term Employees (Prevention of Less Favourable Treatment) Regulations 2002.

Continuity

Most employment rights depend on continuity of employment on the part of the employee. This is governed by s 212 of the ERA 1996. See *Flack v Kodak Ltd* (1986).

National minimum wage

This is governed by the National Minimum Wage Act 1998. The current minimum wage is set at £6.31 per hour for persons aged 22 and over and £5.03 for those aged between 18 and 21. All workers aged 18 years and over are entitled to the minimum wage – this is defined in s 54 of the National Minimum Wage Act 1998. A national minimum wage of £3.72 per hour has been introduced for 16 and 17 year olds. These figures have been set as of 1 October 2013.

The Act is enforced by Inland Revenue officers. Employers are expected to keep up to date and accurate records.

Written statement of terms

Although there are no formalities involved in the formation of the contract of employment, every employee is entitled to a statement of written particulars within two months of the commencement of his or her employment (s 1 of the Employment Rights Act 1996).

Express terms

Express terms are agreed between the employer and employee. Implied terms must be read subject to any express terms in the contract.

Implied terms

Implied terms arise out of custom and practice, by statute or through the courts, which will determine whether an implied term is part of the contract (*Johnstone v Bloomsbury HA* (1991)). The test for establishing implied terms can be found in *Henry v London General Transport Services Ltd* (2001).

The duties imposed on the employer are:

- to provide work (*Collier v Sunday Referee Publishing Co Ltd* (1940));
- to provide wages;
- to indemnify his or her employees;
- to have mutual respect (*Donovan v Invicta Airways Ltd* (1970); *Macari v Celtic Football and Athletic Co Ltd* (1999); *TSB Bank plc v Harris* (2000); *Cox v Sun Alliance Life Ltd* (2001); *Cantor Fitzgerald International v Horkulak* (2004)); and
- to provide for the safety of his or her employees.

The duties imposed on the employee are:

- to obey lawful and reasonable orders (*Pepper v Webb* (1969));
- to act with loyalty (*Faccenda Chicken Ltd v Fowler* (1986); *Hivac Ltd v Park Royal Scientific Instruments Ltd* (1946); *Home Counties Dairies Ltd v Skilton* (1970); *Cranleigh Precision Engineering Co Ltd v Bryant* (1965));
- to act with skill and care (*Lister v Romford Ice and Cold Storage Co Ltd* (1957)); and
- not to take bribes or secret profits (*Reading v Attorney General* (1951); *British Syphon Co Ltd v Homewood* (1956)).

Further Reading

Bogg, A, 'Sham self-employment in the Court of Appeal' (2010) 126 Law Quarterly Review 166–71

Davies, ACL, 'Developments in English Labour/Employment Law 2004–2007' 2 Europaische Zeitschrift fur Arbeitsrecht 267–71

Davies, ACL, 'Casual Workers and Continuity of Employment' (2006) 35 Industrial Law Journal 196–201

O'Cienneide, C, 'Democracy and Rights: New Directions in the Human Rights Era' [2004] 57 Current Legal Problems 175–211

Chapter 17

Individual Employment Rights (2): Equal Pay and Discrimination

Chapter Contents

Law in Context: Equal Pay and Discrimination

One of the most significant developments affecting businesses has been the passing of the Equality Act 2010, which brought together all the previous discrimination legislation. Interestingly, the Act identified protected characteristics, including age and disability, which it is illegal to discriminate against. For example, if in an interview Bob is 60 years old and Carl is 45 years old, and you offer the job to Carl because he is younger, then as age is a protected characteristic this would amount to direct age discrimination. This is also the case with pregnancy; for example Emma has just started a new job and discovers that she is pregnant. When she informs her employer, she is dismissed. This is automatically unfair dismissal but is also direct pregnancy discrimination. Emma was dismissed because of her pregnancy, which is a protected characteristic. An employer cannot discriminate against a person, either directly or indirectly, because they have a protected characteristic. The protected characteristics and forms of discrimination are considered in more detail in the chapter. Over the past years there have been a number of cases relating to equal pay, particularly within the public sector, emphasising the need for businesses to fully evaluate and consider the basis for pay levels awarded to staff undertaking different types of work. You will see that equal pay is actually wider than just financial remuneration, and can also include the terms contained within a contract as well. The key here is establishing if work undertaken by the other person (group) is equivalent or of the same value. In this chapter you will find the legislation setting out the basis for equal pay and claims, and how it is applied through the claim procedure.

17.1 Introduction

There have been fundamental changes in discrimination legislation over recent years with the Equality Act 2010. However, implementation of some aspects of the legislation has been delayed and the Coalition Government recently announced that it will not implement dual discrimination, and the third party harassment provisions are due to be repealed in April 2014.

17.1.1 Equal pay

The legal requirement of ensuring equality between men's and women's terms of employment can currently be found in the Equality Act 2010, having originated in the Equal Pay Act (EPA) 1970, Art 141 (formerly Art 119) of the EC Treaty and EC Directive 75/117 (the Equal Pay Directive). However, on 8 April 2010 the Equality Bill received Royal Assent and thus became the Equality Act 2010. The Act came into effect in 2012, and replaced all existing discrimination legislation with two main aims, first to codify the complex provisions of the existing legislation, and secondly to strengthen the law to support the progress on equality.

Although these legislative provisions protect men and women alike, the evidence suggests that the gender pay gap between men and women still exists but is slowly decreasing, with the gap now at 9.6% (Annual Survey of Hours and Earnings, 2012 ONS). Therefore, in practical terms, most cases for equal pay are brought by women. This is further compounded by the segregation of women into jobs perceived as 'women's jobs', which are traditionally in the service sector and in the lower pay bracket. Job segregation is seen as a major obstacle to equality in employment. The National Minimum Wage Act 1998, discussed in Chapter 10 above, may have had an impact in this area. However, there is an argument that the current national minimum wage has been set too low to be effective. (See Sachdev, S and Wilkinson, F, *Low Pay, the Working of the Labour Market and the Role of the Minimum Wage*, 1998.)

See Chapter 10 →

17.2 European Community Law and Equal Pay

The continued impact of European Community (EC) law in the area of equality cannot be underestimated. Article 141 (now Article 157 of the Treaty on the Functioning of the European Union) had direct effect and, therefore, domestic law must be applied and interpreted in the light of the Article.

Equal work is defined in s 65 Equality Act 2010 in the following terms:

> (1) A's work is equal to that of B if it is—
>
> (a) like B's work,
> (b) rated as equivalent to B's work, or
> (c) of equal value to B's work.
>
> (2) A's work is like B's work if—
>
> (a) A's work and B's work are the same or broadly similar, and
> (b) such differences as there are between their work are not of practical importance in relation to the terms of their work.
>
> (3) So on a comparison of one person's work with another's for the purposes of subsection (2), it is necessary to have regard to—
>
> (a) the frequency with which differences between their work occur in practice, and
> (b) the nature and extent of the differences.
>
> (4) A's work is rated as equivalent to B's work if a job evaluation study—
>
> (a) gives an equal value to A's job and B's job in terms of the demands made on a worker, or
> (b) would give an equal value to A's job and B's job in those terms were the evaluation not made on a sex-specific system.
>
> (5) A system is sex-specific if, for the purposes of one or more of the demands made on a worker, it sets values for men different from those it sets for women.
>
> (6) A's work is of equal value to B's work if it is—
>
> (a) neither like B's work nor rated as equivalent to B's work, but
> (b) nevertheless equal to B's work in terms of the demands made on A by reference to factors such as effort, skill and decision-making.

This contains several important concepts which have rolled over from the Equal Pay Act, so previous case law is still relevant. The decision in *Jenkins v Kingsgate (Clothing Productions) Ltd* (1981) upholds this principle. Article 157 requires each Member State to ensure that the principle of equal pay for both male and female workers, and for equal work or work of equal value, is applied (Art 1). 'Pay' for this purpose means the ordinary basic or minimum wage or salary and any other consideration, whether in cash or kind, which the worker receives, directly or indirectly, in respect of his or her employment (for example, a company car).

The right to equal pay is enforceable by an individual (see *Kowalska v Freie und Hansestadt Hamburg* (1990)). It is supplemented by the Equal Pay Directive. Generally, such directives are not enforceable by an individual, as it is left to the Member State to comply with the directive, using whatever form or method they choose. However, the Equal Pay Directive is an exception to this, as, first, it gives meaning and clarity to Art 141 and, as a result, is applied through Art 141; secondly, it fulfils the test in *Van Duyn v Home Office* (1975), where it was held that a directive could be enforced by an individual if it was 'sufficiently clear, precise, admitted of no exceptions and, therefore, of its nature, needed no intervention by the national authorities'. The Directive states that:

> . . . the principle of equal pay for men and women outlined in Article 141 . . . means, for the same work or for work to which equal value has been attributed, the elimination of all discrimination on grounds of sex with regard to all aspects and conditions of remuneration.

Where a Member State fails to comply with the Article or Directive, the European Commission may make a challenge, in the form of legal action, against that Member State. An important and successful legal action was taken by the Commission against the UK for failing to implement the equal value provision in the EPA 1970. This led to an amendment to that Act, providing a new head of claim for equal value (see *Commission v United Kingdom* (1982)).

Where two groups of employees, one predominantly female, the other male, perform for the most part identical work, different training and qualifications may result in the two groups using different knowledge and skills acquired through their different disciplines to carry out their job. As a result, they may not be employed to do the same work within Art 141 (*Angestelltenbetriebstrat der Wiener Gebietskrankenkasse v Wiener Gebietskrankenkasse* (1999)).

A wide interpretation has been given to the meaning of 'pay'. It has been found to include occupational pension schemes (see *Barber v Guardian Royal Exchange Assurance Group* (1990)); piecework pay schemes (see *Specialarbejderforbundet i Danmark v Dansk Industri (acting for Royal Copenhagen A/S)* (1995)); sick pay (see *Rinner-Kuhn v FWW Spezial-Gebaudereinigung GmbH* (1989)); and Christmas bonus (see *Lewen v Denda* (2000)).

The European Court of Justice (ECJ) in *Lommers v Minister Van Landbouw Natuurbeheer en Visserij* (2002) concluded that 'a scheme under which an employer makes nursery places available to employees is to be regarded as a "working condition" within Dir 76/207 rather than as "pay", notwithstanding that the cost of the nursery places is partly born by the employer'.

Although certain working conditions may have pecuniary consequences, such conditions may not fall within Art 141 (now Article 157) unless there is a close connection existing between the nature of the work done and the amount of pay.

17.3 Equality Clause

The Equality Act 2010 incorporates a sex equality clause into all contracts of employment. As a result of this clause, any term in the contract of employment which is less favourable to the woman (or man) as compared with a similar clause in a man's contract (or vice versa) will be deemed to be no less favourable. Similarly, if the woman's contract does not contain a beneficial term which is to be found in the man's contract, her contract will be deemed to contain such a clause.

A claim is not restricted to purely claims for pay, but applies to any terms in the applicant's contract which are less favourable than the comparator's. Each term must be considered individually, rather than as part of the remuneration package, as decided in *Hayward v Cammell Laird Shipbuilders Ltd* (1988). Furthermore, a collective agreement may be only one aspect in adducing evidence of remuneration – *Brunnhofer v Bank der Österreichischen Postsparkasse* (2001). In theory, the equality clause should operate automatically, without recourse to the employment tribunal system, although, in reality, many complainants have had to resort to the tribunals.

17.3.1 Claiming equality

In order to bring a claim for equal pay under the Equality Act 2010, the claim must date from 1 October 2010 onwards. Acts prior to this are issued under the EPA 1970. As outlined in section 17.2 earlier, The applicant must show that he or she is employed under a contract of service, a contract of apprenticeship, or contract for services where there is a requirement for them personally to do the work (s 83(2)). This provides the opportunity for a greater number of people to be afforded some equality protection. In *Mirror Group Newspapers Ltd v Gunning* (1986) (a sex discrimination case), it was held that the question to be asked is: is the sole or dominant purpose of the contract the execution of work or labour by the contracting party? If the answer is no, then clearly the applicant is not employed.

The scope of applicant is quite wide and covers holders of public offices, although not elected officials, holders of public office or peers (ss 52, 64(1)(b) Equality Act 2010) as well as Crown employees (s 83(2)), House of Commons and House of Lords staff and armed forces personnel.

The applicant must be in the same employment as her comparator, that is, she should be employed by the same employer at the same establishment, or by the same employer or an associated employer at an establishment where common terms and conditions are observed. This subsection recognises the need for as wide a choice as possible in selecting a comparator within the acceptable confines of the legislation; that is, it would be totally unreasonable to allow a comparison between unrelated employers or industries. The term 'common terms and conditions' was considered in *Leverton v Clwyd CC* (1989). Ms Leverton, the applicant, was a nursery nurse employed by Clwyd County Council. She selected, as her comparators in her equal value claim, male clerical staff who were employed by the county council but who worked at a different establishment. This comparison would only be valid, therefore, if she and her comparators were subject to 'common terms and conditions'. It was held that s 1(6) of the EPA 1970 required a comparison between the terms and conditions observed at the establishment at which the woman was employed and the establishment at which the men were employed, applicable either generally or to a particular class of employee to which both the woman and the men belonged. In this particular case, they were both employed under the same collective agreement, which was applied generally. It was irrelevant that there were some differences between the actual terms of their contracts. Section 1(6) was therefore satisfied.

Furthermore, in *British Coal Corp v Smith* (1996), the House of Lords concluded that 'common terms and conditions' meant terms and conditions which are comparable substantially on a broad basis. It is sufficient for the applicant to show that her comparators at both another establishment and her own establishment were, or would be, employed on broadly similar terms.

EC law provides further scope by allowing an applicant to avoid the restrictive nature of s 1(6), in so far as it confines 'associated employer' to private employers. Article 141 of the EC Treaty allows the applicant to select a comparator in the same establishment or service, so held the Employment Appeal Tribunal (EAT) in *Scullard v Knowles and South Regional Council for Education and Training* (1996). This, in turn, would allow public sector employees to compare themselves for the purpose of making equal pay claims. One possible limitation on this interpretation can be seen in *Lawrence v Regent Office Care Ltd* (2002), in which former employees of the county council who were now employed by private contractors were not permitted by the ECJ to compare themselves with current employees of the county council. The reason for this was that the differences identified in the pay of workers performing equal work or work of equal value could not be attributed to a single source and as a result there was nobody who could be held responsible for the inequality.

Whilst the case of *Allonby v Accrington & Rossendale College* (2004) is primarily a sex discrimination case, the employment tribunal at the initial hearing was asked to consider whether s 1(6) of the EPA 1970 provided grounds for an equal pay claim. The tribunal held that, as s 1(6) was not satisfied, there could be no equal pay case. However, the Court of Appeal referred the equal pay issue to the ECJ for it to consider whether Art 141 had direct effect so as to entitle the applicant to bring an equal pay claim against ELS, the agency which found her employment at the college, the argument being that in comparing herself with a lecturer employed by the college at a time when she was employed there, she was working in the same employment for the purposes of Art 141. The ECJ held that although Art 141 is not limited to situations in which men and women work for the same employer and may be invoked in cases of discrimination arising directly from legislative provisions or collective agreements, as well as in cases in which work is carried out in the same establishment or service, where the differences identified in the pay conditions of workers performing equal work or work of equal value cannot be attributed to a single source, there is no body which is responsible for the inequality and which could restore equal treatment. Such a situation does not come within the scope of Art 141. This in effect follows the decision in *Lawrence*.

The decision in *Scullard* has been applied in *South Ayrshire Council v Morton* (2002), in which the Court of Session held that a claimant in an equal pay claim can now use a comparator who is not employed by the 'same employer' as defined in s 1(6). In the *Morton* case, a female headteacher employed by a local education authority in Scotland was permitted to compare herself with a male headteacher employed by a different Scottish education authority, using Art 141. This type of comparison is restricted to the public sector on the basis that 'any pay settlement conducted under statutory authority and under overall government control constitutes a national collective agreement of the kind contemplated in the *Defrenne* case'. However, the impact of the decision in *Morton* has been limited by the decision in *Lawrence*.

17.3.2 Comparator

The applicant must select a comparator of the opposite sex. The choice of comparator is a decision for the applicant, as can be seen in *Ainsworth v Glass Tubes Ltd* (1977), and she may apply for an order of discovery in order to select the most appropriate comparator (see *Leverton v Clwyd CC* (1989) (above)). However, and more importantly, the comparator must be, or have been, in existence. While, therefore, comparison with a predecessor of the opposite sex is allowed, as decided by the ECJ in *Macarthys v Smith* (1980), comparison with a hypothetical comparator is not permitted. This, in effect, prevents any claim from applicants in segregated industries where there is no one of the opposite sex falling within s 1(6) of the EPA 1970. However, comparison with a successor is now permitted by virtue of *Diocese of Hallam Trustees v Connaughton* (1996).

The Court of Session in *South Ayrshire Council v Milligan* (2003) recognised the validity of contingency claims. In this case, a male primary school teacher was allowed to claim equal pay with a male secondary school head teacher, by naming as his comparator a female colleague on the same or less pay than himself, who, in her own equal pay claim, had cited as comparator the male secondary head teacher. The court in this case adopted a purposive approach in interpreting the legislation, to ensure compliance with Art 141 and the Equal Pay Directive. Failure to allow a claim on a contingent basis to proceed could result in the applicant suffering prejudice in relation to back pay, since he or she could lodge a claim only after the comparative claim had succeeded.

The Equal Pay Act 2010 (part of the Equality Act 2010, largely mirroring the 1970 Act) also requires claimants to name a comparator of the opposite sex who is employed 'in the same employment as them'. However, recent case law has shown that there may be exceptional cases where comparators employed by a different employer can be used if the inequality in pay originates from one single source, for example a piece of legislation that is binding on both employers. It is required that the claimant and the comparator have to be employed normally within the previous six years at the same time.

17.3.3 Grounds of claim

Equality can only be claimed on the grounds of:

- like work;
- work rated as equivalent; or
- work of equal value.

Like work (s 65(1) of the Equality Act 2010)

'Like work' was defined by s 1(4) of the EPA 1970 as either the same work or work of a broadly similar nature, where the differences (if any) between the applicant's and comparator's jobs are not of practical importance in relation to the terms and conditions of employment. This concept is seen in the definition of s 65(1–6) Equality Act 2010 (see 17.2 above).

The application of the original s 1(4) of the Equal Pay Act 1970 can be seen in *Capper Pass Ltd v Lawton* (1977), where Mrs Lawton was a cook employed in a directors' dining room, where she provided lunches for up to 20 directors each day. She claimed equal pay on the basis of 'like work' with two male assistant chefs in the works canteen, which provided some 350 meals per day. It was held that a two-stage test should be applied:

- Is the work the same or, if not, is it of a broadly similar nature? The EAT suggested that a broad approach should be adopted to this question, without a minute examination of the differences between the jobs.
- If the work is broadly similar, are the differences of practical importance? In applying this test, it was concluded that Mrs Lawton was employed on 'like work', as both her work and that of her comparator fell within s 1(4).

Additionally, there may be other factors that have a bearing on whether s 1(4) of the EPA 1970 is satisfied. Additional responsibility may justify a difference in pay (see *Eaton Ltd v Nuttall* (1977)) whereas, in general, the time at which work is done should be ignored (*Dugdale v Kraft Foods Ltd* (1977)) unless it brings with it additional responsibilities, as in *Thomas v NCB* (1987). There, a male chef working permanent nights on his own was found not to be on 'like work' because of the extra responsibilities and the lack of supervision. This amounted to a 'difference of practical importance in relation to terms and conditions of employment', as illustrated in *Calder and Cizakowsky v Rowntree Macintosh Confectionery Ltd* (1993).

Finally, the tribunal is concerned with what the applicant and the comparator actually do in practice, not necessarily what their job descriptions are under their contracts. See *E Coomes (Holdings) Ltd v Shields* (1978), where a woman employed in a betting shop claimed equal pay with a male employee who appeared to be doing the same job as a counterhand. She was paid 62p per hour, while he received £1.06. The employer claimed that the difference in pay resulted from the fact that the man was also required to deal with troublemakers. The reality was that he had never been called upon to cope with a disturbance and had never received any training in respect of this. The applicant was, therefore, found to be doing 'like work'.

Work rated as equivalent (s 65(2) Equality Act 2010)

An applicant may bring an equality claim if her job has been rated as equivalent with that of her male comparator by virtue of a job evaluation scheme. This can only be used where there is in existence a complete and valid scheme, the validity of which has been accepted by the parties who agreed to its being carried out. Indeed, in *Arnold v Beecham Group Ltd* (1982), it was held that there could be no implementation of a job evaluation scheme until the parties who agreed to it had accepted its validity. It would appear, therefore, that even if it supports the position of the applicant, the employer is not compelled to implement it. Such schemes must comply with s 1(5) of the EPA 1970. The interpretation of this, resulting from the case of *Bromley v H and J Quick Ltd* (1988), is that all valid schemes, as well as being non-discriminatory, must be analytical and must not involve the subjective views of management as to the grading of an employee. Comparisons must, therefore, be made of the various demands upon the employees under the headings laid down in s 1(5), that is, effort, skill, decision, etc. As a result, some job evaluations will not satisfy the decision in *Bromley* or s 1(5) and can therefore be challenged.

Some guidance on analytical schemes is offered in *Eaton v Nuttall* (1977) and the Advisory Conciliation and Arbitration Service (ACAS) *Job Evaluation* booklet.

Work of equal value (s 65(6) Equality Act 2010)

This head of claim originated from a case brought by the European Commission against the UK Government for failing to comply with Art 119 (now Art 141) of the EC Treaty and Directive 75/117, in that there was no provision in UK law for claims of equality where jobs were of equal value. This was highlighted by the fact that there was no right on the part of the employee to compel an employer to carry out a job evaluation scheme under s 1(2)(b) (see *Commission v United Kingdom* (1982)). As a result, the UK was forced to amend the EPA 1970 by inserting a provision on equal value. This had the effect of making the equality law available to a greater number of claimants.

From the wording of the EPA 1970, it was thought that this head of claim could only be used if there was no 'like work' or 'work rated equivalent' claim available. However, a potential loophole was spotted by at least one employer, which involved the use of the token man employed on 'like work' to prevent an equal value claim proceeding. In *Pickstone v Freemans plc* (1988), where the employer attempted to block an equal value claim in this way, the House of Lords concluded that the presence of a man doing like work to the applicant did not prevent the applicant bringing an equal value claim using another male comparator. In making this decision, consideration was had of EC law, with the conclusion that any other construction would:

> . . . leave a gap in the equal work provision, enabling an employer to evade it by employing one token man on the same work as a group of potential women claimants who were deliberately paid less than a group of men employed on work of equal value with that of the woman. This would mean that the UK had failed yet again to fully implement its obligations under EC law.

The claims that can be made remain to be the same under the Equality Act 2010 and these provisions can be found in s 65.

17.3.4 Equal value procedure

The procedure in equal value claims is complex. An initial decision has to be made as to whether the claim is a claim for equal pay or indeed a sex discrimination or maternity discrimination pay claim, and appropriate claims issued. Either claim would have to be issued at the employment tribunal, a process which now requires a fee. An earlier and less contentious action would be for an employee to raise a grievance under the employer's internal grievance procedure.

If a claimant makes an application to an employment tribunal, they have the option of raising a questionnaire to be sent to the employer. Whilst there is no power to order an employer to answer the questionnaire, the tribunal may draw adverse inferences from their failure to do so. Initially, a claim is sent to ACAS with a view to settling the claim. If this does not occur, the claim is then the subject of a preliminary hearing, where it is decided whether there are reasonable grounds for determining that the work is of equal value. The purpose of this hearing is to weed out hopeless cases, for example, where the jobs have been deemed unequal under a valid job evaluation scheme. Alternatively, the employment tribunal may refer the claim directly to an independent expert. Where a case is referred to an independent expert, he or she must provide the employment tribunal with an estimation of the length of time it will take him or her to prepare the report. The employer may introduce the genuine material factor defence (see below) at the preliminary stage but, if he or she does so, he or she will not be allowed to plead it after the independent expert has reported back to the tribunal. If the tribunal is then satisfied that there are reasonable grounds on which the claim may proceed, the claim is then referred to an independent expert appointed from the ACAS panel. The expert carries out a thorough investigation of the jobs for comparison and reports in writing to the tribunal. Interestingly, the tribunal is not obliged to accept the report, as held in *Tennants Textile Colours Ltd v Todd* (1989). The onus is on the applicant to prove that her job is of equal value to that of the comparator.

Tribunals may determine the question of equal value themselves rather than refer to an independent expert. Also, job evaluations are presumed to be reliable unless there are reasonable grounds for suspecting that they have been conducted in a discriminatory way. The Employment Tribunals (Constitution and Rules of Procedure) (Amendment) Regulations 2004 (SI 2004/1861) provide tribunals with greater case management powers in equal pay cases and simplify equal value claims.

What amounts to 'equal value'?

One of the problems for the tribunal has been what amounts to work of equal value. At employment tribunal level, there has been some inconsistency; for example, in *Wells v F Smales and Son (Fish Merchants)* (1985), the tribunal adopted a broad brush approach in concluding that female fish packers were engaged in work of equal value to that of a male labourer, even though some of the women's work was assessed at only 75% of the value of the men's work. The tribunal concluded that the differences were not material. In *Brown and Royal v Cearn and Brown Ltd* (1985), however, the independent expert concluded that the applicant's work was worth 95% of her comparator's work, yet the tribunal declined to conclude that this was work of equal value, as it was not 'precisely equal value'. In *Pickstone v Freemans* (1988), the industrial tribunal concluded that equal value does not have to be 100% value. Equal value also includes higher value, as can be seen in *Murphy v Bord Telecom Eireann* (1988), where the applicant was found to be on less pay yet on work of higher value than her comparator.

Genuine material factor defence (s 69 Equality Act 2010)

There is a defence in equal pay cases if the employer can show that the variation between the women's and the men's contract is genuinely due to a real need on the part of the employer, is a proportionate means of achieving that objective and is necessary. Proportionality needs to be considered with whether it is necessary and appropriate. In the case of 'like work' or 'work rated equivalent' claims, that factor must be a material difference whereas, in 'equal value' claims, it *may* be such a difference. The distinction has, in reality, been removed by the decision in *Rainey v Greater Glasgow Health Board* (1987), which went on to apply the criteria in *Bilka-Kaufhaus GmbH v Weber von Hartz* (1986) for establishing this defence. This is now codified in s 69 Equality Act 2010. This requires the employer to show objectively justified grounds for the different treatment. There must be a real need on the part of the undertaking for the difference; it is not sufficient merely to show that the reason for the difference was not discriminatory. However, the need to justify any inequality in pay only arises where the disparity in pay is based on gender – see *Strathclyde Regional Council v Wallace* (1998). This has been supported in *Glasgow CC & Others v Marshall* (2000), although this interpretation has been challenged in *Brunnhofer v Bank der Österreichischen Postsparkasse* (2001), in which it was held that there was a need for objective justification where a difference in pay between men and women is established.

The criteria in the *Bilka* case have been successfully used to uphold 'market forces' as a defence, as in *Rainey v Greater Glasgow Health Board* (1987), but can no longer be used to justify inequalities arising out of collective bargaining agreements, as was held in *Enderby v Frenchay HA* (1993). This case further confirms that the burden of proof moves to the employer to show that the pay differential is not discriminatory and is based on an objectively justified factor. (See also *Glasgow CC & Others v Marshall* (2000) for a restatement of this principle and a detailed explanation of what the employer must do to establish the defence.) The burden of proof is on the applicant to establish that the employer's explanation for the variation between her pay and that of her male comparator indirectly discriminated against women – *Nelson v Carillion Services Ltd* (2003).

The following are examples of genuine material factors: the location at which the applicant and her comparator work may justify the difference in terms, for example, work in London as compared with the provinces (see *Navy, Army and Air Force Institutes v Varley* (1976)); 'red circling' – this occurs where the contractual terms of an employee or group of employees are legitimately preserved, for example, where the job may have been downgraded but existing staff have their terms protected. This is a legitimate defence, as long as the red circling is genuine and only applies to an existing person or pool of employees (*Snoxell v Vauxhall Motors Ltd* (1977)). The same is true of economic necessity (see *Benveniste v University of Southampton* (1989)), although once the economic situation improves, the employer is bound to redress the disparity in terms. Following the decision in *Ratcliffe v North Yorkshire DC* (1995), competitive tendering may not amount to a genuine material difference/factor unless it can be shown to be gender neutral. (See Gill, D, 'Making equal pay defences transparent' (1990) 33 EOR 48.)

17.3.5 Remedies

The applicant must make her claim either whilst still in employment, or within six months of leaving that employment. EC law does not impose a time limit for claims. However, the case law suggests that any claim based on EC law should be subject to the limits set for tribunal claims under domestic legislation (*Emmott v Minister for Social Welfare* (1991)). This was successfully challenged in *Preston v Wolverhampton Healthcare NHS Trust* (2000). The ruling by the ECJ in *Levez v TH Jennings (Harlow Pools) Ltd* (1999) also confirms that the two-year limitation on arrears of remuneration is in breach of EC law – see also *Levez v TH Jennings (Harlow Pools) Ltd (No 2)* (1999). As a result of the decision in *Levez*, the Equal Pay Act 1970 (Amendment) Regulations 2003 (SI 2003/1656) have extended the limit on pay claims to six years. In addition, if an employer has deliberately concealed information about inequality from their employee, no limit to backdated claims is imposed.

In determining where a successful applicant should be placed on an incremental scale, any entitlement is to join the scale at the point where his or her comparator stood at the relevant date and to enjoy the same entitlement to incremental progression (*Evesham v North Hertfordshire HA* (2000)).

In conclusion, there was previously some debate as to the continued efficacy of the discrimination legislation, including the EPA 1970 (*Equal Pay for Men and Women; Strengthening the Acts*, EOC report, 1990). However, recent proposals and the implementation of the Equality Act 2010 are fairly radical, in that these proposals are now contained within a single statute covering all aspects of equal treatment for men and women, including gender reassignment and sexual orientation. In respect of pay, it was proposed that employers be placed under a statutory duty to review their pay structures, in order to identify any areas of potential pay inequality and eliminate them; however, the Coalition Government has decided to neither implement nor repeal this power under the Equality Act, but it is very unlikely to be enacted. Whilst there has been discussion about the introduction of equal pay audits for private companies regardless of their size, it is unlikely to be implemented.

17.4 The Protected Characteristics

The Equality Act 2010 is now the main source of discrimination legislation. It has codified the different pieces of legislation such as the Sex Discrimination Act 1975 and Disability Discrimination Act 2005. The key concepts from previous discrimination legislation has been largely retained, so that the concept of less favourable treatment for direct discrimination is the same in the Equality Act as it was in the Sex Discrimination Act 1975. The definition of a disability was established in case law and has now been encompassed into the statutory definition at s 6 of the Equality Act 2010. This means that many of the cases decided before the Equality Act was implemented are still of some relevance, if only showing the development of discrimination legislation from an historical context. Although matters such as the Part Time Workers Regulations retain separate protection for part-time workers, the majority of discrimination legislation is now found in the Equality Act. The Equality Act lists nine protected characteristics in s 4 which form the basis of the discriminatory acts which are also described in separate sections further in the Act. In basic terms, unless the characteristic is protected under s 4 of the Equality Act, it is unlikely that the act is discriminatory.

The protected characteristics listed in s 4 are age, disability, gender reassignment, marriage and civil partnership, pregnancy and maternity, race, religion or belief, sex and sexual orientation. Each is then defined more specifically in individual sections.

Previously the level of protection was found in a variety of different acts. Now the protected characteristics are in essence a checklist which anyone can refer to and interpret relatively easily. Prior to the Equality Act, the Sex Discrimination Act covered not just sex discrimination but also gender reassignment, pregnancy and maternity discrimination, as well as discrimination based on a woman's marital status. These are all now separate protected characteristics.

Age

The first protected characteristic defined in the Act is age, defined in s 5 as follows:

> (1) In relation to the protected characteristic of age—
>
> (a) a reference to a person who has a particular protected characteristic is a reference to a person of a particular age group;
>
> (b) a reference to persons who share a protected characteristic is a reference to persons of the same age group.
>
> (2) A reference to an age group is a reference to a group of persons defined by reference to age, whether by reference to a particular age or to a range of ages.

In basic terms, age is given the straightforward definition. If someone is being treated in a particular way because they are of an age or age group this may potentially establish the protected characteristic of age. There then needs to be a discriminatory act (discussed at 17.4.2 below) in order to have a successful claim.

Disability

The definition of a disability found in s 6 follows the definition from *Goodwin v Patent Office* (2005) and will be discussed in greater depth at 17.4.4, as it is more complicated and has special considerations.

Gender reassignment

Gender reassignment is defined in s 7 as:

> (1) A person has the protected characteristic of gender reassignment if the person is proposing to undergo, is undergoing or has undergone a process (or part of a process) for the purpose of reassigning the person's sex by changing physiological or other attributes of sex.
>
> (2) A reference to a transsexual person is a reference to a person who has the protected characteristic of gender reassignment.

This definition is wider than previously given in the amendments to the Sex Discrimination Act 1975. It covers people proposing to undergo treatment, whether an operation or merely psychological treatment rather than surgery. This has widened the protection available.

Marriage and civil partnership

Civil partners have the same protection against discrimination as married people do. Marriage and civil partnership is defined in s 8 as:

> (1) A person has the protected characteristic of marriage and civil partnership if the person is married or is a civil partner.

Originally, protection for women who were married was developed because of the sort of assumption made in the example given at the beginning of this chapter. Attitudes may have changed, but many employers and managers still have a similar approach to young married women now.

Race

Race Discrimination has been developed as a protected characteristic over the decades since the original race discrimination legislation in 1976. The Equality Act has widened the scope in principle to cover discrimination on the basis of caste, although an exact date for implementation is still outstanding, theoretically this is a significant development.

Race is defined in s 9:

> (1) Race includes—
>
> (a) colour;
> (b) nationality;
> (c) ethnic or national origins.
>
> (2) In relation to the protected characteristic of race—
>
> (a) a reference to a person who has a particular protected characteristic is a reference to a person of a particular racial group;
> (b) a reference to persons who share a protected characteristic is a reference to persons of the same racial group.
>
> (3) A racial group is a group of persons defined by reference to race; and a reference to a person's racial group is a reference to a racial group into which the person falls.
> (4) The fact that a racial group comprises two or more distinct racial groups does not prevent it from constituting a particular racial group.
> (5) A Minister of the Crown may by order—
>
> (a) amend this section so as to provide for caste to be an aspect of race;
> (b) amend this Act so as to provide for an exception to a provision of this Act to apply, or not to apply, to caste or to apply, or not to apply, to caste in specified circumstances.
>
> (6) The power under section 207(4)(b), in its application to subsection (5), includes power to amend this Act.

Section 9(6) is significant only in terms of the possibility of the definition being extended further in the future. The crucial part of the definition is really only in s 9(1).

The previous test for establishing 'ethnic origin' can be found in *Mandla v Dowell Lee* (1983), in which it was decided that Sikhs constituted an ethnic group. It was stated by Lord Fraser that in order for a group to constitute an 'ethnic group', it must be regarded as a distinct community by virtue of certain characteristics, some of which are essential:

> . . . a long, shared history; a cultural tradition of its own; a common geographical area or descent from a number of common ancestors; a common language; a common literature; a

> common religion different from that of neighbouring groups or from the general community surrounding it; being a minority or being an oppressed or dominant group within a larger community . . .

The test has been applied with some success to bring gypsies within the RRA 1976 (see *CRE v Dutton* (1989)), but not Rastafarians (*Dawkins v Department of the Environment* (1993)), as the latter were deemed to be no more than a religious sect and, in any event, there was no 'long, shared history'. However, Jews may fall within the RRA 1976, although whether an action will succeed depends upon the reason for the discrimination; that is, if a Jew is discriminated against because of his or her religion, he or she will not be protected (see *Seide v Gillette Industries* (1980) and *Simon v Brimham Associates* (1987)). Each case must be considered on its merits. Note that gypsies and Jewish communities are now identified as protected ethnic groups within the Code of Practice.

Religion and belief

Region and belief is defined in s 10 as:

> (1) Religion means any religion and a reference to religion includes a reference to a lack of religion.
>
> (2) Belief means any religious or philosophical belief and a reference to belief includes a reference to a lack of belief.
>
> (3) In relation to the protected characteristic of religion or belief—
>
> (a) a reference to a person who has a particular protected characteristic is a reference to a person of a particular religion or belief;
>
> (b) a reference to persons who share a protected characteristic is a reference to persons who are of the same religion or belief.

Belief is given a wide definition, and includes Druidism. The explanatory notes to the Equality Act state that this is 'a broad definition in line with the freedom of thought, conscience and religion guaranteed by Article 9' of the ECHR. The main limitation on what constitutes a 'religion' for the purposes of Art 9 of the European Convention is that it must have a clear structure and belief system (see *X v UK* (1977)).

Sex discrimination

Sex is defined in s 11 as:

> (1) In relation to the protected characteristic of sex—
>
> (a) a reference to a person who has a particular protected characteristic is a reference to a man or to a woman;
>
> (b) a reference to persons who share a protected characteristic is a reference to persons of the same sex.

This means it is as appropriate for a man to bring a sex discrimination claim as for a woman. In *James v Eastleigh BC* (1990), free swimming was provided for children under the age of three and for persons who had attained the state retirement age. Mr and Mrs James were both aged 61 and were both retired. When they went to the swimming baths owned by the defendant council, Mrs James was able to take advantage of free swimming, whilst her husband had to pay. Mr James alleged an act of direct discrimination, which breached s 29 of the SDA 1975, relating to discrimination in the provision of goods, facilities and services. Initially, the Court of Appeal held that there was no act of discrimination, as it was necessary to look at the reason for adopting the discriminatory policy, which, in this case, was to help the needy; therefore, the discrimination was not on grounds of sex. However, on appeal to the House of Lords, it was decided to apply the 'but for' test and ask the question, 'but for the complainant's sex, would he have received the same treatment?'; the answer was in the affirmative and, as a result, Eastleigh Borough Council had to alter their policy.

Sexual orientation

Sexual orientation is defined in s 12 as:

> (1) Sexual orientation means a person's sexual orientation towards—
>
> (a) persons of the same sex,
> (b) persons of the opposite sex, or
> (c) persons of either sex.

This is a straightforward definition and one that requires little explanation. It is a new development that sexual orientation is no longer contained with sex discrimination and is a separate protected characteristic.

There is also protection from harassment on the grounds of homophobia (se discriminatory acts, later). Whilst a comparator is needed, the comparator can be a heterosexual of the same gender. There are specific exceptions in the form of genuine occupational requirements, and specific exemption for benefits exclusively for married couples. This is paralleled in the Equality Act and the Statutory Code of Practice 2010, which defines the meaning of sexual orientation, which can include orientation towards someone of their own sex, someone of the opposite sex or persons of either sex.

Some redress may also be available as a result of the HRA 1998. Indeed, the European Court of Human Rights (ECtHR) has held that the Ministry of Defence was in breach of Art 8 (right to a private life) of the ECHR in banning homosexuals from the armed forces (*Smith and Grady v UK* (1999)).

Considerable doubt has been cast on the applicability of Art 14 of the ECHR by the decision in *Secretary of State for Defence v MacDonald* (2001). The Court of Session in this case confirmed that 'sex' within the meaning of s 1(1) of the SDA 1975 does not include sexual orientation. Nor does the decision of the ECtHR in *Salgueiro da Silva Mouta v Portugal* (2001) result in Art 14 of the ECHR including sexual orientation. Once again, in the *MacDonald* case, the issue of comparison in s 5(3) was considered, and the conclusion reached was that the comparator was a person of the opposite sex attracted to the same sex, rather than a heterosexual. As Michael Rubenstein has pointed out on a number of occasions, this comparison does not equate to the same circumstances but is merely analogous – see 'Highlights' [2001] IRLR 413.

The continued impact of the need for a 'like with like' comparison to be made under the SDA 1975 is problematic in harassment cases, particularly where the applicant is subjected to verbal abuse. This was highlighted in *Pearce v Governing Body of Mayfield Secondary School* (2001), in which a teacher was forced to resign from her post due to a campaign of homophobic abuse from her students. The Court of Appeal restricted the comparator to a male homosexual who would have been treated to the same sort of sexual harassment. However, *Pearce* provided some hope regarding the application of the HRA 1998, in that Hale LJ (at p 675) concluded that the acts of homophobic abuse were capable of contravening Art 8 when read with the prohibition of discrimination under Art 14. She suggested, therefore, that 'a remedy might lie against a public authority under ss 6 and 7 of the Human Rights Act 1998 in respect of acts taking place on or after 2 October 2000'.

Pregnancy and maternity

Pregnancy and maternity discrimination is defined in s 18 in relation to the workplace rather than generally. Section 18 states that:

(2) A person (A) discriminates against a woman if, in the protected period in relation to a pregnancy of hers, A treats her unfavourably—

(a) because of the pregnancy, or
(b) because of illness suffered by her as a result of it.

(3) A person (A) discriminates against a woman if A treats her unfavourably because she is on compulsory maternity leave.
(4) A person (A) discriminates against a woman if A treats her unfavourably because she is exercising or seeking to exercise, or has exercised or sought to exercise, the right to ordinary or additional maternity leave.
(5) For the purposes of subsection (2), if the treatment of a woman is in implementation of a decision taken in the protected period, the treatment is to be regarded as occurring in that period (even if the implementation is not until after the end of that period).
(6) The protected period, in relation to a woman's pregnancy, begins when the pregnancy begins, and ends—

(a) if she has the right to ordinary and additional maternity leave, at the end of the additional maternity leave period or (if earlier) when she returns to work after the pregnancy;
(b) if she does not have that right, at the end of the period of 2 weeks beginning with the end of the pregnancy.

(7) Section 13, so far as relating to sex discrimination, does not apply to treatment of a woman in so far as—

(a) it is in the protected period in relation to her and is for a reason mentioned in paragraph (a) or (b) of subsection (2), or
(b) it is for a reason mentioned in subsection (3) or (4).

Discrimination related to pregnancy or maternity is part and parcel of direct discrimination. As a result, a pregnant woman can, at least in theory, challenge unfavourable treatment because of her pregnancy as an act of direct discrimination. Through the Equality Act 2010, the law relating to pregnancy and maternity discrimination is found in s 17 for non-work cases and s 18 for work cases. At one time, it was thought that such treatment was not protected by the SDA 1975, on the basis that there could be no male comparator. This approach was supported in *Turley v Allders Department Stores Ltd* (1980). However, some redress was provided by cases such as *Hayes v Malleable Working Men's Club* (1985) and *Webb v EMO Cargo Ltd* (1993), although both of these cases required comparison of the treatment of the pregnant woman with that of the sick man or, at the very least, a male employee who would be absent for an equivalent period. However, the ECJ, in considering Webb's case, ruled that this comparison was no longer acceptable and that dismissal on account of pregnancy constituted direct discrimination (see also *Dekker v Stichting Vormingscentrum voor Jong Volvassen (VJW Centrum) Plus* (1991)).

Webb was referred back to the House of Lords (*Webb v EMO Air Cargo Ltd* (No 2) (1995)), where it was concluded that the ECJ ruling should be limited to permanent contracts rather than those existing or intending to exist for a fixed term only, for example, maternity cover. It is therefore arguable that if this distinction is maintained, the UK provision does not comply with EC law. However, in *Caruana v Manchester Airport plc* (1996), the EAT decided that the ruling in *Webb* applied equally to fixed term contracts. This has been clarified by the decision in *Mahlburg v Land Mecklenburg-Vorpommern* (2000). In *Mahlberg*, the ECJ, in applying *Dekker* and *Habermann* (1994), concluded that it was contrary to Art 2(1) of the Equal Treatment Directive for an employer to refuse to appoint a pregnant woman to a post of an unlimited duration on the ground that a statutory prohibition on employment arising on account of her pregnancy would prevent her from being employed in that post from the outset and for the duration of the pregnancy.

To replace an employee on maternity leave with a permanent employee, knowing that the pregnant employee wanted to return to her post, amounted to less favourable treatment within the SDA – (NICA) *Patefield v Belfast CC* (2000). She was therefore disadvantaged in the circumstances in which she had to work.

The ECJ has confirmed that protection of the pregnant woman under Art 5 of the Equal Treatment Directive and Art 10 of the Pregnant Workers Directive is not restricted to a woman employed for an indefinite period, but extends to one employed for a fixed term, even though, because of her pregnancy, she may be unable to work for a substantial part of the term of the contract. Dismissal of a worker on account of pregnancy constitutes direct discrimination on grounds of sex, whatever the nature and extent of the economic loss incurred by the employer as a result of her absence because of pregnancy. Whether the contract was concluded for a fixed or an indefinite period has no bearing on the discriminating character of the dismissal. In either case, the employee's inability to perform her contract of employment is due to pregnancy – *Tele Danmark A/S v Handels-Og Kontorfunktiunaerernes Forbund i Danmark acting on behalf of Brandt-Nielsen* (2001).

We can see the use of the purposive approach by the ECJ in considering whether the non-renewal of a fixed term contract on grounds related to pregnancy fell within Art 10 of the Pregnant Workers Directive or Arts 2(1) and 3(1) of the Equal Treatment Directive.

While the ECJ concluded that non-renewal of a fixed contract when it comes to the end of its stipulated term cannot be regarded as dismissal within Art 10, it can be viewed as a refusal of employment which, if it relates to a worker's pregnancy, constitutes direct discrimination contrary to Arts 2(1) and 3(1) of Directive 76/207 – *Jiménez Melgar v Ayuntamiento de los Barrios* (2001).

Whilst the 'sick man' comparator has no role in the treatment of the pregnant woman or woman on maternity leave, it still has a limited role to play (see *Brown v Rentokil Ltd* (1998)). For example, it has been held that a woman who was dismissed on grounds of absence due to an illness which arose from pregnancy was not necessarily discriminated against on grounds of sex. In this case, it was thought to be quite legitimate to compare the treatment of the woman with how a sick man would have been treated, although it was decided that protection for the pregnant woman extended to the end of the maternity leave period (*Handels og Kontorfunktionaernes Forbund i Danmark (acting for Hertz v Dansk Arbejdsgiverforening)* (1991)). Where, therefore, a woman is dismissed due to an illness originating from her pregnancy which occurs outside the maternity leave period, her treatment by her employer should be compared to that of the hypothetical sick man – see *Handels og Kontorfunktionaerenes Forbund i Danmark (acting on behalf of Larson) v Dansk Handel and Service (acting on behalf of Fotex Supermarket)* (1997).

In *Busch v Klinikum Neustadt GmbH & Co Betriebs – KG* (2003), the ECJ held that not allowing a woman to return to work following parental leave because she was pregnant and could not carry out all of her duties was contrary to Art 2(1) of Directive 76/207 as amounting to direct discrimination.

Even where national legislation allows an employer to send home a pregnant employee on the basis that she is unfit for work, the employer is still required to pay her full pay – see *Handels og Kontorfunktionaernes Forbund i Danmark (acting on behalf of Hoj Pedersen) v Faellesforeningen for Danmarks Brugsforeringer (acting on behalf of Kvickly Skive)* (1999).

Finally, the courts have established that a woman has the rights to return to the same job or as similar to as possible to which she was employed before her absence (see *Blundell v Governing Body of St Andrew's Catholic Primary School* (2007)).

❖ **KEY CASE** *Blundell v Governing Body of St Andrew's Catholic Primary School* (2007)

Facts:

The claimant teacher had taught a reception class before taking maternity leave. Upon her return, she was offered a role either as a floating teacher or taking a class of older children. The claimant took the role of teaching older children, but considered it to be a particularly onerous duty, as she had not previously taught that age group, who were subject to national assessment tests. The claimant argued that the employer had committed acts of less favourable treatment towards her due to her pregnancy, and that the employer had failed to return her to the same job.

Decision:

The tribunal dismissed the claim, finding no detriment, as the claimant was contractually required to teach whatever class she was allocated. The job in which she had previously been employed was that of teacher, not of reception class teacher. The EAT held that the right to return to 'the job in which she was employed before her absence' provided by reg 18 of the Maternity and Parental Leave etc Regulations 1999 meant that the employee should be able to return to a work situation as near as possible to that which she left. In this case the return post was within the normal range of variability which the claimant could reasonably have expected.

Some of these issues may have less significance as a result of the Employment Rights Act 1996, which provides protection from dismissal for all pregnant employees and in connection with childbirth. Further rights relating to maternity and parental leave can be found in the Employment Relations Act 1999 and the Maternity and Parental Leave Regulations 1999, as amended by the Employment Act 2002 and the Maternity and Parental Leave (Amendment) Regulations 2002.

A major change introduced by the Equality Act 2010 was the introduction of perception and association. For example if someone was discriminated against because they were perceived to be gay although they were not, they would have a potential claim of sexual orientation discrimination.

Discrimination by association has effectively closed a loophole in previous discrimination legislation. Previously if you were not disabled, you could not claim disability discrimination. Now if you are treated less favorably because of your association with a disabled person, you may claim.

Perceptive and associative discrimination can be relied upon in support of a claim of direct discrimination or harassment. Association and perception cannot apply to claims of indirect discrimination because the claimant has to possess the actual protected characteristic.

17.4.1 Who is protected?

The legislation covers anyone who seeks employment under a contract of service or who is employed under a contract of service. It covers job applicants, those already employed seeking promotion or training opportunities as well as employees subjected to harassment or assisting a colleague with a complaint against another employee. It extends to those employed under a contract for services where there is a requirement for them personally to do the work (see *Mirror Group Newspapers Ltd v Gunning* (1986)). Protection from discrimination is also extended to discrimination by trade unions and employers' associations, employment agencies and qualifying bodies such as the Association of Chartered Accountants, The Law Society and partnerships. EC law also encompasses 'workers' and is therefore wider in scope than the domestic provisions.

Specific protection is now afforded to part time employees by virtue of s 19 of the Employment Relations Act 1999, which provides that the Secretary of State for Employment shall make regulations for ensuring that part-time employees are treated no less favourably than persons in full-time employment. This has led to the Part-Time Workers (Prevention of Less Favourable Treatment) Regulations 2000 (SI 2000/1551). These Regulations also implement the EC Part-Time Workers Directive (97/81).

The Regulations make it unlawful to treat part-time workers less favourably than full-time workers, and cover pay, pensions, training and holidays. The right of employers to objectively justify the different treatment is enshrined in the Regulations. Rights are extended to workers who become part-time having worked full-time. The rise in sex discrimination claims is a direct result of these Regulations.

The first case to consider the Part-Time Workers (Prevention of Less Favourable Treatment) Regulations 2000 has construed the permissible comparisons narrowly. The EAT, in *Matthews v Kent & Medway Town Fire Authority* (2003) held that reg 2(4) limits the comparison of a part-time worker with a full-time worker to those workers who are employed by the same employer under the same type of contract, and that it is reasonable of the employer to treat them differently. The decision was upheld by the Court of Appeal (2004). It is suggested that this encourages segregation of part-time workers to avoid equalising their rights with those of full-time workers.

Although there are no immediate plans for a Code of Practice, employers are recommended to review posts to determine whether they could be performed by part-time workers. For a critique of the impact of the Part-Time Workers (Prevention of Less Favourable Treatment) Regulations 2000, see McColgan, A, 'Missing the point? The Part-Time Workers (Prevention of Less Favourable Treatment) Regulations 2000 (SI 2000/1551)' (2000) 29 ILJ 260.

Similar protection is also afforded to fixed term workers by virtue of the Fixed-Term Employees (Prevention of Less Favourable Treatment) Regulations 2002 (SI 2002/2034).

17.5 Discriminatory Acts

We have established that a successful claim of discrimination firstly requires a relevant protected characteristic. The second requirement is for a discriminatory act. These are defined in ss 13, 19, 26 and 27. They are direct discrimination, indirect discrimination, harassment and victimisation. Additionally these discriminatory acts may be related to the perception of the claimant as having a protected characteristic when they do not, or an association with someone who does have a protected characteristic. These may be relevant when considering direct discrimination and harassment in particular.

17.5.1 Direct discrimination

Direct discrimination is defined in s 13 thus: 'A person (A) discriminates against another (B) if, because of a protected characteristic, A treats B less favourably than A treats or would treat others'.

The action must be 'because of' a protected characteristic. This language has changed from 'on the grounds of' and also contains the 'but for' test commonly referred to. 'But for' the protected characteristic, the claimant would not have been subjected to discrimination.

In order to establish this type of discrimination, comparison must be made with a person of the opposite sex or another race; however, a hypothetical person can be used for this comparison. Following the decision in *Badamoody v United Kingdom Central Council for Nursing, Midwifery & Health Visiting* (2002), where the applicant failed to establish an actual comparator, the employment tribunal must go on to construct a hypothetical comparator and test the case against that benchmark. Although this head of claim has been difficult to establish in the past, in recent years the following test has been formulated, which has helped the complainant and reinforces the fact that intention and motive, no matter how good, are not relevant. The test is as follows:

- Has there been an act of discrimination?
- If so, but for the sex or race of the complainant, would he or she have been treated differently, that is, more favourably? If the answer to this is in the affirmative, an act of direct discrimination has taken place (see *R v Birmingham CC ex p EOC* (1989), followed in *James v Eastleigh BC* (1990) (17.4.1 above)).

However, the 'but for' approach has been questioned, particularly in cases where discrimination is inferred. In *Zafar v Glasgow CC* (1998), it was held that the guidance provided in *King v The Great Britain China Centre* (1991) should be applied when inferring that discrimination had taken place. This places the burden of proof squarely on the applicant, but allows the tribunal to draw any inferences which it believes are just and equitable. The employer will then be required to give an explanation, which, if unsatisfactory or inadequate, will allow the tribunal to infer that an act of discrimination has taken place. The decision in *Zafar* goes on to support the dissenting judgment in *James*, which allows the tribunal to consider reason, intention and motive. Whether this decision will now make it harder for the applicant to establish direct discrimination remains to be seen. (See Watt, B, 'Goodbye "but-for", hello "but-why?"?' (1998) 27 ILJ 121, which provides a detailed analysis of the possible impact of *Zafar*.) The Sex Discrimination (Indirect Discrimination and Burden of Proof) Regulations 2001 shift the burden of proof in direct discrimination cases to the extent that, once the complainant has established a *prima facie* case, that is, that there is sufficient evidence to infer discrimination, the burden will move to the respondent to offer a non-discriminatory reason for his actions. It is unclear at this stage whether it will have a significant impact on the guidance provided by the decision in *King*.

The decision in *Shamoon v Chief Constable of the Royal Ulster Constabulary* (2003) offers revised guidance on establishing direct discrimination. The House of Lords suggest that there are circumstances where the questions raised in the two stage test (see *James*) should be reversed; the first question would then be 'Why was the complainant treated less favourably?' This would allow the employment tribunal to infer discrimination at this stage, or to conclude that it was not on grounds of sex or race. This decision questions the decision in *Zafar* in so far as it relates to the inference of discrimination.

Further assistance in establishing direct discrimination can be found in the case of *Noone v North West Thames Regional HA* (1988), which concluded that once the complainant has shown that there is a *prima facie* case of discrimination, even though actual evidence may be lacking, discrimination will be inferred unless the employer can show good reason for his or her actions which are not connected to the sex or race of the complainant.

The Court of Appeal in *Anya v University of Oxford* (2001) stresses the importance of looking for indicators from a time before or subsequently which may demonstrate that a decision to appoint, or not, was affected by racial bias. For example:

> . . . evidence that one of the panel was not unbiased, or that equal opportunities procedures were not used when they should have been, may point to the possibility of conscious or unconscious racial bias having entered into the process.

Direct discrimination is usually the most obvious and easily observed form of discrimination, as it is in essence direct. Direct discrimination covers both overt and covert acts against the individual and is not confined to hostile or intentional acts of discrimination. Indirect is more problematic.

It should be noted that the Equality Act 2010 (s 23(1)) requires a 'like with like' comparison to be made, so that the 'relevant circumstances between the comparators are the same or not materially different' (*Bain v Bowles* (1991)). However although the Equality Act 2010 replicates similar provisions in previous legislation, it originally contained the new concept of dual discrimination. This is where claims for discrimination on two combined grounds are to be allowed (but no more than two). Thus, the treatment of the claimant must be compared with that of an actual or a hypothetical person – the comparator – who does not share the same protected characteristic as the claimant (or, in the case of dual discrimination, either of the protected characteristics in the combination) but who is (or is assumed to be) in not materially different circumstances from the claimant. In cases of direct or dual discrimination, those circumstances can include their respective abilities where the claimant is a disabled person. However the Coalition Government have announced that the concept of dual discrimination is not going to be implemented so whilst an interesting and some would say crucial concept, is currently on the statute books, is not going to be available to claimants.

Finally, the Human Rights Act (HRA) 1998 provides some protection from discrimination on the grounds of 'religion, politics, or other opinion, national or social origin, association with national minority, property, birth and other status'. Discrimination is prohibited under the HRA 1998 in so far as it relates to other Articles of the European Convention on Human Rights (ECHR), such as freedom of association, right to respect for private life, etc. All primary legislation must be read subject to the ECHR, and such legislation must be interpreted in the light of legal decisions in respect of the Convention.

The HRA 1998 is likely to have an impact on areas of discrimination which are either not currently protected or are inadequately protected. For example, the right to have respect for one's private life (Art 8) is likely to encompass sexual orientation, sexual activity, dress codes and family life – such as working hours. Article 9 embodies the right to religious and political freedom. However, Art 14 does not provide a free-standing right not to be discriminated against. It prohibits discrimination solely in relation to the enjoyment of the substantive Convention rights:

> **Article 14 – Prohibition of Discrimination**
> The employment of the rights and freedoms set forth in this Convention shall be secured without discrimination on any ground such as sex, race, colour, language, religion, political or other opinion, national or social origin, association with a national minority, property, birth or other status.

An individual may challenge existing legislation on the basis of incompatibility; such a challenge will be heard by the High Court. The Secretary of State has the power to amend legislation deemed to be incompatible by an Order in Council. (See Ewing, KD, 'The Human Rights Act and labour law' (1998) 27 ILJ 275 for an analysis of the application of the HRA 1998 to employment law.)

17.5.2 Indirect discrimination

Indirect discrimination covers conduct which, on the face of it, does not treat people differently; that is, it is neutral. However, it is the impact of this treatment which amounts to discrimination. It can, therefore, be subtle in nature and may be difficult to prove.

Indirect discrimination is defined in s 1(2)(b) of the Equality Act 2010 as occurring:

> where a provision, criterion or practice is applied equally to men and women, but which is to the detriment of a considerably larger proportion of women than men, and which cannot be shown to be justifiable irrespective of the sex of the person to whom it is applied, and which is to the woman's detriment.

Indirect discrimination occurs in race cases where a provision, criterion or practice is applied equally to persons not of the same race or ethnic or national origins of the complainant, but which puts persons of the same race or ethnic or national origins as the complainant at a particular disadvantage when compared with other persons and which is an actual disadvantage for the complainant and which cannot be justified as being a proportionate means of achieving a legitimate aim (s 1(1A) of the RRA 1976). The definition of indirect discrimination will be found in s 19 of the Equality Act 2010 when it comes into force.

Under the Sex Discrimination (Indirect Discrimination and Burden of Proof) Regulations 2001 (SI 2001/282), the complaint need only establish facts from which the tribunal can conclude that the respondent has committed an act of discrimination. The burden of proof then moves to the respondent to show that he did not commit such an act, or that his actions were not tainted by discrimination.

In *Barton v Investec Henderson, Crosthwaite Securities Ltd* (2003), the EAT concluded that the respondent must show that sex or race, etc, did not form part of the reasons for the discriminatory treatment. If the respondent does not discharge the burden of proof, the employment tribunal must find that there has been unlawful discrimination. The guidelines in *Barton* have been amended by the EAT in *Chamberlins Solicitors & Another v Emokpae* (2004), in that 'employers will no longer have to show that their action/treatment was not tainted with any discrimination whatsoever, but only that, if gender or race was a factor, it had no significant influence on such action/treatment' – see [2004] IRLR 743.

It is expected that the new definition of indirect discrimination will provide greater flexibility. There may, for example, be less dependence on statistical evidence, although the employment tribunal is encouraged to focus on the discriminatory effect of the particular provision or criterion, etc, and determine whether the employer has objectively justified it – *Sibley v The Girls Public Day School Trust & Norwich High School for Girls* (2003). Again, the intention of the employer is irrelevant in establishing indirect discrimination, although it becomes important to the tribunal in deciding whether compensation should be awarded, as both statutes provide that no compensation is payable for unintentional, indirect discrimination. There has yet to be any case law on the new provisions. However, some existing case law may assist in interpreting them.

In isolating a requirement or condition, the complainant has in the past had to show that it operates as an absolute bar, in that it amounts to 'a must', without which an applicant could not proceed. This is highlighted by *Perera v Civil Service Commission* (1983). Perera was a barrister from Sri Lanka who applied for a post with the defendants. The selection criteria, which were applied to all candidates, included age, practical experience in the UK, spoken and written English, etc. Perera argued that these were requirements or conditions. It was held that they were not a 'must', without which an applicant could not succeed. The only relevant condition was that the applicant should be a barrister or solicitor, and Perera fulfilled this condition.

This interpretation allowed an employer to apply a wide range of criteria in making selections for employment or promotion and, as long as they did not constitute a 'must', how he or she applied them was not called into question under the SDA 1975 or the RRA 1976. However, the decision in *Perera* has been challenged by the EAT in *Falkirk Council v Whyte* (1997). The EAT in this case confirmed that a 'desirable' qualification could amount to a requirement or condition where it was clear that the qualification operated as the decisive factor in the selection process. The EAT not only chose not to follow *Perera*, but also welcomed a more liberal approach to determining 'requirement or condition' and avoiding the need to establish an absolute bar. Past cases show that age limits may be discriminatory, as in *Price v Civil Service Commission* (1977), as may requirements to work full-time (*Home Office v Holmes* (1984); *Briggs v North Eastern Education and Library Board* (1990)); a mobility clause which requires an employee to move to new locations may also amount to requirement or condition, as in *Meade-Hill and National Union of Civil and Public Servants v British Council* (1995). The new definition in employment cases is in line with this more liberal approach as seen in *Falkirk*.

In determining what amounts to a 'considerably smaller proportion', the complainant must show, usually by the use of statistical evidence, that there is an adverse impact on his or her particular race or sex (see *London Underground Ltd v Edwards (No 2)* (1998) for a flexible application of adverse impact). Many complainants fail by selecting the wrong pool for comparison.

In *Pearse v City of Bradford Metropolitan Council* (1988), Ms Pearse, a part time lecturer at Ilkley College, was unable to apply for a full time post at the college because the only persons eligible to apply were full time employees of the local authority. She alleged that this amounted to indirect discrimination and submitted statistics which showed that only 21.8% of the female academic staff employed at the college were employed on a full time basis, compared with the 46.6% of the male academic staff who could comply with the requirement/condition regarding full time employment. It was held that Ms Pearse should fail in her claim because she had selected the incorrect pool for comparison; the correct pool would have been those with the appropriate qualifications for the post, without reference to the requirement/condition in question, rather than those eligible.

Whether the complainant has selected the correct pool for comparison is a question of fact to be decided by the tribunal. However, as can be seen in *Kidd v DRG (UK) Ltd* (1985), statistical evidence is usually necessary to support claims and this must specifically relate to the pool for comparison. For example, if the requirement or condition affects part time workers and the applicant wants to show that the majority of part time workers are female, her statistical evidence must show this.

In deciding whether the complainant has selected the correct pool, the tribunal will not allow the complainant to limit the pool just because it suits her case. In *Jones v University of Manchester* (1993), the Court of Appeal held that the appropriate pool for comparison was all those with the required qualifications for the post, not including the requirement complained of. So, Mrs Jones' attempts to narrow the pool failed. The new wording is unlikely to require a comparison based on statistical evidence. A more theoretical comparison may suffice.

The term 'can comply' has also been open to interpretation by the tribunals. It has been determined that the words mean 'can in practice', rather than 'can as a theoretical possibility'. This is supported by the decisions in *Price v Civil Service Commission* (1977) and *Mandla v Dowell Lee* (1983).

Be careful not to confuse indirect discrimination with third party discrimination. Third party harassment is when the employers knows that the employee has been harassed by another person who is not an employee of the company – for example, this could be an employee from another company that they do business with, or a customer. Where the employer does nothing to stop this harassment the employer would be liable.

Third party harassment is included within the Equality Act 2010, but in the Enterprise and Regulatory Reform Act 2013, this section was to be repealed. This repeal was due to take effect from 1 October 2013.

Has the condition or requirement operated to the detriment of the complainant?

The complainant must show that he or she has suffered a detriment, that is, that the requirement or condition has disadvantaged him or her; in effect, the complainant must have *locus standi*. The following have been held to amount to a disadvantage: requiring a woman to work part time (*Home Office v Holmes* (1984)); transfer to a less interesting job (*Kirby v MSC* (1980)); and conduct amounting to sexual harassment (*Wileman v Minilec Engineering Ltd* (1988)).

The decision in *Shamoon v Chief Constable of the Royal Ulster Constabulary* (2003) confirms that 'detriment' amounts to suffering a disadvantage; however, it must relate to the employment field. The House of Lords supported the test as outlined in *Ministry of Defence v Jeremiah* (1980): 'Is the treatment of such a kind that a reasonable worker would or might take the view that in all the circumstances it was to his detriment?' Nevertheless, it is not necessary to demonstrate some physical or economic consequence. The Court of Appeal in *London Borough of Ealing v Rihal* (2004), in applying *Shamoon*, found that an Indian Sikh, although having the same, if not better, qualifications and more experience than other applicants, was passed over for promotion on a number of occasions. The court found that Ealing in effect operated a 'glass ceiling' in the Housing Department where Mr Rihal worked, which made it difficult for those who were not white to obtain posts in senior management.

Justification

Once the complainant has established the above requisites, the onus of proof moves to the employer to show that the requirement or condition is justified irrespective of the gender, race or marital status of the complainant. The criteria for establishing justification were clarified by the Court of Appeal in *Hampson v Department of Science* (1989), in which it was made clear that the test requires a balance to be struck between the discriminatory effect of the requirement or condition and the needs of the employer. The employer must show a real need on the part of the undertaking to operate such a practice (this must be objective; it will then be balanced against the discriminatory impact of the practice). If there is a less discriminatory alternative, the employer must take it.

The fact that a requirement or condition is not inherently discriminatory does not amount to justification within s 1(1)(b). As the operation of s 1(1)(b) is based on gender neutral requirements which have a disparate impact on a particular sex (or race), it is not acceptable justification of the practice to argue that it may operate in a non-discriminatory manner – *Whiffen v Milham Ford Girls' School* (2001).

The Equality Act 2010 harmonises the concept of justification in discrimination cases as a 'proportionate means of achieving a legitimate aim'. The key change here for employment lawyers is the imposition of an objective justification test in relation to the two new disability claims of indirect discrimination and discrimination arising from a disability. (For more detail on these changes please see the section on disability discrimination below.) It is important to note that for most of the protected characteristics it is not possible to justify direct discrimination.

17.5.3 Harassment

The Equality Act 2010 also covers the law on harassment and widens the definition of what is meant by the term 'harassment' (s 26). The definition of sexual harassment as interpreted by the courts is also wide and encompasses any conduct meted out in a particular way because of the complainant's gender or race; that is, it is not confined to conduct of a purely physical nature, even though many of the cases involve this type of conduct.

In *Strathclyde Regional DC v Porcelli* (1986), Mrs Porcelli was a laboratory assistant at a school under the control of the council. She was subjected to a variety of treatment from two male laboratory assistants, who were intent on driving her from her job. This conduct involved brushing against her and making suggestive remarks, as well as putting heavy equipment on the top shelves of the store. She made her claim and asked to be transferred. It was held that she had been discriminated against, as the type of treatment was related to her sex and a man in a similar position would not have been treated the same way. The employer was found to be vicariously liable for the actions of the male laboratory assistants by virtue of s 41 of the SDA 1975.

The courts have gone further, in holding that harassment need not be a course of conduct but can manifest itself in a single act of a serious nature. In *Bracebridge Engineering v Darby* (1990), it was held that employees committing such acts might be within the course of their employment, resulting in the employer being vicariously liable for such acts. Racial harassment is akin to sexual harassment and, to that extent, racial insults may also be a form of harassment. However, in establishing either type of discrimination, the complainant must show that the treatment is to their detriment, as that term is used in s 6 of the SDA 1975 and s 4 of the RRA 1976 (see *De Souza v Automobile Association* (1986)).

The EC has intervened on the question of sexual harassment by, first, adopting a resolution relating to sexual harassment at work (Resolution No 6015/90) and, secondly, agreeing to a recommendation and Code of Practice on the Protection and Dignity of Women and Men at Work (92/C 27/04). As a result, although the recommendation is not directly enforceable, the ECJ has ruled that the national courts must take such measures into account in applying national and Community law (*Grimaldi v Fonds des Maladies Professionelles* (1990)). The amended Equal Treatment Directive will give further legitimacy to this and will result in amendments to the SDA 1975. The proposed provision on sexual harassment extends harassment to sex-related and sexual harassment, including verbal and non-verbal images such as pornography or sexually explicit emails.

Harassment is defined in three ways. There is what we will call type 1 harassment, which is available in connection with all protected characteristics save for marriage and civil partnership and pregnancy and maternity, and then types 2 and 3, which are specifically in relation to sexual harassment:

- Type 1 harassment – unwanted conduct on the grounds of race/sex which has the purpose or effect of violating another person's dignity or creating an intimidating, hostile, degrading, humiliating or offensive environment for that person.
- Type 2 harassment (only in the case of sexual harassment) – harassment by virtue of unwanted sexual conduct which has the effect of type 1.
- Type 3 harassment – sexual harassment that has an additional strand in that if a person is treated less favourably as a result of having rejected or submitted to a sexual advance, they may claim sexual harassment.

In *Wadman v Carpenter Farrer Partnership* (1993) it was held that the tribunal should look at the employer's implementation of the code of practice on harassment. It should be noted that the Criminal Justice and Public Order Act 1994 introduced a criminal provision against harassment. The Protection from Harassment Act 1997 also creates a criminal offence of harassment, as well as providing civil remedies in the form of damages or an injunction. It is unclear how far this Act covers harassment in the workplace. The Act is limited, in that one act of harassment will not support an action and there is no vicarious liability provision.

As with all acts of discrimination, the employer may be found to be vicariously liable unless all reasonable precautions are taken to prevent the act of discrimination from taking place. Employers are expected to take preventative action even though such action may not have prevented the act complained of from taking place – *Canniffe v East Riding of Yorkshire Council* (2000). See Roberts, P, 'Employer's liability for sexual and racial harassment: developing the reasonably practicable steps defence' (2001) 30(4) ILJ 388. Although it was thought that the common law test for determining whether an employee was acting outside the course of the employment was also applicable to this statutory form of vicarious liability, it is clear from the current case law that the tribunals will not necessarily apply such a stringent test. In *Burton v DeVere Hotels Ltd* (1996), the employer was found to be vicariously liable where the harasser was a third party who subjected the employer's employees to racial insults as part of his nightclub act. In these circumstances, it was found that the employer would be vicariously liable, provided he could have prevented the harassment from taking place by applying the standards of good practice. However, the decision in *Burton* has now been overruled by the House of Lords in *Pearce v Governing Body of Mayfield Secondary School* (2003), in which it was concluded that in the *Burton* case, whilst there was a failure on the part of the employer to prevent the act of discrimination, this failure had nothing to do with the sex or race of the employees. The failure to protect the employee on the part of the employer must be related to their sex or race for the employer to be vicariously liable. In *Tower Boot Co Ltd v Jones* (1997), the Court of Appeal overruled the decision of the EAT by finding that the employer was vicariously liable for extreme acts of racial harassment perpetrated by his employees on a fellow employee, such as branding with a screwdriver and whipping, even though the EAT had felt that the employees were outside the scope of their employment. The Court of Appeal felt that a purposive construction should be given to s 32 of the RRA 1976 and s 41 of the SDA 1975, so as to deter acts of sexual and racial harassment in the workplace. (See also *Sidhu v Aerospace Composite Technology Ltd* (2000), in which an act of discrimination occurring on a works trip was found to be outside the course of employment, and Roberts and Vickers, 'Harassment at work as discrimination: the current debate in

England and Wales' (1998) 3 IJDL 91.) The common law approach resulted in a restrictive interpretation, which would allow employers to avoid liability for more heinous acts of discrimination.

17.5.4 Victimisation

Victimisation occurs where the complainant is treated less favourably because he or she has: brought proceedings against the discriminator or another person under the Equality Act 2010 or has assisted someone who is doing so.

Previously, the complainant had to show a clear connection between the action of the discriminator and his or her own conduct (presuming that it falls under one of the above); if there was no more than a casual connection, then the tribunal would be reluctant to find that victimisation had taken place. (See *Aziz v Trinity Street Taxis Ltd* (1988).) However, the decision in *Nagarajan v London Regional Transport* (1999) overturned the decision in *Aziz*. As a result, the alleged victim no longer has to show that the discriminator had a motive which was consciously connected with the discrimination legislation. It would suffice to show that the discrimination provisions in the discrimination legislation had consciously or subconsciously influenced the discriminator.

❖ KEY CASE *Nagarajan v London Regional Transport* (1999)

Facts:

Mr Nagarajan had brought a number of race cases against his employer London Regional Transport over the years, largely unsuccessfully. He applied for a vacant post within LRT, and failed at interview. He had performed the duties of the job for several months previously without any complaints. One of the interview panel scored him one out of ten for articulacy and noted that he was 'very anti-management', even though the sole source of such a conclusion must have been the panel member's previous knowledge of his discrimination complaints.

Decision:

The Tribunal found that Mr Nagarajan had been victimised 'consciously or subconsciously' and awarded compensation of £2,500. The employers were successful at the Employment Appeal Tribunal and the Court of Appeal, on the basis that victimisation could only ever be conscious. Victimisation, by definition, involves a subjective analysis of the mind of the person in question. 'I do not understand how one can victimise someone "subconsciously"?', the Court had said. With these two decisions of the Employment Appeal Tribunal and the Court of Appeal it was much harder for victimisation cases to succeed. However, that worrying state of affairs has now been conclusively overturned by the House of Lords. In a majority decision, the possibility of subconscious influence amounting to victimisation is confirmed. Arguing that the victimisation provisions of the Race Relations Act should be interpreted consistently with the s 1 direct discrimination provisions, Lord Nicholls points to the fact that what matters in discrimination cases is not the reason for the decision made. Motive has long been recognised as irrelevant, and therefore whether the decision was conscious or subconscious is not the point. 'Members of racial groups need protection from conduct driven by unrecognised prejudice as much as from conscious and deliberate discrimination.' Therefore whether the panel member who scored Mr Nagarajan for articulacy was influenced consciously or not mattered little: the fact is that they were significantly influenced and the score was 'ridiculous'. Accordingly, the Tribunal were entitled to draw the inference that she had been significantly influenced by his previous race claims.

The House of Lords in *Chief Constable of West Yorkshire Police v Khan* (2001) held that whilst failure to provide a reference may amount to victimisation, the withholding of the reference must be linked to a protected act on the part of the applicant. In the present case, the reason why the reference was withheld was not because the applicant had brought discrimination proceedings, but rather because the employer temporarily needed to preserve his position in the outstanding proceedings. The evidence established that, once the litigation was concluded, a reference would have been supplied. From this case, it is clear that the reason for the alleged act of victimisation is relevant and must be identified.

17.6 Bringing a Claim

An applicant must bring a claim to the employment tribunal within three months of the date on which the act complained of was committed. A single act of discrimination is easier to date than a series of continuing acts. A different consideration with discrimination claims is often the date of knowledge of the discriminatory act. Initially the claimant may not realise that they have been discriminated against until after they have left their employment some time. It is when they discover that they have been subjected to discrimination that the time limit starts to run. A complaint brought after this limit will only be heard by the tribunal if it is just and equitable to do so. The employment tribunal is generally more flexible with discrimination claims than other types of claim.

It should be noted that under the Enterprise and Regulatory Reform Act 2013 a system of employment tribunal fees was introduced on 29 July 2013, amid considerable controversy. At present there are two applications for the judicial review of the new fees system. Interestingly one judicial review is being heard in Scotland but will bind English and Welsh employment tribunals. A further fundamental change was the introduction of compulsory mediation by ACAS in April 2013. The exact details are unclear, save that without a referral to ACAS for mediation, no tribunal claim will be issued.

17.7 Remedies

There are three potential remedies available to claimants in discrimination cases: a declaration, recommendation and compensation. It is worth noting at this stage that a claimant does not have to have actually left their employment in order to bring a claim of discrimination. For a claim of unfair dismissal a claimant generally needs to have been dismissed, while for a discrimination claim, the claimant does not.

A successful complainant may receive an award of compensation, which may include a sum for actual losses, such as expenses and wages, injury to feelings and future losses. However, no compensation will be awarded for indirect race discrimination unless it is intentional. An amount of not less than £500 should be awarded for injury to feelings, which should always form part of the award (*Sharifi v Strathclyde Regional Council* (1992)). The upper limit for compensation was £11,000. This was challenged in *Marshall v Southampton and South West Hampshire AHA* (No 2) (1993), where it was held by the ECJ that the limit on compensation contravened EC law and should, therefore, be removed; in addition, it was in order to award interest on compensation. Following *City of Bradford v Arora* (1991), an employment tribunal may award aggravated damages but, following *Deane v London Borough of Ealing* (1993), can no longer award exemplary damages. The heads of damages and their respective limits are defined in *Vento v Chief Constable of West Yorkshire Police* (2000) and have been updated in *Da'Bell v NSPCC* (2009). They are known generally as the Vento guidelines.

The Court of Appeal in *Sheriff v Klyne Tugs (Lowestoft) Ltd* (1999) has recognised a new head of damages for personal injury in discrimination cases. As a result, where an applicant can show that an act of discrimination resulted in personal injury, the employment tribunal must award compensation for it. Compensation may be awarded for injury to feelings and psychiatric injury resulting from an act of discrimination. Whilst they are distinct forms of injury, it is recognised that they are not always easily separable – *HM Prison Service v Salmon* (2001). There has also been controversy over whether a claimant is entitled to claim compensation during a period of receipt of incapacity benefit (see *Sheffield Forgemasters v Fox* (2009)).

The employment tribunal also has the power to:

- make a declaration with respect to the rights of the complainant under the respective legislation – such a declaration is not enforceable and, at the most, can only be persuasive as far as the employer is concerned; and
- make a recommendation for the employer to take specific action, for example, order the employer to cease discrimination with respect to an individual complainant. However, this does not extend to a general order to cease a discriminatory practice, nor, failing the decision in *Noone v North West Thames RHA (No 2)* (1988), does it extend to positive discrimination such as recommending that the applicant who has been the victim of discriminatory selection be awarded to the next available post.

17.8 The Equality and Human Rights Commission

The Equality and Human Rights Commission was established in 2006 to bring together all the independent equality bodies together, such as the Equal Opportunities Commission and the Commission for Racial Equality (CRE). The EHRC took on this role from 1 October 2007, and has powers to issue guidance on and enforce all the equality enactments (covering race, sex, disability, religion and belief, sexual orientation and age).

The mission of the Equality and Human Rights Commission is to be 'a catalyst for change and improvement on equality and human rights', with a statutory mandate from Parliament to 'challenge discrimination and protect and promote human rights'. This can include challenging individuals and employers and bringing cases to court if required.

The Commission regularly assesses progress, and reports back to the Government, through its Annual Report.

17.9 Disability Discrimination

Disability is a protected under s 6 of the Equality Act 2010. The disabled employee is protected at all stages of the employment process, that is, recruitment and selection, during the contract's existence and with respect to termination. It includes constructive dismissal – *Nottinghamshire CC v Meikle* (2004). In effect, the disabled employee has to show that he or she has been treated less favourably on grounds relating to his or her disability (s 5) (now s 3A). There is, however, no need to make a 'like with like' comparison, as this is not required by the DDA 1995. In assessing whether the treatment is less favourable, comparison is with another person, not another disabled person – see *Clark v TDG Ltd (t/a Novacold)* (1999).

In assessing whether there had been a breach of s 5 (now s 3A), one contentious point was whether there was a need for knowledge of the disability on the part of the employer. The tribunals moved from the position in *O'Neill v Symm & Co* (1998), which required such knowledge, as a result of the decision in *Clarke v TDG* (knowledge being irrelevant in assessing less favourable treatment within s 5(1) and (9) and in respect of justification in s 5(3) – see *London Borough of Hammersmith and Fulham v Farnsworth* (2000)).

However, the issue of 'knowledge' on the part of the employer has been revisited in *HJ Heinz Co v Kenrick* (2000). In this case, Mr Kenrick was employed by Heinz from 1979 until his dismissal in 1997. He became ill in 1996, but his condition was never satisfactorily identified. He was warned by his employer that he risked being dismissed if he did not indicate a likely date of return to work. In April 1997, the company's medical adviser noted that he was still unfit for work and he was dismissed. After his dismissal, a diagnosis of chronic fatigue syndrome (CFS) was confirmed. In the subsequent legal action under the DDA 1995, Heinz argued that they could not be liable because they were not aware of his disability at the time of the dismissal. It was, however, accepted that CFS was a disability within the meaning of the DDA 1995. The EAT held that the employer had sufficient knowledge, through their medical adviser, of Kenrick's illness so as to be held to have treated him less favourably for a reason related to his disability. The tribunal further concluded that s 5 does not require the employer to have knowledge of the disability in order to have acted for a reason that relates to the disability. It is not anticipated that this case will open the floodgates. The intention of the tribunal is to '. . . require employers to pause to consider whether the reason for a dismissal might relate to disability'.

Such a lack of knowledge of the disability did not discharge the onus of establishing justification under s 5(3) of the DDA 1995. 'A justification defence cannot be thought up after the event when it has never been considered during the period of employment', that is, an employer could not say that there was nothing they could have done because they did not know of the disability – *Quinn v Schwarzkopf Ltd* (2001). However, the decision in *Quinn* was qualified by the decision in *Callagan v Glasgow CC* (2001). The EAT did not rule out the provision of the justification issue where the employer was unaware of the disability. In considering justification, the emphasis was placed on consideration of the treatment meted out by the employer and this did not depend upon the tribunal being satisfied that all possible protection had been given to the employee.

There is a further duty on the employer by virtue of s 6 (now s 4A) of the DDA 1995 to make adjustments to premises to ensure that the disabled person is not placed at a substantial disadvantage as compared with persons who are not disabled. The performance of the duty under s 6 (now s 4A) may require the employer to treat a disabled person more favourably in order to remove the disadvantage attributable to the disability – so held the House of Lords in *Archibald v Fife Council* (2004). In this particular case, this might have involved transferring the employee to a sedentary job that she was qualified to undertake even if it was at a higher grade. Restricting the consideration of 'reasonable adjustments' to the existing job was unacceptable.

The duty to make reasonable adjustments is to be judged on whether the employer was aware of, or could reasonably be expected to know of, the person's disability (*Rideout v TC Group* (1998)). The duty under s 6 (now s 4A) does not extend to the provision of a personal carer (*Kenny v Hampshire Constabulary* (1999)). However, it includes adjustments to working arrangements. The employer is provided with a justification defence. The test of whether the employer must make adjustments is one of reasonableness, which permits consideration of the cost and nature of the adjustments, as well as the practicability of making them. An employer is duty-bound under s 6 (now s 4A) to consider the adjustments proposed by the applicant, whether they were reasonable and whether their implementation would have avoided the discriminatory act (*Fu v London Borough of Camden* (2001); *Johnson and Johnson Medical Ltd v Filmer* (2002)). However, the onus is on the employer to assess the employee's needs (*Mid-Staffordshire General Hospital NHS Trust v Cambridge* (2003)). Section 6 (now s 4A) places the duty on the employer (*Cosgrove v Caesar and Howie* (2001)). An example of the steps which might need to be taken by an employer can be found in the new s 18B(2).

The Equality Act 2010 brings about two fundamental changes in the area of disability discrimination in the form of two new types of disability discrimination claim. The Act widens the concept of indirect discrimination to encompass disability (even though doubts over this were raised during the consultation process). Secondly, the Act introduces the new concept of 'discrimination arising from disability', which will in reality replace the outgoing disability-related discrimination provisions. As a result of the House of Lords' decision in *London Borough of Lewisham v Malcolm* (2008), it has become much more difficult for a claimant to establish disability-related discrimination because of the Court's ruling on the correct comparator in such cases. In essence the new provisions prohibit an employer from treating a disabled employee in a way which, because of the employee's disability, is to their detriment and which cannot be objectively justified. The employer has a defence if he can show that he did not know and could not reasonably be expected to know that the employee had a disability. This new claim is broadly equivalent to that of disability-related discrimination as it existed before *Malcolm* with the difference that lack of knowledge is a potential defence and the new form of discrimination is subject to the standard objective justification test discussed above. Also, the new Act prohibits employers from asking about health issues pre-employment (Talibart, Griffin, Darbourne and Sanders, 2010).

Greater detail on disability discrimination is contained within the statutory Code of Practice

Meaning of disability

One contentious issue is what is meant by 'disability' and 'disabled'. The Equality Act 2010 states at s 6(1) that:

> (a) P has a physical or mental impairment, and
> (b) the impairment has a substantial and long-term adverse effect on P's ability to carry out normal day-to-day activities.

This largely mirrors the definition which emanated from *Goodwin v Patent Office* (1999). They are cumulative conditions. Each must be satisfied for a claimant to fall within the definition.

In assessing whether a person's ability to carry out such activities is affected, the employment tribunal may consider evidence relating to the performance of their duties at work, where these duties include 'normal day to day activities', for example, nursing (*Law Hospital NHS Trust v Rush* (2001)); and also whilst not at work (*Cruickshank v Vaw Motor Cast Ltd* (2002)). The focus for the employment tribunal should be on what the applicant cannot do, or can only do with difficulty, not what he can do (see *Leonard v Southern Derbyshire Chamber of Commerce* (2001)). Also, the impairment and its effect should be considered holistically; for example, an impairment to the hand should be considered in the light of an adverse effect on manual dexterity, ability to lift and carry everyday objects, instead of focusing on particular tasks or issues. Nor should tasks which are gender specific – for example, applying make up – be discounted as not being a normal day to day activity as it is carried out almost exclusively by women – see *Ekpe v Commissioner of Police of the Metropolis* (2001).

The onus is on the employment tribunal to make its own assessment from the evidence before it, and avoid being over-influenced by medical opinion rather than fact. However, it should not be trying to establish the cause of the disability – see *Power v Panasonic UK Ltd* (2003). Also, where the applicant is receiving medical treatment for the condition, so that the final outcome cannot be determined or the removal of the treatment would result in a relapse, the medical treatment must be disregarded in determining whether there is a substantial adverse effect – see *Abadeh v British Telecommunications plc* (2001).

Where the expert medical evidence demonstrates that the applicant has a disability which is controlled by medication, it still falls within the definition of disability – see s 1 of the DDA 1995 and *Kapadia v London Borough of Lambeth* (2000).

Finally, a difficult area for the employment tribunals is where the alleged disability is actually due to a functional or psychological 'overlay', that is, where a person claims to be suffering from a physical injury, which the doctor states is due to the individual's psychological state and is not related to any physical pathology. The problem for the tribunal is that the applicant is claiming a physical impairment (which does not in fact exist) whilst the tribunal must assess whether the mental impairment falls within s 1 of the DDA 1995 – that is, is a 'clinically well-recognised illness'. Interestingly, 'functional overlay' does not appear in the World Health Organisation's International Classification of Diseases or the American Psychiatric Association's *Diagnostic and Statistical Manual of Mental Disorders* – see *Rugamer v Sony Music Entertainment Ltd* (2001) and *McNicol v Balfour Beatty Rail Maintenance Ltd* (2001), in which the employment tribunals concluded that the applicants, both with 'functional overlay', did not have a mental impairment. In *College of Ripon & York St John v Hoggs* (2002), the EAT concluded that 'impairment' is something that results from an illness as opposed to being the illness itself; it can therefore be cause or effect. It is not necessary to consider how impairment is caused, be it physical or mental.

Since the Disability Discrimination Act 2005, conditions such as depression, HIV/AIDS and cancer have been established as relevant conditions to satisfy the mental or physical impairment as relevant. Furthermore, there have also been problems for the tribunals regarding the assessment of the disability and whether or not the disability is likely to recur.

❖ KEY CASE — *Richmond Adult Community College v McDougall* (2008)

Facts:

M had suffered from psychological disorders but recovered after medical treatment. M was offered a job as a database assistant for the College. When the College learned of M's medical history it withdrew the offer. M brought a disability discrimination claim.

Decision:

The employment tribunal accepted that M had a mental impairment but held that she was not disabled within the meaning of s 1 of the Disability Discrimination Act 1995, as the impairment did not have a substantial and long-term adverse effect and there was no evidence that the condition was likely to recur. The EAT reversed the decision, stating that the tribunal ought to have taken into account medical evidence between the date of the discrimination and the hearing of the claim, which showed a relapse. The College appealed on the basis that when considering whether the effect of a medical condition was likely to recur the employer had to base its decision on the circumstances existing at that date, and that what actually happened after that date was not relevant to the tribunal's decision. The Court of Appeal allowed the appeal. On the facts, there was no evidence at the time of the decision that M's condition was likely to recur. The tribunal should only consider evidence available at the relevant time.

The word 'likely' has caused several issues in recent years which can also be seen in the case *SCA Packaging v Boyle* (2009).

However, the Equality Act 2010 brings about some small changes in relation to the definition of disability, although there is no change to the list of characteristics currently provided under the law. For example, the test for establishing whether someone has a disability has been amended slightly. The Act no longer lists these capacities but relies on the general requirements in the original definition that the impairment must be long-term and have a substantial effect on a person's ability to carry out normal day-to-day activities (Talibart, Griffin, Darbourne and Sanders, 2010).

These proposals should not, in theory, lead to a significant widening of the definition of disability in the employment context, but removing the list of capacities should make it less onerous for employees to prove their case.

The Equality Act generally carries forward the protection provided for disabled people by the DDA. However, there are key differences.

- The DDA provided protection for disabled people from direct discrimination only in employment and related areas. The EA protects disabled people against direct discrimination in areas beyond the employment field (such as the supply of goods, facilities and services).
- The EA introduced improved protection from discrimination that occurs because of something connected with a person's disability. This form of discrimination can be justified if it can be shown to be a proportionate means of achieving a legitimate aim.
- The EA introduced the principle of indirect discrimination for disability. Indirect discrimination occurs when something applies in the same way to everybody but has an effect which particularly disadvantages, for example, disabled people. Indirect discrimination may be justified if it can be shown to be a proportionate means of achieving a legitimate aim.
- The EA applies one trigger point at which there is a duty to make reasonable adjustments for disabled people. This trigger point is where a disabled person would be at a substantial disadvantage compared to non-disabled people if the adjustment was not made.The obligation to make reasonable adjustments is a continuing one so a disabled person's needs must be subject to regular review by the employer.
- The EA extends protection from harassment that is related to disability. Previously, explicit protection only applied in relation to work. The EA applies this protection to areas beyond work.
- The EA provides protection from direct disability discrimination and harassment where this is based on a person's association with a disabled person, or on a false perception that the person is disabled.
- The EA contains a provision which limits the type of enquiries that a recruiting employer can make about disability and health when recruiting new staff. This provision will help prevent disabled candidates from being unfairly screened out at an early stage of the recruitment process.

(Source: Office for Disability Issues, available from: http://odi.dwp.gov.uk/disabled-people-and-legislation/equality-act-2010-and-dda-1995.php)

Summary

Individual Employment Rights (2): Equal Pay and Discrimination

European Community law

The Equal Pay Act 1970 (now the Equality Act 2010) incorporates an equality clause into every contract of employment, which has the effect of equalising unfavourable terms between men's and women's contracts and, should a claim for equal pay be pursued, the applicant must select a comparator of the opposite sex and show he or she is employed by:

- the same employer or associated employer;
- the same establishment or an establishment where common terms and conditions are observed (*Leverton v Clwyd CC* (1989); *British Coal Corp v Smith* (1996));
- *Allonby v Accrington and Rossendale College* (2004);
- *Lawrence v Regent Office Care Ltd* (2002); or
- *South Ayrshire Council v Milligan* (2003).

There are three heads of claim:

- like work;

- work rated equivalent;
- work of equal value.

Compensation in the form of backdated pay may be made for up to six years.

Ocupational requirement

The employer must objectively justify any differing terms between the contracts of male and female employees:

- *Rainey v Greater Glasgow Health Board* (1987);
- *Glasgow CC & Others v Marshall* (2000).

Protected characteristics

There are nine protected characteristics defined in s 4 Equality Act 2010: sex, race, disability, sexual orientation, religion or belief, pregnancy and maternity, gender reassignment and age.

Direct discrimination

The test for establishing direct discrimination is the 'but for' test (*James v Eastleigh BC* (1990)).

The definition has been made 'more accessible' with the introduction of the Equality Act 2010. The words 'on the grounds of' or 'on the ground of' in the current definition of direct discrimination have been replaced with the words 'because of', thus meaning that the definition will be interpreted more widely as it does not refer to the protected characteristic of any particular person.

The law relating to direct discrimination is covered in s 13 of the Equality Act 2010. The law remains the same as in previous legislation in regard to the meaning of the definition of direct discrimination.

Burden of proof

Once the complainant has established the facts from which the tribunal can conclude that an act of discrimination has been committed, the onus moves to the employer – *Barton v Investec Henderson, Crosthwaite Securities Ltd* (2003); *Chamberlins Solicitors v Emokpae* (2004).

Indirect discrimination

This occurs where, on the face of it, all employees or potential employees are treated the same, but in effect there is a disparate impact on one group because of their sex or racial group. The applicant must establish a provision, criterion or practice:

- which is to the detriment of a considerably larger proportion of women than men; and
- which cannot be justified irrespective of the gender of the complainant.

In cases of racial discrimination, the applicant must establish a provision, criterion or practice:

- which puts or would put persons of the same race, or ethnic or national origins as that other, at a particular disadvantage when compared with other persons;
- which puts that other at that disadvantage; and
- which he cannot show to be a proportionate means of achieving a legitimate aim.

The applicant must also show that the provision, criterion or practice operates to the detriment of the complainant because he or she cannot comply with it: *London Borough of Ealing v Rihal* (2004).

Finally, even where the complainant has been able to establish these elements, the employer has the opportunity to justify the requirement or condition by showing that there is an objective necessity for the requirement or condition which is not based on the sex or race of the complainant.

The Equality Act 2010 harmonises the definitions of indirect discrimination regarding all protected characteristics. The main difference between the current law and the new Act is that the concept of indirect discrimination is extended to cover both disability and gender reassignment for the first time.

Victimisation

Victimisation occurs where the complainant is treated less favourably because he or she has brought relevant proceedings under the Equality Act 2010. Victimisation is defined at s 27 of the Equality Act 2010.

Occupational requirement

The employer has the opportunity to defend the act of discrimination on the basis that there is an 'occupational requirement' (OR) defence across all protected characteristics and removes the job-specific genuine occupational qualifications in sex, gender reassignment and nationality cases.

Remedies

Remedies are in the form of compensation. Compensation may be provided for injury to feelings and psychiatric injury resulting from an act of discrimination (*HM Prison Service v Salmon* (2001)).

Sexual orientation

It is unlawful to discriminate on grounds of sexual orientation – Employment Equality (Sexual Orientation) Regulations (2003); and on grounds of gender reassignment – Sex Discrimination (Gender Reassignment) Regulations 1999, although these provisions are now consolidated into the Equality Act 2010.

Disability discrimination

This is currently governed by s 6 Equality Act 2010. The definition requires satisfaction of the cumulative conditions.

The Equality Act 2010 introduced two fundamental changes in the area of disability discrimination. In short, it introduces two new types of disability discrimination claim. The Act widens the concept of indirect discrimination to encompass disability (even though doubts over this were raised during the consultation process). Secondly, the Act introduces the new concept of 'discrimination arising from disability', which replaces the outgoing disability-related discrimination provisions.

Summary of the Equality Act 2010

One of the key aims of the Equality Act is to harmonise current equality legislation; however, the scope of discrimination law has also been widened and reinterpreted in a number of key respects.

The following notes provide a brief summary of some of the provisions of the Equality Act 2010.

Harmonisation and extension of existing legislation

The Equality Act extends the prohibition for directly or indirectly discriminating to all 'protected characteristics' that will cover:

- age;
- disability;
- gender reassignment;

- marriage and civil partnership (in many but not all instances);
- pregnancy and maternity;
- race;
- religion or belief (including lack of belief);
- sex;
- sexual orientation.

Extended scope

- inclusion of discrimination by association or based on perception;
- indirect discrimination extended to disability and gender reassignment;
- protection against harassment by third parties extended;
- hypothetical comparators now allowed in some gender pay claims;
- ban on health questionnaires in recruitment;
- wider tribunal powers to make recommendations.

Disability

The Act provides for 'detriment arising from disability', which clarifies and widens protection against disability discrimination. The Act abandons the current list of capacities, relying instead on the general requirement that an impairment has a substantial and long-term effect on a person's ability to carry out normal day-to-day activities.

Gender reassignment

This is given a broader definition than under the Sex Discrimination Act 1975. Under the Equality Act a person is protected if that person is proposing to undergo, is undergoing or has undergone a process (or part) for the purpose of reassigning their sex by changing physiological or other attributes of sex. The provision removes the previous requirement for the process to have to be undertaken under medical supervision. So it covers, for example, someone who is born physically male but who decides to live permanently as a woman.

Discrimination by association or perception

Extends the scope of the legislation to protect people who 'associate' with others with the protected characteristics, for instance people who are related to or who care for someone who is disabled. Protection includes perception (eg discrimination based on the belief that someone is gay or disabled or has a particular belief).

Positive action on recruitment and promotion

Extends the range of lawful positive action enabling employers to choose someone for a job from an underrepresented group when there is a choice between two or more candidates who are equally qualified.

Recommendations by tribunals

Allows employment tribunals to make recommendations in discrimination cases which apply to the whole workforce.

Pre-employment health questionnaires

Section 60 of the Act prohibits employers asking job applicants questions about their health and whether they have a disability.

Equal pay

The Act provides for increased transparency in respect of equal pay.

Further Reading

Clayton, D, 'Employment law: the Equality Act 2010 – pressing the launch button', 2010, Law Society Gazette, available at www.lawgazette.co.uk/in-practice/employment-law-equality-act-2010-pressing-launch-button

Equality Act 2010, available at www.equalities.gov.uk/equality_act_2010.aspx

Fredman, S, 'Reforming equal pay laws' (2008) 37 Industrial Law Journal 193–218

Lawson, A and Gooding, C, *Disability Rights in Europe*, 2005, Oxford: Hart

O'Cienneide, C, 'Comparative European Perspectives on Age Discrimination Legislation', in S Fredman and S Spencer, *Age as an Equality Issue*, 2003, Oxford: Hart Publishing, 195–218

O'Cienneide, C, 'The Commission For Equality And Human Rights: A New Institution For New And Uncertain Times' (2007) 36(2) Industrial Law Journal 141–162

Talibart, Griffin, Darbourne, & Sanders, 19 May 2010, 'The Equality Act 2010 – one statute to cover all discrimination laws', retrieved 1 June 2010, from Lexology: www.lexology.com/library/detail.aspx?g=7d353d53-b503-4e4a-b86c-c13940875143

Chapter 18

Individual Employment Rights (3): Termination

Chapter Contents

Law in Context: Termination

Terminating a job can be a difficult and often emotional task, as it affects many people. Termination can take many forms, such as dismissal or being made redundant, and it is vital that employers are clear about the reasons for termination of employment, and that these are clearly set out and explained to the employee. In this chapter we will consider dismissal and redundancy in greater detail. Dismissal can occur for a number of reasons, such as gross misconduct, and in this case the employer would have a duty to investigate any misconduct through a set procedure. For example, If Mary, a secretary, is dismissed for falsifying her time records this is misconduct which is a potentially fair reason to dismiss. However, her employer should have considered the alleged misconduct and investigated the allegation before deciding on a disciplinary sanction. Not all dismissal is managed effectively or fairly, and the employee may be wrongfully, unfairly or constructively dismissed. In these cases, there is an expectation that the issues should be solved informally if possible, such as by addressing the issues and reaching a conclusion, or using conciliation or negotiation. If an employer is expecting that redundancies are likely to be made, it is recommended that the employer develops a procedure for handling the redundancies in advance, taking all possibilities into consideration. This procedure should be available to employees and be followed when required. Alternative employment is one option which could be considered within any procedure, with the employer offering alternative employment opportunities if possible. You will find further detail on dismissal and redundancy procedures as you read through this chapter.

18.1 Introduction

The contract of employment may be terminated at common law in various ways, some of which do not amount to a dismissal, for example, death, mutual agreement (see *Birch and Humber v University of Liverpool* (1985) and *Igbo v Johnson Matthey Chemical Ltd* (1986)), expiry of a fixed term contract (although this may amount to a statutory dismissal) and frustration. Frustration occurs where there is an unforeseen event which either makes it impossible for the contract to be performed at all, or at least renders its performance as something radically different from what the parties envisaged when they made the contract. The event must have occurred without the fault of either contracting party, for example, imprisonment or sickness. With respect to the former, in *Shepherd & Co Ltd v Jerrom* (1986), the applicant had entered into a four year apprenticeship when, after 21 months, he was sentenced to a minimum of six months in borstal. On his release, his employers refused to take him back and he complained of unfair dismissal. The tribunal rejected the employer's argument that the contract had been frustrated by reason of the custodial sentence, but the Court of Appeal allowed the employer's appeal.

The criteria for allowing frustration of a contract of employment were laid down in *Williams v Watsons Luxury Coaches Ltd* (1990). The factors to be taken into account are:

- length of previous service;
- how long it had been expected that the employment would continue;
- the nature of the job;
- the nature, length and effect of the illness or disabling event;
- the need of the employer for the work to be done and the need for a replacement to do it;
- the risk to the employer of acquiring obligations in respect of redundancy payments or compensation for unfair dismissal to the replacement employee;
- whether wages given continued to be paid;

- the acts and the statements of the employer in relation to the employment include the dismissal of, or failure to dismiss, the employee; and
- whether, in all the circumstances, a reasonable employer could be expected to wait any longer.

In addition, the Employment Appeal Tribunal (EAT) in this case recommended that any court should guard against too easy an application of the doctrine.

Frustration automatically terminates a contract without the need for affirmation or acceptance by the innocent party. If frustration is established, there will be no dismissal and, therefore, no right to claim unfair dismissal or redundancy payments. For this reason, the courts have shown a degree of reluctance in applying the doctrine of frustration fully to contracts of employment. Termination by dismissal occurs where there is dismissal by notice.

As you work through this chapter, be aware that there are moves to make it easier for employers and employees to talk with each other about employment issues, and to come to a joint agreement, for example if the employment is not working out on either side. These discussions can take place without the fear of a claim being bought on the basis of the discussions. This is called a pre-termination discussion and applies only to unfair dismissal claims.

This was due to come into force in 2013, but as yet has not been challenged or had test cases followed through the Tribunal system, which may occur over the coming years.

18.2 Dismissal for Fundamental Breach or Wrongful Dismissal

18.2.1 Notice

If the employer wishes to terminate an employee's employment, the minimum period of notice (as stated in the contract of employment) must be given or, if there is nothing in the contract, the amount of notice required by s 86 of the Employment Rights Act (ERA) 1996. Section 86 states that where an employee has been continuously employed for between one month and two years, he or she shall be given one week's notice; if employed for more than two years, he or she is entitled to one week's notice for each year of employment, subject to a maximum of 12 weeks.

Either party may waive their right to notice or terminate without notice in response to a serious breach of the contract by the other. The employer may give wages or salary in lieu of notice and s 49 does not prevent the employee from accepting such payment. Generally an employer must have included a payment in lieu of notice clause in their employees' contracts of employment to be able to insist on paying in lieu of notice. Such a clause is an express term and generally referred to as a PILON clause. In order to avoid legal action by the employee, the employer must have a legitimate reason in the eyes of the law for terminating the contract of employment. Where the employee wishes to terminate the contract of employment, the minimum period of notice, as stipulated in his or her contract, must be given. If this is not stated, a minimum of one week's notice must be given (s 86(2) of the ERA 1996).

18.2.2 Summary dismissal for fundamental breach of contract

An employer may summarily dismiss an employee (that is, dismiss without notice) for conduct which is judged to be sufficiently serious. In these circumstances, the employee will lose the right to contractual and statutory notice. Conduct such as theft, violence, etc, will warrant such action on the part of the employer, and even misconduct may do so. However, in *Wilson v Racher* (1974), where the plaintiff was dismissed for using bad language in a row with his employer, his summary dismissal was found to be unfair, as the evidence was that, in general, he was a good employee and this had been a solitary incident. However, in *Denco Ltd v Joinson* (1991), the applicant was instantly dismissed for unauthorised access to computer information which the employer considered was done to assist the employee in his capacity as a union representative. The tribunal refused to accept that such conduct could justify dismissal without prior warning. The EAT allowed the employer's appeal, as there was a clear analogy with dishonesty. If the summary dismissal is not justified, the employee may bring an action at common law for wrongful dismissal.

There is an issue of whether the breach automatically ends the contract, or whether it is only so effective once the innocent party elects to accept the breach. The decision in *Boyo v London Borough of Lambeth* (1995) attempted to clarify the position by determining that an unaccepted dismissal did not bring the contract to an end, nor should acceptance be readily inferred. The Court of Appeal chose to follow the decision in *Gunton v London Borough of Richmond-upon-Thames* (1995).

18.3 Wrongful Dismissal

A claim for wrongful dismissal is a separate claim from a claim of unfair dismissal although they may be issued together on the same facts at an employment tribunal. Essentially it is a claim for breach of contract, most commonly for failure to pay the correct notice period or benefits in kind due under the contract of employment. A claim for breach of the employment contract may be commenced in the employment tribunal, subject to a maximum award limit of £25,000. Compensation in the form of wages and damages can, in general, only be awarded for the notice period and will be subject to the calculation of damages in contract. This may include the monetary value of the benefits in kind due for the notice period. This has been confirmed by the decision in *Johnson v Unisys Ltd* (2001), where the applicant argued that his claim for dismissal should include compensation for breach of various implied terms which led to his mental breakdown. It was held that, if wrongful dismissal is the only cause of action, nothing can be recovered for mental distress or damage to reputation.

In *McCabe v Cornwall CC* (2004), a teacher who was suspended after allegations of inappropriate sexual conduct and dismissed 10 months later sought damages for psychiatric injury in respect of an alleged breach of trust and confidence. In respect of his suspension, it was alleged that the employer's failure to inform him of the allegations or to carry out a proper investigation resulted in psychiatric injury. In the High Court, his claim was struck out on the grounds that the actions complained of were 'part and parcel' of the events leading up to the dismissal and therefore precluded by the decision in *Johnson v Unisys*. However, the House of Lords held that *Johnson* did not exclude a claim for damages for psychiatric injury arising from an alleged breach of the trust and confidence term, whenever a dismissal eventuates. The test is whether the wrongful conduct by the employer formed part of the process of dismissal; if it did, no compensation would be available.

Whilst the case of *Johnson v Unisys* limits the implied terms of trust and confidence to the pre-dismissal employment relationship, the Court of Session in *King v University Court of the University of St Andrews* (2002) makes it clear that the duty is to be implied throughout all aspects of the ongoing relationship of employer and employee. As a result, it subsists 'during the stage at which the employers were investigating allegations against the employee and considering whether there were grounds for dismissal'.

The limitation imposed by *Johnson* is confined to a situation where the decision to dismiss has been taken. The decision in *Malik* is further supported by *Gogay v Hertfordshire CC* (2000), in which it was held by the Court of Appeal that where there has been a breach of the implied duty of trust and confidence, damages for a recognised psychiatric illness could be awarded. However, this limitation is not applicable where there is a breach of the duty of trust and confidence which makes it more difficult for an employee to obtain further employment (see *Malik v BCCI SA (In Liq)* (1997)). How far other contractual remedies such as specific performance and injunctions are available is open to debate. Injunctions restraining a dismissal have been issued where the rules of natural justice have not been followed in circumstances where the employee is in public employment.

In *Irani v SouthWest Hampshire HA* (1985), the plaintiff was an ophthalmologist who was employed part-time in an outpatient eye clinic. He was dismissed with six weeks' notice because of irreconcilable differences with the consultant in charge of the clinic. No criticism at all was made of his competence or conduct. In dismissing him, the employers were in breach of the disciplinary procedure established by the Whitley Council and incorporated into his contract of employment. He sought an injunction to prevent the employers from dismissing him without first following the appropriate disciplinary procedure. The employers argued that this would be contrary to the general rule that injunctions cannot be issued to keep a contract of employment alive. The plaintiff successfully obtained his injunction on the basis that, first, the case fell within the exception to the general rule, in that trust and confidence remained between the employer and the employee – the breakdown in confidence between the consultant and Irani did not affect the latter's relationship with the employer; and, secondly, damages were not an adequate remedy in this case, since Irani would become virtually unemployable throughout the National Health Service.

There have been further important decisions in this area, for example, *Ridge v Baldwin* (1964), in which a chief constable was dismissed without a proper opportunity to be heard in his own defence. He obtained a declaration that the decision to dismiss him was a nullity, as it was in breach of the rules of natural justice. See also *Powell v London Borough of Brent* (1987), in which an interlocutory injunction for specific performance was obtained. It had previously been thought that an order for specific performance could not be awarded in respect of a contract of employment because the requisite mutual trust and confidence has generally been destroyed. It is quite clear that the courts will be sympathetic to the issue of injunctions where the employee has not yet exhausted all of his or her rights under grievance and disciplinary procedures (see *Wadcock v London Borough of Brent* (1990) and *Robb v London Borough of Hammersmith and Fulham* (1991)).

In most cases the employer may prevent a claim by ensuring they pay their employee the correct notice period and benefits due to them.

18.4 Unfair Dismissal

Employees who qualify for protection under the ERA 1996 have the right not to be unfairly dismissed; that is, the employer must show that the reason for the dismissal was reasonable. The ERA 1996 provides greater protection and a wider range of remedies for the unfairly dismissed employee and, in this respect, is a much-needed provision in the light of the inadequacies of the common law. Whilst a claim for unfair dismissal is primarily concerned with the fairness of the dismissal, this now incorporates an aspect of procedural fairness.

The disciplinary proceedings which an employer should follow have been amended significantly over the last 10 years or so. The most recent changes have been the repeal of the statutory disciplinary and grievance procedures introduced by the Employment Act 2002 and the introduction of a simplified procedure known as the ACAS Code of Practice on Disciplinary and Grievance Procedures. This code was introduced by the Employment Act 2008 and is not compulsory or as prescriptive as the statutory code. If an employer fails to follow the ACAS Code of Practice then it does not render the dismissal unfair, but if the employee is successful in their claim, they may be awarded an increase of up to 25% for their failure to follow the code. Likewise an employee who should have raised a grievance under the code may have their compensation reduced by up to 25% for failing to follow the code.

However, there is now a further significant step in that a compulsory form of mediation will be introduced in April 2014 by a new s 18A Employment Tribunals Act 1996. This will make it mandatory that the parties refer the dispute to ACAS before the employment tribunal will issue any claim for unfair dismissal. It will have a significant impact in terms of the time limit for issuing any claims, as a referral to ACAS will 'stop the clock' for limitation purposes.

18.4.1 Who qualifies under the Employment Rights Act 1996?

Protection from unfair dismissal is only available to employees, that is, those employed under a contract of service. The basic rule is that any employee employed on or after 6 April 2012 must have at least two years' continuous employment in order to qualify to bring a claim. Those employed prior to 6 April 2012 only have to have one year's continuity of employment. The proposal for a one-year qualifying period arose out of the Government's White Paper, *Fairness at Work* (Cm 3968, 1998), which resulted in the Unfair Dismissal and Statement of Reasons for Dismissal (Variation of Qualifying Period) Order 1999 (SI 1999/1436). However, in 2012 this change was reversed back to a two-year qualifying period, for employees starting work on or after 12 April 2012. However, note that if the dismissal is for an automatically unfair reason, no continuity of employment is required. For example a woman dismissed because she announces she is pregnant on her first day cannot be fairly dismissed for her pregnancy, as it is an automatically unfair reason as well as being maternity and pregnancy discrimination. Another automatically unfair reason would be the assertion of a statutory right, such as complaining about not being given breaks in line with the Working Time Regulations.

18.5 Claims

An applicant must bring a claim within three months of the effective date of termination (s 111 of the ERA 1996). The employment tribunal may extend this limit if it considers that it was not reasonably practicable for the applicant to present it in time (*Palmer v Southend-on-Sea BC* (1984)). However, the time limit tends to be rigorously applied. Such is the stringency of the approach that it has been held that an applicant may not use the excuse that his or her failure to claim was due to a mistake of 'a skilled adviser' such as a lawyer, trade union official or Citizen's Advice Bureau worker (see *Riley v Tesco Stores Ltd* (1980)). Thus, the date of termination, as well as the length of service, etc, is of importance in deciding whether a claim is made in time.

18.6 Effective Date of Termination

The same rules apply for unfair dismissal and redundancy, although with respect to redundancy it is known as 'the relevant date':

- Where the contract of employment is terminated by notice, whether by the employer or employee, the date of termination is the date on which the notice expires (s 97(1) of the ERA 1996). If an employee is dismissed with notice but is given a payment in lieu of notice, the effective date of termination is the date when the notice expires, as illustrated in *Adams v GKN Sankey* (1980).
- Where the contract of employment is terminated without notice, the date of termination is the date on which the termination takes effect, that is, the actual date of dismissal, not the date on which the notice would expire. In *Robert Cort & Sons Ltd v Charman* (1981), where an employee was summarily dismissed with pay in lieu of notice, the effective date of termination was the actual date on which he was told of his dismissal, not the date on which the notice would expire. The exception to this rule is provided by s 97(2) of the ERA 1996, by which the effective date is extended either where summary dismissal has occurred, despite the employee

being entitled to the statutory minimum notice, or where the actual notice given was less than that required by statute. In both cases, the effective date is the expiration of the statutory notice period.

- Where the employer is employed under a contract for a limited term, the date of termination is the date on which the term expires.

One important issue has been what the effective date of termination is where the employee invokes an internal appeals procedure. It appears that, if the appeal is subsequently rejected, the effective date is the date of the original dismissal (*J Sainsbury Ltd v Savage* (1981)), unless the contract provides for the contrary (*West Midlands Cooperative Society v Tipton* (1986)).

The introduction of compulsory mediation is relevant here again, as outlined at 18.4, as it has the effect of 'stopping the clock' for the purposes of limitation on a claim. However, if mediation fails, the clock starts again.

18.7 What is Meant by Dismissal?

The onus is on the employee to show that he or she has been dismissed within the meaning of the Act (s 95 of the ERA 1996). There are three ways in which dismissal can take place, which are as follows:

- *Express termination of the contract of employment by the employer*
  The employer may terminate the contract with or without notice. Such a dismissal may be made orally or in writing; however, if it is made orally, the words used should be unambiguous. For example, in *Futty v Brekkes Ltd* (1974), in a row with his foreman, the employee was told, 'If you do not like the job, fuck off'. This was interpreted by the employee as a dismissal and he left and found a job elsewhere. The employer argued that there had been no dismissal, as the words were to be interpreted in the context of the workman's trade. Furthermore, if a dismissal had been intended, the words used would have been formal. This argument was accepted by the tribunal, which concluded that the employee had terminated his own employment. Where the words are ambiguous, the effect of the statement is determined by an objective test; that is, would the reasonable employer or employee have understood the words to be tantamount to a dismissal? One of the problems for the courts has been deciding whether there has been a dismissal within the meaning of the ERA 1996. What may be acceptable language in one industry may not be in a different working environment.

  A termination which is mutually agreed between the employer and employee is not a dismissal. However, the courts have, with some reluctance, upheld this practice, as it may work to the advantage of the employer in avoiding employment rights and thereby lead to an abuse of a dominant position. The courts will look closely to see whether there is genuine mutual agreement; this will be a question of fact in each case.

  In *Igbo v Johnson Matthey Chemicals Ltd* (1986), the applicant requested extended leave to visit her husband and children in Nigeria. This was granted by her employers on the condition that she signed a document which stated that she agreed to return to work on 28 September 1986 and, if she failed to do so, her contract of employment would automatically terminate on that date. She signed the document. She failed to return on the due date because she was ill and, as a result, her contract was terminated. The Court of Appeal held that the contract had been terminated, not by mutual agreement, but by dismissal. The document amounted to a means of avoiding employment rights and was, therefore, void by virtue of s 140(1) of the Employment Protection (Consolidation) Act 1978 (now s 203 of the ERA 1996).

It should be noted that, where the employee is under notice of termination and gives the employer a counter notice indicating an intention to leave before the expiry of the employer's notice, the employee is still deemed to have been dismissed for the purposes of the ERA 1996. Any counter notice must be in writing with respect to a claim for redundancy, but this is not a requirement in respect of unfair dismissal.

- *Where the employee invites a termination of his contract either by his inaction or conduct*
In *Martin v Yeoman Aggregates Ltd* (1983), Martin refused to get a spare part for the director's car. The director angrily told the employee to get out. Five minutes later, the director took back what he had said and instead suspended Martin without pay until he could act more rationally. Martin insisted that he had been dismissed. It was held that it was vital to industrial relations that both the employer and employee should have the opportunity to withdraw their words. It was up to a tribunal to decide whether the withdrawal had come too late to be effective. Certainly, immediate retraction is effective. However, a subsequent retraction will only be effective with the consent of the other party. Where the employer invites the employee to resign, this may amount to a dismissal. In *Robertson v Securicor Transport Ltd* (1972), Robertson had broken one of the works rules by signing for a load which had not actually been received. When his employers discovered what he had done, they gave him the option of resignation or dismissal. He chose resignation. It was held that resignation in these circumstances amounted to a dismissal by the employer because, in effect, there was no alternative action open to the employee. He would have been dismissed if he had not opted to resign on the invitation of his employer.
- *Expiration of a fixed or limited term contract*
If a fixed term contract is not renewed, the failure to renew amounts to a dismissal (whether it is a fair dismissal is another issue). Section 95 of the ERA 1996 states that an employee is dismissed by his employer if he is employed under a limited term contact and that contract terminates by virtue of the limiting event, without being renewed under the same contract. Although historically fixed term contracts could exclude claims for unfair dismissal this was removed in October 1999.
Similarly if a fixed term contract is not renewed after two years and the reason is redundancy, the employee would be entitled to a redundancy payment. Furthermore, at one time, it was thought that a fixed term contract must run for the whole of the term and must not be capable of termination before the term expired, for example, by a clause giving either party the right to terminate (see *BBC v Ioannou* (1975)). However, in *Dixon v BBC* (1979), it was held that a fixed term contract could exist even though either party could terminate it before it had run its full term.

18.7.1 Constructive dismissal

Constructive dismissal is an important concept, since the law recognises that an employee may be entitled to protection where he or she is put in a position in which he or she is forced to resign. Constructive dismissal arises where the employee is forced to terminate the contract with or without notice due to the conduct of the employer (s 95(1)(c) of the ERA 1996).

One issue for the courts is whether the words or actions of the employee in resigning are unambiguous. In *Sovereign House Security Services Ltd v Savage* (1989), Savage, a security officer, was told that he was to be suspended pending police investigations into the theft of money from the employer's offices. Savage told his immediate superior to pass on the fact that he was 'jacking it in'. The Court of Appeal held that the employer was entitled to treat these words as amounting to a resignation.

The courts will, however, make some allowance for 'heat of the moment' utterances (see *Tanner v Kean* (1978)). The main focus for the courts is to decide whether the employer's conduct warrants the action taken by the employee. It is now firmly decided that, in order to permit the employer to constructively dismiss him or her, the employee's actions must amount to a breach of contract and must, therefore, be more than merely unreasonable conduct.

The basic test as to whether the employer's actions do entitle the employee to resign are contained in the leading case of *Western Excavating Ltd v Sharp* (1978), Sharp took time off from work without permission. When his employer discovered this, he was dismissed. He appealed to an internal disciplinary board, which substituted a penalty of five days' suspension without pay. He agreed to accept this decision but asked his employer for an advance on his holiday pay, as he was short of money; this was refused. He then asked for a loan of £40, which was also refused. As a result, he decided to resign, since this would at least mean that he would receive his holiday pay. At the same time, he claimed unfair dismissal on the basis that he was forced to resign because of his employer's unreasonable conduct. Initially, the tribunal found in Sharp's favour; that is, the employer's conduct was so unreasonable that Sharp could not be expected to continue working there. However, the case eventually went to the Court of Appeal, where it was decided that, before a valid constructive dismissal can take place, the employer's conduct must amount to a breach of contract such that it entitles the employee to resign. In this particular case, there was no breach by the employer and, therefore, there was no constructive dismissal.

It would appear that if the breach by the employer is to allow the employee to resign, it must be a breach of some significance and must go to the root of the contract, for example, a unilateral change in the employee's terms (express or implied) and conditions of employment. For example, in *British Aircraft Corp v Austin* (1978), a failure to investigate a health and safety complaint was held to be conduct amounting to a breach of contract on the part of the employer which was sufficient to entitle the employee to treat the contract as terminated. If the employee does not resign in the event of a breach by the employer, the employee will be deemed to have accepted the breach and to have waived any rights. However, the law recognises that he or she need not resign immediately but may, for example, wait until he or she has found another job (see *Cox Toner (International) Ltd v Crook* (1981)).

It is also recognised that a series of minor incidents can have a cumulative effect, which results in a fundamental breach amounting to repudiation of the contract by the employer. In *Woods v WM Car Services (Peterborough)* (1982), it was held that the general implied contractual duty that employers will not, without reasonable or proper cause, conduct themselves in a manner calculated as being likely to destroy the relationship of trust and confidence between employer and employee, is an overriding obligation independent of and in addition to the literal terms of the contract. See also *London Borough of Waltham Forest v Omilaju* (2004).

In *Simmonds v Dowty Seals Ltd* (1978), Simmonds was employed to work on the night shift. His employer attempted to force him to work on the day shift by threatening to take industrial action if he refused to be transferred from the night shift. He resigned. It was held that he was entitled to resign and could regard himself as having been constructively dismissed because the employer's conduct amounted to an attempt to unilaterally change an express term of his contract, namely, that he was employed to work nights.

The employee may also be able to claim where he or she is forced to resign when the employer is in breach of an implied term in the contract of employment. However, it must be stressed that the employee must be able to show not only the existence of the implied term, but also what is required by the implied term, that is, its scope (see *Gardner Ltd v Beresford* (1978)). An implied term in a contract which provided for demotion in the event of incompetence defeated a claim of constructive unfair dismissal when applied to a helicopter pilot who was demoted following a dangerous incident (*Vaid v Brintel Helicopters Ltd* (1994)).

It is also possible for the conduct of an immediate superior to amount to a fundamental breach on the part of the employer, as long as the test for establishing vicarious liability is satisfied (*Hilton International Hotels (UK) Ltd v Protopapa* (1990)).

The case law illustrates that a wide range of conduct on the part of the employer may entitle the employee to resign. For example, in *Bracebridge Engineering Ltd v Darby* (1990), failing to properly investigate allegations of sexual harassment or failing to treat such a complaint with sufficient seriousness was held to be constructive dismissal.

❖ KEY CASE *Bracebridge Engineering Ltd v Darby* (1990)

Facts:
Mrs Darby had worked for 13 years for Bracebridge Engineering, a small company. One evening as she was washing her hands, the chargehand and works manager grabbed her and took her into an office, where she was indecently assaulted. Mrs Darby reported this to the general manager but, as the harassers denied the incident, the employer took no action. Mrs Darby resigned and claimed constructive dismissal.

Decision:
The EAT held that a single incident of sexual harassment of this severity would amount to discrimination. Mrs Darby was entitled to resign when her employers failed to investigate her complaint properly. She was awarded compensation for loss of earnings and injury to feelings.

The employee is not expected to tolerate abusive language from his or her employer, particularly when he or she is being accused of something which he or she did not do (*Palmanor Ltd v Cedron* (1978)). Even where the employer orders his or her employee to relocate as a result of a mobility clause in the employee's contract, if the employee is given very short notice and no financial assistance, he or she may resign and claim constructive dismissal (*United Bank Ltd v Akhtar* (1989)). Finally, where an employee lodges a grievance which is not investigated because of a failure to implement a proper procedure, the employee's resignation may be justified (*WA Goold (Pearmak) Ltd v McConnell & Another* (1995)).

As a result of the decision in *Western Excavating Ltd v Sharp*, it is clear that unreasonable conduct alone which makes life difficult for the employee, so that he or she is put in a position where he or she is forced to resign, will not automatically be deemed to be a constructive dismissal, unless it can be found to be a breach of the express or implied terms on the part of the employer. The employee may have to depend on the generosity of the courts in establishing a breach of an implied term.

In the case of *Pepper and Hope v Daish* (1980), in December 1978, Pepper, who was employed by the defendants, negotiated for himself an hourly wage rate. In January 1979, his employers increased the hourly rate of all workers by 5%, with the exception of Pepper. As a result, Pepper resigned and claimed constructive dismissal. It was held that Pepper would succeed in his claim. The tribunal was prepared to imply a term into his contract that he would be given any wage increases received by the hourly rate workers. Such a term had therefore been broken by his employer, forcing him to resign. Whether the courts will always be as generous in their interpretation is open to debate.

It is however crucial when considering whether an employee should resign and claim constructive dismissal, to be aware of the ACAS Code of Practice on disciplinary and grievance procedures, and that if the employee is successful they may lose 25% of their compensation if they did not raise a grievance prior to their resignation.

18.8 Reasons for the Dismissal

An employee who is dismissed within the meaning of the ERA 1996 is entitled to a written statement of the reasons for his dismissal (s 92 of the ERA 1996). He or she must, however, have been continuously employed for one year (s 92(3) of the ERA 1996). However, this qualifying period is not applicable where a female employee is dismissed while she is pregnant or in connection with childbirth (s 92(4) of the ERA 1996). The employee must request the statement and it must be supplied within 14 days of this request. Failure to do so or providing particulars which are inadequate or untrue will allow the employee to make a complaint to an employment tribunal. If the tribunal finds in favour of the employee, it may declare the real reason for the dismissal and award the employee two weeks' pay. It has been held that a 'conscientiously formed belief that there was no dismissal was a reasonable ground for refusing to provide a written statement' (*Brown v Stuart Scott & Co* (1981)). The written statement is admissible in proceedings and any inconsistency between the contents of the statement and the reason actually put forward could seriously undermine the employer's case.

18.9 Fair Dismissals – substantive and procedural fairness

Once the employee has established dismissal, be it by the employer or constructively, the onus moves to the employer to show that he or she acted reasonably in dismissing the employee and, therefore, that the dismissal was fair (s 98 of the ERA 1996). Prior to 1980, the burden of proof in unfair dismissal claims at this stage was on the employer.

The test of reasonableness requires consideration of what a reasonable employer would have done in the circumstances; that is, does it fall within 'the band of reasonable responses to the employee's conduct within which one employer might take one view, another quite reasonably another?' (*Iceland Frozen Foods v Jones* (1982), *per* Browne-Wilkinson J). Whether the test is satisfied is a question of fact in each case. In *Haddon v Van Den Bergh Foods Ltd* (1999), the EAT held that the 'range of reasonable responses' test was an unhelpful gloss on the statute and should no longer be applied by employment tribunals. The EAT qualified its decision in *Haddon* in the case of *HSBC v Madden* (2000). In this case, the EAT stated that, whilst only the Court of Appeal or a higher court can discard the range of reasonable responses test, a tribunal is free to substitute its own views for those of the employer as to the reasonableness of dismissal as a response to the reason shown for it. Instead, the test of fairness should be applied 'without embellishment and without using mantras so favoured by lawyers in this field'. The EAT recommended the approach adopted in *Gilham v Kent CC (No 2)* (1985), in which the Court of Appeal emphasised that whether a dismissal was fair or unfair is a pure question of fact for the tribunal. However, the Court of Appeal in *Post Office v Foley; HSBC Bank v Madden* (2000) has now restored the 'band of reasonable responses' test. The proper function of the employment tribunal is to determine objectively whether the decision to dismiss the employee fell within the band of reasonable responses which a reasonable employer might have adopted. In practice, this may not be required in every case; nor is there a requirement to show that the employer's decision was so unreasonable as to be perverse.

In *Sainsbury's Supermarkets Ltd v Hitt* (2003), the Court of Appeal held that the range of reasonable responses test applied to the question of whether the employer's investigation into suspected misconduct was reasonable in the circumstances. As a result, a dismissal which occurs without an opportunity for the employee to explain his conduct is fair unless no reasonable employer could take the view that no explanation was necessary.

However, employment tribunals continue to have regard to the substantive merits of a case, for example, length of service, previous disciplinary record and any other mitigating circumstances, with a view to maintaining consistency of treatment and procedural fairness. In other words, they will ask whether the employer has adhered to the ACAS Code of Practice on Disciplinary and Grievance Procedures, which involves the provision of formal warnings, internal hearings, appeals procedures, etc.

The leading case on procedural fairness is *Polkey v AE Dayton Services Ltd*. Polkey was employed as a van driver. In order to avoid more financial losses, his employer decided to make three van drivers redundant. There was no prior consultation; Polkey was merely handed a letter informing him that he was being made redundant. Polkey claimed that this amounted to unfair dismissal, as the failure to consult showed that the employer had not acted reasonably in treating redundancy as a sufficient reason for dismissing him. It was held that, in deciding whether the employer had acted reasonably, the tribunal should have regard to the facts at the time of the dismissal and should not base their judgment on facts brought to light after the dismissal, such as whether the failure to consult would have made any difference to the dismissal or whether the employee had in practice suffered an injustice. The points made in this case have been expanded by further case law, see for example, *Mofunanya v Richmond Fellowship and anor EAT* (2003), *Compass Group UK & Ireland Ltd t-a ESS Support Services Worldwide v Baldwin and EAT* (2006) and *Lambe v 186 Ltd CA* (2005).

The implementation of the disciplinary procedure is also of paramount importance. In *Westminster CC v Cabaj* (1996), the council's disciplinary code required three members of the council to be in attendance to hear appeals. The complainant's appeal was heard by the Chief Executive and two other members. The EAT held that this amounted to a significant error, as the appeals panel should have been constituted in a particular way. As a result, the dismissal was unfair.

The grounds on which a dismissal is capable of being fair are laid down in s 98 of the ERA 1996. In *Wilsorky v Post Office* (2000), the Court of Appeal held that it was a question of legal analysis to determine in which part of s 98 of the ERA 1996 a reason for dismissal falls. If it was incorrectly 'characterised', this was an error of law which would therefore be corrected on appeal.

18.9.1 The fair reasons – capability or qualifications

There are five potentially fair reasons which an employer may cite as the reason for dismissal. They are conduct (misconduct), capability and qualifications, statutory illegality, redundancy and some other substantial reason.

Section 98(3) states that capability is 'assessed by reference to skill, aptitude, health or any other physical or mental quality', whereas qualifications means 'any degree, diploma, or other academic, technical or professional qualification relevant to the position which the employee held'. In *Blackman v Post Office* (1974), Blackman was a telegraph officer. He was required to pass an aptitude test. He was allowed the maximum number of attempts (three), and he still failed. He was then dismissed. It was held that, as the taking of an aptitude test was a qualification requirement of that job, his dismissal was fair.

Before dismissing an employee for incompetence, the employer should have regard to the ACAS Code of Practice which offers some guidance on improving poor performance; certainly, no dismissal should take place without formal warnings providing the employee with an opportunity to redress his or her position, unless the potential consequences of the incompetence are so serious that warnings are inappropriate. In *Taylor v Alidair* (1978), a pilot was dismissed for a serious error of judgment when he landed a plane so badly that it caused extensive damage. The Court of Appeal held that the company had reasonable grounds for honestly believing that he was incompetent.

The employer must not only be able to show that, for example, the employee was incompetent or inadequately qualified, but also that, in the circumstances, it was reasonable to dismiss him or her – that is, what would the reasonable employer have done? The court will have regard to all the surrounding circumstances, such as training, supervision and what alternatives were available, for example, could the employee have been redeployed in another job, etc? The employer may also have to show that the employee was given a chance to improve his or her standing. If the employer is to be deemed to have acted reasonably, he or she must be able to show that dismissal was the last resort.

In *Davison v Kent Meters Ltd* (1975), Davison worked on an assembly line. She was dismissed as a result of assembling 500 components incorrectly. She alleged that she had merely followed the instructions of the chargehand. The chargehand maintained that he had not given her any instructions. It was held that the dismissal was unfair. Davison should have received supervision and training in the assembly of the components. It was clear from the evidence that she had not received any; therefore, her employer had not acted reasonably in dismissing her.

Persistent absenteeism may be treated as misconduct and should be dealt with under the disciplinary procedure. However, a long-term absence, such as long term sickness, should be treated as incapability. Whether the employer's action to dismiss for long term sickness absence is reasonable will depend on the particular circumstances of each case, for example, the nature of the illness, the length of the absence, the need to replace the absent employee and the carrying out of an investigation of the illness (*London Fire and Civil Defence Authority v Betty* (1994)). The employer will be expected to make a reasonable effort to inform him or herself of the true medical position of the employee, although the consent of the employee is needed before access to medical records can be gained.

18.9.2 Conduct

In deciding whether a dismissal for misconduct is to be regarded as fair, attention must be paid to the nature of the offence and the disciplinary procedure. For example, gross or serious misconduct may justify instant dismissal, whereas a trivial act may only warrant a warning in line with the disciplinary procedure. In *Hamilton v Argyll and Clyde Health Board* (1993), it was found that the fact that the employer was prepared to offer the employee an alternative post did not mean that the misconduct could not be classified as 'gross'. The word 'misconduct' is not defined in the ERA 1996, but it is established that it covers assault, refusal to obey instructions, persistent lateness, moonlighting, drunkenness, dishonesty, failing to implement safety procedures, etc.

Before any dismissal for misconduct takes place, the employer must have established a genuine and reasonable belief in the guilt of the employee. The leading case on this point is *British Home Stores v Burchell* (1978). This set a three-strand test. The employer must have a genuine belief in the employee's guilt. Secondly that belief must be based on reasonable grounds. Thirdly there must have been a reasonable investigation. A false accusation without reasonable foundation may result in the employee resigning and claiming constructive dismissal (*Robinson v Crompton Parkinson Ltd* (1978)). It should be remembered that reference must also be made to whether the action is within the band of reasonable responses.

In *Taylor v Parsons Peebles Ltd* (1981), a works rule prohibited fighting. It was also the policy of the company to dismiss anyone caught fighting. The company had employed the applicant for 20 years without complaint. He was caught fighting and was dismissed. It was held that the dismissal was unfair. Regard must be had to the previous 20 years of employment without incident. The tribunal decided that the reasonable employer would not have applied the sanction of instant dismissal as rigidly, because of the mitigating circumstances.

In *Whitbread & Co v Thomas* (1988), it was held that an employer who could not identify which member of a group was responsible for an act could fairly dismiss the whole group, even where it was probable that not all were guilty of the act, provided that the following three conditions were satisfied:

- the act of misconduct warranted dismissal;
- the industrial (now employment) tribunal is satisfied that the act was committed by at least one of the group being dismissed and all were capable of committing the act; and
- the tribunal is satisfied that the employer had carried out a proper investigation to attempt to identify the persons responsible.

In *Parr v Whitbread plc* (1990), Parr was employed as a branch manager at an off-licence owned by the respondents. He and three other employees were dismissed after it was discovered that £4,000 had been stolen from the shop in circumstances which suggested that it was an inside job. Each of the four had an equal opportunity to commit the theft and the employers found it impossible to ascertain which of them was actually guilty. It was held, applying the test in the *Thomas* case, that the dismissals were fair.

In the case of *Salford Royal NHS Foundation Trust v Roldan* (2010), the Court of Appeal studied the approach that employers should follow when investigating allegations of misconduct, specifically where a dismissal can have serious implications for an employee. Ms Roldan, a nurse from the Philippines received a complaint from her colleague Ms Denton, a health care assistant that Ms Roldan had mistreated a patient. As a result, Ms Roldan was suspended whilst an investigation was carried out by a senior manager who concluded that Ms Roldan's evidence was vague and unclear whilst Ms Denton provided clear and concise information on the matter. The senior manager advised that the investigation should be referred to a disciplinary hearing which also found Ms Denton's evidence preferable to Ms Roldan's, and thus Ms Roldan was dismissed on the grounds of gross misconduct. The implications for Ms Roldan were huge; she lost her job, her work permit and the right to remain in the UK. Furthermore, she was also the subject of a criminal investigation by the police. Ms Roldan brought a claim for unfair dismissal and race discrimination. While the race discrimination claim was unsuccessful, the employment tribunal upheld the claim for unfair dismissal.

Recent developments in the case law have indicated that in incidences of misconduct dismissals, employers should consider the career implications for the individual.

18.9.3 Redundancy

Redundancy is *prima facie* a fair reason for dismissal. However, the employer must show that the reason for the dismissal was due to redundancy (s 98(2) of the ERA 1996). He or she must, therefore, be able to establish redundancy within the meaning of the ERA 1996. A dismissal for reason of redundancy will be unfair if the employer had not acted as the reasonable employer would have acted in the circumstances. The following matters, as laid down in *Williams v Compair Maxim Ltd* (1982), should be considered before the redundancies are put into effect:

- to give as much warning as possible;
- to consult with the trade union (see ss 188–92 of the TULR(C)A 1992, as amended by the Collective Redundancies and Transfer of Undertakings (Protection of Employment) (Amendment) Regulations 1995 (SI 1995/2587));
- to adopt an objective rather than a subjective criteria for selection;
- to select in accordance with the criteria; and
- to consider the possibility of redeployment rather than dismissal.

In *Allwood v William Hill Ltd* (1974), William Hill Ltd decided to close down 12 betting shops. Without any warning, they made all the managers redundant. They offered no alternative employment. The managers, as employees, complained that this amounted to unfair dismissal. It was held that, in the circumstances, this amounted to unfair dismissal. The employer should have considered possible alternatives, such as transfers to other betting shops. Furthermore, the way in which the redundancies had taken place was not the way in which a reasonable employer would have acted.

It is important to realise that just because there is a redundancy situation within the meaning of the ERA 1996, it does not automatically follow that any dismissal due to redundancy will be fair. An important issue is whether the criteria used for selection of those employees who are to be made redundant are fair, for example, first in, first out (FIFO); last in, first out (LIFO); or part time staff first, which may also amount to discrimination. Contravention of customary practices may be evidence that the dismissal is unfair.

In *Hammond-Scott v Elizabeth Arden Ltd* (1976), the applicant was selected for redundancy because she was close to retirement age. The defendants had employed her for many years, but this was not taken into account when she was selected for redundancy. It was held that her selection for redundancy amounted to unfair dismissal because the employer had not acted reasonably in the circumstances. In view of her age, the length of service and the fact that she was close to retirement age, it would have had little financial effect on the company if they had continued to employ her until she retired. Now, with the prohibition against age discrimination, this case might be decided differently.

Transferring the responsibility for deciding who will be made redundant from the employer to the employees involved in the redundancy may also amount to unfair dismissal. In *Boulton and Paul Ltd v Arnold* (1994), when an employee complained about her selection for redundancy, the employer offered to retain her, but on the terms that another employee would be made redundant in her place. She rejected this offer and claimed unfair dismissal. Her claim was upheld, as the EAT did not accept the employer's defence that she could have remained in employment. It also declared that it was unfair to move the onus to the employee in order to decide whether she or another employee would be selected for dismissal.

Where employees in similar positions are not made redundant and the reason why a particular employee was selected for redundancy was because he or she was a member or non-member of a trade union or participated in trade union activities, dismissal will be deemed to be automatically unfair (s 153 of the TULR(C)A 1992). This is no longer subject to any qualifying period of service.

18.9.4 Statutory restrictions/illegality (s 98(2)(d) of the Employment Rights Act 1996)

If the dismissal is because the continued employment of the employee would result in a contravention of a statute or subordinate legislation on the part of either the employer or the employee, the dismissal will be *prima facie* fair, for example, if the employee has been banned from driving, yet the job requires him or her to hold a current driving licence – if the employee continues to fulfil the job specification, he or she would be in breach of the Road Traffic Acts (*Fearn v Tayford Motor Co Ltd* (1975)); or if the employer, in continuing to employ someone, was found to be contravening the Food and Drugs Act 1955.

As with all cases of dismissal, the employer must act as the reasonable employer and must, therefore, consider any possible alternatives if the dismissal is to be regarded as fair (*Sandhu v Department of Education and Science and London Borough of Hillingdon* (1978)). Another example would be employing someone who had a visa to work in the UK but whose visa was subsequently withdrawn. Continuing to employ them would be a criminal offence and so their dismissal would be considered fair.

18.9.5 Some other substantial reason

Where the employer is unable to show that the reason for the dismissal was one of those referred to above, he or she may show 'some other substantial reason' (s 98(1)(b) of the ERA 1996). There is no exhaustive list of what is recognised in law as some other substantial reason. The employer must show not only that his or her actions were reasonable, but also that the reason was 'substantial'. The following have been held to be valid reasons for dismissal, although it should be appreciated that it is a question of fact in each case:

- a conflict of personalities which is primarily the fault of the employee. In *Tregonowan v Robert Knee and Co* (1975), the atmosphere in the employer's office was so bad, due to the complainant constantly talking about her private life, that her fellow employees could not work with her. Accordingly, she was dismissed and the tribunal upheld the dismissal. Dismissal should be a last resort after attempts to improve relations have taken place;

- failure to disclose material facts in obtaining employment, for example, mental illness (see *O'Brien v Prudential Assurance Co Ltd* (1979));
- commercial reasons, for example, pressure from important customers to dismiss the employee (*Grootcon (UK) Ltd v Keld* (1984));
- failure to accept changes in the terms of employment (see *Storey v Allied Brewery* (1977)). Any change must be justified by the employer as being necessary;
- non-renewal of a fixed term contract – the employer must show a genuine need for temporary contracts and that the employee knew of the temporary nature of the contract from the outset (*North Yorkshire CC v Fay* (1985)); and
- a dismissal which satisfies reg 8(2) of the Transfer of Undertakings (Protection of Employment) Regulations 1981 (SI 1981/1794) in so far as the dismissal is for an 'economic, technical or organisational reason entailing changes in the workforce and the employer is able to show that his actions were reasonable'. Where the employer can satisfy reg 8, the employee may be able to claim redundancy, as in *Gorictree Ltd v Jenkinson* (1984). Any other dismissal in connection with the transfer of the business is automatically unfair: see *Litster & Others v Forth Dry Dock and Engineering Co Ltd* (1989), considered below.

18.10 Automatically Unfair Dismissals

The following are situations where dismissal is automatically unfair:

- *Trade union membership or activity (s 152(1) of the TULR(C)A 1992)*
  Where the employee is dismissed because of an actual or proposed membership of an independent trade union, or because he or she is not a member of a trade union or refuses to become a member, the dismissal is automatically unfair. This is also the case where the employee has taken part or proposes to take part in any trade union activities. The employee need not have the required qualifying period of employment in order to bring an action for unfair dismissal under this section.
- *Pregnancy or childbirth*
  Section 99 of the ERA 1996 provides that an employee is automatically unfairly dismissed where the principal reason for the dismissal is pregnancy or a reason connected with pregnancy; or, following maternity leave, dismissal for childbirth or a reason connected with childbirth, adoption leave, parental leave, paternity leave, etc. In *O'Neil v Governors of St Thomas Moore RCVA Upper School* (1996), a religious instruction teacher was dismissed whilst on maternity leave when it was discovered that the father of her child was the local Roman Catholic priest. The employer argued that the reason for the dismissal was the paternity of the child and her particular post at the school. The EAT declined to accept this and held that the main reason related to pregnancy and was, therefore, unlawful.
- *Industrial action*
  Dismissals during strike or lock-out are governed by s 238 of the TULR(C)A 1992. Generally, dismissal of the participants during a strike, lock-out or other industrial action is not unfair, as long as all those participating are dismissed and none are reengaged within three months of the dismissal. However, if only some of the participants are dismissed or have not been offered re-engagement within the three month period, an unfair dismissal claim may be brought. This exception is subject to the action being regarded as official by trade unions (s 20 of the TULR(C)A 1992).

- *Industrial pressure*
  Where an employer dismisses an employee because of industrial pressure brought to bear by other employees, the dismissal may be unfair. Section 107 of the ERA 1996 provides that industrial pressure such as the threat of a strike if the applicant continues to be employed by the employer should be ignored by the tribunal, which must consider the dismissal on the basis of whether the employer had acted reasonably.
  Where pressure is put on an employer to dismiss the applicant by a trade union, because the applicant was not a member of a trade union, the trade union may be joined by the employer or applicant as party to the proceedings. The tribunal may then make an award against the trade union if it finds that the dismissal was unfair.

Sections 99 and 105 of the ERA 1996 made it automatically unfair to select an employee for redundancy on grounds of pregnancy or childbirth, or because he or she has made a health and safety complaint or has asserted a statutory right.

Section 100 of the ERA 1996 provides that an employee has the right not to be dismissed:

- for carrying out, or proposing to carry out, any health and safety activities which he or she is designated to do by the employer;
- for bringing to his or her employer's attention, by reasonable means and in the absence of a safety representative or committee who could do so on his or her behalf, a reasonable health and safety concern (see *Harris v Select Timber Frame Ltd* (1994));
- in the event of danger which he or she reasonably believes to be serious and imminent and which he or she could not reasonably be expected to avert, for leaving or proposing to leave the workplace or any dangerous part of it, or (while the danger persisted) refusing to return; or
- in circumstances of danger which he or she reasonably believes to be serious and imminent, for taking or proposing to take appropriate steps to protect him or herself or other persons from danger. In *Lopez v Maison Bouquillon Ltd* (1996), an assistant in a cake shop complained to the police that a chef, who was married to the shop manageress, had assaulted her. She was then dismissed from her job. She claimed unfair dismissal, stating that it was reasonable for her to leave the workplace because of the assault. The tribunal found that the incident came within s 100 and, therefore, the dismissal was unfair.
- *Dismissal for exercising rights under the Part-Time Workers (Prevention of Less Favourable Treatment) Regulations* 2000
  Part-time employees will be held to be unfairly dismissed (or selected for redundancy), regardless of length of service or age, if the reason, or the main reason, for the dismissal is: that they exercised or sought to enforce their rights under the Regulations, refused to forgo them or allege that the employer had infringed them; they requested a written statement; they gave evidence or information in connection with proceedings brought by an employee under the Regulations; or that the employer believed that the employee intended to do these things. The same rights are provided for a dismissal for exercising rights under the Fixed-Term Employees (Prevention of Less Favourable Treatment) Regulations 2002.
- *To dismiss someone because they are entitled to working tax credits, or they took any action with a view to enforcing or securing their rights to working tax credits, also amounts to an unfair dismissal*
- *A dismissal for making an application for flexible working arrangements, if this is the main reason for the dismissal, also amounts to unfair dismissal. However, an employer does not have to accept an application for flexible working arrangements, if there is a business reason why.*

The ERA 1996 also extends protection to the following: workers who refuse to comply with working hours which would contravene the Working Time Regulations 1998 (s 101A of the

ERA 1996); workers who are dismissed on the grounds of asserting a statutory right, for example, bringing proceedings against an employer to enforce a statutory right (s 104 of the ERA 1996) – see *Mennell v Newell and Wright (Transport Contractors) Ltd* (1997); employees who are dismissed for making protected disclosures (s 103A of the ERA 1996) – protective disclosures are defined in ss 43A–J of the ERA 1996 and cover such matters as crime, protection of the environment, disclosure to a legal adviser, to the Crown or to a prescribed person. This protection arises from the Public Interest Disclosure Act 1998. Finally, s 25 of the National Minimum Wage Act 1998 amends the ERA 1996 by inserting new ss 104A and 105(7A), which provide that employees who are dismissed or selected for redundancy will be regarded as unfairly dismissed if the sole or main reason for the dismissal or selection was that, *inter alia*, they had asserted their right to the national minimum wage; or the employer was prosecuted for an offence under the National Minimum Wage Act 1998; or they qualify for the national minimum wage.

18.11 Remedies

Where the dismissal is found to be unfair, the tribunal has the power to make an order for reinstatement, re-engagement or compensation (ss 112–124 of the ERA 1996).

18.11.1 Reinstatement

Reinstatement is the same job with the same employer. In the case of reinstatement, the tribunal must ask the applicant whether he or she wishes such an order to be made. The effect of an order for reinstatement is that the employer must treat the employee as if he or she had not been dismissed, that is, as if his or her employment is on the same or improved terms and conditions.

18.11.2 Re-engagement

Re-engagement is returning to work for the same employer, but in a different role or at a different location. If the applicant so wishes, the tribunal may make an order for re-engagement (s 115 of the ERA 1996). The effect of this is that the applicant should be re-engaged by the employer, or by an associated employer in employment which is comparable to the previous employment or amounts to other suitable employment. The tribunal will specify the terms on which the applicant should be re-engaged and this may make provision for arrears of pay. The making of orders for reinstatement and re-engagement is at the discretion of the tribunal, which will consider whether it is just and equitable to make such an order considering the conduct of the employee and whether it is practicable to do so.

Failure to comply fully with the terms of an order for reinstatement or re-engagement will result in an award of compensation being made by the employment tribunal, having regard to the loss sustained by the complainant, which is usually the basic award plus an additional award. The employer may raise 'impracticability' as a defence to such a claim.

18.11.3 Compensation

Certain employment protection awards are now automatically index-linked – see the Employment Relations Act 1999 (Commencement No 3 and Transitional Provision) Order 1999 (SI 1999/3374). It should be noted that compensation for unfair dismissal cannot include any award for non-economic loss – see *Dunnachie v Kingston-upon-Hull CC* (2004).

❖ KEY CASE *Dunnachie v Kingston-upon-Hull City Council, CA* (2004)

Facts:
Dunnachie was employed by the council as an environmental health officer. However he resigned in March 2001 as a result of a prolonged campaign of harassment and bullying by his line manager in which he argued he had been constructively and unfairly dismissed.

Decision:
He succeeded in his tribunal claim for constructive unfair dismissal. In addition to compensation for his economic losses (including loss of earnings), the tribunal awarded him £10,000 for injury to his feelings. The EAT upheld the council's appeal against the decision to award a sum for non-economic losses, holding that an employee could only be compensated for quantifiable economic losses. The Court of Appeal allowed Dunnachie's appeal by a majority, overruling the principle established in *Norton Tool Co Ltd v Tewson* that only economic losses can be awarded for unfair dismissals. The Court decided that the relevant legislation was drafted widely enough to include non-pecuniary loss, so damages for injury to feelings were available in principle for successful unfair dismissal claims. However, the court made it clear that not every unfair dismissal claim will carry such an award, and employment tribunals were advised to require firm proof that an applicant has suffered real injury to his or her self-respect. This is only likely to become material in some cases of constructive dismissal. The case was later heard in the House of Lords, and it was found that the court should not have included an element of non-financial loss.

However, where the injury, including psychiatric harm, resulted prior to and separately from the act of dismissal, a cause of action will exist at common law – see *Eastwood & Another v Magnox Electric plc; McCabe v Cornwall CC & Others* (2004).

An award of additional compensation may be made where an order for reinstatement or re-engagement is not complied with or it is not practicable to make such an order. The various types of compensation are described below.

Basic award (s 118 of the ERA 1996)

The calculation of the basic award is dependent upon the number of years of continuous service which the applicant has attained:

Entitlement:	21 and under	Half a week's pay for each year of employment
	22–40	1 week's pay for each year of employment
	41–65	1.5 weeks' pay for each year of employment

The maximum number of years which can be counted is 20 and the maximum amount of weekly pay is currently £450. The maximum basic award is at present £13,500. The tribunal may reduce the basic award on the grounds of contributory conduct on the part of the applicant. Where there is also an award of a redundancy payment, the basic award will be reduced by the amount of that payment, as long as it is established that the dismissal was for reason of redundancy.

The basic award will be two weeks' pay where the reason for the dismissal was redundancy and the employee unreasonably refuses to accept a renewal of the contract or suitable alternative employment.

Any statutory limits placed on awards have been index-linked and reviewed each year (s 34 of the Employment Relations Act 1999).

Compensatory award (s 123 of the ERA 1996)

A compensatory award is in addition to the basic award and is awarded at the discretion of the tribunal. The amount of the award is decided upon by the tribunal by reference to what is 'just and equitable in all the circumstances, having regard to the loss sustained by the applicant in consequence of the dismissal'. At present, the maximum amount of this award is £72,300. The amount of the award may be reduced by failure on the part of the employee to mitigate his or her loss, contributory conduct and any *ex gratia* payment made by the employer.

In making the award, the tribunal will take into account loss of wages; expenses incurred in taking legal action against the employer; loss of future earnings; loss of pension rights and other benefits, for example, a company car; and the manner of the dismissal.

However, the Unfair Dismissal (Variation of the Limit of Compensatory Award) Order 2013 introduced a new upper limit for unfair dismissal claims issued after 29 July 2013. The new limit will be £74,200 or 52 weeks' pay, whichever is the lower.

Additional award

An additional award can be made where the employer fails to comply with an order for reinstatement or re-engagement and fails to show that it was not practicable to comply with such an order. The amount of this additional award will be between 13 and 26 weeks' pay; if the dismissal is unfair because it is based on sex or race discrimination, the additional award will be between 26 and 52 weeks' pay.

Interim relief

There are now minimum awards of compensation for dismissal in 'special situations'. For example, the minimum amount for contravening s 100 is £3,600.

Where an employee alleges dismissal for union/non-union membership or trade union activities, he or she can apply to the employment tribunal for an order for interim relief (s 128 ERA 1996).

Such an order will preserve the status quo until a full hearing of the case and has the effect, therefore, of reinstating or re-engaging the employee. In order to obtain an order for interim relief, an application must be made to the employment tribunal within seven days immediately following the effective date of termination. This must be supported by a certificate signed by an authorised trade union official where the allegation relates to dismissal for trade union membership or taking part in trade union activities. Finally, it must appear to the employment tribunal that the complaint is likely to succeed at a full hearing.

Even where these conditions are satisfied, the employment tribunal must then determine whether the employer is willing to reinstate or re-engage the employee. If the employer is not so willing, then the employment tribunal must make an order for the continuation of the employee's contract of employment until the full hearing, thus preserving continuity, pay and other employment rights.

Where the employer fails to comply with an interim relief order, the employment tribunal must:

- make an order for the continuation of the contract; and
- order the employer to pay such compensation as the tribunal believes is just and equitable, having regard to the loss suffered by the employee.

Where an employer fails to observe the terms of a continuation order, the employment tribunal shall:

- determine the amount of any money owed to the employee; and
- order the employer to pay the employee such compensation as is considered to be just and equitable.

There has been much academic debate about the success or otherwise of the unfair dismissal provisions. It has been said that the law has been unsuccessful in providing effective control over what is seen as managerial prerogative in relation to dismissals (see, for example, Collins, H, 'Capitalist discipline and corporatist law' (1982) 11 ILJ 78). One general weakness expounded by academics is the attitude of the appeal court judges to the legislation. They perceive that judges feel that they are being asked to intervene in areas which they believe individuals should resolve; as a result, judges end up endorsing the ordinary practices of employers, even though these may be flawed (see *Saunders v Scottish National Camps Association Ltd* (1980)). The right to protection from unfair dismissal can be seen as a fundamental human right, which therefore demands a complete overhaul of the current legislative provisions (see Hepple, R, 'The fall and rise of unfair dismissal', in McCarthy, W (ed), *Legal Intervention in Industrial Relations: Gains and Losses*, 1992, p 95).

18.12 Redundancy

When an employee's services are no longer required by the business, either through the closing down of that business or perhaps because of the introduction of new technology, he or she will in general have been made redundant. Whether or not the employee is entitled to redundancy pay will depend upon whether the qualification rules and the key essentials are satisfied. The law in this area is weighted in favour of the employer, who, in order to avoid the higher compensation limits for unfair dismissal, may well try to disguise an unfair dismissal situation as redundancy. The law relating to redundancy can be found in the ERA 1996. The purpose of the ERA 1996 is to provide for the payment of compensation based on an employee's service and wages, in order to tide the employee over during the period in which he or she is without a job. However, any entitlement to redundancy payments only exists where it is established that the employee's dismissal was by reason of redundancy within the meaning of the ERA 1996.

18.12.1 Qualifications

In assessing whether an employee qualifies for redundancy payment, the rules are similar to the unfair dismissal provisions. The qualifying period for redundancy is two years. The final outcome of the decision in *R v Secretary of State for Employment ex p Seymour-Smith and Perez (No 2)* (2000) does not change this, even though a two year qualifying period was found by the House of Lords to discriminate indirectly against women and was contrary to EC law. The onus is on the employer to show that continuity has been broken or that there are weeks which do not count towards continuity; once again, the same rules apply regarding continuity. Certain categories of employee are excluded from the provisions of the ERA 1996 (as referred to earlier), in some cases because existing arrangements between their employer and their trade union are better than the protection afforded by the ERA 1996.

18.12.2 Dismissal

The burden of proof in the initial stages of any claim for redundancy is on the employee to show dismissal. There is then a presumption that the dismissal was for reason of redundancy and the burden moves to the employer to show that redundancy was not the reason for the dismissal.

Where an employee meets the basic qualification requirements, it must be shown that he or she has been 'dismissed' within the meaning of s 136 of the ERA 1996. Again, the provisions which determine dismissal are the same as for unfair dismissal. According to s 139 of the ERA 1996, an employee shall be treated as dismissed by the employer if, but only if:

- the contract of employment is terminated by the employer with or without notice; or
- it is a fixed term contract which has expired without being renewed; or
- the employee terminates the contract with or without notice in circumstances such that he or she is entitled to terminate it without notice by reason of the employer's conduct; or
- the contract is terminated by the death of the employer or on the dissolution or liquidation of the firm.

It is clear, however, that the initiative to dismiss the employee must come from the employer. An employee who resigns is not entitled to redundancy payment unless the constructive dismissal provision is satisfied (*Walley v Morgan* (1969)).

Whether a dismissal is within s 136 or s 139 is a question of fact in each case. For example, a variation in the terms of the employee's contract will amount to a dismissal if he or she does not agree to the new terms. If, however, the employee accepts the new terms, there can be no dismissal and continuity is preserved.

In *Marriot v Oxford and District Co-operative Society Ltd* (1970), the defendants employed Marriot as a foreman. He was informed that, from a certain date, he would be employed on a lower grade and his rate of pay would be reduced accordingly. It was held that the variation in the terms of the existing contract amounted to termination by the employer, which Marriot could treat as a dismissal.

Clearly, there may be a term in the contract which allows the employer to vary the terms. If the employee in this situation does not like the new terms and chooses to leave his or her employment, this will not amount to a dismissal for the purposes of the ERA 1996. One type of contentious term has proved to be the 'mobility clause' which many executive contracts contain. Where an employee refuses to comply with an express mobility clause requiring him or her to move, the refusal amounts to misconduct and, therefore, any dismissal cannot be treated as redundancy, but it could leave the employer open to a claim of unfair dismissal. Furthermore, if the employee attempts to anticipate the employer's actions and resigns, the resignation will not amount to a dismissal.

In *Morton Sundour Fabrics v Shaw* (1966), Morton employed Shaw as a foreman. He was informed that there might be some redundancies in the near future, but nothing specific was decided. In the light of what he had been told, he decided to leave the firm in order to take another job. It was held that he had not been dismissed and, therefore, was not entitled to redundancy payments. His precipitous action could not be shown to relate to the subsequent redundancies made by his employer.

Obviously, he would have succeeded had he waited until he received his notice of redundancy. However, when he resigned, there was no way of knowing exactly who would be made redundant (see *Doble v Firestone Tyre and Rubber Co Ltd* (1981), which followed the decision in *Morton*).

18.12.3 Dismissals for reasons of redundancy

In order for the employee to be entitled to redundancy payments, he or she must have been dismissed 'for reason of redundancy'. There is a presumption that, once the employee has shown dismissal, the reason for the dismissal was redundancy (s 163(2) of the ERA 1996). The onus is on the employer to show that the dismissal was for some reason other than redundancy.

Section 139(1) of the ERA 1996 provides a definition of 'redundancy':

> [This is where] dismissal is attributable wholly or mainly to:
>
> (a) the fact that his employer has ceased, or intends to cease, to carry on the business for the purposes of which the employee was employed by him, or has ceased, or intends to cease, to carry on that business in the place where the employee was so employed; or
>
> (b) the fact that the requirements of that business for employees to carry out work of a particular kind, or for employees to carry out work of a particular kind in the place where they were so employed have ceased or diminished or are expected to cease or diminish.

In effect, there are three situations in which the dismissal can be said to be for redundancy. These are as follows.

Cessation of the employer's business

This covers both temporary and permanent closures of the employer's business in respect of the type of work carried on at the premises and is, on the whole, straightforward. In *Gemmell v Darngavil Brickworks Ltd* (1967), a brickworks closed for a period of 13 weeks in order for substantial repairs to be carried out. Some of the employees were dismissed. It was held that the dismissal was for reason of redundancy, even though part of the premises was still in use.

Closure or change in the place of work

Where the employer ceases to trade at a particular place, as opposed to the cessation of the type of work, the dismissal of any employees will usually be for reason of redundancy. This is subject to any term in the contract of employment which contains a 'clear and unambiguous mobility clause'. Such clauses will rarely be implied.

In *O'Brien v Associated Fire Alarms Ltd* (1969), O'Brien was employed by the defendants at their Liverpool branch. There was a shortage of work and he was asked to work in Barrow-in-Furness. He refused and was dismissed by his employer. He contended that the dismissal amounted to redundancy. It was held that, as there was no clause in O'Brien's contract of employment which would have allowed his employer to move him to a different location, the dismissal was for reason of redundancy.

In these cases and if the employer is insolvent, the employee can apply to the National Insurance Fund, which can offer payments for redundancy claims in specific circumstances.

Where the employer only moves his place of work a short distance and/or remains within the same town or conurbation, any offer of work to his existing employees at the new place of employment may prevent any dismissal from being for reason of redundancy. Obviously, this will depend on accessibility to the new premises, as well as the terms on which the offer is made – it should be remembered that the terms must not be worse than existing terms. It can, therefore, be within the employer's expectations that his or her employees will move to different premises without there being a redundancy situation if such an expectation is reasonable in all the circumstances of the case.

In *Managers (Holborn) Ltd v Hohne* (1977), the defendants occupied premises in Holborn, of which Hohne was a manageress. They decided to move their business to Regent Street, which was only a short distance away. Hohne refused to move there and claimed redundancy, on the basis that there was no term in her contract which required her to move. It was held that the new premises were just as accessible as the old ones and, therefore, it was reasonable for her employer to expect her to move without there being any issue of redundancy. There was no evidence of any additional inconvenience to Hohne if she agreed to move to the new premises. She did not, therefore, succeed in her action.

Finally, this provision has been interpreted in such a way that it will only be satisfied if the place where the employee actually works, rather than is expected to work, closes or changes. In *High*

Table Ltd v Horst (1997), Mrs Horst was employed as a silver service waitress. Her letter of appointment specified that she was appointed as waitress to one particular client and she worked at their premises from July 1988 until she was dismissed. The staff handbook stated:

> Your place of work is as stated in your letter of appointment, which acts as part of your terms and conditions. However, given the nature of our business, it is sometimes necessary to transfer staff on a temporary or permanent basis to another location. Whenever possible, this will be within reasonable travelling distance of your existing place of work.

The client for whom Horst worked reduced its catering needs and, as a result, Horst was dismissed as redundant. She claimed unfair dismissal. The main issue for the Court of Appeal was, what is the test for determining redundancy? It held that the test was primarily a factual one and, on the facts, the place where she was employed no longer needed her. There was, therefore, a redundancy situation, which caused her to be dismissed. This decision casts doubt on the decision in *UK Automatic Energy Authority v Claydon* (1974). In that case, Claydon's contract of employment included a mobility clause. When he was asked to move from his employer's Suffolk plant to their Aldermaston premises, he refused and was dismissed. It was held that the mobility clause was valid and, although the work had ceased in Suffolk, it was reasonable for the employer to request a transfer to Aldermaston. The dismissal was therefore fair.

Whilst the decision in *Horst* appears to recognise the importance of an employee's redundancy rights and the desire to ensure that those rights are not negated by the unscrupulous use of mobility clauses, in real terms the employer in this case wanted it to be a redundancy situation without any obligation to redeploy staff or increase the amount of compensation payable.

Diminishing requirements for employees

As a general rule, where the employer is forced to dismiss employees because of a reduction in the work available, such employees are surplus to the requirements of the business and any dismissal is for reason of redundancy. Furthermore, where there is a change in systems of work so that fewer employees are actually needed to do the job, this, too, can amount to redundancy. The courts are, from time to time, faced with the difficult task of deciding whether dismissal for failing to keep up with modern working practices is for reason of redundancy.

In *North Riding Garages v Butterwick* (1967), Butterwick had been employed at the same garage for 30 years and had risen to the position of workshop manager. The garage was taken over by the appellants and Butterwick was dismissed for inefficiency, on the ground that he was unable or unwilling to accept new methods of work, which would involve him in some administrative work. It was held that the dismissal was not for reason of redundancy because the employee was still expected to do the same type of work, subject to new working practices. As far as the court was concerned, employees who remain in the same employment for many years are expected to adapt to new techniques and methods of work and even higher standards of efficiency. It is only when the new practices affect the nature of the work so that, in effect, there is no requirement to do that particular kind of work, that a redundancy situation may arise.

In *Hindle v Percival Boats Ltd* (1969), Hindle had been employed to repair wooden boats for many years. This type of work was in decline because of the increasing use of fibreglass. He was dismissed because he was 'too good and too slow' and it was uneconomical to keep him. He was not replaced; his work was merely absorbed by existing staff. It was held that Hindle's dismissal was not for reason of redundancy. The court felt that the employer was merely shedding surplus labour and that this was not within the ERA 1996.

In *Haden Ltd v Cowen* (1982), Cowen was employed as a regional supervisor. He was based in Southampton and had to cover a large part of southern England as part of his job. He suffered a mild heart attack. His employer then promoted him to divisional contracts surveyor, as it was thought that this would make his life less stressful. One of the terms of his contract required him to undertake, at the discretion of the company, any duties which reasonably fell within the scope of his capabilities. The company was later forced to reduce the number of employees at staff level. Cowen was not prepared to accept demotion and was dismissed. He claimed both redundancy and unfair dismissal. It was held that Cowen was dismissed for reason of redundancy because there was no other work available within the terms of his contract, that is, as divisional contracts manager.

It is suggested that the true test of redundancy is to be found in this case and the issue to be considered is 'whether the business needs as much work of the kind which the employee could, by his contract, lawfully be required to do'. This is a question not of the day-to-day function of the employee, but of what he or she could be expected to do under his or her contract of employment (see *Pink v White & Co Ltd* (1985)). Recent case law suggests that, even where a contract contains a 'flexibility clause', for example, 'and any work which may be required by the employer', there may still be a redundancy situation. In *Johnson v Peabody Trust* (1996), Johnson was employed as a roofer. A flexibility clause was introduced into his contract, which stated that he was expected to undertake general building work. By 1993, Johnson was doing more general work than roofing. He was then laid off. The EAT concluded that he was redundant. In looking at the basic task which he was expected to perform, it was determined that he was first and foremost a roofer and the need for such employees had diminished. However, a move from day shift to night shift work or vice versa may be 'work of a particular kind', as was held in *Macfisheries Ltd v Findlay* (1985).

In *Shawkat v Nottingham City Hospital NHS Trust (No 2)* (2001), the Court of Appeal held that the mere fact of a reorganisation of the business, as a result of which the employer requires one or more employees to do a different job from which he or she was previously doing, is not conclusive of redundancy. The tribunal must go on to decide whether that change had any, and if so what, effect on the employer's requirements for employees to carry out work of a particular kind. It does not necessarily follow from the fact that a new post is different in kind from the previous post or posts that the requirements of the employer's business for employees to carry out work of a particular kind must have diminished. Nor does the fact that an employee of one skill was replaced by an employee of a different skill compel the conclusion that the requirements for work of a particular kind have ceased or diminished. That is always a question of fact for the tribunal to decide.

In *Shawkat's* case, a tribunal was entitled to find that dismissal of a thoracic surgeon, following a reorganisation as a result of which he was asked to carry out cardiac surgery in addition to thoracic surgery, was not by reason of redundancy. The requirements for employees to carry out thoracic surgery had not diminished even though the reorganisation changed the work which the employees in the thoracic department, including the applicant, were required to carry out.

Finally, the definitive test, which upholds an earlier decision in *Safeway Stores plc v Burrell* (1997), can be found in *Murray & Another v Foyle Meats* (1999). The House of Lords in this case determined that a dismissal must now be regarded as being by reason of redundancy wherever it is attributable to redundancy; that is, did the diminishing requirement for employees cause the dismissal? This is a straightforward causative test.

18.12.4 Change in ownership and transfer of undertakings

Where there is a change in the ownership of a business and existing employees either have their contract renewed or are re-engaged by the new employer, this does not amount to redundancy and continuity is preserved (s 218(2) of the ERA 1996); an example of this is where the business is sold as a going concern, rather than a transfer of the assets. However, if the employee has reasonable grounds for refusing the offer of renewal, he or she may be treated as redundant (s 141(4)).

The Transfer of Undertakings (Protection of Employment) Regulations 2006 (also referred to as TUPE) apply to the sale or other disposition of commercial and non-commercial undertakings (bringing the UK in line with EC Directive 77/187 – the Acquired Rights Directive). The transfer must be of the whole or part of a business, not merely a transfer of assets (*Melon v Hector Powe Ltd* (1980)); nor do the Regulations apply to a change in ownership resulting from a transfer of shares. Since 2006 this also applies to the provision of services when they are transferred from one company to another. Where there is the transfer of a business which falls within the Regulations, the contracts of employment of the employees are also transferred, as if they had been made by the transferee. This not only protects continuity, but also puts the new employer in the same position as the original employer. As a result, all existing rights, etc, attained by employees are preserved and become enforceable against the new business. Such transfers are subject to the consent of the employee. If the employee objects, the transfer will in effect terminate the contract of employment, but this termination will not amount to a dismissal (s 33(4) of the TURERA 1993). If, following a transfer, there is a subsequent dismissal, the employee may claim unfair dismissal, or, if it is for 'an economic, technical or organisational reason', redundancy payment may be claimed.

KEY CASE *Celtec v Astley* (2006)

Facts:

The case concerned civil service employees performing vocational training and enterprise activities who were seconded to a Training and Enterprise Council (TEC) to carry out the same tasks. After three years, they resigned from the civil service, thereby ending their secondments, and immediately signed up to fresh contracts with the TEC. The TEC argued that the TUPE transfer had taken place at the time of the secondment and so, at the time of the transfer they remained employees of the civil service. On this basis, the TEC refused to recognise continuity of employment. Following this line of argument, the employees were not taken on by the TEC until three years later. The employees, on the other hand, argued that the secondment formed part of the transfer process which took place gradually over the three-year period.

Decision:

The ECJ ruled that it is not possible for a transfer to take place over a period of time. For the purposes of legal certainty the claimants must be able to point to a specific date at which the transfer is alleged to have taken place. The date of transfer is to be determined as the date on which the employer's responsibility switches to the transferee with references to the circumstances in each case. This precludes employers from postponing or agreeing the date on which the contracts of employment transfer, rather this will be a matter of fact which may be objectively determined.

The Court of Appeal in *RCO Support Services v Unison* (2002) held that there can be a TUPE transfer even where there is no transfer of significant assets and none of the relevant employees were taken on by the new employer. In the present case, there was a change in hospitals providing inpatient care within the same NHS trust area and new contractors took over the provision of cleaning and catering. In determining whether there had been a transfer of an undertaking, the tribunal had correctly applied the retention of identity test as well as considering the reasons why the employees were not taken on by the new employer.

The contentious issue concerning the position of employees who are dismissed prior to a transfer (thus potentially enabling the employers to evade the Regulations) has been resolved by *Litster & Others v Forth Dry Dock and Engineering Co Ltd* (1989), in which it was decided that where employees are dismissed in these circumstances, they must be treated as if they were still employed at the time of transfer. As a result, the Regulations are to be applied to such employees. The transferee employer will be responsible for any unfair dismissals, unless they can be shown to be for an 'economic, technical or organisational' reason entailing a change in the workforce.

By virtue of reg 8(2), such dismissals are deemed to be for a substantial reason for the purposes of s 98(1) of the ERA 1996 and are fair, provided that they pass the statutory test of reasonableness. If the employer successfully establishes the 'economic, technical or organisational' (ETO) defence, an employee can claim a redundancy payment if the transfer was the reason for the redundancy dismissal. The Court of Appeal considered the scope of the ETO defence in *Berriman v Delabole Slate Ltd* (1985). The court held that in order to come within reg 8(2), the employer must show that a change in the workforce is part of the economic, technical or organisational reason for dismissal. It must be an *objective* of the employer's plan to achieve changes in the workforce, not just a possible consequence of the plan. So, where an employee resigned following a transfer, because the transferee employer proposed to remove his guaranteed weekly wage so as to bring his pay into line with the transferee's existing workforce, the reason behind the plan was to produce uniform terms and conditions and was not in any way intended to reduce the numbers in the workforce.

A further contentious issue relating to the position of contracted out services has been resolved by the decision in *Dines & Others v Initial Health Care Services & Another* (1994). The Court of Appeal held that where employees are employed by the new contracting company, the new company is obliged to take over the contract of employment on exactly the same terms (following the decision in *Kenny v South Manchester College* (1993)).

Following *Dines*, cases have extended the meaning of 'relevant transfer'. In *Betts v Brintel Helicopters and KLM* (1996), Brintel had, until 1995, exclusive rights to provide and service Shell's helicopter requirements for all of their North Sea oil rigs. In 1995, Shell decided to split the contract between Brintel and KLM, and 66 Brintel employees were left without jobs. Betts and six others claimed successfully that they were now employed by KLM. The High Court held that there had been a transfer of the 'activity' from Brintel to KLM, even though there was no transfer of employees or assets. (See also *ECM (Vehicle Delivery Service) Ltd v Cox & Others* (1999).)

An attempt to avoid the application of the first regulations in 1981 (Transfer of Undertakings (Protection of Employment) Regulations 1981 (SI 1981/1794)) by 'hiving down' the transfer first to a subsidiary company and then to the ultimate transferee has been thwarted. In *Re Maxwell Fleet and Facilities Management Ltd (No 2)* (2000), the High Court held that liability for employees dismissed before the purported 'hive down' passed to the ultimate transferee by virtue of the application of the *Litster* principle. The employees in this situation were dismissed for a reason connected with the transfer and were, therefore, deemed to have been employed immediately before the transfer.

Following the decision in *Abler & Others v Sodexho MM Catering Gesellschaft mbH* (2004), the courts make a clear distinction between 'asset reliant' businesses and 'labour intensive' businesses. For there to be a transfer in respect of the former, all of the key assets must be transferred; in respect of the latter, the labour force must be transferred. In this particular case, catering was held to be asset intensive.

Finally, the Government reformed the Transfer of Undertakings (Protection of Employment) Regulations 1981 and issued a Consultation Paper: *Government Proposals for Reform (Employment Relations Directorate)* (DTI, September 2001). Draft regulations and a further Consultation Paper have been produced (see www.dti.gov.uk).

The Collective Redundancies and Transfer of Undertakings (Protection of Employment) (Amendment) Regulations 1995 have amended the 1981 Regulations. In particular, reg 8(5) was introduced to reverse the decision in *Milligan v Securicor Cleaning Ltd* (1995) to the effect that an employee did not need to have two years' continuous employment in order to claim unfair dismissal on a transfer pursuant to reg 8. The effect of the decision was that someone who was dismissed after one week's employment because of a transfer could claim unfair dismissal, whereas an employee of

23 months' duration who was dismissed in a non-transfer situation could not! The decision has been overruled by the High Court in *R v Secretary of State for Trade and Industry ex p Unison* (1996).

However, concern has been expressed that companies find these TUPE arrangements to be over-bureaucratic, leading to a Government consultation on the effectiveness of the regulation. The Government's response to the consultation is awaited, and it is expected that there will be alterations of some type of the regulation, probably the removal of the service provision change to trigger TUPE.

18.12.5 Offer of alternative employment

The offer of alternative employment is covered by s 141 of the ERA 1996. The general rule is that where the employer makes an offer of suitable alternative employment, which is unreasonably refused by the employee, the employee will be unable to claim redundancy. This contract, which is either a renewal or a re-engagement, must take effect on the expiry of the old contract or within four weeks. Clearly, the main issue is what amounts to 'suitable'. Consideration must be had of the old terms and conditions as compared with the new ones, that is, the nature of the work; remuneration; hours; place; skills; and experience, including qualifications, etc. Where the conditions of the new contract do not differ materially from the old contract regarding place, nature of the work, pay, etc, then the question of suitability does not arise. It is a question of fact in each case as to whether an offer can be deemed 'suitable', with the onus resting on the employer to establish suitability. However, the facts must be considered objectively.

In *Taylor v Kent CC* (1969), Taylor was made redundant from his post as headmaster of a school. He was offered a place in the pool of supply teachers from which temporary absences were filled in schools. There was no loss of salary or other rights, other than status. Taylor refused the offer. It was held that his refusal was reasonable. The offer was not suitable because of the loss of status, since he was being removed from a position as head of a school to an ordinary teacher.

A loss of fringe benefits has been held to be a reasonable refusal (*Sheppard v NCB* (1966)). However, the refusal of an offer of a job which may only last a short period could be deemed to be unreasonable (*Morganite Crucible v Street* (1972)). It was decided in *Spencer and Griffin v Gloucestershire CC* (1985) that the issue for the industrial (now employment) tribunal is twofold: first, whether the job offered is suitable; and, secondly, whether the employee has acted reasonably in refusing the offer.

In considering whether a refusal by the employee is reasonable, regard must be had for the personal circumstances of the employee, such as housing and domestic problems. It may be reasonable for an employee to refuse a job offer which involves a move to London when he or she lives in the Midlands, because of the housing problems associated with a move to the Home Counties. However, a refusal based upon a personal whim will be unreasonable. In *Fuller v Stephanie Bowman (Sales) Ltd* (1977), the applicant refused to move with her employers from a West End address to one in Soho, where the new business premises were above a sex shop. After a site visit to the premises, it was decided that the dislike of the sex shop was not enough to make the refusal of the offer reasonable, as it was not one of the worst streets in Soho and it was unlikely that the applicant would be mistaken for a prostitute. In *Rawe v Power Gas Corp* (1966), it was held to be reasonable to refuse a move from the south-east of England to Teesside because of marital difficulties.

Finally, even where the employment tribunal finds that the offer was suitable, it does not automatically follow that a refusal by the employee is unreasonable. For example, in *Cambridge and District Co-operative Society Ltd v Ruse* (1993), although the job was deemed to be suitable by the industrial tribunal, the employee had personal objections to the job offered, as he perceived a lack of status which supported his refusal of the offer.

It must be remembered that the onus is on the employer to show that the employee's rejection of the offer is unreasonable. Where the offer of alternative employment is accepted by the employee, there is deemed to be continuity of employment between the former contract and the new contract.

The offer of alternative employment following the transfer of an undertaking must not be on less favourable terms than the original contract. If the alteration of the employment relationship is connected to the transfer, it is invalid – see *Martin v South Bank University* (2004).

By virtue of s 132 of the ERA 1996, the employee is entitled to a trial period of four weeks (or longer, if agreed with the employer) if the contract is renewed on different terms and conditions. If the employee terminates his or her employment during the trial period for a reason connected with the new contract, he or she will be treated as having been dismissed on the date that the previous contract was terminated. Whether he or she will be entitled to redundancy will depend on whether it was a suitable offer of alternative employment and whether the refusal to accept it was reasonable (see *Meek v Allen Rubber Co Ltd and Secretary of State for Employment* (1980)). If the employer dismisses the employee during the trial period for any reason, the dismissal is to be treated as redundancy.

An employee is entitled to a reasonable amount of time off to seek work or retrain once notice of redundancy has been received (s 52 of the ERA 1996). This right is confined to those employees who meet the qualifying periods. Failure to provide time off may result in the employee making a complaint to an employment tribunal, which may award two-fifths of a week's pay.

18.12.6 Calculation of redundancy payment

The employee must inform the employer, in writing, of any intention to claim a redundancy payment. If the employer does not make the payment or there is a dispute over entitlement, the matter is referred to an employment tribunal. As a general rule, the claim must be made within six months of the date of termination of the contract of employment. This period can be extended at the discretion of the employment tribunal but cannot exceed 12 months.

Method of calculation

There is now no upper or lower age limit on the entitlement of statutory redundancy pay, an employer will have to pay you the statutory minimum redundancy payment even if you are under 18 or over 65 (or after an individuals' normal retirement age, if this is lower). The method of calculation is the same as for unfair dismissal (considered above). The maximum award at present is, therefore, £13,500. An employee may lose entitlement to all or part of his or her redundancy payments in the following circumstances:

- if the claim is made out of time, that is, after a period of six months from the relevant date. However, as with unfair dismissal, an employment tribunal may allow an extension within the time limit if it is just and equitable to do so (s 164 of the ERA 1996);
- if employment is left prematurely, the employee having been warned of the possibility of redundancy in the future. An employee under notice of dismissal who leaves before the notice expires may also lose the right to payment. This will depend on whether the employer objects to the premature departure (s 142 of the ERA 1996);
- where the employee is guilty of misconduct, allowing the employer to terminate the contract for this reason (s 140(1) of the ERA 1996); and
- strike action – if the employee is involved in a strike during his or her period of notice, he or she will still be entitled to redundancy payment. However, if his or her notice of dismissal is received whilst on strike, he or she will not be entitled to claim redundancy payment.

18.12.7 Procedure for handling redundancies

This is governed by s 188 of the TULR(C)A 1992 (as amended by the Trade Union Reform and Employment Rights Act (TURERA) 1993) and the Collective Redundancies and Transfer of Undertakings (Protection of Employment) (Amendment) Regulations 1995 (SI 1995/2587). There is an obligation on the employer to consult a recognised trade union or elected employee representative 'in good time', as opposed to 'at the earliest opportunity'. Such consultation must take place even if only one employee is being made redundant. Where consultation cannot take place at the earliest opportunity, the fall back rules are as follows:

- at least 90 days before the first dismissal takes effect, where he or she proposes to make 100 or more employees redundant at one establishment within a period of 90 days or less; or
- at least 30 days before the first redundancy takes effect, where he or she proposes to make 20 or more employees redundant at one establishment within a 30 day period.

Consultation must include consideration of the ways in which the redundancies can be avoided; a possible reduction in the numbers of employees being dismissed; anything which might mitigate the effects of the redundancy *ex gratia* payment. During the consultations, the employer must also disclose (s 188(4) of the TULR(C)A 1992):

- the reasons for the proposed redundancies;
- the number and description of the employees whom it is proposed to make redundant;
- the total number of employees of that description employed at that establishment;
- the method of selection, for example, FIFO, LIFO, part-timers first, etc; and
- the method of carrying out the redundancies, having regard to any procedure agreed with the trade union.

During these consultations, the trade union may make any representations which it sees fit. The employer may not ignore these representations and must give the reasons if he or she chooses to reject them. However, in considering the fairness of the employer's conduct, in *British Aerospace plc v Green* (1995) the Court of Appeal adopted a broad brush approach in judging the overall fairness of the employer's conduct of the selection procedure and did not feel that it was necessary to examine individual applications of it too closely. Where there are special circumstances, such as insolvency, the employer need only do what is reasonably practicable to comply with the consultation requirements.

Effect of non-compliance with the procedure

Where the employer fails to comply with the consultation procedure in circumstances where it was reasonably practicable to expect him or her to do so, the trade union can complain to the employment tribunal. If the tribunal finds in favour of the trade union, it must make a declaration to this effect and may make a protective award to those employees who were affected. This award, which is discretionary, takes the form of remuneration for a protected period. The length of the protected period usually reflects the severity of the breach by the employer. However, the protected period:

- must not exceed 45 days, where it was proposed to make 100 or more employees redundant within 90 days; or
- is 30 days, where it was proposed to make 20 or more redundant.

All employees covered by the protective award are entitled to up to 13 weeks' pay (Collective Redundancies and Transfer of Undertakings (Protection of Employment) (Amendment) Regulations 1995 (SI 1995/2587)).

18.12.8 Notification of redundancies to the Secretary of State

By virtue of s 193 of the TULR(C)A 1992, an employer must notify the Secretary of State of his or her intentions where he or she proposes:

- to make 100 or more employees redundant at one establishment within a 45 day period – here, the notification must take place within 45 days; or
- to make 20 or more employees redundant within a 30 day period – in which case the notification must take place within 30 days.

Failure to meet these requirements may result in prosecution. However, there is a 'special circumstances' defence where it is not reasonably practicable for the employer to comply with the law on notification.

Summary

Individual Employment Rights (3): Termination

The contract of employment may be terminated by agreement, death, frustration or performance. As a general rule, an employer must give notice if he or she wishes to terminate an employee's contract. The minimum periods of notice are laid down in s 86 of the ERA 1996. An employee wishing to terminate his or her contract must give at least one week's notice.

Employers should have a basic disciplinary and grievance procedure following the ACAS Code of Practice as a minimum requirement.

Summary dismissal

Summary dismissal is dismissal without notice for a serious breach of the contract.

Wrongful dismissal

Wrongful dismissal is summary dismissal without just cause (*Irani v South West Hampshire HA* (1985)). Compensation in the form of wages and damages will generally only be awarded for the notice period unless there has been a breach of the implied term of trust and confidence (*Malik v BCCI SA* (1997); *Gogay v Hertfordshire CC* (2000)). However, no compensation can be awarded for mental distress or damage to reputation (*Johnson v Unisys Ltd* (2001)). This is qualified by *McCabe v Cornwall CC* (2004).

Unfair dismissal

Protection for unfair dismissal is provided by the Employment Rights Act 1996. All employees employed on or after 6 April 2012 must now satisfy the qualifying period of at least two year's continuous service and must not belong to the excluded groups. Anyone employed prior to that must demonstrate just one year's employment.

Effective date of termination (s 97 of the Employment Rights Act 1996)

Rules are the same for redundancy and unfair dismissal where:

- termination is with notice and the effective date/relevant date is the date on which the notice expires; and
- termination is without notice and the effective date is the date on which termination takes effect.

Dismissal

The employee must show that he or she has been dismissed within the meaning of the Employment Rights Act 1996. This may amount to the following:

- Express termination by the employer:
    - *Igbo v Johnson Matthey Chemicals Ltd* (1986);
    - *Martin v Yeoman Aggregates Ltd* (1983);
    - *Robertson v Securicor Transport Ltd* (1972).
- Expiration of a fixed term contract which is not renewed.
- Constructive dismissal where the employee is entitled to terminate his or her contract:
    - *Western Excavating Ltd v Sharp* (1978);
    - *Simmonds v Dowty Seals Ltd* (1978);
    - *Pepper and Hope v Daish* (1980).
- Written reasons for the dismissal: where the employee makes a written request for a statement of the reasons for his or her dismissal, the employer must supply this information within 14 days (s 92 of the ERA 1996).

Fair dismissals

Once the employee has established dismissal, the onus moves to the employer to show that he or she acted reasonably and that, therefore, the dismissal was fair (s 98 of the ERA 1996).

The employer must show the following:

- That the actions were a reasonable response:
    - *Polkey v AE Dayton Services Ltd* (1987);
    - *Haddon v Van Den Bergh Foods Ltd* (1999);
    - *Post Office v Foley* (2000);
    - *Sainsbury's Supermarkets Ltd v Hitt* (2003).

  ACAS Code of Practice on Disciplinary and Grievance Procedures.
- That the capability or qualifications of the employee were inadequate:
    - *Davison v Kent Meters Ltd* (1975).
- That the conduct of the employee merited dismissal:
    - *Taylor v Parsons Peebles Ltd* (1981);
    - *Parr v Whitbread plc* (1990).
- That there was a redundancy situation:
    - *Allwood v William Hill Ltd* (1974);
    - *Hammond-Scott v Elizabeth Arden Ltd* (1976).
- That there were statutory restrictions/illegality.
- That there was some other substantial reason.

Automatically unfair

The following dismissals are automatically unfair:

- trade union membership or activities;
- pregnancy and childbirth;
- industrial action;
- health and safety matters;

- protected disclosures;
- selection for redundancy in respect of the above;
- covered by the Part-Time Workers Regulations 2000 or the Fixed-Term Employees Regulations 2002; and
- Assertion of a statutory right.

Remedies

The remedies available for unfair dismissal are:

- reinstatement;
- re-engagement;
- compensation, comprising:
  - basic award;
  - compensatory award;
  - additional award; and
  - interim relief order.

Redundancy

Redundancy occurs when an employee is dismissed because his or her services are no longer required or the business ceases. The employee may have a claim for redundancy payments. The employee must show:

- that he or she satisfies a qualification period of two years' continuous employment and does not fall within excluded classes (*R v Secretary of State for Employment ex p Seymour-Smith and Perez (No 2)* (2000)); and
- dismissal by his or her employer – *Marriot v Oxford and District Co-operative Society Ltd* (1970).

Once dismissal has been established, there is a presumption that the reason for the dismissal was redundancy. There are three situations which are deemed to be 'for reason of redundancy':

- cessation of the employer's business (*Gemmell v Darngavil Brickworks Ltd* (1967));
- closure or change in the place of work (*O'Brien v Associated Fire Alarms Ltd* (1969); *Managers (Holborn) Ltd v Hohne* (1977)); and
- diminishing requirements for employees (*North Riding Garages v Butterwick* (1967); *Hindle v Percival Boats Ltd* (1969); *Shawkat v Nottingham City Hospital NHS Trust (No 2)* (2001)).

Lay-off and short time

Redundancy payment may be made where an employee has been laid off or kept on short time.

Change in ownership and transfer of undertakings

Change in ownership occurs where there is a transfer of a whole or part of the business (*Melon v Hector Powe* (1980)).

The Transfer of Undertakings (Protection of Employment) Regulations 2006 apply to employees dismissed prior to the transfer (*Litster & Others v Forth Dry Dock and Engineering Co Ltd* (1989)). A transfer of an undertaking may occur even where there is no transfer of significant assets and none of the relevant employees are taken on by the new employer (*RCO Support Services v Unison* (2002); *Abler and Others v Sodexho MM Catering Gesellschaft mbH* (2004)). It may also apply to the change of provision of services.

Offer of alternative employment

- *Taylor v Kent CC* (1969) – an unsuitable offer may be refused.
- *Martin v South Bank University* (2004) – an offer on less favourable terms following the transfer of an undertaking will not be acceptable.

Trial period

A trial period is four weeks.

Procedure for handling redundancies

The correct procedure for handling redundancies is to consult with representatives of a recognised independent trade union. Failure to consult may result in a protective award. Notification of redundancies should be given to the Secretary of State within set time limits.

Further Reading

Bogg, A, 'The right to paid annual leave in the Court of Justice: the eclipse of functionalism' (2006) 31 European LR 892

Freedland, MR and Davies, PL, 'The role of EU employment law and policy in the de-marginalisation of part-time work', paper presented at Cambridge University Press 63–82

O'Cienneide, C, 'Fumbling Towards Coherence: The Slow Evolution of Equality Law in England and Wales' (2006) Northern Ireland Legal Quarterly 57–102

Chapter 19

Health and Safety Law

Chapter Contents

Law in Context: Health and Safety Law

Health and safety at work can be easily ridiculed, but if not followed can have significant impacts on both employees and the liability of the business itself. Health and safety can have a significant financial cost to a business, whether this be down-time as a result of an accident, or an employee being injured and taking sick leave. Health and safety law is broad, and includes areas that you may not initially identify as being related to health and safety, such as Manual Handling Operations Regulations (1992) and the Control of Substances Hazardous to Health Regulations 2002. However, the role of health and safety is changing, largely as a consequence of societal changes and technological changes, and this can result in legal requirements and guidance for employers to follow. Employers have a duty of care towards their staff, visitors and other people who may be affected by the employer's business. As such, the employer must take reasonable actions to minimise the risk of harm. Many employers use risk assessment to assess the level of risk posed, and while a risk assessment can help to reduce the risk of accidents and keep employees safer, accidents can still happen. Therefore, a risk assessment can reduce the level of risk, but not eliminate it altogether. Employers may also find it useful to include the general duties of employees at work within a workplace health and safety policy, which should be communicated to all staff. This enables employees to be aware of their own responsibilities, and put in place any requirements in their system of working and general conduct in the workplace. As you work through this chapter, you will see an emphasis on the prevention of accidents and maintaining a healthy and safe workplace. This is also the case at a European level, where the emphasis is placed on changing employers' and workers' perceptions to prevent accidents occurring in the workplace.

19.1 Introduction

Health and Safety in Britain rose from humble beginnings in the 19th century Victorian era. With the emergence of the Industrial Revolution, its aim was to minimise the working hours of women and children and until the 1970s, continued to evolve in a piecemeal manner, giving minimal protection to employees. Today, we have a plethora of health and safety regulation that has emerged most significantly since the 1970s with the passing of the Health and Safety at Work Act 1974 (HASAWA) including impressive enforcement agencies who oversee every aspect of occupational health and safety. However during the 1980s when Britain became a member of the European Union (EU), the European Commission set up Action Programmes specifically to develop health and safety standards within the EU. This resulted in it becoming far more heavily regulated with the passing of many Directives and Regulations, which have been implemented into UK law. The EU continues to revise and develop health and safety regulation within the EU and Health and Safety in the UK is more tightly regulated than ever before. More recently, the Corporate Manslaughter and Corporate Homicide Act 2007 (CHCHA), came into force changing the way in which organisations are liable for the death of their employees resulting from health and safety issues. This piece of legislation is demonstrative of a well-overdue change of the law, in which companies can be held liable for causing a person's death due to a gross breach of a relevant duty of care. Health and safety at work is a common target of criticism by the popular media and by sections of the public. However, breaches of health and safety law can have highly significant consequences for businesses through financial loss in the payment of fines, loss of production and financial compensation in the payment of damages to employees who have been injured at work.

19.2 The Health and Safety Executive

The HSE was established in 1975 and is a government body appointed by the Health and Safety Commission (HSC) responsible for Health and Safety regulation in Britain including implementing policy. The HSE works within a coalition of other regulators as well as possessing regulatory powers in the field of occupational health and safety as an enforcement authority. Its jurisdiction is primarily in the high risk fields such as industry and other high risk sectors of employment. HSE essentially aims to prevent people from being killed, injured or made ill by work. Injuries at work are now at their lowest and the UK is proud to have one of the lowest accident rates in the EU because of the HSE. In spite of these improvements there is no need for complacency. In 2011/12 1.1 million working people were suffering from work-related illness. 172 workers were killed at work and 111,000 other injuries to employees were reported under statutory reporting requirements. However, there are still large numbers of people affected by work related illnesses or injuries. This is increasingly evident now due to advances in new technology which pose new and serious risks.

The HSE is continually looking for ways in which to tighten and improve health and safety methods by issuing Improvement Notices, Prohibition Notices and providing Action Plans for employers. In addition to this, the HSE carry out awareness campaigns working with businesses in assisting them to improve their health and safety regimes. It also acts as an advisory agency, working with specialist high-risk industries, for example the nuclear industry, as well as providing Government advice on applying EU law. Lastly, it undertakes research on a range of issues (the Health and Safety Executive, 2010).

The HSE and local government work in support of the HSC. They are also responsible for maintaining the Employment Medical Advisory Service (EMS), which provides advice on occupational health matters.

19.2.1 Local Authorities (LA)

Local authorities are responsible for health and safety enforcement. The Local Authority has the power to approve building plans but can refuse them if the fire safety arrangements are inadequate. The LA can issue certificates where public entertainment is carried out, including aspects such as: food safety, licenses in relation to environmental matters, for example serving Abatement Notices (Environmental Protection Act 1990), and, in conjunction with the Fire Brigade, issuing fire safety certificates in premises situated within their area.

19.3 The Beginning of Health and Safety Regulation

The 1800s saw the birth of the Industrial Revolution. Factories were rapidly being built due to the use of steam-powered machines. Young children were forced to work in the factories, working incredibly long hours and often operating dangerous machinery. Widespread concern emerged over the treatment of these child workers at a time when wider humanitarian concerns developed in other sectors, including the penal system. Addressing this disquiet, the Government decided to bring legislation and regulation into the area.

19.3.1 The Ten Hour Movement and the Factory Act 1833

In 1833 the Government introduced the Factory Act to improve the conditions for children who were working in the factories.

In 1833 they passed a law for the Textile Industry, which stated that:

> . . . no person under eighteen years of age shall [work] between half-past eight in the evening and half-past five in the morning, in any cotton, woolen, worsted, hemp, flax, tow, linen or silk mill . . .
>
> . . . No person under the age of eighteen shall be employed in any such mill . . . more than twelve hours in . . . one day, nor more than sixty-nine hours in . . . one week . . .
>
> There shall be allowed . . . not less than one and a half hours for meals.
>
> It shall not be lawful for any person to employ . . . in any factory . . . as aforesaid for longer than forty-eight hours in one week, nor for longer than nine hours in one day, any child who shall not have completed his or her eleventh year . . .
>
> It shall be lawful for His Majesty to appoint four Inspectors of factories where . . . children and young persons under eighteen years of age [are] employed, empowered to enter any . . . mill, and any school . . . belonging thereto, at all times . . . by day or by night, when such . . . factories are at work.
>
> The Inspectors shall have power to make such rules as may be necessary for the execution of this act, binding on all persons subject to the provisions of this act; and are authorised to enforce the attendance at school of children employed in factories according to the provisions of this Act.

With regulation now in force, an Inspectorate of Factories was created in order to ensure that these regulations were being complied with and to distribute penalties for failing to meet the requirements of the regulations. Unfortunately, the Act was not widely complied with, as the inspectorate was unable to deal with the large number of factories. However, the Act did pave the way for further regulation.

In 1884 the Government passed another Factories Act, which was the first Health and Safety Act in Britain.

The Factories Act 1844

The Factories Act 1844 further reduced hours of work for children and applied the many provisions of the Factory Act of 1833 to women. The Act applied to the textile industry and included the following provisions:

- Children of 9–13 years could work for 9 hours a day with a lunch break.
- Women and young people now worked the same number of hours. They could work for no more than 12 hours a day during the week, including one and a half hours for meals, and 9 hours on Sundays.
- Factory owners must wash factories with lime every 14 months.
- Ages must be verified by surgeons.
- Accidental death must be reported to a surgeon and investigated.
- Thorough records must be kept regarding the provisions of the act.
- Machinery was to be fenced in.

Hours of Labour of Young Persons and Females in Factories Act 1847

The Government passed a further Factories Act in 1847. This Act limited the hours of the working day to 10 hours for women and children under the age of 18 years old in the working week.

The Factory Act 1850

The Factory Act 1850 was passed in order to amend the 1847 Act particularly in relation to:

- Employers could no longer decide on the hours people had to work.
- Women and children could only work from 6 am to 6 pm in the summer and from 7 am to 7 pm in the winter.
- All work on a Saturday would end at 2 pm.
- The working week was extended to 60 hours from 58 hours.
- The hours of work for 9 to 18 years of age were changed to 10.5 hours day and night from 10 hours previously.

Factory Act 1878

This Act consolidated all the previous Acts and now applied to all trades:

- No children under the age of 10 were allowed to be employed anywhere.
- Education now became compulsory for children up to the age of 10 years old.
- Children between the ages of 10–14 could only work for half-days.
- Women were not allowed to work for more than 56 hours per week.

Factory Act 1891

The Factory Act 1891 made the requirements for fencing machinery much more regulated and more strict. The 1891 Act added further conditions to the Conditions of Employment such as:

- The minimum age from which a child could be employed changed from 10 years to 11 years of age.

Factory and Workshop Act 1901

The minimum working age was raised to 12 years of age. The Act also introduced legislation regarding the education of children, meal times and fire escapes.

Factories Act 1937

The 1937 Act (1 Edw. 8 & 1 Geo. 6 c. 67) consolidated and amended the Factory and Workshops Acts from 1901 to 1929. It was introduced to the House of Commons on 29 January 1939 and given the Royal Assent on 30 July 1939.

Factories Act 1961

The 1961 Act consolidated the legislation on workplace health and safety. However, it has largely been superseded by the Health and Safety at Work Act 1974.

19.4 The Transformation of Health and Safety Legislation in the UK

In 1974, the Government published a consultative document with a view to consolidating health and safety legislation into one Act and extending it to all workplaces. The Robens Report (1972, Cmnd 5034) reviewed workplace health and safety. Its findings became the basis for the Act. This is still considered to be one of the most important pieces of legislation in health and safety. There is a requirement that certain information is to be displayed (this has changed over time) to anyone working in any environment.

In the 1990s the European Union (EU) passed directives on health and safety heralding the start of a comprehensive set of revised provisions, which harmonised, updated and simplified health and safety legislation.

In addition to this, the health and safety enforcement bodies were brought together under the remit of the HSE and under the supervision of the HSC. In April 2008, both of these bodies were replaced by a single body, HSE, which has taken over the statutory functions. The HSE is responsible for initiating research, training and the publishing of information (Ford and Clarke, 2008: 2).

The Health and Safety at Work Act 1974 (HSAW) made provisions for appointing various safety representatives and committees to consult with employee safety representatives, in order to create a safer working environment. Under The Safety Representative and Safety Committee Regulations 1977, trade unions have a right to be consulted with regard to health and safety matters, and the Health and Safety (Consultation with Employees) Regulations 1996 governs when the employer does not have a union.

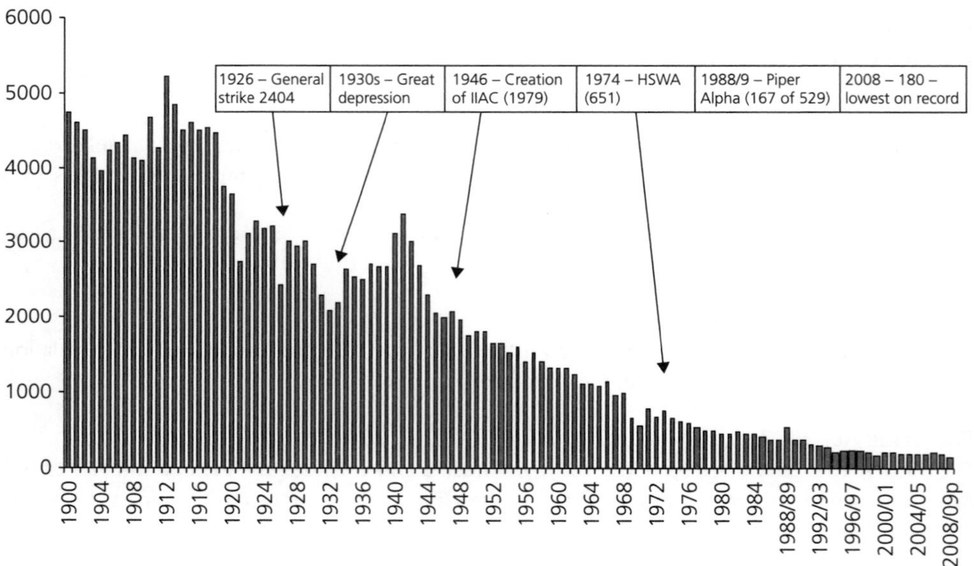

Figure 19.1 Employee fatalities – HSE

19.5 The Health and Safety at Work Act 1974

Employers are under a legal duty to ensure their employees are safe at work. This is achieved through conducting risk assessments, taking into account the many hazards that could arise, which could affect the physical and mental wellbeing of an employee or even cause death (The Key Consulting Element 1, 2008: 2).

As discussed previously, employers have a common law responsibility to take reasonable care for their employees' safety as laid down in the leading House of Lords case of *Wilson's and Clyde Coal Co v English* (1937).

❖ KEY CASE *Wilson's & Clyde Coal Co Ltd v English* (1937)

Facts:

Mr English, a miner, was injured at work when he was crushed by haulage plant. He claimed damages from his employer, the mine owner. The employer argued that, at the time of the accident, responsibility for the safety of the mine had been delegated to his agent. In an action by a miner against his employers for damages for personal injury alleged to be due to the negligence of the employers in that they had failed to provide a reasonably safe system of working the colliery, questions were raised (1) whether the employers were liable at common law for a defective system of working negligently provided or permitted to be carried on by a servant to whom the duty of regulating the system of working had been delegated by the employers, the employers' board of directors being unaware of the defect, and (2) if they were liable, whether the employers were relieved of their liability in view of the prohibition contained in the Coal Mines Act 1911, s 2(4), against the owner of a mine taking any part in the technical management of the mine unless he is qualified to be a manager.

Decision:

It was held by the House of Lords that (1) the employers were not absolved from their duty to take due care in the provision of a reasonably safe system of working by the appointment of a competent person to perform that duty. Although the employers might, and in some events were bound to, appoint someone as their agent in the discharge of their duty, the employers remained responsible. (2) the doctrine of common employment does not apply where it is proved that a defective system of working has been provided. To provide a proper system of working is a paramount duty, and, if it is delegated by a master to another, the master still remains liable.

As well as the Health and Safety and Work Act, there are also legislation and codes of practice relating to specific areas of the workplace. Legislation and codes of practice are used to focus on specific areas of work, such as the code of practice on installing gas boilers, or legislation relating to Health and Safety (of) (Display Screen Equipment) Regulations 1992 (as amended in 2002).

Employers are encouraged to consider which legislation and codes of practice may apply to their area of work, and to also consider those which are relevant to the majority of workplaces.

Other legislation important to note includes the Management of Health and Safety at Work Regulations 1999 which require employers to undertake risk assessments, and the Workplace (Health, Safety and Welfare) Regulations 1992 which look at the physical/material objects in the workplace and the importance of maintenance, signing etc.

19.5.1 Criminal responsibility for health and safety at work

Duties of employers

The Health and Safety at Work Act 1974 is the most important of all health and safety legislation. It imposes a general duty on employers, self-employed, employees, suppliers and owners of premises to make sure that their premises are risk-free and safe.

Section 2(2) states:

> (1) It shall be the duty of every employer to ensure, so far as is reasonably practicable, the health, safety and welfare at work of all his employees.

(2) Without prejudice to the generality of an employer's duty under the preceding subsection, the matters to which that duty extends include in particular—

(a) the provision and maintenance of plant and systems of work that are, so far as is reasonably practicable, safe and without risks to health;
(b) arrangements for ensuring, so far as is reasonably practicable, safety and absence of risks to health in connection with the use, handling, storage and transport of articles and substances;
(c) the provision of such information, instruction, training and supervision as is necessary to ensure, so far as is reasonably practicable, the health and safety at work of his employees;
(d) so far as is reasonably practicable as regards any place of work under the employer's control, the maintenance of it in a condition that is safe and without risks to health and the provision and maintenance of means of access to and egress from it that are safe and without such risks;
(e) the provision and maintenance of a working environment for his employees that is, so far as is reasonably practicable, safe, without risks to health, and adequate as regards facilities and arrangements for their welfare at work.

19.5.2 Powers of inspectors

Policy statements

A safety policy is a written statement of the employer's intent to ensure the safety of their employees. Employers are required to prepare the statement and make it available to their employees and revisions are also required to be made.

The policy should consist of three parts: i) a general statement of the employer's intent, ii) the organisation for safety and iii) the arrangements in force for carrying out the policy. The objectives are to be met by the most senior management in order to ensure that health and safety is maintained at all times. (The Key Consulting Element 2, 2008: 2.)

Standards

Standards are what companies work towards and the policy should set the overall aims of the company. The standards that companies set must be achievable, measurable and realistic. Some companies even ensure that all managers are qualified to NEBOSH standard.

Targets

Once the company has set its standards, the next stage is to evaluate how close they are to achieving these standards. Companies usually find that there is always room for improvement, therefore targets are then set.

Benchmarking

The company will then use a technique called Benchmarking in order to compare their performance with others and learn how to improve health and safety practices. (The Key Consulting Element 2, 2008: 4.)

Section 2(3) states:

(3) Except in such cases as may be prescribed, it shall be the duty of every employer to prepare and as often as may be appropriate revise a written statement of his general policy with respect to the health and safety at work of his employees and the organisation and arrangements for the time being in force for carrying out that policy, and to bring the statement and any revision of it to the notice of all of his employees.

Enforcement and prohibition notices

Inspectors have the power to issue Improvement and Prohibition Notices where necessary.

An Inspector will serve an Improvement Notice when they have come to the decision that a statutory requirement has been, or is about to be carried out. The person, on whom the Notice has been served, has to make the improvements and take other remedial action. The employer has not less than 21 days to comply with the Improvement Notice.

Section 21 states:

> If an inspector is of the opinion that a person—
>
> (a) is contravening one or more of the relevant statutory provisions; or
> (b) has contravened one or more of those provisions in circumstances that make it likely that the contravention will continue or be repeated,
>
> he may serve on him a notice (in this Part referred to as 'an improvement notice') stating that he is of that opinion, specifying the provision or provisions as to which he is of that opinion, giving particulars of the reasons why he is of that opinion, and requiring that person to remedy the contravention or, as the case may be, the matters occasioning it within such period (ending not earlier than the period within which an appeal against the notice can be brought under section 24) as may be specified in the notice.

19.5.3 Prohibition notice

An inspector will serve a Prohibition Notice if they feel that an activity that is being carried out or is about to be carried out may cause serious personal injury – this can require that the activity in question be halted immediately. The requirement that a statutory requirement has been breached does not apply in this case. The Notice takes effect on the date specified in the Notice or immediately. If the employer wishes to appeal he has 21 days to do so, but this will not suspend the Prohibition Notice as it would an Improvement Notice. (The Key Consulting Element 1, 2008: 8.)

Section 22 states:

> (1) This section applies to any activities which are being or are [likely] to be carried on by or under the control of any person, being activities to or in relation to which any of the relevant statutory provisions apply or will, if the activities are so carried on, apply.
>
> (2) If as regards any activities to which this section applies an inspector is of the opinion that, as carried on or [likely] to be carried on by or under the control of the person in question, the activities involve or, as the case may be, will involve a risk of serious personal injury, the inspector may serve on that person a notice (in this Part referred to as "a prohibition notice").
>
> (3) A prohibition notice shall—
>
> (a) state that the inspector is of the said opinion;
> (b) specify the matters which in his opinion give or, as the case may be, will give rise to the said risk;
> (c) where in his opinion any of those matters involves or, as the case may be, will involve a contravention of any of the relevant statutory provisions, state that he is of that opinion, specify the provision or provisions as to which he is of that opinion, and give particulars of the reasons why he is of that opinion; and

(d) direct that the activities to which the notice relates shall not be carried on by or under the control of the person on whom the notice is served unless the matters specified in the notice in pursuance of paragraph (b) above and any associated contraventions of provisions so specified in pursuance of paragraph (c) above have been remedied.

Appeal

The employer may apply to an Employment Tribunal and this may take two forms:

1. Appeal on the grounds that the notice and remedial action is unreasonable.
2. The time given in which to comply is insufficient.

Failure to comply with both Notices is an indictable offence. The case will be heard in the Crown Court, which could impose an unlimited fine and/or imprisonment not exceeding two years. An Inspector could also prosecute the employer directly in the Magistrates' Court, rather than serving a Notice. However, if the case gets referred to the Crown Court, a Barrister will have to be employed. (The Key Consulting Element 1, 2008: 8.)

Inspectors have substantial powers to investigate breaches of Health and Safety under s 20 of the Act:

> (1) Subject to the provisions of section 19 and this section, an inspector may, for the purpose of carrying into effect any of the relevant statutory provisions within the field of responsibility of the enforcing authority which appointed him, exercise the powers set out in subsection (2) below.
>
> (2) The powers of an inspector referred to in the preceding subsection are the following, namely—
>
> (a) at any reasonable time (or, in a situation which in his opinion is or may be dangerous, at any time) to enter any premises which he has reason to believe it is necessary for him to enter for the purpose mentioned in subsection (1) above;
> (b) to take with him a constable if he has reasonable cause to apprehend any serious obstruction in the execution of his duty;
> (c) without prejudice to the preceding paragraph, on entering any premises by virtue of paragraph (a) above to take with him—
>
> (i) any other person duly authorised by his (the inspector's) enforcing authority; and
> (ii) any equipment or materials required for any purpose for which the power of entry is being exercised;
>
> (d) to make such examination and investigation as may in any circumstances be necessary for the purpose mentioned in subsection (1) above;
> (e) as regards any premises which he has power to enter, to direct that those premises or any part of them, or anything therein, shall be left undisturbed (whether generally or in particular respects) for so long as is reasonably necessary for the purpose of any examination or investigation under paragraph (d) above;
> (f) to take such measurements and photographs and make such recordings as he considers necessary for the purpose of any examination or investigation under paragraph (d) above;
> (g) to take samples of any articles or substances found in any premises which he has power to enter, and of the atmosphere in or in the vicinity of any such premises;

(h) in the case of any article or substance found in any premises which he has power to enter, being an article or substance which appears to him to have caused or to be likely to cause danger to health or safety, to cause it to be dismantled or subjected to any process or test (but not so as to damage or destroy it unless this is in the circumstances necessary for the purpose mentioned in subsection (1) above);

(i) in the case of any such article or substance as is mentioned in the preceding paragraph, to take possession of it and detain it for so long as is necessary for all or any of the following purposes, namely—

 (i) to examine it and do to it anything which he has power to do under that paragraph;
 (ii) to ensure that it is not tampered with before his examination of it is completed;
 (iii) to ensure that it is available for use as evidence in any proceedings for an offence under any of the relevant statutory provisions or any proceedings relating to a notice under section 21 or 22;

(j) to require any person whom he has reasonable cause to believe to be able to give any information relevant to any examination or investigation under paragraph (d) above to answer (in the absence of persons other than a person nominated by him to be present and any persons whom the inspector may allow to be present) such questions as the inspector thinks fit to ask and to sign a declaration of the truth of his answers;

(k) to require the production of, inspect, and take copies of or of any entry in—

 (i) any books or documents which by virtue of any of the relevant statutory provisions are required to be kept; and
 (ii) any other books or documents which it is necessary for him to see for the purposes of any examination or investigation under paragraph (d) above;

(l) to require any person to afford him such facilities and assistance with respect to any matters or things within that person's control or in relation to which that person has responsibilities as are necessary to enable the inspector to exercise any of the powers conferred on him by this section;

(m) any other power which is necessary for the purpose mentioned in subsection (1) above.

(3) The Secretary of State may by regulations make provision as to the procedure to be followed in connection with the taking of samples under subsection (2)(g) above (including provision as to the way in which samples that have been so taken are to be dealt with).

(4) Where an inspector proposes to exercise the power conferred by subsection (2)(h) above in the case of an article or substance found in any premises, he shall, if so requested by a person who at the time is present in and has responsibilities in relation to those premises, cause anything which is to be done by virtue of that power to be done in the presence of that person unless the inspector considers that its being done in that person's presence would be prejudicial to the safety of the State.

(5) Before exercising the power conferred by subsection (2)(h) above in the case of any article or substance, an inspector shall consult such persons as appear to him appropriate for the purpose of ascertaining what dangers, if any, there may be in doing anything which he proposes to do under that power.

(6) Where under the power conferred by subsection (2)(i) above an inspector takes possession of any article or substance found in any premises, he shall leave there, either with a responsible person or, if that is impracticable, fixed in a conspicuous position, a notice giving particulars of

that article or substance sufficient to identify it and stating that he has taken possession of it under that power; and before taking possession of any such substance under that power an inspector shall, if it is practicable for him to do so, take a sample thereof and give to a responsible person at the premises a portion of the sample marked in a manner sufficient to identify it.

(7) No answer given by a person in pursuance of a requirement imposed under subsection (2)(j) above shall be admissible in evidence against that person or the [spouse or civil partner] of that person in any proceedings.

(8) Nothing in this section shall be taken to compel the production by any person of a document of which he would on grounds of legal professional privilege be entitled to withhold production on an order for discovery in an action in the High Court or, as the case may be, on an order for the production of documents in an action in the Court of Session.

19.5.4 Section 3: Duties of employers to persons other than their employees

Employers and self-employed persons are under a duty not to expose other persons who are not employed by them to risks while on their premises. It also includes the activities of other persons.

(1) It shall be the duty of every employer to conduct his undertaking in such a way as to ensure, so far as is reasonably practicable, that persons not in his employment who may be affected thereby are not thereby exposed to risks to their health or safety.

(2) It shall be the duty of every self-employed person to conduct his undertaking in such a way as to ensure, so far as is reasonably practicable, that he and other persons (not being his employees) who may be affected thereby are not thereby exposed to risks to their health or safety.

(3) In such cases as may be prescribed, it shall be the duty of every employer and every self-employed person, in the prescribed circumstances and in the prescribed manner, to give to persons (not being his employees) who may be affected by the way in which he conducts his undertaking the prescribed information about such aspects of the way in which he conducts his undertaking as might affect their health or safety.

19.5.5 Section 4: Duties of the controllers of premises to other persons

This section concerns persons (controllers of premises) who are non-employees but use non domestic premises as a place of work. They have a duty not to expose others to any risks created by their premises or any equipment (The Key Consultancy Ltd Element 3, 2008: 3):

(1) This section has effect for imposing on persons duties in relation to those who—

- (a) are not their employees; but
- (b) use non-domestic premises made available to them as a place of work or as a place where they may use plant or substances provided for their use there,

and applies to premises so made available and other non-domestic premises used in connection with them.

(2) It shall be the duty of each person who has, to any extent, control of premises to which this section applies or of the means of access thereto or egress there from or of any plant or substance in such premises to take such measures as it is reasonable for a person in his position to take to ensure, so far as is reasonably practicable, that the premises, all means of access thereto or egress therefrom available for use by persons using the premises, and any plant or substance in the premises or, as the case may be, provided for use there, is or are safe and without risks to health.

(3) Where a person has, by virtue of any contract or tenancy, an obligation of any extent in relation to—

(a) the maintenance or repair of any premises to which this section applies or any means of access thereto or egress there from; or
(b) the safety of or the absence of risks to health arising from plant or substances in any such premises;

that person shall be treated, for the purposes of subsection (2) above, as being a person who has control of the matters to which his obligation extends.

(4) Any reference in this section to a person having control of any premises or matter is a reference to a person having control of the premises or matter in connection with the carrying on by him of a trade, business or other undertaking (whether for profit or not).

19.5.6 Section 6: Manufacturers' and suppliers' duties

This covers the responsibilities of suppliers, designers, manufactures, importers, and installers (including fairground equipment).

(1) It shall be the duty of any person who designs, manufactures, imports or supplies any article for use at work or any article of fairground equipment—

(a) to ensure, so far as is reasonably practicable, that the article is so designed and constructed that it will be safe and without risks to health at all times when it is being set, used, cleaned or maintained by a person at work;
(b) to carry out or arrange for the carrying out of such testing and examination as may be necessary for the performance of the duty imposed on him by the preceding paragraph;
(c) to take such steps as are necessary to secure that persons supplied by that person with the article are provided with adequate information about the use for which the article is designed or has been tested and about any conditions necessary to ensure that it will be safe and without risks to health at all such times as are mentioned in paragraph (a) above and when it is being dismantled or disposed of; and
(d) to take such steps as are necessary to secure, so far as is reasonably practicable, that persons so supplied are provided with all such revisions of information provided to them by virtue of the preceding paragraph as are necessary by reason of its becoming known that anything gives rise to a serious risk to health or safety.

(1A) It shall be the duty of any person who designs, manufactures, imports or supplies any article of fairground equipment—

(a) to ensure, so far as is reasonably practicable, that the article is so designed and constructed that it will be safe and without risks to health at all times when it is being used for or in connection with the entertainment of members of the public;

(b) to carry out or arrange for the carrying out of such testing and examination as may be necessary for the performance of the duty imposed on him by the preceding -paragraph;

(c) to take such steps as are necessary to secure that persons supplied by that person with the article are provided with adequate information about the use for which the article is designed or has been tested and about any conditions necessary to ensure that it will be safe and without risks to health at all times when it is being used for or in connection with the entertainment of members of the public; and

(d) to take such steps as are necessary to secure, so far as is reasonably practicable, that persons so supplied are provided with all such revisions of information provided to them by virtue of the preceding paragraph as are necessary by reason of its becoming known that anything gives rise to a serious risk to health or safety.

19.5.7 Section 7: General duties of employees at work

Employees also have duties in order to safeguard their health and safety and also for the safety of others it shall be the duty of every employee while at work—

(a) to take reasonable care for the health and safety of himself and of other persons who may be affected by his acts or omissions at work; and

(b) as regards any duty or requirement imposed on his employer or any other person by or under any of the relevant statutory provisions, to co-operate with him so far as is necessary to enable that duty or requirement to be performed or complied with.

19.5.8 Section 8: Duty not to interfere with or misuse things

Everyone in the workplace has a duty not to interfere or misuse anything that has been provided in order to safeguard health and safety.

No person shall intentionally or recklessly interfere with or misuse anything provided in the interests of health, safety or welfare in pursuance of any of the relevant statutory provisions.

Section 37 states that where a corporate body makes or neglects to make decisions that affect health and safety, they will be guilty of an offence. The Key Consultancy Ltd Element 3 (2008:4).

(1) Where an offence under any of the relevant statutory provisions committed by a body corporate is proved to have been committed with the consent or connivance of, or to have been attributable to any neglect on the part of, any director, manager, secretary or other similar officer of the body corporate or a person who was purporting to act in any such capacity, he as well as the body corporate shall be guilty of that offence and shall be liable to be proceeded against and punished accordingly.

(2) Where the affairs of a body corporate are managed by its members, the preceding subsection shall apply in relation to the acts and defaults of a member in connection with his functions of management as if he were a director of the body corporate.

19.6 The European Dimension

When the Single European Act 1986 came into effect, this pushed forward the emphasis on health and safety measures, for example Art 118 was inserted into the Treaty of Rome. The EU then had the power to introduce health and safety standards. Each EU State had the authority to implement Directives that were binding; States were given the freedom to implement these Directives into their own laws by whichever way practical. This Article led the way on health and safety measures throughout the EU. It was a step in harmonising the laws of health and safety across Member States and to make sure that States lacking in up to date policies were brought into line.

Before 1987, six Directives had been passed on health and safety at work under the European Commissions, first two action programmes on Health and Safety at work.

The Third Programme from 1988–92 was put forward. This was based on the improvement of health and safety for workers and making sure they had enough protection even though the market was facing competitive pressures. This led to a further fifteen new health and safety Directives with more Directives being added under the influence of the 1989 Social Charter and Action Programme. Following this came the principle Directives known as the 'Six Pack' of new regulations in the UK and then yet further regulations.

The Framework Directive gives employers duties of evaluating and dealing with, avoiding risks to health and safety, drafting a prevention policy, issuing appropriate instructions to workers (Art 6) and improvement in the protection Art 6(3). New technology in the workplace must be reviewed with employees and their representatives (Art 6(3)(c)).

The Framework Directive was then followed by six Directives which were enforced by 1 January 1993, followed by six other Directives which were enacted later along with further Directives, see Ford and Clarke (2008) for some interesting commentary on the EU development of health and safety.

Regulation (2062/94) was passed in order to establish a European Agency for Safety and Health at Work for research at European level and also Regulation (EC) 1907/2006 which deals with the Registration, Evaluation, Authorisation and Restriction of Chemicals (REACH). This Regulation implemented a new system for the control of chemicals that are manufactured and imported in Europe.

The Commission will be putting forward a new agenda, based on new risks within the workplace and safeguarding workers who are not protected adequately. This is aimed at reducing accidents in the workplace and implementing new strategies for the prevention of breaches of health and safety.

Similar to British law, the EU Health and Safety law includes regulations and decisions covering more detailed health and safety issues, such as the regulation on classifying, labelling and packaging of substances and mixtures (1272/2008), which is being progressively implemented into UK law in various stages between December 2010 and June 2017. The EU is also looking to the future, with an Occupational Safety and Health Strategy, which will set the tone and direction for future UK legislation.

19.7 The Common Law: Employers' Liability

Employers have a duty to protect their employees from physical injury, invoking the application of the law of negligence (please see previous chapter for more detailed discussion on negligence). However in other cases, it was held that where an employee was injured overseas, he could sue his employer under contract law in order to sue in the UK (*Matthews v Kuwait Bechtel Corporation* (1959)). The court was more in favour of employees bringing an action against their employees in Contract rather than Tort, if a contractual relation existed. An example of this is demonstrated in *Tai Hing Cotton mill Ltd v Liu Chong Rush and Tompkins* (1989). The employee had been sent overseas to Ethiopia, to work on a project when he was injured in a road accident through the negligence of an unknown party. Ethiopia did not require compulsory third party insurance; therefore the employee was not insured against the accident. He based his claim on the fact that his employers had not insured him, nor did they advise him on insurance and therefore were in breach of the implied term in his contract. It was held that there were no grounds for implying a term of the contract that the employer should have insured him or advised him to get insurance and that a duty of care in tort could be imposed to enlarge the employer's contractual obligation.

In the case of *Scally v Southern Health and Social Services Board* (1991) doctors claimed that the board had been negligent in failing to inform them of the benefits they could purchase under their pension scheme which was now too late for them to apply for. They suffered pure economic loss and this cannot usually be recovered under the law of tort. The House of Lords considered that a term could be implied into the contract that the employer should draw employees' attention to it, see Pit (2009). In the case of *Johnstone v Bloomsbury HA*, the Court of Appeal accepted that the employer could exclude liability for breach of the duty of care. However, under the Unfair Contract Terms Act 1977, this would be void if employers tried to exclude liability for an employees' death or injury. The duty of care is covered by the law of negligence.

At common law, employees may claim against the employer in two ways: by using the action of Vicarious Liability. This applies when the employee is injured by another employee, whom the employer is responsible for, then the employer is vicariously liable for the employees' actions or by the breach of the employer's own duty to take reasonable care for the safety of its employees.

19.7.1 Direct Duty of Care

The duty that is owed by the employer to the employee could be an implied term in the contract of employment, see *Wilsons & Clyde Coal Co v English* (1938). The question to be asked is whether the employer took reasonable care for the employee's safety.

Competent fellow-employees

In the case of *Hudson v Ridge Manufacturing* (1957) an employee broke his wrist when wrestled to the ground by another employee who had a reputation for habitually engaging in horseplay of this kind and had done so within the workforce for a number of years. The argument was centred on the fact that the employer had failed to maintain discipline and prevent dangerous conduct. However, where the employer is unaware of the propensity for this kind of behaviour, it could be argued that there was no breach of a direct duty of care. With this is mind though, the employer could still be found to be vicariously liable for the employees' actions if it was done during the course of his employment, *Harrison v Michelin Tyres* (1985).

Safe plant and equipment

The employer is responsible for making sure that tools and machinery are safe. Not only must they be safe for work they must also be suitable for the task that is to be carried out. The issue is that many employers do not have the necessary skills to check to see if machinery is safe itself. In order to discharge this duty then the employer can purchase machinery and keep it in good repair. In the case of *Coltman v Bibby Tankers* (1988) the House of Lords held that 'equipment' was wide enough to include a ship. As you can see the scope of what is deemed 'equipment' can be interpreted widely. This is an essential point when health and safety is discussed in the context of business. Many businesses do not realise that certain equipment is classified as such and that they have responsibility for making sure it is in good working order and suitable. If an employee injures themselves on a piece of machinery then it would be tough for the employer to negate their responsibility. Only if it is a fault or something that has been used in a negligent way (which could throw the question of training into dispute) would the employer be able to remove their liability. If they do manage to remove their liability then it could fall to the manufacturer or the employee themselves depending on the situation. This is why it is important that accurate health and safety records are kept and that managers are clear about their own policy. Many businesses have a health and safety committee where issues such as accident reports, training, risk assessments etc can be discussed. This is imperative to keep a safe working environment for all employees.

Safe system of work

The employer is responsible for making sure that the methods used to do the work and the system of supervision is a safe system of work. This, again, is something that you find often gets overlooked in many businesses. For example, some employers will take on skilled employees and not think about aspects of training/health and safety training. This could be incredibly dangerous down the line and it is something that they do need to address.

Standards have changed with regards to newly recognised injuries. In the case of *Pickford v ICI* (1998) this concerned a claim for repetitive strain injury (RSI). The claimant was a secretary who spent most of her time typing without a break. The HSE in 1983 supplied an advisory booklet on avoiding health risks, which included taking breaks. In 1987 the company advised typists to take breaks before their hands and arms became tired. However, this information was not passed on to the secretaries as the employer believed their typing duties comprised of only 50% of their workload.

Use of safety equipment

Employers are under a duty to provide employees with safety equipment. In some cases the use of safety equipment is required by law and employers as well as employees could be subject to criminal sanctions if these requirements are not met.

❖ KEY CASE *McWilliams v Arrol* (1962)

Facts:

An erector fell to his death, he was not wearing a safety belt, nor was one provided. However, safety belts had previously been provided but the employee had never worn one.

Decision:

The court held that he would not have worn one on the day of the accident therefore the employer was not at fault of causing death. If there had been a provision to ensure the use of safety equipment, then the employer would have been held liable for the death. Therefore it is the employees' conduct that can also give rise to fault in health and safety, as it does in tort law.

Employers are liable where: (i) they have not properly instructed employees in the use of the equipment, (ii) when the equipment was awkward to use, was not intended for that particular job or affected the way they conducted their work. This can be demonstrated in the case of *Couch v British Rail Engineering* (1988). In this case a fitter damaged their eye through not wearing the appropriate protective clothing (in this case goggles). The employer did provide goggles, in a separate room, however the fitter decided to carry on without them. The court stressed that the employer would still be liable as they had not put the goggles into the hand of the fitter, so there would be some liability on both parties (contributory negligence on the part of the fitter).

Employer's duties extend to assessing the risks of a particular individual, in line with their characteristics, i.e. younger workers are higher risks. *Paris v Stepney BC* (1951) illustrates this point where the employee was blind in one eye and was employed as a mechanic. A piece of metal flew off while removing a bolt and damaged his good eye. It was not normal practice to provide goggles for this kind of work, as the risk of injury was very small, however the risk for this particular employee was very high compared to an employee with normal sight and was held therefore that he should have been provided with goggles. As you can see, a business must take account of any characteristic of an employee that could result in some issues with regards to health and safety. Do also bear in mind that it is not just employees that you also may have these duties for. It could be students, for example at a university or college, where their needs for health and safety must also be addressed at an individual level. This could even be something like a PEEP (Personal Emergency Evacuation Plan). For example a disabled student may, in the event of an emergency, need extra help in order to evacuate a building.

❖ KEY CASE *Pape v Cumbria CC* (1991)

Facts:

The claimant argued that their dermatitis was caused by contact with cleaning products. Although the employers had provided protective gloves they had failed to warn them about the danger of sustained exposure of the cleaning products to the skin, and had also failed to advise them to wear gloves at all times.

Decision:

It was held that a failure to warn employees of dangers not obvious to them was a breach of the duty of care. It appears that the court will find it acceptable for an employer to dismiss an employee if their health would suffer.

In the case of *Page v Freight Hire* (1981) a woman was employed as a HGV driver delivering chemicals. The haulage company was informed that the chemicals could be dangerous to an unborn child; therefore a woman of child-bearing age should not be doing this particular work. The claimant was aged 23, divorced and did not intend to have any children. She was willing to take any risks associated with the job. It was held that the employer was justified in removing her from this line of work for her own safety.

Risk assessments

The Management of Health and Safety at Work Regulations 1999 reg 3 states that an employer must carry out a risk assessment depending on the size of the organisation. Risk assessments are there to help employers identify any issues of risk for employees/public etc. There are 5 steps in a risk assessment. Step 1 – Identify the Hazard, Step 2 – Decide who might be harmed and how, Step 3 – Evaluate the risks and decide on precautions, Step 4 – Record your findings and implement them, Step 5 – Review. As you can see, it is a basic evaluation of risks and assessing the possible consequences of risks. The Health and Safety Executive publish numerous leaflets and forms for companies to carry out the assessments. This is part of the law and something which companies must adhere to. One important note is that with a risk assessment it doesn't mean that the risk will be completely negated (sometimes this can be impossible) what it does mean is that the risk is accounted for and all precautions that can be taken are taken.

19.7.2 Liability for psychiatric injury

Walker v Northumberland CC (1995) was the first reported case of an employer being liable for the stress of an employee in the workplace. This case concerned a social services manager suffering two nervous breakdowns brought on by the stress of too much work which his superiors declined to alleviate along with the stress he was experiencing as a result. It was held that the first breakdown was not foreseeable but the second breakdown was foreseeable as they did not alleviate the stress at work. The council was held to be in breach of their duty for not providing a safe system of work. *Hatton v Sutherland* (2002) involved appeal cases concerning stress at work. It was held that an employer was entitled to assume that an employee was able to cope with the normal pressures of their job. It was only if there were indications that would lead a reasonable employer to come to the decision that a problem did exist, that a duty to take action arises. Foreseeability in this case would mean that the employer knew or should have known that the employee had a particular condition to stress-related illnesses. The employer then has a duty to take positive action to alleviate the employee's stress. The court would need to take into consideration whether the employee would have suffered this in any event, whether the workload was abnormally heavy, too demanding intellectually for the employee and a comparison of the demands made on other employees would also need to be considered. The court would further consider what other options were available to the employer. The court also held that if the employer decided to dismiss the employee in order to make the employee safe, they would not be in breach of duty. The employee also needed to know that the stress was caused by the employer's breach of duty.

The court has to consider whether the psychiatric illness occurred solely because of work or if there were other contributing factors. The employee must prove that the breach was the cause of the harm. *Hartman v South Essex* (2005) provided that the employee must show that the breach of duty by the employer substantially contributed to the harm. The employer will have to prove that other causes were the contributing factor to the injury. This will result in damages being reduced.

❖ KEY CASE — *Hartman v South Essex Mental Health and Community Care NHS Trust* (2005)

Facts:

Mrs Hartman, who had a history of depression, had been a nursing auxiliary at a children's home since 1989. Following an accident in 1996 in which a child was killed, her hours increased significantly, putting her under great pressure (of which the trust was aware). In early 1999, she applied for ill health retirement because of depression.

Decision:

The Court of Appeal did not think that the trust was in breach of its duty of care to Mrs Hartman. It said that working in a children's home was not in itself unduly stressful, and that she worked without any problems for a number of years, including the post-accident period. As for the issue of overwork, it said that there was nothing to indicate she was unable to cope.

19.7.3 Duty to independent contractors

The employer does not owe a contractor the same level of duty as it does employees. Contractors are expected to guard against any risks and take care of their own safety. The only duty on the employer is to safeguard them from less obvious risks when they enter the premises under Occupiers' Liability Act 1957 s 2(3). However, there are exceptions. If the employer specifically requests the contractor to perform a tortious duty, the employer is liable. Also, employers are liable for actions that have strict liability. Under the strict liability rule of *Rylands v Fletcher* (1866) it established that an occupier of land who brings onto it anything likely to do damage if it escapes, and keeps that thing on the land, will be liable for any damage caused by an escape. Landowners employed contractors to build a reservoir on their land, the water escaped and flooded a mine on neighbouring land. The landowners were viewed as employers to the contractors and were therefore found to be held liable.

19.8 Vicarious Liability

An employee and third parties can hold an employer liable if the injury was caused by another employee for whom the employer is responsible. The employee must have been acting in the course of his employment when he committed the negligent act. The employer will not be liable if the employee was acting outside the scope of their contract (Pit 2009: 439). In *Limpus v London General Omnibus Co* (1862) bus drivers were forbidden to race drivers from other bus companies. A driver decided to engage in a race and caused an accident for which the employer was liable, even though he was racing, as he was doing his job, but doing it badly. In *Rose v Plenty* (1976) a milkman was forbidden to allow children on the milk float to help in delivering milk. The milkman allowed a 13 year old to help and the child was subsequently injured. It was held that the employer was liable as the milkman was still performing his duties although in the wrong way. However, if the standard of work has dropped so badly that it cannot be viewed as in the course of their employment, then the employer will not be deemed liable. In *General Engineering Services v Kingston & St Andrew Corp* (1989) firemen had decided to institute a go-slow, with regards to a pay claim. They decided not to attend to a burning building until it had completely burnt down. This action was held to be outside their course of employment. The court applies the 'close connection test' and asks whether or not the employee's action had a close connection with what he was employed to do.

In the case of *Smith v Stages* (1989) Lord Goff stated:

> the fundamental principle is that an employee is acting in the course of his employment when he is doing what he is employed to do . . . or anything which is reasonable incidental to his employment.

Travelling to and from work will be in the course of their employment if they are using a vehicle provided by their employer. Deviations made to a journey will not be within their course of employment.

Difficulties may arise in trying to ascertain whether or not the main employer is liable for negligence, especially where an employee is lent to another firm. In the leading case of *Mersey Docks and Harbour Board v Coggins & Griffith* (1947) the test involves deciphering which employer had control of the situation, which employer was 'directing and supervising' at the time of the act? However, if the employee was supplied to the other company temporarily, because of a special skill, the main employer remains vicariously liable (Pitt 2009: 441).

19.8.1 Liability for breach of statutory duty

Difficulties may arise for an employee who needs to prove that the employer, or a person which the employer was responsible for, was negligent. The employee may also have an alternative claim, by showing that the employer was in breach of a statutory duty. The employee need only show that the breach was the cause of injury. The Health and Safety at Work Act 1947 s 47 states that if there is a breach of the duties laid down in ss 2–8, there is no civil liability, but if there is a breach of the regulations, this will give rise to civil liability unless it states otherwise. If there is no express provision, the court will look at the interpretation of the statute. In *Lonrho v Shell* (1982) the House of Lords stated that:

> for civil liability, it had to be shown either that the relevant provision was intended for the benefit or protection of a particular class of person, including the claimant, or that it created a

public right and this particular claimant suffered damage over and above that suffered by the general public because of its breach.

19.8.2 Defences

Employers may rely on two defences, that of contributory negligence and consent.

Contributory negligence

If the claimant is partly to blame for the accident, the employer may rely on this defence under the Law Reform (Contributory Negligence) Act 1945. The court will decide the extent of fault by the claimant and damages will be reduced accordingly by a certain percentage.

Consent

Volenti non fit injuria is a defence which states that if you willingly consent to take a risk, you cannot complain if the danger materialises. However, the courts have recognised that you do not consent to a risk because you are aware of it (*Smith v Baker* (1891)). (Please see the Tort chapters for more discussion on defences.)

19.9 Corporate Manslaughter

Corporate liability has been developed in a piecemeal fashion, taking over ten years for the Corporate Manslaughter and Corporate Homicide Act 2007 (CMCHA) to be passed. Prior to the enactment of the (CMCHA) 2007, a corporation could be convicted of 'manslaughter by gross negligence'. However, there were problems with securing a conviction with large and medium-sized companies and successful convictions have tended to involve small companies. Much of this is due to the fact of who to hold accountable in large organisations. Many places have committees/health and safety managers etc which have responsibility for health and safety, therefore it can be argued that the directors of organisations have passed on their liability. This is, obviously, not satisfactory, as there were many prosecutions that resulted in failure, and the Law Commission published a report in 1996 which put forward a recommendation for a new offence of Corporate Manslaughter. This need existed particularly following the failed prosecutions after the disaster of the capsizing of the Herald of Free Enterprise. In 2005 the Government published a draft Corporate Manslaughter Bill and the CMCHA 2007 came into force on 6 April 2008.

An incorporated company and a limited liability partnership under the Limited Liability Partnership Act 2000 have separate legal personality. Therefore the business is a separate entity and one which can then be held accountable. A limited company is distinct from its shareholders, directors and employees. It can be made criminally liable for an offence that requires *mens rea*, if it is proved that an individual, who is part of the directing mind and will of the corporation, committed the *actus reus* for that offence with appropriate *mens rea* when acting within the scope of his office.

This Act creates an offence whereby if a company, by its activities, causes the death of a person, it is a gross breach of the duty of care, which is owed to the deceased person, by the organisation.

19.9.1 The offence

CMCHA 2007 s 1(1) provides:

> (1) An organisation to which this section applies is guilty of an offence if the way in which its activities are managed or organised—

> (a) causes a person's death, and
> (b) amounts to a gross breach of a relevant duty of care owed by the organisation to the deceased.

Organisations the Act Covers

The term 'organisation' in s 1(2) of the Act, covers different types of organisations that the Act applies to:

> (2) The organisations to which this section applies are—
>
> (a) a corporation;
> (b) a department or other body listed in Schedule 1;
> (c) a police force;
> (d) a partnership, or a trade union or employers' association that is an employer.

Section 1(3) of the Act specifically states that persons who will be made liable for the manslaughter, will be persons who hold senior management positions and persons who have management of activities. The 'senior management failure' must have caused the death. Causation will apply to determine this, meaning that the management failure does not have to be the main cause of death; it only needs to be a cause:

> (3) An organisation is guilty of an offence under this section only if the way in which its activities are managed or organised by its senior management is a substantial element in the breach referred to in subsection (1).
>
> (4) For the purposes of this Act—
>
> (a) 'Relevant duty of care' has the meaning given by section 2, read with sections 3 to 7;
> (b) a breach of a duty of care by an organisation is a 'gross' breach if the conduct alleged to amounts to a breach of that duty falls far below what can reasonably be expected of the organisation in the circumstances;
> (c) 'senior management', in relation to an organisation, means the persons who play significant roles in—
>
> (i) the making of decisions about how the whole or a substantial part of its activities are to be managed or organised, or
> (ii) the actual managing or organising of the whole or a substantial part of those activities.

The standard of care for 'gross negligence' is a standard whereby the breach falls below what should be reasonably expected, taking all the circumstances into account.

19.9.2 The relevant duty of care

Under s 2(1) the standard of duty of care that is owed comes under the law of negligence. However, this duty of care is owed not just to employees of the company, but to anybody who supplies goods and services to the company and even persons who are engaged in unlawful activity. Even though a person accepts certain risks, this does not prevent the Act from applying.

> (1) A 'relevant duty of care', in relation to an organisation, means any of the following duties owed by it under the law of negligence—

(a) a duty owed to its employees or to other persons working for the organisation or performing services for it;
(b) a duty owed as occupier of premises;
(c) a duty owed in connection with—

(i) the supply by the organisation of goods or services (whether for consideration or not),
(ii) the carrying on by the organisation of any construction or maintenance operations,
(iii) the carrying on by the organisation of any other activity on a commercial basis, or
(iv) the use or keeping by the organisation of any plant, vehicle or other thing;

(d) a duty owed to a person who, by reason of being a person within subsection (2), is someone for whose safety the organisation is responsible.

(4) A reference in subsection (1) to a duty owed under the law of negligence includes a reference to a duty that would be owed under the law of negligence but for any statutory provision under which liability is imposed in place of liability under that law.

(5) For the purposes of this Act, whether a particular organisation owes a duty of care to a particular individual is a question of law.

The judge must make any findings of fact necessary to decide that question.

(6) For the purposes of this Act there is to be disregarded—

(a) any rule of the common law that has the effect of preventing a duty of care from being owed by one person to another by reason of the fact that they are jointly engaged in unlawful conduct;
(b) any such rule that has the effect of preventing a duty of care from being owed to a person by reason of his acceptance of a risk of harm.

***Hsaio* (2009)**

Section 8 sets out some factors that the jury must consider. Even though a company had safeguards in place, there is no issue of liability, as a death has still occurred.

19.9.3 Factors for the jury

(1) This section applies where—

(a) it is established that an organisation owed a relevant duty of care to a person, and
(b) it falls to the jury to decide whether there was a gross breach of that duty.

(2) The jury must consider whether the evidence shows that the organisation failed to comply with any health and safety legislation that relates to the alleged breach, and if so—

(a) how serious that failure was;
(b) how much of a risk of death it posed.

(3) The jury may also—

(a) consider the extent to which the evidence shows that there were attitudes, policies, systems or accepted practices within the organisation that were likely to have encouraged any such failure as is mentioned in subsection (2), or to have produced tolerance of it;
(b) have regard to any health and safety guidance that relates to the alleged breach.

(4) This section does not prevent the jury from having regard to any other matters they consider relevant.

(5) In this section 'health and safety guidance' means any code, guidance, manual or similar publication that is concerned with health and safety matters and is made or issued (under a statutory provision or otherwise) by an authority responsible for the enforcement of any health and safety legislation.

Section 9 states that when a company has been found guilty of corporate manslaughter, the court has the power to make a 'remedial order' to compel them to remedy the breach and anything that flowed from it, i.e. health and safety deficiencies, etc.

19.9.4 Power to order breach etc to be remedied

(1) A court before which an organisation is convicted of corporate manslaughter or corporate homicide may make an order (a 'remedial order') requiring the organisation to take specified steps to remedy—

- (a) the breach mentioned in section 1(1) ('the relevant breach');
- (b) any matter that appears to the court to have resulted from the relevant breach and to have been a cause of the death;
- (c) any deficiency, as regards health and safety matters, in the organisation's policies, systems or practices of which the relevant breach appears to the court to be an indication.

(2) A remedial order may be made only on an application by the prosecution specifying the terms of the proposed order.

Any such order must be on such terms (whether those proposed or others) as the court considers appropriate having regard to any representations made, and any evidence adduced, in relation to that matter by the prosecution or on behalf of the organisation.

(3) Before making an application for a remedial order the prosecution must consult such enforcement authority or authorities as it considers appropriate having regard to the nature of the relevant breach.

(4) A remedial order—

- (a) must specify a period within which the steps referred to in subsection (1) are to be taken;
- (b) may require the organisation to supply to an enforcement authority consulted under subsection (3), within a specified period, evidence that those steps have been taken.

A period specified under this subsection may be extended or further extended by order of the court on an application made before the end of that period or extended period.

(5) An organisation that fails to comply with a remedial order is guilty of an offence, and liable on conviction on indictment to a fine.

Section 10 states that a court will make a 'Publicity Order' compelling the company to publicise their conviction, the details surrounding it and the outcome of the court case.

19.9.5 Power to order conviction etc to be publicised

(1) A court before which an organisation is convicted of corporate manslaughter or corporate homicide may make an order (a 'publicity order') requiring the organisation to publicise in a specified manner—

- (a) the fact that it has been convicted of the offence;
- (b) specified particulars of the offence;
- (c) the amount of any fine imposed;
- (d) the terms of any remedial order made.

(2) In deciding on the terms of a publicity order that it is proposing to make, the court must—

- (a) ascertain the views of such enforcement authority or authorities (if any) as it considers appropriate, and
- (b) have regard to any representations made by the prosecution or on behalf of the organisation.

(3) A publicity order—

- (a) must specify a period within which the requirements referred to in subsection (1) are to be complied with;
- (b) may require the organisation to supply to any enforcement authority whose views have been ascertained under subsection (2), within a specified period, evidence that those requirements have been complied with.

(4) An organisation that fails to comply with a publicity order is guilty of an offence, and liable on conviction on indictment to a fine.

As you can see, the legislation is fairly straightforward in essence. It is important to note that relevant health and safety legislation and gross negligence manslaughter will still apply alongside the Act. They are NOT replaced by the Act.

19.10 Conclusion

Health and safety often receives 'bad press'. Many people have conceptions and misconceptions about what health and safety is and why it is there. What is important to remember is that it is there to protect employees, the public and employers. It is there to make a safe working environment. As you can see from the history it was an important step to make sure that people's welfare at work was considered. Many people work in a safe environment and can be thankful for the development of these principles for this. There are still concerns and there are still issues regarding health and safety. It is an area that will continue to grow and develop and adapt to the change in working patterns and society. As we have now seen more reliance is placed upon technological working, working from home and flexible working. With these considerations health and safety will need to continue to grow and develop. In order to keep updated the Health and Safety Executive highlight the important changes, new developments and leaflets on dealing with amendments on their website (www.hse.gov.uk). It will also give an idea of future developments and report on cases that have been investigated as well as outcomes.

Summary

Health and Safety Law

The Ten Hour Movement and the Factory Act 1833

In 1833 the Government introduced the Factory Act to improve the conditions for children who were working in the factories.

The Factories Act 1844

In 1844 the Government passed another Factories Act, which was the first Health and Safety Act in Britain. This Act further reduced hours of work for children and applied the many provisions of the Factory Act of 1833 to women.

Factories Act 1961

The 1961 Act consolidated the legislation on workplace health and safety. However, it has largely been superseded by the Health and Safety at Work Act 1974.

The Health and Safety at Work Act 1974

The Robens Report (1972, Cmnd 5034) reviewed workplace health and safety, and this report became the basis for the Act. It imposes a general duty on employers, self employed, employees, suppliers and owners of premises to make sure that their premises are risk-free and safe. This duty is achieved through conducting risk assessments, taking into account the many hazards that could arise, which could affect the physical and mental wellbeing of an employee or even cause death (The Key Consulting Element 1, 2008: 2).

As discussed previously, employers have a common law responsibility to take reasonable care for their employees' safety as laid down in the leading House of Lords case of *Wilson's and Clyde Coal Co v English* (1938).

Section 3: employers and self-employed persons are under a duty not to expose other persons, who are not employed by them, to risks while on their premises. Section 4: this section concerns persons (controllers of premises) who are non-employees but use non domestic premises as a place of work.

Section 7: General duties of employees at work

Employees also have duties in order to safeguard their health and safety, and also for the safety of others: it shall be the duty of every employee while at work—

(a) to take reasonable care for the health and safety of himself and of other persons who may be affected by his acts or omissions at work; and

(b) as regards any duty or requirement imposed on his employer or any other person by or under any of the relevant statutory provisions, to co-operate with him so far as is necessary to enable that duty or requirement to be performed or complied with.

The European dimension

Before 1987, six Directives had been passed on health and safety at work under the European Commissions, first two action programmes on Health and Safety at work.

The Framework Directive gives employers duties of evaluating and dealing with and avoiding risks to health and safety, drafting a prevention policy, issuing appropriate instructions to workers (Art 6) and improvement in the protection offered Art 6(3).

Regulation (2062/94) was passed in order to establish a European Agency for Safety and Health at Work for research at European level and also Regulation (EC) 1907/2006 which deals with the Registration, Evaluation, Authorisation and Restriction of Chemicals (REACH).

The Common law – employers' liability

Employers have a duty to protect their employees from physical injury, invoking the application of the law of negligence. However in another case, it was held that where an employee was injured overseas, he could sue his employer under contract law in order to sue in the UK (*Matthews v Kuwait Bechtel Corporation* (1959)).

At common law, employees may claim against the employer in two ways: by using the action of Vicarious Liability. This applies when the employee is injured by another employee, whom the employer is responsible for, then the employer is vicariously liable for the employee's actions or by the breach of the employer's own duty to take reasonable care for the safety of its employees.

Direct duty of care

The duty that is owed by the employer to the employee could be an implied term in the contract of employment, see, *Wilson's & Clyde Coal Co v English* (1938).

Risk assessments

The Management of Health and Safety at Work Regulations 1999 reg 3 states that an employer must carry out a risk assessment depending on the size of the organisation.

Vicarious liability

An employee and third parties can hold an employer liable if the injury was caused by another employee for whom the employer is responsible. The employee must have been acting in the course of his employment when he committed the negligent act.

In the case of *Smith v Stages* (1989), Lord Goff stated,

> the fundamental principle is that an employee is acting in the course of his employment when he is doing what he is employed to do . . . or anything which is reasonable incidental to his employment.

Defences

Contributory negligence

If the claimant is partly to blame for the accident, the employer may rely on this defence under the Law Reform (Contributory Negligence) Act 1945. The court will decide the extent of fault by the claimant and damages will be reduced accordingly by a certain percentage.

Consent

Volenti non fit injuria is a defence which states that if you willingly consent to take a risk, you cannot complain if the danger materialises. However, the courts have recognised that you do not consent to a risk because you are aware of it (*Smith v Baker* (1891)).

Corporate manslaughter

Corporate liability has been developed in a piecemeal fashion, with it taking over ten years for the Corporate Manslaughter and Corporate Homicide Act 2007 (CMCHA) to be passed. This Act creates an offence whereby if a company, by its activities, causes the death of a person, it is a gross breach of the duty of care, which is owed to the deceased person, by the organisation.

CMCHA 2007 s 1(1) provides:

> (1) An organisation to which this section applies is guilty of an offence if the way in which its activities are managed or organised—

(a) causes a person's death, and
(b) amounts to a gross breach of a relevant duty of care owed by the organisation to the deceased.

Factors for the jury:

(1) This section applies where—

(a) it is established that an organisation owed a relevant duty of care to a person, and
(b) it falls to the jury to decide whether there was a gross breach of that duty.

(2) The jury must consider whether the evidence shows that the organisation failed to comply with any health and safety legislation that relates to the alleged breach, and if so—

(a) how serious that failure was;
(b) how much of a risk of death it posed.

Further Reading

Allen, J *et al*, *Festival Special Events Management*, 3rd edn, 2007, London: John Wiley and Sons Ltd
Labour Research Department, *Health and Safety Law 2010*, London: LRD Publications
Stranks, J, *Health and Safety Law*, 5th edn, 2005, London: Prentice Hall
Tolley's Health and Safety at Work Handbook 2008, London: Butterworths

HSE Books

Managing health and safety aspects of research in higher and further education, Education Service Advisory Committee, HSE Books, 2000
Everyone's guide to RIDDOR, HSE31, HSE Books, 1999
Guide to the Reporting of Injuries, Diseases and Dangerous Occurrences, Regulations 1995, HSE Books, 1999
5 Steps to risk assessment, INDG163 HSE Books, 1998
Consulting employees on health and safety: A guide to the law, INDG232, HSE Books, 1996
Safe work in confined spaces. Confined Spaces Regulations 1997; Approved Code of Practice and guidance, LIOI, HSE Books, 1997
Safe use of lifting equipment. Lifting Operations and Lifting Equipment Regulations 1998. Approved Code of Practice and guidance, L113, HSE Books, 1998
Manual Handling. Manual Handling Operations Regulations 1992. Guidance on Regulations, L23, HSE Books, 1998
Slips and trips. Guidance for employers on identifying hazards and controlling risks, HSG155, HSE Books, 1996
Safe use of work equipment. Provision and Use of Work-Equipment Regulations 1998. Approved Code of Practice and guidance, L22, HSE Books, 1998
Health and Safety (Display Screen Equipment) Regulations 1992 as amended by the Health and Safety (Miscellaneous Amendments) Regulations 2002. Guidance on regulations: L26 (Second edition) HSE Books, 2002.

Index

D

G

H

I

N

Z